CAPSTONE REFERENCE

THE
CAPSTONE
ENCYCLOPAEDIA
OF BUSINESS

D0891240

THE CAPSTONE ENCYCLOPAEDIA OF BUSINESS

THE MOST UP-TO-DATE AND ACCESSIBLE GUIDE TO BUSINESS EVER!

CAPSTONE

Copyright © Capstone Publishing, 2003

The right of the authors to be identified as the authors of this book has been asserted in accordance with the Copyright, Designs and Patents Act 1988

First published 2003 by

Capstone Publishing Limited (a Wiley company)
8 Newtec Place
Magdalen Road
Oxford
OX4 1RE
United Kingdom
http://www.capstoneideas.com

CIP catalogue records for this book are available from the British Library and the US Library of Congress

ISBN 1-84112-053-7

Typeset in 10/13 pt Minion
by Sparks Computer Solutions Ltd
http://www.sparks.co.uk
Printed and bound by
TJ International Ltd, Padstow, Cornwall

Substantial discounts on bulk quantities of Capstone Books are available to corporations, professional associations and other organizations. For details telephone Capstone Publishing on (+44-1865-798623), fax (+44-1865-240941) or email (info@wiley-capstone.co.uk)

CAPSTONE ENCYCLOPAEDIA ADVISORY BOARD

Julian Birkinshaw

Julian Birkinshaw is Tenured Associate Professor and Co-Chair of the Department of Strategic and International Management at the London Business School.

He gained a PhD in business from the Richard Ivey School of Business, University of Western Ontario in 1995. He has also worked at the University of Toronto and the Stockholm School of Economics.

He is the author of five books, including *Inventuring* (2003), *Leadership the Sven-Goran Eriksson Way* (2002) and *Entrepreneurship in the Global Firm* (2001), and over 40 articles. He is active as a consultant and executive educator to many large companies. In addition, he is a member of the Council of Economy Advisors to the Invest in Sweden Agency, and on the board of governors of the London Business School.

In 1998 the leading British management magazine *Management Today* profiled Julian Birkinshaw as one of six of the 'Next Generation of Management Gurus'. He is regularly quoted in international media outlets, including CNN, the BBC, *The Economist,* the *Wall Street Journal,* and *The Times.*

Peter Cohan

Peter Cohan is president of Peter S. Cohan & Associates, a management consulting and venture capital firm. His strategy consulting practice helps managers to identify, evaluate, and profit from opportunities created by changing technology. His private equity practice helps entrepreneurs build successful companies through capital, advice, and contacts.

Cohan has written seven books including *Value Leadership: Seven Principles That Define Corporate Value in Any Economy* (2003). He earned an MBA from the Wharton School, did graduate work in computer science at MIT and earned a BS in Electrical Engineering from Swarthmore College.

Stuart Crainer and Des Dearlove

Stuart Crainer and Des Dearlove are the founders of Suntop Media. They write columns for *The Times* and *Chief Executive* and are contributing editors to *Strategy & Business*. Their work appears in leading business magazines throughout the world and their syndicated interview series is sold to 20 countries.

Stuart and Des's book credits include *Firestarters!* (2001) and *Generation Entrepreneur* (2000). They are the editors of the *Financial Times Handbook of Management.*

In addition to their writing, Stuart and Des are sought after trainers, speakers and consultants. Suntop Media's Business Writing Masterclass has been delivered to corporate, academic and student audiences.

Andrew Kakabadse

Andrew Kakabadse is Professor of International

Management Development, Deputy Director of the School of Management at Cranfield University. He is ACT Visiting Professor at the Australian National University, Canberra, Visiting Professor at Hangzhou University, China, Visiting Fellow at Babson College, Boston, USA and was Honorary Professorial Fellow, Curtin University of Technology, Perth. He is a Fellow of the International Academy of Management, Fellow of the British Psychology Society and Fellow of the British Academy of Management.

His current areas of interest focus on improving the performance of top executives and top executive teams, excellence in consultancy practice, corporate governance and conflict resolution and international relations. His top team database covers 14 nations and over 10,000 private and public sector organisations. His books include the bestselling *Essence of Leadership*, *Politics of Management*, *Working in Organisations* and *The Wealth Creators*. His two most recent books are *Geopolitics of Governance* and *Smart Sourcing: International Best Practice*. He holds positions on the boards of a number of companies, edits the *Journal of Management Development* and sits on the editorial board of the *Journal of Managerial Psychology* and the *Leadership and Organisation Development Journal*.

W. Chan Kim

W. Chan Kim is the Boston Consulting Group Bruce D. Henderson Chair Professor of Strategy and International Management at INSEAD Business School, France. Prior to joining INSEAD, he was a professor at the University of Michigan Business School. He has served as a board member as well as an advisor for a number of multinational corporations and has published numerous articles on strategy and managing the multinational which can be found in *Academy of Management Journal*, *Management Science*, *Organization Science*, *Strategic Management Journal*, *Administrative Science Quarterly*, *Journal of International*

Business Studies, *Harvard Business Review*, *Sloan Management Review*, and others.

Professor Kim's current research focuses on strategy and management in the knowledge economy. His recent work, with Renée Mauborgne, includes: 'Charting Your Company's Future' (*Harvard Business Review*, June 2002), 'Knowing a Business Idea When You See One' (*Harvard Business Review*, September–October, 2000), 'Creating New Market Space' (*Harvard Business Review*, January–February, 1999), 'Value Innovation: The Strategic Logic of High Growth' (*Harvard Business Review*, January–February, 1997) and 'Fair Process: Managing in the Knowledge Economy' (*Harvard Business Review*, July–August, 1997).

He is a Fellow of the World Economic Forum at Davos and the winner of the Eldridge Haynes Prize, awarded by the Academy of International Business and the Eldridge Haynes Memorial Trust of Business International, for the best original paper in the field of international business.

Renée Mauborgne

Renée Mauborgne is the INSEAD Distinguished Fellow and Professor of Strategy and Management at INSEAD in Fontainebleau, France and Fellow of the World Economic Forum. She has served as an advisor for a number of multinational corporations in Europe, the US and Pacific Asia. She has published numerous articles on strategy and managing the multinational which can be found in *Academy of Management Journal*, *Management Science*, *Organization Science*, *Strategic Management Journal*, *Administrative Science Quarterly*, *Journal of International Business Studies*, *Harvard Business Review*, *Sloan Management Review*, and others.

Professor Mauborgne's current research focuses on strategy, innovation and wealth creation in the knowledge economy. Her recent work, with W. Chan Kim, includes the newly released article, 'Charting your Company's Future' (*Harvard Business Review* June, 2002), as well as the worldwide best-selling articles 'Knowing a Winning Business Idea When You See One' (*Harvard Business Review*, September–October, 2000), 'Creating New Market Space' (*Harvard Business Review*, January–February, 1999), 'Value Innovation: The Strategic Logic of High Growth' (*Harvard Business Review*, January–February, 1997) and 'Fair Process: Managing in the Knowledge Economy' (*Harvard Business Review*, July–August 1997).

Georgina Peters

Georgina Peters is senior editor at Suntop Media. Her work appears in business publications around the world including *Business Life* and *Silver Kris*, the Singapore Airlines in-flight magazine. She is a contributor to the *Financial Times Handbook of Management*.

Jonas Ridderstråle

Jonas Ridderstråle works as an assistant professor at the Centre for Advanced Studies in Leadership at the Stockholm School of Economics. Jonas has a doctorate and an MBA from the same school. His research focuses on new organizational models and leadership styles in the information age and has been published in leading academic journals, magazines and newspapers. Dr. Ridderstråle was recently recognized as Sweden's outstanding young academic of the year. He has also run the School's Advanced Management Program, a five-week top-management programme that attracts the elite of Scandinavian business leaders.

Jonas is at the forefront of the new generation of European-based business gurus. The Thinkers 50, the world's first ranking of management thinkers, ranked him number 17. He is an advisor, lecturer and consultant to a number of international corporations. His book *Funky Business: Talent makes capital dance* (co-authored with Kjell A. Nordström) is an international bestseller that has been translated into more than 25 languages.

Fons Trompenaars

Fons Trompenaars studied economics at the Free University of Amsterdam and later earned a PhD from Wharton School, University of Pennsylvania. He experienced cultural differences firsthand at home, where he grew up speaking both French and Dutch, and then later at work, with Shell in nine countries.

In 1989 he founded the Centre for International Business Studies, a consulting and training organization for international management. Since 1998 it has operated as Trompenaars Hampden-Turner.

Fons Trompenaars is the author of *Riding the Waves of Culture, Understanding Cultural Diversity in Business*, which has sold over 120,000 copies. He is co-author of *Seven Cultures of Capitalism, Building Cross-Cultural Competence* and *21 Leaders for the 21st Century* with Charles Hampden-Turner. His most recent book is *Did the Pedestrian Die?* published in 2002.

Bruce Tulgan

Bruce Tulgan is internationally recognized as the leading expert on young people in the workplace. He is an advisor to business leaders all over the world, the author of twelve different books and numerous management training programmes including *Winning The Talent Wars* (2001) and *Managing Generation X* (2000). He is also a sought-after keynote speaker and seminar leader. Bruce's writing has appeared in numerous periodicals, including the *Harvard Business Review, BusinessWeek*, the *New York Times*, the *Los Angeles Times*, and *USA Today*. His work has been the subject of more than 1000 news stories around the world.

Editorial

Research for the *Encyclopaedia* was carried out by Stephen Coomber. Melissa Master edited the manuscript.

A

Above the line

In marketing, 'above the line' is the term used to describe the promotion or advertising of a product or service through media such as television, radio, magazines and the press. This is promotion or advertising using the services of an agency – public relations, advertising, etc. – to which a fee or commission is paid. Contrast this with sales promotions, direct mail and similar marketing tactics, which are deemed '**below the line**'.

In the United Kingdom, above-the-line accounting was a term used to distinguish exceptional from extraordinary items. In corporate accounts, a line was drawn to separate out the figures that demonstrated how a profit (loss) was arrived at and those that demonstrated how that profit (loss) was distributed. Exceptional items, classified as occurring within the purposes of the business, were included above the line. Extraordinary items, those incurred outside the usual purposes of the business, were included below the line.

This led to creative accounting practices whereby profits on the sale of an item that perhaps should have fallen below the line were entered above the line, inflating profits and increasing the earnings per share. Similarly, losses that should, when considering the nature of the transaction, have been entered above the line found their way below the line as extraordinary items, thus flattering the profit figure. Financial Reporting Standard 3 'Reporting Financial Performance' (and its subsequent amendments), introduced in the United Kingdom in October 1992, changed all this. The effect of the new accounting standard was to outlaw extraordinary items, requiring that they be included in the earnings figure used to calculate earnings per share.

Key link

- www.asb.org.uk/technical/current.cfm – for current position on standard intended to supersede FRS 3.

Absenteeism

Defined as 'absence from work without a legitimate reason', absenteeism involves employees sporadically taking a few days off, usually citing ill health as the reason. The small number of days means they do not need a doctor's certificate to support their absence. Absenteeism can be expressed as the amount of deliberate absenteeism in proportion to the total number of employees. Many organizations have introduced policies to alleviate absenteeism, such as flexible working practices, job sharing and other efforts to improve job enrichment.

A number of theoretical models have been proposed as a means of explaining and examining absenteeism. These include the withdrawal model (the employee is absent in order to avoid an unpleasant situation in the workplace); the medical model (absence due to illness, which, while popularly cited by the absent individuals themselves, stands up less well to verification by independent means); and the deviance model (absence due to deviant or negative traits in the individual, such as unreliability or slacking).

Regardless of the real reasons for absenteeism, there is no question that it costs business a large amount of money each year. In the United Kingdom in 2000, for example, British employees averaged 7.8 days' absence from the workplace, equivalent to 192 million days in total, or 3.4 per cent of total working time. The estimated cost to British business was £10.7 billion.

Key text
- *Pulling together: 2001 absence and labour turnover survey*. CBI 2001

Accelerator

The accelerator theory of investment holds that investment spending is a function of consumer demand. As consumer demand increases, there is an excess demand for goods. A firm is thus faced with two choices: it can raise prices and attempt to throttle demand or meet increased demand by increasing supply. In accelerator theory, the latter is held more likely, as corporate spending on materials and plants increases to enable the firm to meet increased demand.

The term 'accelerator' is also used to describe a company that acts as a catalyst to boost another company's growth rate. Most commonly, but not exclusively, associated with the high-tech industry, as with **incubators**, accelerators are usually early-stage investors nurturing a start-up through the first months/years of its life. They facilitate access to the experience, funds and contacts necessary to speed up the growth process.

Key text
- Albert Aftalion. 'La Réalité des surproductions générales: Essai d'une théorie des crises générales et périodiques.' *Revue d'Economie Politique*, 1909
- Colin Barrow. *Incubators: A Realist's Guide to the World's New Business Accelerators*. John Wiley, 2001

Accountability

Accountability is the responsibility ascribed to an individual for a particular task or function. In a flat organizational structure, individuals have more autonomy and power, but with empowerment comes increased accountability. In hierarchical organizations, accountability is passed along the chain of management, resting with the **CEO**. However, when a company's actions are called into question, the theoretical chain of accountability to the top often proves less complete in practice, with those at the top claiming not to know what those at the bottom are doing on their behalf. Clear lines of accountability are important in providing the motivating factors, such as achievement, identified by American clinical psychologist **Frederick Herzberg** and developed in his two-factor theory.

Accrual

A standard method of accounting in which income or expenses are accounted for when they occur, regardless of whether cash has been received or parted with, or even whether there is supporting evidence such as a bill or invoice. This might occur, for example, when gas charges have been incurred but no bill has been received yet. In such a case, the expense credit would be entered into the accruals account and the debit into the gas expenses account. The accruals basis of accounting is to be contrasted with the cash basis, in which transactions are accounted for when cash is received or expended.

Key link
- www.nolo.com/lawcenter/ency/article.cfm/ objectID/08E205EE-E8B6–4D25- A2B01C3AC318E291

Acid test ratio

Also known as the quick asset or quick ratio, the

acid test ratio measures a company's liquidity. It is calculated by taking **current assets** (cash, accounts receivable, etc.), subtracting inventory and dividing by current liabilities.

Key link
- www.inc.com/finance_and_capital/advice/ 20662.html

Action learning

A simple yet powerful management concept introduced by British industrialist and academic **Reg Revans**. Influenced by the cooperative learning environment of Cambridge's Cavendish Laboratories, where he worked during the 1920s, Revans's theory of action learning suggests that managers learn best when they work on real issues in a group, rather than in the traditional classroom. His formula to explain action learning is L = P + Q: learning (L) occurs through a combination of programmed knowledge (P) and the ability to ask insightful questions (Q). Action learning is, essentially, based upon releasing and reinterpreting the accumulated experiences of people in the group. Originally implemented between organizations, today it is more likely to be implemented within an organization between teams or individuals. The benefits of action learning are supposed to be reducing the time between learning and implementation, reducing costs, increasing organizational commitment and delivering innovative solutions.

Key text
- Reginald Revans (foreword by David Botham, Mike Pedler). *ABC of Action Learning*. Lemos & Crane, 1998

Key link
- www.it.bton.ac.uk/staff/rng/teaching/IS307/ ALbookmarks.html – Action Learning Bookmarks.

Activity-based costing (ABC)

The concept of activity-based costing traces its roots back to Harvard Business School, and in particular to the work of HBS professor **Robert Kaplan,** inventor of the **balanced scorecard**. With ABC, direct and indirect costs are allocated to specific products or market segments. The company identifies core processes and analyses the costs at each stage of the process. It can then determine how much a specific activity – R&D for example – costs and what element of a product's total cost consists of R&D. In theory, the benefit of ABC is that it allows companies to understand and streamline cost structures. ABC was particularly popular during the mid-1980s. Yet by 1998, Robert Kaplan was quoted as saying, 'ABC has stagnated over the last five to seven years.' Why? Possibly because companies found the results fell short of their expectations. Supporters of the technique counter that many companies were not prepared to implement the costing method adequately.

Key texts
- R. Cooper and R.S. Kaplan. *Cost & Effect: Using Integrated Cost Systems to Drive Profitability and Performance*. Harvard Business School Press, 1998
- R. Cooper and R.S. Kaplan. *The Design of Cost Management Systems*. Prentice Hall, 1991

Key link
- www.offtech.com.au/abc/Activity_Based_ Costing.html – activity-based costing portal with helpful links, information, a magazine and forums, all devoted to ABC

Actuary

An actuary is an individual who specializes in forecasting outcomes, usually financial, using statistics and probability theory. These kinds of calculations frequently require complex mathematical modelling. Actuaries are commonly employed in industries in which financial risk and forecasting assume great importance, such as life insurance or pension fund management. Actuaries produce actuarial tables for underwriters and insurance brokers to use as quick risk reference guides for the calculation of, for example, life insurance premiums.

Key links
- www.actuary.com
- www.actuaries.org.uk

Adams, Scott

American cartoonist; creator of Dilbert empire (b. 1957)

Cartoonist and sometime corporate staffer Scott Adams is the creator of the eponymous Dilbert cartoon strip. Dilbert, with its wry take on the abject tedium of much of corporate life, is now syndicated to 2000 newspapers in more than 56 countries and has spawned a series of bestsellers.

Adams is a failed inventor with an MBA from the University of California at Berkeley ('I'm far more of the businessman who draws cartoons,' he says) who found much of his inspiration working as an engineer for Pacific Bell. (He also worked at Crocker National Bank and is a certified hypnotist.) It is amazing to think that he actually hung onto this job until 1995: 'I really didn't know until about 1994 that the cartooning was going to work. For the first several years it just limped along at fewer than 100 newspapers.'

Adams, now based in Danville, California, receives around 350 e-mails per day from readers, which give him much of his material. With Dilbert everywhere, Adams has signed a reputed $20 million contract for five more Dilbert books.

Not everyone is a fan. 'Dilbert is the bestselling business book of all time. It is cynical about management. Never has there been so much cynicism,' laments Gary Hamel. Such comments tend to overlook the fact that managers tend to be among the most cynical people on the planet.

But Adams serves up a lot more than comic jabs at corporate jaws. He's got a track record of creating success in a variety of diverse businesses. His first book, *The Dilbert Principle*, became a number-one *New York Times* bestseller and one of the top-selling business books of all time.

Adams created the first advertiser-supported comic Web site, managed by United Media, and one of the first Web sites to become profitable. Other cartoonists have since followed suit. He became one of the most popular and highly compensated public speakers in America. Before phasing out his public speaking business to focus on other ventures, he was getting five to ten speaking requests each day, primarily from word-of-mouth referrals. Dilbert has also spawned a vast character-licensing business.

Capitalizing on his global fame, Adams created Scott Adams Foods to create and market convenient, tasty food containing 100% of the daily values of vitamins and minerals. The Dilberito – a frozen vegetarian burrito product – is in 2000 food stores and growing. Adams and a business partner also own Stacey's Cafe, which has rapidly become one of the most popular eateries in the Pleasanton, California, area.

Key links
- http://my.linkbaton.com/bibliography/ adams/scott – for a listing of 86 titles by Scott Adams
- www.dilbert.com
- www.dilberito.com
- www.staceyscafe.com

Adding value

An essential element of the **brand**ing process, adding value aims to increase the perceived value of a good or service in the eyes of the consumer. Ideally, it should lead to product differentiation. A company may increase the value of a product through its presentation and packaging, or by providing an after-sales service, for example. In the case where a consumer knows very little about a product or service, a company's reputation or image alone may be sufficient to confer added value. Added value may cost the company providing the product or service little but is often enough to confer a competitive advantage in a crowded market.

Adhocracy

The opposite of a bureaucracy, an adhocracy is an organization that disregards the classical principles of management, in which each member of the organization has a clearly defined and permanent role. Instead, it advocates a more fluid organization, in which individuals are free to deploy their talents as required. The opposite of traditional big-business organizational structures, an adhocracy is a highly organic organizational design, representing the idea of an open, flexible, creative and spontaneous business. It has similar characteristics to horizontal or flat organizations, in which teams of knowledge workers work largely under their own initiative and direction.

The term was possibly coined by American leadership expert **Warren Bennis** in the 1960s; he described the formation of ad hoc project teams that are 'adaptive, problem-solving, temporary systems of diverse specialists linked together … in an organic flux'. Creation of the concept has also been attributed to American futurist **Alvin Toffler** in the 1970s.

The concept of adhocracy was popularized by US management guru Robert Waterman, who defines adhocracy as 'any form of organization that cuts across normal bureaucratic lines to capture opportunities, solve problems, and gets results'. US academic **Henry Mintzberg** cites adhocracy as one of his four forms of organizational structure, further distinguishing between adhocracies by how they relate to administrative and operating structures within the organization. Operating adhocracies, according to Mintzberg, work on behalf of their clients, e.g. an advertising agency. Administrative adhocracies, however, serve themselves.

Key text
- Robert H. Waterman. *Adhocracy: The Power to Change*. W.W. Norton, 1993

ADSL (asymmetric digital subscriber line)

ADSL is a technology that allows faster data transfer rates to be squeezed from existing copper telephone wire. Transfer rates of up to 9 Mbps (megabytes per second) are possible when receiving data – the downstream rate – and up to 640 kbps when sending data – the upstream rate. This is fast enough to provide high-quality Internet provision, video on demand and other high bandwidth services.

A special ADSL modem is required. Although the technology promises to fundamentally improve the Internet browsing experience of 56k modem users, its rollout, in the United Kingdom at least, has been slow, partly due to pricing issues.

Key link
- www.redherring.com/mag/issue66/news-explain.html

Advertising elasticity

Advertising elasticity is the percentage change in quantity demanded as a result of a 1 percent change in advertising expenditure. It demonstrates the relationship between spending on advertising and demand. A product is said to be 'advertising elastic' if a small increase in advertising spending on a product results in a large increase in demand for that product.

Advertising Standards Authority (ASA)

In the United Kingdom, the advertising industry is self-regulated. The UK-based organization that administers and enforces the Code of Advertising Practice is the Advertising Standards Authority (ASA), founded in 1962. The first edition of the Advertising Code was published in 1961 in an effort to prevent legislation being applied to advertising in the same way that the Broadcasting Act of 1955 legislated for television. The Sales Promotion Code was added in 1974 and in 1995 the two Codes were merged into one comprehensive set of rules for advertisements and sales promotions.

The basic principles of the Codes are that advertisements should be legal, decent, honest and truthful; prepared with a sense of responsibility to consumers and to society; and in line with the principles of fair competition generally accepted in business.

The ASA regulates all advertisements and promotions in non-broadcast media (broadcast advertisements are covered by the Independent Television Commission). These include press – (newspapers and magazines, including free newspapers); outdoor (posters, transport placards and aerial announcements); direct marketing (direct mail, leaflets and brochures); cinema commercials; sales promotions; Internet (advertisements in paid-for space); and other electronic media, including advertisements on computer games, videos and CD-ROMs.

The ASA receives its funding, some £4 million for the year 2002, from the advertising industry through a small levy on display-advertising and direct-mail expenditure. To protect its independence from the advertising industry, this income is collected via a separate body, the Advertising Standards Board of Finance.

The ASA's potential sanctions include the refusal of further advertising space, adverse publicity for the offender and the threat of legal proceedings via the Office of Fair Trading. Because of the close relationship between the ASA and the advertising industry, there has been some criticism that the ASA lacks teeth and does not provide sufficient deterrent to advertisers who contravene the Code.

Key link

- www.asa.org.uk

Advertising

Communication through the media between an organization and its target audience or the public at large. Although some aspects of advertising will be dealt with in-house, the advertising of a company's products, services, or corporate brand is usually handled by a specialized advertising agency.

Advertising can be divided into two broad categories: informative advertising and persuasive advertising. Advertising can also be broken down into the message delivered and the medium carrying the message.

The execution of an advertising strategy during a specified period of time is known as an advertising campaign. An ad campaign will consist of several distinct phases, including identifying and analysing the advertising target, defining the objectives of the campaign, determining the total amount of money to be allocated to the campaign, creating the advertising message, developing a media plan and executing the campaign. They may encompass many different media, from television to specialist print.

The history of advertising dates back to Roman times and beyond. One of the earliest methods of advertising was signage, usually painted on buildings. Examples of this type of advertising have been unearthed in excavations at Pompeii – a sign advertising an inn in another town painted on a wall, for example.

With the invention of the printing press with Johannes Gutenberg in 1445, advertising began to reach a wider audience, with printed ads soon replacing the 'town criers' employed to shout out the virtues of various products. Mass communication in the United States, with the completion of the transnational railroad and the invention of the telegraph, spurred on the development of advertising so that specialized agencies sprang up focusing solely on the creation of advertising, a function that had until then remained in-house.

Finally, with the help of great advertising pioneers such as James Walter Thompson, Raymond

Rubicam and David Ogilvy, advertising grew into the sophisticated industry it is today.

The effectiveness of advertising is notoriously difficult to quantify. As Frank Woolworth once said, 'I know that half of my advertising budget is wasted. The problem is that I don't know which half.' Marketing departments, which often take responsibility for a company's advertising budget, will usually attempt to gauge the success of product or service advertising through market research.

Key texts

- Juliann Sivulka. *Soap, Sex, and Cigarettes: A Cultural History of American Advertising.* Wadsworth Pub Co, 1997
- Philippe Lorin. *5 Giants Of Advertising.* Assouline, 2001

Affiliate marketing

Affiliate marketing is one of the earliest marketing models used on the Internet, championed by companies such as Amazon.com. The affiliate is a company that is connected to, or associated with, another company that has agreed to carry the affiliate's advertising, particularly on a Web site, in exchange for a fee.

The affiliate model works like this. An e-tailer sets up a Web site, selling Indian furniture for example, then contacts another Web site, such as an interior design portal or a furniture e-store, that prospective furniture purchasers are likely to visit. The e-tailer then persuades the other Web site to carry its own advertising banner on its Web site. In return, the affiliate receives a reward for displaying the banner. This reward could be linked to the number of surfers clicking through the banner ad, or to the number of leads produced. Alternatively, it may be linked to actual sales made, in the form of a paid commission. Through affiliate marketing, a company can build an extensive advertising network in prime positions for no upfront costs. In turn, the affiliate gets money for nothing other than giving over an unused space on its site to an advertising banner.

Setting up an affiliate marketing programme can be difficult for companies without significant marketing resources. Therefore a number of companies offer to manage, to a lesser or greater extent, affiliate programmes on behalf of companies who cannot or do not wish to set up their own. These companies (including BeFree, LinkShare and Click Trade) plug a would-be affiliate marketer straight into their affiliate network, numbering anywhere between 50,000 and 250,000 companies, and make their money, in the main, by charging commissions on affiliate earnings.

Key links

- www.clickz.com/aff_mkt/aff_mkt/
- www.i-revenue.net/

Affirmative action

Consisting of policies aimed at increasing the numbers of people from certain social groups in employment, education, business, government and other areas, affirmative action has its origins in the United States. It supports segments of the population that are discriminated against, such as women, African Americans, Asian Americans, Hispanic Americans, American Indians, disabled people and Vietnam veterans.

The roots of affirmative action lie in the civil rights programmes enacted during the late 1800s to help African Americans attain full US citizenship. The US Constitution outlawed slavery with the Thirteenth Amendment; the Fourteenth Amendment guaranteed equal protection under the law; and the Fifteenth Amendment prohibited racial discrimination in access to voting. The Civil Rights Act of 1866 guaranteed every citizen 'the same right to make and enforce contracts … as is enjoyed by white citizens'. The resulting situation, however, was not one of homogenous equality, but segregation and separation, as Southern states adopted so-called Jim Crow laws, such as this one from Mississippi: 'Separate free schools shall be established for the education of children of African descent; and it shall be unlawful for any coloured child to attend any white school, or any white child to attend a coloured school.'

Black trade union leader A. Philip Randolph made some inroads into apartheid in the 1940s. In 1941, as a result of his lobbying, President Franklin D. Roosevelt signed Executive Order 8802 outlawing segregationist hiring policies by defence-related industries that held federal contracts.

It was the Civil Rights Act of 1964 that kick-started the move to affirmative action. Title VI declared, 'No person in the United States shall, on the ground of race, colour, or national origin, be excluded from participation in, be denied the benefits of, or be subjected to discrimination under any program or activity receiving federal financial assistance.'

The phrase 'affirmative action' was first used in Executive Order 11246, implemented during President Lyndon Johnson's term in 1965. Federal contractors were required to 'take affirmative action to ensure that applicants are employed, and that employees are treated during employment, without regard to their race, creed, colour, or national origin'. This was extended to include women in 1967.

During the administration of President Richard Nixon, the wording was broadened to require all federal contractors to develop 'an acceptable affirmative action program', including 'an analysis of areas within which the contractor is deficient in the utilization of minority groups and women, and further, goals and timetables to which the contractor's good faith efforts must be directed to correct the deficiencies'. 'Minority groups' was to refer to 'Negroes, American Indians, Orientals, and Spanish Surnamed Americans'. 'Underutilization' meant 'having fewer minorities or women in a particular job classification than would reasonably be expected by their availability'.

Critics of affirmative action argue that some groups benefit unjustly from affirmative action as a result of their political influence. They argue that it leads to 'reverse discrimination and unwarranted preferences' although in reality only a small percentage of cases before the Equal Employment Opportunities Commission are for reverse discrimination.

In 1995, the United States Supreme Court ruled that a federal programme requiring preference based on a person's race is unconstitutional unless the preference is designed to make up for specific instances of past discrimination. This meant that affirmative action could no longer be used to counteract racial discrimination by society as a whole, but must be aimed at eliminating specific problems. In 1989, the court had made a similar decision regarding state and local programmes, which leaves affirmative action in a state of flux.

Key text

- Gertrude Ezorsky. *Racism and Justice: The Case for Affirmative Action.* Cornell University Press, 1991

Key link

- www.affirmativeaction.org

After-sales service

A means of providing added value to a transaction, after-sales service is the service provided to a consumer following the conclusion of a transaction. After-sales service, which includes service such as technical helplines in the case of technology products, or repairs and servicing in the case of new vehicles, or free fitting check-ups after buying a pair of glasses, is of particular importance in highly competitive markets.

Ageism

In broad terms, ageism can be defined as any attitude, action, or institutional structure that subordinates a person or group because of age or any assignment of roles in society purely on the basis of age. With reference to age and employment, discriminating against job applicants on the grounds of age has been legislated against in the United States.

The Age Discrimination in Employment Act of 1967 (ADEA) provides that:

'It shall be unlawful for an employer:

(1) to fail or refuse to hire or to discharge any individual or otherwise discriminate against any individual with respect to his compensation, terms, conditions, or privileges of employment, because of such individual's age;

(2) to limit, segregate, or classify his employees in any way which would deprive or tend to deprive any individual of employment opportunities or otherwise adversely affect his status as an employee, because of such individual's age; or

(3) to reduce the wage rate of any employee in order to comply with this chapter.'

Under the ADEA, it is unlawful to discriminate against a person due to age with respect to any term, condition, or privilege of employment, including, but not limited to benefits, compensation, firing, hiring, job assignments, layoff, promotion and training. The act applies to employers with 20 or more employees and to employment agencies and to labour organizations, as well as to the federal government.

In the United Kingdom, however, there is no similar legislation and none is planned until 2006, when the UK government will have to introduce law to comply with a European directive. As is often the way in the United Kingdom, the government at the time chose to introduce a voluntary code of practice rather than legislating against ageism. The code of practice, drawn up in consultation with the Confederation of British Industry, the Trades Unions Congress and Age Concern, urges companies, among other things, not to use age limits or phrases such as 'young graduates' in job advertisements and to promote staff on merit regardless of age. Unfortunately, two years after the voluntary code was introduced in 1998, the government's evaluation of the Voluntary Code of Practice on Age Diversity suggested it was having little impact.

Key text
- Todd D. Nelson. *Ageism: Stereotyping and Prejudice against Older Persons.* The MIT Press, 2002

Agency

An arrangement where one party, the agent, is authorized to, or implied to, act on behalf of another, the principal, in dealings with third parties. When it comes to responsibility in law, the principal is deemed to 'stand in the shoes' of the agent, and is therefore bound by the actions of the agent, providing that the agent is acting within their authority. The law of agency is based on the Latin maxim *Qui facit per alium, facit per se* or 'He who acts through another is deemed in law to do it himself'. Typical examples of an agency relationship include estate agents and lawyers granted power of attorney.

Key text
- R.J.C. Munday. *Outline of the Law of Agency.* Butterworths, 1998

Agility

Agility, as defined by internationally recognized American competitiveness expert Dr Roger N. Nagel, is the ability of a company to operate profitably in a competitive environment of continually and unpredictably changing customer opportunities. The concept stems from the work done by experts such as Rick Dove, Steven L. Goldman, Roger N. Nagel and Kenneth Preiss at the Iacocca Institute of Lehigh University in Bethlehem, Pennsylvania. It was first expressed in academic papers, such as *21st Century Manufacturing Enterprise Strategy*, which was written by Dove and Nagel in 1991 and examined the competitiveness of US manufacturing.

In the 1995 book *Agile Competitors and Virtual Organizations*, Nagel and co-authors Steven Goldman and Kenneth Preiss present agile competition as a system with four strategic dimensions: organizing to manage change and uncertainty; leveraging the impact of people and information; cooperating to enhance competitiveness; and enriching the customer. The concept of the agile company recognizes that speed of response to market opportunities and threats, plus flexibility, are what separate many successful companies from their competitors.

Key text
- Steven L. Goldman, Roger N. Nagel and Kenneth Preiss (contributor). *Agile Competitors and Virtual Organizations*. Van Nostrand Reinhold, 1995

AIDA (awareness, interest, desire, action)

AIDA is one of the most enduring and successful marketing models, designed to help marketers understand the wants and needs of consumers and provide an insight into their decision-making process. The concept's origins lie in the work of pioneering psychologists such as Walter Dill Scott, who developed the 'attention-comprehension-understanding' model in 1913 at Northwestern University. By the 1950s, this model had evolved into AIDA.

AIDA predicts that before consumers make a purchase decision, they go through four stages, all of which need to be addressed for an advertising campaign to be effective. The consumer needs to be aware that the product exists and know what it is/does; the consumer's interest in the product needs to be stimulated; once stimulated, that interest must be transformed into desire; and finally, that desire must result in the action of purchasing.

Key text
- Walter Dill Scott. *Influencing Men in Business*. The Ronald Press, 1911

AIM (alternative investment market)

Created in 1995, the alternative investment market is a UK securities market specially tailored to suit growing businesses – companies that cannot, or do not wish to, obtain a full listing on the **London Stock Exchange**. Companies listed on AIM tend to be smaller and higher-risk than their LSE counterparts. The companies trading on AIM in April 2001, for example, had a total market capitalization of £11.1 billion, with individual market capitalizations ranging from less than £2 million to more than £100 million. Because of the size and nature of many of the businesses on AIM, there is less liquidity in the market than in the LSE and, as a result, shares tend to be more volatile.

Key link
- www.londonstockexchange.com/aim/default.asp

Allen, Paul

American entrepreneur; co-founder of Microsoft (b. 1953)

Paul Allen attended Lakeside School, a school for gifted children in Seattle, with fellow computer enthusiast Bill Gates. After Lakeside, Allen went on to work as a programmer at Honeywell in Boston. It was during his time at Honeywell that he noticed an ad for a microcomputer kit in an issue of *Popular Electronics*. He contacted Bill Gates and persuaded him to join forces to develop software for the microcomputer, and Microsoft was born. As more powerful processors emerged, PC manufacturers looked to Microsoft to supply with them with software applications that turned the computer from an enthusiast's hobby to a commercial tool. At Microsoft, Allen was head of research and worked on products like MS-DOS, Windows and the Microsoft Mouse.

In 1983, a serious illness caused Allen to take stock of his life, and he left Microsoft to follow other interests. Today, Allen's activities are both commercial – he invests in a wide variety of independent companies, many technology-based – as well as philanthropic. He is also a keen musician. Allen remains Microsoft's second-largest stockholder and retains a position on the board of directors.

Allen is also one of the richest men on the planet – actually, the third-richest according to *Forbes*. When he left Microsoft, it had 476 employees and revenues of $50 million. His stock in the company is now estimated to be worth some $22 billion.

Allen could have elected to take it easy and count his money. Instead, he has given more than $100 million to worthy causes and has dabbled – in a fairly serious financial sort of way, it must be said – in a number of companies through the Paul Allen Group, which he founded. He clearly believes that money is there to be used.

Upside magazine has labelled him 'high-tech's fairy godmother'. This title has been earned through a stream of high-profile and huge investments in high-tech companies since Allen collected his Microsoft golden egg. During 1998, he spent $2.8 billion on Marcus Cable and $4.5 billion on Charter Communications.

Key link

- www.paulallen.com

Andreessen, Marc

American entrepreneur; founder of Netscape and Loudcloud (b. 1971)

Today the Internet is so pervasive that it's hard to believe that pre-1993 it was relatively inaccessible to the majority of ordinary computer users, let alone the unwired masses. Two key events changed that: the creation of the **World Wide Web** by **Tim Berners-Lee** and the development of the Mosaic point-and-click graphical browser, invented by a team of students led by Marc Andreessen. The new Mosaic software made the World Wide Web accessible to anyone with a computer and a telephone line.

Andreessen was born in Cedar Falls, Iowa, in 1971 and was brought up in the small village of New Lisbon, Wisconsin, in the heart of the Mid-

west. At the age of 8, he taught himself computer programming. At the age of twelve, his talent blossomed when his parents bought him a computer to keep him busy while he was recuperating from an operation. Computer programming helped make rural life more exciting and allowed Andreessen to express himself creatively. While at the University of Illinois, he got a computer programming job at the National Center for Supercomputing Applications (NCSA), a university-affiliated, federally funded research centre.

Andreessen created 'Mosaic X' while working at NCSA. Frustrated at his inability to develop his software commercially from within the NCSA, he left, and in 1994 founded Netscape with the help of entrepreneur **James Clark**. At Netscape, Andreessen worked on a new browser called Navigator. It was rushed out before the rival Mosaic browser – by this time licensed to a company called Spyglass – could gain a dominant market share. To help boost Netscape's chances of succeeding, Andreessen and Clark adopted a radical business model. The plan was to give the browser away as a loss leader – the profits would come from selling server software to work with Navigator. The strategy worked. The Netscape Navigator was a huge success.

Just as Bill Gates and Steve Jobs became icons for a generation of entrepreneurs, so Marc Andreessen has become a role model for a new generation. With his Internet browser, the tall whizz-kid from Wisconsin democratized the Internet, which had previously been the province of fusty academics and geeks. The Mosaic browser and Netscape Navigator opened a door onto cyberspace. This process was accelerated by the radical business plan that Andreessen implemented at Netscape.

When Netscape was floated on Wall Street in August 1995, the stock price rocketed. Virtually overnight, Andreessen was worth some $171 million. But Netscape's virtual monopoly in the browser market was to be short-lived. It soon dawned on others, including Microsoft CEO Bill Gates, that the browser could hold the key to the next generation of computing. Microsoft took the shortest route to market, sourcing its own browser from Spyglass, the company that had licensed the Mosaic browser. What followed was a period known as 'the Browser Wars', in which Microsoft's Internet Explorer battled it out with Netscape's Navigator/Communicator browser. By mid-1998, Netscape's revenues had risen to $534 million, but its share of the browser market had slumped from 80 percent to some 60 percent.

After a bruising battle with Microsoft, Netscape finally threw in the towel and in 1998 was swallowed up by America Online for $4.2 billion. Andreessen lasted six months at AOL as chief technology officer before leaving to found another Internet start-up, Loudcloud, with fellow Netscapee Ben Horowitz. Loudcloud provides mission-critical hosting services to companies such as Ford and Nike.

With Loudcloud, Andreessen produced something of an errant child. The Sunnyvale, California-based company had an uninspiring **IPO** in March 2001, followed a few weeks later by layoffs of over 15 percent of its staff. As the United States enters into a full-blown recession, Andreessen will need all his entrepreneurial experience and skill to keep the company going. If he can make a success of Loudcloud, then his reputation as one of the great entrepreneurs of his generation will be secure. Even if he does not, he will be remembered as the man whose Web browser helped make the Internet the medium it is today.

Key texts
- Jim Clark and Owen Edwards. *Netscape Time: The Making of the Billion-Dollar Start-Up That Took on Microsoft.* Saint Martin's Press, 1999
- Daniel Ehrenhafte. *Marc Andreessen: Web Warrior.* Twenty-First Century Books, 2001

Key link
- www.loudcloud.com

Angel investor

Angel investors are wealthy private individuals who invest in start-up companies, usually during the early stages of financing. Angels invest for a variety of reasons, the primary one being financial. For an angel to invest, there must be sufficient prospects for growth, plus an exit strategy. In return for his investment, the angel will receive an equity stake, usually a minority stake (less than 50 percent), in the company. Although attracted by above-average rates of return on capital, angels are often actively interested in the type of businesses they invest in and are often willing to participate in a non-executive director capacity.

It is estimated that in the United States, one-seventh of the approximately 300,000 start-up or early-growth companies receive funding from angel investors. A profile of angel investors involved with the Texas Capital Network revealed the following details: angel investors are typically well educated; prefer to invest within one day of travel; like to be involved in the venture; tend to invest in a group; are not in a rush to reap their returns; make investments in the $10,000–$500,000 range; make an average investment of between $50,000 and $500,000; and make one investment every two years. One advantage of dealing with angels is speed. Angels will usually make investment decisions more quickly than **venture capitalists.** Often entrepreneurs use angels to raise **seed capital**, leaving venture capitalists for later-stage financing.

Key links
- www.angelinvestors.org
- www.nationalbusangels.com
- www.bhpcapital.com/treasury.html
- www.bvca.co.uk

Annual report

The annual report must be produced each year by private and public limited companies. Usually, reports will contain common elements such as details about the company's activities over the previous year (the director's or chairman's report), financial highlights, details of directors and officers, and financial accounts – at least a profit-and-loss account and a balance sheet.

As well as the full annual report, there is usually a cut-down version containing the salient financial details. A copy of the annual report must be distributed to shareholders. In addition, a public limited company must allow anyone to inspect its annual report.

Key link

- www.onlineannualreports.com/how_to_read_an_ar.html

Annuity

An annuity is a contract, usually with an insurance company, under which the recipient of the annuity receives payments on a regular basis for the rest of his life or for another specified period of time. The annuity is often purchased with the proceeds from a pension fund. The amount of income paid depends on the annuity rates at the time that the annuity is purchased, which in turn depends on factors such as prevailing interest rates. The annuity may be deferred so that the recipient need not convert the lump sum into an annuity immediately upon retirement, waiting instead for the most favourable market conditions. The company paying the annuity retains the lump sum after the person purchasing the annuity has died. In return, it provides a fixed and regular payment for the duration of the purchaser's life.

Ansoff, Igor

American educator (b. 1918)

Igor Ansoff was one of the key figures in the formulation of a clear concept of strategic management. He was born in Vladivostok in 1918, a year after the Russian Revolution, the son of an American father and a Russian mother. In 1936, the Ansoff family moved to New York. Ansoff trained as an engineer and mathematician; he worked for the RAND Corporation and then the Lockheed Corporation, where he was a vice-president.

In 1963, he left industry for academia, joining Carnegie Mellon's Graduate School of Business Administration. He joined the San Diego-based US International University in 1983, where he became Distinguished Professor of Strategic Management.

Ansoff's first – and most important – book was *Corporate Strategy*, in which he sought to make sense of the broader implications of what he had learned at Lockheed. Ansoff believed that there was 'a practical method for strategic decision making within a business firm' that could be made accessible to all.

Ansoff's work struck a chord. Until then, strategic planning was a barely understood, ad hoc concept. It was practised, while the theory lay largely unexplored.

The result of Ansoff's research was a rational model by which strategic and planning decisions could be made. The model concentrated on corporate expansion and diversification rather than strategic planning as a whole. From this emerged the Ansoff Model of Strategic Planning, an intricate and somewhat daunting sequence of decisions.

Central to this was the reassuringly simple concept of gap analysis: see where you are; identify where you wish to be; and identify tasks that will take you there. Ansoff can also lay claim to introducing the word 'synergy' into the management vocabulary. He explained it with uncharacteristic brevity as '2 + 2 = 5.' In addition, Ansoff examined 'corporate advantage' long before Michael Porter cornered the field 20 years later.

To the contemporary observer, Ansoff's work can appear excessively analytical and highly prescriptive. In an era in which corporate change is increasingly recognized as a fact of life, thinkers argue that solutions are ever more elusive. Ansoff's model was better suited to a world of answers than one beset by turbulence and uncertainty.

Key texts

- Igor Ansoff. *Corporate Strategy*. McGraw Hill, 1965

- Igor Ansoff. *Strategic Management.* Macmillan, 1979
- Igor Ansoff. *Implanting Strategic Management.* Prentice Hall, 1984

Key link
- www.cspp.edu/usicb/ansoff.htm

Ansoff matrix

Developed by the Russian-born, US-based 'father of strategy' **Igor Ansoff**, the Ansoff matrix is a tool for assessing the risks of strategic options. The matrix demonstrates the relationship between new and existing products and new and existing markets. Divided into four quadrants, the matrix shows existing and then new products along the horizontal axis, and existing and then new markets along the vertical axis. Risk increases along the x=y line. Thus a strategy that involves introducing a new product into a new market carries the highest risk, and an existing product in an existing market has the least risk.

Anti-dilution clause

When financing a new venture, it is common practice for investors to reserve the right to make further investments in future financing stages. To protect an investor's equity from being diluted in further financing rounds, an anti-dilution clause may be inserted into the financing agreement, protecting his stake at the expense of the other shareholders.

This is because in the event of the company raising more funding, the investor who has the benefit of the anti-dilution clause will keep the same proportion of equity without making a proportionately larger investment. If an investor starts with 60 percent of the equity and another funding round takes place, he will still have 60 percent of the equity after that funding round. The people who suffer are the other unprotected investors – often the founders.

Anti-virus program

An anti-virus program is a software program designed to detect, eradicate and/or neutralize computer viruses. Programs that detect computer viruses are called scanning software; those that eliminate viruses are called disinfecting software. Anti-virus programs can be general catch-all programs or programs designed to catch viruses delivered by a particular method, such as e-mail. They must be regularly updated with new signature files that enable the software to recognize the latest viruses; otherwise they will be vulnerable to attack. Updating can usually be done over the Internet.

Symantec and McAfee are two of the biggest names in anti-virus software, while the NCSA (National Computer Security Association) is an organization that tests different anti-virus programs. It certifies them if the programs successfully identify all of the 'in-the-wild' viruses and 90 percent or more of a 6000-virus sample.

Key links
- www.symantec.com
- www.mcafee.com
- www.ncsa.com

Applet

An applet is a small software program, usually written in the **Java** programming language (or ActiveX), that can be incorporated into an **HTML** page, in a similar manner to the way images are included. When the viewer uses an appropriate technology-enabled browser to view a page containing an applet, the applet's code is transferred to his system and executed by the browser's Java Virtual Machine (JVM). Examples of applets include animations, such as a moving ticker tape of stock prices. Companies will often prevent applets from being downloaded through the firewall. This is because, as software programs, they present a potential malicious threat.

Appraisal

An employee's performance review, usually conducted as a one-to-one interview with an immediate superior. Appraisals are usually held at regular intervals annually, or more frequently, and are linked to pay where a company operates a performance-related pay policy. Predetermined subjects such as timekeeping, time off for ill health and task completion are likely to be discussed. Appraisal meetings will also cover training needs, career progression and the ambitions of the appraisee.

Types of appraisal include the 360-degree performance review, in which opinions of an individual's performance are taken from a multitude of sources, including immediate managers, colleagues, subordinates and even customers and suppliers; the ranking in which review managers are required to rank their subordinates – also know as 'rank-and-yank' and famously used at General Electric; and the very rare 'bottom-up' approach, in which the employee conducts his own research, identifies his own training needs, conducts his own round of performance interviews with whomever he thinks appropriate, and presents his report to his boss.

Key text
- Walter W. Tornow (ed). *Maximizing the Value of 360-Degree Feedback: A Process for Successful Individual and Organizational Development* (Jossey-Bass Management Series). Jossey-Bass, 1998

Arbitrage

Arbitrage is the exploitation of a difference in value between two markets to make a profit. An arbitrageur – the person carrying out the arbitrage – may, for example, benefit from the minute difference between a stock price and the futures contract for that stock. Or he might exploit a marginal difference between a quoted price for sterling in two countries by buying sterling in the cheaper country, selling it in the more costly country and pocketing the difference. The risk is minimal, as all costs are known and, providing the transaction costs do not exceed the difference between the currencies, a profit is guaranteed. The only slight risk is that the price could move against the arbitrageur during the time it takes to do the deal. Arbitrage helps keep worldwide values of a commodity or currency at similar values.

Arbitrage is also used to describe the speculative purchase of a large number of shares in a corporation, with the buyer hoping to profit from an anticipated merger or takeover.

Argyris, Chris
American educator (b. 1923)

Chris Argyris is a long-time researcher into learning and the failure to learn in organizations. He is a formidable thinker even by the lofty standards of his employer, Harvard Business School.

Argyris was brought up in New York's suburbs and spent some time in Greece with his grandparents. Prior to joining Harvard, he was a professor of administrative science at Yale. His qualifications embrace psychology, economics and organizational behaviour.

Argyris's early work concentrated on the then-innovative field of behavioural science. Indeed, his 1957 book, *Personality and Organization*, has become one of the subject's classic texts. Argyris argued that organizations depend fundamentally on people and that personal development is and can be related to work. The problem, Argyris believed, in many organizations is that the organization itself stands in the way of people fulfilling their potential.

Central to his work has been the entire concept of learning. Argyris has examined learning processes, both in individual and corporate terms, in huge depth. His most influential work was carried out with Donald Schön in their 1974 book, *Theory in Practice*, and their 1978 book, *Organizational Learning*.

Argyris and Schön originated two basic organizational models. In Model 1, managers concentrate on establishing individual goals. They keep to themselves and don't voice concerns or disagreements. Model 1 managers are prepared to inflict change on others, but resist any attempt to change their own thinking and working practices. Model 1 organizations are characterized by what Argyris and Schön labelled '**single-loop learning**,' in which 'the detection and correction of organizational error permits the organization to carry on its present policies and achieve its current objectives.'

In contrast, Model 2 organizations emphasize '**double-loop learning**,' in which 'organizational error is detected and corrected in ways that involve the modification of underlying norms, policies, and objectives.' In Model 2 organizations, managers act on information. They debate issues, respond to change and are prepared to change. A virtuous circle emerges of learning and understanding. 'Most organizations do quite well in single-loop learning but have great difficulties in double-loop learning,' concluded Argyris and Schön.

Corporate fashions have moved Argyris's way. With the return of learning to the corporate agenda in the early 1990s, his work became slightly more fashionable.

Key texts

- Chris Argyris. *Personality and Organization.* Harper & Row, 1957
- Chris Argyris. *Understanding Organizational Behavior.* Dorsey Press, 1960
- Chris Argyris. *Overcoming Organizational Defences.* Allyn & Bacon, 1990
- Chris Argyris (with Donald Schön). *Organizational Learning: A Theory of Action Perspective.* Addison-Wesley, 1978
- Chris Argyris. *On Organizational Learning.* Blackwell, 1993
- Chris Argyris. *Knowledge for Action.* Jossey-Bass, 1993

Key link

- www.actionscience.com/argbib.htm – Chris Argyris, bibliography of works

Arm's length

Some commercial transactions are required to be conducted at arm's length. This is to ensure that the parties entering the transaction are acting in their own best interests, are financially unconnected to one another and are unable to exert undue influence or control over one another.

Thus a transaction between two divisions of the same company would not be at arm's length, and neither would a transaction between members of the same family. In the case of related parties, such as companies within the same group, there is a provision in UK accounting practice for the parties to disclose their relationship, partly to give notice to third parties who may wish to scrutinize the deal to ensure it was conducted at arm's length.

Arthur, W. Brian
American economist (b. 1945)

Economist W. Brian Arthur is based at the Santa Fe Institute, where he is Citibank Professor. He has an MA in mathematics from the University of Michigan (1969) and a PhD in operations research from the University of California at Berkeley (1973). He was later Dean and Virginia Morrison Professor of Population Studies and Economics at Stanford and Professor of Biology at Stanford (1983–96).

Given his multiskilled CV, it is perhaps just as well that Arthur now refers to himself as an 'applied mathematician'. Arthur's central gripe about economics as a discipline is that it has become distanced from reality. 'I would like to see economics become more of a science, and more of a science means that it concerns itself more with reality,' he says. 'We're facing a danger that economics is rigorous deduction based upon faulty assumptions.'

This is of concern, says Arthur, because we are moving to a 'technically based economy' in which the rules of economics are being challenged and changed. Understanding of the new commercial realities requires radical new insights from radical new economists.

Underpinning Arthur's arguments is a move away from solutions and foolproof models to questions and frameworks. 'Economics has always taken a shortcut and said, assume there is a problem and assume that we can arrive at a solution. Now, I would say, assume there's a situation, how do players cognitively deal with it? In other words, what frameworks do they wheel up to understand the situation?' Making sense of the situation is the critical first step. Assuming there is an economic model that will spit out a solution is a sure route to diminishing returns.

Key text
- Brian Arthur, Steven Durlauf and David Lane (eds). *The Economy as an Evolving Complex System II, 1997; Increasing Returns and Path Dependence in the Economy*. University of Michigan Press, 1994

Key link
- www.santafe.edu/%7Ewba

ASB (Accounting Standards Board)

Established in 1990 following a review by the Consultative Committee of Accountancy Bodies (CCAB), the ASB issues the guidelines for accounting standards – financial reporting standards (FRSs) – in the United Kingdom. The ASB took over the task of setting accounting standards from the Accounting Standards Committee (ASC; 1976–1990).

Accounting standards apply to all companies that prepare accounts intended to provide a true and fair view of the company's underlying financial situation. They are first issued as Financial Reporting Exposure Drafts (FREDs) for consulta-tion and include the Financial Reporting Standard for Smaller Entities (FRSSE).

Key links
- www.asb.org.uk – the Accounting Standards Board
- www.frc.org.uk – the Financial Reporting Council

ASEAN (Association of South East Asian Nations)

The Association of South East Asian Nations is a regional alliance formed in Bangkok in 1967; it took over the non-military role of the Southeast Asia Treaty Organization in 1975. Its members are Indonesia, Malaysia, the Philippines, Singapore, Thailand, (from 1984) Brunei, (from 1995) Vietnam, (from 1997) Laos and Myanmar, and (from 1999) Cambodia; its headquarters are in Jakarta, Indonesia. North Korea took part in the organization for the first time at the 2000 annual meeting of foreign ministers.

Ash, Mary Kay

American entrepreneur; founder of Mary Kay Cosmetics (1918–2001)

Mary Kay Ash was born Mary Catherine Wagner in 1918 (or so it is believed – there is some mystery about this) in Hot Wells, Texas. A bout of tuberculosis had left her father an invalid. As a result, her mother was the principal breadwinner in the family. With her mother working long days as a restaurant manager, the young Ash was left to cook, clean and look after the home and her father.

Although a bright pupil – she gained straight As at school – money and marriage meant college was delayed, permanently as it turned out. Three children swiftly followed and Ash, like her mother before her, was forced to take a job to help support the family. Opportunities for a mother with only a high school education were limited; opportunities in depression-ridden Texas almost non-existent.

Salvation came in the form of a door-to-door saleswoman who turned up on Ash's doorstep in the mid-1930s. The saleswoman, who was selling books, offered to give Ash a free set if she could sell ten sets herself. Soon the ambitious Ash was persuading her friends from the local church that the children's books were an essential purchase. The ten sets were gone in less than two days. For the next few months, she did little else except sell books, and by the end of nine months she had accumulated $25,000 in sales. Ash had found her vocation.

Ash moved on to Stanley Home Products, a direct sales company. Her success continued as she was crowned 'sales queen' in 1938. Following World War II, her husband asked for and received a divorce, leaving Ash to support three children alone. Undeterred, Ash continued to make great progress as a saleswoman. At Stanley, she was entrusted with recruiting and managing other sales staff, and in 1959 she joined the World Gift Company. However, she resigned from the World Gift Company when in 1963 her male assistant was promoted above her. Ash had hit the **glass ceiling** with a resounding thud.

It was a tough time for Ash. She was 45 years old, jobless, and, despite a recent remarriage, was still supporting two children. But rather than give up, she decided to write a book in which she would distil her direct sales knowledge. After sketching out her thoughts, she decided instead to put her ideas into action and start her own business. The result was Beauty by Mary Kay (later renamed Mary Kay Cosmetics).

The business got off to an inauspicious start. First, tragically, her husband died of a heart attack. Then her lawyer tried to persuade her against the new venture. But Ash was determined. She formulated a company to provide women with business opportunities not previously available. She bought the rights to a face and hand cream and devised a business model based on consultants who demonstrated products at 'Mary Kay beauty shows' held in their own homes. This strategy was designed to provide additional value to the customer above that of the service given by her greatest competitor, Avon. Business commenced on Friday, 13 September 1963. She improved her chances of success by getting her first employees – nine consultants – to contribute 50 percent of the retail price of the cosmetic packages they were selling.

By the end of the first year of trading, sales totalled $198,000 and the number of employees had grown to 200. Ash threw a celebration party, handing out wigs to her best sales people. After her demoralizing experience at the World Gift Company, she was determined to ensure that her staff felt motivated and fully rewarded. Salespeople who achieved a certain level of sales were recognized in a 'ladder of success' where each rung bought a new token to signify success, from ribbons to pink Cadillacs.

Way ahead of her time, Ash was an avowed equal-opportunity employer, valuing the contribution that her female staff could make to the organization. She was a benevolent employer, sending birthday cards to all of her employees and often inquiring about their circumstances. Employees were well rewarded: the company's mark-up was above average and the commissions of the staff generous; consultants could also earn commissions on the sales of staff that they recruited; and those who signed up a significant number of consultants were promoted.

In 1968 Ash raised $2,340,000 by selling 195,000 shares on the New York stock market. She used the money to finance the building of a new production facility in Dallas, which allowed the company to manufacture nearly all of its own products. By 1972, the company was one of the nation's largest private employers, with sales of $18 million and several thousand employees. Between 1963 and 1978, sales grew at an average of 28 percent annually.

In the 1980s, Ash's crusade to give women business opportunities began to backfire as more and more of her consultants, who were still paid on a commission-only basis, began to take full-time paid positions at other companies. Sales fell from $323 million in 1983 to $260 million by the end of 1984. In 1985, Ash took the opportunity to purchase the outstanding 70 percent of shares that weren't owned already by her family. In a leveraged buyout, Ash and her son Richard paid a reported $350,000 for the outstanding shares. This put Ash back in the driving seat of the company.

Under the direction of the founder and her son, the company quickly turned round and in 1991 achieved $487 million in sales. With over 475,000 consultants in 25 countries, the company she founded is the largest direct sales cosmetics company in the world.

Key texts

- Mary Kay Ash. *Mary Kay: The Story of America's Most Dynamic Businesswoman*. Harper & Row, 1981
- Mary Kay Ash. *You Can Have It All – Lifetime Wisdom From America's Foremost Woman Entrepreneur*. Prima Publishing Rocklin, 1995

Key link

- www.marykaytribute.com

ASP (active server page)

Active server pages are dynamic Web pages created on the fly, such as the page generated for the browser to view. ASP is a scripting language, meaning that before a Web server returns a Web page called by an Internet browser, it goes through the script line by line and executes any commands requested. This may, for example, be to obtain certain information from a database. This means that, instead of a static **HTML** Web page, the viewer may get a different Web page each time it is requested, depending on what the ASP script says. Most Web sites that use constantly changing information, such as news sites, utilize some form of scripting like ASP.

ASP (application service provider)

An application service provider provides software

services to third parties, with software stored and run from the ASP's servers rather than from the client's. The theory is that companies who sign up for ASP services can concentrate on their core business without worrying about implementing the latest technology, outsourcing that function to the ASP.

The term was coined in 1996 by Jostein Eikeland, a Norwegian video and movie producer who started up one of the first ASPs. Eikeland was working for a Norwegian bank at the time and suggested that the bank's desktop applications could be run remotely with the help of new technology from a company called Citrix. Eikeland now runs one of the largest companies in the ASP business, Telecomputing Inc., based in Fort Lauderdale, Florida.

ASP services cover a range of software applications, from e-mail – such as Microsoft's Hotmail – to online stores. The software-application market is predicted to be worth some $50 billion by 2006.

Key link

- www.telecomputing.net

Asset

An asset is anything owned by or owed to the company that is cash, or can be turned into cash. Assets are divided into fixed assets and current assets. Fixed assets are those assets bought by a company for use over an extended period of time. Fixed assets include tangible assets (plants, machinery, land and buildings); intangible assets (goodwill and trademarks); and investments in other companies. Over a period of time, the value of fixed assets can be written off against profits by depreciating the book value of the asset in the accounts. Current assets are those that are easily turned into cash, such as those frequently turned over in the course of business, like stock.

Assets can also be divided into physical assets, such as the land or property of a company or individual, and financial assets, such as cash, payments due from bills and investments. On a company's balance sheet, total assets must be equal to total liabilities (money and services owed).

Asset stripper

'Asset stripper' is a term that became fashionable during the 1960s. It was used to describe a person who identified an undervalued company, organized a takeover of that company (often hostile or leveraged) and then proceeded to sell the assets to make a profit. This was possible when the parts of the business were more valuable separately than together. 'Corporate raiders' is another term used to describe asset strippers (particularly during the 1980s).

Famous asset strippers included James Goldsmith, Carl Icahn and Jim Slater. Asset strippers were lambasted by many, especially the unions, as job losses invariably followed a takeover. It is true, however, that they unlocked shareholder value tied up in large, cumbersome and often ineffective companies. Asset stripping is a major force for the more efficient use of assets.

Key texts

- Jim Slater. *Return To Go – My Autobiography*. Weidenfeld & Nicolson, 1977
- Geoffrey Wansell. *Tycoon: The Life of James Goldsmith*. Atheneum, 1987

Asset turnover

An important measure of business efficiency, the asset-turnover ratio is a measure of a company's ability to generate sales turnover from its asset base. Asset turnover is calculated by dividing sales revenue by total net assets. The result is the amount of sales revenue generated by each monetary unit of asset – pounds or dollars, for example.

During the 1990s, the asset-turnover ratio assumed heightened importance as companies strived to obtain greater efficiencies from existing plants rather than build new infrastructure, a practice known as '**sweating the assets**'.

Asset value

In theory, the asset value represents the proportion of assets allotted to each share in the event of a company break-up. In practice, certain parties such as preference shareholders and other creditors have priority over ordinary shareholders and would be first in line in any distribution. Therefore, in calculating asset value, the amount due to these parties should also be deducted from total assets available. Thus asset value is the total value of the assets minus liabilities, divided by the number of ordinary shares in issue. The value of assets shown in a company's balance sheet is not necessarily the true value of a company's assets. To determine the asset value, a full appreciation of the company's assets would need to be undertaken.

Astor, John Jacob

American entrepreneur (1763–1848)

Born in Germany in 1763, John Jacob Astor emigrated to America in 1783. Arriving with a few dollars and seven flutes, he amassed a fur and property empire that made him one of the richest men of his day. Astor's story is a lesson for all entrepreneurs: excellent customer service, closeness to markets and the maxim of 'buy cheap, sell wherever the price is best'. In a battle with Astor, the state-subsidized fur trade looked a definite winner, but it was a mismatch and Astor won by a knockout.

The lucrative fur trade was important not only commercially but politically. Canada's patronage from France was dependent on its revenues. American, French-Canadian and British companies, like the Hudson Bay Company and the Northwest Company, dominated the fur trade. In 1796, a treaty between the United States and Great Britain demarcated trading boundaries along national boundaries, excluding the Canadians from American territories. Into the vacuum left by the Canadians moved Astor.

By 1800, Astor was the leading American fur trader. It was a considerable achievement. As well as competition from other private traders, Astor successfully competed with the American government. Unlike the government, Astor shipped his furs around the world to whatever market paid the best price. The folly of the government's attempts to control the fur trade were revealed when it passed legislation to close down the fur factories and sell their assets. The sales realized $50,000 against an investment of $300,000.

Already wealthy, Astor expanded his commercial horizons. He obtained permission to trade through ports owned by the East India Company, sent a ship to China in a joint venture, and pocketed $50,000 in profit. The profit was invested in New York property.

In 1808, Astor consolidated his holdings and incorporated the American Fur Company. This was a precursor to an attempt to control the developing fur trade in the West. Most companies planned to extend their territories to the West: The key would be finding and controlling a route through to the Pacific. A Canadian expedition had set out cross-country and was rumoured to be making good progress. Astor thought it more sensible to make his way around the Cape of Good Hope by ship and head for the mouth of the Columbia River. To finance his enterprise, he took up with some of the members of the Northwest Company and founded the Pacific Fur Company in 1810.

Astor's party arrived at the Columbia River in 1811. Six weeks after they raised the US flag over a hastily erected stockade christened Astoria, the Canadian expedition arrived. Astoria was to be an essential cog in Astor's international trading plans. No one could accuse Astor of lacking ambition. His intention was to send goods from New York to Astoria, trade them for furs with the Indians, ship the furs to the Orient and trade them for goods, ship the Oriental goods to Europe and trade them for European goods, and ship the European goods to America, taking a profit at every stage. It was a brilliant plan that fell at the first hurdle when one of his ships sank and the war of 1812 between the United States and England broke out. The British forced Astor to hand over his fort in Astoria for $58,000.

Other than this setback, Astor did well out of the war. Like fellow entrepreneur Commodore Vanderbilt, Astor exploited the opportunities that the inevitable disruption to the fur trade offered. Even in his worst year during the war, his revenues were $50,000. By the end of the conflict, he had substantially increased his property holdings. After the war, with the help of some friendly government officials and some helpful legislation that forbade Canadian involvement in the American fur trade, Astor gained control of all the Northwest Company's holdings that lay within American borders. He continued to take over the interests of other companies, inching his way West. But by the late 1820s, fashions had changed, silk was all the rage, and profits were falling. Never failing to spot a trend, Astor got out while he could. In June 1834 he sold all his fur trading holdings and retired.

Moving onto something more fashionable, he bought up property lots like most people buy groceries. In doing so, he helped shape the development of one of the greatest cities on the planet: New York City. When he died in 1848, he was the richest man in America, worth over $20 million.

Astor is an important figure in business history for a number of reasons. As a champion of private enterprise, Astor's endeavours clearly illustrated the shortcomings of state monopolies. Ultimately, he demonstrated that the disincentivized, bureaucracy-ridden, heavily subsidized state-run fur factories were no match for an agile private enterprise that paid close attention to its customers' needs and promoted innovation as a means to increasing profitability. Astor's actions also helped open the western frontiers of America for development. Finally, regardless of his motivation, he was responsible for shaping the development of New York City.

Key texts
- Washington Irving. *Astoria; or, Enterprise Beyond the Rocky Mountains*. Richard Bentley, 1839

- Walter R. Houghton. *Kings of Fortune or the Triumphs and Achievements of Noble, Self-made Men.* The Loomis National Library Association, 1888
- Arthur D. Howden Smith. *John Jacob Astor: Landlord of New York.* Lippincott, 1929
- John Upton Terrell. *Furs by Astor (John Jacob Astor).* Morrow & Co., 1963

Key link

- www.libertyhaven.com/theoreticalorphilosophicalissues/protectionismpopulismandintervntionism/johnjacob.shtml

B

Babbage, Charles

British political economist, innovator and pioneer (1791–1871)

Charles Babbage was one of the great minds of the first industrial revolution. Born in London, Babbage went to Cambridge University in 1810. He and others helped introduce the Leibnitz notation for calculus, which had a major impact on the study of mathematics. Among many other activities, Babbage also pioneered signalling for lighthouses and investigated mathematical code-breaking.

Babbage's most substantial achievement was the plans he made for Calculating Engines: the Difference Engines and the Analytical Engines. Babbage's engines, though never actually built by him, were the precursors of the modern computer. In recent years, Babbage has increasingly been accepted as the 'pioneer of the computer.' (See Hyman, Anthony, *Charles Babbage: Pioneer of the Computer*, Princeton University Press, Princeton (NJ), 1982.) In the 1970s, a team at London's Science Museum successfully built Babbage's Second Difference Engine.

In parallel to his career as an innovator, Babbage was also a political economist. In his book *On the Economy of Machines & Manufactures*, his professed aim was to look at 'the mechanical principles which regulate the application of machinery to arts and manufactures.'

Babbage's fundamental approach was highly scientific: first, gather the evidence. Babbage did so through touring factories exhaustively in the United Kingdom and Europe. Indeed, in his book,

Babbage provides helpful hints and a checklist of questions on how to find the best information when touring a factory. 'Political economists have been reproached with too small a use of facts, and too large an employment of theory,' he reflects. 'If facts are wanting, let it be remembered that the closet-philosopher is unfortunately too little acquainted with the admirable arrangements of the factory; and that no class of persons can supply so readily, and with so little sacrifice of time, the data on which all the reasoning of political economists are founded, as the merchants and manufacturer; and, unquestionably, to no class are the deductions to which they give rise so important. Nor let it be feared that erroneous deductions may be made from such recorded facts: the errors which arise from the absence of facts are far more numerous and more durable than those which result from unsound reasoning respecting true data.'

Babbage encourages managers to follow his example and gather their own data: 'The importance of collecting data, for the purpose of enabling the manufacturer to ascertain how many additional customers he will acquire by a given reduction in the price of the article he makes, cannot be too strongly pressed upon the attention of those who employ themselves in statistical inquiries,' he writes.

To his data, Babbage adds masterly logic and the anticipatory instincts of the best futurist. *On the Economy of Machinery and Manufactures* is one of the first books to recognize the importance of factories, economically and socially. It is akin to the first book on the potential of the Internet.

Contrasts can be made with Adam Smith, whose economic viewpoint remained stuck in the agricultural era. Babbage beckons in the industrial era and, in doing so, lays the intellectual groundwork for Marx, Engels and John Stuart Mill.

Babbage recognized that the factory required an entire system of operation. It needed to be organized in a vastly different way to the conventional means of production. He provides insights in two central areas: economies of scale and the division of labour. 'Perhaps the most important principle on which the economy of a manufacture depends, is the division of labour amongst the persons who perform the work,' he writes.

Babbage's approach to labour bears more than a passing resemblance to that later adopted by the American champion of scientific management, **Frederick Taylor**. While touring factories, he closely observed the actions of workers. 'The number of operations performed in a given time may frequently be counted when the workman is quite unconscious that any person is observing him,' he notes. 'Thus the sound made by the motion of a loom may enable the observer to count the number of strokes per minute, even though he is outside the building in which it is contained.'

Among the many other issues raised by Babbage is the life expectancy of capital equipment. 'Machinery for producing any commodity in great demand, seldom actually wears out; new improvements, by which the same operations can be executed either more quickly or better, generally superseding it long before that period arrives: indeed, to make such an improved machine profitable, it is usually reckoned that in five years it ought to have paid itself, and in ten to be superseded by a better,' he writes. *On the Economy of Machinery and Manufactures* was a bestseller of its times. Babbage was not only the pioneer of computing, but also a true pioneer of modern management.

Key text
- Doron Swade and Charles Babbage. *The Difference Engine: Charles Babbage and the Quest to Build the First Computer*. Viking Press, 2001

Key links
- http://ei.cs.vt.edu/~history/Babbage.html
- www.systemtoolbox.com/article.php?articles_id=43

Baby boomers

The baby boomers are a demographic segment of the population born during a post-World War II increase in births. This major boom in births spanned the period from the end of the war in 1946 to the early 1960s and is known as the post war bulge in population. Because of the sheer number of baby boomers – their generation peaked at 79 million in the US in 2000 – marketers have targeted them from the very start. In the 1940s and 1950s it was baby equipment and toys, in the 1950s and 1960s cars and records, and in the 1980s technology. The baby boomers are still driving consumer trends, although as their influence wanes – the last boomer is predicted to survive until about 2070 – **Generation X**ers will no doubt supersede them.

Bhatia, Sabheer

Internet entrepreneur

If you want a model for the new career, Sabheer Bhatia provides it. Bhatia changed the face of e-mail by co-founding the first Web-based e-mail company, Hotmail Corporation in 1996. Formerly with Apple, Bhatia's bright idea was to offer a free e-mail service supported by advertising. Bhatia worked on the idea in his garage *à la* Hewlett and Packard circa 1937. He then sat in his car and recruited staff. The company instantly became the market leader, with Bhatia at its helm as **CEO** and president. Before long, Hotmail had 1 million subscribers and was sucked into the Microsoft empire in 1997 for around $400 million, making Bhatia some $200 million dollars richer. Today, Hotmail is still the largest Web-based e-mail service provider, with over 50 million registered users. With ad revenue increasing by a massive 15 to 20 percent per month, Hotmail is an e-business that makes money.

Bhatia, meanwhile, has gone on to become one of a growing band of second-generation serial Internet entrepreneurs, along with the likes of **Jim Clark** and **Marc Andreessen**.

Bhatia's achievements have been widely recognized. *Upside* magazine, for example, named Bhatia as one of it's 'Elite 100', trendsetters who have had made the greatest impact on the Internet industry.

Key links
- www.hotmail.com
- www.lrb.co.uk/v21/n19/lanc2119.htm

Balance of payments

This term refers to the balance of all payments into a country and all payments out of that country during a specified period; i.e., an account of a country's debit and credit transactions with other countries. The balance of payment is made up of the current account, which includes both visible trade (imports and exports of goods) and invisible trade (services such as transport, tourism, interest and dividends), and the capital account, which includes investment in and out of the country, international grants and loans, and the movement of gold. Deficits or surpluses on these accounts are brought into balance by buying and selling reserves of foreign currencies.

An extreme deficit in the balance of payments may cause problems by affecting the stability of the nation's currency. In the past, notably after World War II, the International Monetary Fund was forced to step in and deal with balance-of-payments problems.

The United States in particular, during the latter half of the twentieth century, has run a balance-of-payments deficit. This is partly because of the investment by the United States in post-war Europe and other US investment abroad, compounded by rising oil prices in the 1970s and government borrowing. For example, as of 1999, the US current account deficit was an all-time record of $338.9 billion, up from 1998 level of $220.6 billion. In the United Kingdom, the balance-of-payments deficit tends to be much narrower.

Key links
- www.ons.gov.uk/
- www.bankofengland.co.uk
- www.statistics.gov.uk/themes/economy/Articles/bop.asp
- www.census.gov/foreign-trade/www/ – US information

Balance of trade

A component of a country's balance of payments, and therefore a narrower economic measure, is the balance of trade: the relationship between the trade imports and exports of a country. When imports exceed exports, the country has a trade surplus. When exports exceed imports, the country is operating a trade deficit.

During the 1600s and 1700s, the major trading nations favoured an economic system – mercantilism – based upon maximizing exports in return for gold and other precious metals. Universally valued gold could always be relied upon to finance the construction of an army or navy, which in turn could secure trade. To ensure that the trade surplus was maintained, legislation was passed to restrict imports, encourage exports and prevent bullion from leaving the country. It wasn't until economists and philosophers such as **Adam Smith** and David Ricardo began to study the theory of political economy more closely that the benefits of positive trade balance were called into question.

Today many Western countries run a trade deficit in goods, which is in many cases balanced, as it is in the United Kingdom, by trade surplus on services, such as music royalties and insurance.

Key links
- www.ons.gov.uk/
- www.bankofengland.co.uk

- www.statistics.gov.uk/themes/economy/ Articles/bop.asp
- www.census.gov/foreign-trade/www/ – US information

Balanced scorecard

To take companies beyond the often limiting measurement of financial criteria, David Norton and **Robert Kaplan** developed the balanced scorecard: 'A strategic management and measurement system that links strategic objectives to comprehensive indicators.' Norton is co-founder of the consulting company Renaissance Solutions, and Kaplan is Marvin Bower Professor of Leadership Development at Harvard Business School. The duo developed the balanced scorecard concept at the beginning of the 1990s, in research sponsored by KPMG.

The result was an article in the *Harvard Business Review* ('The Balanced Scorecard,' January/February 1993). The article had a simple message for managers: what you measure is what you get. Norton and Kaplan compared running a company to flying a plane: the pilot who relies on a single dial is unlikely to be safe. Pilots must utilize all of the information contained in their cockpits. 'The complexity of managing an organization today requires that managers be able to view performance in several areas simultaneously,' said Norton and Kaplan. 'Moreover, by forcing senior managers to consider all the important operational measures together, the balanced scorecard can let them see whether improvement in one area may be achieved at the expense of another.'

Norton and Kaplan suggest that four elements need to be balanced: the customer perspective – companies need to ask how customers perceive them; the internal perspective – companies need to ask what is it that they must excel at; the innovation and learning perspective – companies must ask how they can improve and create value; and the financial perspective – companies need to ask how their shareholders perceive them.

According to Norton and Kaplan, by focusing energy, attention and measures on all four of these dimensions, companies become driven by their mission rather than by short-term financial performance. Applying measures to company strategy is crucial to achieving this goal. Instead of being beyond measurement, the balanced scorecard argues that strategy must be central to any process of measurement: 'A good balanced scorecard should tell the story of your strategy.'

Identifying the essential measures for an organization is not straightforward. One company produced 500 measures on its first examination. This was distilled down to seven measures (20 is par for the course). According to Norton and Kaplan, a good balanced scorecard contains three elements. First, it establishes cause-and-effect relationships: rather than being isolated figures, measures are related to each other and the network of relationships makes up the strategy. Second, a balanced scorecard should have a combination of lead and lag indicators. Lag indicators are measures, such as market share, that are common across an industry and, though important, offer no distinctive advantage. Lead indicators are measures that are company- and strategy-specific. Finally, an effective balanced scorecard is linked to financial measures. By this, Norton and Kaplan mean that initiatives such as reengineering or lean production need to be tied to financial measures rather than pursued indiscriminately.

In many ways, the concept of the balanced scorecard is brazen common sense. Balance is clearly preferable to imbalance. (The counterintuitive reality is that unbalanced companies, usually driven by a single dominant individual, have often proved short-term successes.) The Balanced Scorecard is now widely championed by a variety of companies. Indeed, it has, somewhat ironically, become a management fad. Its argument that blind faith in a single measurement or a small range of measures is dangerous is a powerful one. However, effective measures of elements, such as management competencies or intellectual capital, remain elusive.

Key texts
- Robert S. Kaplan and Robin Cooper. *Cost and effect: Using integrated cost systems to drive profitability and performance*. Harvard Business School Press, 1998
- Robert S. Kaplan and David P. Norton. *The Balanced Scorecard: Translating strategy into action*. Harvard Business School Press, 1996

Key link
- www.people.hbs.edu/rkaplan/

Balance sheet

A statement of the financial position of a company or individual at a point in time, the balance sheet reveals a great deal about a company's finances, such as whether the company has the necessary liquid assets to reward the shareholder through dividends and whether the company is likely to need to issue debt or stock to fund its growth.

For US corporations, the balance sheet is available in either the 10-K – a cut-down version of the full annual report verified by accountants – or the 10-Q, a quarterly report filed for the first three quarters of the year (the fourth-quarter filing is the 10-K).

The balance sheet consists of a number of important financial components. Current assets are those assets that can be easily and quickly converted into cash. The specified time period is usually within one operating cycle, this being the time taken to sell the product and collect the proceeds. Current assets are an important financial indicator, as they are the assets used to fund the day-to-day operations of the company. If there are insufficient funds available, the company will have to look to other means to fund its operations, which may incur costs through interest payments or affect the shareholder adversely by diluting the stock.

There are six main kinds of current assets: accounts receivable, cash and equivalents, inventory, prepaid expenses, short-term investments and current liabilities.

- *Accounts receivable* indicates the amount allocated for products/services delivered to customers but not yet paid for. Although in theory accounts receivable should be translated into cash as customers pay for the goods and services they received, this is not always the case in practice. Where the company feels it is unlikely that a customer will pay, a figure in brackets may be included to signify bad debts written off by the company. Inevitably, these figures are an estimate and may prove an inadequate reflection of the true position of bad debts, especially in a difficult economic climate.
- *Cash and equivalents* reflect cash in the bank or similar items, such as bearer bonds. A positive cash figure is good for shareholders in that it increases the chance of being paid a dividend. However, if there is too much cash, questions are likely to be asked as to whether the company is using its assets effectively on behalf of the shareholders.
- *Inventory* reflects components and finished products not yet sold. For some companies, such as service companies, inventory is irrelevant. High stock figures, or stock growing faster than revenue, may indicate problems shifting product.
- *Prepaid expenses* are, as the name suggests, expenditure already paid on credit.
- *Short-term investments* are investments that earn more for the company than cash in the bank but can still be converted into cash comparatively easily, such as bonds with a lifetime of less than one year.
- *Current liabilities* are the amount a company owes currently to its creditors and suppliers. Disclosed in a company's accounts on the balance sheet as short-term debts, they normally require a company to convert some its current assets into cash to pay them off. The five main categories of current liabilities are accounts payable (money owed to suppliers, employees, etc); accrued expenses (debts racked up but not yet payable); income tax payable is a specific type of accrued expense (tax owed but not yet due); short-term notes payable (the amount

drawn from an arranged line of credit that falls due in the following twelve-month period); and long-term debt (the element of long-term debt that falls due in the near term, i.e. within the following twelve-month period). Current liabilities are not to be confused with long-term liabilities, such as debt that is not due for over a year.

Other items appearing on the balance sheet include total plant, assets; non-liquid assets (plants, property, land, etc.); and long-term liabilities (loans not falling due within a year and often secured against assets of the company).

A balance sheet should always balance; that is, the sum of all of the assets must equal the sum of all of the liabilities.

Bank of England

Sometimes known as the Old Lady of Threadneedle Street, as it is situated on Threadneedle Street in the City of London, the Bank of England is the central bank of the United Kingdom. It was founded by William Paterson in July 1694 to bail out King William and Queen Mary. Paterson and others loaned the government £1,200,000 and in return the subscribers were incorporated as the Governor and Company of the Bank of England.

The government's banker and debt manager, the Bank moved to Threadneedle Street in 1734. It was entrusted with issuing bank notes in 1844, nationalized in 1946, and gained operational independence in 1997. It is banker to the UK clearing banks and government. As well as providing banking services to the UK banking system, the Bank of England manages the United Kingdom's foreign exchange, the gold reserves and the government's stock register.

In addition to the issue of banknotes, for which it has had a monopoly since the mid-1800s, the bank's most high-profile role is the setting of UK interest rates, a decision made by the Bank's Monetary Policy Committee.

Another role of the bank is to maintain the stability of the financial system. To do this, it works in close cooperation with the government's Treasury department and the Financial Services Authority (the regulator of banks and other financial institutions in the United Kingdom) and constantly monitors the economic situation in the United Kingdom. It also operates as the financial system's lender of last resort if necessary.

The bank's business is controlled by a governor, a deputy and 16 directors.

Key text
- Sir John Clapham. *The Bank of England a History* (2 volumes). Cambridge University Press, 1944

Key link
- www.bankofengland.co.uk

Banking covenant

See Loan.

Bankruptcy

Bankruptcy is the process by which the property of a person (in legal terms, an individual or corporation) unable to pay debts is taken away under a court order and divided fairly among the person's creditors, after preferential payments such as taxes and wages. Proceedings may be instituted either by the debtor (voluntary bankruptcy) or by any creditor for a substantial sum (involuntary bankruptcy). Until 'discharged', a bankrupt person is severely restricted in financial activities, at least theoretically.

When an individual or company is made bankrupt, a trustee or administrator is appointed to manage the bankrupt's assets. The only assets the individual will control will be the tools of his trade and clothing, bedding and other basic items for the bankrupt and his family. The trustee will also control how much income the bankrupt is entitled to.

The bankrupt has certain legal duties, which include not obtaining credit over a certain amount; not carrying on business in a different name to that under which they were made bankrupt; and not being involved in forming or managing a company without the court's permission. The bankrupt is also prevented from holding certain public offices.

A bankrupt is usually 'discharged' after a set period of time, usually three years. This means the bankrupt will be free of all of his debts other than those arising from fraud.

There are alternatives to bankruptcy in the United Kingdom, including an informal or 'family' arrangement arrived at by contacting the individual creditors and making acceptable arrangements for payment; administration orders, under which the court administers the repayment in regular amounts, providing the total debts do not exceed £5000; and individual voluntary arrangements, which are similar to informal arrangements.

In the United States, there tends to be a slightly more lenient attitude toward bankruptcy. Bankruptcy is controlled by legislation such as the Chandler Act (1938) and the Bankruptcy Reform Act (1978).

This attitude manifests itself in Chapter 11 bankruptcy. In a Chapter 11 bankruptcy, a company in debt that might otherwise cease trading is allowed to continue its business operations by means of a plan of reorganization, which must meet certain statutory criteria. When a company gets into financial difficulties, it may consider filing a Chapter 11 bankruptcy at the bankruptcy court. If it can then reduce its debts through reorganization, it may be able to return to trading as a viable concern. The rationale behind the legislation is that it is often more cost-effective in both financial and human terms to return a company to viability, saving jobs and assets, than to liquidate it. Cooperation between creditors, the company and all other interested parties is vital to the successful outcome of a Chapter 11 bankruptcy.

A Chapter 7 bankruptcy is harsher. A provision of the US Federal Bankruptcy legislation, it deals with companies that are in financial difficulties and can no longer reasonably be expected to trade viably. Unlike Chapter 11, the debtor under a Chapter 7 bankruptcy does not remain in control of the company; a trustee is appointed to prevent further losses. Before a company is liquidated under the provisions of Chapter 7, a company will normally file for protection from creditors under Chapter 11.

Revisions to US bankruptcy law in 1978 made it easier for managers of a company to remain in control during a bankruptcy. This resulted in an increase in bankruptcy filings in the 1980s and 1990s and, as a result, there is talk of law reform to remedy this situation.

Banner ads

Banner ads are one of the earliest and best-established forms of Internet advertising. In its standard form, a banner ad is a **GIF** graphic on a Web site hot-linked to the advertiser's site. The link to the advertiser is then used to send potential customers to the advertiser's site, and to provide metric data for pricing the cost of the advertising and judging the success of the ad. The most commonly used data is the click-through rate; i.e., the number of surfers who click through the banner ad. Research has shown that click-through rates on the average banner are declining. Yet despite their apparent ineffectiveness they remain a ubiquitous form of Internet advertising. Technological advances have allowed more interactive forms of banner ads, incorporating animation, audio, and **Java** to grab the surfer's attention.

Banner ads are usually priced using the click-through model. In this model the owner of the Web site displaying the banner ad receives a payment each time a customer clicks through the banner ad to whatever lies beyond (usually the advertiser's Web site). The payment per click-through is higher than the CPM (cost per mille – or cost per thousand) rate, reflecting the higher level of risk to the Web site displaying the ad. There is an inherent problem in this model for the company displaying the banner ads on their Web site. Regardless of whether surfers click-through the banner, the advertisement is still displayed. Advertisers have used this to their advantage by gearing their banner ads to brand awareness campaigns instead of using them to generate sales directly.

Banners come in eight standard sizes, as suggested by the Internet Advertising Bureau (IAB) and the Coalition for Advertising Supported Information (CASIE) in December 1996. They are (with all sizes in pixels) button ads (120x60), button ads (120x90), full banners (468x60), full banners with vertical navigation bar (392x72), half banners (234x60), micro-buttons (88x31), square button ads (125x125) and vertical banners (120x240).

Key links
- www.banneradmuseum.com/Mission.html
- www.iab.net/

Barnard, Chester

American executive (1886–1961)

A senior executive, Chester Barnard was a rarity: a management theorist who was also a successful practitioner. As such, he was one of the first to examine the nature and extent of executive responsibilities.

Barnard won an economics scholarship to Harvard, but before finishing his degree, he joined American Telephone and Telegraph to begin work as a statistician. He spent his entire working life with the company, eventually becoming president of New Jersey Bell in 1927.

Though he was the archetypal corporate man, Barnard's interests were varied, and he also found time to lecture on the subject of management. His best-known book, *The Functions of the Executive*, collected together his lectures. The language is dated and the approach is ornate, but it's a comprehensive study. Much of what Barnard argued

strikes a chord with contemporary management thinking. For example, he highlighted the need for communication so that every single person could be tied into the organization's objectives. He also advocated lines of communication that were short and direct.

To Barnard, the chief executive was not a dictatorial figure geared to simple short-term achievements. Instead, part of his responsibility was to nurture the values and goals of the organization. However, for all his contemporary-sounding ideas, Barnard was a man of his times, advocating corporate domination of the individual and regarding loyalty to the organization as paramount.

Even so, Barnard proposed a moral dimension to the world of work: 'The distinguishing mark of the executive responsibility is that it requires not merely conformance to a complex code of morals but also the creation of moral codes for others,' he wrote. In arguing that there was a morality to management, Barnard played an important part in broadening the managerial role from one of simply measurement, control and supervision to one also concerned with more elusive, abstract notions, such as values.

Key texts
- Chester Barnard. *The Functions of the Executive.* Harvard University Press, 1938
- Chester Barnard. *Organization and Management.* Harvard University Press, 1948

Key link
- http://ollie.dcccd.edu/mgmt1374/book_contents/1overview/management_history/mgmt_history.htm

Barnevik, Percy

Former CEO of Asea Brown Boveri (ABB) (b. 1941)

Born in Sweden in 1941, Percy Barnevik obtained an **MBA** from the School of Economics, Gothenburg, in 1964 before travelling to the United States to study at the Stanford Graduate School of Business. Early in his career he worked at Sandvik AB, where he was head of administration and group operations. He became president of the company's US operations in 1975 and chairman of the board in 1983. However, Barnevik is best known for his role at the Swedish company Asea, which he joined in 1980 as president and **CEO**.

For the next few years, Barnevik concentrated on turning Asea around. By 1987, Barnevik had transformed Asea from a $2 billion company into a $9 billion company ranked in the top 10 companies in its field worldwide. It was a credible performance, but Barnevik had bigger things on his mind. Swiss-German-Italian company Brown Boveri had competed with Asea for more than a century. Why be rivals, thought Barnevik, when together they could be the dominant force in their market?

When the merger was announced on 10 August 1987, the corporate world was stunned. *The Wall Street Journal* said that it was a merger 'born of necessity, not of love'. This overlooked the uncanny fit between the two companies. It was truly a marriage made in corporate heaven. Brown Boveri was international; Asea was not. Asea excelled at management; Brown Boveri did not. Whether by luck or by insight, their technology, markets and cultures fitted together. Then, quite simply, Barnevik made it work.

Four months after the deal was signed, Barnevik called a meeting in Cannes. Attending were over 300 executives handpicked by Barnevik to manage the new company. Barnevik and his directors had spent hours interviewing hundreds of executives and sifting through corporate documents to distil the strengths of the two companies. From this they compiled ABB's 'bible' – a corporate blueprint containing the goals and values of the organization. This was what Barnevik presented to the troops in Cannes.

The ink on the merger was barely dry when the new company acquired 15 companies. Within two years, it had added the power transmission and distribution operations of the Westinghouse Electric Corporation and purchased the Combustion Engineering Group, along with about 38 other companies. Focus then shifted to Eastern Europe, parts of the former Soviet Union and Asia. By 1998, ABB had 213,000 employees in 1000 companies in 150 countries around the world. Its major business segments include power generation; power transmission and distribution; industrial and building systems; financial services; and rolling stock.

Incorporating more than 1000 companies within one streamlined entrepreneurial organization with as few management layers as possible was a major challenge for Barnevik. It required a radical rethinking of organizational structure and management practice. To enable it to happen, Barnevik introduced a complex matrix structure – what his successor as CEO, Göran Lindahl, called 'decentralization under central conditions'. An executive committee ran the company with the organization below divided by business areas, company and profit centres, and country organizations. The aim was to reap the advantages of being a large organization while also having the advantages of smallness.

ABB's matrix structure has been the source of much debate. Though it has been hailed as a new organizational model and Barnevik as GM's **Alfred P. Sloan** reincarnated, Barnevik himself argues that the matrix system is simply a formal means of recording and understanding what happens informally in any large organization.

Barnevik's changes in the company are inspirational in other ways. ABB's management style and philosophy could be summarized as management by and for grown-ups. The company is seemingly free of pointless in-fighting. Constructive debate is welcomed. Managers from different countries work together effectively. One gets the impression that decisions are thought through, backed by analysis, then made and carried out decisively. ABB is a ringing endorsement for professional management. Barnevik has been compared favourably with General Electric's **Jack Welch**.

In 1997, Barnevik moved on to new challenges. He remained an executive chairman of ABB, but handed over the day-to-day running of the conglomerate to Göran Lindahl (Lindahl was succeeded in 2000 by Jörgen Centerman). Barnevik now runs the powerful Swedish investment group Investor AB, owned by the Wallenberg family. His role as chairman involves overseeing an empire that includes companies such as Scania, Astra-Zeneca, Incentive, ABB, Enso Stora, Ericsson, Atlas Copco, SKF, Electrolux and SAS. In 1999, he became chairman of pharmaceuticals company AstraZeneca.

Key texts

- Manfred F.R. Kets de Vries with Elizabeth Florent-Treacy. *The New Global Leaders – Richard Branson, Percy Barnevik and David Simon and the Remaking of International Business.* Jossey-Bass , 1999
- Kevin Barham and Claudia Heimer. *ABB: The Dancing Giant.* Financial Times Prentice Hall, 1998

Key links

- www.abb.com
- www.investorab.com

Barriers to entry and exit

Barriers to entry and exit are those barriers that deter an organization from entering a new market. These obstacles may include:

1 technological advantages held by existing companies in the market and secured through patents;
2 high marketing expenditure by existing companies in a market that makes it difficult for new entrants to build public awareness; and
3 difficulty securing contracts with members of the supply chain because of exclusive contracts that they have already signed with companies operating in the same market.

A market dominated by a few large corporations – the oil refining market for example – is particularly difficult for a small company to enter, as the larger companies benefit from economies of scale and may operate such a competitive pricing policy that it is impossible for an entrant to make a profit.

In addition to those barriers preventing a company from entering a market, there are barriers that deter companies from leaving markets. These may include location in an industry-specific cluster and a highly specialized workforce that would prove difficult to retrain.

Bartlett, Christopher

Harvard Business School professor and author (b. 1943)

Australian-born and educated at University of Queensland and Harvard University, Christopher Bartlett has worked as a marketing manager with Alcoa, as a London-based McKinsey consultant, and as general manager of Baxter Laboratories' French operations. He joined the Harvard Business School faculty in 1979 and is now the MBA Class of 1966 Professor of Business Administration at Harvard Business School.

Bartlett has authored five books with **Sumantra Ghoshal**, their most recent being *The Individualized Corporation* (1997), and the second edition of their now classic *Managing Across Borders: The Transnational Solution* (1998). *The Individualized Corporation* is based on six years of research and hundreds of interviews with managers at every level of companies such as Intel, ABB, Canon, 3M and McKinsey. It examines the rapid rise of a fundamentally different management philosophy – one based on the power of the individual as the driver of corporate value creation, and the central importance of individuality in management.

In *Managing Across Borders* (first published in 1989), Bartlett and Ghoshal identify a number of organizational forms prevalent among global companies. The first is the multinational or multidomestic firm. Its strength lies in a high degree of local responsiveness. It is a decentralized federation of local firms (such as Unilever or Philips) linked together by a web of personal controls (expatriates from the home country firm who occupy key positions abroad).

The second is the global firm, typified by US corporations such as Ford earlier this century and Japanese enterprises such as Matsushita. Its strengths are scale efficiencies and cost advantages. With global scale facilities, the global firm seeks to produce standardized products; it is often centralized in its home country with overseas operations considered as delivery pipelines to tap into global market opportunities. There is tight control of strategic decisions, resources and information by the global hub.

The third type of firm is the international one. Its competitive strength is its ability to transfer knowledge and expertise to overseas environments that are less advanced. It is a coordinated federation of local firms, controlled by sophisticated management systems and corporate staffs. The attitude of the parent company tends to be parochial, fostered by the superior know-how at the centre of the organization.

Bartlett and Ghoshal argue that global competition is forcing many of these firms to shift to a fourth model, which they call the *transnational*. This firm combines local responsiveness with global efficiency and the ability to transfer know-how better, cheaper and faster.

The transnational firm was the model many companies aspired to during the 1990s. The transnational firm is made up of a network of specialized or differentiated units, with attention paid to managing integrative linkages between local firms as well as with the centre. The subsidiary becomes a distinctive asset rather than simply an arm of the parent company. Manufacturing and technology development are located wherever it makes sense, but there is an explicit focus on leveraging local know-how in order to exploit worldwide opportunities.

In transnational organizations, say Bartlett and Ghoshal, there are three techniques crucial to forming an organization's 'psychology'. First, there must be 'clear, shared understanding of the company's mission and objectives'. Second, the actions and behaviour of senior managers are vital as examples and statements of commitment: 'Particularly in a transnational organization, where other signals may be diluted or distorted by the sheer volume of information sent to foreign outposts, top management's actions have a powerful influence on the company's culture. When Sony's founder and chief executive, Akio Morita, relocated to New York to build the company's US operations, he sent the most convincing possible message about Sony's commitment to its overseas businesses.' Third, corporate personnel policies must be geared up to 'develop a multidimensional and flexible organization process'.

With its emphasis on networking across the global organization and transferring learning and knowledge, *Managing Across Borders* effectively set the organizational agenda for a decade. It created a new organizational model. Unfortunately, such is the complexity and cautiousness of the modern organization that many have chosen to remain one-dimensional and inflexible rather than embrace Bartlett and Ghoshal's transnational alternative.

While *Managing Across Borders* was concerned with bridging the gap between strategies and organizations, Ghoshal and Bartlett's sequel, *The Individualized Corporation*, moved from the elegance of strategy to the messiness of humanity. In their latest book, Bartlett and Ghoshal contend that revitalizing a company's people is fundamentally about changing those people. The trouble is that adults don't change their basic attitudes unless they encounter personal tragedy. Things that happen at work rarely make such an impact. If organizations are to revitalize people, they must change the context of what they create around people. To do so requires a paradoxical combination of what Bartlett and Ghoshal label 'stretch' and 'discipline'.

These factors do not render attention to strategy, structure and systems obsolete. Businesses can still be run by strict attention to this blessed corporate trinity. These are, in Bartlett and Ghoshal's eyes, the legacy of the corporate engineer, **Alfred P. Sloan**, and the meat and drink of business school programmes. The way out of the smog is through purpose ('the company is also a social institution'); process ('the organization as a set of roles and relationships'); and people ('helping individuals to become the best they can be'). Undoubtedly these factors are less hard and robust than the three 'S's, but Bartlett and Ghoshal believe that they are the way forward.

Key texts
- Sumantra Ghoshal and Christopher A. Bartlett. *The Individualized Corporation: A Fundamentally New Approach to Management.* HarperBusiness, 1997
- Sumantra Ghoshal and Christopher A. Bartlett. *Managing Across Borders: The Transnational Solution.* Second edition, Harvard Business School Press, 1998

Key link
- www.jboyett.com/GuruAB.htm

Base rate

The base rate is the rate set, usually by a national central bank, to determine the cost of borrowing. In the United Kingdom, the base rate is the rate at which the Bank of England lends to other financial institutions. The Monetary Policy Committee sets the base rate according to economic conditions. Retail banks usually follow the lead of the Bank of England by adopting the base rate, although they are under no obligation to do so. Similarly, mortgage lenders may pass on the base rate to their borrowers or not, as they think fit. Historically, the Minimum Lending Rate set by the **Bank of England** ended on the 20 August 1981. The government then set the base rate through the Bank of England in an attempt to regulate the economy through monetary policy. The new Labour government restored the responsibility for setting the base rate to the Bank of England in 1997.

In the United States, the Federal Reserve Board, currently chaired by Alan Greenspan, sets the discount interest rate, which governs the rate of interest that banks pay to the Federal Reserve

Banks for short-term borrowing of reserves. As in the UK, the announcement of a change in the discount rate is often most significant for the message it sends to the financial markets about the direction of monetary policy.

In the European Union, interest rates for all members that adopted the Eurosystem single currency (Austria, Belgium, Finland, France, Germany, Greece, Ireland, Italy, Luxembourg, Netherlands, Portugal and Spain) are set by the European Central Bank.

Key links
- www.ecb.int/ – European Central Bank
- www.bankofengland.co.uk – Bank of England
- www.federalreserve.gov. – US Federal Reserve

Basis point

A commonly used unit in finance, one basis point is equivalent to one hundredth of one percent (0.01 percent). For example, if a bond's yield rises from 10.50 percent to 10.55 percent, it is said to have risen by 5 basis points.

Bathtub curve

The bathtub curve depicts the failure rate of a piece of equipment/product over time. The outline of the curve typically assumes the shape of a bathtub. The leading edge of the curve (infant mortality) shows how the failure rate becomes progressively lower as the equipment/product is worn-in and faults mended. The curve is then flat until the equipment draws to the end of its normal working life. The trailing edge of the curve (wearout) shows an increasing failure rate as the equipment/product begins to wear out.

BATNA (best alternative to a negotiated agreement)

The concept of BATNA or the 'best alternative to

a negotiated agreement' was developed by Roger Fisher and William Ury in their book *Getting to Yes* (1981). BATNA reflects 'the course of action a party would take if the proposed deal were not possible'. It is a key factor in negotiation strategy. In order to know whether or not to accept a negotiated settlement, it is essential to know if a better outcome is obtainable by alternative means. If the settlement obtained through negotiation is better than the BATNA, then the settlement should be accepted. If a party to negotiations has a good BATNA, or even if they only perceive it to be, it will be difficult to arrive at a negotiated settlement. The better the BATNA, therefore, the stronger the negotiating position. Knowing both your own and your adversary's BATNA is crucial to successful negotiating.

As Fisher says: 'Which would you prefer to have in your back pocket during a compensation negotiation with your boss: a gun or a terrific job offer from a desirable employer who is also a serious competitor of your company?'

Key text

- William Ury and Roger Fisher. *Getting to Yes: Negotiating Agreement Without Giving In.* Houghton Mifflin, 1981

Bearer bond

Also called a coupon bond, a bearer bond is an unregistered financial instrument that is legally owned by whoever possesses it. Interest and principal are payable to the holder, regardless of to whom the bond was issued. This is unusual for financial securities that normally require registration in the owner's name, and registration in the case of transferral. The bond has coupons attached. These are removed and submitted by the holder to the issuer or paying agent at regular intervals, usually twice annually, in return for payment of interest. Eurobonds are an example of a bearer bond. As ownership passes with possession, bearer bonds are usually kept under lock and key, in bank deposit boxes for example.

Beaverbrook, Lord (William Maxwell Aitken)

Newspaper proprietor and politician (1879–1964)

Born the son of a poor Presbyterian minister in Northern Ontario, Canada, as William Maxwell Aitken, Lord Beaverbrook was brought up in the town of Newcastle, New Brunswick. It was a religious upbringing in austere surroundings. But while his father may have been a minister, Beaverbrook was the pupil most acquainted with the schoolmaster's strap. His teacher described him as 'the wildest imp of mischief I ever knew,' adding tellingly, 'but a born leader of men from the day he left he cradle'.

After failing to get into college, Beaverbrook became a clerk for a local barrister. In 1897, he became involved in politics, helping future Canadian Prime Minister Richard Bedford Bennett win a seat on the Legislative Assembly of the Northwest Territories. Moving to Halifax in 1898, Beaverbrook made friends with a leading businessman, J.P. Stairs. Stairs and several other investors formed the Royal Securities Corporation and put Beaverbrook in charge. Soon he had set up a number of companies with wide-ranging interests, both in Canada and abroad, moved the company's head office to Montreal, and, by 1906, was worth a small fortune.

Beaverbrook's biggest deal in Canada was to consolidate the cement industry and create a cement trust. Although the deal made Beaverbrook even richer, it also made him some powerful enemies. Sensing that sentiment was turning against him, Beaverbrook made the decision that would set him on the path to his career as a media baron. In 1910, he moved to England.

When Beaverbrook arrived in London, it was to raise money in the financial markets for another of his deals. But he found a new interest in British politics. Influential friends in England, such as Scottish-Canadian Bonar Law, encouraged him to run for Parliament. He stood as Conservative candidate for the seat of Ashton-under-Lyne in Lancashire. With only ten days to go until the election, standing against an experienced local man, no one gave Beaverbrook a chance. He won by 196 votes. It was a remarkable rise to favour for this young upstart from Canada. Incredibly, in 1911, having been in the country for less than two years, he was knighted in the Coronation honours.

Reluctant to return to Canada because of investigations into his business affairs, and enjoying the influence his money and connections secured, Beaverbrook settled in England. He continued to act as a catalyst for behind-the-scenes political manoeuvring. In 1916, against the backdrop of World War I, he helped Lloyd George and Bonar Law depose Herbert Asquith as prime minister. As a reward, Beaverbrook was given a peerage. Remembering the name of a place he had seen on a map of New Brunswick, Aitken became the first Lord Beaverbrook.

All the time Beaverbrook had been pulling the political strings, he had also been steadily acquiring stock in one of Britain's main newspapers, the *Daily Express*. By 1916, he had obtained a controlling interest in the paper, which he subsequently used to wield political influence. By then, a major falling-out with Lloyd George had forced Beaverbrook to resign from his position as Minister of Information and Chancellor of the Duchy of Lancaster. Bloodied but unbowed, he retreated to the safety of his newspaper, from where he continued to wage war on Lloyd George.

For a time, Beaverbrook concentrated on his newspaper interests. He introduced the *Sunday Express* in 1918 and bought the *Evening Standard* in 1923. The circulation of the flagship *Daily Express* increased from 400,000 in 1919 to 2,329,000 by 1938. He ruled his growing media empire from his country house, Cherkley Court, near Leatherhead in Surrey.

Beaverbrook often showed poor judgement in international affairs. His newspapers toed the appeasement line as Hitler rose to power and threatened to rampage through Europe. Right up until September 1938, Beaverbrook and the *Daily Express* were proclaiming that there would be no war in Europe, 'this year, or next year either'.

Beaverbrook made up for his lack of judgement with a sterling performance as Minister of Aircraft Production during World War II. He was given the position by Winston Churchill against the advice of King George VI. It was an inspired decision by Churchill and a particularly unselfish one, as Churchill and Beaverbrook had not always seen eye to eye. Churchill said that it was Beaverbrook's 'vital and vibrant energy' that convinced him that he was the right man for the job.

After the war, Beaverbrook's interest in politics waned, as did his influence. Beaverbrook disliked Clement Attlee, who had succeeded Churchill as Prime Minister. The feeling was mutual. Opinion was also moving against Beaverbrook's pervasive influence in British society. In 1947, a Royal Commission was appointed to look into Beaverbrook's activities. 'I run the paper purely for propaganda purposes,' was Beaverbrook's provocative response. Despite his comments, he somehow managed to avoid serious censure.

Beaverbrook gradually withdrew from the day-to-day management of his business interests and took to travelling the world, writing, and spending time with his family. His last years were spent at Cherkley Court, from where he continued to make his presence felt by constantly checking up on his editors. The *Daily Express* continued to go from strength to strength. By 1960, its circulation was 4.3 million, making it the number one British newspaper. Beaverbrook died at home in June 1964, shortly after his 85th birthday.

Key texts

- Lord Beaverbrook. *My Early Life*. Brunswick Press, 1965
- A.J.P. Taylor. *Beaverbrook; A Biography*. Simon & Schuster, 1972
- Anne Chisholm and Michael Davie. *Lord Beaverbrook A Life*. Alfred A. Knopf 1993

Key link

- www.beaverbrookfoundation.org/bbrook.htm

Behlendorf, Brian

*CTO of Collab.net; co-founder of Apache
Software Foundation; open-source advocate*

Brian Behlendorf was one of the driving forces
behind the open-source movement. The Apache
Software Foundation, which developed the code
for the Apache Web server, was co-founded by
Behlendorf. Sixty percent of all Internet sites run
on Apache servers.

While Behlendorf was perfecting Apache code
for fun, he was earning his money as chief engineer
at HotWired; he also co-founded the Web design
firm, Organic. In early 1999, he joined O'Reilly
& Associates as **CTO** of new ventures. In turn,
O'Reilly spun off Collab.net with Behlendorf as
founder and president.

Collab.Net is an example of how the open-
source model is maturing. Its first service is
sourceXchange, an online matchmaking service
for companies and coders. The companies post
details of the job they need to be done and the
price they are willing to pay for a piece of software
that will do it. The registered developers decide
what projects they want to work on. The new twist
is that they get paid for participating in an open-
source project.

Key text

- Chris Dibona, Mark Stone and Sam Ockman
  (eds). *Open Sources: Voices from the Open
  Source Revolution (O'Reilly Open Source)*.
  O'Reilly & Associates, 1999

Key link

- http://sanfrancisco.bcentral.com/sanfrancisco/
  stories/2001/05/21/newscolumn8.html

Belbin, Meredith

Academic and author (b. 1926)

Meredith Belbin is the doyen of the theory of
teamworking. He majored in classics and psychology at Cambridge University before becoming a

researcher at the Cranfield College of Aeronautics.
He worked in Paris for the Organization for Eco-
nomic Cooperation and Development, with the
Industrial Training Research Unit at University
College, London, and in a number of manufac-
turing companies.

In 1967, the United Kingdom's Henley Management College introduced a computer-based
business game into one of its courses. In this
game, known as the Executive Management
Exercise, 'company' teams of members competed
to achieve the best score according to the criteria
laid down in the exercise. Henley arranged to
collaborate with Meredith Belbin, then with the
Industrial Training Research Unit at University
College, London.

Belbin was interested in group performance
and how it might be influenced by the kinds of
people making up a group. Members engaging
in the exercise were asked, voluntarily and confi-
dentially, to undertake a personality and critical-
thinking test. From his observations, based on the
test results, Belbin discovered that certain combi-
nations of personality types performed more successfully than others. Belbin began to be able to
predict the winner of the game and realized that,
given adequate knowledge of the personal characteristics and abilities of team members through
psychometric testing, he could forecast the likely
success or failure of particular teams. As a result,
unsuccessful teams can be improved by analysing their team-design shortcomings and making
appropriate changes.

Belbin's first practical application of this work
involved a questionnaire that managers filled
out for themselves. The questionnaire was then
analysed to show the functional roles that the
managers thought they performed in a team. This
had one drawback: what you think you do is not
of much value if the people with whom you work
think differently. Belbin refined his methods and
worked with others to design a computer program
to do the job. (His work is now available online
and on CD-ROM.)

From his first-hand observation at Henley's unique 'laboratory,' Belbin identified nine archetypal functions that go to make up an ideal team. They are:

- *Plant* – creative, imaginative, unorthodox; solves difficult problems. Allowable weakness: bad at dealing with ordinary people.
- *Coordinator* – mature, confident, trusting; a good chairman; clarifies goals, promotes decision-making. Not necessarily the cleverest.
- *Shaper* – dynamic, outgoing, highly strung; challenges, pressurizes, finds ways around obstacles. Prone to bursts of temper.
- *Teamworker* – social, mild, perceptive, accommodating; listens, builds, averts friction. Indecisive in crunch situations.
- *Completer* – painstaking, conscientious, anxious; searches out errors; delivers on time. May worry unduly; reluctant to delegate.
- *Implementer* – disciplined, reliable, conservative, efficient; turns ideas into actions. Somewhat inflexible.
- *Resource investigator* – extrovert, enthusiastic, communicative; explores opportunities. Loses interest after initial enthusiasm.
- *Specialist* – single-minded, self-starting, dedicated; brings knowledge or skills in rare supply. Contributes only on narrow front.
- *Monitor evaluator* – sober, strategic, discerning. Sees all options, makes judgements. Lacks drive and ability to inspire others.

These categories have proved robust and are still used in a variety of organizations. The explosion of interest in teamworking during the last decade has prompted greater interest in Belbin's work. He has since continued to refine and expand his theories in a series of books.

Key texts
- Meredith Belbin. *Beyond the Team*. Butterworth-Heinemann, 2000
- Meredith Belbin. *Managing Without Power: Gender Relationships in the Story of Human Evolution*. Butterworth-Heinemann, 2001

Key link
- www.belbin.com

Benchmarking

Benchmarking is the comparison of one company's performance against that of another company, or against an industry average. A concept that gained currency during the 1980s and 1990s, benchmarking involves the detailed study of productivity, quality and value in different departments and activities in relation to performance elsewhere. Three different techniques can be used in benchmarking: best demonstrated practice (BDP) – the comparison of units within one firm, comparing sales per square unit of one retail outlet with another, for example; relative cost position (RCP) – this technique looks at each element of the cost structure per pound sterling of sales in firm A and compares it with the same element in competitor B; and best related practice (BRP) – similar to BDP but with a comparison between related firms that are willing to cooperate to make the necessary data available.

Below the line
See Above the line.

Bennis, Warren
American academic (b. 1925)

Born in 1925, Warren Bennis was the youngest infantry officer in the European theatre of operations during World War II, an early student of group dynamics in the 1950s, a futurologist in the 1960s and the world's premier leadership theorist in the 1970s and 1980s.

Bennis received his PhD in economics and social science at the Massachusetts Institute of Technology (MIT); he later served on the school's faculty and was chairman of the Organization Studies Department. Bennis studied under

Douglas McGregor at Antioch College and later became an academic administrator – he was provost at SUNY Buffalo from 1967 to 1971 and president of the University of Cincinnati between 1971 and 1978. He is now Distinguished Professor of Business Administration at the University of Southern California, as well as founder and chairman of the school's Leadership Institute.

Psychologist **Abraham Maslow** described Bennis as 'one of the Olympian minds of our time'. In his book *Future Shock*, **Alvin Toffler** claimed: 'If it was Max Weber who first defined bureaucracy, and predicted its triumph, Warren Bennis may go down as the man who first convincingly predicted its demise and sketched the outlines of the organizations that are springing up to replace it.'

Best known for his work on leadership, Warren Bennis's intellectual roots lie with the work of Douglas McGregor on motivation and the human-resources school of the 1950s. Perpetually tanned, with a shining, white-toothed smile, Bennis appears to be the archetype of the Californian popular academic. His lengthy career has involved him in education, writing, consulting and administration. Along the way, he has made contributions to an array of subjects and produced a steady stream of books, including the bestselling *Leaders: Strategies for Taking Charge* and, more recently, *Organizing Genius: The Secrets of Creative Collaboration*.

From being an early student of group dynamics in the 1950s, Bennis became a futurologist in the 1960s. His work – particularly *The Temporary Society* (1968) – explored new organizational forms. Bennis envisaged organizations as adhocracies – roughly the direct opposite of bureaucracies – freed from the shackles of hierarchy and meaningless paperwork.

Despite his varied career, Bennis remains inextricably linked with the subject of leadership. With the torrent of publications and executive programmes on the subject, it is easy to forget that leadership had been largely forgotten as a topic worthy of serious academic interest until it was revived by Bennis and others in the 1980s.

Bennis's work stands as a humane counter to much of the military-based hero worship that dogs the subject. Bennis argues that leadership is not a rare skill; leaders are made rather than born; leaders are usually ordinary – or apparently ordinary – people, rather than charismatic; leadership is not solely the preserve of those at the top of the organization – it is relevant at all levels; and, finally, leadership is not about control, direction and manipulation.

Bennis's best-known leadership research involved 90 of America's leaders. From these leaders, he identified four common abilities. The first is management of attention. This is, said Bennis, a question of vision. Successful leaders have a vision that other people believe in and treat as their own.

The second skill shared by Bennis's selection of leaders is management of meaning, which encompasses communications. A vision is of limited practical use if it is encased in 400 pages of wordy text or mumbled from behind a paper-packed desk. Bennis believes effective communication relies on the use of analogy, metaphor and vivid illustration as well as emotion, trust, optimism and hope.

The third aspect of leadership identified by Bennis is trust, which he describes as 'the emotional glue that binds followers and leaders together'. Leaders have to be seen to be consistent.

The final common bond between the 90 leaders studied by Bennis is 'deployment of self'. The leaders do not glibly present charisma or time management as the essence of their success. Instead, the emphasis is on persistence, self-knowledge, taking risks, commitment and challenge but, above all, learning. 'The learning person looks forward to failure or mistakes,' says Bennis. 'The worst problem in leadership is basically early success. There's no opportunity to learn from adversity and problems.'

Most recently, Bennis has switched his attention to the dynamics of group working. The relationship between groups and their leaders is clearly of fundamental interest to Bennis: 'Greatness starts with superb people. Great groups don't exist without great leaders, but they give the lie to the persistent notion that successful institutions are the lengthened shadow of a great woman or man.'

Indeed, the heroic view of the leader as the indomitable individual is now outdated and inappropriate. Says Bennis, 'He or she is a pragmatic dreamer, a person with an original but attainable vision. Ironically, the leader is able to realize his or her dream only if the others are free to do exceptional work.'

A rich strand of idealism runs through Bennis's work. He is a humanist with high hopes for humanity. To accusations of romanticism, Bennis puts up a resolute and spirited defence: 'I think that every person has to make a genuine contribution in their lives and the institution of work is one of the main vehicles to achieving this. I'm more and more convinced that individual leaders can create a human community that will, in the long run, lead to the best organizations.'

Key texts
- Warren Bennis (with Burt Nanus). *Leaders: The Strategies for Taking Charge*. Harper & Row, 1985
- Warren Bennis. *On Becoming a Leader*. Addison-Wesley, 1989
- Warren Bennis. *Why Leaders Can't Lead*. Jossey-Bass, 1989
- Warren Bennis. *An Invented Life: Reflections on Leadership and Change*. Addison-Wesley, 1993

Key link
- www.managementskills.co.uk/articles/ap98-bennis.htm

Berners-Lee, Tim

Lead developer of the World Wide Web (b. 1955)

Tim Berners-Lee is widely credited as the man who developed the World Wide Web. After graduation from Queen's College, Oxford in 1976, Berners-Lee had brief stints at Plessey Communications and DG Nash Ltd. in the UK. Eventually, however, he set up as an independent consultant.

It was during a six-month period at the Conseil Européen pour la Recherche Nucléaire (CERN) that he wrote a never-published programme, Enquire, for storing information using random associations. It was this programme that was to form the conceptual foundations for development of the World Wide Web.

In 1984, Berners-Lee took a full-time research position at the CERN laboratories in Geneva, Switzerland. In 1989, he wrote a proposal entitled 'Hypertext and CERN', circulating it among his colleagues for comment. His proposals, partly inspired by the work of Ted Nelson on the Xanadu project, incorporated three new technologies: **HTML** (Hypertext Mark-up Language), the language used to write Web documents; **HTTP** (Hypertext Transfer Protocol), the protocol to deliver the page; and a Web browser client, 'WorldWideWeb', which allowed the Web page to be viewed and edited.

By May 1991, an information-sharing system including these three key features was operational on the multiplatform network run at the CERN laboratories. In August of the same year, the files were made available to the external world, served up by the main file storage computer at CERN – the first Web server.

Instead of going on to make millions out of the commercial potential of his invention, Berners-Lee joined the Laboratory for Computer Science (LCS) at the Massachusetts Institute of Technology (MIT) in 1994. He didn't abandon development of the World Wide Web, however; he became director of the World Wide Web Consortium (W3C), which oversees and coordinates the global development of the Web. As one of the inventors of the Internet – perhaps the inventor – Berners-Lee is qualified for the job. To help things along, he has recently been given a $270,000 'genius grant', courtesy of a helpful foundation.

Key texts
- Tim Berners-Lee, Mark Fischetti (contributor) and Michael L. Dertouzos. *Weaving the Web:*

The Original Design and Ultimate Destiny of the World Wide Web. HarperBusiness, 2000

- Melissa Stewart. *Tim Berners-Lee: Inventor of the World Wide Web (Ferguson's Career Biography Series)*. Ferguson Publishing, 2001

Key links

- www.scientificamerican.com/2001/0501issue/0501berners-lee.html
- www.ora.com/www/info/wj/issue3/tbl-int.html

Beta

Beta is an indicator of the risk associated with a particular share in relation to the risk of the equity market as a whole. It is a reflection of the volatility of return on a share compared to a 1 percent return from the whole market. If, over a set period of time, when the market moves up 10 percent a particular stock does likewise, that stock is said to have a beta of 1. If, however, the market moves 10 percent but the share moves 25 percent, then the beta will be 2.5. A beta of 0.5 will represent a movement of 5 percent against the market's 10 percent shift. The lower the value of the beta, the less risk is associated with the stock. The higher the beta value, the riskier the share is. Shares with a low beta are also known as defensive stocks.

Bezos, Jeff

Founder of Amazon.com; Time *Magazine 1999 'Person of the Year' (b. 1964)*

Born in Albuquerque, New Mexico, Jeffrey Preston Bezos was a clever child. At a young age he took a screwdriver to his crib, dismantling it into its component parts. This set a pattern. A few years later, when his grandfather bought him a Radio Shack electronic kit, he concocted a 'burglar alarm' to keep his siblings out of his bedroom. Moving on to the garage, the venue of choice for so many budding entrepreneurs, the ingenious

Bezos went onto to build a microwave oven driven by solar power.

After graduating from Princeton University with a degree in electrical engineering and computer science in 1986, Bezos headed for a high-tech start-up company, Fitel, in New York, where he built a computer network for financial trading. After Fitel, Bezos joined Bankers Trust, becoming its youngest vice-president in February 1990. From there, he moved to D. E. Shaw. The Wall Street firm interviewed him on the strength of a recommendation from one of its partners, who suggested that Bezos was 'going to make someone a lot of money someday'. At Shaw, Bezos described his role as a 'sort of an entrepreneurial odd-jobs kind of a person', effectively looking for business opportunities in the insurance, software and Internet sectors. He excelled in the role, helping to set up one of the most successful quantitative hedge funds on Wall Street and becoming senior vice-president in 1992.

Then came his epiphany. Sitting at his computer in the office, surfing the Internet, Bezos came across an astounding fact. According to the Internet usage statistics, the Internet was growing at a rate of 2300 percent per year. Bezos sensed an opportunity. Online commerce, he realized, was a natural next step. A combination of Wall Street insider and computer **nerd**, Bezos was perfectly positioned to cash in.

He compiled a list of 20 products that were suitable for selling online. On the list were items such as CDs, magazines, PC software and hardware – and books. The shortlist was quickly whittled down to two contenders – books and music. In the end, Bezos opted for books. His logic was twofold. For one thing, with more than 1.3 million books in print as against 300,000 music titles, there was more to sell. And, perhaps more importantly, the major book publishers appeared less intimidating than their record company counterparts. The six major record companies had a stranglehold on the popular music distribution business, but the biggest book chain, Barnes & Noble, had only 12 percent of the industry's total sales.

Quitting his job, Bezos headed out West and, after evaluating several locations, chose Seattle. With no state tax, a wealth of high-tech talent and a major book distributor on the doorstep – Ingram's Oregon warehouse – it seemed a perfect place to start his new business. From the garage of his rented home, Bezos and his first three employees set up their computers and began writing software for the new business. Originally, he planned to call the company Cadabra – a reference to the magic incantation. Fortunately, Bezos's friends convinced him that while the name may have spell-binding connotations, it also sounded very similar to 'cadaver'. Instead, Bezos opted for Amazon, after the world's largest river.

The company, according to its Web site, 'opened its virtual doors in July 1995 with a mission to use the Internet to transform book buying into the fastest, easiest, and most enjoyable shopping experience possible.' By the beginning of 1999, Amazon.com Inc. had a market capitalization of an astonishing $6 billion – more than the combined value of Barnes & Noble and Borders, its two largest bookstore competitors. The fourth quarter of 1998 brought net sales of $252.9 million, an increase of 283 percent over the same period in 1997. With Amazon awash with revenue, analysts and e-commerce commentators seemed unperturbed by the absence of profits.

For a while, investors were more than happy to go along for the ride. Then in June 2000, cracks began to appear in the almost unanimous support enjoyed by the star child of the Internet revolution. Holly Becker, e-commerce analyst at Lehman Brothers and long-time Amazon believer, switched her recommendation on the company from a buy to a neutral. She was, she said, 'throwing in the towel on Amazon'. Many saw Becker's change of heart as a turning point in the company's fortunes.

Yet Bezos may well have the last laugh. With some 21 million satisfied customers in June 2001, revenue over the same period up by 16 percent, and a strategic alliance with America Online in the bag, Amazon finally achieved pro forma operating profitability early in 2002. Whether, in the final analysis, Bezos will go down in the business history books as the creator of a viable and long-lived Internet business or simply as an e-business pioneer, remains to be seen.

Amazon is the totem stock of the Internet evangelists. What Bezos has created, after all, is nothing more or less than a virtual bookshop, and one that in its first five years didn't turn a profit. But Amazon.com isn't a bellwether stock without reason. Bezos is the quintessential dotcom icon. He proved to the business world that the Internet was about more than the dissemination and exchange of knowledge. He proved that it was possible to overcome fears about purchasing online; that it was possible to drive down transaction costs; that it was feasible to build an international e-commerce business over the Internet. Bezos is one of the great business pioneers. He had the courage to attempt something that people doubted could be done. Amazon has firmly entrenched itself as a dominant force in e-commerce. The question is whether it can profitably exploit its position.

Key texts

- Rebecca Saunders. *Business the Amazon.com Way. Secrets of the World's Most Astonishing Web Business.* Capstone, 1999
- Robert Spector. *Amazon.com: Get Big Fast – Inside the Revolutionary Business Model That Changed the World.* HarperBusiness, 2000

Key link

- www.amazon.com

Big Mac Index

Started by *The Economist* magazine in September 1986, the Big Mac Index is a measure of the comparative valuation of international currencies against the dollar. The Index was originally calculated to show the over- or undervaluation of the dollar itself. However, in 1993, it was changed to track the over- or undervaluation of each currency against the dollar.

The idea is that a dollar should have equal purchasing power in all countries. Therefore, over a period of time, the exchange rate between two countries should move toward a rate that equalizes the prices of an identical basket of goods and services in each country. *The Economist* chose a basket containing just one item – the Big Mac. The ubiquitous nature of the McDonald's burger – it is produced in over 120 countries – makes it a perfect candidate for this type of exercise and led to what *The Economist* lightheartedly refers to as 'Burgernomics'. The Big Mac purchasing power parity (PPP) is the exchange rate that would mean the hamburger costs the same in the United States as elsewhere. A comparison of actual exchange rates to PPPs shows whether a currency is under- or overvalued.

Key link
- www.economist.com/markets/Bigmac/ Index.cfm

Black and Scholes Model

Invented by American economists Fischer Black and Myron Scholes in 1973, the Black and Scholes Model was the first successful model for pricing options. The original model was used for simple put and call options on equities, but it has since been expanded to cover more complex transactions. The complex mathematical formula relates the price of an option to five inputs: time to expiration, strike price, value of the underlier (the underlying asset delivered under the contract), the implied volatility of the underlier and the **risk-free rate**.

Key link
- http://invest-faq.com/articles/deriv-black-scholes.html

Black knight

A black knight is a company that mounts a hostile takeover bid, as opposed to a **white knight**, which rescues the target company from the black knight through an agreed takeover or merger. A good example of one such unwanted suitor in recent corporate history is Vodafone AirTouch, which dramatically engineered a hostile takeover of German telecom giant Mannesmann in 2000.

Blake, Robert and Jane Mouton

Developers of the Managerial Grid (b. 1918)

Robert Blake co-founded Scientific Methods Inc. with Jane Mouton in 1961. He has a psychology degree from Berea College (1940), an MA from the University of Virginia (1941), and a PhD in psychology from the University of Texas at Austin (1947), where he later worked as a professor. Jane Mouton was a mathematician and a student of Blake's at the University of Texas. She led T-Groups at the National Training Laboratories in the 1960s.

In the 1950s, the American oil company Exxon employed Robert Blake and Jane Mouton as consultants. They brought refined sensibilities to the dirty and macho oil business. As they examined the behaviour of the people at Exxon, Blake and Mouton concluded that there was a sizeable gap in management theorizing, especially in terms of leadership and motivation.

Popular among the theories of the time was that of **Douglas McGregor** and his motivational extremes of X and Y. The trouble that Blake and Mouton found was that many behaviours and motivations fell in the middle of these extremes. They saw with their own eyes that theories X and Y were only a part of the overall picture of organizational behaviour.

Blake and Mouton's conclusion was that a model with three axes was a more accurate representation of reality. The three crucial axes, they determined, were concern for productivity, concern for people and motivation. Concern for production and people were both measured on a scale of one to nine, with nine being high. Blake explains: 'The reason you have to have a people axis is that managers achieve things indirectly. They don't produce nuts and bolts themselves, they organize others so that the production line can be productive.' Motivation was measured on a scale from negative (driven by fear) to positive (driven by desire).

Work by Blake and Mouton's company, Scientific Methods, found that when left to rank themselves, some 80 percent of people give themselves a 9.9 rating. Once this is discussed and considered, this figure is routinely reduced to 20 percent. Given such capacity for self-deception (and the figures are drawn from experience in more than 40 countries), Blake has reflected that it is little wonder that change programmes often hit the buffers.

Five key manager styles emerge from the grid:

- 1 (production); 1 (people): Do-nothing manager. The leader exerts a minimum of effort to get the work done with very little concern for people or production.
- 1 (production); 9 (people): Labelled the 'Country Club Manager'. This manager pays a lot of attention to people, but little to production. Can be seen in small firms that have cornered the market and some public sector organizations.
- 9 (production); 1 (people): This manager emphasizes production and minimizes the influence of human factors.
- 5 (production); 5 (people): Organization man who diligently fosters mundanity.
- 9 (production); 9 (people): Managerial nirvana. The ultimate manager, with an emphasis on teamworking and team-building. Personal and organizational goals are in alignment; motivation is high.

Key text
- Anne Adams McCanse. *Leadership Dilemmas – Grid Solutions*. Gulf Professional Publishing Company, 1991

Key link
- www.lib.uwo.ca/business/blake.html

Bloomberg, Michael

Founder and CEO of Bloomberg LP; author; mayor of New York City (b. 1942)

Michael Bloomberg was educated at John Hopkins University and **Harvard Business School**. After running Salomon Brothers' equity trading and technology systems, Bloomberg left the company in 1981. With a group of fellow ex-Salomon employees, Bloomberg founded Innovative Market Systems. The company was later renamed Bloomberg. It now has annual revenues in excess of $1 billion and Bloomberg is CEO. The company includes Bloomberg Financial Markets, Bloomberg News Radio, Bloomberg Business News, and Bloomberg Information TV.

His public pronouncements suggest arrogance: 'I could literally walk up to any crowd anytime, and speak for as long as you like, and they would love it,' he told the *Financial Times* for no apparent reason. His autobiography is accurately entitled *Bloomberg on Bloomberg*. This is tempered by fears of individual and corporate mortality. 'If you don't keep improving, someone else will; clean your clock,' he says. 'No company in history has gone on forever. It's scary. Of the *Fortune* 500 when we started the business in 1981, only 160 are left.' Bloomberg has prepared for the company's demise, or at least purchase, after his death: his will stipulates that the business will be sold to the highest bidder within two years of his death.

Bloomberg retains 80 percent of the business (the remaining share is owned by Merrill Lynch). He remains resolutely blunt in his managerial philosophy: 'Management, accountants, and other outsiders can say anything they want. Clients and employees never lie.'

Key texts
- Mac Barnes. *Total Wealth: Lifetime Wealth and Lifelong Security*. Capital Press, 2001
- Matthew Winkler (contributor). *Bloomberg by Bloomberg*. John Wiley & Sons, 2001

Key link
- www.bloomberg.com

Blow-out round

The blow-out round, also called the wash-out round, is venture capital jargon used to describe a situation in which a start-up company has received its first round of funding but requires more money. Unfortunately for the initial investors, another round of financing at a lower price will dilute their stake substantially (unless they have the benefit of an **anti-dilution clause**).

Blue-sky law

Introduced by 47 of the 48 US states between 1911 and 1931, blue-sky laws hand the responsibility for regulating and policing the issue of securities to the state in which the securities are being issued. The justification for these laws was ostensibly to prevent the sale of fraudulent securities to unsophisticated investors. The term 'blue sky' is said to originate from the supporters of the laws, who claim that some securities were so dishonest they would sell 'building lots in the sky'. Its use in law is first noted in an opinion of Justice McKenna of the United States Supreme Court in Hall vs. Geiger-Jones Co., 242 US 539 (1917). Justice McKenna wrote:

> 'The name that is given to the law indicates the evil at which it is aimed, that is, to use the language of a cited case, "speculative schemes which have no more basis than so many feet of 'blue sky"; or, as stated by counsel in another case, "to stop the sale of stock in fly-by-night concerns, visionary oil wells, distant gold mines and other like fraudulent exploitations."'

As Justice McKenna never referenced the 'cited case' to which he referred, the Hall cases have become known as the Blue Sky Cases, and Justice McKenna as the author of the phrase.

Boat anchor

A boat anchor is venture capital jargon used in start-up financing to describe a factor that acts as a brake on a company's early growth, such as a maverick manager, technology problems, or lack of product awareness.

Boeing, William

Aeronautical pioneer (1881–1956)

William Boeing was one of the great business pioneers of the twentieth century. Fascinated by aviation as a young man, Boeing turned a passion for flying into a business. The birth of William Boeing in Detroit, Michigan, on the first day of October 1881 goes down in history as one of the most significant days in the development of air travel. After an education in Detroit and Switzerland, Boeing studied at Yale Engineering College. His father was a wealthy lumberman so, in 1902, Boeing went to work for the family timber interests in Aberdeen, Washington, working his way up to become president of Greenwood Logging Company.

In 1908, he travelled to Seattle. It was here that Boeing became interested in aeronautics. On the University of Washington campus during the Alaska-Yukon-Pacific Exposition in 1909, he saw a manned flying machine for the first time. To the modern eye, the contraption that J.C. 'Bud' Mars took to the skies in would have seemed laughable, as well as downright dangerous. To Boeing the sight of the small gasoline-powered dirigible ascending above the university buildings was a marvel.

In the ensuing years Boeing discovered all he could about aeronautics. He joined the Seattle University Club, where he picked the brains of students like Navy engineer Conrad Westervelt. In 1915, with the help of Westervelt and another engineer, Herb Munter, Boeing established the Pacific Aero club in a boathouse at Lake Union. Together they began work on the B&W – a new twin-float seaplane.

Boeing anticipated that World War I would mean the US government would need more planes. He produced two prototype seaplanes *Bluebill* and *Mallard*; and Boeing took the controls at *Bluebill* on its maiden flight. Encouraged by the trials, Boeing founded Pacific Aero Products Co. in July 1916. When America entered the war in April 1917, Boeing changed the name of Pacific Aero Products to Boeing Airplane Co., and obtained orders from the Navy for 50 planes. A workforce of over 300 was assembled to construct the new planes in the 'Red Barn' on the Duwamish River.

The end of World War I was celebrated throughout the Allied nations. For Boeing it was a bittersweet moment. Victory in Europe meant the end of an intense period of activity; without the war to fuel production, prospects looked bleak. Orders dried up and Boeing turned to speedboat and furniture manufacture. Small military contracts kept the company ticking over but it was an entirely different type of business that was to save Boeing from bankruptcy.

Boeing's future lay in the hands of a man called Eddie Hubbard. Hubbard was Boeing's chief test pilot. Hubbard was convinced that the future of the aeroplane lay in transporting passengers and goods. In March 1919 he delivered the first international airmail to America flying in from Vancouver, Canada. While Boeing struggled for survival, Hubbard organized an aerial taxi offshoot of the company. In 1920, Hubbard was awarded a contract to carry mail between Seattle and Canada. He left Boeing and started his own firm, and he bought a Boeing B1 seaplane to use as the delivery plane. It was Boeing's first commercial aeroplane sale. In 1926 the Post Office invited tenders for its Chicago-San Francisco route. Hubbard personally persuaded Boeing to bid. Boeing won, founded a new subsidiary, the Boeing Air Transport Corporation, and welcomed Hubbard back into the fold to help organize the new company.

Boeing rushed out over 20 Model 40s in time to start the new airmail contracts on 1 July 1927. In 1928 he brought airline and aircraft manufacturing operations under the aegis of a new company – the Boeing Airplane and Transport Company – and then bought out one of his main rivals, Gorst's Pacific Air Transport. He introduced larger planes that were capable of carrying up to 18 passengers, attended by registered nurses, the first air stewardesses. In 1929, Boeing changed the name of his company to United Aircraft and Transport Corp. and proceeded to buy out most of the competition. When the balance of the Post Office mail contracts were handed out to private carriers, United picked up the Northern routes.

Boeing's acquisitive activities had, however, brought him onto the radar of President Franklin Roosevelt and a new Democratic administration. The US government in a show of strength were determined to rid the country of the monopolistic practices that dominated industry throughout the late nineteenth and early twentieth century. All airmail franchises were cancelled with effect from March 10, 1934. When the contracts were offered to private carriers again aircraft manufacturers were prevented from bidding. As a result of the government's actions, United Aircraft and Transport was divided into three separate companies: United Aircraft Co., Boeing Airplane Company and United Air Lines.

Although Boeing's company was in a strong enough position to survive without the mail contracts, Boeing was disgusted with the government's actions. The loss of the mail contracts sapped his resolve. After the breakup of United Aircraft and Transport, the prospect of restructuring and steering his company through another difficult period depressed him. At the age of 50 he retired from the company he had founded and had little more to do with it, other than acting as a consultant during World War II. He died in 1956.

Key texts
- Harold Mansfield. *Vision: A Saga of the Sky.* Duell, Sloan and Pearce, 1956

- Carl M Cleveland. *Boeing Trivia*. CMC Books, 1989
- Robert J. Serling. *Legend & Legacy: The Story of Boeing and Its People*. Martins Press, 1992

Bond

A bond is financial security issued by a company (or government) for the purposes of borrowing money. The bond is the certificate of indebtedness issued by the borrower, corporation or government in return for the loan. Bonds are issued for a fixed period, at a fixed (nominal) value, are repayable on a fixed date (the maturity date) and pay a set rate of interest during that period. At the end of the fixed period, some bonds may be convertible into the issuing company's stock. Bonds are bought and sold in a similar way to equities. To make them attractive to purchasers, their price will take into account the prevailing interest rates.

Historically, bonds have been a popular method of raising finance for funding wars. During World War II, the US government raised more than $185 billion from the sale of war bonds to more than 85 million Americans – over half the population of the United States at the time.

Key links
- www.wall-street.com/bonds.html – US bond links
- www.dmo.gov.uk/gilts/retail
- www.savingsbonds.gov/

Boo.com

Boo.com will go down in the annals of e-commerce history as one of the first and most public of a wave of dotcom company failures. The online fashion retailer jumped out onto the Internet in November 1999. Its launch was accompanied by a fanfare familiar to Internet observers, including a marketing campaign that highlighted an impressive range of established fashion brands, which would be available on Boo.com.

Unfortunately for Boo and its Swedish founders – Ernst Malmsten, Kajsa Leander and Patrik Hedelin – the site's launch was not as smooth as they might have hoped. Boo had already been criticized in the press for a delayed launch, with fingers pointed at bugs in the site structure. Post-launch, others jumped on the bandwagon, complaining that the site was difficult to browse if the viewer had a slow Internet connection or lacked the correct plug-ins. Plus – a cardinal sin to many – the site lacked Mac support. Boo responded with site redesigns and said it intended to build a Mac-compatible version.

Boo's aim of delivering the first truly global online retail site for fashion and sportswear was an attractive one. Had it gained momentum as a first mover, it might have been a lucrative one as well. Sadly, none of these scenarios materialized. Instead, when the hype had settled, Boo was left torn and tattered.

Apart from the lack of customers, the problem was the company's **burn rate**: the founders were not afraid to spend money, conducting themselves in some style, but at a cost. When the money ran out, the crowd of venture capitalists and banks clamouring to invest in the golden child of Internet fashion shopping had long since dispersed.

Key text
- Ernst Malmsten, Erik Portanger and Charles Drazin. *Boo Hoo: a Dot-com Story*. Random House Business Books, 2001

Book value

Similar to net asset value (NAV), book value is a ratio that reflects the amount of a shareholder's funds per unit share; i.e. shareholders' equity divided by the number of shares issued.

A company's stock usually trades above its book value. The difference between the book value and price paid, the premium paid by the investor, reflects future earnings and goodwill. Where there is doubt over the valuation of company's assets, or other problems associated with that company's trading, the company's stock may trade under the book value. However, in a depressed stock market, it is possible to find the stock of quality companies trading below the book value.

Another problem with using book value as a guide to stock value is how companies value their assets. In some cases, the value of a company's assets will not be fully reflected in the balance sheet. This is often the case, for example where a company has a valuable brand, valuable intellectual property or items like software, which do not always make their way onto the balance sheet.

In a more restricted sense, the book value represents the value of an asset on the balance sheet. This is normally the historic cost of the asset, less the amount written off for depreciation. The book value rarely reflects the market value of the asset.

Bootstrap finance

Bootstrap finance is a term used to describe the way the majority of businesses form themselves in the start-up stage. The term is derived from the strap on boots that is used to pull them on. Thus the bootstrapper pulls their business up by the bootstraps.

The bootstrapper uses a variety of means to fund the company, with the emphasis on imagination. It may mean focusing on a non-core product to bring in early revenue, employing guerrilla marketing tactics, tapping up friends and relatives or maxing out credit cards. The objective is to raise as much cash and grow as quickly as possible to a size where raising finance by more conventional means will be feasible.

Boston Matrix

The man who can be largely credited with bringing business models into the mainstream is Australian **Bruce Henderson** (1915–92). Henderson

was an engineer who worked as a strategic planner for General Electric. From GE, he joined the management consultancy Arthur D. Little. In 1963, Henderson left to set up his own consultancy, the Boston Consulting Group (BCG).

At the time, management consulting was beginning to establish itself as a profession and BCG is regarded by some as the first pure strategy consultancy. It quickly became a great success. Within five years, it was in the top group of consulting firms, where it has largely remained. It has been called the most idea-driven major consultancy in the world.

BCG went on to originate or develop concepts such as sustainable growth, time-based competition, segment-of-one marketing, value-based strategy, total shareholder value and even disease management. However, the model for which Henderson and BCG are best known is the Boston Matrix, which measures market growth and relative market share for all of the businesses in a particular firm. The hypothesis of the Boston Matrix is that companies with higher market share in faster-growing industries are more profitable. The further to the left a business is on the Boston Matrix, the stronger a company should be.

As with most such models, refinements have been added along the way. On its original matrix, BCG superimposed a theory of cash management that included a hierarchy of uses of cash, numbered from one to four in their order of priority. This identified the top priority as cash cows, characterized by high market share and low growth. Investment in cash cows is easily justified, as they are dull, safe and highly profitable. Next in line are the stars (high growth; high market share), though their investment requirements are likely to be significant. More problematic is the third category, question marks (or wildcats in some versions), where there is high growth and low share. Any investment in them is risky. The final category is the aptly titled dogs, where low market share is allied to low growth. Dogs should not be approached.

Celebrated in the 1960s, the Boston Matrix proved a highly popular innovation. From a business point of view, the matrix had the characteristics of any great model: It was accessible, simple and useful. However, it was also limiting. Measuring corporate performance against two parameters is straightforward, but potentially dangerous if these are the only two parameters against which performance is measured. A creature of its times, the matrix offered a blinkered view of a world where growth and profitability were all.

The Boston Matrix encouraged a preoccupation with market share.

Not surprisingly, other consulting firms were quick to respond with their own variations on the Boston Matrix. The most credible response came in the form of the General Electric and McKinsey matrix. This measured performance against two variables – industry attractiveness and business strength – and was effectively a dandified version of the original.

As a business tool, the Boston Matrix had a significant and long-term impact. It provides a useful way of looking at the world. Of equal significance was its influence on the management-consulting business, as it spawned a host of imitators. Now, it seems, no consultant's report is complete without a matrix of some sort. More importantly, BCG effectively introduced off-the-shelf consulting (though it wouldn't see it that way). Companies required the company's big idea. They wanted to see how they fared on the Matrix and how it could shape their strategies. The consulting firm product was born.

Previously, consultants had gone in to client companies to solve specific business problems. The success of the Boston Matrix marked a change in tactics. As well as problem solving, consultancy became concerned with passing on the latest ideas – the frameworks, models, and matrices that were the height of fashion. Problem solvers became peddlers of big ideas. This opened up huge new vistas for the management consultancy profession, which it has been assiduously – and profitably – chasing ever since.

Key text

- Carl W. Stern, George Stalk and John S. Clarkeson. *Perspectives on Strategy: From the Boston Consulting Group.* John Wiley, 1998

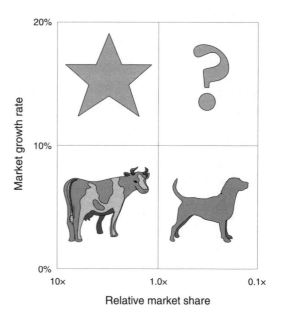

Figure 1 The Boston Matrix

Bot

Also known as agents or **intelligent agents**, bots (short for robot, from the Czech *robota* – to work) are automated pieces of software that sniff out information on the Web. One common use of bots is in directory classification and search engine rankings. Search engines send out bots (also called 'spiders') to crawl through the Internet, compiling information on the **URLs** they visit. This information is then used to help compile the ranking of Web sites that is returned when an individual searches for a term using a **search engine**.

Brainstorming

A creative process used to generate ideas, brainstorming is a group activity that involves encouraging members of the group to contribute any idea they have about the subject selected for discussion, no matter how wild it may seem. All ideas are written down and then, when the initial brainstorming process is completed, each is examined in more detail. This process aims to overcome social barriers that may stifle unusual or unorthodox suggestions from being made in a group situation.

Brand

When the McKenna Group, the firm of the celebrated 'father of high-tech marketing', Regis McKenna, conducted a survey of 100 CEOs, the results made alarming reading for brand managers everywhere. The CEOs, many of whom were leaders of high-tech companies in the driving seat of the new economy, were asked, 'What is a brand?' To this one question, they gave a 100 different answers. And therein lies the dilemma.

The unpleasant truth is there is no pat answer, no one definition of a brand. A legal definition might be approximately 'a sign that distinguishes the goods of a company from those of another while guaranteeing its origins'. But a brand is much more than its dry legal definition. A brand has many different attributes and the importance and nature of those attributes change according to whom you ask and when you ask them. The opinions of experts can offer some clues.

Historically, a brand was a mark on a product – a signature or symbol – signifying its origin or ownership. The traditional view of what constitutes a brand is summed up by marketing guru **Philip Kotler** in his classic textbook *Marketing Management*. He writes: '[A brand name is] a name, term, sign, symbol or design, or a combination of these, which is intended to identify the goods or services of one group of sellers and differentiate them from those of competitors.'

A more recent definition comes from Richard Koch in his book *The Dictionary of Financial Management*. Koch defines a brand as 'a visual design and/or name that is given to a product or service by an organization in order to differentiate it from competing products and that assures consumers that the product will be of high and consistent quality.' Koch stresses differentiation – making a product or service different (or seemingly different) – and achieving consistent quality.

More recently, and perhaps more usefully, three American consultants – Sam Hill, Jack McGrath and Sandeep Dayal – have defined branding as 'creating a mutually acknowledged relationship between the supplier and buyer that transcends isolated transactions or specific individuals'. It is a significant sign of our times that the brand is now pinned around a 'relationship' rather than a product.

Leslie de Chernatony, professor of brand marketing at the United Kingdom's Open University Business School, writing in *Marketing Business* in May 1999, echoes this perception of brands: 'The brand is, through the staff, an active participant in any relationship, be it between customer and brand, employee and employee, employee and customer, or employee and other stakeholders ... Inadequate communication of the corporation's values and individual's roles in delivering them can quickly result in inconsistencies between the brand's espoused values and the values perceived by stakeholders when dealing with staff.'

One of the most practical and contemporary definition of brands comes from the consultants Booz Allen & Hamilton: 'Brands are a shorthand way of communicating critical data to the market to influence decisions. Across a multitude of consumer-focused industries, brands are an important means for differentiation and competitive advantage, although they are most influential when customers lack the data to make informed product choices and/or when the differentiation between competitors' versions of the same product are small to non-existent. Additionally, brands take on more significance when consumers place great importance on the decision being made.'

Issues associated with brands include:

- **Branding:** Adding value to a product or service (which becomes the brand) over and above its retail price. This is achieved through a variety of branding strategies, which include creating a psychological and physical relationship between the consumer and the product, a brand identity and brand values.

- **Brand architecture:** A corporate structure delineating relationships between different parts of the brand. It explicitly defines the relationship between the master brand, sub-brands and products/services.
- **Brand awareness:** Degree to which a consumer recognizes and recalls a particular brand. Brand awareness is not just about recalling a brand's name but involves strategic awareness; i.e. the reason for which the consumer recalls the brand. Building brand awareness means creating a broad sales base and can involve operating outside the normal media channels – by using events promotion, **product placement**, **guerrilla marketing**, and other less conventional methods of reaching the consumer.
- **Brand equity:** The perceived added value that a brand confers on a good or service. There are three distinct components that intertwine to form brand equity. The first is the notion of the financial value of a brand as a distinct asset capable of representation on a company's balance sheet; this can be thought of as 'brand valuation'. The second is the consumer's degree of attachment to the brand, or 'brand loyalty'; finally, there is the description of the associations and beliefs that a consumer has about a brand, which is sometimes referred to as 'brand description'.
- **Brand extension:** Extension of a brand to products and services not normally associated with the core brand. Producing sub-variants of an existing branded product is line extension; applying a brand to an entirely different product is brand extension. The Virgin brand is the most commonly cited example of how to extend a brand successfully.
- **Brand image:** The mental perception of the brand in the minds of consumers. This is developed through communications and experience of the brand, and includes the distinguishing 'human' characteristics of brand personality (e.g. warm, friendly, fun, strong, etc.). The concept of brand identity is also closely aligned with that of brand positioning. However, positioning tends to suggest action on the part of the company in assigning the brand with attributes, as opposed to brand image, which is more about consumer perception.
- **Brand loyalty:** Attachment to a particular brand even if that brand is more expensive than competing brands. Brand loyalty is the target of all marketers. It is hard to win and easy to lose. Brand loyalty is a product of the psychological contract between the brand and the consumer. If the brand moves in a direction that is out of character with its brand identity, betrays its brand values or extends itself too far, it will breach the psychological contract and lose the loyalty of its consumers.
- **Brand U:** Application of corporate branding strategy to the individual. The concept was outlined by management guru **Tom Peters** in a 1997 article in *Fast Company*. An individual, argued Peters, should establish his own brand by going through the type of procedures that a company would. This includes identifying his brand identity, determining key differentiating characteristics and marketing himself at every available opportunity.
- **Brand values:** The essence of the brand, often expressed in key words, such as quality, creativity, luxury and integrity. Tom Blackett of media agency Interbrand has suggested that brand values can be divided into three classes: functional (what the brand 'does' for the consumer); expressive (what the brand 'says' about the consumer); and central (what the brand and the consumer 'share' at a fundamental level).

Another facet of branding is *co-branding*. This is where two or possibly more independent brands, often from different companies, join forces to support a new product or service. This practice is becoming increasingly popular, in order to squeeze the last drop of competitive advantage from a brand. Co-branding enables brands to increase their sphere of influence, enhance their reputation by association, deliver economies of scale and utilize new technologies more efficiently.

It often takes place where the economics of the market do not justify the launch of a new brand or formal joint venture. All brands involved will retain their individual brand names and usually the brands will be roughly equal in terms of public recognition.

Table 1 The world's most valuable brands 2001

Brand	Brand value ($ billion)
Coca-Cola	68.9
Microsoft	65.1
IBM	52.8
GE	42.4
Nokia	35.0
Intel	34.7
Disney	32.6
Ford	30.1
McDonald's	25.3
AT&T	22.8

Source: Interbrand

Key texts

- Philip Kotler. *Marketing Management: Analysis, Planning and Control.* Eighth edition, Prentice Hall, 1993
- Richard Koch. *The Financial Times Guide to Management and Finance.* Financial Times/ Pitman Publishing, 1994
- Sam I. Hill, Jack McGrath and Sandeep Dayal. 'How to brand sand.' *Strategy & Business,* second quarter 1998
- Harry Totonis and Chris Acito. "Branding the bank: the next source of competitive advantage", *Insights* series, 1998

Branson, Richard

UK entrepreneur; founder, CEO and chairman of the Virgin Group (b. 1950)

Richard Charles Nicholas Branson was born to an affluent middle-class family. He had a privileged private education: first at Scaitcliffe preparatory school and then at Stowe, one of England's foremost private schools.

Branson took little interest in academic studies, and only slightly more in sports. But he had a sense of confidence and self-belief. This was evident from Branson's assertion that despite failing his elementary math test three times, he could make a better job of running the school than the headmaster. He dispatched a memo to the headmaster outlining his suggestions on how the school should be run, which included a recommendation to allow senior students to drink two pints of beer a day.

Branson was never to profit from his suggestion since he dropped out of school at 16, keen to make his way in the world of business. His headmaster of the time commented that Branson would end up either a millionaire or behind bars. Fortunately, it was the former.

Branson's first serious business was a magazine called *Student*, which he launched when he was only 16 years old. He already had two failed schoolboy businesses behind him; one breeding budgerigars, another growing Christmas trees. The magazine business wasn't a resounding success either. But somehow Branson, despite his scant knowledge of pop music, came up with the idea of a mail-order record company. When the cheques began flooding in, Branson knew he had his first hit on his hands. Casting around for a name for his company, Branson came up with 'Virgin', which won out over alternatives such as 'Slipped Disc Records'. 'I had some vague idea of the name being catchy and applying to lots of other products for young people,' said Branson.

The next move for Branson was into record stores. This move was a fortuitous one, forced on him by a postal strike that decimated his mail-order business. It was in the early days of his record business that Branson had a chastening encounter with the law. Attempting to exploit a tax loophole, Branson was arrested and threatened with prosecution; the threat was only withdrawn when a repentant Branson agreed to pay back the money he owed.

Branson's charmed business life continued when he launched the Virgin record label and signed up Mike Oldfield, whose first album, *Tubular Bells*, remained on the UK album charts for the next ten years. Cash flowed into the company from

Tubular Bells and enabled Branson to expand his company. The Virgin record label continued to sign up hit artists. The label became synonymous with a radical new wave of musicians, including the Sex Pistols and Boy George.

In 1984, Branson, for the first time but certainly not for the last, stretched the Virgin brand beyond its normal territory of music and media and launched Virgin Atlantic Airways. Branson cleverly positioned Virgin Atlantic as a David taking on the Goliath of British Airways. The theme of sticking up for the little guy was one carried through future Virgin start-ups. In the case of Virgin Atlantic, it was an apt metaphor; Branson spent many of the ensuing years pursuing British Airways through the courts over allegations of 'dirty tricks' and subsequent libel actions. In the end Branson beat his Goliath when British Airways settled for £610,000 plus all legal costs in 1993.

A charismatic character, Branson used his own flair for publicity to help extend the Virgin brand to a host of other businesses. Mates condoms, Virgin Publishing, Virgin Cola, Virgin Direct personal financial services, Virgin Trains, Virgin Internet and Virgin Bride were all businesses that became part of the Virgin empire between 1984 and 2000. During this time, Branson has attempted to circumnavigate the globe in a hot air balloon; appeared at the inaugural press conference for the launch of his airline wearing a brown leather aviator's helmet; driven a tank down a busy New York City street to demolish a wall of cola cans during the US launch of Virgin Cola; dressed up as an air stewardess and as a bride, complete with the full regalia of wedding dress and high heels; and skied down a mountainside naked (not on camera). His PR genius has earned the company millions of dollars' worth of publicity for next to nothing. His column inches are only matched by his wealth.

Branson's gifts are many. He is an entrepreneur whose timing is often impeccable. He has a talent for publicity. His business secret is simply to go into stuffy markets where the customer has been consistently ripped off or underserved, and the competition is complacent. He then shakes things up, casting Virgin as the cheeky underdog, faster on its feet and nipping at the heels of big business. His marketing strategy appeals to millions.

Richard Branson is the ultimate brand-builder. Through his company, the Virgin Group, he has created a unique business phenomenon. Never before has a single brand been so successfully deployed across such a diverse range of goods and services. His personal wealth has been estimated at $2.7 billion, but it's hard to get an accurate tally, since his companies are private, constantly dividing and multiplying, and are controlled via a series of tax-efficient offshore trusts. Remarkably, he has also managed to keep a veil around the inner workings of his financial empire. In 1986, he floated his Virgin business on the London Stock Exchange, only to buy it back because he didn't like the constraints a market listing brought with it.

According to Tim Jackson, author of *Virgin King*, the unofficial Branson biography, Branson's motto should be *Ars est celare artem* – the art lies in concealing the art. This is the essence of the Branson management style, and the cornerstone of the Virgin empire.

Key text
- Des Dearlove, Stuart Crainer. *Business the Richard Branson Way: 10 Secrets of the World's Greatest Brand-Builder.* Amacom, 1999

Key links
- www.business2.com/webguide/0,1660,22172, FF.html
- www.virgin.net

Breakeven

Breakeven is the level of output where costs equal revenue and no profit or loss is made.

To determine the levels of activity required to generate a certain level of profit, and how changes in fixed and variable costs impact on profit levels, a management accounting technique relating to breakeven called 'breakeven analysis' is used. The technique involves analysing costs according to cost behaviour – fixed and variable costs – and comparing them with the total revenue to determine the breakeven point.

From this analysis, a breakeven chart may be produced. This is a line graph showing fixed costs, total revenue and total costs for a given activity over the entire range of possible output levels. The point at which the total revenues and total cost curves meet is the breakeven point. As well as showing the breakeven point, a breakeven chart allows the profit or loss to be determined for any level of output.

Brown goods

The term 'brown goods' is used to describe televisions, hi-fis, video machines and other similar electronic goods. It stems from the fact that these types of goods were often housed in wooden or simulated wooden cabinets, although silver plastic or tubular steel is more likely today.

Browser

A browser is a program that allows the user to search for and view data. Browsers are usually limited to a particular type of data; thus a graphics browser will display graphics files stored in many different file formats. Browsers usually do not permit the user to edit data, but are sometimes able to convert data from one file format to another.

Web browsers allow access to the World Wide Web. Mosaic was one of the first of the Web browsers, swiftly superseded by Netscape Navigator and Microsoft's Internet Explorer. Today, Microsoft's Internet Explorer dominates the market, despite some run-ins with the US Department of Justice over monopoly issues. Browsers act as a graphical interface to information available on the Internet – they read **HTML (hypertext mark-up language)** documents and

display them as graphical documents, which may include images, video, sound and hypertext links to other documents.

Key links
- www.microsoft.com/windows/i.e./default.htm
- http://home.netscape.com/computing/download/index.html

BSI (British Standards Institute)

Founded in 1901, the British Standards Institute assumed its present name in 1931 after receiving a royal charter in 1929. The government-funded but independent institute interprets international technical standards for the United Kingdom. Its remit also includes responsibility for setting standards in a variety of industries, including construction, electrical products, engineering and textiles. Products and companies meeting the standards set by the British Standards Institute are permitted to display the kitemark symbol. The symbol is used under licence, on condition that the BSI is able to inspect the product or company on a regular basis to ensure that standards are maintained.

One important quality standard is BS5750 – the standard applied to processes. Under BS5750, a company sets quality targets and then monitors performance against those targets. The level of quality guaranteed by the BS5750 certificate therefore depends on the level at which a company sets its quality targets. Once acknowledged as the industry standard in the United Kingdom, BS5750 has been somewhat superseded by **ISO** 9000.

Bubble

A bubble is an unsustainable rise in the price of an asset, such as a raw material, product or company share. Bubbles recur throughout trading history and are not a new phenomenon.

The South Sea Bubble is possibly the most famous example. The South Sea Company was proposed by George Caswall, a London merchant and stockbroker, and John Blunt, also a London stockbroker. It was chartered in 1711 by Robert Harley, Chancellor of the Exchequer, and formed as a joint stock company to assume government short-term debt. The idea was that the company would benefit from a monopoly on British trade to the South America and the South Seas. The trade was expected to arise out of concessions given by the Spanish in the peace negotiations that concluded the War of the Spanish Succession. Although the concessions ceded were not as lucrative as hoped and although trade was difficult, the company offered to assume the remainder of the government's debt in return for South Sea stock. The agreement of the government triggered a wave of investor speculation, which in turn drove up the stock price.

The stock price, which was £128 on 1 January 1720, reached £1050 on 24 June. But by December, the stock was back to £128. In the interim, thousands of individuals had been ruined, many borrowing heavily to finance their share purchases. Many banks went bust, unable to collect loans.

Shareholders who lost money included swathes of society's elite as well as famous figures, including authors Daniel Defoe, Alexander Pope and Jonathan Swift.

Other examples of bubbles are the tulip-bulb bubble, which deflated in 1637, and the Internet bubble of the 1990s. After a period of rapid price growth, the bubble inevitably bursts amid frantic selling, leaving many individuals with near-worthless goods or shares.

Buffer stock/inventory

Buffer stock is the stock required to meet contingencies. The level of buffer stock should be sufficient to cover problems such as a break in supply or damaged stock. In some production systems, such as **just-in-time**, the aim is to eradicate the need for buffer stock.

Buffett, Warren

Consummate investor; CEO of Berkshire Hathaway (b. 1930)

Born in Omaha, Nebraska, Warren Buffet exhibited the talents that were to make him a wealthy man at an early age. Aged only six, he would buy six packs of Coca-Cola for a quarter, break them up, and sell the individual bottles for a nickel each. When the young Buffet was stricken with a mysterious illness, he lay in bed figuring how to get rich.

On his recovery, he roped his friends into a number of money-making enterprises he had thought up. He looked for lost golf balls, packaged up those he found, and sold them. He also became one of the youngest racing tipsters in the United States when he published the *Stable Boy Selections* – Buffet's information on the hot horses of the moment. His record for picking winners is not known, but if it was anything approaching his later success with picking stocks, he must have made a few gamblers very rich.

When he was twelve, his father, Howard Buffet, won a seat in Congress, and Warren moved with his family to Washington, DC. The move was initially unpopular with Buffet, who registered his protest by running away from home. However, when he realized the commercial potential of the US capital, he changed his mind. He took on five paper routes at once, delivering a staggering 500 papers each morning and earning the equivalent of a man's full-time salary of $175. When he was still only 14, he had earned $1200, enough to buy 40 acres of farmland in Nebraska and rent them out.

After another business foray in high school – installing renovated arcade games in barber's shops – Buffet decided to add to his natural flair for commerce with a formal business education. He landed a place at the prestigious Wharton School of Finance and Commerce at the University of Pennsylvania. But Buffet did not complete his course. He found the theoretical aspects of business dull, and discovered nothing in the curriculum to slake his thirst for practical knowledge.

So he left Wharton for the University of Nebraska, where he finished his studies in business and economics while organizing the paper routes for the *Lincoln Journal* on the side. At 19, he applied to Harvard Business School but was refused admission. Giving up on Harvard, he turned to Columbia Business School. But it was in reading the stock market that Buffet found his true vocation.

Determined to make a living by investing, Buffet put his energy and all of the savings amassed from his various schemes into the stock market. Between 1950 and 1956, he turned $9800 into $140,000. News spread about the new whizz-kid investor, and more and more people asked him to invest their money for them. What started with friends spread to the general public, and soon Buffet was forming limited partnerships and taking a 25 percent cut of any return above 4 percent.

Once Buffet started investing as a career, he soon developed his own personal investment strategy. He began by looking for stocks that offered outstanding value – those that were relatively cheap given their asset value – and then holding those shares for the long term. 'Lethargy, bordering on sloth should remain the cornerstone of an investment style,' he has said. He was heavily influenced by the theories of Ben Graham, co-author of the investment classic *Security Analysis* (1934) and his former tutor at Columbia.

Buffet eventually took Graham's value-investing strategies a step further by seeking out companies whose shares were inexpensive compared to their growth prospects. This approach required assessing a company's intangible assets, such as brand value. In this, Buffet was ahead of his time. The whole area of intangible assets is now receiving growing interest from business academics, but back then it was largely neglected.

Between 1957 and 1966, the investment partnership that Buffet managed posted an incredible 1156 percent return against 122.9 percent over the same period for the Dow Jones average. A partner's investment of $10,000 would, after deducting Buffet's share, have returned $80,420. Buffet continued to outperform the market with a 36 percent return in 1967 and a 59 percent return in 1968; this was in a speculative market, not particularly suited to Buffet's investment strategy.

In 1969 Buffet, to the surprise of his managers, called it a day. Concerned about maintaining his performance in an unsuitable investment climate. Buffet decided to wind up the partnership.

Since 1969, Buffet's attentions have been focused entirely on his investment vehicle Berkshire Hathaway, a publicly listed company that he acquired in 1965. The markets may go up or down but over time, Buffet has consistently delivered for his shareholders. His legendary, almost uncanny knack of picking stocks has earned him the epithet 'the Sage of Omaha'. It's a tag the unassuming man from Omaha undoubtedly deserves on the strength of his company's performance. A $10,000 investment in Berkshire Hathaway in 1965 would have been worth more than $50 million by the end of 2000. (Investors who backed the S&P 500 Index would have accumulated some $500,000, a paltry amount by comparison.)

Buffet himself has remained relatively unaffected by the plaudits heaped upon him. A modest man, he has few indulgences other than the corporate jet owned by his company. Even this was something he stoutly resisted for many years. He lives in an average home in Omaha, famously drives an old car, and maintains a fairly small office with few staff. His main hobby, it seems, is reading company reports – something in which he maintains an avid interest, despite the many thousands he must have ploughed through.

Warren Buffet is one of the greatest investors of all time. What lifts him above his peers is a determination to stick to his investment principles. Companies have risen and fallen, one minute the height of fashion, the next discarded on the bankrupt company pile. Buffet has steadfastly refused to jump on the fashionable company bandwagon. Famously, he refuses to invest in companies that he doesn't understand – this includes most high-tech companies. Instead, Buffet has made a fortune for himself and his shareholders by investing in undervalued companies for the long term. It's

Buffet's willingness to buck the trend that makes him worthy of his 'Sage of Omaha' tag.

Key texts
- Roger Lowenstein Buffett. *The Making of an American Capitalist.* Doubleday, 1996
- John Train. *The Midas Touch: the Strategies That Have Made Warren Buffett America's Pre-eminent Investor.* Harper & Row, 1987

Key link
- www.berkshirehathaway.com

Building society

A building society is a financial institution in the United Kingdom and Ireland. It attracts investment in order to lend money, repayable at interest, for the purchase or building of a house on security of a mortgage.

The origins of the building society date back to the industrial revolution, when members of local organizations pooled funds in order to purchase land and build houses. The first building society, Richard Ketley's at the Golden Cross Inn, Birmingham, was formed in 1775, and like most of the early building societies was 'terminating' – it closed when its members had been housed.

Then, when members began to invest without wanting to buy property, the building societies became permanent. The first permanent society, The Metropolitan Equitable, was formed in 1845.

The largest building societies in the United Kingdom in 1996, in order, were the Halifax, Nationwide, Woolwich, Alliance and Leicester, Bradford and Bingley, Britannia, Bristol and West, and Northern Rock. In 1997, five of these became banks or were taken over by banks in order to extend their range of financial services: the Halifax, Woolwich, Alliance and Leicester, Bristol and West, and Northern Rock. In 2001, the top 5 building societies were Nationwide, Britannia, Yorkshire, Portman and Coventry.

Key link
- www.bsa.org.uk

Bulk-decreasing good

A bulk-decreasing good decreases in size and/or weight during the manufacturing process. The resulting reduction in transportation costs means that bulk-decreasing goods tend to be manufactured close to the raw materials they use and then transported to market.

Contrast this with a bulk-increasing good, which increases in size and/or weight during the manufacturing process. The resulting increase in transportation costs means that bulk-increasing goods tend to be manufactured close to the markets they are sold in.

Bulls, bears and stags

The stock market (and other trading markets) seem to be obsessed with animals. If investors are not queuing up like lambs to the slaughter, they are joining the ranks of the bulls, bears or stags – all animals traditionally associated with stock markets.

A bull is an optimist – a trader in a stock, currency or other market who believes that the market is going to rise. Such positive sentiments are said to be bullish.

A bull market is a market in which traders are buying or expecting to buy and so pushing the market up. In a bull market, a trader will go long in a stock, predicting that it will rise in value so that it can be sold at a profit.

Where the use of the term 'bull' comes from is unknown, although there are suggestions that it is related to the tendency of bulls to charge ahead or toss their heads upwards.

On the other side of the pen are bears. A bear is a trader in a stock, currency or other market who believes that the market is going to fall. Such negative sentiments are said to be bearish.

A bear market is a market in which traders are selling or expecting to sell and so depressing the market. In a bear market, a trader may short stock – that is, sell stock they do not possess – then buy the stock to fulfil the contract when the price has fallen and pocket the difference between the two prices.

The use of the term 'bear' comes from the days when traders used to sell bearskins before the bears were caught.

Finally, there are stags – investors who buy up new issues in the hope of selling them quickly for a profit. Stagging, as the practice is known, was rife in the United Kingdom during the 1980s, when a number of publicly owned companies were privatized.

The last word to all those who predict the way the world's markets will move goes to economist John Kenneth Galbraith: 'We have two classes of forecasters: Those who don't know – and those who don't know they don't know.'

Bundling

The practice of giving one product away with another, bundling is usually used by manufacturers and retailers as a marketing tactic to promote the good being given away. Bundling can also be used to encourage consumers to use one retailer's product instead of a competitor's. Microsoft bundled its Web browser software, Internet Explorer, with its operating system, Windows. This was to encourage the use of Explorer instead of Netscape Navigator, its principal competitor's product. Using bundling in this way may fall foul of anti-competition legislation.

Bureaucracy

A bureaucracy is an organization whose structure and operations are governed to a high degree by written rules and a hierarchy of offices; in its broadest sense, all forms of administration, and in its narrowest, rule by officials. The individuals who operate within such a centralized, hierarchical organization, or bureaucracy, including government officials and other officials of large organizations, are known as bureaucrats.

Bureaucracies were declared by **Max Weber** (1864–1920) to be technically superior to all other forms of organization and therefore essential to large, complex enterprises. Today, however, *bureaucracy* and *bureaucrat* are used as mildly derogatory terms associated with overadministration, overstaffing and inefficiency. New organizational models, such as the matrix model, have sprung up to replace the traditional top-down hierarchical models.

Key text
- Max Weber. *The Theory of Social and Economic Organization*. Oxford University Press, 1947

Burnett, Leo

Advertising guru; founder of the 'Chicago school' (1891–1971)

Simply put, Leo Burnett changed the face of advertising in the United States. After working his way through a number of agencies, including Homer McKee and Erwin Wasey, he resisted the lure of New York's Madison Avenue agencies and in 1935 set up his own in Chicago. After a hesitant start, Burnett's distinctive style of advertising soon attracted major clients, such as Procter & Gamble. The Leo Burnett advertising agency went on to produce some of the most distinctive advertising of its time, including the Marlboro Man campaign. Burnett's advertising philosophy gave rise to the Chicago School of advertising and by his death in 1971, he was universally acknowledged as one of the most influential figures in his industry.

Burnett started out young in advertising. His father owned a drapers store and Burnett would design and draw the display cards, little realizing how advertising would come to play such an important part in his life. Burnett attended the local high school, moonlighting as a reporter for several weekly newspapers in the area.

Immediately after graduation, he briefly took up a position as a teacher in St Johns' single-classroom village school before heading for the University of Michigan at Ann Arbor, where he earned a journalism degree. Once again, he continued to work throughout his studies, this time both as a night editor at the *Michigan Daily* and producing display cards for a department store. After graduation Burnett worked at the *Peoria Journal* in Illinois as a reporter for eighteen dollars a week. He remained there for about a year, until the lure of the burgeoning car industry proved too great and Burnett set off for Detroit.

In Detroit, Burnett joined the Cadillac Motor Car Company as editor of an in-house magazine. He had been tipped off about the job by one of his old college professors and, as part of his application, wrote an essay on neatness that had sufficiently impressed the people at Cadillac to win Burnett the job. Soon, Burnett had been handed responsibility for Cadillac's advertising. The pattern for Burnett's social and professional life was set.

After a brief stint in the US Navy during World War I, Burnett, with several other Cadillac employees. broke away from Cadillac to form LaFayette Motors. Burnett followed LaFayette to Indianapolis but, when the company moved to Wisconsin, remained in Indianapolis as creative head at the Homer McKee advertising agency.

Burnett settled at Homer McKee for ten years as a copywriter. In 1929, the stock market crash affected advertising agencies badly. Homer McKee was no exception, losing one of its major car accounts. Now with a young family, Burnett needed a secure job and decided to move on. The Burnett family moved to Chicago in 1930 and Burnett signed up for Erwin Wasey as creative vice-president. At the time, Erwin Wasey was one of the leading advertising agencies in the world. Shortly after Burnett joined, the firm moved its headquarters to New York. The New York ad agencies had developed a reputation for a hard-sell approach to advertising. They were also perceived by their West and Midwest clients to favour companies based on the East Coast.

Several of Burnett's clients approached him and suggested he open his own agency. Initially, Burnett's loyalty prevailed. Then Art Kudner left Wasey to start his own agency, taking several car manufacturing clients – including General Motors – with him. Burnett relented. It was 1935, Burnett was 44, and on 5 August, his own agency opened for business.

Burnett's agency made a name for itself through its distinctive style of advertising, what Burnett called 'stressing the inherent drama in the product'. The trickle of clients became a flood after Procter & Gamble chose Burnett for an institutional campaign in 1950.

In 1955, Burnett was retained by Philip Morris to develop a campaign for Marlboro cigarettes. The Marlboro campaign, with its imagery of the rugged Marlboro man, was one of the most memorable campaigns of the twentieth century. There were many other memorable campaigns in the years that followed. Clients included Schlitz Beer, Maytag and United Airlines.

Burnett's influence on the advertising industry was so great that the term 'the Chicago School of Advertising' was coined to describe his and his followers' distinctive approach. It was a style that tried to capture the essence of the product in its advertising rather than just using clever words. It was also an inclusive approach that didn't try to play to either the East or the West Coast.

In the late sixties, suffering increasingly from illness, Burnett took a back seat in the business he had created. He retired in 1967, although he continued to come into the office at least twice a week. On 7 June 1971, after a spell in the office, Burnett suffered a heart attack at his home and died that night. He was 79.

Praised by competitors and clients alike, Leo Burnett made a unique contribution to the advertising industry. He was driven by a consuming passion for excellence and creativity that shone through in the work of his agency. He also adopted a socially responsible approach to business, demonstrated through the firm's pro bono work, carried out in part under the auspices of the Advertising Council. The pressures of winning business never drove Burnett to employ unscrupulous or cut-throat practices, which was not true for every agency. It was a testimony to his even-handed approach that he was often fêted by his closest rivals.

Key text

- Simon Broadbent. *Leo Burnett Book of Advertising*. Business Books, 1984

Key link

- www.leoburnett.com

Burnout

Burnout markedly impairs the performance of employees and may even incapacitate them. Some jobs are known by employer and employee to cause burnout and employees only expect to be in that position for a limited period. These types of jobs tend to be very well-rewarded financially. Traders in financial markets are a typical example. In other industries, burnout is unpredictable and companies take measures to guard against it, such as enforcing vacation time and introducing stress-management programmes.

Burnout is the physical or psychological condition induced in workers by overwork or overexposure to stress in the workplace. In the United States, the phenomenon of career burnout has long been recognized. Employees who work too hard, for too long, can become demotivated, depressed and, in extreme cases, suffer nervous breakdowns or worse. Comparative figures are hard to come by, but anecdotal evidence suggests that the problem may be getting worse in the United Kingdom. The situation in the United States is so bad that almost one-third of the workforce feels overworked or overwhelmed by the amount of work they have to do.

'Feeling Overworked: When Work Becomes Too Much' is a survey conducted by the non-profit Families and Work Institute, supported by international accountancy firm PriceWaterhouse-Coopers. 'Overworked' was defined by the authors of the study as 'a psychological state that has the potential to affect attitudes, behaviour, social relationships, and health both on and off the job'.

The study looked at a sample of 1003 adults who performed paid work for an employer (as opposed to being self-employed). When asked how often they felt overworked and/or overwhelmed by work over a period of three months, over half said that they felt overworked and overwhelmed sometimes and a significant number said they felt that way most of the time.

Professor Andrew Kakabadse at the Cranfield School of Management has also investigated the phenomenon of burnout as part of a worldwide study of executive performance. His data, based on a detailed survey of 6500 managers from ten countries, suggests all leaders are prone to burnout, but their organizations are often embarrassed by the phenomenon and don't know what to do about it.

'Corporate life requires deadlines to be met and inevitably workloads are unevenly shared, meaning that organizations generate their share of workaholics irrespective of the wishes of the individual,' he says. 'In addition, organizational chaos is rife, yet most workplaces still implicitly demand employees be "corporate people", living and dreaming about attaining success in organizational life.'

Serious attention, Kakabadse says, should be given to how burnout happens, how to recognize and cope with it, and how to combat it. The symptoms include increasing fatigue, not listening effectively, feeling saturated with work and feeling unable to participate in routine operational conversations.

What make the tell-tale signs hard to spot, however, is that declining morale and feelings of personal vulnerability usually emerge slowly and insidiously.

'Increases in stress, job pressure, competition, higher work complexity, faster pace of life, and the greater likelihood of redundancy all make for an inevitable drip, drip of negativity which leads many top managers to burnout,' says Kakabadse. 'Prolonged demotivation leads to an emotional deterioration which is worsened by a realization that to some extent current lifestyle traps us in our jobs. Age, difficulty in matching remuneration packages, and the continuity needed to support family life contribute to a sense of being trapped.'

It is often worse for those further down in the organization. Evidence suggests that stress is more pronounced among those who are not in control of their own destiny. Employees who are suffering burnout and feeling overworked and overwhelmed by work are detrimental to an organization. According to the Families and Work Institute study, overworked employees are more likely to make mistakes at work, resent their employers for expecting them to do so much, resent co-workers who do not work as hard as they do, and look for a new job.

While these effects are bad for the employers, it gets worse for the employee. The study also found that employees who feel overworked are more likely to suffer from sleep loss, are more likely to neglect themselves, are less likely to report very good or excellent health, feel less successful in personal relationships, experience more work/life conflict, have higher stress levels and are less able to cope with everyday life.

Key text
- E. Galinsky, S. Kim and J. Bond. *Feeling Overworked: When Work Becomes Too Much*. Families and Work Institute, 2001

Burn rate

The burn rate is the rate at which a company uses available cash. Burn rate became an important metric for analysing the fortunes of nascent dotcom companies. With phenomenal growth fuelled by huge advertising expenditures, but little or no earnings, analysts looked at how long the company could survive on existing funds in the bank, assuming costs remained at the same level. This measurement became critical when investors became reluctant to provide later-stage funding for dotcom companies.

The burn rate is usually expressed in terms of the amount of cash spent per month. A burn rate of 1 million, for example, would mean the company is spending $1 million per month. If revenue fails to meet projections, the first step the company usually makes is to reduce the burn rate.

Burns, James MacGregor

Political scientist and author on leadership (b. 1918)

James MacGregor Burns is a political scientist. Not simply a theorist, he has run, unsuccessfully, for Congress as a Democrat and worked in John F. Kennedy's presidential campaign.

His books include *Congress on Trial* (1949); *Government by the People* (with Jack Peltason, 1950); *Roosevelt: The Lion and the Fox* (1956); *John Kennedy: A Political Profile* (1960); *The Deadlock of Democracy* (1963); *Presidential Government: The Crucible of Leadership* (1965); *Roosevelt: The Soldier of Freedom* (1970); *Uncommon Sense* (1972); and *Edward Kennedy and the Camelot Legacy* (1976).

In the prologue to his 1985 book *Leadership*, Burns observes, 'The crisis of leadership today is the mediocrity or irresponsibility of so many of the men and women in power, but leadership rarely rises to the full need for it. The fundamental crisis underlying mediocrity is intellectual. If we know all too much about our leaders, we know far too little about leadership.'

There are literally hundreds of definitions of leadership. Burns suggests that, as a result, 'leadership as a concept has dissolved into small and discrete meanings. A superabundance of facts about leaders far outruns theories of leadership.' Undaunted, in *Leadership*, Burns provides yet another theory – but one that has proved more enduring: 'Leadership over human beings is exercised when persons with certain motives and purposes mobilize, in competition or conflict with others, institutional, political, psychological, and other resources so as to arouse, engage, and satisfy the motives of followers.'

To Burns, leadership is not the preserve of the few or the tyranny of the masses. 'The leadership approach tends often unconsciously to be elitist; it projects heroic figures against the shadowy background of drab, powerless masses,' he writes. 'The followership approach tends to be populistic or anti-elitist in ideology; it perceives the masses, even in democratic societies, as linked with small, overlapping circles of conservative politicians, military officers, hierocrats, and businessmen. I describe leadership here as no mere game among elitists and no mere populist response but as a structure of action that engages persons, to varying degrees, throughout the levels and among the interstices of society. Only the inert, the alienated, and the powerless are unengaged.' To Burns, leadership is intrinsically linked to morality and 'moral leadership emerges from, and always returns to, the fundamental wants and needs, aspirations, and values of the followers.'

Aside from his thoughtful definition in *Leadership*, Burns identifies two vital strands of leadership: transformational and transactional leadership.

Transformational leadership 'occurs when one or more persons engage with others in such a way that leaders and followers raise one another to higher levels of motivation and morality. Their purposes, which might have started out separate but related ... become fused. Power bases are linked not as counterweights but as mutual support for common purpose,' writes Burns. 'Various names are used for such leadership: elevating, mobilizing, inspiring, exalting, uplifting, exhorting, evangelizing. The relationship can be moralistic, of course. But transforming leadership ultimately becomes moral in that it raises the level of human conduct and ethical aspiration of both the leader and the led, and thus has a transforming effect on both ... . Transforming leadership is dynamic leadership in the sense that the leaders throw themselves into a relationship with followers who will feel "elevated" by it and often become

more active themselves, thereby creating new cadres of leaders.'

Transformational leadership is concerned with engaging the hearts and minds of others. It works to help all parties achieve greater motivation and satisfaction and a greater sense of achievement. It is driven by trust, concern and facilitation rather than direct control. The skills required are concerned with establishing a long-term vision, empowering people to control themselves, coaching and developing others, and challenging the culture to change. In transformational leadership, the power of the leader comes from creating understanding and trust.

Alternatively, transactional leadership is built on reciprocity – the idea that the relationship between the leader and their followers develops from the exchange of some reward, such as performance ratings, pay, recognition or praise. It involves leaders clarifying goals and objectives, communicating to organize tasks and activities with the cooperation of their employees to ensure that wider organizational goals are met. Such a relationship depends on hierarchy and the ability to work through the mode of exchange. It requires leadership skills, such as the ability to obtain results, to control through structures and processes, to solve problems, to plan and organize and work within the structures and boundaries of the organization.

In their apparent mutual exclusiveness, transformational and transactional leadership are akin to **Douglas McGregor**'s X and Y theories. The secret of effective leadership appears to lie in combining the two elements so that targets, results and procedures are developed and shared.

Burns's book provides an important link between leadership in the political and business worlds. In all of the books on leadership, the two have usually been regarded as mutually exclusive. His examination of transformational and transactional leadership also stimulated further debate on leadership at a time when it was somewhat neglected. In the 1980s, it returned to prominence in management literature as a subject worthy of study.

Key text

- James MacGregor Burns. *Leadership*. Harper-Collins, 1985

Key link

- www.academy.umd.edu/home/index.htm

Business bites

The corporate catchphrase 'business bite' is a relatively recent development. Business bites distil complex issues into punchy one-liners. Forget the detailed academic argument; the idea is to capture the very essence of your business philosophy or message into a simple but highly memorable sentence. 'IBM was yesterday; Microsoft is today; Oracle is the future,' says **Larry Ellison** with customary élan. In so doing, the owner and originator hopes to achieve two not entirely unrelated objectives. First, to become instantly recognizable to managers around the globe; and second, to sell business books and consultancy services.

These intellectual sound bites are phrases such as *Only the Paranoid Survive*, which became the title of a bestseller for **Andrew Grove**, head of Intel. We can only guess at how the book might have fared had his original, altogether less snappy title, *Navigating Strategic Inflection Points*, not been rejected by the publisher. 'Managers do things right; leaders do the right things' is a hardy perennial from leadership guru **Warren Bennis**. 'Don't automate, obliterate' was the reengineering call to arms. **James Champy** and Michael Hammer also produced 'Good products don't make winners; winners make good products.'

Meanwhile, in the high-tech arena, 'A PC in every home' could only be **Bill Gates**. There is also 'Trade not Aid' from **Anita Roddick** of The Body Shop, and the slightly less sassy but no less true 'Corporations are not things, they are the people who run them' from **Charles Handy**.

Business bites differ sharply from mission statements, which are typically bland corporate statements. They belong to the individual rather than the company. So, for example, the phrase

'Any colour you like as long as it's black' goes with **Henry Ford** and not with the eponymous car company he founded.

Some have been quicker on the uptake than others. The man who coined the phrase 'nanosecond nineties', **Tom Peters**, has had more bites than just about anyone. More recently, his bite has been 'Crazy times call for crazy organizations'.

Business bites are important business weapons. No business leader ever achieved anything if he wasn't understood. At their best, business bites communicate complex ideas simply, quickly and understandably. At worst, they are meaningless bastardizations.

Such is the premium placed on business bites that it is not unheard of for them to be followed by the copyright symbol or even the letters TM, denoting trademarks of the author. This is more likely where there are consultancy products and services to be sold on the back of the intellectual property they represent.

Business books

Over the last 15 years, the business book market has been revolutionized. Once, business books were dull and unreadable; they even looked dull and unreadable. Today, a small segment of the publishing world has been turned into a global market, with publishers hurrying to find the latest purveyor of managerial jargon. Business books even look like novels, with their garish covers, punchy titles and hard sales lines.

Thanks to *The Dilbert Principle*, by **Scott Adams**, business books have gone mainstream with a vengeance. Their titles are hip, or at least would like to be. Harvard's John Kao wrote *Jamming*, a eulogy to jazz creativity and how it could be the future of business. Then there are the bright and zany titles. This trend was established with the success of *When Giants Learn to Dance*, by another Harvard star, **Rosabeth Moss Kanter**. Kanter is a serious academic who prides herself – justifiably – on the quality of her research. She is, however, responsible for a steady stream of books with silly names.

Charles Handy picked up on Kanter's example early on – he wrote *The Age of Unreason* and, more biblically, *Waiting for the Mountain to Move*. A title like Handy's *The Empty Raincoat* is – in this market at least – pure genius. It defies analysis and begs a number of important questions: Why is the raincoat empty? What can and should be inside? The fact that the answer is 'doughnuts and shamrocks' only adds to the confusion.

Things have got a little out of hand. Now, no business book is complete without a surreal title and a detailed subtitle that attempts to tell you its contents in less than twelve words. Alternatively, for those who don't thrive on subtlety and ambiguity, there is the shocking title that has blockbuster and bestseller written all over it. **Tom Peters** has cornered this particular market with titles such as *Thriving on Chaos* and *Liberation Management*. These give managers the impression that the contents are all about action, and action is managers' fatal attraction.

Yet while business books are fond of silly names, they appear to make a serious difference. Every intricate detail of the latest business blockbuster is being put to work somewhere. Helped by the fact that business is increasingly global and the skills of management often universal, books make their way around the world, shaping the management of the future. At this very moment, a factory in China could be contemplating reengineering, a start-up in Stockholm may be coming to terms with one-to-one marketing, and a Polish conglomerate examining the merits of intellectual capital.

Books are being put to work. Look at the big idea of the 1990s – reengineering. The idea was popularized by a book – *Reengineering the Corporation* by **James Champy** and Michael Hammer. It was hailed as a revolution. The book sold in the hundreds of thousands. People everywhere began reengineering. At one time, most of the world's leading companies were reengineering.

Then there is the part played by **W. Edwards Deming** in the renaissance of Japan, or the impact of **Michael Porter**'s work on the value chain, which has been taken up by companies throughout the world. Porter's work on national competitiveness has altered the economic perspectives of entire countries. Porter has been called in by countries as far apart as Portugal and Colombia to shed light on their competitiveness. And who thought customer service was a key competitive weapon before Peters and Waterman's *In Search of Excellence*?

However, such a significant impact is the province of just a few titles. The practical usefulness of much that is published is questionable. Over 2000 business book titles emerge every year, but only a handful are worth reading. Few influential business books are written by practising managers (or by women). Books by actual managers largely provide proof of why the individuals chose a career in business rather than in the media. They tend to be riddled with egotism and poor writing. There are a few exceptions, such as **Alfred P. Sloan** or, more recently, **Ricardo Semler**. (The readability of **Jack Welch**'s autobiography was helped by the writing acumen of *BusinessWeek*'s **John Byrne**). But the vast majority of business bestsellers are written by academics from the leading US business schools and American consultants.

Critics of business books would suggest that therein lies the problem. Academics and consultants are routinely condemned as being out of touch with business reality. In some cases, this is undoubtedly true. But the individual experiences of a single executive in a particular organization are unlikely to provide a rich vein of inspiration for executives in wildly different situations.

The trick of timelessness is to write something that is universal in appeal rather than constrained by context. **Sun Tzu**'s wisdom may be 2500 years old, but it is still routinely quoted, pinned on notice boards and enshrined on laminated cards. **Dale Carnegie**'s books are still selling and the training organization he created is still thriving. Ideas live on.

Business cycle

A business cycle is a period of time that includes

a peak and trough of economic activity, as measured by a country's national income. The economy passes through phases of boom and recession, causing changes in the levels of output, unemployment, and inflation. For example, between 1854 and 1991, the US economy went through 31 cycles.

Key links
- www.cris.com/~netlink/bci/bci.html – US business cycle indicators
- www.stern.nyu.edu/~nroubini/bci/bcibase.htm
- www.nber.org/cycles.html – with historical dates back to 1854

Business model

A company's business model is the means by which it plans to conduct its business and make a profit. Business models were put under the spotlight during the Internet boom. Many companies were operating with business models that relied on advertising revenue to support other activities. This is the business model adopted by most magazines in the physical world. On the Internet, however, it has proved difficult to sustain. Other common business models include the age-old retail business model, in which goods are sold at a sufficient margin to make a profit.

Business plan

The business plan is an essential business tool used as an aid to secure financing for a new venture. The dotcom start-up frenzy of the 1990s led to a reappraisal of business-plan contents and format. As venture capitalists were buried under a deluge of business plans from would-be dotcommers, the business plan became shorter and shorter, until it was frequently being presented as a PowerPoint display only.

Even after the dotcom slowdown, there remain conflicting opinions as to whether business plans should be long and detailed or short and concise,

delivered in writing or in PowerPoint. In-depth or brief, a business plan will usually contain the following ingredients: an executive summary (the summary of the business plan in a couple of pages, including a summary of the summary – known as the **elevator pitch**); the space (a description of what market the business is in); marketing (an outline of marketing strategy and projected costs); management team (details of the management team, their areas of expertise and relevant experience); financials (realistic financial predictions such as **breakeven** point and cash **burn rate**); and an exit strategy (an appraisal of how the investors will recoup their investment).

Business process reengineering (BPR)

See Reengineering.

Business school

A business school is an institution for training in management and marketing. In recent years, the emphasis has shifted to include study of such issues as environmental policy, corporate responsibility, business ethics and internationalism. The master's in business administration (**MBA**) has become a highly prized degree in many professions.

Business schools are a huge international business. The global executive education market has been calculated at some $12 billion. A place in the nine-week Advanced Management Program at Harvard Business School will cost in excess of $40,000. Over the last 50 years, business schools have created a formidable industry.

Today, however, after more than 20 years of booming business, business schools face intensifying competition and fundamental questions about their role. Competition comes from a number of fronts. There is a growing number of corporate universities – centres funded by companies to train their staff. Then there are consulting firms. Once the big business ideas came out of business schools. Now, they tend to emerge from consulting firms like McKinsey & Co., which increasingly consider themselves to be in the ideas market. There are also many start-ups specializing in distance learning delivered by the latest technology.

The final source of competition to business schools comes, somewhat surprisingly, from their own faculty. Business school faculty can increasingly be found running their own lucrative consulting businesses. Then there is the seminar and conference merry-go-round.

The end result of growing competition is likely to be a shakedown in business school numbers. At the moment, there are approximately 800 business schools in the United States and Europe producing well over 100,000 MBA graduates per year. The future may well see a three-tier system, with a small elite of global schools at the top, nationally competing schools below, and a final tier of local competitors.

The trouble is that business schools have never quite established whether they wish to be considered as academic institutions or businesses. The result is that they tend to perform badly on both counts. As academic institutions, business schools have to increasingly acknowledge an indifferent record in generating new thinking. Then there are matters of academic impartiality. The business school habit of seeking corporate funding for everything from chairs (professorial and others) to wallpaper means that anomalies can arise. The holder of a professorship sponsored by a particular company is hardly likely to publish a damning case study of the company's management techniques. Little wonder that much business literature is banal and self-congratulatory.

If business schools are to be treated as businesses, their record is equally questionable. Business schools appear adept at shooting themselves in the foot and remain perpetual hostages to charges of not running themselves according to the precepts they champion in the lecture theatre. Business schools may protest about the unfairness of being judged by their practical application of the theories they so eloquently espouse. But how many business schools reengineered themselves at the beginning of the 1990s? How many have identified their core competencies and, as a result, changed their organizational structure? How many really know what business they are in?

If business schools have led managers to believe that running a business can be a precise, measurable and, therefore, manageable science, it is no surprise that they are being measured by their own yardsticks. Those that fail to come up to the mark are likely to find the going tough.

Key link
- www.usnews.com/usnews/edu/beyond/bcrank.htm – business school rankings

Byrne, John A.

Author, BusinessWeek *columnist, senior writer and B-school ranking wizard*

John Byrne is the *BusinessWeek* columnist who ran the magazine's bi-annual survey of business schools. 'Some deans refer to John Byrne, the *BusinessWeek* journalist responsible for compiling the rankings, not altogether jokingly as "the most important man in North American management education",' wrote George Bickerstaffe in *Which MBA?*. Byrne no longer has this onerous responsibility, but remains a senior writer at the magazine.

Byrne is also known for extensive coverage of Al Dunlap's career over the years. He is the author of several books, including *Informed Consent* and *The Whiz Kids*, and is the co-author, with John Sculley, of *Odyssey*. Most recently he teamed up with celebrity CEO **Jack Welch** for the hit book *Jack: Straight from the Gut*.

Key texts
- Jack Welch and John A. Byrne. *Jack: Straight from the Gut.* Warner Books, 2001
- John Sculley and John A. Byrne. *Odyssey: Pepsi to Apple … a Journey of Adventure, Ideas & the Future.* Diane Publishing Co, 2000
- John A. Byrne. *Informed Consent*, McGraw-Hill, 1996

- John A. Byrne and Cynthia Greene. *Business Week's Guide to the Best Executive Education Programs*. McGraw-Hill Companies, 1992

Key link
- www.businessweek.com

Byte

A byte is sufficient computer memory to store the set of binary digits – 0 and 1 – that represent a character, such as a letter of the alphabet. Usually a byte is comprised of eight bits.

C

CAD (computer-aided design)

Computer-aided design is real-time graphic design carried out using a computer. Originally, CAD just automated the drafting process. In the late 1970s and early 1980s, however, CAD developed into a three-dimensional modelling system. It was developed and pioneered in scientific institutions such as the CERN particle physics laboratories in Switzerland, where the EUCLID 3D CAD system was used for the design of particle accelerators and detectors.

CAD has paved the way for advanced computer graphics and computer animation. Powerful CAD software allows designers to build virtual designs and manipulate them onscreen. An architect can, for example, use CAD, combined with virtual reality and other graphics programs, to 'walk' people through a virtual model of a planned building. CAD software has also become cheaper and is available for home computer users.

Key link
- www.autodesk.com/siteselect.htm

Call centre

A call centre is a dedicated office that deals with customer telephone enquiries. The first call centres (although they were not known as such) were created in the United States during the 1970s, when the travel and hospitality industry began to centralize its reservation centres. This move came about because new phone technology ena-

bled large-scale, high-volume telephone traffic at single premises.

The practice was soon adopted by banks and mail-order companies. But it wasn't until the 1990s that the management of call centres was recognized as a stand-alone industry rather than an adjunct to the business it was serving.

The 1990s have been a boom time for call centres. The number of call centres in North America has been estimated at up to 200,000, although the correct figure is probably closer to 100,000.

Often employing several hundred staff in a tightly regulated environment, call centres have been described as the developed world's version of the sweatshop or Taylorism – **scientific management** – in the twenty-first century.

Employees are frequently required to read from a predetermined script and deal with enquiries within prescribed time limits while supervisors listen to conversations. While the United States and the United Kingdom took a lead in the provision of call centres, in theory call centres can be sited wherever the cheapest competent labour is found.

Key links
- www.callcentres.com.au
- www.callcenternews.com

CAM (computer-aided manufacturing)

Computer-aided manufacturing refers to the use of computers to control manufacturing processes. In this form of automation, it is computers that give instructions directly to the manufacturing machinery, rather than people.

Advanced systems even manage tasks such as tool replacement and parts ordering.

CAM systems are often linked to **CAD (computer-aided design)** systems. The CAD data helps with various stages of the CAM process, including tool and fixture design (the stage that creates the hardware required to make a product) and manufacturing planning and control (the creation of inventory lists and similar documents).

Computers are commonly used to control industrial processes in many industries, from petrochemicals and steel to electronic engineering and food processing. CAM can be used as part of a computer-integrated manufacturing system.

Campbell, Andrew

Director, Ashridge Strategic Management Centre; author (b. 1950)

Andrew Campbell is one of three directors (with Michael Goold and Marcus Alexander) of the Ashridge Strategic Management Centre (ASMC) in London. He was a Baker Scholar and Harkness Fellow at **Harvard Business School**, and earned his degree in economics and statistics at Eton and Edinburgh University.

ASMC is associated with Ashridge Business School. The *Financial Times* ranked the school's executive **MBA** programmes as 7th in the United Kingdom, 12th in Europe, and 43rd in the world as of October 2001. Ashridge dates back to 1283, when Earl Edmund of Cornwall founded it as a monastery.

Prior to his tenure at Ashridge, Campbell was a Fellow in the Centre for Business Strategy at the London Business School. His research on corporate strategic decision-making processes resulted in the publication of *Strategies and Styles*, co-authored with Michael Goold. In total, his research to date has resulted in the publication of nine books and numerous articles, including four for *Harvard Business Review*. Campbell had previously worked for six years with McKinsey & Co.

in their Los Angeles and London offices, and for three years as a loan officer with the Industrial and Commercial Finance Corporation (now Investors in Industry).

The basic, and accurate, realization behind Michael Goold, Marcus Alexander, and Andrew Campbell's *Corporate-Level Strategy* is that most large companies are now multibusiness organizations. The logic behind this fact of business life is one that is generally assumed rather than examined in any depth. Multibusiness companies through their very size offer economies of scale and synergies between the various businesses that can be exploited to the overall good.

While this is a truth universally acknowledged, Goold, Campbell and Alexander's research suggests that this *raison d'être* does not, in reality, exist. They calculate that in over half of multibusiness companies, the whole is worth less than the sum of its parts. Instead of adding and nurturing value, the corporation actually negates value. It is costly and its influence, though pervasive, is often counterproductive.

This condemnation is not restricted to what we would normally consider to be conglomerates. Goold, Campbell and Alexander suggest that the baleful influence of the corporate parent also applies to companies with portfolios in a single industry, or in a series of apparently related areas.

One of the primary causes of this phenomenon is that while the individual businesses within the organization often have strategies, the corporation as a whole does not. It may pretend otherwise, but the proclaimed strategy is often an amalgam of the individual business strategies given credence by general aspirations.

If corporate-level strategy is to add value, Goold, Campbell and Alexander suggest that there needs to be a tight fit between the parent organization and its businesses. Successful corporate parents focus on a narrow range of tasks, create value in those areas, and align the structures, processes and central functions of the parent accordingly. Rather than being all-encompassing and constantly interfering, the centre is akin to a specialist medical practitioner – intervening in its areas of expertise when it knows it can suggest a cure.

From their detailed analysis of 15 successful multibusiness corporations, Goold, Campbell and Alexander identify three essentials to successful corporate strategies. First, there must be a clear insight about the role of the parent. If the parent does not know how or where it can add value, it is unlikely to do so. Second, the parent must have distinctive characteristics: it, too, has a corporate culture and personality. Third, there must be recognition that 'each parent will only be effective with certain sorts of business' – described as its 'heartland'.

'Heartland businesses are also well understood by the parent; they do not suffer from the inappropriate influence and meddling that can damage less familiar businesses. The parent has an innate feel for its heartland that enables it to make difficult judgements and decisions with a high degree of success,' say the authors. Heartlands are broad-ranging and can cover different industries, markets and technologies. Given this added complexity, the ability of the parent to intervene on a limited number of issues is crucial.

The concept of heartland businesses is, they make clear, distinct from core businesses. Though core businesses may be important and substantial, say Goold, Campbell and Alexander, the parent may not be adding a great deal to them. 'A core business is often merely a business that the company has decided to commit itself to,' they write. 'In contrast, the heartland definition focuses on the fit between a parent and a business: Do the parent's insights and behaviour fit the opportunities and nature of this business? Does the parent have specialist skills in assisting this type of business to perform better?'

Corporate strategy should be driven by what Goold, Campbell and Alexander label 'parenting advantage': 'to create more value in the portfolio of businesses than would be achieved by any rival'. To do so requires a fundamental change in basic perspectives on the role of the parent and of the nature of the multibusiness organization.

Key texts

- Andrew Campbell and Michael Goold. *The Collaborative Enterprise: Why Links Between Business Units Often Fail and How to Make Them Work*. Perseus Books, 1999
- David Sadtler, Andrew Campbell and Richard Koch. *Breakup! Why Large Companies are Worth More Dead Than Alive*. Capstone, 1997
- Andrew Campbell and Kathleen Sommers Luchs. *Core Competency-Based Strategy*. International Thomson Business Press, 1997
- Michael Goold, Andrew Campbell and Marcus Alexander. *Corporate-Level Strategy: Creating Value in the Multibusiness Company*. John Wiley & Sons, 1994
- Andrew Campbell and Kathleen Sommers Luchs. *Strategic Synergy*. Butterworth-Heinemann, 1992

Key links

- http://freespace.virgin.net/andrewcampbell/index.htm
- www.ashridge.org.uk

Candlestick chart

A candlestick chart is a graphic representation of the performance of a traded commodity, usually a stock, so called because of its resemblance to a candle.

Candlestick charts have a well-established history. They are sometimes referred to as Japanese candles because the Japanese used them hundreds of years ago to depict the price of rice contracts.

Favoured by stock analysts, the candlestick chart shows a stock's opening, closing, high, and low prices. A vertical rectangular box, known as the body of the candle, joins the opening and closing prices – opening at the top and closing at the bottom. If the closing price is higher than the opening, the box is left empty; if the opening price is higher than the closing, the box is coloured in. Alternatively, different colours are used to show whether the stock was up or down over the day. At either end of the body of the candle are thin lines (imagine a wick at either end) that represent the highest price (at the top of the candle) and lowest price (beneath the box).

There are several patterns easily recognizable by interpreters of candlestick charts. One pattern is 'the hammer' – a small body with a large range – which is a bullish pattern that occurs when the stock price has fallen for several days. Another pattern is the star, supposedly indicating a reversal or change in the current trend.

Key link
- www.altavest.com/candlesticks.html

Cannibalization

Cannibalization is the undesired situation in which an increase in sales for one branded product sold by a company results in a decrease in sales for another branded product sold by the same company. The reason for this corresponding reduction in sales is usually insufficient product differentiation between the two products affected. Thus, if a manufacturer of shampoo introduces a new shampoo on the market with only minor modifications to that product over existing products, sales of the new product are likely to be at the expense of existing product sales.

Capacity planning

In its broadest sense, capacity planning involves analysis and decision making in order to balance capacity for producing a product or service with the demand from customers.

Capacity planning is conducted over the long, medium, and short terms, with day-to-day adjustments being vital to its success. Regardless of the nature of operations involved, the principles and considerations of capacity planning remain similar. They include forecasting (the consideration of dependent and independent demand); output strategy (the relative merits of chasing demand or utilizing level output production); and planning systems (aggregate planning methods, including master production schedules and others).

The company conducting the capacity planning exercise will need to have knowledge of and understand a range of factors, including the possibilities of outsourcing, the technology available, the operational situation at major suppliers and staffing availability.

Capacity planning for a Web site will, for example, involve measuring the ability of the Web site to deliver content to its customers at an acceptable speed. The number of site visitors will be analysed, as well as the demand each user places on the server. The resources required to meet existing and future usage are then determined. This involves assessing adequacy of resources such as network bandwidth, disk space and processor speeds. Factors that affect the capacity of a Web site include the site content (content that uses a lot of bandwidth, such as video and static graphics, have an adverse effect on performance); user numbers (as site use grows, so capacity must keep pace with user growth in order to continue to deliver acceptable levels of service); and hardware and software infrastructure (upgrading infrastructure such as hard disk space and processing speed can increase capacity).

Capital

In classical economics, capital – financial capital (money) or physical capital (machinery and plant) – is considered one of the non-human factors of production, along with land. Capital is also used to describe investment in a company as either share capital or debt (loan capital).

Capital asset pricing model (CAPM)

The capital asset pricing model, first introduced in the 1960s by William Sharpe, then a researcher at the RAND Corporation, is a mathematical pricing model used in portfolio theory; it models the systemic risk in a particular asset. By systemic risk, we mean risk that cannot be avoided by a trader. Even though traders can avoid much risk by diversifying their portfolios, there will always be some risk associated with the market. This risk is the systemic risk.

By using the CAPM, a trader can examine the relationship between investment risk and expected return and attempt to evaluate and minimize investment risk.

The return on an investment is its risk premium added to its risk-free rate. The risk premium is the difference between the market rate of return and the risk-free rate (the rate of return on an investment with no risk, such as a treasury bill), multiplied by the **beta** of the share.

The capital asset pricing model requires several assumptions, including that a riskless security exists; that all assets in the world are traded; that for each lender, there is a borrower; and that all investors borrow and lend at the riskless rate.

Key text
- Diana R. Harrington. *Modern Portfolio Theory, the Capital Asset Pricing Model & Arbritrage Pricing Theory: A User's Guide.* Prentice-Hall Canada,1987
- William F. Sharpe. *Portfolio Theory & Capital Markets: The Original Edition.* McGraw-Hill Professional, 1999

Key link
- www.moneychimp.com/articles/valuation/capm.htm

Capital gain

If an asset is bought and later sold at a profit, the increase in value is deemed a capital gain. The capital gain is nominally the sale price less the purchase price.

In many countries, individuals are liable to capital gains tax on gains above a specified level. Arriving at the amount of capital gain for tax purposes is complicated by indexation. This is a process in which the original purchase price is

adjusted to take into account the effect of inflation in the years between purchase and sale. In the case of corporations, a capital gain is listed in the shareholders' funds on the balance sheet.

The effects of capital gains taxation vary from country to country. For example, capital gains taxes are higher in Canada than in the United States. Also, in the United States, holding an asset for longer than 18 months entitles the recipient of the capital gain to a lower tax rate.

Key link
- www.cato.org/pubs/pas/pa-242.html – in the US
- www.inlandrevenue.gov.uk/rates/cgt.htm – in the UK
- www.netaccountants.com/taxsummary/taxdata-cgt.html

Capitalization

See Market capitalization.

Career

From the Latin *carraria*, which means carriageway, a career is a progression of jobs throughout an individual's life. A 'career' is more than 'a job'. A job is an increasingly transient phenomenon. Most individuals will do several different jobs during their lifetime; some will do many, not all necessarily in the same field. A career is the collective experience of a working life. A job is a part; a career is the sum of the parts.

Careers were once spent mainly with one company, moving from each job to a better job in that organization. Today, careers can involve working for one company, working for many different companies, working in different industries or even working for different companies and industries at the same time.

The planning of an individual's career, by the individual or by a specialist company, is known as career management. Professional career managers act as consultants, offering their services to individuals who need assistance planning their careers, as well as to companies as an added-value service for the human resources department.

A new phenomenon, career management includes issues such as **employability**, career coaching, **work/life balance** and personal development. It aims to identify and improve an individual's unique skills, and then to find jobs, or assignments, which match those skills and the individual's values.

There is also a term for a person for whom personal advancement in a career assumes a great importance – some might say too great an importance – in his life: careerist.

Key link
• www.wetfeet.com/careers/home.asp

Carlzon, Jan

Former President and CEO, SAS Group; IT Investor; chairman, CEO and co-owner of Transpool AB (b. 1941)

Jan Carlzon was president and **CEO** of the airline SAS during the 1980s. SAS had been an indifferent performer until Carlzon introduced it to customer service. It had lost money in 1979 and 1980 but while other airlines went on to lose record amounts of money, SAS returned to high profitability under Carlzon's tutelage and became Airline of the Year.

Most notably, Carlzon came up with the phrase 'moments of truth': the sequence of critical transactions across each stage of the ownership or use cycle. 'Anytime a customer comes into contact with any aspect of a business, however remote, is an opportunity to form an impression,' Carlzon writes.

These were broken down into initial contact; first use; problem solving; ongoing support; further purchases; and recommendations to others. Evaluating the degree to which satisfaction and value are affected at these different points in the cycle, and how they vary by customer type, can be the key to understanding customer behaviour.

Carlzon truly understood the process and decided to dramatically prove the company's dedication to moments of truth by sending tens of thousands of SAS managers on training programmes. It was a dramatic but meaningful statement. In doing so, Carlzon set in motion SAS's revival and became a benchmark for international best practice in customer service, celebrated by many, including **Tom Peters** in *A Passion for Excellence*. For a time, with a neat line in phrase-making and a great story to tell, Carlzon was hardly out of the business magazines. Carlzon's *Moments of Truth (Riv Pyramiderna!* – 'flatten the pyramids' – in Swedish) was an international bestseller, selling 3 million copies.

Carlzon reversed the normal pyramid view of organizations, which shows the boss at the top and the people who actually meet customers at the bottom. Carlson believed that management's only justification is to enable and facilitate the people in contact with the customers to do their jobs well. Thus he inverted the typical organizational pyramid, and drew himself at the bottom and the customers on top, with the customer-contact people just below them.

In November 1993, Carlzon left SAS and become chairman, CEO and co-owner of an integrated leisure, travel, and airline company (Transpool AB). He also co-founded a customer-driven telecommunications company – NETnet – that has successfully been introduced throughout Europe. Carlzon is also directly or indirectly involved in more than a dozen new IT ventures through venture capital firm Ledstiernan AB, where he is the chairman and senior partner.

Key texts
• Gary Heil, Tom Parker and Deborah C. Stephens. *One Size Fits One: Building Relationships One Customer and One Employee at a Time.* John Wiley & Sons, 1999
• Jan Carlzon and Tom Peters. *Moments of Truth.* Harper Collins, 1989

Key link
- www.ledstiernan.com

Carnegie, Andrew

Industrialist; philanthropist, founder of Carnegie Steel Company (1835–1919)

Born in Dunfermline, Scotland, the son of a handloom weaver, Andrew Carnegie emigrated with his family to the United States in 1848 during an economic depression. Settling in a colony of Scots gathered at Slabtown, Pennsylvania (near Pittsburgh), the twelve-year-old Carnegie took work in a local cotton mill.

Leaving the cotton mill, Carnegie got a job at the local Pittsburgh Telegraph Office as a messenger boy. Thomas A. Scott, superintendent of the western division of the Pennsylvania Railroad at the time, spotted Carnegie's potential and appointed Carnegie as his secretary at $50 a month, then a handsome salary for one so young. It was Scott who set Carnegie on the path to riches by showing him the potential of investing in start-up companies. Acting on a tip from Scott, Carnegie bought stock in Adams Express Company with money from his mother, who had re-mortgaged her house. Shortly afterward, he borrowed money to invest in a venture commercially exploiting the invention of the sleeping car for the railway.

During the American Civil War, Carnegie served with Scott in Washington. Then, with the Union victory secured, Carnegie took Scott's old position as superintendent of the western division of the Pennsylvania Railroad. But Carnegie's entrepreneurial instincts soon got the better of him and he left the railroads to set up the Keystone Bridge Company to build iron bridges. He was also involved in several other speculative ventures that proved successful.

While Carnegie was busy hustling in the United States, inventor and businessman Henry Bessemer was working on an industrial process in England that would change industry the world over. The Bessemer process allowed for the industrialized production of steel from iron. Carnegie often visited the United Kingdom, and on one visit he came across the Bessemer converter. It was a revelation.

Hurrying back to the United States, Carnegie formed Carnegie, McCandless & Co., built his first blast furnace in 1870, and began experimenting with the Bessemer process. Carnegie opened a steel furnace in Braddock, Pennsylvania; by 1880, the plant was operating 24 hours a day with annual profits of $2 million. In 1881, the company reorganized, becoming Carnegie Bros. & Co., with Carnegie holding the controlling interest. In 1882, Carnegie acquired the coke-producing interests of Henry C. Frick. Frick became Carnegie's most trusted associate.

In 1889, Carnegie moved to New York to continue his research into the steel manufacturing process. He also spent six months of the year with his family in Scotland. In his absence from the day-to-day running of the company, Carnegie left Frick in charge as chairman of Carnegie Bros. When Frick took over, the company was effectively a collection of disparate threads, mills and furnaces dotted about Pittsburgh. Frick wove these threads together to create the fabric of a company that would become the biggest steel company in the world. He centralized the management structure and integrated production to form the Carnegie Steel Company, valued at $25 million.

Unfortunately for Carnegie, Frick also presided over one of the most notorious incidents in US corporate history. In an attempt to drive down costs and boost profits, Frick reduced piecework rates. Incensed, the Amalgamated Iron and Steel Workers Union called its members at the Carnegie Homestead plant out on strike. Instead of settling through negotiation, Frick further inflamed the situation by planning to bring in 300 strikebreakers.

When the day came and the strikebreakers arrived on barges down the Monongahela River, complete with armed guard, all hell broke loose. At the end of a day of pitched battle, ten men lay dead with a further 60 wounded. The Homestead plant was placed under martial law.

Carnegie, in Scotland at the time, was irate. It was not just the disruption to the company that he rued: Frick had countermanded Carnegie's explicit instructions not to use strikebreakers. For Carnegie, it was a matter of personal ethics. For many years after the debacle, Carnegie as the controlling owner, and as such responsible, would have to bear the dark stain of the workers' blood on his reputation.

Although Carnegie refrained from criticizing Frick in public, their relationship never recovered. The company continued to thrive, improving annual production of steel from 332,111 tons in 1889 to 2,663,412 in 1899, and profits from $2 million to $40 million. Carnegie and Frick's relationship, however, deteriorated. In 1899, Carnegie took an opportunity to buy Frick out for a handsome $15 million. Even this act of severance failed to quell the personal animosity between the two men. In 1901, Frick returned with the backing of the notorious **J. Pierpont Morgan** and purchased the Carnegie Company for $500 million, establishing the US Steel Corporation. Valued at $1.4 billion, it was the biggest steel company in the world.

Carnegie will be remembered as much for his philanthropy as his business adventures. In later life, Carnegie, guided by his ethical beliefs, gave away the majority of his fortune. He set up a trust fund 'for the improvement of mankind'. Three thousand public libraries, the Carnegie Institute of Pittsburgh, the Carnegie Institute of Technology and the Carnegie Institution of Washington were built with the trust's money.

When the king of steel died in August 1919, he had already given away $350 million of his fortune.

Key texts
- James Mackay. *Andrew Carnegie: His Life and Times*. Wiley, 1998
- Harold C. Livesay. *Andrew Carnegie and the Rise of Big Business*. Little, Brown & Co., 1979
- Joseph Frazier Wall. *Andrew Carnegie*. OUP, 1970
- John K. Winkler. *Incredible Carnegie; the Life of Andrew Carnegie (1835–1919)*. The Vanguard Press, 1931
- Andrew Carnegie. *Autobiography of Andrew Carnegie*. Houghton Mifflin, 1920
- Bernard Alderson. *Andrew Carnegie; the Man and His Work*. Doubleday, Page & Co., 1905
- Andrew Carnegie. *The Empire of Business*. Doubleday, Doran & Co., 1902
- Andrew Carnegie. *The Gospel of Wealth and Other Timely Essays*. The Century Company, 1901

Key link
- www.carnegie.org

Carnegie, Dale

Trainer; author; first motivational guru (1888–1955)

Born on a Missouri farm, Dale Carnegie (originally Carnegey) began his working life selling bacon, soap and lard for Armour & Co. in south Omaha. He turned his sales territory into the company's national leader, but then went to New York to study at the American Academy of Dramatic Arts, after which he toured the country as Dr Harley in *Polly of the Circus*. Realizing the limits of his acting potential, Carnegie returned to salesmanship, selling Packard cars. It was then that Carnegie persuaded the YMCA schools in New York to allow him to conduct courses in public speaking.

Carnegie's talks became highly successful. He wrote *Public Speaking and Influencing Men in Business* and a variety of other variations on his theme – *How to Stop Worrying and Start Living, How to Enjoy Your Life and Your Job, How to Develop Self-Confidence and Influence People by Public Speaking*. He is best known, however, for *How to Win Friends and Influence People*, which has sold over 15 million copies (its first edition had a print run of a mere 5000).

How to Win Friends and Influence People is the original self-improvement book. 'If by the time you have finished reading the first three chapters of this book – if you aren't then a little better equipped to meet life's situations, then I shall consider this book to be a total failure,' Carnegie writes in its opening. He wrote it as a textbook for his courses in 'Effective speaking and human relations'. Carnegie's aim was to write 'a practical, working handbook on human relations'.

To do so, Carnegie eagerly explains that no stone was left unturned. He read extensively and hired a researcher to spend 18 months reading the books he had missed – 'I recall that we read over one hundred biographies of Theodore Roosevelt alone'. Carnegie then interviewed famous personalities – from Clark Gable to Guglielmo Marconi, Franklin D. Roosevelt to Mary Pickford.

Carnegie was a salesman extraordinaire: Throughout the book, names are dropped and promises made. Upbeat and laden with sentiment, *How to Win Friends and Influence People* is a simple selling document: 'The rules we have set down here are not mere theories or guesswork. They work like magic. Incredible as it sounds, I have seen the application of these principles literally revolutionize the lives of many people.'

The result is a number of principles from which friends and influence should, Carnegie anticipates, surely emerge. First, there are the 'fundamental techniques in handling people': 'don't criticize, condemn or complain; give honest and sincere appreciation; and arouse in the other person an eager want'. Then Carnegie presents six ways to make people like you – 'become genuinely interested in other people; smile; remember that a person's name is to that person the sweetest and most important sound in any language; be a good listener. Encourage others to talk about themselves; talk in terms of the other person's interests; make the other person feel important – and do it sincerely.'

It is easy to sneer at Carnegie's work – it is homespun wisdom adorned with commercial know-how. But it is difficult to sneer at the enduring popularity of his books and his company's training programmes. Long after his death, they continue to strike a chord with managers and aspiring managers, because they deal with the universal challenge of face-to-face communication.

Dale Carnegie was the first superstar of the self-help genre. Go forth with a smile on your face and a song in your heart and sell, sell, sell. His successors – from **Anthony Robbins** to **Stephen Covey** – should occasionally doff their caps in Carnegie's direction.

Key text
- Dale Carnegie. *How to Win Friends and Influence People*. Simon & Schuster, 1937

Key links
- www.dale-carnegie.com
- www.dale-carnegie.co.uk

Cartel

A cartel is a group of organizations that agree, formally or informally, not to compete with each other. Cartels may be formed within or across national boundaries. A cartel may be formed to fix the price of a product at an artificially low level to deter new competitors, or to restrict production of a commodity and maintain prices at an artificially high level and thereby boost profits. It may also indulge in bid rigging – agreeing who should win a contract—or the members may agree among themselves on how to divide the markets and customers they will supply. **OPEC** is an example of a transnational cartel restricting the output of a commodity – oil. In many countries, including the United States and the United Kingdom, companies operating a cartel may fall foul of legislation designed to abolish anti-competitive practices.

Another well-known example of a cartel is the De Beers-led marketing cartel for diamonds. Throughout the twentieth century, the majority of major diamond producers in the world belonged to, or cooperated with, this cartel to maintain the price of diamonds at a high level.

Key links

- www.diamondregistry.com/Debeers.htm
- www.debeers.com/

Case, Stephen McDonnell

Chairman, AOL Time Warner; co-founder of America Online (AOL) (b. 1958)

Steve Case, born in Honolulu, Hawaii, is a world apart from the likes of **Marc Andreessen** (Netscape) and David Filo (Yahoo!), other geniuses of the **New Economy**. Instead of the standard geekster's path to billionaire status – studying computer sciences or engineering in some West Coast tech hotspot like Stanford – Case graduated with a degree in political science from Williams College, Massachusetts.

After completing his studies, Case worked in marketing and sales, first at Procter & Gamble (hair-care products) and then at PepsiCo (the Pizza Hut division). It was only then that Case paid any attention to the Internet.

After his taste of the corporate world, Case joined a small video games service company called Control Video in 1983. He had always had a touch of the entrepreneur about him. As a kid, he sold lime juice from his backyard at two cents a cup, took charge of the obligatory paper route and started a mail-order company, Case Enterprises, with his brother Dan.

While the video company wasn't a storming success, it did introduce Case to Jim Kinsey and Mark Seriff. It was the perfect combination: Seriff had technology in his blood – he had worked on Arpanet, the forerunner of the Internet; Kinsey was a finance man; and Case provided the sales and marketing know-how. Together the trio founded Quantum Computers. The company provided online services to users of the soon-to-be-defunct Commodore computer. Commodore imploded, but America Online (AOL), as the Quantum business was renamed in 1989, went from strength to strength.

Case instinctively knew what the customer wanted. Not being burdened with a technologi-cal background, he could pitch the product to the average consumer and make the experience as simple and user-friendly as possible. 'Our strategy has always been crystal clear,' Case said in a 1998 interview. 'Consumers want one place where they can find good Internet content and meet interesting people. And they want someone to make it easy for them.'

America Online went to the market in 1992. At the time, it had a membership of approximately 150,000. By 1996, with the help of an innovative marketing strategy involving the shipping of AOL CDs offering a free trial, 4.6 million had signed up. The company's marketing guru, Jan Brandt, even put discs on the office wall, bearing the message 'Resistance is futile'.

AOL dominated its main rivals, CompuServe and Prodigy, though Microsoft's MSN was still a distant threat. Yet success brought its problems: AOL replaced usage charges with a flat fee structure and usage figures shot up. People spent more time online, the systems couldn't cope and the service caved in under the pressure.

Case hired Bob Pittman, co-founder of MTV, to take over the day-to-day running of the company. Pittman was a media man who understood content delivery. He also knew how to deal with a corporation the size of AOL. Making money out of the subscriptions, however, proved a tough nut to crack. The more users AOL signed up, the more AOL spent on infrastructure and maintaining quality of service. Case and Pittman formulated a business model where content sucked in subscribers who then spent money. They figured that surely if they had a captive audience, advertisers would be falling over themselves to get onto AOL. They were right.

Pittman attacked costs, driving down customer-acquisition costs from nearly $400 per new subscriber to less than $100. The company sold concessions to bring in money: 1-800-Flowers bought the flower concession for $25 million; Amazon paid $19 million to be the exclusive bookseller on the external aol.com Web site; Barnes & Noble went one better, paying $40 million to be the exclusive bookseller inside.

Active on the acquisitions trail, Case engineered a takeover of rival CompuServe in 1998 (adding 2.5 million subscribers), and in the same year took the opportunity to acquire Netscape for $4.2 billion. Then, in early 2000, AOL made the shock announcement of a planned $166 billion merger with media giant Time Warner. Analysts weren't convinced that the Time Warner deal made sense and dumped stock, causing a 20 percent drop in AOL's share price. But the analysts called it wrong: the main prize for AOL was the distribution and content.

The combination of Time Warner's movie and music business – with its publishing and television channels – all efficiently managed and running at Internet speed over AOL's Internet network is an apparently perfect fit with Case's take on the future of AOL. He explains, 'What we're trying to be is a global leader in interactive service – the concept of interactive service is really a concept that embraces media and communication in a pretty central way – and commerce, too. If we're successful, we believe the AOL brand will stand for the way lots of people connect to this interesting new interactive world … we really want to be their gateway into this exciting future.'

So far, so good for Case and AOL. Roughly 80 percent of the world's online users log on to AOL in some way. And while they are there, traipsing around the online shopping malls, they part with more than $10 billion dollars per year. AOL itself saw revenues of more than $4.5 billion in 1999 and nearly $6.9 billion in revenues in 2000. As of September 2001, AOL had 30 million subscribers worldwide (nearly 6 million outside of the United States, with services available in 16 countries and eight languages). And the best is yet to come as AOL continues its rollout over the Time Warner Cable network and launches the new, improved AOL 7.0.

Case – not your standard e-commerce techie – made the Internet experience easy for millions worldwide and in doing so built a company that was able to effectively take over one of the world's largest media companies.

Key text

- Kara Swisher. *Aol.com: How Steve Case Beat Bill Gates, Nailed the Netheads, & Made Millions in the War for the Web.* Random House, 1998

Key link

- www.aoltimewarner.com

Cash cow

A cash cow is a brand (or company) that has a high share of a mature or declining market. Because investment has already been made and revenue streams established, cash cows are used (milked) to generate money for investment in other products. The term comes from Bruce Henderson's **Boston Matrix**.

Key link

- www.bcg.com

Cash flow

The cash flow is the amount of money coming into and flowing out of an organization. Money may be received through cash sales of products or assets and receipts of debts. Money may flow out through purchase of raw materials, the settlement of debts and the payment of salaries.

For an organization to survive, it must have sufficient cash to meet its obligations. Many businesses each year become insolvent due to insufficient cash being available to meet short-term obligations such as the payment of bills.

In order to ensure sufficient funds are available, it is essential to understand how cash is generated and flows through the business. Cash is expended purchasing the raw materials and services required to produce finished goods or deliver services, as well as paying amounts owed to suppliers. Cash is generated through the sale of goods and services. When cash is received from customers, the cash account increases.

Net working capital represents the change in value of cash available to meet obligations as calculated by subtracting current liabilities from current assets. Changes over a period of time can be calculated using a cash flow statement. This is an analysis of the cash inflows and outflows.

Key link

- www.businessweek.com/2001/01_04/ b3716159.htm

Category killer

Category killers are retailers that offer such an extensive and comprehensive range of products of a particular type that they threaten to eliminate the competition. A category killer will usually dominate its market on price, product selection, store appearance or any combination of these elements. A retail phenomenon that has grown substantially in the 1990s, category killers in the United States include stores such as Wal-Mart, Toys "R" Us, Home Depot and Barnes & Noble.

In the United Kingdom, out-of-town super-store retailers such as IKEA could be described as category killers.

Caveat emptor

Latin for 'buyer beware', the doctrine of *caveat emptor* is the overriding principle governing contracts for the sale of goods and services where the vendor is acting in good faith. The implication is that the contract is at the purchaser's risk. The purchaser must satisfy himself that the goods are complete and in order and that the vendor has title to them. In the United Kingdom, legislation – such as the Sale of Goods Act 1979, the Sale and Supply of Goods Act 1994 and the Unfair Contract Terms Act 1977 – overrides the general principle of caveat emptor to offer the purchaser a degree of protection in certain cases, such as the right to expect that a good is fit for the purpose it as advertised for.

Cell production

In manufacturing processes such as **just-in-time** manufacturing, continuous-flow production is broken up into a functional layout based on several separate cells. Each cell is a self-sufficient entity carrying out a specific part of the manufacturing process, such as the production of a component or product.

This enables the workers to more be committed to their contribution and cell team than if they were small cogs in a huge production line.

Centralization

In early corporate organizational structures, decision-making powers tended to be concentrated in one part of an organization, usually the head office (even in one person). With power concentrated in one place, centralization results in less empowerment for the workforce but ensures that an organization takes a consistent policy line.

As early as the 1920s, however, there was a move towards the dispersal of authority away from the centre of an organization and its headquarters. This move was led by **Alfred P. Sloan**, CEO at General Motors in the 1920s, who pioneered decentralization by restructuring GM along divisional lines and in so doing conferred on his organization the advantages of quick decision making, the empowerment of line managers and corporate flexibility at a local level. Since Sloan's bold move, the arguments for and against centralization have waxed and waned. Through the late 1980s and early 1990s, the move toward empowering the workforce favoured decentralization. With the increase in globalization and global branding, the need to apply a coherent policy to support the corporate brand may reverse this trend.

CEO (chief executive officer)

'CEO' is the term widely used in the United States to refer to the most senior manager in a company.

In the United Kingdom, the term 'managing director' is more common, although 'CEO' is growing in use. The roles of the CEO include communicator (they provide an interface with the external world, such as shareholders and the press, as well as between the board and employees); decision maker (they make high-level decisions regarding company policy and strategy); leader (they advise the board of directors, motivate employees and drive change within the organization); and manager (they manage human resources, physical and financial resources such as budgets, and the implementation of strategic plans). As well as presiding over the day-to-day operations of their companies, many CEOs sit on the boards of other companies as **non-executive directors**.

Key link

- www.presidentandceomag.com/

Cerf, Vinton G.

Senior Vice President for Internet Architecture and Technology, MCI WorldCom (b. 1943)

When Vinton Cerf was 10 years old, he read a book called *The Boy Scientist* and knew he wanted to be one. He got bored in fifth-grade maths and his teacher, Mr Tomaszewski, gave him a seventh-grade algebra book, which he loved. He spent the summer working through every problem in the book. Then he got a chemistry set and concocted incendiary devices with his best friend.

Cerf went on to study at Stanford and UCLA. Between 1976 and 1982, he worked at the US Department of Defense's Advanced Research Projects Agency; from 1982 until 1986, he was vice-president of MCI Digital Information Services. He has also been vice-president of the Corporation for National Research Initiatives.

Cerf is one of the founding fathers of the Internet and senior vice-president of Internet Architecture and Technology for MCI WorldCom. He unravels the technological future, and the future is 'seamless interaction'.

Cerf co-designed the TCP/IP protocol, the computer language that effectively gave birth to the Internet. He was founding President of the Internet Society (1992–95). Contrary to popular speculation, however, his name is not the source of the now-ubiquitous pet e-phrase, 'surfing the Net'.

According to Cerf, 'In 1989, a company called General Atomics started an intermediate-level network to link universities and other research and educational institutions to the NSFNET backbone. They planned to call themselves SURF-NET (they were in San Diego), but they discovered that another organization already existed in the Netherlands called SURFNET, which essentially did the same thing. SURF was a Dutch acronym. So they decided to call themselves the California Education and Research Foundation Network or CERFNET. They had already worked out an advertising campaign based on Surfing the Net, so they just spelled it differently in their advertisements. The result was a delicious coincidence.'

Equally delicious, as Cerf points out, is the fact that despite the Internet's explosive growth, there is still plenty of room for growth in Internet usage. For example, 60 percent of US homes do not have Internet access. Explosive growth disguises the fact that the Internet has grown since the 1960s. Behind the revolution is a story of diligent evolution. He is also quick to refute notions that the Internet is a limited commercial tool laden with security problems. **Dell**, says Cerf, records daily sales of $6 million through the Internet and Cisco Systems totals annual sales of $2 billion through its site.

He envisages a future where access to the Internet is constant. 'The idea of having to dial a phone to make a temporary Internet connection – which is the way many people use the Net today – will seem pretty odd. We're going to evolve to the point where network access is provided like electricity – in other words, always on.'

Not only will it be always on; it will be interplanetary. Cerf is working with the US Jet Propulsion Laboratory on creating the Interplanetary Internet (www.ipnsig.org).

Key texts

- Eric Hall and Vinton G. Cerf. *Internet Core Protocols: The Definitive Guide with CD-ROM*. O'Reilly & Associates, 2000
- Mark J. Stefik and Vinton G. Cerf. *Internet Dreams*. MIT Press, 1997

Key links

- www.mci.com
- www.worldcom.com/generation_d/cerfs_up

Ceteris paribus

Financial and economic modelling and analysis are frequently based on the assumption that the scenario under analysis is free from any influence other than that of the factors under consideration. The phrase used to describe this assumption is *ceteris paribus*, which is Latin for 'other things being equal'.

CFO (chief financial officer)

The CFO is the executive with responsibility for financial planning and record keeping in a company. The CFO may also be the company treasurer and is often considered the second most important person in a company after the **CEO**. In the United States, the term 'comptroller' is sometimes used as an alternative for a financial director or financial head of a group of companies.

The two most important functions of the CFO are the control function and the treasury function. The control function stems from the budget. The budget is a financial appraisal of the goals of the company: it outlines the necessary financial resources to achieve the corporate goals. The CFO implements the systems required to monitor the performance relating to those goals.

The treasury function is connected with identifying and obtaining financing for a company and keeping stakeholders in the picture regarding the performance of the company. The CFO is also responsible for allocating the budget and assess-

ing the financial needs of departments within the company.

Although traditionally the CFO's role was restricted to the balance sheet and finances, the demands of modern, fast-moving markets and sophisticated investors have led to a broadening of the CFO's role. In addition to their traditional duties, modern CFOs are required to make their companies' financial position understandable and palatable to the external world, and in particular the media.

Key link

- www.cfo.com

Chairman

The chairman is the most senior executive in a company. He presides over the annual general meeting and may chair board meetings. Traditionally, chairmen were concerned primarily with the long-term strategy of a company, with the managing director (or CEO) dealing with the day-to-day running of the organization. In the United Kingdom, the chairman is often a non-executive director. In the United States, the position of chairman is also known as president, and may be held by the chief executive. Alternatively, the president in US corporations may be the equivalent of a vice-chairman, acting as the number-two in an organization.

Champy, James A.

Chairman, Perot Systems consulting practice; co-founder and former chairman and CEO of CSC Index (b. 1942)

James A. Champy received both his bachelor's and master's degrees from MIT, and his law degree from Boston College Law School. He was one of the co-founders of Index, a $200 million consulting practice that CSC (Computer Science Corporation) acquired in 1988. As chairman and CEO of CSC Index, Champy grew the company's consulting practice at a rate of 25 percent per year. CSC became one of the largest consultancy companies in the world, with more than 2000 consultants worldwide and revenues in excess of $500 million.

In 1996, Champy left CSC to join Perot Systems as chairman of its consulting practice. He is also responsible for providing strategic direction and guidance to the company's team of business and management consultants. Champy is most famous, however, for co-authoring (with Michael Hammer) *Reengineering the Corporation*, a *New York Times* bestseller that sold more than 2 million copies and was translated into 17 languages.

Reengineering was unquestionably the business idea of the first half of the 1990s. Champy and Hammer's *Reengineering the Corporation* was the manifesto for a promised revolution, one that – except in a few instances – largely failed to materialize. The claims made for reengineering and for Champy and Hammer's book were large. 'When people ask me what I do for a living, I tell them that what I really do is I'm reversing the Industrial Revolution,' proclaimed Hammer with apparent sincerity. Indeed, the opening of the book positions it as the ready replacement for Adam Smith's *The Wealth of Nations*.

Cutting away the hype and hyperbole, the basic idea behind reengineering is that organizations need to identify their key processes and make them as lean and efficient as possible. Peripheral processes (and, therefore, peripheral people) need to be discarded. Champy and Hammer define reengineering as 'the fundamental rethinking and radical redesign of business processes to achieve dramatic improvements in critical measures of performance such as cost, quality, service, and speed'.

To Champy and Hammer, reengineering is more than dealing with mere processes. They eschew the popular phrase 'business process reengineering', regarding it as too limiting. In their view, the scope and scale of reengineering goes far beyond simply altering and refining processes. True reengineering is all-embracing.

Champy and Hammer recommend that companies equip themselves with a blank piece of paper and map out their processes. Having come up with a neatly engineered map of how their business should operate, companies can then attempt to translate the paper theory into concrete reality.

The concept is simple. (Indeed, critics of reengineering regard it as a contemporary version of Taylor's **scientific management** with its belief in measurement and optimal ways of completing particular tasks.) Making it happen has proved immensely more difficult.

The first problem is that the blank piece of paper ignores the years, often decades, of cultural evolution that have led to an organization doing something in a certain way. Such preconceptions are not easily discarded. Indeed, discarding them may well amount to corporate suicide.

Champy and Hammer say that reengineering is concerned with 'rejecting conventional wisdom and received assumptions of the past ... it is about reversing the industrial revolution ... tradition counts for nothing. Reengineering is a new beginning.'

In *Leaning into the Future*, British academics Colin Williams and George Binney are dismissive of such talk: 'The last time someone used language like this was Chairman Mao in the Cultural Revolution. Under the motto "Destroy to build," he too insisted on sweeping away the past. Instead of such wanton destruction, successful organizations do not deny or attempt to destroy the inheritance of the past. They seek to build on it. They try to understand in depth why they have been successful and they try to do more of it. They are respectful of the learning accumulated from experience and recognize that much of this learning is not made explicit at the top of the organization.'

The second problem is that reengineering has become a synonym for redundancy. Champy and Hammer cannot be entirely blamed for this. Often, companies that claim to be reengineering are simply engaging in cost-cutting under the convenient guise of the fashionable theory. **Downsizing** appears more publicly palatable if it is presented as implementing a leading-edge concept. In research covering 624 companies in 1994, CSC Index found that on average, 336 jobs were lost per reengineering project in the United States and 760 in Europe.

The third obstacle is that corporations tend to reengineer the most readily accessible process and then leave it at that. Related to this issue, and the subject of Champy's sequel, *Reengineering Management*, reengineering usually fails to impinge on management. Managers are all too willing to impose the rigours of a process-based view of the business on others, but often unwilling to inflict it upon themselves. Champy suggests reengineering management should tackle three key areas: managerial roles, styles and systems.

It is the human side of reengineering that has proved the greatest stumbling block. 'Most reengineering efforts will fail or fall short of the mark because of the absence of trust – meaning respect for the individual, his or her goodwill, intelligence, and native, but long shackled, curiosity,' observed **Tom Peters**.

Champy and Hammer would counter that true reengineering is actually built on trust, respect and people. 'It is astonishing to see the extent to which the term reengineering has been hijacked, misappropriated, and misunderstood,' Hammer lamented. By cutting away peripheral activities, companies provide an environment that places a premium on the skills and potential of those it employs. This, as yet, has not been supported by corporate experience – though James Champy believes the best may be yet to come. 'There are at least another ten years of genuine reengineering to run,' he said in 1995.

Key texts
- James Champy. *X-Engineering the Corporation*. Warner Books, 2002
- James Champy and Nitin Nohria. *The Arc of Ambition: Defining the Leadership Journey*. John Wiley, 2001
- James Champy and Nitin Nohria. *Fast Forward: The Best Ideas on Managing Business Change*. Harvard Business School Press, 1996

- James Champy. *Reengineering Management: The Mandate for New Leadership*. Harper Business, 1995
- Michael Hammer and James Champy. *Reengineering the Corporation*. HarperCollins, 1993

Key links
- www.perotsystems.com/frmbase.asp?URL=/ content/AboutUs/Leadership/james.asp
- w w w . p e r o t s y s t e m s . c o m / C o n t e n t / N e w s a n d E v e n t s / A r t i c l e s / c h a m p y / Reengineering_Dead-Dont_Be.htm

Chandler, Alfred

Business historian (b. 1918)

Pulitzer Prize-winning business historian Alfred Chandler brought strategy into the modern age and championed the multidivisional organizational form. After graduating from Harvard, he served in the US Navy before becoming, somewhat unusually, a historian at MIT in 1950. He has been Straus Professor of Business History at Harvard since 1971.

Chandler's hugely detailed research into US companies between 1850 and 1920 has formed the cornerstone of much of his work. Chandler observes that organizational structures in companies such as Du Pont, Sears Roebuck, General Motors and Standard Oil were driven by the changing demands and pressures of the market place. He concludes that the market-driven proliferation of product lines led to a shift from a functional, monolithic organizational form to a more loosely coupled divisional structure.

Chandler was highly influential in the trend among large organizations for decentralization in the 1960s and 1970s. In his classic book, *Strategy and Structure*, Chandler praises **Alfred P. Sloan**'s decentralization of General Motors in the 1920s. He argues that the chief advantage of the multidivisional organization was that 'it clearly removed the executives responsible for the destiny of the entire enterprise from the more routine operational responsibilities and so gave them the time, information, and even psychological commitment for long-term planning and appraisal.'

While the multidivisional form has largely fallen out of favour, another of Chandler's theories continues to raise the blood pressure of those who care about such things. Chandler argues that strategy comes before structure. Having developed the best possible strategy, companies could then determine the most appropriate organizational structure to achieve it. In the early sixties, this was speedily accepted as a fact of life.

More recently, Chandler's premise has been regularly questioned. In a perfect world, critics say, companies would hatch perfect strategies and then create neat structures and organizational maps. Reality, however, is a mess in which strategy and structure mix madly.

Contemporary strategist **Gary Hamel** provides a more positive perspective on Chandler's insights. 'Those who dispute Chandler's thesis that structure follows strategy miss the point,' Hamel argues. 'Of course, strategy and structure are inextricably intertwined. Chandler's point was that new challenges give rise to new structures. The challenges of size and complexity, coupled with advances in communications and techniques of management control, produced divisionalization and decentralization. These same forces, several generations on, are now driving us toward new structural solutions – the federated organization, the multicompany coalition, and the virtual company. Few historians are prescient. Chandler was.'

Strategy and Structure also contributed to the 'professionalization of management'. Chandler traces the historical development of what he labels 'the managerial revolution' fuelled by the rise of oil-based energy, the development of the steel, chemical and engineering industries, and a dramatic rise in the scale of production and the size of companies. Increases in scale, Chandler observes, led to business owners having to recruit a new breed of professional manager.

Chandler believes that the roles of the salaried manager and technician are vital, and talks of the 'visible hand' of management coordinating the flow of product to customers more efficiently than **Adam Smith**'s 'invisible hand' of the market. The logical progression from this is that organizations and their managements require a planned economy rather than a capitalist free-for-all dominated by the unpredictable whims of market forces. In the more sedate times in which *Strategy and Structure* was written, the lure of the visible hand proved highly persuasive.

Key texts
- Alfred Chandler. *Scale and Scope: The Dynamics of Industrial Capitalism*. Harvard University Press, 1990
- Alfred Chandler and H. Deams (eds). *Managerial Hierarchies*. Harvard University Press, 1980
- Alfred Chandler. *The Visible Hand: The Managerial Revolution in American Business*. Harvard University Press, 1977
- Alfred Chandler. *Strategy and Structure*. MIT Press, 1962

Key link
- www.lib.uwo.ca/business/chandler.html

Channel management

The product/service channel refers to how and where a product or service is delivered to the consumer. CDs, for example, can be bought through a traditional channel – the record store – or a non-traditional channel – on the Internet through an online CD store.

Channel management involves managing a channel in order to reach and take care of a company's customers. The concept covers three areas: information flow, inward and outward, through the channel; the logistics to deliver products and services to the consumer; and value-added services, which augment the product or service. Steven Wheeler and Evan Hirsh, two management consultants at consultancy Booz Allen & Hamilton, emphasized the importance of channel management in their book *Channel Champions*.

Key text
- Steven Wheeler and Evan Hirsh. *Channel Champions: How Leading Companies Build New Strategies to Serve Customers.* Jossey-Bass, 1999

Chaordic organization

Dee Hock, founder and CEO Emeritus of VISA USA and VISA International, left VISA in 1984 to pursue his interest in the evolution of organizations and management practices.

In 1993, Hock made his first speech on 'chaords' at the Sante Fe Institute.

He also articulated four conditions necessary for catalyzing institutional change. They were creation of a dozen or more examples of new, successful chaordic organizations; development of visual and physical models of chaordic organizations; development and dissemination of an impeccable intellectual foundation for chaordic organizations; and creation of a global institution.

Hock coined the word 'chaord' by borrowing the first syllables from the words 'chaos' and 'order.' He uses the term chaordic to describe any system of organization that exhibits characteristics of both chaos and order, dominated by neither. In his book *Birth of the Chaordic Age*, Dee defines chaordic as '1. The behavior of any self-governing organism, organization, or system that harmoniously blends characteristics of order and chaos. 2. Patterned in a way dominated by neither chaos nor order. 3. Characteristic of the fundamental organizing principles of evolution and nature.'

Key text
- Dee Hock. *Birth of the Chaordic Age*. Berrett-Koehler Publishers, Incorporated, 1999

Key link
- www.chaordic.org

Chapter 11 bankruptcy

See Bankruptcy.

Chapter 7 bankruptcy

See Bankruptcy.

Chartist

Chartists (also known as technical analysts) are investment analysts who use charts based on the past performance of a stock, market sector or index to predict future price movements. Contrary to the universal warning attached to investment advice that past performance is not necessarily a guide to future performance, chartists rely on the premise that past performance is indeed a strong indication, if not an irrefutable guide, to future performance. Using the fluctuations and patterns of charts depicting key historic stock indicators, such as **P/E ratios** and price movements, chartists predict the future movements of those indicators. Patterns identified by the chartists include 'double tops', 'rising bottoms' and 'head-and-shoulders formations'. Some financial analysts and commentators regard chartists as the equivalent of astrologers. Many analysts, however, use some chartist techniques along with other investment analysis techniques.

Key links
- www.equis.com/free/taaz
- www.stern.nyu.edu/~adamodar/New_Home_Page/invphillectures/tech.html

CGI (common gateway interface)

The common gateway interface (CGI) is a means by which a Web server communicates with another piece of software. A software program, in the form of a CGI script, will communicate with the Web server according to CGI standards. It will usually take data from the server and process it in some way, such as parsing the content of Web form into an e-mail message. For example, a company may want visitors to their Web site to be able to access and query a database running on one of their **UNIX** servers. With CGI scripts, a program can be written to act as a link between the client's browser and the UNIX database. CGI scripts are written in a variety of languages, with **PERL** being one of the most common. The CGI scripts are located in a special directory on the Web server: the /cgi-bin directory.

Key link
- http://cgi.resourceindex.com/

Chase demand strategy

See Managing demand.

CIO (chief information officer)

Traditionally, the CIO is the manager who runs IT within a company, with the focus on operations. The Internet boom, however, has led to a persistent confusion over acronyms and roles, with the role of the **CTO** overlapping or even replacing that of the CIO.

As knowledge management is increasingly recognized by companies as a central component of strategic planning, the IT function is expanding and consequently, so is the role of the CIO. The role of the CIO is moving from one of technical planning and implementation to one of strategic planning.

According to some studies, however, the CIO is more sidelined from major decision making than other board-level positions, such as the **CFO**. Additionally, the move from CIO to CEO is not seen as a natural one in the same way as the progression of CFO to **CEO** is perceived.

Key link
- www.cio.com

Chinese wall

A Chinese wall is a virtual barrier between differ-

ent departments within an organization. Usually required by law, the idea is that no information should pass between the departments separated by the Chinese wall. Chinese walls are common in merchant banks where one department has access to privileged information. A corporate financing department, for example, would not be expected to pass on price-sensitive information about a pending merger or acquisition to an in-house share-dealing department. Equally, an analyst at an investment bank should refrain from recommending stock in a new issue underwritten by the same investment bank, other than on that stock's merits.

In the wake of the dotcom meltdown in 2000 and 2001, the efficacy of Chinese walls at some of the firms underwriting the dotcom **IPO** issues between 1998 and 2000 was called into question. Government concern over conflicts of interest between stockbrokers and investment bankers is nothing new. After the Wall Street crash in 1929, the US government moved to separate investment bankers and stock brokerage firms and avoid conflicts of interest over objectivity and the desire to have a successful new stock issue. The regulations introduced by the government became known as the Chinese wall. The idea was to erect a barrier as imposing as the Great Wall of China between stock analysts and corporate financiers.

After the dotcom fiasco, the Securities Industry Association introduced a new code of ethics for Wall Street analysts. The intention of the code was to prevent analysts from being influenced by a need to get a new stock launch successfully underway, where the same firm was underwriting the new issue.

Christensen, Clayton M.

Harvard Business School professor; author (b. 1952)

Professor of business administration at Harvard Business School, Clayton Christensen's research and writing interests focus on managing technological innovation and locating new markets for leading-edge technologies.

Before returning to Harvard, where he obtained his **MBA**, Christensen worked as chairman and president of Ceramics Process Systems Corp. (CPS) and also with the Boston Consulting Group as a consultant and project manager.

Christensen has been published in a number of prestigious publications including the *Harvard Business Review* and *The Wall Street Journal*. His acclaimed book *The Innovator's Dilemma: When New Technologies Cause Great Firms to Fail*, won the Global Business Book Award for best business book published in 1997.

Key text
- Clayton M. Christensen. *The Innovator's Dilemma: When New Technologies Cause Great Firms to Fail*. Harvard Business School Press, 1997

Key link
- http://dor.hbs.edu/fi_redirect.jhtml?facInfo= bio&facEmId=cchristensen

Chrysler, Walter Percy

Founder of Chrysler Motors (1875–1940)

Shortly after Walter Chrysler was born, his family moved from Wamego, Kansas, to Ellis, Kansas, where his father worked as an engineer for the Kansas Pacific Railroad. Chrysler attended the local school in Ellis but also spent a great deal of time with his father in the engineering workshops of the Kansas Pacific Railroad, where he developed a fascination with engineering.

After leaving school, he became an engineer with the Union Pacific Railroad (previously the Kansas Pacific Railroad) and by the age of 18 had already designed and built a miniature steam engine that ran on a homemade track.

When Chrysler finished his apprenticeship, aged 22, he set out across the country looking for work. He moved from job to job – from the Rio Grande & Western Railroad, to the Colorado &

Southern Railroad, to the Chicago & Great Western Railroad – all the while enhancing his reputation as a skilled engineer.

It was in Oelwein, Iowa, while Chrysler was working as the superintendent of motive power for the Chicago & Great Western Railroad, that he first saw the contraption that would change his life. Walking the streets of Oelwein one day, Chrysler came across several horseless carriages. Curiosity aroused, he made a point of attending the 1905 Chicago Auto Show.

At the Auto Show, Chrysler was entranced by a Locomobile Phaeton, with its red leather upholstery and white bodywork. Putting $700 down and financing the balance, Chrysler bought the car, had it shipped home, and then proceeded to take it to pieces – not once but several times. By the time Chrysler was done with dismantling and reassembling his new car, he had a perfect understanding of how it was engineered.

Chrysler's next career move took him to Pittsburgh, Pennsylvania, as works manager for the American Locomotive Company. It was an executive there who tipped Chrysler off about a job at the Buick Automobile Company. Chrysler met Buick's president, Charles W. Nash, and was taken on as works manager. It was 1911 and Chrysler had entered the car industry.

The Buick plant in Flint, Michigan, was the cornerstone of **William Crapo Durant**'s General Motors, founded in 1908. Durant was ousted as president of GM in 1910 but staged a comeback, regaining the presidency in 1916 and firing Charles W. Nash. As Durant's fortunes rose, so too did Chrysler's. Chrysler began by sorting out production at the Buick plant. Before long, he was president and general manager of Buick. When Durant got wind of a rumour that Chrysler was planning to take over another auto company, Packard Motors, Durant made Chrysler an offer he couldn't refuse. He increased his salary from $50,000 a year to an astonishing $500,000.

Chrysler's meteoric ascent continued. As General Motors' vice-president in charge of production and then executive vice-president, Chrysler worked alongside Durant. But Chrysler wasn't impressed with Durant's handling of the company. Predicting disaster, he left GM in 1920. Shortly after, Durant was forced out by GM's financiers over the company's $80 million debt. Chrysler, however, had restored the good name of Buick and increased production from 40 to more than 500 cars per day. In 1920, aged 45 and financially secure, Chrysler put away his desk diary and retired.

It was a brief retirement. A group of bankers approached Chrysler and asked him to rescue the ailing Willys-Overland company. He would have a two-year contract, the position of executive vice-president, and a free hand. Chrysler asked for one extra thing – an annual salary of $1 million. The desperate bankers agreed and Chrysler set about saving the company.

Chrysler's strategy was to build a brand new car – new design, new engineering – to revive W-O's fortunes. Chrysler assembled a team of automotive experts that included the independent engineering team of Carl Breer, Owen Skelton and Fred Zeder. Work was well advanced on the new car when the bankers got cold feet and withdrew their support. Chrysler, however, motored on, forming the Chrysler Corporation as a separate entity within W-O and retaining the original design team at the production facility in Elizabeth, New Jersey. The new car was christened the Chrysler Six.

Before long, Chrysler was on the move again when bankers called him in to save yet another car company in trouble – Maxwell-Chalmers. Chrysler negotiated with W-O to be allowed to work with Maxwell and took a $100,000 salary and stock options. When his two-year contract was up at W-O, Chrysler left for Maxwell-Chalmers.

When he arrived, Maxwell-Chalmers was in a mess. After some wheeling and dealing, Chrysler merged Maxwell and Chalmers. Then, at the helm of the new Maxwell Motors, Chrysler refocused his attention on the Chrysler Six. He brought the Chrysler Six engineering team to Maxwell and in 1923, the new car appeared in prototype. With its fast top speed, high compression engine and hydraulic brakes, the Chrysler Six car was truly revolutionary.

For once, Chrysler struggled to raise the financing to put the car into production. Bankers were reluctant to bankroll an unproven and experimental product. Undaunted, Chrysler took the car to the 1924 New York Auto show. On discovering that, as a prototype, the car was ineligible for the show, he displayed it in the foyer of the Hotel Commodore – the show's headquarters – creating enough interest to persuade financiers Chase Securities to put up production money.

The Chrysler Six was in production by 1924. In that year alone, 32,000 were sold. Maxwell Motors was restructured in 1925, emerging as the Chrysler Corporation with Chrysler as president and chairman of the board. In 1925, the company turned a profit of $17 million. New car models rolled off the Chrysler production line. In 1928, Chrysler Corporation bought Dodge Brothers, with its extensive dealership network, and changed its name to Chrysler Motors. With Chrysler in command, the company flourished, survived the Great Depression, and outlasted many competitors with a combination of astute management and innovative products. Chrysler remained president until 1935 and chairman until his death in 1940.

The list of recipients of *Time* magazine's Man of the Year award is dominated by politicians and statesmen, with a few notable exceptions. One of those exceptions is the *Time* Man of the Year in 1928 – Walter P. Chrysler (the same year his namesake skyscraper was erected in Manhattan). Alongside **Henry Ford** and William Crapo Durant, Chrysler was one of the greatest car manufacturing industrialists of the first half of the twentieth century.

Of the three men, Chrysler arguably represented the most complete combination of technical, entrepreneurial and managerial ability. Few men have taken on such demanding corporate challenges so frequently. It was no coincidence that whenever an car company was ailing, the man the bankers called in to save it was Chrysler.

Key texts
- Vincent Curcio. *Chrysler: the Life and Times of an Automotive Genius*. Oxford University Press, 2000
- Carl Breer. *The Birth of Chrysler Corporation and its Engineering Legacy*. Society of Automotive Engineers, 1995
- Walter P. Chrysler in collaboration with Boyden Sparkes. *Life of an American Workman*. Dodd, Mead, 1950

Key link
- www.chrysler.com

Churning

Churning is the practice of excessive trading by a broker on his client's account. The intention is usually to increase his commission income and the trading is usually unauthorized. Most churning is conducted on discretionary accounts – accounts where the broker doesn't have to obtain prior approval from the client every time he makes a trade. A court may still hold that churning has taken place, even in an account where a client's approval is required prior to dealing. Investors are often unsophisticated and will give approval for a trade without realizing the implications. The court will look for dealing that is not in the client's best interest. The term is also used to describe providers of mortgages who encourage mortgage holders to take out new mortgages rather than top up an existing mortgage, in order to increase income from mortgage charges. Naturally, both practices are frowned upon.

CIF (cost insurance freight)

'Cost insurance freight' is a term applying to an export contract that stipulates that the goods are at the seller's risk until they reach the dock at the destination port. The documents that give title to the goods are sent to the purchaser, who pays the purchase price on receipt of the documents. If the goods subsequently do not arrive or are damaged, the purchaser may claim on the insurance. This is in contrast to the position where the goods are at the seller's risk until they are loaded onto the ship – **free on board (FOB)**.

Civil Rights Act of 1964

The Civil Rights Act of 1964 outlawed discrimination in the United States on the grounds of a person's colour, race, national origin, religion, or sex. Rights protected under the act include a person's freedom to seek employment. Complaints against discrimination in the workplace are filed with the Equal Employment Opportunity Commission (EEOC), which was established by the act. The EEOC will take the complaint to court.

One of the most significant sections of the act was Title VII, which prohibited 'private employers from refusing to hire or from firing or discriminating against any person because of race, color, sex, religion, or national origin.' When originally introduced by President John F. Kennedy, the section was only intended to apply to government employment. However, after Congress had fully debated the matter, it was changed to apply to private sector employment only. Federal, state and local government employment were excluded from the law. The Civil Rights Act was the precursor to attempts to redress discrimination against minorities, such as the affirmative action programme.

Key link
- http://usinfo.state.gov/usa/infousa/laws/majorlaw/civilr19.htm

Clark, James H.

Founder of Silicon Graphics, Netscape and myCFO.com (b. 1944)

Jim Clark, born in Plainview, Texas, dropped out of high school at the age of 16 and joined the US Navy. Clark's disinterest in school wasn't due to a lack of aptitude – he had a gift for math and technology. He simply wasn't ready to study at that point in his life. Military service changed that.

While still in the Navy, Clark was required to take a standard math test. He scored so high that the administrators suspected him of cheating and insisted he retake the test. When he repeated the feat, they moved him into an area that might tax his mind a little more – computers. The Navy was also the proving ground for Clark's shrewd business brain. He ran a surreptitious loans business on the side, lending money to the other sailors to tide them over until payday. At 40 percent interest, it was a lucrative operation.

After the Navy, Clark went to Louisiana State University, where he excelled. He graduated in 1971 with an MS in physics. In 1974, he obtained a PhD in computer science at the University of Utah. At Utah, Clark met Ivan Sutherland, widely regarded as the man behind interactive computer graphics. It was a field in which Clark was to have a big impact.

The pattern of Clark's early working life was that of a bright if somewhat restless individual, seeking a challenge that would hold his attention. Seduced by the romantic notion of academic life, he embarked on a teaching career at the University of Santa Cruz. The romance soon wore off and he quit to take up consulting, which he found even less to his liking.

In 1978, returning to academia, Clark took up a teaching position at Stanford University. In addition to his teaching duties, he had obtained funding from the Defense Advanced Research Projects Agency (DARPA) to lead a team of students conducting research into computer graphics technology.

Clark worked with his team for three years. During that time, they made several important technological breakthroughs. The team created a 'geometry engine' shifting 3-D graphics processing from software to hardware, with the instruction set embedded into a computer chip. Clark attempted to sell the technology to established computer companies.

When no one showed any interest, Clark determined to go it alone. 'I concluded after talking to DEC and IBM and all these companies,' he said, 'that they didn't understand how to use what we had in the first place, so they would surely screw it up.' Taking six of the Stanford team with him, he left Stanford in 1982 to found Silicon Graphics (now SGI).

At Silicon Graphics, an ambitious Clark drove his team to create the ultimate 3-D engine, delivering 3-D computer graphics to the humble PC. When Clark resigned from SGI in 1994, the company had eight years of annual growth at an astonishing 40 percent with annual revenues reaching the $2 billion mark. The company employed more than 5000 people, and the name Silicon Graphics was synonymous with the high-end computer graphics market.

In February 1994, Clark left the company that had made him rich. The split was the result of his growing frustration. SGI had become a large company. It was no longer able to move at the speed Clark wanted. His vision was to bring the expensively priced SGI technology within the grasp of the average consumer. Others at the company were unconvinced. So Clark left.

He was unemployed for approximately 24 hours. On the same morning he resigned, he sent an e-mail to **Marc Andreessen**, a brilliant young computer programmer. Clark thought that an invention of Andreessen's, the NCSA Mosaic browser, would be perfect for interactive television. At the time, the Internet was in its infancy, and many saw interactive television as 'the next big thing'. Andreessen persuaded Clark that the Internet was the best market for the browser and in 1994 they set up Mosaic Communications Corporation with $6 million of Clark's money and $6 million venture capital. It was the company that became Netscape.

Clark's genius was evident in the business plan. The strategy was a radical one: give the product – the Netscape browser – away. It was a masterstroke and it worked. Soon the Netscape Navigator browser was familiar to virtually every

Internet user. By 1996, Clark and Andreessen's company had captured over 80 percent of the market. When the company had its **IPO** in August 1995, it was valued at some $2 billion, making Clark the first Internet billionaire. Had it not been for Microsoft, Netscape Navigator would have become the dominant browser on the Internet. Although initially slow to recognize the potential of the Internet, Microsoft moved decisively into the browser market. With the might of the Redmond-based computer giant arrayed against it, Netscape eventually lost ground and was sold to America Online. Having played a significant role in making the Internet the pervasive means of communication it is, Clark became an even wealthier man due to the AOL deal.

Since then, Clark's enterprising spirit has seen him involved in several start-ups, including Healtheon, Shutterfly.com and myCFO.com. In the space of two decades, he built two incredibly successful companies. The first, Silicon Graphics, was part of the personal computer revolution; the second, Netscape, played a pivotal role in the development of the Internet. Clark attributes his fortune to 'a combination of being persuasive; believing in what you're doing; having integrity … and knowing how to judge good people, because you can't afford to have anything but good people early on in a company.'

Clark knows the value of a good team, surrounding himself with the right people. He then acts as a catalyst, fomenting the creativity and hard work that are needed in a start-up. It is a formula that has made him one of the stars of the New Economy.

Key text
- Jim Clark and Owen Edwards (contributor). *Netscape Time: The Making of the Billion-Dollar Start-Up That Took on Microsoft*. St Martin's Press, 1999

Key link
- www.mycfo.com

Classical management theory

It was French industrialist **Henri Fayol** (1841–1925) who first recognized the importance of the function of management in an organization. Fayol rejected the purely scientific examination of work and the organization espoused by **Frederick W. Taylor** (1856–1917) and his followers. Instead, Fayol proposed that any industrial undertaking had six functions: accounting, commercial, financial, managerial, security and technical. Of these, Fayol saw management – defined as 'to forecast and plan, to organize, to command, to co-ordinate and control' – as distinct from the other five. In addition to his six functions of management, Fayol also identified a number of general principles of management: division of work; authority and responsibility; discipline; unity of command; unity of direction; subordination of individual interest to general interest; remuneration of personnel; centralization; scalar chain of authority; order; equity; stability of tenure of personnel; initiative; and *esprit de corps*. Fayol's views on management remained popular throughout most of the twentieth century.

Von Clausewitz, Karl

Prussian general and military strategist (1780–1831)

Karl von Clausewitz fought in the Napoleonic Wars and in the Rhine campaigns (1793–94). Working on behalf of Russia from 1812 until 1814, von Clausewitz helped negotiate the convention of Tauroggen in 1812. This laid the ground for an alliance of Prussia, Russia and Great Britain in opposition to Napoleon. In his later career, von Clausewitz rejoined the Prussian army, fought at the Battle of Waterloo, and became director of the Prussian war college in 1818. *On War* was unfinished and published posthumously.

Von Clausewitz was firmly of the mind that comparisons between the military and commercial worlds were both valid and useful. 'Rather than comparing it [war] to art we could more accurately compare it to commerce, which is also a conflict of interests and activities; and it is still closer to politics, which in turn may be considered as a kind of commerce on a larger scale,' he writes in *On War*.

As one would expect of a military theorist, von Clausewitz possesses a strong strain of pragmatism. 'To be practical, any plan must take account of the enemy's power to frustrate it; the best chance of overcoming such obstruction is to have a plan that can be easily varied to fit the circumstances met; to keep such adaptability, while still keeping the initiative, the best way is to operate along a line which offers alternative objectives,' he advises. Mere theory will get you nowhere. (In this, and other areas, von Clausewitz was heavily influenced by the wily power politics so potently mapped out by **Machiavelli**.) 'Knowing is different from doing and therefore theory must never be used as norms for a standard, but merely as aids to judgement,' von Clausewitz writes. Pragmatism is combined with a desire to achieve results through minimal effort: 'A prince or general can best demonstrate his genius by managing a campaign exactly to suit his objectives and his resources, doing neither too much nor too little.'

Most famously, von Clausewitz observes that war 'is merely the continuation of policy by other means'. Instead of being catastrophic, he views war as a normal and acceptable part of politics.

Von Clausewitz differentiates between strategy – the overall plan – and mere tactics – planning of a discrete part of the overall plan, such as the battle. Above this, von Clausewitz placed what he labelled 'grand strategy': the overall political aims. Arguments over the difference between strategy and tactics have raged inconclusively ever since.

Von Clausewitz's view was that success comes through concentrating on one battle at a time. This is the distant precursor of the managerial theory of management by objectives. 'By looking on each engagement as part of a series, at least insofar as events are predictable, the commander is always on the high road to his goal,' he writes.

Key text
- Karl von Clausewitz. *On War*. Viking Press, 1983

Key link
- www.mala.bc.ca/~mcneil/cit/citlcclaus.htm

Click-through

See banner ad.

Clicks-and-mortar

See Internet business models.

Client

In a client-server arrangement, the server is the provider and the client is the recipient of whatever passes between the two. In the case of information technology and the transmission of data, the client is the software program used to contact and retrieve data from a server program. Client programs often require a specific type of server program. A Web browser client, such as Netscape Navigator, Microsoft Internet Explorer or Opera, is an example of a client program on a personal computer. The Web browser client communicates with a Web server to send and retrieve data.

Closed question

A technique used in **quantitative research** for product and service marketing, a closed question is a one that limits the answer to a particular response. 'Do you like football?' is an example of a closed question, eliciting a 'yes' or 'no' answer. Contrast this with an **open question**, such as 'What kind of sports do you like?', which allows for a range of responses. Closed questions are often used in 'mark-the-box' type questionnaires. Open questions are used for **qualitative research**.

Closed shop

'Closed shop' is the term used to describe an organization in which all employees are required to be members of a union in order to join the organization. This is slightly different from a union shop, where employees are not required to be a member of a union when hired but must become one within a specified period of time to remain employed.

In the United Kingdom, the power of the trade unions was progressively eroded throughout the latter half of the twentieth century, notably as a result of legislation passed under Margaret Thatcher's Conservative government in 1988, when closed shops were made illegal.

In the United States, the closed shop was made illegal in the Taft-Hartley Labor Act of 1947, which also prohibited union shops unless authorized in a secret poll by a majority of the workers. The need for a vote was dropped in 1951. The present situation in the United States is that several states have outlawed union shops.

One of the last examples of the closed shop in the United Kingdom was the acting profession, in which actors, in order to obtain acting work, were required to be a member of Equity, the actors' union. The term 'closed shop' is also used to describe the situation in which only a person holding certain qualifications is permitted to carry out a particular task. Barristers, for example, have sole rights of representation in some courts, something solicitors would like to change. Solicitors, in their turn, protested when licensed conveyancers were permitted to conduct the conveyancing of property.

Cluetrain Manifesto

The Cluetrain Manifesto began life as an online protest against soulless corporate Web sites. Addressed to 'The people of Earth', the manifesto consists of 95 theses or principles that were posted on the site. They include:

- Markets are conversations.
- Markets consist of human beings, not demographic sectors.
- Conversations among human beings *sound* human. They are conducted in a human voice.
- Whether delivering information, opinions, perspectives, dissenting arguments, or humorous asides, the human voice is typically open, natural, uncontrived.
- People recognize each other as such from the sound of this voice.
- The Internet is enabling conversations among human beings that were simply not possible in the era of mass media.
- Hyperlinks subvert hierarchy.

The manifesto began life in early 1999 when the authors – Rick Levine, **Christopher Locke**, Doc Searls, and David Weinberger – decided to vent their frustration about insipid corporate Web sites.

'We all got talking one day not too long ago about what essential realities many businesses are missing as they attempt to play in the Internet headspace,' the four self-proclaimed ringleaders explain. 'We got tired of invoking clichéd refrains like "clueless companies" and "they just don't get it". The Cluetrain Manifesto is our attempt at articulating a set of principles and dynamics we believe will determine the future experience of both individuals and institutions online. We're lobbing some bombs here. But we're also optimistic. We hope not too much so.'

The manifesto was posted on a Web site, www.cluetrain.com. The quartet invited those who read their manifesto to sign up to it. The response was emphatic. News of the site spread virally, the Net equivalent of word of mouth, and quickly developed a cult following.

Key text
- Rick Levine, Christopher Locke, Doc Searls and David Weinberger. *The Cluetrain Manifesto*. Perseus, 1999

Key link
- www.cluetrain.com/signers.html

Cluster

Cluster is a term used to describe a collection of businesses operating in the same industry gathered in a single geographical location. The phenomenon of clusters, such as the Internet clusters in Silicon Valley, California, in the United States and Silicon Fen in Cambridge and the surrounding area in the United Kingdom, is examined in some depth by Harvard Business School strategy guru **Michael Porter**. (Porter's five forces framework, developed in the 1980 bestseller *Competitive Strategy*, is one of the most popular business models in history.)

Theory suggests that the globalization of markets, rapid transportation and high-speed communications capability should allow companies to source anything from anywhere, anytime. But, argues Porter, the reality is very different. The global theory fails to explain the remarkably high success rate of firms specializing in the same disciplines operating in close geographical proximity.

Porter points to clusters – critical masses of linked industries and institutions in a particular place – that enjoy unusual competitive success in a particular field. The most famous examples, he says, are computer firms in Silicon Valley and the Hollywood film industry, but other such clusters are dotted around the globe.

The proximity of organizations within these clusters – including suppliers, academic institutions and government agencies – appears to affect competition in three broad ways. First, it increases the productivity of companies in the region. Second, it drives the direction and pace of innovation. Third, it stimulates and triggers the genesis of new businesses within the cluster.

According to Porter, this phenomenon is probably best explained by the notion of a closer-knit community; one in which geographical, cultural and institutional closeness confer insiders with special access to each other's skills and ideas.

Porter's hothouse theory is hard to refute, though it does not explain the success of a company such as Microsoft, which deliberately chooses to position itself out of Silicon Valley.

Key text

- Michael Porter. 'Clusters and the New Economics of Competition.' *Harvard Business Review*, November/December 1998

Cluster sample

A cluster sample is a small selected sample chosen by market researchers to represent a particular target market. Clusters are often chosen on a geographic basis, as this cuts down costs. A cluster sample from the Scottish Highlands, for example, might be asked to test midge repellent.

Co-branding

See Brands.

Codec

A codec is technology that compresses and decompresses (encodes and decodes) data (*com*pression/*de*compression). Most streaming media relies on compression and decompression. This is because, due to their size, sound and video files, for example, can take a long time to download over the Internet and occupy a large amount of space on a hard drive. Formats such as Real Audio and Video, Windows Media Player, and Apple's Quicktime use codecs to enable the efficient transfer of audio and video and information. **MPEG**, which converts analogue video signals into compressed video files, is an example of a popular codec.

Cognitive dissonance

Cognitive dissonance is the mental state caused in a consumer by a difference between the consumer's perception of, and expectations for, a product or service and the reality; the greater the difference, the greater the mental conflict and anxiety. Advertising uses this cognitive dissonance to induce consumers to buy, and to reward them for buying. Cognitive dissonance can be used to induce a purchase by sowing the seeds of doubt in a consumer's mind by suggesting they need to purchase a product in order to close the gap between the consumer's self-perception and the reality suggested by the ad. For example, if an ad suggests that you need product A in order to be a good parent, then a consumer who does not have the product but perceives himself as a good parent will be encouraged to purchase the product. Cognitive dissonance can also be used to reassure consumers who are in a post-purchase state of doubt that their purchase was indeed the correct one.

Cold-calling

A favoured sales technique, cold-calling involves approaching consumers with a view to selling them goods or services even though the consumer has not given their permission to be approached, explicitly or implicitly, and may even be unfamiliar with the product or service. Telephone canvassing is a common method of cold-calling, as are door-to-door selling and direct mail.

Collins, James C.

Author; academic; thought leader (b. 1958)

James Collins runs a management learning laboratory in Boulder, Colorado and is a visiting professor at the University of Virginia. He has also taught at Stanford and worked at McKinsey & Co. and Hewlett-Packard.

While the term 'corporate values' is a relative newcomer to the business lexicon, the concept of values as an important aspect of corporate life is not. Although not always described as such, many companies have long recognized the importance of possessing a set of guiding principles. The evolution of the concept can be traced through some of the most influential business books over the last 50 years.

In his 1963 book *A Business and Its Beliefs*, Thomas Watson Jr, CEO of IBM, observed: 'Consider any great organization – one that has lasted over the years – I think you will find it owes its resiliency not to its form of organization or administrative skills, but to the power of what we call beliefs and the appeal these beliefs have for its people.' When Watson talks about beliefs, he is talking about fundamental principles or standards, about what is valuable or important to IBM, the organization. He is talking about values.

Similarly, **Tom Peters** and Robert Waterman thought corporate values important enough to warrant an entire chapter in their 1982 book *In Search Of Excellence*. For them, the terms 'beliefs' and 'values' were interchangeable. Other writers touched on the subject with varying degrees of interest.

But the debate took a leap forward in 1994 with *Built to Last* by James C. Collins and **Jerry I. Porras**. The two business academics from Stanford University set out to identify the qualities essential to building a great and enduring organization; what the authors called 'successful habits of visionary companies.' The 18 companies they wrote about had outperformed the general stock market by a factor of 12 since 1925.

Core values, they say, are: 'The organization's essential and enduring tenets – a small set of guiding principles; not to be confused with specific cultural or operating practices; not to be compromised for financial gain or short-term expediency.' For Collins and Porras, values are timeless guiding principles that drive the way the company operates – everything it does – at a level that transcends strategic objectives. For Hewlett-Packard, for example, values include a strong sense of responsibility to the community. For Disney, they include 'creativity, dreams, and imagination' and the promulgation of 'wholesome American values'.

'Companies that enjoy enduring success have core values and a core purpose that remain fixed while their business strategies and practices endlessly adapt to a changing world,' write Collins and Porras. This, they say, is a key factor in the success of companies such as Hewlett-Packard, Johnson & Johnson, Procter & Gamble, Merck and Sony. Collins and Porras recommend a conceptual framework to cut through some of the confusion swirling around the issues. In their model, vision has two components – core ideology and envisioned future.

Core ideology, the Yin in their scheme, defines what the company stands for and why it exists. Yin is unchanging and complements Yang, the envisioned future. The envisioned future is what the company aspires to become, to achieve, to create – something that will require considerable change and progress to attain.

Core ideology provides the glue that holds an organization together through time. Any effective vision must embody the core ideology of the organization, which in turn has two components – core values (a system of guiding principles and tenets) and core purpose (the organization's most fundamental reason for existence).

Key text
- James C. Collins and Jerry I. Porras. *Built to Last: Successful Habits of Visionary Companies.* HarperCollins, 1994

Key links
- www.jimcollins.com/pageload.asp?pagename=mai_pubs.html
- www.business2.com/webguide/0,1660,62470, FF.html

Comfort zone

A comfort zone is an area (not physical) in which an individual feels happy that he can perform competently without extending himself. For an individual to perform to his maximum ability, he may need to be challenged. This will inevitably involve operating 'outside the comfort zone': undertaking a task that the individual does not feel absolutely certain that he can perform successfully.

Command economy

A command economy is an economy planned and directed by a government. Such an approach rejects the *laissez-faire* free market in favour of state intervention. Common elements of a command economy include cooperation; collectivization, such as collective farms; central planning; equality, with all members of these states sharing equally in the wealth of the state; the public ownership of property; and the five-year plan (industrial and economic plan).

Command economies, such as communist USSR, Cuba and the post-war Eastern Bloc, do not have a good track record. In practice, most economies tend be mixed, combining free market policies with some state intervention.

Key text
- R.B. Jain (ed). *Command Economy To Market Economy: Restructuring And Transformation.* Deep & Deep Publications, 2000

Commission

The term 'commission' refers to a fee charged for conducting a transaction. A commission is usually calculated as a percentage of the transaction value and is normally paid to an intermediary who deals with both the consumer and the supplier of the good or service. A stockbroker, for example, will be paid a commission based on a percentage of the value of the stock purchased. Both a vendor and purchaser of a stock will be required to pay a commission. In insurance, when the broker sells a policy on an insurance company's behalf, a commission is paid to the insurance broker by the insurer of the risk. The commission was a convenient way of rewarding a broker for introducing business to a company. The advent of direct selling and financial scandals, such as the mis-selling of pensions in the United Kingdom, has led to a reappraisal of the commission method of payment, with many intermediaries offering a flat fee as an alternative.

Community

The advertising model was one of the first business models employed by Internet businesses. The premise was that advertising revenue would be sufficient to pay for running costs and deliver a profit. In e-commerce business models built around advertising revenue, generating eyeballs (Web site visitors) is essential. Any Web site feature that encourages surfers to stick around – **stickiness** – rather than move on to another site is a bonus.

'Community' is a term used in e-business to describe specific Web site functionality that encourages like-minded people to interact. Chat rooms and message boards are popular examples of community-related Web site functions. Message boards allow a user to post a message, a technical query for example, so that other users can post responses. Chat rooms allow Web site users to interact in real time, carrying on an immediate conversation. Chat rooms may be regulated, and have their own rules of etiquette that are standard across the Internet. The idea is that building a community generates a loyal user base, creating the all-important stickiness.

Companies Act 1985

A complex piece of UK legislation, The Companies Act 1985 governs the way companies are set up, run and wound up. The bulk of the Companies Act was introduced in 1985. It was subsequently amended in 1989 to bring the legislation in line with EU legislation.

Company formation

In the United Kingdom, there are four main types of company: a private company limited by the shares; a private company limited by guarantee; a private unlimited company; and a public limited company. A limited company is incorporated by submitting the required documents to the registrar of companies at Companies House. These documents include a memorandum of association and articles of association, along with a fee.

A private company must have at least one director and one secretary, who cannot be the same person. The company secretary does not require formal qualifications. In a public limited company, at least two directors are required, as well as a formally qualified company secretary. The rules governing the formation of companies are contained in the **Companies Act**.

Key link
- www.companies-house.gov.uk/

Competency tracking

Competency tracking enables companies to overcome some of the logistical challenges in ensuring that training and development are constantly related back to competencies, as well as being planned ahead with competencies in mind.

When core competence became popular in management circles, companies set out to identify the competencies required in specific jobs. The downside was that this produced a mountain of paper and a lengthy list of training and development requirements. On the plus side, training could be targeted more appropriately. Clearly defined competencies could result in timely and targeted training.

While the competency-training link makes clear, logical and powerful managerial and competitive sense, it has not always worked in practice. Indeed, as in so many cases, practice lags well behind the theory.

While lots of companies engage in skills-gap analysis, often they do not move forward to the next stage. The gaps inevitably remain as organizations ponder the wisdom of investing in training to fill them.

Then there is the sheer number of actual and potential competencies. While some companies have managed to distil the core competencies they require to a meagre twelve, most finish with far more. This may be entirely accurate, but it means that actually managing them is usually impossible.

For many, the reality is that linking competencies to appraisal and assessment systems, as well as to training, simply produces an array of paperwork. Even companies with carefully mapped-out and understood competency frameworks have struggled with monitoring what has happened, what needs to happen, and what is happening regarding training.

Technology is now bringing new rigour and efficiency to the divide between theories and practices. Use of competency-tracking software is increasing as organizations seek solutions to long-running problems. Competency software aims to halve the administrative workload for those whose job it is to track and record employee development and standards. It breaks down employees' roles into specific areas, such as technical knowledge, processing knowledge, behavioural skills and systems awareness.

As well as taking much of the labour out of the competency process, competency tracking takes the subjectivity out of management assessment and may help companies with their succession planning.

More generally, demand for competency tracking is liable to expand as the quantity of administration and the complexity of compliance issues increase workloads in HR and training administration. Closer ties between competencies and reward and remuneration packages may further stimulate growth. Competency-based pay is a reality in mainland Europe; competency tracking may convince companies elsewhere to follow this route.

Competition Act 1998

The Competition Act 1998 outlaws agreements, business practices and conduct that damage competition in the United Kingdom. The Act prohibits anti-competitive agreements (known as the Chapter I prohibition) and abuse of a dominant position (the Chapter II prohibition). A business in breach of the Act can be fined up to 10 percent of its UK turnover; additionally, third parties may be able to claim for damages. In order to establish whether the Act has been infringed, officials from the Office of Fair Trading can enter premises and demand relevant documents.

'Anti-competitive agreements' includes both informal and formal arrangements, in writing or otherwise. Agreements covered by the Act include an agreement to fix purchase or selling prices; an agreement to limit or control production, markets, technical development or investment; and an agreement to share markets or supply sources. Agreements must have 'an appreciable effect on competition' to be covered by the Act.

For the purposes of 'abuse of a dominant position,' a dominant position means that a business is able to behave independently of competitive pressures on its market. Generally speaking, a company with less than 40 percent market share will not be in a dominant position (although this is not an absolute rule). Examples of abuses of a dominant position given in the Act include the imposition of unfair purchase or selling prices; limiting production, markets or technical development to the prejudice of consumers; and attaching unrelated supplementary conditions to contracts.

As UK competition law is subject to EU competition law, the Competition Act 1998 allows for the referral of proposed mergers and takeovers to the Competition Commission to establish whether they are in the public interest or anti-competitive.

Key link

- www.oft.gov.uk/Business/Legal+Powers/ Competition+Act+1998.htm

Concert party

A concert party consists of individuals or companies that, following an agreement or understanding, informal or formal, cooperate to obtain or consolidate control of a company. In some cases, such as that of a financial adviser and its clients or company and its related companies, the parties will be presumed to be acting in concert until proved otherwise. Where persons acting in concert hold a certain percentage of the voting shares of a public company, they may be required to make a formal bid for the company.

Conglomerate

A conglomerate is a company whose growth is predominantly through an acquisition of or merger with other companies that operate in unrelated markets to that of the acquiring company. Conglomerates became popular during the 1960s with companies such as ITT. Modern examples of conglomerates include Tyco International and General Electric. Conglomerate British American Tobacco (BAT), for example, owns a tobacco company as well as a Californian insurance company. A conglomerate merger is a merger between two companies that produce unrelated products.

Conjoint analysis

Conjoint analysis is a sophisticated and versatile marketing research technique for analysing the consumer decision-making process. It can be used to answer questions such as: Which new products are likely to prove successful? Do specific market segments exist for a product or service? What advertising will be most successful with a particular segment?

The technique is based on the idea that consumers make choices about products by trading good product features against bad. They might, for example, choose a small car over a large one if it is capable of a faster speed or is a convertible. Conjoint analysis looks at the feature trade-offs to determine the combination of attributes that will be most attractive to a prospective consumer.

Points are allotted for product features. For example, a computer might be rated on processor speed, memory, monitor size and hard disk size.

A conjunctive purchaser looks for a minimum standard for each feature and rejects brands that fail to reach that level; they would consider jointly all product features. A disjunctive purchaser looks for a minimum standard from a few or one highly valued attribute and does not care about the others. By asking individuals to make choices between products with different configurations, market researchers can explore the factors driving consumers' choices about a product. This information can then be used to design targeted advertising and products.

Connectivity

Understanding connectivity is like coming to terms with the childhood revelation that we are all, somewhere along the line, related. In the information economy, small things are connected in a myriad of ways to create complex adaptive systems. Instantaneous, myriad connections are speeding up the economy and, more critically, changing the way it works.

The difference in the information economy is that the small things are connected in a myriad of ways to create a 'complex adaptive system'. 'We have multiplied the instant connections among individuals, organizations, and information itself. Attention has been focused on the resulting acceleration of business. But connections are doing more than accelerating the economy; they are changing the way it works,' says **Chris Meyer**, co-author of *Blur*. 'As the number of connections among the elements of a system grows, the system no longer behaves predictably – the system as a whole begins to exhibit unforeseen, *emergent* properties.'

The trouble is that the connections are so many and so complex that they can bring things to a grinding, inexplicable halt. 'The stock market crash of October 1987 was caused by computerized trades, none of which were linked explicitly. The damage was done by the interaction of independent investor instructions – a kind of connected network of trading programs,' write **Stan**

Davis and Chris Meyer in *Blur*. Therefore, the stock market crash was not a frenzy of capitalism, but a connectivity short circuit. Such short circuits – akin to butterflies fluttering their wings in Mongolia and changing the climate of the world while also causing a run on the US dollar – are likely to occur with greater regularity.

Key text
- Stan Davis and Christopher Meyer. *Blur: The Speed of Change in the Connected Economy*. Warner Books, 1998

Consortium

A consortium is an alliance between companies for the purpose of undertaking a specific task. A consortium is usually formed because each company offers different expertise, or, alternatively, to allow companies to pool finances for the purposes of a particular project.

Major construction projects are often tended for by companies acting in a consortium. A consortium doesn't have to be formed for profit-making activities, however. Take The Leapfrog Group, for example: a consortium of more than 100 public and private organizations, representing more than 31 million healthcare consumers in the United States. The group works with medical experts throughout the country to improve the provision of health care.

Consumable

A consumable is a good purchased that, as the name suggests, is consumed immediately or shortly thereafter, as opposed to consumer durables, which are goods not consumed immediately or shortly after purchase.

Consumables tend to be frequent purchases and include foodstuffs, beverages, detergents and petrol. Consumer durables are infrequently purchased and tend to be more expensive than consumables; they include items such as tel-

evisions, stereos, washing machines, dishwashers and beds.

C2B (consumer-to-business)

See Internet business models.

C2C (consumer-to-consumer)

See Internet business models.

Content aggregator

Content aggregators are companies that gather, process and distribute online content. Content is supplied to content aggregators by content partners. Proprietary software is used to deliver the content to the client or, alternatively, the client accesses the content on the aggregator's servers. Aggregators include companies such as information aggregator Yahoo! and news aggregator Moreover. As middlemen, content aggregators fall under the label of cybermediaries – organizations that act as intermediaries in e-business.

While aggregators trade on the fact that they offer a conveniently packaged selection of content, sophisticated surfers increasingly head straight for the individual content providers, cutting out the intermediary. Services such as My Yahoo! allow personalized content aggregation tailored to the individual user, providing an effective halfway house.

Key links
- http://my.yahoo.com
- http://w.moreover.com

Contrarian

A contrarian is an individual who acts in the opposite way to popular opinion. Investors adopting a contrarian approach to stock selection would choose stocks and industry sectors that were performing poorly or were out of favour. This is based on the simple premise that what goes down must come up.

Adopting a contrarian approach can be a profitable method of stock selection, provided that investors do not confuse stocks that are out of favour with those of companies that are badly run and unlikely to recover. To avoid the situation, the contrarian applies a number of criteria to the purchasing decisions. He will look at factors such as the momentum of the share and share movement trends, often using technical analysis.

Key link
- www.contrarianinvesting.com/index.php

Cookie

A cookie is an electronic file containing a small piece of computer code, which is sent to a user when a Web page is requested and stored in a text file on the user's hard disk. The transaction is a hidden one, with the recipient often unaware that the cookie has been delivered. Every time thereafter that the user requests a Web page from the same server, the message will pass back to the server.

The purpose of cookies was originally to make the connection between the server and the client (the user) more efficient. Cookies are used by online marketing and advertising companies to gather information about individuals and deliver personalized advertising to individuals. They are also used by Web retailers to deliver personalized services to visitors to a site. Online retailing giant Amazon.com, for example, uses cookies to deliver a personalized Web page and viewing experience. Visitors to its site will see details of books that they have recently expressed an interest in, by viewing a particular page, and also books that they may be interested in – all delivered through the technology of cookies.

The use of cookies has caused some debate about the issue of privacy. As a result, the Euro-

pean Parliament has passed an amendment to data collection and privacy legislation to force Web sites to ask permission of visitors before serving cookies to their computers. It remains to be seen how individual countries will comply with this legislation. However, in the United States, the pro-cookie lobby led by the Interactive Advertising Bureau (IAD) has managed to resist similar legislation.

Many Web browsers, including later versions of the Netscape and Microsoft browsers, allow the user to block acceptance of cookies. Some sites, however, will not admit surfers who will not accept a cookie file.

Cooperative

The cooperative is an organizational structure favoured by command economies. In a cooperative business organization, there is limited liability and each shareholder has only one vote, regardless of how many shares he owns. In a worker cooperative, it is the workers who are the shareholders and own the company. The workers decide on how the company is to be run. In a consumer cooperative, consumers control the company.

Co-opetition

Co-opetition is a business concept introduced by Harvard Business School professor Adam Brandenburger and Yale School of Management professor Barry Nalebuff during the 1990s. The authors acknowledge that some companies prefer a competitive approach to business – treating business like warfare with outcomes seen in terms of winners and losers. Other companies prefer to adopt a cooperative attitude to business – embracing team and partnership approaches. Co-opetition is a combination of both the competitive and cooperative approaches. The word was originally coined by Ray Noorda, founder of the networking software company Novell: 'You have to compete and cooperate at the same time.'

Incorporating elements of game theory, the concept relies on treating business as a game, then developing strategies to shape the game to suit the company. Brandenburger and Nalebuff advocate approaching co-opetition in stages. First, they suggest, construct a map, or Value Net, that identifies 'all the players in the game of business and the interdependencies among them'. The next and most important step is to 'change the game'.

Copyright

A form of intellectual property, copyright is the exclusive right given to the author of a work – including words, music, video, sound, picture, architecture, etc. – to reproduce, distribute, display, license or perform the work. Copyright is an unregistered right, meaning the beneficiary of the copyright need do nothing in order to receive the protection of the law. The copyright comes into effect immediately as soon as the work capable of being copyrighted is created and made permanent.

Copyright law in the United Kingdom has its origins in the Licensing Act of 1662. With the advent of printing, it soon became apparent that the issue of pirate copies of books would be a problem. The Act provided for books to be registered and licensed. Although the legislation was repealed shortly afterward, it established the principle of rights of ownership.

It was the Statute of Anne, 1709, that introduced the first Copyright Act in the world. The Act introduced two new concepts – an author being the owner of copyright and a fixed term of protection for published works (14 years in the case of this Act). Subsequent Copyright Acts, such as those passed in 1911 and 1956, revised and amended the legislation.

In the United States, copyright legislation is enshrined in the Copyright Act of 1976, which offers protection to authors of 'original works of authorship'. The protection is offered to both published and unpublished works. Copyright owners have the exclusive right to reproduce the work, prepare derivative work, distribute copies and perform the work publicly. The provisions of the Act are similar to copyright legislation in the United Kingdom.

Core competence

Core competencies are distinctive and differentiating competencies that lie at the heart of an organization. These include not just the products and services a company sells but also 'soft' areas of a company's activities, such as branding, organizational innovation and service.

A company's core competence is at the very heart of its ability to compete.

The theory is that identifying core competencies allows an organization to nurture and build from its strengths rather than pursuing activities in which it does not possess the necessary skills. It also allows a company to create the exceptional customer value assets that set it apart from its competitors.

The concept of core competencies was championed by American academics **Gary Hamel** and **C.K. Prahalad** in their 1994 book *Competing for the Future*.

Core product benefits

Core product benefits are the key attributes of a product in the mind of a consumer when making a purchasing decision. When buying a car, for example, one purchaser might consider space to be the core product benefit, another speed, and another style. By defining core product benefits, it is possible to differentiate products and so maximize that benefit.

Core values

Core values define the essence of what a company stands for. They act as a reference point for individuals within an organization. Usually numbering more than three and less than ten, they might include qualities such as responsible, ethical, honest, innovative and pioneering. Often a company's values will be exhibited in the company's offices or headquarters or, as in the case of General Electric, printed on a card that employees can carry on their person.

New Economy companies have embraced values as a way to preserve their distinctive cultures and inspire employees. Amazon.com, for example, famously has its six core values: customer obsession; ownership; bias for action; frugality; a high hiring bar; and innovation. These, it hopes, provide the springboard for its vision as 'the world's most customer-centric company. The place where people come to find and discover anything they might want to buy online.'

Values may be popular with up-and-coming companies, but they are not a new idea. The fact is that they have been a staple of successful organizations for decades. Well-managed companies have always found it useful to spell out what they stand for. A set of core values underpins many of the most famous and long-lived of the old-economy companies.

General Electric, one of the outstanding old-economy success stories of recent times, subscribes to a set of core values. Among them are 'setting stretch goals' and 'simplicity'. Other organizations that find it helpful to spell out their core values include Walt Disney, the US Army, and the Federal Bureau of Investigation (FBI).

Values are not only the province of large, well-established businesses. They can and are used as a way to attract bright people to small, growing businesses. Take de Baer Corporate Clothing, for example. Founded by chief executive Jacqueline de Baer, the company designs and manufactures staff uniforms for the likes of Holiday Inn, Boots Opticians and the Odeon Cinema in Leicester Square.

De Baer sees itself as an international company with personality. It aims to create a culture that will attract young talent looking for an informal and fun environment to work in. The company's values include fun, integrity, openness and learning. Says CEO Jacqueline de Baer: 'If you start a company then the company takes on a lot of your personality. As it gets bigger it's very important to identify the personality of the company. It might still be 75 percent the personality of the founder but there may be other elements. Defining the values is very powerful. The values can guide you in all sorts of ways, especially in speeding up decision making. We are very clear on what we are trying to do.'

The company also uses values to guide recruitment decisions. Every new person to join at management level has a telephone interview to discuss his values before being asked to the first formal interview. At other levels within the organization, questions aimed at identifying values are incorporated into the first interview. 'It's more than just empowering decision making. I recruit against the values,' says de Baer.

Although many companies have corporate values from the outset, not all do. Companies that have not expressly stated their values can conduct an exercise to 'discover' them. Commentators, such as UK business writers Stephen Coomber and Des Dearlove, authors of the report on core values 'Heart and Soul', are divided on whether it is possible or desirable for a company to change or reinterpret its values.

Corporate anorexia

When corporate restructuring involves layoffs, a company may shed too many employees and lose some of the crucial creative staff and knowledge workers that gave the company a competitive advantage. This undesirable side-effect of **downsizing** or **rationalization** is termed 'corporate anorexia'. Companies that downsize have to be careful not to let go of key teams and personnel that would prevent them from carrying out their business profitability. Rehired employees who act as consultants in performing specialized tasks are known as ghost workers.

Corporate citizenship

Covering issues such as corporate social responsibility and business ethics, corporate citizenship is a broad term used to describe the corporation's role in society. Corporations have a significant impact on their stakeholders, including customers, shareholders, employees and communities, in the location of the business. The concept of corporate citizenship has become increasingly important as a wealth of research suggests responsible business attitudes, policies and practices have a beneficial effect on the bottom line.

Key link
- www.greenleaf-publishing.com/jcc/ jcchome.htm

Corporate culture

Corporate culture is a combination of factors, including company values, working conditions, employee benefits and even office design. Over time, these reflect the underlying conscious and subconscious values and beliefs shared by the employees of a company. Different industries have a reputation for particular types of corporate culture. Accountancy firms are typically painted as having formal, stuffy, regimented corporate cultures while advertising agencies are supposed to have vibrant, fun-loving, lively cultures. It is not always easy to identify corporate culture. One indicator is the type of behaviour encouraged and rewarded by management. Risk taking, acting on initiative, employee participation, change; the management's attitude to all of these will provide important clues to the nature of the corporate culture. In reality, lines are not so clearly defined. As firms struggle to find talented employees, corporate culture becomes increasingly important in attracting and retaining the best staff.

Corporate governance

Corporate governance is the examination of the control of a company as exercised by its directors. The directors of public companies are accountable for their actions to the company shareholders. However, in practice, the power of the shareholders to affect the behaviour of the directors is limited and rarely exercised. As a result, unlike a government that is restrained from certain action by the people it governs and the institutions of government, directors are relatively unfettered, with considerable power to act however they wish.

In the United Kingdom, following a series of corporate scandals during the 1980s and 1990s, including the Mirror Group pensions scandal, the issue of corporate governance came under close scrutiny. The result was the Cadbury Report (1992), which set out a Code of Practice that companies should adhere to, an important element of which was the separation of power between the CEO and the chairman. The Greenbury Report on directors' pay followed in 1995, the Hampel Report covering implementation of Cadbury and Greenbury in 1998, and the Combined Code on Corporate Governance (1998/1999) from the **London Stock Exchange**.

Although there is no equivalent approach to corporate governance in the United States, large investors such as CALPERS, the California Pensions organization, have brought pressure to bear on US corporate boards. The repercussions of the Enron affair may also affect attitudes toward corporate governance in the United States.

Corporate image

Corporate image refers to the way a company is perceived by those outside the company. A company's image is conveyed to the consumer in a variety of ways. In the case of a retail store, for example, interaction with the staff, advertising, location, corporate identity (representation of a company by its emblem, logo, livery and other visual and aural means) and company values will all influence consumer perception.

The corporate image has a strong impact on market performance. Positive corporate image can overcome temporary setbacks. For example, poor sales performance will be better tolerated by the financial markets in companies with a positive corporate image. Similarly, if a company with a positive corporate image has a problem with one of its products, it will be given some leeway by consumers – more so than a company with a negative corporate image.

Building, creating, and moulding a corporate image is not something that can be done in a short time. It requires planning and implementation over many months, even years. It also requires management buy-in and consistent behaviour in accordance with the image created. Creating a positive corporate image is not always an easy task. However, the effect on the bottom line may suggest it is well worth taking the trouble.

Corporate legacy

The idea of corporate legacy asserts that senior management is the custodian of the values that underpin the culture, conserving them on behalf and for the benefit of the company in the future. It goes right to the heart and soul of the business – what it exists for and the values it holds most dear.

The concept came from research by UK business writers Des Dearlove and Stephen Coomber examining the impact of values on business. The values handed down from one generation to the next are an important dimension of the legacy. Clearly defined corporate values can play an important role in the success of a business by engaging the energy, enthusiasm and loyalty of employees.

The notion of corporate legacy, however, extends beyond the here and now. It raises the issue of what one generation of management should pass on to the next. In any long-lived company, generations of CEOs will preside over the culture of the organization, inheriting it from their predecessors, passing it on to their successors.

Ex-director of Shell International and business author Arie de Geus looked at corporate longevity in his book *The Living Company*. De Geus writes about the managers of long-lived companies: 'They succeeded through the generational flow of members, and considered themselves stewards of the longstanding enterprise. Each management generation was only a link in a long chain.'

Stewardship is an idea that is increasingly relevant to business. How successive leaders deal with this corporate legacy, however, is rarely discussed. It goes beyond traditional ideas of succession planning – deciding whom the baton will be passed to and developing the next generation of managers – or even the work on corporate memory carried out by the American management writer **Art Kleiner**.

Corporate legacy is particularly critical when the founder or founders of a company hand over control. What marks out the great CEOs from the rest is their ability to ensure that the company goes on after them. **Bill Gates** and **Richard Branson** are both great leaders in their own right, but what legacy will they leave behind?

Another critical dimension to the legacy issue is the immutability of corporate values. As economic conditions change with the passage of time, there is often pressure within companies to deviate from the values, drop them altogether, or take on new ones. The question that then has to be answered is: Can values change or be replaced, or are they sacrosanct?

Opinion varies on this point. 'Our basic principles have endured intact since our founders conceived them,' said John Young, former CEO of Hewlett-Packard in 1992. 'We distinguish between core values and practices; core values don't change, but the practices might.'

Writing in *Fortune* magazine, **Thomas A. Stewart** draws a different conclusion: 'Over time self-interest distorts corporate values … To bring them back, top management must constantly reiterate, refresh, reinterpret, and rename.'

If the original sense of the values has been lost or if the values have evolved in the wrong direction, it is the top team's role to redefine and reinterpret the values so that they are relevant.

Corporate memory

Corporate memory is a readily accessible fund of useful knowledge about how and why the company has done things. Corporate memory aims to allow an organization to transfer experience from one generation to the next – and, more mundanely, from one office to the next. It is based on the understanding that intellectual capital is not simply a contemporary phenomenon. Knowledge is – or should be – cumulative. All of our insights come from retrospect; we just have to make the past available and then be able to put the past into perspective.

To help create and sustain a corporate memory, American researchers and writers **Art Kleiner** and George Roth suggest that companies use a tool called the *learning history* – 'a narrative of a company's recent set of critical episodes, a corporate change event, a new initiative, a widespread innovation, a successful product launch, or even a traumatic event like a downsizing'. Other techniques to organize and gather together corporate experiences are being explored. For example, technology enables databases of personal experience to be assembled.

Corporate social responsibility (CSR)

CSR has been defined by the World Business Council as 'the continuing commitment by business to behave ethically and to contribute to economic development while improving the quality of life of the workforce and their families, as well as of the local community and society at large'. The intention of companies adopting a socially responsible corporate attitude is to ensure a positive social, environmental, and economic impact on the communities within which they operate and on all other **stakeholders**.

Business ethics – the consideration of how business and businesspeople should behave toward each other and toward the public – plays a large part in CSR.

Some industries, particularly law and medicine, have a clearly defined code of professional ethics. In other industries, appropriate behaviour has been established over time by practice. At its most complex, business ethics touches on the role of the company in society. Issues such as the effect of a petrochemical company's actions on the environment, or the obligation of a pharmaceutical company to make its drugs available to third-world nations, are difficult and contentious areas of business ethics. As lobbyists and pressure groups become more powerful, companies are forced to pay greater attention to corporate responsibility and business ethics.

Corporate universities

As the name suggests, a corporate university is an educational establishment, akin to a university, run by a corporation, largely for the benefit of its staff. In the United States, for example, there are now more than 1000 corporate colleges in operation. They come in all shapes and sizes, and cover virtually every industry. The Ohio automotive-parts manufacturer, Dana Corporation, has Dana University; Ford has a Heavy Truck University in Detroit; Intel runs a university in Santa Clara, California; Sun Microsystems has Sun U; and Apple has its own university in Cupertino, California.

When they were first established, corporate universities raised a few academic eyebrows and not a little criticism. The criticism has largely subsided and suspicion has taken over. If corporations can train their own executives, their reliance on business schools is reduced.

The scale of the corporate universities is, in many cases, impressive.

McDonald's Hamburger University, located in Oak Brook, Illinois, may not, in the eyes of some, have a great deal of academic credibility, but it has celebrated its 35th anniversary and boasts more than 50,000 graduates. It has 30 resident professors, suggesting that its programmes go a little beyond the art of frying. Indeed, the McDonald's educational empire has spread in tandem with the growth of its business – there are now ten international training centres in the United Kingdom, Japan, Germany, and Australia – and technology enables programmes to be delivered simultaneously in 22 languages.

It's a similar, if less prolific, story in the United Kingdom. In April 1998, British Aerospace, one of Europe's biggest defence and aerospace companies, unveiled plans to create its own virtual university in partnership with outside academic institutions. Called the British Aerospace Virtual University, the initiative involves a massive financial commitment by the company. In the next decade, it is pledged to invest more than £1.5 billion in building up the company's all-important 'knowledge base' for the future. The virtual university marks one of the biggest European investments in workplace development and one of the most significant developments in corporate universities.

Corporate universities are not for the fainthearted. They are highly expensive. Research in the United States by Jeanne Meister calculated that the average operating budget for a corporate university was $12.4 million (though 60 percent reported budgets of $5 million or less).

One of the main criticisms of corporate universities has been that they often do not offer anything other than an internal qualification. However, in an effort to broaden their appeal, corporate universities are establishing partnerships with a wide range of organizations. Courses are increasingly compatible with those of a more traditional academic institution.

Some corporate universities are attempting to develop degree-awarding powers themselves.

Consulting firm Arthur D. Little has already pursued the degree route at its Boston-based school. But a survey of 100 corporate-university deans, carried out for the Association to Advance Collegiate Schools of Business by Corporate University XChange, suggested a change of heart. Rather than going it alone, 40 percent of corporate universities now plan to offer degrees in partnership with institutions of higher education – mostly in business administration, computer science, engineering and finance.

There must be a question mark over whether corporate universities can produce meaningful research. Their close allegiances raise issues of objectivity and independence.

Corporate values

See Core values.

Corporate venturing

Corporate venturing describes the situation in which one company invests in a new or existing venture. Corporate venturing is usually undertaken by large, established firms, which invest in smaller start-ups or rapidly growing companies. The benefits of corporate venturing include that growing firms have access to more venture funding, are able to receive advice from the investing company and can achieve faster and higher growth rates than they might otherwise. A disadvantage is that large companies can use corporate venturing as a means of stifling competition through acquisition.

Corporate vision

Unlike the corporate mission, which is an attainable goal, corporate vision is an unattainable goal toward which a company is striving. Why set an unattainable goal? The idea is that, as the vision is a desirable but unattainable target, it will always drive the company in the desired direction.

Corporate voodoo

A term coined by English authors René Carayol and David Firth, 'corporate voodoo' can roughly be translated as 'business magic'. The term was introduced partly to describe the phenomenon of rapidly growing companies during the Internet boom – both in terms of revenues and share price. In their book of the same name, *Corporate Voodoo*, the authors state that in order to weave corporate magic, companies must possess five essential characteristics: they must be virtual, open-cultured, customer-led, risk-embracing and courageous.

Key text
• David Firth with Rene Carayol. *Corporate Voodoo: Business Principles for Mavericks and Magicians*. Capstone, 2001

Corporation

A corporation is the US legal equivalent of a UK public limited company. Public corporations are state-owned companies. Multi-national corporations are companies that are usually owned in one country but produce and sell in many countries. In the United Kingdom, there are some public limited companies, such as the British Sugar Corporation, that call themselves corporations but in this context the name has no legal meaning.

Cosmocrat

Popularized in the book *A Future Perfect: The Challenge and Hidden Promise of Globalization*, written by British journalists John Micklethwait and Adrian Wooldridge, 'cosmocrat' means a cosmopolitan businessperson and member of an alleged global ruling elite. The term is a contraction of cosmopolitan and bureaucrat.

Key text
• John Micklethwait and Adrian Wooldridge. *A Future Perfect: The Challenge and Hidden Promise of Globalization*. Crown Publishers, 2000

Cost

Where a business spends money in order to meet a specific aim, such as producing goods and services for sale, it is termed a cost. Costs come in three main types. Fixed costs remain relatively unaltered, regardless of a change in the level of activity. Variable costs rise or fall in proportion to a rise or fall in the level of activity. Other costs exhibit characteristics of both fixed and variable costs – semi-variable costs. An analysis of the effect on total costs of a change in the level of a given activity in an organization is known as cost behaviour.

In medium-sized and large businesses, costs are allocated to different parts of a business – cost centres – for the purposes of strategic planning. These cost centres can be large divisions of a business, departments, small teams or even individuals.

Cost-benefit analysis

When planning certain projects, it is common to take consideration of the social and welfare benefits in addition to considering the financial return on investment. This process is known as cost-benefit analysis. For example, this might take into account the environmental impact of an industrial plant or convenience for users of a new railway. A major difficulty is finding a way to quantify net social costs and benefits.

Cotsakos, Christos
*Chairman and CEO, E*Trade (b. 1948)*

There are few leading companies that can boast

a decorated war hero as **CEO**; E*Trade is one of them. Christos Cotsakos made the transition from an errant schoolboy who helped himself to the communion wine to successful businessman with the help of a few wise words from a church priest. He served in the US military during the Vietnam War, and was honoured for his bravery with a Purple Heart and a Bronze Star. A stint at the marketing research firm ACNielsen proved he had the management savvy to succeed in business. Hired by Bill Porter in 1996 to put some fizz into the Internet operations of stock-brokerage firm E*Trade Securities, Cotsakos had, by 2000, built the company into the number-two Web-based brokerage.

E*Trade, the Internet share-trading company, started life as an electronic trading network, Trade Plus & Co., founded in 1982 by Bill Porter, an MIT **MBA** graduate. The company was created to provide trading services to stock brokerages Fidelity, Charles Schwab and Quick & Reilly. By 1992, the company had changed its name to the E*Trade Group and under the name of E*Trade Securities was providing share-dealing services to the public via AOL and CompuServe. Porter's aim was to offer a low-cost service on the back of high-volume business. Economies of scale allowed E*Trade to reduce its commission charge seven times between 1991 and 1995. In 1996, things really took off when Porter saw the potential of Internet trading and launched E*Trade.com. He brought in Cotsakos to manage the new venture.

Although E*Trade had stolen a march on its competitors, the advantage did not last long. To survive, Cotsakos had to fight a battle on two fronts: on one side were the deep-discount brokers swarming onto the Internet and undercutting E*Trade on price; on the other were the traditional brokerage services, such as Charles Schwab, Morgan Stanley, Merrill Lynch, Prudential, and PaineWebber, which pursued a clicks-and-mortar strategy. The established brokerages charged more but provided added-value services and possessed strong brand images.

Luckily for E*Trade, Cotsakos was no stranger to a fight. In 1998, Cotsakos decided the time was right for drastic action. The company was doing well – turning in a $7 million profit on $72 million sales – but Cotsakos believed that this belied the company's shortsighted strategy. Being a major player in the share-trading market, he realized, was not enough to secure the future of E*Trade. What was required, he decided, was a bigger vision: the transformation into a financial portal covering insurance, financial news, banking and other financial sectors. The company had to become the obvious destination for anyone with an interest in online financial information and products. Such a strategy required an investment of billions of dollars in technology and marketing, at the expense of profits for some time to come. But the result, in Cotsakos's view, would justify the means. It was a bold move and carrying it off would require special qualities – resolve, single-mindedness and excellent managerial skills. But Cotsakos was confident he could see it through.

Cotsakos leads from the front, and he's a tough act to follow. He crams more into a day than many executives manage in a week. He serves on the boards of a number of leading technology companies, and even managed to juggle his job as CEO with studying for a PhD in economics at the University of London. He demands the same uncompromising standards from his employees. 'My job is to make people do the impossible,' says Cotsakos. 'I push people hard and I don't tolerate excuses.'

In the period from 1998 to 2000, Cotsakos and E*Trade made progress – but at a price. As he predicted, the company bled money and posted mounting losses. Yet it also rapidly expanded its consumer base from fewer than 100,000 to more than 2 million, placing it third behind Schwab and Fidelity Investments in terms of online accounts. Despite terrible trading conditions in 2001, the company still managed a small second-quarter operating profit, with revenues down by less than 10 percent – helped by drastic cuts in the marketing budget. With its customer base approaching 4 million, the second-biggest Web-based stockbroker appears to be in good shape to bounce back when stock buying picks up again.

Key link
- www.etrade.com

Covey, Stephen

Founder, Covey Leadership Center (b. 1932)

MBA Stephen Covey spent the bulk of his career at Brigham Young University, first as an administrator and then as professor of organizational behaviour. His doctoral research looked at 'success literature'. In 1984, he founded his Leadership Center, aiming to 'serve the worldwide community by empowering people and organizations to significantly increase their performance capability in order to achieve worthwhile purposes through understanding and living principle-centered leadership'.

Covey reached a huge global audience in 1989 with the success of *The Seven Habits of Highly Effective People*, which has sold over 6 million copies and remained on the *New York Times* bestseller list for ten years. Along the way, the devout Mormon transformed himself into an end-of-the-century **Dale Carnegie**. 'He has sold himself with a brashness that makes the over-excited **Tom Peters** look like a shrinking violet,' noted *The Economist*. Another commentator observed, 'Mr Covey has a knack of dressing up spiritual principles in pinstripes.' In fact, Covey's 'principles' are a mixture of the commonsensical and the hackneyed – 'be proactive; begin with the end in mind; put first things first; think win/win; seek first to understand then to be understood; synergize; sharpen the saw.' Yet it is their very simplicity and accessibility that partly explain Covey's astonishing success.

In 1997, the Covey Leadership Center merged with Franklin Quest Co., training provider and creator of the Franklin Day Planner, to form FranklinCovey Co., perhaps the largest entity in the corporate training industry. Today Franklin-Covey is an international firm with 4500 members and an annual turnover of more than half a billion dollars. The company's mission is to 'inspire change by igniting the power of proven principles so that people and organizations achieve what matters most'. Clients include 82 of the *Fortune* 100 companies, more than two-thirds of the *Fortune* 500 companies, thousands of small and mid-size companies, and government entities at local, state and national levels. FranklinCovey has also created pilot partnerships with cities seeking to become principle-centred communities, and is currently teaching the Seven Habits to teachers and administrators in more than 3500 school districts and universities, through statewide initiatives with education leaders in 27 states.

Key texts
- Covey, Stephen. *The 7 Habits of Highly Effective People*. Simon & Schuster, 1990
- Covey, Stephen. *Principle-Centered Leadership*. Simon & Schuster, 1992

Key link
- www.franklincovey.com

CPM (cost per mille)

See Banner ads.

Credit rating

Credit rating is a measure of the willingness or ability of an individual, company or country to pay for goods, loans or services. The lower the credit rating, the higher the interest charged by banks and other creditors is likely to be. Professional credit ratings agencies, such as **Standard & Poor**'s, give ratings to companies and other institutions depending on their view of the subject's creditworthiness. Ratings are usually within a range from so-called triple-As, AAA (the best), to D. A firm or country with a high credit rating will attract loans on favourable terms.

Credit squeeze

Where there is insufficient money supply to meet

demand, the situation is described in general terms as a credit squeeze. In macroeconomic terms, it describes a government's attempts to dampen economic activity by reducing the money supply. Measures a government may take to reduce money supply include raising interest rates to make borrowing more expensive and discouraging banks from lending money.

Crisis management

Crisis management is the implementation of systems within an organization to deal with potential crises. Lawsuits, environmental disasters, financial collapses, accusations of fraud or sexual harassment: these crises are facts of corporate life. The American Institute for Crisis Management's (ICM) database of business crisis news stories, which has only been compiled since 1990, contains more than 60,000 entries.

Definitions and perceptions about what constitutes a crisis and how it should be managed differ greatly. What can be said is that the word 'crisis' originates from the Greek word *krinein* – to decide. In corporate terms, a crisis is a major, unpredictable event with a potentially negative impact on the company's employees, products, services, financial situation or reputation. It is a decisive moment. The ICM defines a crisis as 'a significant business disruption that stimulates extensive news media coverage. The resulting public scrutiny will affect the organization's normal operations and also could have a political, legal, financial, and governmental impact on its business.' It is perhaps significant that the modern measure of a crisis is column inches rather than lives lost.

Crises are caused by a multitude of events and factors. Some are pure acts of nature – storms destroying a factory – or the result of mechanical malfunctions, such as when metal fatigue causes an airplane to crash. More avoidable are crises precipitated by human error or management. The ICM calculates that 62 percent of business crises can be traced back to management and 23 percent to employees.

As most crises are caused by human frailty rather than dramatic outside intervention, the profession of crisis management has emerged. Over the last decade in particular, crisis management has become a substantial business. Companies increasingly accept that crises, in whatever form, are inevitable.

While there are a variety of theories and opinions on how best to manage a crisis, some fundamentals are common. First, accurate information is essential. Any attempt to conceal relevant facts and to manipulate the situation ultimately backfires and increases the damage to the company. Perrier's management maintained that its mineral water did not contain any toxic element in spite of persuasive evidence to the contrary. When it finally admitted the failure, the damage to Perrier's public image was already done. Honesty is the best policy – even if there is nothing to report.

For some companies, this is easier said than done. If a company has fostered a culture of secrecy and manipulative behaviour, it cannot simply transform itself. The real nature of a company's culture surfaces in a crisis. Usually, management has only limited control over the situation. It cannot prevent all of its employees from talking to the press, or prescribe what finally appears in the media. When faced with unforeseen predicaments, employees have to act according to their own judgement rather than instructions from senior management. Communicating with employees is critical.

Second, the company must react as quickly as possible. Any suggestion that the company is playing for time, unsure as to what is happening or being indecisive is counterproductive. In 1989, Exxon CEO Lawrence Rawl waited two weeks before paying a visit to the scene of the Exxon Valdez oil spill. This sent a clear message about where mass pollution figured on his priorities. For all of the media clamour, action speaks louder than words.

Third, the response must come from the top. Credibility comes from the presence of senior management. Texaco CEO Peter Bijur took control of his company's reaction to a potentially damaging lawsuit; British Midland's Sir Michael Bishop was the company's spokesman after an air crash on the M1 motorway. The level of response is an indication of the importance management places on the problem.

The fourth fundamental is a long-term perspective. The long-term goodwill the company enjoys from its customers should be kept in mind when considering the short-term costs of corrective measures. Immediately withdrawing all products from supermarket shelves if there is a suggestion of contamination sends a clear signal that the problem is taken seriously and the company is intent on sorting it out.

Fifth, predicting problems requires a coherent strategy. Companies need to be prepared for a crisis. Bombs explode; planes crash; products go wrong; boats sink; and people make mistakes – sometimes, disastrous mistakes. Companies need to review and rehearse options in advance. Systems need to be in place. Most large organizations now have crisis management plans covering a variety of eventualities. At a government level, crisis management is well established – much crisis management best practice has its origins in the armed services. The American Federal Emergency Management Agency has 2600 staff as well as a further 4000 who are called on in a crisis.

Whatever an organization's level of preparedness, the central problem with crisis management is that most problems are caused by management. As a result, the people charged with resolving a crisis are often the very same people who made – or did not make – the decisions that got the company into the situation in the first place. To resolve this situation demands a degree of decisiveness, humility and public honesty.

Above all, a coherent strategy is essential. No company, no matter how large, is immune. Exxon, Perrier, Intel, Johnson & Johnson, BA – all of these major corporations have had to deal with corporate crises.

Key texts
- Steve Albrecht. *Crisis Management for Corporate Self-Defense.* AMACOM, 1996
- Kathleen Fearn-Banks. *Crisis Communication: A Casebook Approach.* Lawrence Erlbaum Associates, 1996
- Joe Marconi. *Crisis Marketing: When Bad Things Happen to Good Companies.* NTC Business Books, 1997
- Ian I. Mitroff, Catherine M. Pearson and L. Katharine Harrington. *The Essential Guide to Managing Corporate Crises.* Oxford University Press, 1996
- Geary W. Sikich. *Emergency Planning Handbook.* McGraw-Hill, 1995

Critical-path analysis (CPA)

Critical-path analysis (CPA) is a tool used in the management of complex projects to minimize the amount of time taken. The analysis shows which sub-projects can run in parallel with each other, and which have to be completed before other sub-projects can follow. CPA is used in preparing a work schedule and resource planning, as well as in monitoring of goal achievement during a project.

CPA is predicated on the fact that some tasks cannot be started until others are finished. By identifying the earliest start date, estimated length of time it will take, and whether a task is parallel or sequential, a task list can be built up into a plan. Each activity in the list is represented with circle and arrow diagrams. Circles depict events such as start and finish times and are usually numbered for identification purposes. Arrows between two event circles show the activity needed to complete that task; the task's description is written beneath the arrow.

Float time, the difference between the amount of time a task takes and the amount of time the task is allocated in the critical-path analysis, is an important element of CPA. Float time is also referred to as slack time.

Project managers often use software such as Microsoft's Project to perform critical-path analysis.

Critical risks

An essential element of a business plan is the identification of critical risks – threats to the continued viability of a business. Critical risks go beyond mere competitive threats; they include inadequate cash flow, potential legal liabilities, loss of important intellectual property rights and inadequate personnel. Start-ups and early-stage businesses must be aware of critical risks and draw up contingencies to deal with them.

Cross-currency swap

A cross-currency swap is an agreement to exchange a fixed amount in two different currencies for a fixed period and then re-exchange when the swap matures. Interest is paid on the swapped amount at the prevailing fixed or floating interest rate, which is set in the country issuing the currency for the duration of the swap. Cross-currency swaps allow the participants to obtain the use of a currency at a cheaper rate than might be possible through other means, lock into a specific interest rate, hedge and speculate.

Key link
- http://us.hsbc.com/business/treasury/derivatives/crossswap.asp

Cryptography

Cryptography is the science of creating and reading codes. Examples include those produced by the German Enigma machine used in World War II, those used in the secure transmission of credit card details over the Internet, and those used to ensure the privacy of e-mail messages. The origins

of the word 'cryptography' lie in the Greek words *kryptos*, meaning 'hidden', and *logos*, meaning 'word'. The use of cryptography is equally ancient. Roman Emperor Julius Caesar, for example, used a cipher to conceal the meaning of the messages to his troops. There are two principal fields within cryptology: that of cryptography – the creation of ciphers – and cryptanalysis – the cracking of them.

Unencoded text (known as plaintext) is converted to an unreadable form (known as cyphertext) by the process of encryption, which encodes the message so that it can only be read by the recipient. The recipient must then decrypt the message before it can be read. There are two types of cryptosystem: symmetric and asymmetric. In symmetric systems, the same key is used to encrypt and decrypt a message – the secret key. In asymmetric systems, one key – the public key – is used to encrypt a message, another – the private key – to decrypt it.

No encryption method is completely unbreakable, but cryptanalysis of a strongly encrypted message can be so time-consuming and complex as to be almost impossible.

Key links
- www.rsasecurity.com/rsalabs/faq
- www.cdt.org/crypto

CTO (chief technical officer)

The chief technical officer is the manager responsible for information technology within a company. He acts as a communication point for investment analysts and the media with regards to technological issues, and purchases and implements IT. The role of the CTO used to be subordinate to that of the **CIO**; the CTO rarely reports directly to the **CEO**, but usually to the CIO or Finance Director. Following the dotcom boom, the role of the CTO has become less well defined and the CTO may often find himself responsible for technology on a strategic level, with the CIO dealing with IT purchasing and reporting lines fluid.

Current asset

See Balance sheet.

Current liabilities

See Balance sheet.

Customer loyalty

Customer loyalty refers to the willingness of a consumer to repeatedly purchase the same product or service. Customer loyalty is a valuable commodity for companies, particularly those that have high customer acquisition costs. However, companies must be careful to cultivate customer loyalty so that they can be assured that it is active loyalty to their product, rather than inertia, that is the motivation for repeat purchases.

Customer relationship management (CRM)

Customer relationship management (CRM) is a strategy used to determine customers' needs and behaviours and use this knowledge to develop stronger relationships with them. CRM is facilitated by specialized CRM IT systems. A CRM system will cover the consolidation of the sales force, call centre, field service, help desk and marketing automation applications. CRM systems allow companies to measure the value of their customers. At its most sophisticated, CRM provides integration of all aspects of a business that involve the customer, including sales, marketing, customer service and even product design. Effective CRM can result in better customer service, cost reductions in marketing, the identification

of new customers and, ultimately, increased sales revenues.

Cyert, Richard

President, Carnegie Mellon University (1921–1998)

Richard Cyert was educated at the University of Minnesota and Columbia University. He spent 50 years at Pittsburgh, Pennsylvania-based Carnegie Mellon University as a professor of economics and management; he served as CMU's President from 1972–1990.

An entire academic discipline, decision science, is devoted to understanding management decision-making. As an introduction to the complex world of decision making, Cyert and March's 1963 classic, *A Behavioral Theory of the Firm*, remains powerful and useful. Cyert and March contend that business decision-making theory faces a crucial and immediate problem. Individuals have goals; collective groups do not. The need, therefore, is to create credible and useful organizational goals while not believing there is such a thing as an 'organizational mind.'

Cyert and March regard organizations as coalitions that negotiate goals. Creating goals requires three processes: the bargaining process, which establishes the composition and general terms of the coalition; the internal organizational process of control, which clarifies and develops the objectives; and the process of adjustment to experience, which alters agreements in accord with changing circumstances.

The trouble is that as circumstances change, short-term issues take precedence over long-term objectives. Goals are inconsistent thanks to decentralized decision-making, the fact that short-term goals take most managerial attention, and the disparity between the resources available to the organization and the payments required to maintain the coalition.

Cyert and March identify the five principal goals of the modern organization – production, inventory, sales, market share and profit – and nine steps in the decision process: forecast competitors' behaviour; forecast demand; estimate costs; specify objectives; evaluate plan; re-examine costs; re-examine demand; re-examine objectives; and select alternatives.

To work successfully, this decision-making model demands that there are standard operating procedures – a learned group of behaviour rules. The procedures can be divided into general ones, based on avoiding uncertainty; maintaining the rules; and using simple rules, such as task-performance rules, continuing records and reports, information-handling rules and plans. These procedures are the link between the individual and the organization. They are the means by which organizations make and implement choices.

Key text

- James G. March and Richard Michael Cyert. *A Behavioral Theory of the Firm*. Second edition, Blackwell Publishers, 1992

D

Davis, Stan M.

Author; senior research fellow at CAP Gemini Ernst & Young Center for Business Innovation

Stan Davis is a futurist, author, consultant and expert on e-business. Prior to becoming senior research fellow at CAP Gemini Ernst & Young, Davis served on the faculties of Harvard Business School, Columbia University and Boston University. His books have sold more than 500,000 copies and been published in 15 languages. His book *Future Perfect* won the **Tom Peter**'s Book of the Decade award. *Fortune* magazine named Davis's book *20/20 Vision* as its Best Book of 1991. Davis has also written articles for *Forbes*, *Fast Company* and *Time*. Apple, AT&T, Ernst & Young, Ford, KPMG/Peat Marwick and Sun Microsystems are among his major clients.

Stan Davis and **Christopher Meyer**'s *Blur* is a new breed in business books. Nowhere is this more evident than in the book's title. *Blur* would not even have been considered as a possible title just a few years ago, when blind faith and certainty ruled. It would have been too weak, too suggestive of managerial confusion and impotence; too realistic.

For a book about the future, Davis and Meyer are candid about their lack of answers: 'We are not offering the ultimate word on our topics, but a starting point: provocative ideas, observations, and predictions to get you to think creatively about your business and your future.' There is an array of questions, delivered with a suggestion of urgency in keeping with Davis and Meyer's central themes.

At the heart of *Blur* are three forces: connectivity, speed and intangibles ('the derivatives of time, space, and mass'). According to Davis and Meyer, this triad is 'blurring the rules and redefining our businesses and our lives. They are destroying solutions, such as mass production, segmented pricing, and standardized jobs, that worked for the relatively slow, unconnected industrial world.' The three forces are shaping the behaviour of the New Economy. They are affecting what Davis and Meyer label 'the blur of desires; the blur of fulfilment; and the blur of resources'.

The 'blur of desires' has two central elements: the offer and the exchange. These were once clear-cut. In the product-dominated age, a company offered a product for sale. Money was exchanged and the customer disappeared into the distance. Now, products and services are often indistinguishable from each other and buyers and sellers are in a constantly evolving relationship ('mutual exchange') that is driven by information and emotion as well as by money.

The second aspect of the new economic reality is 'the blur of fulfilment'. As organizations change to meet changing demands, so, too, must the entire theory and practice of competitive strategy. Connectivity produces different forms of organization operating according to different first principles. 'The blur of businesses has created a new economic model in which returns increase rather than diminish; supermarkets mimic stock markets; and you want the market – not your strategy – to price, market, and manage your offer,' write Davis and Meyer.

The third leg to the economic stool is that of resources and the emergence of **intellectual capital** as the key resource. Hard assets have become intangibles; intangibles have become your only assets.

Blur portrays an unsettling world. Strangely, the disturbing element at its core is not the one you most expect: The surprisingly disturbing thing about *Blur* is the concept – and fast emerging reality – of connectivity. Understanding connectivity is like coming to terms with the childhood revelation that we are all, somewhere along the line, related. A whole new family suddenly emerges before you go on to ponder the awful impossibility of it all. In the information economy mapped out by Davis and Meyer, small things are connected in a myriad of ways to create a 'complex adaptive system'. Instantaneous, myriad connections are speeding the economy up and, more critically, changing the way it works.

The trouble is that the connections are so many and so complex that they can bring things to a grinding, inexplicable halt. The randomness is disturbing, but the reality so poignantly mapped out by Stan Davis and Christopher Meyer in *Blur* is one without safety nets.

Key texts
- Stan M. Davis. *Lessons from the Future: Making Sense of a Blurred World from the World's Leading Futurist*. Capstone, 2001
- Stan M. Davis and Chris Meyer. *Blur: The Speed of Change in the Connected Economy*. Warner Books, 1999

Key links
- http://www2.darwinmag.com/learn/guru/guru_details.cfm?ID=44
- www.webcom.com/quantera/davis.html
- www.fastcompany.com/online/12/almanac finance.html

Dead-cat bounce

The dead-cat bounce is a term that refers to the phenomenon that occurs when there is a sudden but temporary upswing in a falling market. The term was coined by market traders in the 1990s. It was based on the expression, 'even a dead cat will bounce if you drop it from high enough'.

The dead-cat bounce is a temporary rally in the market, usually called by technical buying. Traders short stock – sell stock predicting the stock will fall further – and then buy it back at the cheaper price to fulfil the contract. When the shorters close out their positions by buying stock, the market responds to the purchasers by marking stock up, causing a brief rally.

A famous example of the dead-cat bounce was the Wall Street revival that took place on Friday, 13 October 2000. In the six weeks prior to that Friday, the **NASDAQ** had crashed by close to 30 percent and the **Dow** 30 by 12 percent. Then, suddenly, market sentiment got the better of market fundamentals and the NASDAQ rose by 8 percent. Come the next Monday, however, the market had resumed its downward trend, leaving a lot of investors with burnt fingers.

Most commonly associated with capital markets, dead-cat bounce can also be seen in other markets. High-volume, low-unit-priced markets, such as commodity markets, are particularly susceptible.

For investors, the prize comes with separating out the dead-cat bounce from a real market revival. Akin to the holy grail of investing, predicting the bottom of the market is part science, part luck. The trick is not to let sentiment get in the way of market fundamentals. Sentiment can only carry a market so far without supporting evidence from the economy.

Debenture

A debenture is an instrument issued as evidence of a borrower's debt to a lender. The word derives from the Latin *debeo*, meaning 'I owe'. Debentures are used by companies to raise finance repaid over the long term. The holder of debenture will normally receive a fixed rate of interest, regardless of whether the company makes a profit or not.

Debentures come in a variety of different forms. Most debentures are secured against the assets of the issuing company. Thus, a mortgage debenture will be secured against specific property and a floating debenture will be secured as a floating charge against all or any of the assets of the company. Unsecured or naked debentures, however, are backed only by the company's integrity and promise to pay.

Convertible debentures are those under which the debentures are converted into equity shares at the time of issue. Partly convertible debentures are, as the name suggests, partly converted into equity.

The interest on debentures should be paid out prior to the company's using funds to pay a dividend. Should a company fail to either pay interest on or redeem a debenture, then the holder (assuming it is a secured debenture) can force the company to sell assets in order to meet the terms of the debenture.

Debentures can be issued in large numbers as debenture stock. This form of loan is attractive to companies as it does not dilute equity, is cheaper than a conventional overdraft, and is usually repayable over a long period.

De Bono, Edward

Pioneer of concept of creative, lateral thinking (b. 1933)

Born in Malta in 1933, Edward de Bono qualified in medicine at the University of Malta. A Rhodes scholar, de Bono took honours degrees in psychology and physiology and then a D.Phil in medicine at Christ Church, Oxford, as well as a PhD from Cambridge and an MD from the University of Malta. He has held appointments at the universities of Oxford, London, Cambridge and Harvard.

The inventor of the concept of lateral thinking, de Bono is one of the few people who can claim to have changed the way the world thinks. De Bono pioneered the investigation into creative thought, arguing creativity was essential in a self-organiz-

ing system. His key book, *The Mechanism of Mind* (1969), was years ahead of its time, anticipating future work on the link between chaos theory, non-linear and asymmetric patterns, and perception.

One of the world's leading authorities on constructive and creative thinking, de Bono has worked with many senior executives from *Fortune* 500 corporations and advised governments from around the world. He is founder of the International Creative Forum, author of more than 30 books, and has been featured in TV series such as de Bono's *Course in Thinking*. In July 1994, he was awarded the Pioneer Prize in the field of Thinking at the International Conference on Thinking at MIT in Boston.

Key texts
- Edward de Bono. *Six Thinking Hats*. Little, Brown & Co., 1999
- Edward de Bono. *De Bono's Thinking Course*. Checkmark Books, 1994
- Edward de Bono. *Lateral Thinking: Creativity Step by Step*. HarperCollins, 1990

Key link
- www.edwdebono.com

Debt-to-equity ratio

The debt-to-equity ratio is a company's total long-term debt expressed as a percentage of shareholders' equity. The measure is used to assess a company's financial health. The ratio is calculated by dividing the company's long-term debt (capital contributed by creditors) by the shareholders' equity (contributed by owners). The result is often referred to as gearing. A highly geared company has a high proportion of debt in relation to its equity.

In the United States, gearing is known as leverage. If the result is a ratio greater than one, it means assets are financed chiefly with debt. If the result is less than one, then equity provides most of the financing. A high ratio suggests that the company might be in a precarious position, particularly if financing long-term debt becomes more expensive because of interest rate moves or other economic factors.

Decentralization

See Centralization.

Decision making

The theory of decision making holds that business decisions can best be made in the interests of the organization by eliminating intuition and subjective criteria and employing a system of mathematical techniques for analysing decision-making problems.

Decision making is the act of choosing between two or more alternative courses of action. There are many different decision models, including decision trees, discounted cash flow analysis and critical-path analysis, as well as techniques such as game theory, risk analysis and utility theory, and models such as the **Kepner-Tregoe** model and the consensual ring. Indeed, an entire academic discipline, decision science, is devoted to understanding management decision making. Much of it is built on the foundations set down by early business thinkers, who believed that under a given set of circumstances, human behaviour was logical and therefore predictable. The fundamental belief of the likes of computer pioneer **Charles Babbage** and **scientific management** founder **Frederick Taylor** was that the decision process (and many other things) could be rationalized and systematized. Based on this premise, models emerged to explain the workings of commerce, which, it was thought, could be extended to the way in which decisions were made.

The belief in decision theory persists. Most management books and ideas are inextricably linked to helping managers make better deci-

sions. **Strategic management**, for example, was a model by which strategic decisions could be made. Unfortunately, it was a model that demanded vast amounts of data. As a result, enthusiastic managers turned themselves into data addicts rather than better decision makers.

There is now a profusion of models, software packages and analytical tools that seek to distil decision making into a formula. Decision-making models assume that the distilled mass of experience will enable people to make accurate decisions. They enable you to learn from other peoples' experiences. Many promise the world. If you feed in your particular circumstances, out will pop an answer. The danger is in concluding that the solution provided by a software package is *the* answer.

Whether embedded in a software package or buried in a textbook, decision theorizing suggests that effective decision making involves a number of logical stages. This is referred to as the 'rational model of decision making' or the 'synoptic model'. The latter involves a series of steps: identifying the problem, clarifying the problem, prioritizing goals, generating options, evaluating options (using appropriate analysis), comparing predicted outcomes of each option with the goals and choosing the option that best matches the goals.

Such models rely on a number of assumptions about the way in which people will behave when confronted with a set of circumstances. These assumptions allow mathematicians to derive formulae based on probability theory. These decision-making tools include such things as cost-benefit analysis, which aims to help managers evaluate different options.

The difficulty with such theories is that reality is often more confused and messy than a neat model can allow for. Underpinning the mathematical approach is a number of flawed assumptions, such as that decision making is consistent, based on accurate information, free from emotion or prejudice and rational. Another obvious drawback to any decision-making model is that identifying what you need to make a decision about is often more important than the actual decision itself. If a decision seeks to solve a problem, it may be the right decision but the wrong problem.

The reality is that managers make decisions based on a combination of intuition, experience and analysis. This does not mean that decision theory is redundant or that decision-making models should be cast aside. Indeed, a number of factors mean that decision making is becoming ever more demanding. The growth in complexity means that companies no longer encounter simple problems. Furthermore, complex decisions are now not simply the preserve of the most senior managers, but the responsibility of many others in organizations. In addition, managers have to deal with a flood of information: A 1996 survey by Reuters of 1200 managers worldwide found that 43 percent thought that important decisions were delayed and their ability to make decisions affected as a result of having too much information.

These factors suggest that any techniques, models or analytical techniques that enable managers to make more informed decisions more quickly will be in increasing demand. In the past, models were the domain of economists and strategists. Now, there is increasing use of decision support systems. Some show the best types of decisions for a given situation. Typically, these involve how best to use resources. An oil refinery, for example, may use a support system to determine on a daily basis the optimum product that it should produce. Airlines run similar programmes to establish optimum pricing levels. Other systems aim to yield increasingly better decisions based on past results. These learning-based models allow companies to take the data they have gathered and any analysis they have undertaken and gather it up in one place directly related to the decision.

There is little doubt that decision theory and the use of such models is reassuring. They lend legitimacy to decisions that may be based on prejudices or hunches. But, the usefulness of decision-making models remains a leap of faith. None are foolproof, as none are universally applicable.

And none can yet cope with the wilful idiosyncracies of human behaviour.

Key texts

- Jonathan Baron. *Thinking and Deciding.* Second edition, Cambridge University Press, 1994
- Des Dearlove. *Key Management Decisions.* FT/Pitman, London, 1997
- Simon French. *Decision Theory: An Introduction to the Mathematics of Rationality.* Ellis Horwood and John Wiley, New York, 1988
- Ralph L. Keeney. *Value-Focused Thinking: A Path to Creative Decision Making.* Harvard University Press, 1992
- Max D. Richards and Paul S. Greenlaw. *Management Decision Making.* Richard D. Irwin Inc., Homewood, Illinois, 1966
- Frank Yates. *Judgement and Decision Making.* Prentice Hall, Englewood Cliffs, New Jersey, 1990

Decision tree

A decision tree is one of a number of different decision models. It takes the form of a diagrammatic representation of the choices available when making a decision and the possible outcomes, together with their probabilities.

A decision tree starts with the decision to be made represented by a square on the left of a sheet of paper. To the right, branching out from the decision, are lines representing the different possible solutions. At the end of each line is drawn either a circle, to represent uncertain outcomes, or a square, if another decision is required. The process is repeated until all possible solutions and outcomes are represented. The diagram will resemble a tree lying horizontally – hence its name. The next step is to evaluate the various choices by comparing the expected values of the possible outcomes and the probability of the unknown/uncertain outcomes. When this has been done, an informed decision can be made.

Deflation

Deflation, the opposite of **inflation**, is a reduction in the level of economic activity, usually caused by an increase in interest rates and reduction in the money supply, increased taxation or a decline in government expenditure.

Prior to World War II, deflation was the prevailing economic condition in the United States. Between the late 1700s and 1945, the US wholesale price index barely changed amid long periods of mild deflation and occasional bursts of severe inflation and deflation.

The two most damaging episodes of deflation in the last century were immediately following World War I and then again following the sharp downturn in production in 1929. Damaging deflation is about more than declining prices. It is a story of a dramatic reduction in aggregate demand, underpinning a reduction in prices. A fall in prices threatens borrowers and banks alike. Banks withdraw credit, businesses go bankrupt, job-losses mount, wages slump and all of these events feed into a further reduction in demand, creating a dangerous downward deflationary spiral. It was such a reduction in demand and a 25 percent fall in consumer prices following the 1929 Wall Street crash that led to the Great Depression.

Key texts

- Ludwig Von Mises. *Human Action: A Treatise on Economics*. Third edition, Contemporary, 1966
- Gary A. Shilling. *Deflation: Why It's Coming, Whether It's Good or Bad, & How It Will Affect Your Investments, Your Business, & Your Personal Affairs*. Lakeview Economic Services & Publishing, 1998

De Geus, Arie

Former CEO, Royal Dutch/Shell; author; consultant

Arie de Geus gained a Masters in Economics from Erasmus University in Rotterdam and an Honorary Doctorate of Letters from Westminster University in the United Kingdom. He joined Royal Dutch/Shell in 1951 and, the ultimate corporate man, spent 38 years there. (Such loyalty runs in the family – de Geus's father also worked for the company for 26 years.) He lived and worked for periods of time in Turkey, Belgium and Brazil before returning to the United Kingdom in 1979. At that point, he was responsible for Shell's businesses in Africa and South Asia. He became coordinator for group planning in 1981.

During the 1980s, de Geus deepened his understanding of decision making and change-management processes in large corporations and largely originated the now trendy concept of the 'learning organization'. After retiring from Shell in 1989, he became an academic and consultant to the World Bank, as well as government and private institutions. He is a board member of both the Organizational Learning Center at MIT's Sloan School of Management and the Nijenrode Learning Centre in the Netherlands, and visiting fellow at London Business School.

In 1997, de Geus and **Peter Senge** co-authored *The Living Company*, which won the Edwin G. Booz Prize for 'most insightful, innovative management book of the year', and wrote a *Harvard Business Review* article with the same title, which won the McKinsey Award that year.

Companies may be legal entities, but they are disturbingly mortal. In their book, de Geus and Senge quote a Dutch survey of corporate life expectancy in Japan and Europe that came up with 12.5 years as the average life expectancy of all firms. 'The average life expectancy of a multinational corporation – *Fortune* 500 or its equivalent – is between 40 and 50 years,' say de Geus and Senge, noting that one-third of 1970's *Fortune* 500 had disappeared by 1983. De Geus and Senge attribute such endemic failure to the managers' focus on profits and the bottom line rather than the human communities that make up their organizations.

In an attempt to get to the bottom of this mystery, de Geus and a number of his Shell colleagues carried out some research to identify the characteristics of corporate longevity. As you would expect, the onus is on keeping excitement to a minimum. The average human centenarian advocates a life of abstinence, caution and moderation, and the same is true for companies. The Royal Dutch/Shell team identified four key characteristics: long-lived companies were 'sensitive to their environment', 'cohesive, with a strong sense of identity', 'tolerant' and 'conservative in financing'.

Key to de Geus's entire argument is that there is more to companies – and to longevity – than mere money-making. 'The dichotomy between profits and longevity is false,' he says. His logic is impeccably straightforward. Capital is no longer king; the skills, capabilities and knowledge of people are. The corollary to this is that 'a successful company is one that can learn effectively'. Learning is tomorrow's capital. In de Geus's eyes, learning means being prepared to accept continuous change.

Here, de Geus provides the new deal: contemporary corporate employees must understand that the corporation will – and must – change, and it can only change if its community of people changes also. Individuals must change, and the way they change is through learning. As a result, de Geus believes that senior executives must dedicate a great deal of time to nurturing their people. He recalls spending around a quarter of his time on the development and placement of people. **Jack Welch** claims to have spent half of his time on such issues.

According to de Geus, all corporate activities are grounded in two hypotheses: 'The company is a living being; and the decisions for action made by this living being result from a learning process.' With its faith in learning, *The Living Company* represents a careful and powerful riposte to corporate nihilism.

The Living Company proposes that the wisdom of the past be appreciated and utilized rather than cast out in some cultural revolution. Contrast this with reengineering, which (as preached, if not necessarily practised) sought to dismiss the past so that the future could be begun anew with a fresh

piece of paper. De Geus suggests that the piece of paper already exists and notes are constantly being scrawled in the margins as new insights are added.

De Geus's arguments are probably at their weakest when he contemplates why it is that companies deserve to live long lives. After all, the average entrepreneur would probably accept a life expectancy of 12.5 years. 'Like all organisms, the living company exists primarily for its own survival and improvement: to fulfil its potential and to become as great as it can be,' writes de Geus. But life is littered with failed stars. Some fall by the wayside. We can't all be great. We can't all be Shell.

The Living Company is the testimony of someone who practised the human side of enterprise and who believes that companies must be fundamentally humane to prosper, whatever the century.

Key texts
- Arie de Geus. *La Empresa Viviente*. Ediciones Granica Mexico, 1998
- Arie de Geus and Peter M Senge. *The Living Company: Habits for Survival in a Turbulent Business Environment*. Harvard Business School Press, 1997
- Arie de Geus. 'The Living Company.' *Harvard Business Review*, 1997
- Arie de Geus. *Planning as Learning*. Harvard Business School Press, 1988

Key links
- www.speakers.co.uk/featured/arigeu.htm
- www.gbn.org/public/gbnstory/network/individuals/ex_degeus.htm
- www.managementfirst.com/articles/geus.htm

Dell, Michael

Founder of Dell Computer (b. 1965)

Born in Houston, Texas, Michael Dell started his business career at a young age. He came across his first commercial opportunity when he was just twelve years old. Like many children of his age, Dell was a keen collector of stamps. Where Dell differed from his peers was his approach. Dell didn't trade stamps with his friends from school; he contacted the auction houses and sent them his catalogue. When they placed an order, he went out to find the required stamps. The direct sales method and entrepreneurial acumen were early signs of what was to come.

Dell brought new focus and intensity to his early commercial forays. As a summer job, Dell sold newspaper subscriptions for the *Houston Post*. He quickly realized that calling people randomly using the list of telephone numbers supplied by the company was not the best way to win new business. Instead, he targeted two distinct groups: newlyweds and new homeowners. He obtained lists of applicants for wedding licences from the local courthouse. From another source, he compiled a list of people who had recently applied for mortgages. He then wrote a personalized message and carried out his own direct-mail campaign. Subscriptions poured in. When the new school term began Dell was asked, as part of an economics assignment, to complete a tax return. After calculating his profits, Dell estimated his income at $18,000. His teacher, assuming a mistake, corrected his return by moving the decimal point. She was dismayed to discover that the mistake was hers. Dell earned more than she did.

Dell's career really started while he was studying at the University of Texas. By then, the boy who had dismantled and reassembled the motherboard of his Apple II computer at the age of 13 had grown into a fledgling entrepreneur, making money from his computing hobby. Dell would rebuild computers and sell them. While still in college, he started a company called PCs Limited. The headquarters was located in Dell's bedroom. Ignoring his parents' advice to concentrate on his studies, Dell decided the lure of business was too great and concentrated his efforts on his PC company.

In 1984, the Dell Computer Corporation was founded with just $1000 in capital. With such a small investment, Dell was forced to develop a business model that required little capital outlay. He decided to build to order. This eliminated the need to tie up working capital in inventory. The company carried only about eleven days' worth of inventory – and still does. Compare this with the 45 days' worth of inventory in an average non-direct sales channel, and the cost savings are obvious. Building to order also allowed Dell to cut out the middleman, retaining more profit and reducing selling costs from a typical 12 percent of revenue to a mere 4 to 6 percent of revenue.

Low costs and high profit margins is a recipe for an exceptional business. In its first eight years, Dell Computer grew at an astonishing rate of 80 percent. Even when it slowed down, it was still growing at over 50 percent per year. By the middle of 2000, its yearly revenues were up to $27 billion.

Such a successful business model has attracted its imitators. Companies such as Compaq and Gateway have adopted a similar model. None, however, seem to be able to capture the Dell magic. 'There is a popular idea now that if you reduce your inventory and build to order, you'll be just like Dell. Well, that's one part of the puzzle, but there are other parts, too,' Dell has said. He explains the company's success as 'a disciplined approach to understanding how we create value in the PC industry, selecting the right markets, staying focused on a clear business model, and just executing'.

Dell has built more than a simple direct-selling company. His company's success is closely linked to its relationship with the customer. He knows that the company must not only sell but deliver. Dell Computer has made good use of its direct communication with the consumer; the result has been a strong brand, low customer-acquisition costs and high customer loyalty. Dell asks his customers to complain, which allows him to keep the company on the cutting edge of consumer needs. The company once ran an ad that said, 'To all our nitpicky, over-demanding, ask-awkward-questions customers. Thank you, and keep up the good work.' Few computer companies, or any other company come to that, would run a similarly worded ad.

With his innate enthusiasm for technology, Dell was quick to realize the potential of the Internet. Harnessing the Net's power to reach a wide audience at little cost, the company swiftly moved its selling operations online. 'The Internet for us is a dream come true,' Dell has said. 'It's like zero-variable-cost transaction. The only thing better would be mental telepathy.' The figures support the point. In 1997, the company's online sales exceeded $3 million a day. During the year 2000, the online sales figure was $50 million. Some 50 percent of the company's sales are Web-enabled.

Dell's success is founded on a business model rather than a particular product. As if to prove the point, Dell has successfully expanded into areas such as servers and storage network devices. The Dell Computer Corporation has been consistently ranked number two in the world in liquidity, profitability and growth among all computer systems companies, and number one in the United States. With that sort of performance, many CEOs would be pleased to take a bow and enjoy the applause. Dell merely describes it as a 'great start'.

The youngest **CEO** ever to run a *Fortune* 500 company, Michael Dell has joined the ranks of the most revered entrepreneurs in America. He is credited as the man who took the direct sales model and elevated it to an art form. Dell Computer may not be the biggest company in the world – yet. Nor are its products the most innovative. Yet Dell has built a benchmark company demonstrating how best to structure a company in order to reap the most reward from new technologies.

Key text
- Michael Dell with Catherine Fredman. *Direct from Dell: Strategies That Revolutionized an Industry*. Harper Business, 1999

Key link
- www.dell.com

Delphi Technique

The Delphi Technique is a qualitative decision-making process developed in the 1950s by Olaf Helmer and Norman Dalkey, scientists at the RAND Corporation. It derives its name from the oracle of Delphi of ancient Greece. The process is designed to avoid conflict between or undue influence from individual participants in group decision making.

The process is conducted in a series of rounds. A chairman or facilitator asks each participant, often an expert in a particular field, to submit a written answer to a question or series of questions. The chairman or facilitator then considers the replies, writes a summary in the form of opinion statements, and passes the summary on to the group members. This is the end of the first round. The participants then reply to the opinion statements with a rating, usually along the lines of 'strongly agree' or strongly disagree'. This process continues until a consensus is arrived at or stability is obtained (each member's answer varies little from one round to the next). While the technique is especially useful where the participants are separated geographically, it can be a very slow process.

To obtain the best results, the participants must be selected according to carefully selected criteria and not personal preference. The role of the chairman or facilitator is critical, as he has the opportunity to introduce undue influence or bias and steer the group toward a predetermined outcome.

Demerger

A demerger is the creation of two companies from one. It is often used to transform an internal business unit, often run as a profit centre, into a company in its own right. This is known as a spin-off and is particularly common in technology companies where R&D produces a new technology with the potential to create a new product. The spin-off means the resulting company is able to raise money in the markets through venture financing or an **IPO**. A demerger may also be used as a means of dispensing with an unwanted part of a business.

Where two public companies result, shareholders of the original company will receive shares in the demerged company in direct proportion to their original holdings. One example of a demerger is that of Zeneca from ICI in 1993. Shareholders in ICI received one share in Zeneca for every share held in ICI. Another example is the demerger of British Telecom's mobile phone unit in 2001, which subsequently formed two companies: the BT Group and mm02.

Deming, W. Edwards

Academic and consultant (1900–1993)

W. Edwards Deming was born in Iowa and spent his childhood in Wyoming. He trained as an electrical engineer at the University of Wyoming and then received a PhD in mathematical physics from Yale in 1928.

He worked as a civil servant in Washington at the Department of Agriculture. While working at the Department, he invited statistician Walter Shewhart to give a lecture. This proved an inspiration. In 1939, Deming became head statistician and mathematician for the US Census. During World War II, he championed the use of statistics to improve the quality of US production and, in 1945, joined the faculty of New York University as a professor of statistics.

Deming visited Japan for the first time in 1947 on the invitation of General MacArthur. He was to play a key role in the rebuilding of Japanese industry. In 1950, he gave a series of lectures to Japanese industrialists on 'quality control'. 'I told them that Japanese industry could develop in a short time. I told them they could invade the markets of the world – and have manufacturers screaming for protection in five years. I was, in 1950, the only man in Japan who believed that,' Deming later recalled.

In fact, Deming was probably the *only* man in the world to believe that Japanese industry could be revived. But, helped by him, revive it did – in a quite miraculous way. During the 1950s, Deming and the other American standard-bearer of qual-

ity, **Joseph Juran**, conducted seminars and courses throughout Japan. The quality message – and the practice – spread.

The Japanese were highly receptive to Deming's message. The country was desperate and willing to try anything. But, much more importantly, Deming's message of teamwork and shared responsibility struck a chord with Japanese culture.

Deming's message was that organizations needed to 'manage for quality'. To do so required focus on the customer: 'Don't just make it and try to sell it. But redesign it and then again bring the process under control ... with ever-increasing quality ... The consumer is the most important part of the production line.' At the time, such pronouncements would have been greeted with disdain in the West, where production lines ran at full speed with little thought of who would buy the products.

Instead of the quick fix, Deming called for dedication and hard work. His message was never tainted by hype or frivolity. Also difficult for the West to swallow was Deming's argument that responsibility for quality must be taken by senior managers as well as those on the factory floor. Only with senior management commitment could belief in and implementation of quality cascade down through the organization. Quality, in Deming's eyes, was not the preserve of the few but the responsibility of all.

These exhortations were backed by the use of statistical methods of quality control. These enabled business plans to be expanded to include clear quality goals.

While the Japanese transformed their economy and world perceptions of the quality of their products, Western managers flitted from one fad to the next. Deming was completely ignored. His discovery came in 1980, when NBC featured a TV programme on the emergence of Japan as an industrial power. Suddenly, Western managers were seeking out every morsel of information they could find. By 1984, there were more than 3000 quality circles in American companies and many thousands of others appearing throughout the Western world.

Although Deming was in his eighties by the time he was fêted in the West, he dedicated the rest of his life to preaching his quality gospel. Deming's message was distilled down to his famed Fourteen Points:

1 Create constancy of purpose for improvement of product and service.
2 Adopt the new philosophy.
3 Cease dependence on inspection to achieve quality.
4 End the practice of awarding business on the basis of price tag alone. Instead, minimize total cost by working with a single supplier.
5 Improve constantly and forever every process for planning, production and service.
6 Institute training on the job.
7 Adopt and institute leadership.
8 Drive out fear.
9 Break down barriers between staff areas.
10 Eliminate slogans, exhortations and targets for the workforce.
11 Eliminate numerical quotas for the workforce and numerical goals for management.
12 Remove barriers that rob people of pride of workmanship. Eliminate the annual rating or merit system.
13 Institute a vigorous programme of education and self-improvement for everyone.
14 Put everybody in the company to work to accomplish the transformation.

Toyota is the living exemplar of Deming's theories. As working examples go, it remains impressive. **Gary Hamel** has pointed out that its Western competitors have simply followed what Toyota has done for the last 40 years. If Western car manufacturers had listened to Deming, the roles might have been reversed. If Western industry as a whole had listened, who knows what might have happened.

Key texts
- W. Edwards Deming. *Quality, Productivity and Competitive Position.* MIT Center for Advanced Engineering Study, 1982

- W. Edwards Deming. *Out of the Crisis.* Cambridge University Press, 1988

Key links
- www.deming.org
- www.deming.edu
- http://deming.eng.clemson.edu/pub/den;

Demography

Demography is the study of the size, structure, dispersement and development of human populations. From such study, statisticians record criteria including birth and death rates, marriages and divorces, life expectancy and migration. These statistics reveal demographic trends. One such trend, for example, is demographic segment of the population born during a post-World War II increase in births – the **baby boomers**. Another is the generation of young people who were young adults in the early 1990s – **Generation X**. Demography is used by actuaries to calculate life tables, which give the life expectancy of members of the population by sex and age. It is also used extensively in marketing to devise strategies to target specific segments of the population.

Depreciation

An accounting procedure applied to tangible assets, depreciation reflects the decrease in value of the asset due to usage, obsolescence or time. Take the purchase of a van for business use: From the moment that the van is purchased, it begins to lose value. Each year, the van continues to lose value until one day it breaks down and is worth nothing – presuming it is kept for its lifetime. Measuring that loss of value is known as depreciation.

For intangible assets, a technique known as amortization is used; for wasting assets, a technique known as depletion. Depreciation is considered an expense for accounting purposes and included in the income statement. Depreciation is applied to assets yearly, each time reducing the net book value of the asset.

The most common method of depreciation used is straight-line depreciation. This uses the initial cost of the asset and its estimated useful life and then apportions equal amounts of depreciation over the estimated lifetime of the asset.

Depth interview

A depth interview is an extended and formalized form of conversation used as a qualitative analysis tool, predominantly in marketing research. The interviewee is generally a part of a sample selected according to predetermined criteria. The interviewer allows the interviewee to do most of the talking, ensuring only that certain predetermined points are covered. The in-depth interview can be used to gauge individuals' opinions, perceptions, and beliefs. Because it is not quantitative, the value of the in-depth interview is often underestimated.

Key link
- www.pra.ca/resources/indepth.pdf

Derivatives

Derivatives are financial arrangements between two parties, derived from the future performance of underlying assets such as currencies, debt bond shares, commodities or other financial instruments. Futures, options and swaps are all examples of derivatives. The market is huge – the Chicago Mercantile Exchange handles $200 trillion worth – and grew at a phenomenal rate through the 1980s and 1990s. Between 1995 and 1998, turnover in the over-the-counter derivatives market increased by 85 percent.

Traded in derivative markets, derivatives are a specialist, highly geared, high-risk speculative form of trading. The size of the risks is matched by the size of some of the losses. This was a lesson that derivative trader Nick Leeson and his employers, Barings Bank, learned to their cost, when Leeson's losses trading derivatives in 1995 brought about the collapse of the bank. Or as another example, take mining, metals, and industrial group Metallgesellschaft, once one of Germany's top companies: derivative trading led to losses for 1993 of DM 2 billion. By March 1994, the company had total debts of DM 9 billion.

Key texts
- Judith Rawnsley. *Going for Broke, Nick Leeson and the collapse of Barings Bank*. Harper Collins, 1995
- Nick Leeson with Edward Whitley. *Rogue Trader Nick Leeson – His Own Amazing Story*. Little Brown, 1996
- Don M. Chance. *An Introduction To Derivatives and Risk Management*. Harcourt College Publishers, 2001

Deskilling

Deskilling refers to the process whereby the need for individual skill in order to carry out an operation is progressively removed. The term owes much to the work of Marxist theorist Harry Braverman. Technology has continually deskilled operations, from the advent of the production line to the computerization of the service industries. Experienced insurance underwriters, for example, were once required to analyse risks and decide on premiums for all forms of insurance. Today, in many classes of insurance, computers calculate premiums on the basis of input data.

One argument put forward is that, as a result of deskilling, the workforce will be divided into two groups: a small group of highly skilled workers and a large and growing group of unskilled workers consigned to repetitive and boring work. This reality has yet to manifest itself to any significant degree.

Key text
- Harry Braverman. *Labor and Monopoly Capital: The Degradation of Work in the Twentieth Century*. Monthly Review Press, 1974

Digital money

Digital money is electronic currency designed to facilitate e-commerce transactions. It is essentially a payment or transfer of funds that is initiated and processed – usually electronically, but not necessarily – within current interbank payment systems.

Historically, the electronic transfer of money dates back to 1918, when the Federal Reserve Bank moved currency via telegraph. However, the electronic transfer of funds didn't become widespread until 1972, when the US **Federal Reserve** set up the automated clearinghouse (ACH) to provide the US Treasury and commercial banks with an electronic facility for cheque processing. Similar systems sprang up in Europe at about the same time.

Although banks have taken advantage of the ability to move currency electronically for several decades, it was the advent of the Internet that threatened to revolutionize digital money: first, by opening it up to the general public and second, by creating a raft of new experimental proprietary varieties of digital money competing for adoption as the principal online currency. These included beenz, ecash and mondex.

The new currencies soon discovered, however, that the establishment of a new currency is no easy task. To be viable, digital currencies need certain characteristics and supporting mechanisms: there must be instant clearing of funds; there must be no payment risk; transactions must be secure; and the currency must be widely accepted.

These are tough criteria and several widely touted new currencies have since fallen by the wayside. They include the much-lauded beenz, which ceased to conduct business on 11 October 2001, presumably leaving many supporters with worthless beenz rattling about on their hard drives.

Key text
- Pete Loshin, John Vacca and Paul Murphy. *Electronic Commerce: On-Line Ordering and Digital Money*. Charles River Media, Inc. 2001

Digital signature

In the real world, a handwritten signature authenticates a document, for example a contract, as coming from a particular person. In the electronic world, encryption systems provide the same function via digital signatures and other techniques.

A digital signature is a method of using encryption to certify the source and integrity of a particular electronic document. Because all ASCII characters look the same no matter who types them, such methods are necessary to certify the origins of particular messages if they are to be legally binding for electronic commerce or other transactions. To authenticate an electronic document, the sender attaches his encrypted digital signature and sends his public key, with which the message can be unlocked and the signature validated to the recipient.

One type of digital signature commonly seen on the Internet is generated by the program Pretty Good Privacy (PGP), which adds a digest of the message to the signature. Digital signatures play an essential part in authenticating e-commerce transactions.

Even with digital signatures, there is still a possibility for fraud. How does the recipient of the document with the signature know that it has come from the purported sender? This is where the digital certificate comes in.

A digital certificate is a security measure attached to an electronic message. It is used to verify that the sender of the message is the person he claims to be and also provides the means with which to encrypt a reply.

Digital certificates are issued by a certification authority (CA). The digital certificate will include the user's name, the public key of the user, the period over which the certificate is valid, and whether the key is to be used for data encryption, verification of digital signatures, or both.

Dilbert

Dilbert is the star of the eponymous cartoon

series created by hypnotist, engineer, and one-time inventor **Scott Adams**, who, through his cartoon series, has been lampooning the world of management since 1989. The Dilbert cartoon's first appearance in book form was *The Dilbert Principle: A Cubicle's-Eye View of Bosses, Meetings, Management Fads & Workplace Afflictions*. It is a wry, arch, affectionate and a-little-too-true-for-comfort look at the trials of office life. The Dilbert principle states that the most ineffective workers will be moved to a place where they can do the least damage – management.

The most popular cartoon series relating to business ever, Dilbert has even seeped into organizational culture. Witness the Dilbert metric, which involves showing ten Dilbert cartoons, selected at random, to members of an organization. Each member rates the cartoons on a scale of zero to ten: ten means the cartoon is wholly applicable to the organization, while zero means the cartoon is not at all relevant. Each individual's score is then totalled up and an average score of all the totals taken. The resulting figure is an indication of the health of the organization's morale and culture. The closer the figure is to 100, the closer the organization to the Dilbertesque, chaotic view of corporate life; the closer to zero – the better.

Key text
- Scott Adams. *The Dilbert Principle: A Cubicle's-Eye View of Bosses, Meetings, Management Fads & Workplace Afflictions*. Harper, 1996

Key link
- www.dilbert.com

Dilution

When new shares are issued in a company that has already issued shares, there is a corresponding reduction in the value of earnings and asset values to shareholders. A rights issue, for example, results in an increase in the total number of shares issued, with a corresponding dilution of the value of each share. A dilution of earnings, where the increase in

issued shares is unaccompanied by a commensurate increase in profits, may also arise where a less profitable company buys a more profitable one.

Diminishing returns

The law of diminishing returns, also known as the *law of variable proportions*, is not in truth a law but an observation and generalization. It states that when one factor of production is increased and another remains fixed at some point, the resulting increase in output will become smaller and smaller. Thus the additional application of one factor of production, such as an extra machine or employee at first results in rapidly increasing output but eventually yields declining returns, unless other factors are modified to sustain the increase.

The law is relevant to short-run production decisions, as in the long term, the fixed factor of production – be it labour or plant – can usually be increased so as not to constrain production. The law is also important because it underpins economists' expectations that short-run marginal cost curves slope upward as the number of units of output increase.

DINKs (double income, no kids)

DINKs is originally a term coined by marketers to define a particular social stratum. Other similarly brief marketing tags applied to segments of society include: YUPPIEs (young upwardly mobile professionals or young urban professionals); DEWKs (dual employed with kids); and SKIPPIEs – (school kids with income and purchasing power).

Direct marketing

Direct-marketing techniques are those that deal directly with the consumer rather than going through an intermediary such as an advertising agency. Traditional direct-marketing methods include **telephone sales**, direct mail, door-to-door sales, leafleting, **cold-calling**, and junk e-mail. The Internet has opened up a new avenue of opportunity for direct marketers and a number of techniques, such as **permission marketing**, have been pioneered utilizing the interactivity of the medium.

Direct mail, also known as junk mail – solicited or unsolicited advertising sent by mail to individuals – is one of the most popular direct-marketing methods. It is used as a means of targeting potential customers by making use of mailing lists, which specify a range of criteria, including details such as age, income level and profession. It is common, for example, in the selling of insurance, assurance and loans to individuals. Direct mail is not, however, a particularly effective means of advertising; the response rate is generally accepted to be around 2 percent.

Key links
- www.the-dma.org
- www.theidm.co.uk

Discounted cash flow (DCF)

Discounted cash flow is a sophisticated investment appraisal technique that establishes the value of an investment by considering the value of expected cash flow and the opportunity cost of the money invested. DCF takes into account all benefits likely to accrue from the investment, including cash flow, tax credits, net sale proceeds and paper losses as well as cash flow.

Although complex, the basic idea underlying DCF is a simple one: that cash accruing in the future is worth less than money in the bank today. Therefore any investment should produce a greater return than that held. If £100 is invested today, more than £100 will be required in return, in order to justify making that investment. Thus, DCF calculations rely on the analysis of the **Net present value (NPV)** of money, which should be positive if the investment is to justify the opportunity cost.

DCF is used to determine the value of bonds, loans and other fixed-income investments. Venture capitalists use it to predict returns from investments in new companies.

Key text
- Aswath Damodaran. *Damodaran on Valuation: Security Analysis for Investment and Corporate Finance.* John Wiley & Sons, Inc., 1994

Disintermediation

Disintermediation is the elimination of the intermediary or middleman from a transaction. The term was first used during the 1970s, when a financial services upheaval was sparked by high interest rates. Consumers discovered there were better returns available on their money through disintermediation – cutting out the middleman, in this case the banks – and accessing money markets directly.

Technological advances should, in theory, lead to more efficient markets, where buyers and sellers of a commodity or service can transact business directly without the need for a broker. In this new, efficient global economy facilitated by the Internet, consumers can buy insurance directly from insurance companies, investments directly from investment providers and books directly from the author. In reality, however, intermediaries frequently offer independence as well as added-value information relied upon by one or both parties to a transaction and are unlikely to be eliminated from a market. Despite the predictions, the Internet has not so far proved the wholesale demise of intermediaries. What has happened instead, in many cases, is that traditional supply chains have been rearranged in unconventional ways, through online Web-based market places, for example. This rearrangement of the supply chain is termed 'reintermediation'.

Disney, Walter Elias

Founder of the Disney empire (1901–1966)

Born in Chicago, Illinois, Walt Disney was raised by his parents on a farm near Marceline, Missouri. As a child, Disney showed an above-average artistic ability; he sold his sketches to neighbours at the age of seven. His interest in the arts continued at McKinley High School in Chicago, where he concentrated on drawing and photography. In the evenings, he studied at the Chicago Academy of Fine Arts.

When World War I came, Disney tried to enlist in the US Army. Unable to produce his birth certificate, he was rejected for being too young. Instead, he travelled to France with the Red Cross and spent his time driving an ambulance decorated with his own cartoons rather than more conventional camouflage.

Settling in Kansas City, Missouri, after the war, Disney embarked on a career as a cartoonist. In 1920, he created his first original animated characters while working for Kansas City Film Ads. In May 1922, he started his own company, Laugh-O-Grams. The laughs were short-lived – the company soon ran into financial difficulties and Disney decided to skip town. Emboldened with the spirit of youth, he left for Hollywood armed only with his drawing equipment, an idea for a cartoon, and the suit he stood up in.

Disney's new venture began where so many great US corporate dreams have started – in a garage. Together with his brother Roy, who had joined Disney from Arizona, where he had been recuperating from tuberculosis, Disney launched Disney Brothers Studio. Disney started out with $500 borrowed from his uncle, $200 from Roy, and $2500 from his parents, who mortgaged their house to find the money. Before long, Disney was out of the garage and into the back of a Hollywood real estate office. The first work that he sold was a series of featurettes based on Lewis Carroll's Alice character.

Mickey Mouse was born in 1928. There are several versions of how Disney came up with the idea of the little mouse. The most frequently recounted story is that a flash of inspiration came to Disney on the way home from a disastrous business meeting in which he was forced to relinquish control of his most successful character at the time – Oswald the Rabbit. Daydreaming on the train to Hollywood, Disney recalled the mice that had been frequent visitors to his old office. Disney wanted to call his new character Mortimer. His wife, displaying a more acute instinct for marketing, persuaded him to christen his creation Mickey Mouse. Mickey made his sound debut in the first-ever sound cartoon, *Steamboat Willie*. It was November 1928 and Disney was just 26.

Disney continued to innovate within the cartoon medium. *Silly Symphonies* introduced Technicolor to cartoons and in 1937 Disney premiered the first feature-length musical animation, *Snow White and the Seven Dwarfs*. Disney took a huge risk with *Snow White*. The film was the first of its kind. The $2 million it cost to make was an incredible amount in the 1930s, particularly in the middle of the Great Depression. He bet the business on the outcome. Fortunately for Disney, the gamble paid off and the studios followed *Snow White* with other full-length animated classics, including *Pinocchio*, *Dumbo* and *Bambi*.

By 1940, Disney and over 1000 employees occupied the Burbank Studios. For some time, Disney's role had been that of a catalyst; he no longer drew any of the studio's output, nor had he done since the early 1920s. In his own words, he was 'a little bee. I go from one area to another, and gather pollen and sort of stimulate everyone.'

The worker bees in Disney's hive weren't always impressed with Disney's contributions. Many resented his reluctance to acknowledge the contribution of the studio artists. Neither was Disney an easy man to work for. Frequently neurotic and obsessive, he imposed strict rules at his studio. Anyone caught cursing in mixed company was fired on the spot and despite Disney's own preference for a pencil moustache, facial hair was forbidden for all male employees.

During the 1940s, the Disney studio became embroiled in a series of labour disputes. He was also involved to some degree with the FBI, as well as a member of the Motion Picture Alliance for the Preservation of American Ideals, who sought out 'communists, radicals, and crackpots' in the movie business. In 1947, Disney testified before the House Un-American Activities Committee, denouncing a number of employees at his studios as communist sympathizers. The fallout from these events took years to dissipate.

World War II temporarily sidelined the Walt Disney studio's output. After the war, Disney continued to hone his craft and vary the studio's productions. Cartoons were joined by combined live motion/cartoon pictures and 'true-life adventures' that portrayed animals in their natural habitats.

In 1955, Disney took the Disney brand in a new direction. The Disneyland theme park in Anaheim, California, was to be a living embodiment of the Disney movies, a magical land where children and adults could mingle with their favourite cartoon stars from the big screen. Disney's investment was $17 million. It was another big risk for Disney but Disneyland was a big hit, with Mickey and his friends greeting a million people in its first seven weeks and many millions more since.

At the same time, Disney continued to push Disney products on television. Disney supplied television with the Wonderful World of Color, exploiting the lack of programming in what was still a comparatively new medium – colour television.

From the mid-60s onward, one project consumed the final years of Disney's life. The plan was to build a Disney World with a social dimension. Disney was interested in solving the problems afflicting urban living in America. His answer was the Experimental Prototype Community of Tomorrow (EPCOT), the equivalent of a gigantic ideal Home Exhibition for urban life. Disney took a personal interest in all aspects of the project.

Disney World opened in October 1971. Located in Florida, it was built over 43 square miles and included an amusement theme park, hotel complex, airport and Disney's futuristic EPCOT Center. Like its California relation, Disney World was a success. Disney, however, was not present to witness the fruition of his plans. He died on 15 December 1966.

Key texts

- Don Nardo. *Walt Disney*. Lucent Books, 2000
- Henry A. Giroux. *The Mouse That Roared: Disney and the End of Innocence*. Rowman & Littlefield, 1999
- Eleanor Byrne and Martin McQuillan. *Deconstructing Disney*. Pluto Press, 1999
- Dave Smith and Steven Clark. *Disney: The First 100 Years*. Hyperion, 1999
- Bob Thomas. *Building a Company: Roy O. Disney and the Creation of an Entertainment Empire*. Hyperion, 1998
- Robert B. Sherman and Richard M. Sherman. *Walt's Time: From Before to Beyond*. Camphor Tree, 1998
- Richard Schickel. *The Disney Version: The Life, Times, Art, and Commerce of Walt Disney*. Ivan R. Dee, 1997
- Marc Eliot. *Walt Disney: Hollywood's Dark Prince: A Biography*. Carol Publishing Group, 1993

Key link

- disney.go.com/disneyatoz/waltdisney/home.html

Diversification

Diversification is the phenomenon in which a company develops distinctly new products or moves into new markets. There are many reasons for a company to diversify. It may wish to spread its risks, or move from its original area of operation if that is becoming less profitable or overcrowded. Chocolate bar manufacturers, for example, diversified into ice cream versions of their brands to produce revenue at a time – during hot summers – when traditionally their sales were slacker.

There are risks associated with diversification. One of the most significant challenges for a company that is diversifying is to carry its consumer's loyalty to its brand onto its new operations. A company operating in an unfamiliar arena risks losing sight of its core business and core values, losing focus and confusing consumers. Few companies have a brand strong enough to stand the degree of diversification a company like Virgin embraces.

Diversity advantage

Diversity advantage is the supposed competitive advantage conferred by recruiting employees from a diverse background. Historically, companies tried to recruit the same sort of people time and time again. The thinking was that people of the same sort were much easier to control. The end result, however, was more of the same people producing more of the same work. While this was acceptable in the past, the emphasis in modern business is on innovation, speed and flexibility. Managers have to be able to think differently, work with different people and thrive on the difference.

Diversity is a competitive weapon. If companies accept difference, so the theory goes, they are likely to be more responsive to changes in their business environment. They will be more flexible, open-minded, and quicker to react. A Swiss multinational with ten nationalities on the board, including six women, and the ability to make global teams work will have a diversity advantage over an American widget-maker from Cleveland with a board entirely populated by white middle-aged men who believe that Canada is the international market.

While diversity is regarded as a racial issue in the United States, in Europe it is cultural. Multicultural European role models abound – from soccer teams to entire countries. One outstanding European role model is Switzerland, which is highly successful, multi-ethnic and multireligious. It is notable that some of the most successful and international of companies are Swiss – companies like Nestlé, Ciba-Geigy and ABB appear to handle diversity more easily and positively than others in Europe. Indeed, the Swiss-Swedish conglomerate

ABB is often held up as the epitome of the modern organization and is a fervent champion of thinking global, acting local. International teamworking is central to making ABB work successfully. It thrives on diversity and requires that its managers 'have an exceptional grasp of differing traditions, cultures, and environments'. ABB's supervisory board of eight includes four nationalities, while its executive committee goes one further with five. Its former chief executive **Percy Barnevik** argues, 'Competence is the key selection criterion, not passport.'

Other multinationals are similarly diverse as they discover the twin challenges of globalization and teamworking. After its merger, SmithKline Beecham boasted a management group of 13 that included seven nationalities.

Key texts
- David Jamieson and Julie O'Mara. *Managing Workforce 2000: Gaining the Diversity Advantage.* Jossey-Bass, 1991
- John P. Fernandez (with Mary Barr). *The Diversity Advantage; How American Business Can Out-Perform Japanese and European Companies in the Global Marketplace.* Lexington Books, 1993

Dividend

A company's dividend is that element of its after-tax earnings distributed to its shareholders. The dividend, which may be in the form of cash or shares, is recommended by the board of executives and approved by the shareholders in the annual general meeting. There is no guarantee that a dividend payment will be made. Dividend payments may be withheld for many reasons, including poor performance or the reallocation of funds to finance growth. Companies with little or no earnings growth, such as utilities, traditionally pay above-average dividends, as otherwise they would have to recommend the purchase of their stock to investors. Conversely, companies undergoing rapid growth and/or operating in higher-risk industries, such as mining and exploration, tend to pay below-average or no dividends, as the prospect of significant capital growth is sufficient to attract investors. Shares bought with the right to receive a declared dividend payment are said to be cum-dividend, and those without the right, ex-dividend.

Division of labour

The division of labour occurs when a complex production process is split into several parts and done by different workers, each of whom specializes in one (or a few) tasks. For example, on a car assembly line, one worker will fit doors, another will make the engine block and another will work in the paint shop. The advantages of the division of labour from a human productivity perspective were discussed at length in **Adam Smith**'s *The Wealth of Nations*, particularly in his analysis of the pin factory.

Specialization and the division of labour have come under criticism from sociologists, psychologists and philosophers, who have emphasized its dehumanizing effects. Social theorists including Jean-Jacques Rousseau, Karl Marx and **Max Weber** have all discussed the social and economic implications of highly specialized division of labour.

Division of mental labour

Booz Allen & Hamilton consultants Charles Lucier and Janet Torsilieri argue that a process-driven model of management has dominated our minds ever since **Adam Smith**. We have been engaged in maximizing the efficiency of our processes, whether we are widget-makers or McDonald's. Efficient, lean processes with cost-efficient overheads have come to be regarded as the quickest route to profit heaven.

According to Lucier and Torsilieri, good intentions have not been matched by reality. 'Overhead in major corporations is not decreasing,' they

note. One contributory factor to this is the rise of the knowledge worker. As **Peter F. Drucker** has jokingly lamented, 'Knowledge workers are abysmally unproductive.'

This calls for a division of mental labour rather than an overriding emphasis on creating processes to divide physical labour. The route to this requires a number of steps. First, routine work – a depressing 80 percent of what we do – needs to be standardized. This means giving people more responsibility and cutting out middlemen. Second, Lucier and Torsilieri suggest that companies 'outsource the most complex (often most critical) decisions to the real experts'. 'Outsourcing the most complex decisions significantly increases both the quality of decisions and level of service,' they say. The end result will be lower costs (though only slightly). 'Companies will both eliminate expertise-driven overhead and better manage the productivity of knowledge workers,' say Lucier and Torsilieri. They fail to add the most obvious side-effect of outsourcing such work: a boon for management consultants.

As an adjunct to the idea of the division of mental labour, Peter F. Drucker argues that management's great achievement of the century was to increase the productivity of manual workers 50-fold. While this cannot be underestimated, it is not the great challenge of the next century. This, according to Drucker, is to increase the productivity of knowledge workers – dauntingly, he estimates that the productivity of some knowledge workers has actually declined over the last 70 years.

Key text
- Charles Lucier and Janet Torsilieri. 'The end of overhead.' *Strategy & Business*, second quarter, 1999

DMS (database management system)

A database management system is a suite of software applications that facilitates the storage and manipulation of database information.

Database management systems vary in scope and complexity from small programs run on personal computers to large complicated systems run on mainframe computers. Information is retrieved from a database by a request known as a query. This is a stylized way of calling information from a database governed by a set of rules known as a query language, of which there are several, the most common being structured query language (SQL).

DNS (domain name system)

The domain name system is the network system that resolves an alphanumeric common domain name, such as www.moon.com, to its numerical Internet Protocol (IP) address. The Internet is really based not on alphanumeric domain names, but on the underlying numeric IP addresses – usually four sets of numbers separated by periods, i.e., 123.12.123.12. Alphanumeric domain names are used as they are easier to remember and more useful from a business perspective. The Internet Protocol is the accepted format for sending and receiving data between two devices on the Internet.

The specific computer device that resolves the alphanumeric common domain name to its numerical IP address is known as the domain name server.

Double-entry accounting

A standard accounting method, double-entry accounting requires two entries into the accounts for each transaction: one credit and one debit. For example, if an item of stock is purchased for £100, the payment of £100 is reflected in the debit account, whereas the new item of stock value of £100 is entered in the stock account. In this method of accounting, assets will equal liabilities and therefore when a balance sheet is drawn up, the totals for the credit and debits should balance.

Double-loop learning

Double-loop learning is one of three types of learning identified by management academics. The other two types are developing skills (learning and practising new things) and **single-loop learning** (developing better ways of doing things within a field of knowledge, such as improving manufacturing techniques through TQM). Double-loop learning involves challenging and completely re-evaluating the assumptions made about a particular theory or system. It is the most difficult of the three types to undertake, as it requires individuals and teams to overcome defensive attitudes toward new theories of action.

Key text
- Chris Argyris. 'Single-loop and double-loop models in research on decision making.' *Administrative Science Quarterly*, 21(3), 363–375

Dow Jones Industrial Average (DJIA)

The Dow Jones is an index of 30 blue-chip US stocks and one of the oldest and best-known stock market indicators in the world. The value of the index is calculated by adding up the stock prices of the 30 companies that comprise the index, and dividing by a specially calculated divisor.

The unweighted index dates back to 1896, when it was originally made up of twelve stocks. Those twelve were increased to 30 in 1928. The stocks that make up the index are chosen by the editors of *The Wall Street Journal* and are a barometer of the economic health of the United States. Changes to the companies are rare – Sears, Roebuck & Co., for example, was only replaced in 1999, having entered the index in 1924. A few companies have been dropped from the index, only to be selected many years later as their fortunes revived. General Electric, one of the original twelve stocks, has been in and out twice; IBM was ejected in 1939, but readmitted in 1979.

Key text

- John A. Prestbo (ed). *The Market's Measure: An Illustrated History of America Told Through the Dow Jones Industrial Average.* Dow Jones & Company, New York, 1999

Key link

- www.dowjones.com

Downsizing

Downsizing is the euphemistic term given to the restructuring of an organization, usually involving a significant reduction in the workforce. A popular practice during the late 1980s and early 1990s, downsizing was seen as a way to deliver better shareholder value by reducing costs. It was often associated with the practice of delayering. Delayering involves stripping out management layers, usually middle management, from a company.

One person closely associated with the practice of downsizing was US businessman 'Chainsaw' Al Dunlap. Management thought has moved away from wholesale downsizing as a recovery strategy. The stigma associated with the term has led to the use of the equally euphemistic rightsizing instead.

DPI (dots per inch)

A confusing term, dots per inch is used both as a measure of the sharpness of a display screen and a measure of image quality in printing.

With reference to display screens, the dot pitch limits the maximum number of dots per inch (the density of illuminated points). This is usually greater than the screen resolution, which is given in terms of pixels (picture elements), i.e., 800 x 600. The number of dots per inch is dependent on the screen size. Because of the common confusion between DPI and pixels, the term pixels per inch is often preferred as a measure of image sharpness on display screens.

DPI is also the common measurement of image quality in printing. Computer printers will, for example, state that they print at 600 DPI. When very high DPI figures are featured, they may not represent actual DPI, but interpolated DPI, where the location and character of the additional dots are generated by software that guesses what should go in the gaps.

Dress-down Friday

Dress-down Friday refers to the practice of wearing smart casual clothes, as opposed to formal business wear, at work on Fridays. The practice originated in the United States in the mid-1980s and grew – partly as a response to the power dressing of the 1980s, partly due to the increase in popularity of so-called soft management techniques, and partly as a reflection of the casual-dress trend prevalent in the booming Internet industry. Dress-down Friday has since been exported to Europe and other parts of the world and become firmly entrenched in corporate culture; even lawyers, accountants, and management consultants, bastions of the suit, have adopted the policy. Dress-down Friday is undergoing a backlash in some companies. Not without its critics, it is claimed by some to decrease productivity, increase customer dissatisfaction, and give rise to employee stress over what to wear.

Drive-by VC

The term 'drive-by VC' originated during the dotcom start-up frenzy of the 1990s. It refers to the lack of service supplied by some **venture capital** investors to the companies they invested in. In theory, venture capitalists provide added value to the ventures they finance by giving the benefit of their considerable business expertise at board meetings. As the number of start-ups each venture capital firm was involved with rocketed, however, there was less time available to attend board meetings. A drive-by VC is a venture capitalist who pops in briefly to a board meeting and then leaves, or merely drives by.

Drucker, Peter Ferdinand

Journalist, educator and consultant (b. 1909)

Peter F. Drucker is the major management and business thinker of the century. Of that there is little question. Prolific, even in his nineties, Drucker's work is all-encompassing. There is little that executives do, think or face that he has not written about.

Take the contemporary fixation with knowledge management. 'The knowledge worker sees himself just as another professional, no different from the lawyer, the teacher, the preacher, the doctor, or the government servant of yesterday,' wrote Drucker in his 1969 classic *The Age of Discontinuity*. 'He has the same education. He has more income, he has probably greater opportunities as well. He may well realize that he depends on the organization for access to income and opportunity, and that without the investment the organization has made – and a high investment at that – there would be no job for him, but he also realizes, and rightly so, that the organization equally depends on him.'

Far-sighted and always opinioned, Peter Drucker was born in Austria, where his father, Adolph, was the chief economist in the Austrian civil service.

Drucker worked as a journalist in London before moving to America in 1937. His first book, *Concept of the Corporation* (1946), was a groundbreaking examination of the intricate internal working of General Motors. His books have emerged regularly ever since and now total 29. Along the way, he has coined phrases and championed concepts, many of which have become accepted facts of managerial life.

The centrepieces of Drucker's work are two equally huge and brilliant books: *The Practice of Management* (1954) and *Management: Tasks, Responsibilities, Practices* (1973). Both are ency-clopaedic in their scope and fulsome in their historical perspectives. More than any other volumes, they encapsulate the essence of management thinking and practice.

Drucker's book production has been supplemented by a somewhat low-key career as an academic and sometime consultant. He was professor of philosophy and politics at Bennington College from 1942 until 1949 and then became a professor of management at New York University in 1950: 'The first person anywhere in the world to have such a title and to teach such a subject,' he proudly recalls. Since 1971, Drucker has been a professor at Claremont Graduate School in California. He also lectures in Asian art, has an abiding passion for Jane Austen, and has written two novels (less successful than his management books).

Drucker's greatest achievement lies in identifying management as a timeless human discipline. It was used to build the Great Wall of China, to erect the pyramids, to cross the oceans for the first time, to run armies. 'Management is tasks. Management is discipline. But management is also people,' he wrote. 'Every achievement of management is the achievement of a manager. Every failure is the failure of a manager. People manage, rather than forces or facts. The vision, dedication, and integrity of managers determine whether there is management or mismanagement.'

Drucker's first attempt at creating the managerial bible was *The Practice of Management*. He largely succeeded. The book is a masterly exposition on the first principles of management. In one of the most quoted and memorable paragraphs in management literature, Drucker gets to the heart of the meaning of business life. 'There is only one valid definition of business purpose: to create a customer. Markets are not created by God, nature, or economic forces, but by businessmen. The want they satisfy may have been felt by the customer before he was offered the means of satisfying it. It may indeed, like the want of food in a famine, have dominated the customer's life and filled all his waking moments. But it was a theoretical want before; only when the action of businessmen makes it an effective demand is there a customer, a market.'

Drucker also provided an evocatively simple insight into the nature and *raison d'être* of organizations: 'Organization is not an end in itself, but a means to an end of business performance and business results. Organization structure is an indispensable means, and the wrong structure will seriously impair business performance and may even destroy it … The first question in discussing organization structure must be: What is our business and what should it be? Organization structure must be designed so as to make possible the attainment of the objectives of the business for five, ten, fifteen years hence.' With its examinations of GM, Ford and others, Drucker's audience and worldview in *The Practice of Management* is resolutely that of the large corporation. The world has moved on. (And so has Drucker.)

Drucker identified seven 'new tasks' for the manager of the future. Given that these were laid down more than 40 years ago, their prescience is astounding. Drucker wrote that tomorrow's managers must:

1   Manage by objectives.
2   Take more risks and for a longer period ahead.
3   Be able to make strategic decisions.
4   Be able to built an integrated team, each member of which is capable of managing and of measuring his own performance and results in relation to the common objectives.
5   Be able to communicate information fast and clearly.
6   Traditionally, a manager has been expected to know one or more functions. This will no longer be enough. The manager of the future must be able to see the business as a whole and to integrate his function with it.
7   Traditionally, a manager has been expected to know a few products or one industry. This, too, will no longer be enough.

Recent years have seen Drucker maintain his remarkable work rate. In particular, his energies have been focused on non-profit organizations. His ability to return to first principles and question the fundamentals remains undimmed. In the new millennium, Drucker remains worth listening to.

Key texts

- Peter F. Drucker. *Managing in Times of Great Change*. Butterworth Heinemann, 1995
- Peter F. Drucker. *Managing the Nonprofit Organization*. Harper Collins, 1990
- Peter F. Drucker. *The New Realities*. Heinemann, 1989
- Peter F. Drucker. *Innovation and Entrepreneurship*. Heinemann, 1985
- Peter F. Drucker. *Managing in Turbulent Times*. Harper & Row, 1980
- Peter F. Drucker. *Management: Tasks, Responsibilities, Practices*. Harper & Row, 1973
- Peter F. Drucker. *The Age of Discontinuity*. Heinemann, 1969
- Peter F. Drucker. *The Effective Executive*. Harper & Row, 1967
- Peter F. Drucker. *Managing for Results*. Heinemann, 1964
- Peter F. Drucker. *The Practice of Management*. Harper & Row, 1954
- Peter F. Drucker. *The New Society*. Heinemann, 1951
- Peter F. Drucker. *Concept of the Corporation*. John Day, 1946

Key links

- www.pfdf.org
- www.mtspublishers.com
- www.theatlantic.com/issues/99oct/9910drucker.htm

Due diligence

Due diligence is the name given to the process of examining an investment proposition. There are usually two distinct phases to the process of due diligence. First, there is the rough analysis of the business plan. Providing the proposal survives this phase, there follows a closer and more rigorous examination of the business plan. This inspection will include a detailed examination of the financial projections as well as interviews with the proposed management team. Due diligence lasts for several months, although the time period was compressed in many cases during the rush to market of the dotcom start-ups in the 1990s.

Duke, James Buchanan

Founder, Duke Power (1856–1925)

James (Buck) Duke was born near Durham, North Carolina. His education took place at New Garden School in Greensboro, North Carolina and the Eastman Business College in Poughkeepsie, New York – his academic education, that is. His real education took place in the family business. The Duke family farmed and produced tobacco products – chiefly smoking tobacco. Under pressure from local competition, however, they eventually shifted, in 1881, to the production of cigarettes. Initially, this manufacturing process was carried out by hand and was a slow and cumbersome one. Even an expert could only roll four cigarettes a minute.

As cigarettes became more popular, the tobacco companies sought to mechanize the process. The Allen and Ginter Company of Richmond, Virginia, offered $75,000 to any person who could invent a practical cigarette-making machine. The offer was taken up by 18-year-old James Bonsack, who developed such a machine in 1880. Allen and Ginter, however, discarded the machine after a trial period.

Sensing an opportunity, W. Duke, Sons and Co. took up the machine (two, in fact). Once again the invention disappointed, but Buck Duke and a young engineer (William T. O' Brien) were able to alter the machine and make it reliable, cutting the cost of manufacturing cigarettes in half.

At the age of 28, the young Duke was called upon to open a branch of the family business in New York City. Within five years, the New York City factory was rolling out half of the entire country's total production of cigarettes. His talent for marketing helped.

Duke wasn't allowed to celebrate his success for long, however, as the 'tobacco wars' loomed large. Fought between the five principal cigarette manufacturers, the tobacco wars were a bitterly contested battle for supremacy of the market. The four main combatants were the Allen and Ginter Company of Richmond; the F.S. Kinney Company and the Goodwin Company, both of New York City; and William S. Kimball and Co. of Rochester, New York. Together with the Duke company, these five manufacturers produced 90 percent of America's cigarettes in the 1880s. Each company thought that it could dominate the market and an advertising war ensued. When no clear winner emerged, it became clear that the most sensible approach would be to staunch the spending and merge the five companies.

When the smoke cleared in 1890, the five companies had gone. In their place stood the result of the merger – the American Tobacco Company – with president Duke at its helm. This tobacco giant became known as the 'tobacco trust'. During the following decade, the victorious Duke steered the American Tobacco Company to a dominance befitting its nickname as it spread its tentacles across the globe.

In 1901, Duke visited Britain to thwart the transatlantic competition. In the space of a few days, he bid for both Players and Ogdens cigarette manufacturers. He succeeded in buying Ogdens, prompting the formation of the Imperial Tobacco Company to fight off his unwanted attentions. Duke in turn formed the British American Tobacco company.

Eventually, the American Tobacco Company fell victim to its own burning ambition. In 1911, the United States Supreme Court, in the trust-busting spirit of the times, ordered the dissolution of the tobacco trust as a 'combination in restraint of trade'. At the time of its break-up, American Tobacco had 80 percent of the market and revenues of some $325 million. From the ashes of the tobacco trust grew four major tobacco corporations: a new American Tobacco Company; Liggett and Myers; P. Lorillard; and R.J. Reynolds.

While Buck Duke was conquering the tobacco markets, his eldest brother, Benjamin Newton, was wrapping up the textile market. The Duke family had been involved in textiles as far back as 1892. As the textile empire grew, so too did the need for cheap power. This encouraged the Dukes, including Buck, to start up their own hydroelectric generating business, the Southern Power Company (subsequently renamed Duke Power) in 1905. As with everything else the Dukes touched, the energy business took off and before long was supplying electricity to more than 300 cotton mills, plus factories, towns and cities in the Piedmont region of North and South Carolina.

Duke was an ardent Methodist and conducted his professional life in a manner befitting his religious beliefs. The richest member of the Duke dynasty, in later life he embarked on a philanthropic spree. In 1924, he established the Duke Endowment as a permanent trust fund. The prime beneficiary of the fund was Trinity College, a Methodist-related institution founded in part by Duke's father. A new university was built around Trinity and renamed Duke University. The Duke Endowment remains to this day one of the largest foundations in the United States, with offices in Charlotte, North Carolina. It has distributed more than one billion dollars.

James B. Duke died in New York City on 10 October 1925, and is interred on the campus of Duke University. Although he founded a power company that still survives to this day, as well as an endowment trust that has handed out billions of dollars to its beneficiaries, he will always be best remembered for the part he played in establishing the tobacco industry. With the benefit of hindsight, it is clear that Buck Duke was successful in producing and marketing what turned out to be a pernicious product. Even so, he was a tenacious and formidable businessman with considerable marketing acumen.

Key texts
- James O. Nall. *The Tobacco Night Riders of Kentucky and Tennessee, 1905–1909*. McClanahan Publishing House, 1991

- John Kennedy Winkler. *Tobacco Tycoon: The Story of James Buchanan Duke*. Random House, 1942
- John Wilber Jenkins. *James B. Duke, Master Builder: The Story of Tobacco, Development of Southern and Canadian Water-Power and the Creation of a University*. George H. Doran, 1927

Key links
- www.duke-energy.com
- www.dukeendowment.org

Dumbing down

The phrase 'dumbing down' refers to the belief that in many areas of the media and entertainment industries, content is increasingly catering to the lowest common denominator of human taste. In this regard, reference is made to tabloid newspapers (prompted by instances such as 'Zip Me Up Before You Go-Go', *The Sun*'s headline after George Michael's arrest for lewd conduct), violent movies, moronic advertising, soap operas, sound-bite politics and the tell-all talk shows like Jerry Springer Show, among many other sins. Dumbing down is undoubtedly true, but nothing new. Businesspeople have been crassly chasing markets by any means for centuries. The good news is that there is also dumbing up: witness Oprah Winfrey's now-defunct book club.

Durant, William Crapo

Founder of Buick Motors, General Motors, Chevrolet Motors and Durant Motors (1861–1947)

Boston-born William Crapo Durant moved with his mother and sister to Flint, Michigan, a town that would be at the heart of the emerging US car manufacturing industry. Although bright, Durant's academic record was not a distinguished one – he left school at 16 over a dispute with the school principal. Durant obtained work in a lumberyard owned by a relative. He soon moved on, working as a medicine salesman and then a cigar salesman. After a series of jobs covering real estate, bookkeeping, fire insurance and, improbably, a spell as co-owner of an ice-rink, he came to rest at the Flint City Waterworks. An ailing business at the time, Durant soon turned the Waterworks around and restored it to profitability.

Having cut his business teeth on the Waterworks, the young Durant (he was barely 25) went into business with another young man, Dallas Dort. The two bought out a local businessman with $1500 they borrowed from the bank and founded the Flint Road Cart Company in 1886 (eventually the Durant-Dort Carriage Company). Their main product, a new two-wheeled horse-drawn carriage, proved spectacularly popular, with sales peaking at 75,000 units in 1895. Durant and Dort earned enough money to retire, had they wished. But for Durant, still in his 30s, it was just the beginning.

In 1904, sensing that the days of the horse-drawn cart might be coming to an end, Durant bought into the Buick Motor Corporation. On the strength of the car designed by David Buick, he raised $1.5 million of investment. David Buick, the Scots-born inventor, left the company prematurely in 1906, dying a poor man.

From the start, Durant adopted an autocratic management style. As it turned out, his drive and energy and his domineering approach to business would be the perfect recipe to grow companies but rarely the right ingredients for moving those companies on to the next stage of development.

Buick survived an economic crisis in 1907, which bankrupted many other small car companies. To protect the company, Durant sought a merger with other companies in the same industry. He approached auto manufacturers **Henry Ford** and Ransom Olds. Both were interested, but only if Durant put his own money up front. Durant was reluctant to do this; instead, he bought up a disparate collection of smaller companies and, in September 1908, formed the General Motors Company.

As Durant continued to acquire car companies, so GM took on more debt. By 1910, the company owned over 20 percent of the industry, but it had also run into financial difficulties. The financiers' solution was to remove Durant from his position as autocratic leader, although he remained as vice-president. A board of five trustees replaced him.

A resilient Durant merely moved onto his next deal. In August of 1911, he formed Mason Motor Corporation and then the Little Motor Car Company. He then, having persuaded founder William H. Little and racing driver associate Louis Chevrolet to stay with the firm, incorporated the Chevrolet Motor Company in November 1911. Soon the Chevrolet car was in production. By 1915, the Chevrolet Motor Company's net profit was some $1.3 million.

While Durant was building his new company, his old one was in trouble. General Motors was fighting for market share in a business where its rivals were substantially undercutting it. Incredibly, by 1917, with the assistance of the du Pont brothers, Durant had wrested back control of General Motors, by acquiring 450,000 of GM's 768,733 shares. Durant was also fortunate to meet a rising star of the car industry, **Alfred P. Sloan** Jr, who was also to become a business legend.

The General Motors Company was renamed the General Motors Corporation in 1916, and Durant once more assumed dictatorial command of his disparate collection of companies. General Motors continued to prosper. When the US post-war economy hit the buffers, however, Durant once more found himself and GM in financial difficulties. GM stock, which had risen 5500 percent between 1914 and early 1920, nosedived. In the nine months from March to November 1920, GM stock fell by 68 percent, losing over 30 percent of its value in one month alone.

Durant tried to support the share price by buying GM stock on the market, as well as from friends whom he had persuaded to invest in the company. The result for Durant was personal disaster. Not only did he lose control of his beloved company, replaced by du Pont in 1920, he also lost the majority of his personal fortune.

Still, Durant bounced back one last time, founding the eponymous Durant Motors in 1921 with the help of friends' money including, ironically, the du Pont family. By May 1921, the Durant Four was on the market. By the middle of 1921, the company had received 30,000 orders worth some $31 million. Durant continued to produce innovative vehicles, such as the four-cylinder Star. Now in his 60s, Durant steered his company successfully through the 1920s, negotiating personal setbacks, such as the death of his mother in a train crash. During this time, he also campaigned in favour of prohibition and developed an interest in politics.

It was the Wall Street crash in 1929 that finally put paid to Durant's career in business. Once again the bankers came knocking on Durant's door and once again he found himself overextended. This time, with his personal fortune exhausted, he was forced to sell the shares in his company. In 1933, Durant Motors filed for bankruptcy. Finally, in February 1936, Durant filed for personal bankruptcy, declaring debts of $914,000. Although Durant tried to get other ventures off the ground, his entrepreneurial days were over. He died on 18 March 1947, in New York City – the same year as his great rival Henry Ford.

In many ways, Durant was the archetypal entrepreneur. He loved the deal, he loved selling, he loved making things happen. His management style, however, was autocratic and dictatorial, and proved a problem when he was trying to move his companies on from the start-up stage. Durant's life was the perfect example of the tightrope entrepreneurs tread between success and failure. It was his maverick streak that made him a brilliant entrepreneur and led to the creation of the largest car manufacturer in the world, General Motors. It was the same maverick streak that finally bankrupted him.

Key text
- Axel Madsen. *The Deal Makers: How William C. Durant Made General Motors*. John Wiley, 1999

Key link
- www.crapo.org/william_crapo_durant.htm

Dutch auction

A dutch auction is an auction where an auctioneer starts with a high bid price and steadily reduces that price until a bid is received. It is a reverse of the traditional auction model. The name derives from the flower markets in Amsterdam, which operated on this basis, and is traditionally used for goods with a limited life such as cut flowers and fish.

The dutch auction model is also popular with Internet auction companies. Common sense might predict that as the price descends, bidders may enter the bidding at a higher price than they would in a traditional auction, where they have the opportunity to bid low and increase if necessary. Research has shown, however, that with risk-neutral bidders and equal information, the same expected price would be realized by a private bidder buying for private consumption.

Confusingly, the term 'dutch auction' is also used by the financial world to signify an entirely different type of auction – the uniform second-price auction. This auction involves bidders making sealed bids. The highest bid wins but pays the amount of the second-highest bid. This type of auction is better referred to by its academic name: the Vickrey auction.

Dynamic pricing

Dynamic pricing is a flexible pricing model in which the value of goods and services is determined on an individual basis by mutual negotiation. Most contracts for goods and services are fixed-price goods, where the consumer pays a set quoted price. A consumer in a grocery store, for example, will be expected to pay the price advertised on a can of beans without any further negotiation.

With dynamic pricing, the price of a good or service is not fixed but fluid. It depends on the strength of demand from the consumer and the availability of the good or service, as well as a variety of other pricing factors. The point is that the price will shift from moment to moment, always reflecting as closely as possible the best possible outcome for purchaser and vendor.

The Internet is expected to be a proving ground for the dynamic pricing model. Researchers at technology laboratories such as the **Massachusetts Institute of Technology Media Labs** are working on 'intelligent' software agents that will be able to carry out transactions over the Internet remotely. The agents will interact with the vendor's software, which continually monitors and alters the price of goods and services according to external circumstances. In theory, this is a far more efficient pricing model than the traditional fixed pricing model, in which the power lies solely with the vendor. How long dynamic pricing will take to become widely available in practice (outside bazaars and markets, that is) is another matter.

Dyson, Esther

Founder and chair, EDventure Holdings (b. 1951)

When e-guru Esther Dyson speaks, people listen. A Harvard economics graduate and daughter of an English physicist and a Swiss mathematician, Dyson chairs EDventure Holdings. She founded the company after earlier positions as a fact-checker at *Forbes* magazine and as a securities analyst at New Court Securities and then Oppenheimer.

EDventure is a small but diversified company focusing on emerging technologies, emerging markets (particularly Central and Eastern Europe) and emerging companies. EDventure publishes Release 1.0, a highly regarded computer industry newsletter. Dyson also wrote the popular book *Release 2.0: A Design for Living in the Digital Age.*

A multitasking and multitalented woman, in addition to her position at EDventure, Dyson chairs the Internet domain name authority ICANN and is a member of the board at the WPP Group as well as several other institutions. Her articles have been published in the *Harvard Business Review, Forbes, The New York Times* and *The New York Times Magazine*, among many others. She also writes a monthly column for *Computerworld*. She appears frequently on CNN, CNBC, Wall Street Journal TV and the Network News. She is also fluent in Russian.

Dyson's opinions are much sought after. She has advised, among others, Bill Clinton and **Bill Gates**, as well as governments from around the world. Small wonder that *Fortune* magazine named her as one of the 50 most powerful women in US business. Remarkably, she manages all of this without owning a home telephone or a car.

Key text
- Esther Dyson. *Release 2.1: A Design for Living in the Digital Age*. Broadway Books, 1998

Key link
- www.edventure.com

E

Early adopters

Early adopters are the second group following a technological innovation to take up the technology, after the innovators themselves. American academic Everett Rogers suggested in his book *Diffusion of Innovations* that there are several classes of adopters of technological innovation: innovators, early adopters, early majority, late majority and laggards. Rogers documented how these classes were comprised of fundamentally different people, meaning that as a company expands its customer base, it needs also to change its marketing and behaviour. This work was built on by, among others, **Geoffrey Moore** in his 1991 book *Crossing the Chasm*, in which he describes the plight of one company trying to 'cross the chasm' from the early adopter market to the mass market. Early adopters represent 13.5 percent of all adopters. Their role, according to Rogers, is to increase acceptance of a new idea through adoption and dissemination of a subjective evaluation of the innovation.

Key texts

- Everett M. Rogers. *Diffusion of Innovations*. Free Press, 1962
- Geoffrey A. Moore. *Crossing The Chasm: Marketing and Selling Technology Products to Mainstream Customers*. Harper and Row, 1991

EBITDA (earnings before interest, tax, depreciation and amortization)

EBITDA is a financial indicator calculated as revenue, minus expenses, before adjustment for interest, tax, depreciation and amortization. It came into common use when leveraged buyouts were popular in the 1980s, as it was used to judge whether a company was able to service its debts. Since then, it has been used extensively where a company has written down large sums in assets over a long period. Today, however, nearly all companies quote an EBITDA figure and it has become, possibly misguidedly, a common indicator across the board.

EBITDA is used as a financial indicator to analyse a company's core operating profitability. It is a relatively good indicator for providing a profitability comparison between companies. Because it removes large capital investments from analysis, it is also a good tool for comparing profitability trends of companies involved in heavy industry and other business requiring a large capital outlay.

EBITDA is not, however, to be confused with cash flow. Operating cash flow calculations include the changes in working capital that use or provide cash, such as changes in receivables or payables. These changes are a critical part of a cash flow projection, and a vital indicator of the demand for a company's products or services. The changes are not included in EBITDA. The ability of a company to generate cash is a key criterion in appraising that company, so overreliance on EBITDA is unwise.

A more restricted version of EBITDA is EBIT – earnings before interest and tax – which indicates corporate profits as shown on the profit and loss account before the deduction of interest and tax.

Earnings per share (EPS)

Earnings per share is one of the most common indicators used to assess whether a share is under- or overpriced. It is calculated by taking the net profit of a company for a specific period and dividing by the number of ordinary shares outstanding. If a company has after-tax profits of $1 million and 100,000 shares outstanding, the EPS will be $10. The company directors do not have to distribute this amount to shareholders as a dividend, however.

For investors, it is important to know exactly how EPS was calculated in order to judge how effective an indicator it is. Although EPS seems to be straightforward – net earnings divided by shares outstanding – both sides of the equation can be calculated in several different ways, leading to different types of EPS.

Shares outstanding can be taken to mean the number of shares issued and held by investors – the primary EPS – or, more complex, the number of shares outstanding assuming all warrants, options and other instruments capable of conversion into stock were converted – diluted EPS.

Earnings can be manipulated in many ways to produce many different effects. There is the reported earnings figure, derived from the generally accepted accounting principle (GAAP), which is listed in the Securities and Exchange Commission filings. There is EPS based on ongoing net income excluding onetime purchases or expenditures. There is EPS calculated using operating cash flow. And there are others. The important thing is that when using EPS for comparison purposes or evaluation purposes, an individual should be aware which EPS he is comparing or evaluating.

Eastman, George

Founder, Eastman Kodak Company (1854–1932)

The youngest of three children, George Eastman was born in the village of Waterville, 20 miles southwest of Utica, in upstate New York. At age five, Eastman moved with his family to Rochester, where his father pioneered the concept of the business college, establishing Eastman Commercial College. Sadly, his father died unexpectedly and the college failed, leaving the Eastman family in financial straits.

Finishing school at 14, Eastman was forced to get a job to contribute to the family finances. After stints at an insurance firm, Eastman decided to study accounting at home in the evenings to increase his chances of earning more than his salary at the time, which was $5 per week. Five years after starting in insurance, in 1874, his studies paid off when he was offered a position as a junior clerk at the Rochester Savings Bank, with a weekly salary of more than $15.

Eastman's life-changing moment came at the age of 24. He was planning a vacation to Santo Domingo when a colleague suggested making a photographic record of the trip. Eastman bought the bulky equipment needed to take a photograph using state-of-the-art wet-plate technology. The camera was the size of a 21-inch computer monitor and was mounted on a tripod. Then there were the glass plates, chemicals, glass tanks, plate holder and other developing equipment. There was also a tent in which the developing had to take place before the wet plates with the photographic emulsion on them could dry out. To learn how to use all the equipment cost $5 – a week's wages for Eastman only a few years earlier.

Eastman never made it Santo Domingo. Instead, he became obsessed with photography. Before long, he was busy perfecting a dry-plate process in which a photographic plate was covered with a veneer of gelatin emulsion. The emulsion remained sensitive even when it was dry, enabling the plate to be exposed whenever the photographer wished, as opposed to immediately. It was an idea that Eastman had read about in a British magazine. He took the idea, perfected it, and in 1880, after three years of experimentation, patented a dry plate and a machine for mass-producing them. Eastman gave up his job at the bank and at the beginning of 1881 took on a partner, Henry A. Strong.

Quick to recognize the commercial possibilities of his innovation, Eastman leased a building on State Street in Rochester and began to churn out dry plates for other photographers. In 1884, the Eastman Dry Plate and Film Company was incorporated.

It dawned on Eastman that he could do more than make life easier for the professional photographers. He could, in his own words, 'make the camera as convenient as the pencil'. The first advertisements for Kodak film in 1885, however, reveal that he had not yet developed his snappy line in slogans. The early ads stated that 'shortly there will be introduced a new sensitive film which it is believed will prove an economical and convenient substitute for glass dry plates both for outdoor and studio work.'

When Eastman perfected the transparent roll film and roll holder, the days of cumbersome plate photography were numbered. Photography was at last within reach of the amateur. Eastman took a hand in all aspects of promoting his new photographic film. He wrote the ads and came up with the famous slogan: 'You push the button, we do the rest.' He even dreamed up the word 'Kodak', registering the trademark in 1888, and devised the yellow colour scheme associated with it.

The Kodak camera was released in 1888 and before long, Kodak advertising was inescapable. One of the first electric advertising signs in Trafalgar Square, London, bore the legend Kodak. In 1892, the company was renamed the Eastman Kodak company of New York.

Eastman built his business using an enlightened humanitarian management style far removed from that of some of his contemporaries. In 1899, he distributed to his entire workforce a substantial sum from his own pocket. It was the first act of Eastman's 'wage dividend' strategy, a plan to reward employees in proportion to the dividend paid on the company stock. Continuing in the same vein, in 1919 Eastman handed a third of his company holdings – worth some $10 million – to his employees. At the same time, he instituted retirement annuities, life insurance and disability benefits.

George Eastman's philanthropy extended beyond the confines of his corporation. Dental practices, the Massachusetts Institute of Technology (MIT) the city of Rochester – these and many other organizations were recipients of his generosity. On one day alone in 1924, Eastman signed away $30 million to the University of Rochester, MIT, Hampton and Tuskegee. As he laid down the pen he said, 'Now I feel better.'

In his final years, Eastman was plagued by disability resulting from damage to his lower spinal cord. His inability to lead an active life frustrated Eastman so much that he shot himself on 14 March 1932. He was 77.

Eastman took a cumbersome scientific process and turned it into a commercial mass-market product. Through his pioneering and innovative work on photographic technology, Eastman brought the means to capture a moment on film to the general public at a price that they could afford. Eastman was also the father of a particular type of branding: 'Trust what's in the box' branding.

Today, the original Kodak proposition is implicit in the positioning of countless branded gadgets that we now take for granted. With their suggestion that consumers need provide just their imagination to complement its technology, Microsoft's 'Where do you want to go today?' and Intel's 'Intel Inside' are modern echoes of that first Kodak promise. Both draw on Eastman's early inspiration that consumers should trust the brand to take care of the technology side, leaving them free to personalize the product to their own lives.

Like no other slogan, Eastman's captured a turning point in the history of consumerism. Previously, consumers had understood – even if only at a rudimentary level – how the products they bought worked. But in the late nineteenth and early twentieth centuries, an explosion of new inventions – which included the telephone, the electric light bulb and film processing – changed that forever.

Key texts

- Elizabeth Brayer. *George Eastman: A Biography*. Johns Hopkins University Press, 1996

- Douglas Collins. *The Story of Kodak*. Harry N. Abrams, 1990
- Carl W. Ackerman and Edwin R. Seligman. *George Eastman: Founder of Kodak and the Photography Business*. Houghton Mifflin Co., 1930

Key links
- www.kodak.com
- www.eastman.org/2_aboutge/2_index.htm
- www.digitalcentury.com/encyclo/update/eastman.html

E*banners

E*banners are a rich-media form of the standard **GIF** advertising banners used on the Internet. The creation of online market solution-provider BlueStreak, e*banner stands for 'expanding banner'. When a user clicks on an e*banner, the ad enlarges to fill more of the browser window. Once the large window is open, the advertiser can load in promotions, surveys or whatever other type of marketing tool is preferred.

E-business and e-commerce

E-business (electronic business) and e-commerce (electronic commerce) are often used interchangeably but, in fact, have different meanings. Electronic business is the interaction between two or more parties for the purpose of conducting business where the interaction is via an electronic channel mediated by a computer. E-business is conducted through a variety of channels, including video phones, interactive television and the Internet. Generally, e-business is taken to have a wider definition than e-commerce, embracing aspects of business such as marketing, PR and accounting, in addition to the sale and purchase of goods and services.

E-commerce, on the other hand, is generally accepted to mean conducting business online, although there is some confusion over the definition of e-commerce and the relationship between e-commerce and e-business. It is, however, generally accepted that e-commerce is a class of e-business and refers to the transaction of business, and more narrowly, the sale and purchase of goods and services using networked computers. This usually means the Internet, although e-commerce may be conducted over private networks or intranets. E-commerce can fall into a number of classifications. Two of the main categories are B2C – business to consumer – and B2B – business-to-business.

Economies of scale

Economies of scale occur where the average cost of production, and therefore the unit cost, decreases as output increases. If output increased by a factor of two, for example, the cost of production would increase by less than a factor of two. Economies of scale are categorized as internal and external. Internal economies of scale include automation, specialization and bulk-purchasing power. External economies of scale are those that affect an economy, geographical region, or industry as a whole and include general technological advances and industrial clusters.

EDI (electronic data interchange)

The electronic data interchange is a system for managing business-to-business transactions, such as invoicing and ordering, to eliminate the wastefulness of paper-based transaction systems. The standards that govern EDI have been developed over 20 years by the Accredited Standards Committee (ASC) X12, paving the way for worldwide e-commerce. To date, more than 300,000 companies have incorporated EDI into their business operations.

Key link
- http://www.x12.org

Edison, Thomas Alva

Inventor and entrepreneur (1847–1931)

'Genius is one percent inspiration and ninety-nine percent perspiration,' declared Thomas Alva Edison, the American inventor and entrepreneur. It was a maxim Edison clearly lived by. By the end of his extraordinary career, Edison had accumulated 1093 US patents and 1300 foreign patents. The inventor of the phonograph and the incandescent light bulb also found time to start up or control 13 major companies. His endeavours directly or indirectly led to the creation of well-known corporations like General Electric and RCA. Consolidated Edison is still listed on the New York Stock Exchange.

Of Dutch and Scottish extraction, Edison was born in the town of Milan, Ohio. The youngest of seven children, he was effectively an only child as his siblings were much older. His schoolteacher mother was loath to let the young Edison out of her sight and conducted the majority of his education at home.

He was a prodigious reader: he devoured Newton's *Principia Mathematica*, Parker's *Natural and Experimental Philosophy* and Gibbons's *Decline and Fall of the Roman Empire* before the age of twelve. It was a pattern that continued as Edison embarked on a lifetime of discovery and self-tuition.

Telegraphy turned out to be the catalyst for Edison's greatness. Edison was a natural with the Morse key, one of the fastest transcribers of his day. As a night-duty telegrapher, Edison was required to key the number six every hour to confirm he was still manning the wire. Instead, he invented a machine that automatically keyed the number for him and spent the nights indulging himself at the local hostelries. Fired from a succession of jobs, he crossed the United States working as a freelance telegrapher. He passed through Louisville, Kentucky; Memphis, Tennessee; Nashville, Tennessee and Boston, Massachusetts before finally coming to rest in New York. He had by this time filed his first patent – an automatic vote recorder for the Massachusetts Legislature.

It was in New York that Edison formed his first partnership with Frank L. Pope, a noted telegraphic engineer, to exploit their inventions. The partnership was subsequently absorbed by Gold & Stock, a company controlled by Marshall Lefferts, former president of the American Telegraph Company. Lefferts paid $20,000 to the two partners for the privilege. Recognizing Edison's ingenuity, Lefferts conducted a side deal with Edison, securing Edison's independent patents for the then princely sum of $30,000.

In 1870, with the benefit of some financial security, Edison hired the talents of Charles Batchelor, an English mathematician, and the Swiss machinist John Kruesi. He signed patent agreements with Gold & Stock and Western Union, took on a business partner, William Unger, moved into a four-storey building on Ward Street in Newark, New Jersey, and started inventing on a grand scale. The fertile mix of minds at Ward Street quickly produced a stock printer, quadruplex telegraphy and a machine to enable the rapid decoding of Morse.

By 1876, the 29-year-old Edison had 45 inventions to his name and was worth some $400,000. Edison was notorious for his devotion to seeking a solution to the problem at hand. Not only would he work, sleep and eat on the company premises, he would lock the lab doors and tell his staff they were staying until they arrived at an answer.

The 1870s were the most creative phase of Edison's life. Needing to expand his premises, he moved into buildings in Menlo Park, 24 miles from New York City. It was in Menlo Park that Edison and his team perfected the phonograph.

Barely pausing to draw breath, Edison invented on. In early 1877, he began to experiment with incandescent filaments and glass bulbs. He persuaded a consortium that he could produce a commercially viable lighting system based on such a product, though in reality he was far from developing it. As a result, he signed a rights and remuneration agreement that laid the foundation for the Edison Electric Light Company.

It was on Wednesday, 12 November 1879 that Edison finally lit a bulb that lasted long enough to be considered of commercial value. It lasted for 40 hours and 20 minutes and within two months, Edison had extended its longevity to 600 hours. Countless visitors trekked to Menlo Park to gaze in wonder at the lights that lit the roadway. Sadly, what followed for Edison was not the triumph of invention but a period of protracted patent litigation that lasted over ten years.

The invention of the light bulb and formation of the Edison Electric Light Company marks the pinnacle of Edison's achievements. In the years that followed, a succession of new innovations emerged: DC generators; the first electric lighting system; electrical metering systems; alkaline storage batteries; cement manufacturing equipment; synchronized sound and moving pictures; and submarine detection by sound. His labs also threw off a slew of great minds, most notably Nikola Tesla, famed for his work on the Tesla coil and AC induction motors. The wizard of Menlo Park, however, never quite recaptured the brilliance of his earlier years. Edison died, working to the last on Sunday, 18 October 1931.

Part of Edison's genius lay in the realization that innovation alone was insufficient for commercial success. Edison focused on creating a commercially viable product. To do so, he assembled a team of brilliant minds at Menlo Park. In effect, he created the first product research lab – a forerunner of facilities such as the celebrated Xerox PARC in Palo Alto, California. It was a practical and commercial approach to invention that proved immensely successful.

Edison's pragmatism also extended to patenting his ideas. He understood the value of intellectual property and the importance of being able to assert ownership of ideas. A legend in his own lifetime, Edison's achievements were acknowledged shortly before his death in a nationwide celebration attended by luminaries such as President Hoover, Henry Ford, John Rockefeller and George Eastman. Thousands filed past Edison's coffin to pay their final tributes. Edison remains an inspiration for inventors and entrepreneurs to this day.

Key texts
- Paul Israel. *Edison: A Life of Invention*. John Wiley, 1998
- Neil Baldwin. *Edison: Inventing the Century*. Hyperion, 1995
- Andre Millard. *Edison and the Business of Innovation*. Johns Hopkins University Press, 1990
- Reese V. Jenkins *et al.* (eds). *The Papers of Thomas A. Edison*. Johns Hopkins University Press, 1989
- Matthew Josephson. *Edison: A Biography*. McGraw-Hill, 1959
- G.S. Bryan. *Edison: The Man and His Work*. Alfred A. Knopf, 1926

Key links
- www.conedison.com
- http://edison.rutgers.edu
- http://edison.ladygayle.com

EDventure

EDventure is the home of **Esther Dyson**'s online business, including *Release 1.0*, the respected newsletter for the computer industry. Dyson is something of an information guru. Internet pioneer, venture capitalist and an adviser to governments and leaders including as Bill Clinton and **Bill Gates**, Dyson is a Renaissance woman.

Release 1.0, the monthly report from EDventure, takes a look at what is going to change the world and who will make it happen. The report's style is witty and informative and it is renowned for the accuracy of its crystal-ball gazing. Dyson is editor and an occasional contributor to the magazine, which is managed by Kevin Werbach.

Key link
- www.edventure.com

EEA (European Economic Area)

The EEA is an agreement that extends the benefits of the single European market to three of the four non-EU **EFTA** states – Norway, Iceland and Liechtenstein. The agreement, which created a zone of economic cooperation between member states of the European Union (EU) and the European Free Trade Association (EFTA), entered into force in 1994. Switzerland, though a member of EFTA, rejected membership of the EEA in a referendum in 1992 (and also continued to reject membership of the EU in a referendum in March 2001).

The EEA makes up a market of some 380 million consumers, accounting for 18 percent of world imports and 20 percent of world exports, excluding intra-EEA trade. The effect of the EEA is to join the EU states and the three EEA EFTA states into a single market, bound by the same rules underpinned by the four freedoms: free movement of goods, capital, services and persons.

Key link
- http://www.eeassoc.org

EFTA (European Free Trade Association)

The European Free Trade Association was established in 1960 and consists of Iceland, Norway, Switzerland and (as of 1991) Liechtenstein, previously a non-voting associate member. Three of the members – Iceland, Liechtenstein and Norway – are also members of the **European Economic Area**. Through the EEA, the remaining EFTA members share in the common market enjoyed by the EU. Switzerland prefers to negotiate bilateral treaties with its EU trade partners.

The four EFTA countries have a high per capita income. Based on 1999 figures, their combined GDP was equivalent to 5 percent of the combined EU GDP.

Of the original EFTA members, Britain and Denmark left in 1972 to join the European Community (EC), as did Portugal in 1985. Austria, Finland and Sweden joined the European Union (EU) in 1995.

Key link
- www.efta.int/structure/main/index.html

EGM (Extraordinary General Meeting)

An EGM is a general meeting held by a company that isn't an Annual General Meeting. EGMs may be called by directors or shareholders with sufficiently large holdings. Departing auditors also have the right to call an EGM. Examples of matters dealt with at EGMs include approving a rights issue or voting on director's appointments.

Eisner, Michael Dammann
Disney chairman and CEO (b. 1942)

Michael Eisner, chairman and CEO of Disney, is what the famous company had lacked for many years: a true successor to Walt. When Eisner joined Disney as chairman and chief executive, along with Frank Wells as president and COO, in 1984, the entertainment colossus was struggling. Eisner and Wells resurrected the magic kingdom. Eisner's insight was that Disney is in the family entertainment business in all of its manifestations. The Disney brand was stretched to encompass a mountain of merchandising, stores, books, videos, games, movies and theme parks. Eisner's other claim to fame is the size of his pay cheque.

The big cheese that made the mouse roar, Eisner breathed life into a moribund Disney when he arrived in 1984 with his own personal management team. Born during World War II, he got an early taste of the entertainment business when, still a student, he spent three months as a clerk at NBC studios.

By 1966, Eisner had obtained a job working as Barry Diller's assistant at ABC (Diller was to become one of the most respected executives in the entertainment business). ABC proved an excellent training ground for the ambitious Eisner, who became involved in all aspects of the television business. In 1968, he turned down a job offer from advertising agency Foote, Cone & Belding but recommended one of his superiors, who landed the job. Eisner promptly took the position that had been vacated.

Diller, meanwhile, had been promoted to work on a partnership with Universal Studios to produce made-for-television movies. In 1969, Eisner joined him as director of feature films and programme development. In 1971, Eisner became head of daytime and children's programming at ABC. Daytime television improved considerably under his control. After developing several new shows, he was back in prime-time development – this time as vice-president. In 1973, he decided to move out to Los Angeles. After a string of successes, including *Happy Days* and *Starsky & Hutch*, Eisner was headhunted by Barry Diller, now at Paramount, and offered the job of president of Paramount. Eisner was only 34.

Between 1977 and 1982, profits at Paramount increased from $30 million to more than $100 million, largely due to the new culture of aggressive, creative risk taking introduced under Diller and Eisner. Hit TV shows such as *Taxi* and *Mork & Mindy*, together with films such as *Saturday Night Fever*, *Elephant Man*, *Grease*, *Star Trek*, *Ordinary People*, *Airplane* and *Raiders of the Lost Ark*, brought the dollars flooding into the Paramount coffers. In 1984, after some political in-fighting at Paramount, Eisner, by now one of the top film executives in the country, moved on to become CEO of Disney.

When Eisner joined Disney in 1984, the company was in the doldrums. Eisner set about transforming the declining film and theme park company into an entertainment giant. Key to this transformation was an injection of new blood in the form of Jeffrey Katzenberg, still in his early thirties.

Under the labels Touchstone Pictures and Hollywood Pictures, Katzenberg approved a string of hit feature films, including *Down and Out in Beverly Hills* and *Three Men and a Baby*, the latter grossing more than $100 million at the box office, the first Disney film ever to do so. Out of their first 17 films, 15 made money.

Eisner, with his tremendous experience in television, also rejuvenated Disney's TV output, with top 10 shows such as *Ellen* and *Home Improvement*. Eisner and Disney were firing on all fronts. Eisner repackaged classic Disney animation for home video. Titles such as *Bambi*, *Cinderella* and the more modern *Aladdin* and *The Lion King* elevated Disney to the number-one Hollywood studio in home-video sales.

By the early 1990s, Disney, now trading as the more corporate-sounding Walt Disney Company instead of Walt Disney Productions, was posting revenues of more than $5 billion and profits close to $1 billion. The days of Disney built on the fortunes of a small mouse were long gone. From 1985 through 1990, the company posted record profits for 20 quarters in a row.

It was only in the mid-1990s that the Disney magic began to lose a little of its sparkle. Although Eisner pulled off a major coup when he acquired the ABC broadcast network, this was counterbalanced by a spectacular and acrimonious falling-out with Katzenberg, his longtime co-worker at both Paramount and Disney. A little later, Eisner had more executive problems when he hired Mike Ovitz, the talent agent, as his number two, only to see him depart just over a year later.

On top of the problems following Katzenberg's departure, Eisner also had to handle the ongoing saga of Disney America. The proposed site for the park, outside the town of Haymarket, Virginia was blocked by some of the richest families in the United States, who lived in the area. Then, to cap it all off, he had to undergo bypass surgery.

Eisner's troubles were reflected in the balance sheet, with a 28 percent drop in profits from 1998 to 1999. But by 2000, Disney was back on track with a profit of $1.9 billion on revenues of $25 billion. Eisner profited personally from Disney's recovery with a rise in his base salary from $750,000 to $1 million, securing his position as one of the highest-paid CEOs in America.

Key texts

- Ron Grover. *The Disney Touch: How a Daring Management Team Revived an Entertainment Empire*. Business One Irwin, 1991

- Joe Flower. *Prince of the Magic Kingdom: Michael Eisner and the Re-Making of Disney*. John Wiley, 1991
- Michael Eisner with Tony Schwartz. *Work in Progress*. Random House, 1988

Key links
- w w w . f o r b e s . c o m / 2 0 0 1 / 0 1 / 1 6/ 0116faceseisner.html
- www.webcom.com/chotank/disneyrom.html
- www.hollywood.com/celebs/bio/celeb/345118

Elasticity of demand

Elasticity of demand is a measure of the change in demand in response to a change in price, income or any other factor. Price elasticity, for example, is calculated by dividing the percentage change in price by the percentage change in demand.

A good with a price elasticity of greater than one is said to be price-elastic: any change in price will result in a relatively larger change in demand. Luxury goods usually fall into this category; thus, a rise in the price of vacations will result in a fall in demand. In one study, restaurant meals were found to have a price elasticity of 2.3.

A good with a price elasticity of less than one is said to be price-inelastic: any change in price will result in a relatively smaller change in demand. Essential goods usually fall into this category; thus a rise in the price of bread will result in a relatively smaller change in demand and therefore an increase in revenue. In the same study, salt was found to have a price elasticity of 0.1.

Elasticity of supply

Elasticity of supply is the measurement of the change in quantity supplied in response to a change in price. Elasticity of supply is calculated by dividing quantity supplied by percentage change in price. Where the value of elasticity of supply is positive, an increase in price is likely to lead to an increase in supply. Factors that determine the elasticity of supply include spare capacity, which allows for an increase in output without a commensurate increase in costs; inventory, since high levels of stock mean a company can more easily meet an increase in demand; and time, since a longer period available for adjustment means a company can more easily respond to an increase in demand.

Where a shift in the demand curve has no effect on the equilibrium quantity supplied, supply is said to be perfectly inelastic. Theoretically, in this situation, a company can sell an unlimited amount of a good or service at the same price.

Elevator pitch

'Elevator pitch' is the term given to pitching a business proposal in a very short period of time, i.e. as long as it takes to ride in an elevator. Making an elevator pitch was a popular method of pitching movies in Hollywood during the high-concept movie period in the 1980s. The **venture capital** industry appropriated the term and transferred it to Silicon Valley and the venture capital/Internet start-up phenomenon of the 1990s. At the height of the Internet boom, venture capitalists had very little time and the entrepreneur had to be able to pitch his idea wherever an opportunity presented itself. As David Ishag, of the US Internet investment firm Idealab, once put it: 'Plans have to be light as a feather. You have to be able to make your case in an elevator – and I'm talking about an elevator in a very low building.'

Ellison, Larry

Founder and CEO, Oracle Corp. (b. 1944)

Larry Ellison was raised on Chicago's South Side. The neighbourhood is one of the toughest in the United States, yet Ellison says he was unaware that it was a 'bad neighbourhood' until some years after he left.

Ellison's childhood dream was to become an architect. Gifted at math and science, he went to the University of Chicago to study math. While in college, he taught himself to program a computer. Then, like computer billionaire **Bill Gates**, Ellison dropped out of school and, in 1967, headed for California and the nascent computer industry. Arriving armed with little more than his self-taught computing skills, Ellison took a job as a computer programmer.

It was Ellison's good fortune to obtain a job with the company Amdahl. Founded by Gene Amdahl, the company was 45 percent owned by Fujitsu. This gave Ellison the opportunity to travel to Japan on business. It was a trip that was to change Ellison's perspective on life and have a long-lasting influence on his approach to business.

Ellison was intrigued by the apparent contradictions: The Japanese were both aggressive and yet incredibly polite; they were arrogant, yet humble. He was also interested in the emphasis placed on the group rather than the individual. This attitude, the antithesis of individualistic entrepreneurial America, pervaded Japanese corporations and society. Ellison's observations of Japan made a profound impression on him.

In 1976, IBM developed SQL (pronounced 'sequel'), a computer language for accessing databases. Popular opinion at that time said that database programs were not commercially viable. Ellison didn't agree. He was quick to recognize the commercial possibilities. If he moved fast, he thought he could beat IBM to market with a database product.

Ellison is not a man to doubt his instincts. He sought financing for a new company that would specialize in databases. The venture capitalists were less enthusiastic than Ellison about the prospects of his new business. 'They wouldn't even meet with you,' said Ellison of the VCs, 'they would just leave you waiting in the waiting room for 45 minutes, until you finally got the idea they were not going to see you. And then the receptionist would search your briefcase to make sure you were not stealing copies of *BusinessWeek* from the

coffee table. We were *persona non grata* in the venture capital community.'

Frustrated, Ellison, along with partners Bob Miner and Ed Oates, invested $2000 of their own money in the start-up. The company was named System Development Laboratories and later renamed the Oracle Corporation. The company's first product was two years in the making, with Ellison and his colleagues supporting themselves through consulting work.

Once news got out about Oracle's new software, the company never looked back. Profitable from day one, in the period up to 2000, the company only lost money for one quarter, in 1990. Ellison's company grew at an incredible rate. When the company was taken public in March 1986, revenues were some $55 million. By 1989, when the company moved to its new campus-style location in Redwood Shores, California, revenues were $571 million.

Ellison's success and that of Oracle have been built on the strength of the product coupled with an aggressive pursuit of market share. Ellison recalls that his attitude to competitors was informed by his experiences in Japan. On a business trip, Ellison talked to a Japanese executive about competition. 'We believe,' said the executive, 'that our competitors are stealing the rice out of the mouths of our children. In Japan, we think anything less than 100 percent market share is not enough. In Japan, we believe it is not sufficient that I succeed; everyone else must fail. We must destroy our competition.' After recounting the tale to a newspaper reporter, Ellison was greeted with a story featuring his picture accompanied by the words, 'It's not sufficient that I succeed; everyone else must fail.'

Whether or not Ellison needed any lessons in competitive drive is a moot point. Ellison's competitive instincts appear to be well developed. Oracle has for the most part shown itself unwilling to peacefully coexist with its rivals, and has ruthlessly capitalized on its market position.

One element of corporate make-up Ellison did adopt from the Japanese is his fervour for building a team culture. Ellison has said that he would 'never hire anybody you wouldn't enjoy having lunch with three times a week.' If everyone at Oracle gets along, Ellison figures, there will be less destructive internal conflict. This is one of Ellison's greatest strengths – an innate understanding of what motivates people and makes them tick.

In his private life, Ellison has always liked to live life to the fullest. He has flown fast planes, driven fast cars and sailed fast yachts. A good tennis player and a man who likes to be seen with attractive women, Ellison's playboy lifestyle has proved a target for critics, who have accused him of neglecting his corporate responsibilities.

It is a charge that underestimates Ellison's commitment to his business empire. His shrewd business mind is illustrated by his decision in the mid-1990s to refocus the company away from its emphasis on client-server products in favour of products that can run via a browser over the Internet. Ellison virtually bet the company on his vision when Oracle abandoned its flagship software product: the client-server version of Oracle Applications. Ellison's comment was: 'If the Internet turns out not to be the future of computing, we're toast. But if it is, we're golden.'

To date, Oracle8i, the company's new Internet database software, has sold well and, although Oracle was hit along with other tech companies by the slowdown in 2000 and 2001, Ellison continues to vie with Bill Gates for the title of the richest man in the world.

Key text
- Mike Wilson. *The Difference Between God & Larry Ellison: Inside Oracle Corporation*. William Morrow, 1997

Key links
- www.oracle.com
- www.askmen.com/men/may00/24_larry_ellison.html

Emoticon

An emoticon (short for 'emotional icon') is a symbol used in text messages, particularly in e-mail, to signify emotions in a shorthand form. They are useful for avoiding misinterpretation of words in the absence of non-verbal communication such as facial expressions and body gestures. Commonly used emoticons include:

- :-) (happiness or amusement)
- :-Q (confusion)
- :-O (surprise)

In addition to emoticons, a range of acronyms are used to convey meaning in an abbreviated form. These include the ubiquitous IMHO (in my humble opinion), FWIW (for what it's worth) and <L> (laughing).

Key link
- www.emoticon.com

Emotional intelligence/EQ

See Goleman, Daniel.

Employability

Employability is the concept of making employees more employable through continuous learning, training and the development of transferable skills.

This is intended to compensate the employee for short-term contracts and job insecurity. Employability is based on four elements: assets (knowledge, skills and personal attributes); self-promotion and marketing skills; the ability to present an individual's assets; and the individual's ability to use his assets, governed to a degree by external circumstances. The concept was partly as a compensatory response to the widespread downsizing of the 1980s and early 1990s.

Key text
- Richard Pascale. The False Security of 'Employability'. *Fast Company* (2), page 62, April 1996

Employee

An employee is anyone employed under a contract of service to work for some form of payment for an employer (a person or business that makes a payment to another person in exchange for the services of that person).

Payment includes salary, commission and piece rates. Distinguishing between someone who is employed and someone who is self-employed is important in some instances for tax purposes. An employee/employer relationship is suggested in situations in which there is a written agreement to that effect, the employer directs the method of work, the employer provides tools and equipment and the employee is bound to the employer and cannot offer his services elsewhere. The key test is that of control and direction: the employer controls the employee in both the method of carrying out the work as well as the result to be accomplished.

An employee is not someone who performs services in the capacity of an independent contractor. An independent contractor controls the manner of his work – when, where and how he carries out that work.

Empty market share

The accusation levelled against Eckhard Pfeiffer when he was ousted as CEO of Compaq Computer was that he mistook size for success. He established, said one commentator, 'empty market share', meaning that the company became bigger and bigger without organizing itself to reap the economies of scale its size required. The lesson here: profits come before size.

Key text
- D. Kirkpatrick. 'Eckhard's Gone but the PC Rocks On.' *Fortune* (139:10), 1999, pp.153–160

End-game strategies

End-game strategies are a number of strategies that can be adopted when a product, service, division or company begins to falter and come to the end of its lifespan. One strategy is to squeeze as much from the product or service in the time remaining by slashing prices to boost sales and cutting the marketing budget to reduce costs. An alternative strategy is to manoeuvre the product or service into a niche market in order to sustain revenues, even if at a lower level. The term is derived from the alternative courses of action available in the final phase of a game of chess – the end-game.

End user

The end user of product or service is usually the one who requires the product in a workable, defect-free condition. End-user computing, for example, is the use of an application or information service not programmed by the user on a computer. Spreadsheets, word processing and desktop publishing are all popular end-user activities. End users tend to have less technical expertise. Computer developers, for example, are not end users of the products they develop.

Entrepreneur

'Entrepreneur' comes from the French for 'one who undertakes'. An entrepreneur is a person who spots an opportunity to start a business, by creating a new product or offering a new service, for example, and then successfully manages and develops the enterprise through personal skill and initiative. Examples include **John D. Rockefeller**, **Henry Ford**, **Anita Roddick** and **Richard Branson**.

Entrepreneurs have become increasingly important and celebrated during the 1990s. Why? The obvious answer is the spectacular wealth that has accrued to a few individuals. High-tech entrepreneurs like Microsoft's **Bill Gates** and e-Bay founder **Pierre Omidyar** have become rich beyond the imagination of ordinary people. They have become icons.

Their success has spawned imitators, which contributed to the dotcom frenzy. At the height of the gold rush, the entrepreneurial road to riches seemed open to all. For many, we now know, that was a mirage. Many fledgling entrepreneurs have fallen back to earth with a bump. Dotcom millionaires are now an endangered species. But interest in entrepreneurship has not dissipated – far from it. The dotcom crash has focused more attention than ever on the factors that give rise to entrepreneurs and entrepreneurial activity.

There are three possible underlying reasons that entrepreneurship will remain important.

- Wealth creation is increasingly linked to entrepreneurial activity. The future wealth of nations depends on individuals creating new enterprises. Entrepreneurs are essential to economic vitality. They stimulate job creation and play a vital role in the restructuring of industries and whole economies.
- There is a growing recognition that tapping into the entrepreneurial spirit is vital for the long-term viability of established companies. This has focused attention on the role of intrapreneurs – employees who operate within large companies to drive innovation and create new revenue streams. Corporate venturing – companies investing in new business start-ups – is also a growth area.
- There is growing interest in entrepreneurship at the level of the individual. Growing numbers of young people now want to run their own businesses or join start-ups.

The truth is that entrepreneurship has been gaining momentum since the late 1960s. Over the last three decades, the growth in new firm creation, in the United States in particular, has been striking. In the 1950s, approximately 200,000 new US firms were created every year. By the mid-1970s, that number had trebled to 600,000 start-ups per annum. By 1994, it had reached 1.2 million, and by 1996 it had soared to around 3.5 million.

The entrepreneurial trend is not confined to America. Outside the United States, the countries with the highest per capita levels of entrepreneurial start-up activity include Brazil, Australia, Canada, Argentina, Norway and South Korea.

The dotcom gold rush didn't start in earnest until after 1996. Fuelling it was a huge growth in the **venture capital** industry – another significant factor in the new-found interest in entrepreneurs. VC investment in the United States rose from around $3 billion in 1990 to at least $37 billion in 1999, and recorded a further 76 percent increase to $60 billion in 2000. In Europe in 1999, a record $24 billion of venture capital was invested (half of it by the UK VC industry).

The rise of the VC industry itself is based on traditional capitalist principles. Superior return on investment has ensured a plentiful supply of capital. But entrepreneurial activity is no longer confined to making money. A new breed of so-called 'social entrepreneurs' is applying entrepreneurial practices to addressing social issues. They are moving the provision of support for the socially disadvantaged away from the begging-bowl approach to one that pays its way.

In their report on the state of entrepreneurship in 2001, business writers Stuart Crainer and Des Dearlove identified a number of common characteristics shared by entrepreneurs:

- **Energy and enthusiasm:** Entrepreneurs are dynamic, restless creators. They buzz. 'I always run through the office,' says Amazon's Jeff Bezos. 'I mean physically I'm a little bit hyperkinetic. That's why I like this environment.'
- **More than money:** Entrepreneurs who succeed rarely start off with the sole intention of making money. They want to change the world, solve a problem or maximize the potential of their brilliant idea. Money is a welcome by-product of success.
- **Communicating the essence:** Entrepreneurs possess an ability to focus energy and thinking on the issues, trends, and people that really matter. They channel energy into the essence of what is important.

- **Maximizing technology:** Entrepreneurs regard technology as a tool. It is a tool to make money, have a better quality of life and enjoy yourself. Entrepreneurs see technology in an entirely practical light.
- **Failing persistently:** Failure is increasingly recognized as an essential part of personal and professional development because, simply, it provides learning. Entrepreneurs recognize that, though painful, failure is good for you.
- **Constant learning:** More than ever before, education equals money. In the new economy, it pays to have an education. Where once entrepreneurs pooh-poohed a formal business education, they are now trained to the max.
- **The human touch:** Entrepreneurs value the human dimension. They ooze empathy, easily and effortlessly. Previous generations just paid lip service to the idea, but entrepreneurs know that people make the difference. Their greatest commitment is to their immediate colleagues and staff. Entrepreneurs are 'people' people.

Entrepreneur.com

The fact that entrepreneur.com is one of the most extensive and frequently visited sites on the Internet is a measure of the entrepreneurial spirit at large in the business world. The company's Web site has over 500,000 unique users and racks up more than 3 million page views a month.

As you might expect, entrepreneur.com's content is aimed at would-be dotcom millionaires. But it's not simply a site for dotcom start-ups. It offers interesting and practical information for anyone thinking of, or in the process of, starting a business.

In April 2000, entrepreneur.com overhauled, redesigned and relaunched its Web site. Content on the site is both wide-ranging and deep. Business travellers can check out the 'Quick Guide to Business Travel', for example, and learn how to make their travel budgets stretch a little further. Executives in unchallenging, comfortable jobs dithering about joining the free-agent society

can consult a motivation expert to help them take those first steps to relinquishing the company car.

Elsewhere, there are areas where you can chat online to other businesspeople and experts. You can use the onsite search facility to search through a list of *Entrepreneur* magazine's 100 Best Web Sites For Small Business. And, should you need to buy anything, head for the marketplace, where you can even locate vacant office space to start the next Microsoft or Amazon.

Key link
- www.entrepreneur.com

Equity capital

Equity capital is capital derived from the issue of ordinary and preference shares by a limited company. The word 'equity', which means equal, is used because each share entitles its holder to one vote, to a share of the profits of the company, and to any assets remaining when a company is wound up.

Ergonomics

Ergonomics is derived from the Greek *ergon* – work – and *nomoi* – natural laws. It refers to the study of the relationship between people and the furniture, tools and machinery they use at work.

A mismatch between the physical capabilities of the employee and the demands of a job may result in one of a number of musculoskeletal disorders (MSDs). Commonly reported work-related MSDs include back problems, carpal tunnel syndrome, tendonitis, vibration white finger and repetitive strain injury. These types of injury are usually caused or aggravated by stress on the body through repeated activities like bending, lifting, pushing and stretching.

Through the study of ergonomics in the workplace, work performance can be improved and musculoskeletal disorders reduced by implementing company-wide programmes to remove sources of muscular stress and general fatigue; for example, by presenting data and control panels in easy-to-view form, making office furniture comfortable and creating a generally pleasant environment.

Key links
- www.iea.cc/
- www.cdc.gov/niosh/ergopage.html
- www.hse.gov.uk/hthdir/noframes/musculo.htm

ERP (enterprise resource planning)

Traditionally, each department in a company – finance, marketing, etc. – would have its own computer software, separate from and often incompatible with any other department. Enterprise resource planning software is a business management system that integrates all aspects of the business. Sales, finance, quality control, accounting, manufacturing and all other enterprise functions are integrated and managed, usually with the aid of a collection of software applications. ERP has been extended to cover the entire value chain, from supplier to customer. This is known as **supply chain management**. With ERP, each department still has its own software or software modules. The difference is that they can now communicate with each other, as they are all part of the same system.

Key text
- Murrell G. Shields. *E-Business & ERP: Rapid Implementation & Project Planning*. John Wiley & Sons, 2000

Key link
- www.cio.com/research/erp

Escalation clause

An escalation clause is a provision in a contract that allows for an increase in price, of a contrac-

tor's goods and/or services for example, in the case of certain events. Such a clause is common in contracts that cover long periods of time, as an escalation clause can protect a contractor against the effects of inflation. Thus a rental contract could be drawn up so that the rent increases in step with any increase in the inflation rate.

Similarly, escalation clauses can be written into publishing contracts to provide for an increase in royalties if sales reach a certain level. Understandably, they are not popular with publishers.

ESOPs (employee share-ownership programmes)

Employee share-ownership programmes are a means by which a company can reward its employees. The company that wishes to distribute shares forms the ESOP, which then purchases the required number of company shares. The shares are then distributed to the employees. The advantage of distributing shares in this way is that the company's share capital is not diluted.

The difficulties with ESOPs arise when a company has operations in several different countries. As legislation regarding tax, share ownership and accounting varies from country to country, implementing an ESOP becomes a complex matter. The problems may be worth overcoming, however, as there are suggestions that ESOPs help build company loyalty among the workforce by providing employees with an active interest in the financial fortunes of the company that employees them. There is also some anecdotal evidence that ESOPs help raise a company's value in the market.

Ethernet

Ethernet is the most widely used **local area network** technology in the world. The most common version permits data transfer at rates up to 10 Mbps. However, it is fast being superseded by the 100 Mbps Fast Ethernet – often called 100Base-T – which is already in widespread use, while 1000

Mbps Gigabit Ethernet systems are being introduced. Ethernet, Fast Ethernet and Gigabit Ethernet are all IEEE standards.

The first Ethernet system was developed by Bob Metcalfe (founder of 3Com) and David Boggs while working at the Xerox Palo Alto Research Center (PARC) during the 1970s. In 1976, Metcalfe and Boggs published the ground-breaking paper 'Ethernet: Distributed Packet Switching for Local Computer Networks'. In 1979, Digital Equipment Corporation, Intel and Xerox joined forces to standardize the Ethernet, releasing the first standard specification in 1980.

Key texts

- Seth Kenvin. 'Networking With Bob Metcalfe.' *Red Herring*, November 1994
- Bob Metcalfe, David Walden and Peter H. Salus. *Packet Communication*. Peer to Peer, 1996

Ethical investment

Ethical investment, also known as socially responsible investment, is investment based on ethical, social, environmental, and moral considerations rather than solely financial criteria.

The first ethical unit trust in the United States was the Pax World Fund, set up in 1971. The first in the United Kingdom, the Friends Provident Stewardship Fund, was set up in 1984. But the origins of the socially responsible investment movement goes back further than the 1970s, to the Quaker and Methodist movements of the nineteenth century.

Today, ethical investment is big business. In the United Kingdom, the value of investments in more than 50 retail ethical funds grew from £199.3 million in 1989 to £3.7 billion in 2000.

Ethical investment funds invest only in companies that meet their ethical criteria. The criteria might, for example, prohibit investment in tobacco companies, arms manufacturers, nuclear power stations, areas of the world where there are repressive regimes, and companies that engage in animal experimentation. Investment might be encouraged in companies that have good energy conservation policies, are open about their activities, have an established safety record and generally behave in an environmentally responsible manner.

The theory behind ethical investment is that an increase in ethical investment will in turn reward socially responsible companies.

EU (European Union)

The European Union is a political and economic grouping with 15 countries as member states. The 15 members consist of the six original members – Belgium, France, (West) Germany, Italy, Luxembourg, and the Netherlands – plus the United Kingdom, Denmark, the Republic of Ireland, Greece, Spain, Portugal, Austria, Finland and Sweden (which joined in that order). East Germany was incorporated on German reunification in 1990.

The origins of the EU lie in the European Community (EC), which was made up of the European Coal and Steel Community (set up by the 1951 Treaty of Paris), the European Economic Community, and the European Atomic Energy Community (both set up by the 1957 Treaties of Rome).

Following intergovernmental arrangements for a common foreign and security policy and for increased cooperation on justice and home affairs policy issues set out in the Maastricht Treaty (1992), the EU superseded the EC in 1993.

The basic aims of the EU are to foster trade cooperation and expansion of trade, abolish restrictive economic practices and encourage the free movement of capital, labour and goods, as well as the establishment of a closer union among the members of the EU.

To this end, twelve member states abolished the legal use of their national currencies and instead adopted a single currency, the euro, which became the sole legal tender as of 28 February 2002.

Key link

- http://europa.eu.int/index_en.htm

Evans, Philip

Senior vice-president, Boston Consulting Group; co-leader of BCG's practice focused on the new economics of information

Philip Evans has a glittering academic record. He graduated from Cambridge University with a Double First Class Honours in economics and followed up as a Harkness Fellow in the economics department at Harvard and with an **MBA** (honors) from the Harvard Business School.

Co-author of the book *Blown to Bits: How the New Economics of Information Transforms Strategy* (1999), Evans's work on the new economics of information and the deconstruction of traditional strategy has earned him a number of accolades. As co-author of the *Harvard Business Review* article 'Strategy and the New Economics of Information', Evans was awarded a McKinsey Prize in 1997 for the best contribution to the *Review*.

Evans is a pioneer in thinking strategically about the central business challenge of the coming decade: the seismic confrontation between the old economy and the new. Practitioners in the 'old' economy need to abandon their traditional assumptions about information channels and the relationships, hierarchies and organizational boundaries that they create.

Practitioners in the 'new' economy need to move beyond experimentation and growth for their own sake to a hard-edged focus on competitive advantage. Evans's award-winning writings on the new economics of information and the deconstruction of traditional strategy provide the unifying principles that enable both groups to understand and master their futures. His thinking lays the foundations not just for the next generation of electronic commerce, but for strategy, organization and the concept of the corporation itself in the coming decades.

Key text

- Philip Evans and Thomas S. Wurster. *Blown to Bits: How the New Economics of Information Transforms Strategy*. Harvard Business School Press, 1999

Key link

- www.bcg.com

Execution orders

It might be thought that instructing a stockbroker to buy shares was as easy as calling the broker and specifying the company and the number of shares required. There are, however, more ways than one to leave a purchase instruction with a broker. Take the following examples:

- **At best (also known as market order):** An instruction to buy or sell commodities, stocks, currency, etc. at the best possible price available at the moment the broker receives the instruction. At best instructions must be executed in the appropriate market immediately.
- **At limit (also known as limit order):** An instruction to buy or sell commodities, stocks, currency, etc. up to but not beyond a particular price limit. In the case of a purchase, this will be an instruction not to sell above a specified price, and in the case of a sale of stock, not to sell below.
- **All or none:** An instruction to buy or sell a security in which a broker must fulfil an entire order or none of it at all. The broker need not execute the order immediately.
- **Fill or kill:** An instruction to buy or sell a security, which must be executed in the market immediately. If it cannot be, then it is automatically cancelled.
- **Day order:** An instruction to buy or sell a security, which is automatically cancelled if it is not fulfilled by the end of the trading day.
- **GTC (Good till cancelled):** An instruction to buy or sell a security, which remains in force

until cancelled by the person instructing the transaction or executed by the broker.

Executive churn

Executive churn is the name given to the turnover of senior executives – a phenomenon that is accelerating. The upper-middle reaches of US corporations are coming to resemble a game of musical chairs in which the music gets faster and faster, and chairs are left emptier for longer.

Research carried out by the Center for Creative Leadership in Greensboro, North Carolina, and the executive search firm Manchester Partners International found that 40 percent of new executive hires fail within the first 18 months. A daunting two out of every five newly recruited managers don't make it past the first year and a half, 'being terminated for poor performance, performing significantly below expectations, or voluntarily resigning from the position'.

Executive programme

While the educational qualification most commonly associated with business schools is the **MBA**, they also offer a range of other full-time and part-time qualifications and courses. These include educational programmes that provide employees of companies with the opportunity to study in a variety of business-related courses while still working or taking a short time off from work.

Executive programmes are delivered in a number of different ways to suit the executive market, including distance learning; short, intensive courses at the school; and part-time learning over a period of time. Particularly useful for keeping abreast of management theory, executive programmes tend to reflect the latest economic and management trends.

BusinessWeek's 2001 Executive Education rankings rated the following business schools as the top providers of executive education: Harvard Business School, INSEAD (France), Michigan, Stanford, University of Pennsylvania, Northwestern Kellogg, London Business School, IMD (Switzerland), Columbia and IESE-Institute de Estudios Superioures de la Empresa in Spain.

Key link
- www.businessweek.com/bschools/01/exec_ ed_rank.htm

Executive shortages

One major public company anticipates that it will lose 60 percent of its executives within the next three years. Another predicts 40 to 50 percent of its management will walk out the door, never to return. Once upon a time, an orderly line of ready-made replacements stood in the wings. Now, the corporate corridors are empty. Thanks to **downsizing**, tomorrow's leaders are already yesterday's men.

William C. Byham is president and CEO of Bridgeville, Pennsylvania-based Development Dimensions International, which specializes in HR issues. He says bluntly, 'There will be a shortage of executive talent. Demographics mean that there are a lot of people nearing retirement age. Downsizing has meant that companies no longer tend to have developmental roles, like assistant or deputy jobs, from which people were traditionally promoted. At the same time, the experience, qualifications and skills needed to become a senior executive have increased.'

Trends suggest that this talent shortfall may be no mere blip on the radar; the problem could be with us for decades to come. Three trends, in particular, threaten to exacerbate the situation in the next few years.

First, and in many ways most serious, demand for executives appears to be moving in the opposite direction to supply. Remember the demographic time bomb? Back in the 1980s, everyone was talking about it. But it didn't go away when the magazine articles halted. It just kept on ticking and may be about to detonate. Demographic predictions suggest the number of 35- to 44-year-olds in the United States will fall by 15 percent between 2000 and 2015, while the number of 45- to 54-year-olds will increase.

The second factor in the escalating talent shortage is that the demands companies place on executives are increasing. Complex global markets require more sophisticated management skills, including international sensitivity, cultural fluency, technological literacy, entrepreneurial flair and, most critically, leadership. The proliferation of business-school educated managers, especially MBAs, suggests that executives are better trained than ever before. The trouble is that business schools are good at turning out business analysts but have a more questionable record in producing leaders.

The third factor is the rise of many high-potential small and medium-sized companies. For the first time, large companies have to compete with – and provide career opportunities and earnings on a par with – their smaller brethren. A host of high-tech start-ups, especially Internet-based businesses, are likely to draw off a growing proportion of the high-fliers who might otherwise have joined the blue chips. Who wants to work for a faceless corporation when you can earn more and have more fun working for an exciting upstart?

There appears little doubt that it will become much harder for established companies to attract the brightest and the best. 'There will continue to be, for the foreseeable future, greater demand than supply of the best people – the most knowledgeable, skilled, innovative, experienced, entrepreneurial, creative, risk-taking super talent,' says Bruce Tulgan of RainmakerThinking Inc., a think-tank studying changes in the workplace. 'Every business leader and manager in every organization I talk with says that they are spending more time, energy, and money on recruiting at all levels.'

The demographic alarm bells are ringing. The stats don't lie. And they begin with the post-war **baby boom**. The boomers are growing old. This led to a surplus of middle managers in the late 1980s and is now creating an aging workforce – and an aging executive population. By 2000, there were more US workers in their late 40s than in their late 20s. In 1990, there were 53 million 40- to 59-year-olds in the United States. By 2000, there were 73 million, and in 2010 there will be about 83 million. Add in factors like a booming stock exchange and boosting retirement nest eggs, and there are an awful lot of people eyeing condos in Florida.

'The American labour force will shrink in the middle,' says Paul Wallace, author of *Agequake*, a new book examining demographic trends. 'The baby-boom echo and immigration mean that the United States does not face youth deficits. Even so, the bulging portion of the labour force will consist of people over 50. If companies are increasingly looking to younger executives, there will be a problem.'

The numbers don't look good. Broad demographic statistics are backed by research and surveys. In 1998, research by management consultants **McKinsey & Co.** covered nearly 6000 managers in 77 companies and concluded that the battle to recruit talented people was already intensifying. The McKinsey report, appropriately entitled *The War for Talent*, concluded, 'Many American companies are already suffering a shortage of executive talent.' It found that 'three-quarters of corporate officers surveyed said their companies had "insufficient talent sometimes" or were "chronically talent-short across the board".'

Executive summary

If you don't like reading long corporate documents, then the executive summary is the place to start. The executive summary is a section at the beginning of a document that is in effect a miniature version of the document that follows. It should contain all the salient points, which is fortunate as it is often the only part of the report a time-pressed executive manages to read.

Exit interview

The exit interview is a formal or informal interview that takes place when an individual leaves an organization. The interview may take the form of an informal chat or something more structured, such as a questionnaire. There are several reasons for conducting an exit interview. It allows the HR department, as well as the employee's immediate managers, to assess the implementation of any training and education the employee has received. More importantly, it allows a company to assess an individual's reasons for leaving an organization. The interview may reveal important information about the organization, such as stress levels, conflict with corporate culture, personality issues or dissatisfaction with pay levels.

Key text
- www.uncc.edu/ragiacal/exitframes.html

Exit strategy

The exit strategy is an investor's plan for getting out of a company and receiving a return on his investment. Exit strategies will vary according to the type of investor. **Venture capitalists** usually require a quick return on their investment. Ideally, this will be from an **initial public offering**; however, if the economic climate or business is not suitable, they will seek a trade sale, MBO or merger. Venture capital firms can be ruthless in obtaining their return, even forcing through their preferred strategy against the wishes of management if they have sufficient voting power. In extreme cases, VCs may seek liquidation of a company's assets in order to safeguard their investment. Business **angels**, often private investors, may have a more relaxed attitude toward timeframes and be prepared to wait longer to see a return on investment. Founding owners who are also involved in the running of the business may have restrictions placed on the manner of their exit in the terms of the IPO. There may, for example, be an earn-out clause in operation, which means the manager will have to remain at the company after selling his shares in order to ensure continuation until a new manager is appointed. There may also be stipulations on how early after an IPO a director/shareholder may sell his shareholding.

Expectancy theory

Expectancy theory is a motivational theory proposed by Canadian Victor Vroom, professor of management and psychology at Yale University. Vroom is one of the world's leading authorities on the psychological analysis of behaviour in organizations. His book *Work and Motivation* is a seminal work in its field.

Vroom defines motivation as 'a process governing choices … among alternative forms of voluntary behavior'. If a person has a choice of actions A and B, which lead to two different outcomes, then one might expect the individual to take the course of action that leads to the most desirable outcome or avoids the least desirable outcome at any given moment. Vroom, however, suggests there may be indirect motivation at work during the decision-making process.

Vroom's theory postulates that motivation is determined by three factors: the perception that effort will result in success; the perception that a successful performance will lead to a valued outcome – a reward of some kind; and that personal satisfaction will be derived from the outcome. All three elements must be present for an individual to be motivated. That motivation may be a level beyond the immediate outcome of the action. So if a person needs to achieve X sales to be top salesperson, it might be assumed that being top salesperson is the motivation. In reality, the salesperson sees top salesman as the means to further promotion and is motivated by the desire to be promoted.

Key text
- Victor H. Vroom. *Work and Motivation*. John Wiley & Sons, 1964

Experience curve

The experience curve describes the relationship between unit costs, cumulative production and experience. The term was coined by **Bruce D. Henderson**, founder of the Boston Consulting Group, in 1966 and was extended to the area of corporate strategy. The concept came out of observations of the growth rate in the semiconductor industry in the 1960s. Using price data supplied by the Electronic Industries Association, the Boston Consulting Group could make a comparison with industry volume. Two patterns were noted. In one pattern, prices remained constant for long periods before steeply declining over a long period. In the other, prices declined at a constant rate of some 25 percent each time accumulated experience doubled. This effect was the experience curve.

The experience curve describes the observed phenomenon that as cumulative production increases, productivity costs decline. This effect is ascribed to the fact that, as processes are repeated more often, workers become better at their jobs and therefore processes within the organization run more smoothly. Thus, in theory, the faster production capacity is increased, the quicker competitive advantage is obtained.

Key text
- Bruce D. Henderson. *Henderson on Corporate Strategy*. Abt Books, 1979

External constraints

While a business can control its workforce, production capacity, borrowing and other aspects of its business, there will always be some factors that could affect the business that lie outside of its control. These factors are known as external constraints. They might include economic circumstances, such as currency exchange rates, interest rates and inflationary pressures; changing fashion and consumer preferences; political factors, such as governments enacting legislation; climatic conditions, such as floods, water shortages, and the like; and war. An example of an external constraint affecting business on a wide scale was the outbreak of foot-and-mouth disease that occurred in the United Kingdom during 2001.

Extranet

An extranet is an extended **intranet**. It retains the internal networking aspects of the intranet, protected behind a firewall, but extends access to the intranet from beyond the firewall, often utilizing the Internet, although private networks may also be used. An extranet may be extended to permit password-protected access by customers, suppliers and other third parties.

F

Factors of production

The factors of production are those resources used to produce goods and services. Economists group the factors of production into broad categories: land (natural resources and raw materials); labour (human effort); and capital (employees' wages, as well as the other machinery, plant, tools, etc. that have been acquired with money). Other factors, such as enterprise capital and human capital, may also be included by some academics. Goods and services are created by a combination of the factors of production.

In a command or planned economy, central planners determine how the factors of production should be used to provide the best outcome for society. In a market economy, **entrepreneurs** use the factors of production to make goods and services, which are sold for profit.

Fair process

Fair process is a concept initially developed in the field of social psychology and law, and first applied to the strategic business setting by INSEAD business school academics **W. Chan Kim** and **Renée Mauborgne**. It involves *engaging* employees in decisions that affect them, *providing a sound explanation* for why decisions are made as they are, and *setting clear expectations* of the rules of the game and what is required of employees in the executing of decisions. Kim and Mauborgne found that when fair process is exercised, employees' trust and commitment grow and employees are inspired to go beyond the call of duty and exercise voluntary cooperation in the execution of decisions. But when fair process is violated, even favourable decisions are often rejected by employees.

Key text
- W. Chan Kim and Renée Mauborgne. 'Fair Process: Managing in the Knowledge Economy.' *Harvard Business Review*, July/August 1997

Fannie Mae

The Federal National Mortgage Association (FNMA – Fannie Mae) is a private shareholder company, operating under a congressional charter, which provides funds for the mortgage market.

The company was created by Congress in 1938. Its role then was to shore up the housing industry during the Great Depression. Fannie Mae remained a government organization until the 1950s, when it became partly privately owned. But it wasn't until 1968 that the company became completely privatized. Today, Fannie Mae's stock is traded on the New York Stock Exchange, and it is one of the largest corporations in the United States.

The company aims to ensure that low-, moderate- and middle-income families can afford to buy their own homes. It does not offer mortgages directly, but works with lenders to make sure funds are available.

Key link
- www.fanniemae.com

Fast Company

Fast Company magazine is widely acknowledged to be the bible of the **New Economy** and **free agents** in particular. The magazine was launched in November 1995 by Alan Webber and Bill Taylor, who had spent a combined total of eleven years at the *Harvard Business Review* prior to starting *Fast Company*.

Webber and Taylor could see from their perspective at the *Harvard Business Review* that a global revolution was changing the nature of business. They set out to invent a new magazine to show how companies were transforming to compete in the new world. The idea struck a chord, and the magazine received the backing of luminaries including business guru **Tom Peters** and esteemed Harvard academic **Michael Porter**.

In the first issue, the co-founders outlined their manifesto: '*Fast Company* aims to be the handbook of the business revolution. We will chronicle the changes under way in how companies create and compete, highlight the new practices shaping how work gets done, showcase teams who are inventing the future and reinventing business.'

Fast Company set out not only to report the business revolution, but to play a part in shaping it by creating a vocabulary for the **New Economy**. Many issues later, the magazine can justifiably claim a spectacular success. Despite changing ownership twice – Webber and Taylor sold the magazine to New York real estate and media businessman Mort Zuckerman, who in turn sold it sold to Gruner & Jahr USA Publishing, part of German media giant Bertelsmann – the magazine continues to prosper. A new generation of entrepreneurs has grown up on its diet of cutting-edge informative reporting.

Key link
- www.fastcompany.com

Fast-moving consumer goods (FMCG)

Fast-moving consumer goods are branded goods that are turned over quickly. They include many everyday products found in supermarkets, including cereals, candy, detergent, and bread.

Fayol, Henri

French businessman and management thinker (1841–1925)

Henri Fayol was educated in Lyon, France and at the National School of Mines in St Etienne. In 1860, he graduated as a mining engineer and joined the French mining company Commentry-Fourchamboult-Décazeville. He spent his entire working career with the company and was its managing director between 1888 and 1918. During that time, he produced the 'functional principle', the first rational approach to the organization of enterprise. His studies led to lectures at the Ecole Supérieure de la Guerre and to an examination of the public services.

Fayol's work was important for two reasons. First, he placed management at centre stage. Frederick Taylor's **scientific management**, developed from his examination of steelworkers' tasks, emasculated the working man, but still treated managers as stopwatch-holding supervisors. Fayol emerged from a similar background in heavy industry. His conclusion, however, was that management was critical and universal. 'Management plays a very important part in the government of undertakings; of all undertakings, large or small, industrial, commercial, political, religious, or any other,' he wrote. It was not until 1954, and **Peter Drucker's** *The Practice of Management*, that anyone else made such a bold pronouncement in management's favour.

The second contribution of Fayol was to ponder the question of how best a company could be organized. In doing so, Fayol took a far broader perspective than anyone else had previously done. Fayol concluded, 'All activities to which industrial undertakings give rise can be divided into the following six groups.' The six functions that he identified were technical activities, commercial activities, financial activities, security activities, accounting activities and managerial activities.

Such functional separations have dominated the way companies have been managed throughout the twentieth century. It may be fashionable to talk of an end to functional mindsets and of free-flowing organizations, but Fayol's functional model largely remains.

The origins of Fayol's *General and Industrial Management* can be traced back to 1900, when he delivered a speech at a mining conference. When he gave a developed version of his ideas at a 1908 conference, 2000 copies were immediately reprinted to satisfy demand. By 1925, 15,000 copies had been printed and a book was published.

Fayol also offered 14 'universal' principles of organization based upon his extensive experience as an executive. Some of those principles are that work becomes more efficient when divided into separate tasks and jobs; communications should flow from the top to the bottom of the hierarchy, along what Fayol called the 'scalar chain'; decision making should be centralized to the optimal degree; managers must have authority commensurate with their level of responsibility; and they must also treat their subordinates equitably.

Fayol's observations and conclusions are important. He talks of 'ten yearly forecasts … revised every five years' – one of the first instances of business planning in practice. He writes: 'The maxim, "managing means looking ahead," gives some idea of the importance attached to planning in the business world, and it is true that if foresight is not the whole of management at least it is an essential part of it.'

In many respects, Henri Fayol was the first management thinker. While others concentrated on the workman and the mechanics of performance, he focused on the role of management and the essential skills required of managers.

Key text

- Henri Fayol. *General and Industrial Management*. Pitman, 1949 (originally published in French as *Administration Industrielle et Générale*, 1916)

Key link

- www.lib.uwo.ca/business/fayol.html

Federal Reserve System

Known as the Fed, the Federal Reserve System, established by legislation passed in 1913, is the central banking system of the United States. It is responsible for formulating and implementing US monetary policy and issues US banknotes (coins are issued by United States Treasury Department).

The Federal Reserve System was set up as a quasi-independent regulatory commission; the intention was to hand the Fed a degree of autonomy and freedom from outside influence. The principal decision-making body of the Fed is the Board of Governors, which consists of seven members. Members tend to be selected from the financial community. Their appointments are not the responsibility of the President, and therefore all members are free to act without the constraints of party politics affecting their decision-making.

The US federal banking system is comprised of twelve Federal Reserve Banks and all of their member banks. The twelve banks are situated in Atlanta, Boston, Chicago, Cleveland, Dallas, Kansas City, Minneapolis, New York, Philadelphia, Richmond, San Francisco and St Louis. The system is governed by the Federal Reserve Board, which is located in Washington, D.C. The twelve district Federal Reserve Banks are structured in a similar manner to private banks, with their shareholders consisting chiefly of private banks in their areas and the government having a minority shareholding only.

Federal Reserve Banks are not banks in the consumer sense. They are the banks for their member banks, in that the member banks maintain deposits at the Federal Reserve Bank and receive loans from it. The duties of the Federal Reserve Banks include making loans to member banks, deciding whether member banks should be allowed to merge with each other, issuing paper currency, and withdrawal of currency from circulation. They are also a lender of last resort, available to bail out the member banks in the case of a liquidity crisis.

Key text
- *Federal Reserve System Purposes and Functions.* Board of Governors of the Federal Reserve System, 1994

Key link
- www.federalreserve.gov

Ferrari, Enzo

Founder, Scuderia Ferrari (1898–1988)

Enzo Ferrari roared into the world on 18 February 1898, in Modena, northern Italy. His father was a metal fabricator who owned his own factory, so it was no surprise that Ferrari took a keen interest in engineering. As a young boy of 10, he was taken to his first motor race at the Via Emilia, Bologna. Entranced by the fast motorcars, he vowed that he would learn to drive, a feat that he accomplished by the age of 13. In 1914, as war broke out in Europe, Ferrari was forced to leave school and take a job in the workshop of the local fire station.

Ferrari enlisted during World War I. He survived the conflict, only to be brought close to death by the flu epidemic that raged through Italy in 1918. When he had made a full recovery, he set out to find a job associated with racing cars. He applied to Fiat but was rejected. Disappointed but reluctant to give up on his dream, he took work as a delivery driver for a local garage and raced cars in his spare time with moderate success. With the help of a friend, and on the strength of his growing reputation as a driver, he eventually landed a job at the Italian car company Alfa Romeo, which employed him initially as a test driver, and then as a racing driver for the Alfa Romeo works team.

Ferrari's big opportunity came when he was selected to drive for Alfa Romeo at the French Grand Prix. It was one of the most prestigious races in the racing calendar, but Ferrari blew his big chance when he mysteriously pulled out of the race. Ferrari's reasons for withdrawing from the Grand Prix are a mystery: there was speculation that he had lost his nerve and suffered a sudden crisis of confidence. If true, it was nothing to be ashamed of. Ferrari was the best person to judge his own ability, and he would have been foolish to risk his life. If it was an attack of self-doubt, it didn't affect his success as a businessman.

Despite this setback, Ferrari continued to work for Alfa Romeo, and in 1929 started his own company, Scuderia Ferrari. The company provided racing services to its members, delivering the racecars to the track and providing engineering backup, as well as other support services. As most of the cars were Alfa Romeos and Alfa Romeo was also a client of Scuderia, Ferrari maintained his close relationship with the car company. He even struck a deal whereby Alfa Romeo provided technical expertise in return for shares in his company. Shell and Pirelli also obtained stock in Scuderia.

For a company emblem, Ferrari selected the prancing horse, the squadron badge of Italian World War I flying ace Francesco Baracca. The yellow background of the now-familiar symbol came from the colour of Modena.

At first, Ferrari and his team met with great success. Ferrari had signed up the best drivers. He could afford this because to avoid a massive salary bill, he agreed to hand over a share of the prize money. With several victories coming in the first year, it turned out to be a lucrative time for both the drivers and Ferrari.

The company ran into trouble in 1933, however, when Alfa Romeo decided to withdraw from racing. Suddenly Ferrari was without cars, an essential part of any racing team. For a while, Ferrari managed to negotiate a halfway-house deal whereby Alfa Romeo continued to supply cars to Ferrari. Ferrari's Scuderia became, to all intents, the Alfa Romeo racing team. But even this unsatisfactory arrangement came to an end in 1937, when Alfa Romeo decided to run its own racing team once more. Ferrari found himself answering directly to Alfa Romeo management, even though he ran his own company. It was an untenable situation, and in 1939 Ferrari left – but only after Alfa Romeo insisted Ferrari sign a contract agreeing not to use the Ferrari name in motor racing for two years. The contract was rendered meaningless when World War II intervened.

During World War II, Ferrari moved the Scuderia premises from Modena to Marinello. The new factory was razed to the ground during the war and rebuilt from scratch. After the war, at the age of 50, Ferrari set about creating his own racing car. Production was revved up and the first car, the 12-cylinder 125S, emerged in 1947. Before long, Ferrari cars were winning Grand Prix races across Europe. Yet Ferrari was not satisfied. One problem was that constructing racing cars consumed a great deal of cash. His solution to this problem was to build sports cars, and so by default the Ferrari sports car was established.

Ironically, the success of the Ferrari sports car only caused more problems for Ferrari. Now he was struggling to meet demand for road cars at the same time as he was keeping the racing team going. In 1963, Ford Motor Company made an offer for the business, but Ferrari turned it down because of the onerous terms. Instead, in 1969 he turned to a fellow Italian, Gianni Agnelli, who controlled the industrial giant Fiat. Agnelli agreed to acquire a 50 percent share in Ferrari Scuderia.

Throughout the 1970s and 1980s, Ferrari continued to build on the company's reputation as the most exclusive sports car manufacturer in the world. At the same time, the Ferrari racing team sped to victory after victory. The last car created under Ferrari's control was the F40. In 1988, Fiat increased its holding in Ferrari to 90 percent. The Ferrari family retained the balance. Ferrari died at the age of 90 that same year.

Key texts
- Brock Yates. *Enzo Ferrari: The Man, The Cars, The Races, The Machine.* Doubleday, 1991
- Stan Grayson. 'Ferrari: The Man, the Machines'. *Automobile Quarterly Pub.,* 1975

Key links
- www.maranellorosso.com
- www.ferrari.it/cgi-bin/fworld.dll/ferrariworld/scripts/home/home.jsp?language=ENGLISH

Financial plan

The financial plan is an essential part of any business plan in a business proposal for a new start-up; it is the part of the business plan in which the **entrepreneur** outlines the expected financial performance of the business. Inevitably, the figures will be financial projections, as no business has been conducted yet. However, though they are only projections, the potential investor will pay a great deal of attention to them since the financial plan shows where the money is coming from, what the projected cash flow is like, and when the business is likely to turn a profit. All of these factors have a direct impact on the investor's return from his investment.

Financial projections should always be prepared and set out according to current accounting practices. Balance sheets, income statements and cash flow statements represent the bare minimum. An explanation of how the figures were arrived at – the assumptions that underpin them – as well as break-even analysis, financial ratios and investment structure and projections should also be provided.

Financing stages

Financing a start-up is a structured process and usually involves different parties at different stages. The terms used vary from country to country, but there are several distinct stages of funding:

- **Seed funding:** This is used at the very beginning of the project, when the entrepreneur has an idea but little else. Finance is needed to research and develop that idea. This stage is often financed by the **entrepreneurs** themselves, by friends and family, or by business angels. It is also known as friends and family finance.
- **Start-up/early stage:** This is required when the company has started up but as yet is unproven. Finance is required to trade on a commercial basis while the company establishes itself in the

market. If the company is promising, then it may be able to attract the interest of a venture capital firm that specializes in funding start-ups in that particular industry.

- **Expansion/development stage:** Now the company is set up, trading and established. It may not be making a profit yet, but further financing is required to expand during what is usually a period of rapid growth. Several rounds of financing may be required during this stage, often tied into the business plan. Investors may also push for an **initial public offering**: obtaining finance by offering shares to the public. There are many factors that will determine if this is a suitable course of action, not least of which is whether market sentiments are well-disposed to IPOs at that time.

A company's financing troubles do not necessarily end with a successful IPO either. The question that faces many of the firms that have gone to IPOs in the last few years is whether they will be able to attract additional funding if profits do not materialize.

Firewall

The Internet equivalent of the Berlin Wall, a firewall sits between an **intranet** and the outside world. All information heading in or out passes through the firewall. The firewall's job is to act as a security system, blocking access to a particular computer or network while still allowing some types of data to flow in and out onto the Internet. It acts a sentry, making sure no unauthorized data traffic gets through. It is often the first line of defence against hackers.

There are both hardware and software firewall solutions: packet filtering, which accepts or rejects each packet of information according to set criteria; circuit gateways, which allow information to flow freely once a connection has passed the security test; application gateways, where security checks are made on an application basis, e.g. Telnet; and proxy servers, which intercept all traffic, acting as a

false front for the Internet and concealing the true network addresses that lie beyond.

Firmware

A hybrid between software and hardware, firmware is programming held permanently in a computer's ROM (read-only memory) chips, as opposed to a program that is read in from external memory as it is needed. The BIOS in a personal computer is an example of firmware. Firmware is created, tested and distributed in a similar manner to software. Devices that use firmware, such as printers, modems and sound-studio hard-disk recorders, can often have the latest version of the firmware uploaded.

First-mover advantage

An idea that was elevated to beyond-question status during the dotcom boom of the 1990s, first-mover advantage is the competitive advantage conferred upon companies who are first to operate in a particular market.

In an industry where there are economies of scale, first-mover advantage may be significant. The benefits of being a first mover supposedly lie in being able to capture a substantial user base and gain public recognition before the competition, preventing the competition from ever getting a foothold in the market. Management guru **Tom Peters** traces the origins of the first-mover concept back to the oil and gas industry 100 years ago. 'He who builds the first pipeline controls the flow of hydrocarbons,' he says. 'Only an idiot would build the second one nearby.'

The dotcom crash, however, provoked a reappraisal of first-mover advantage.

There are many examples among Internet companies in which the first company into a market did not end up as the dominant player in that market. (This includes many Internet **pure plays** that have lost out to **clicks-and-mortar** companies.) Webvan, pets.com, eToys and Netscape are all examples of Internet companies that were first to the market with a particular business concept or product and were subsequently ousted from their positions as top dog.

A cursory examination of history demonstrates that this phenomenon of first-movers falling by the wayside is not a new one. Cyrus Hall McCormick was not the first or only person to invent a horse-drawn threshing machine. Microsoft may dominate the market with its Windows graphical user interface, yet Apple Computers got there first.

Several terms were coined for the phenomenon of profiting from being a follower, rather than a trailblazer in a market, including late-mover, last-mover and second-mover advantage.

In fact, despite the contrary perception, investors like to invest in **me-too** companies, comforted by the thought that there is a proven market for that particular product or service.

Firth, David

British consultant, author and corporate fool

There's always one joker. David Firth revels in the role. He spent eight years running the theatre company Lords of Misrule. Now, his company is called Treefrog; his book, *The Corporate Fool*. His current project is the Fool School. 'Fools have existed in all world cultures throughout history; now it is time to bring them into modern business,' he says. 'Fools speak out against those who have power, question accepted wisdom, embody controversy and taboo, cast doubt in the face of certainty, bring chaos to order, point out the obvious, throw a spanner in the proverbial works, turn the world upside down.' Great job description.

But there is a serious side to Firth's various activities. He works with companies on a variety of aspects of organizational life – including communication, building trust, creativity and 'learning communities'. His clients include some equally serious big names, including British Airways and Unilever. Firth's *The Fool Show* mixes a traditional business conference with multimedia

and theatre. To prove that business really is the new rock and roll, Firth is touring throughout the world. The end piece comes at the Melbourne Comedy Festival in Australia.

Key texts

- David Firth with Alan Leigh. *The Corporate Fool*. Capstone, 2001
- David Firth with Rene Carayol. *Corporate Voodoo: Business Principles for Mavericks and Magicians*. Capstone, 2001
- David Firth. *Smart Things to Know About Change*. Capstone, 2000

Key link

- www.foolweb.com

Fishbone diagram

See Ishakawa diagram.

Five forces framework

See Porter, Michael.

Fixed asset

See Asset.

Flame

A flame is a rude, offensive, angry, public or private electronic message, usually sent by e-mail. A flame may be sent for several reasons; it is often in response to something posted on a Web site or message board that the person sending the flame objects to, or to express disapproval over breaches of **netiquette**. An offensive message posted to, for example, a Usenet newsgroup will cause those offended to flame the culprit. Flames are often used as an informal method of policing the Internet.

Flash

Flash is a browser-independent vector-graphic animation technology developed by Macromedia. It allows complex multimedia animations to be displayed as a Web page or part of a Web page, providing the browser is equipped with the necessary Flash plug-in. Web sites use Flash animations to attract attention and to provide unique interfaces. The file sizes for Flash animations tend to be smaller than other forms of graphics, making it easier to download and run on the viewer's browser.

Flexible manufacturing system (FMS)

Flexible manufacturing systems are totally automated manufacturing systems that integrate robotics, automated guided vehicles for transferring components between machines and **computer-aided manufacturing**. Flexible manufacturing offers considerable advantages, including increased productivity, cost reduction, the performance of menial mundane tasks to free up personnel for more complex tasks, the ability to switch between types of production while still running and the production of one or many production units in an agreed response time. Notable companies that use FMS include Dell Computers and Levi Strauss.

Flexible working

One way of addressing work/life balance issues is through flexible working. Whereas once regular fixed hours, nine-to-five office hours for example, and a five- or six-day week were *de rigeur*, today the working week has been shattered into a myriad different permutations. Flextime, jobsharing, part-time, full-time, shift time, homeworking, staggering hours, annual hours, temping; these are all flexible working methods. Employees appear never to have had such a choice of how to work their hours.

Reasons for wanting to work a flexible working schedule vary. They include childcare (wanting to spend more time with your children, needing to be at home to take care of your child); study (gaining more skills and qualifications); caring (needing time to care for family or friends); health (when health problems place limitations on your ability to work); travel (when geographical location makes it difficult to travel to work); leisure (taking time off to pursue leisure activities, such as competitive sports); voluntary work (giving your time to others on an unpaid basis); retirement (taking time to prepare for a retirement, winding down); and quality of life (not wanting to work as many hours).

Key text
- S. Shipside. *Flexible & Virtual Working.* John Wiley, 2001

Flotation

A flotation occurs when a company is launched onto the stock market, usually to raise capital for expansion purposes and to reward early-stage investors. There are two methods of floating a company: a private placing, in which shares are placed with institutional investors, such as pension funds; or a public offering, in which shares are offered for sale to the public. When the flotation is completed, then the shares can be traded on the open market.

Companies that are contemplating a flotation will require the services of a number of professionals: investment bankers (who will market the company to potential investors), experienced legal representation and a good firm of accountants are essential.

FOB (free on board)

Free on board is a shipping term that indicates at which point a title of goods passes from the seller to the purchaser. This in turn indicates who is responsible for the goods in transit. That party will need to obtain insurance to cover their risk. If goods are free on board, the goods being shipped remain at the seller's risk until they cross the ship's rail at the docks. Up to this point, the seller pays for the transport of the goods and for their insurance. If sending by rail, then the term FOR (free on rail) applies.

Focus group

Focus groups are small, specially selected discussion groups, usually set up for marketing purposes or to solicit opinions on organizational matters.

A focus group will normally consist of 15 or fewer members, selected for their relevance to a particular topic. Focus groups concerned with the issue of the abolition of foxhunting might contain members of the anti-hunt brigade and/or members of regional hunts.

Discussions in a focus group will be led by a group moderator, whose task is to facilitate the discussion and will, as the name suggests, focus on a limited subject area. The discussion may be recorded in video or audio and may be spread over a period of several months. Focus groups have become increasingly popular in politics for gauging public opinion.

Follett, Mary Parker

American academic (1868–1933)

American political scientist Mary Parker Follett was ahead of her time. She was discussing issues such as teamworking and responsibility (now reborn as empowerment) in the first decades of the twentieth century. Follett was a female liberal humanist in an era dominated by reactionary males intent on mechanizing the world of business.

Born in Quincy, Massachusetts, Mary Parker Follett attended Thayer Academy and the Society for the Collegiate Instruction of Women in Cambridge, Massachusetts (now part of Harvard University). She also studied at Newnham College, Cambridge in the United Kingdom and in Paris.

The simple thrust of Follett's thinking was that people are central to any business activity – or, indeed, to any other activity. Follett explained, 'I do not think that we have psychological and ethical and economic problems. We have human problems, with psychological, ethical, and economical aspects, and as many others as you like.'

In particular, Follett explored conflict. She pointed out three ways of dealing with confrontation: domination, compromise or integration. The last, she concluded, is the only positive way forward. This can be achieved by first 'uncovering' the real conflict and then taking 'the demands of both sides and breaking them up into their constituent parts'. Follett wrote, 'Our outlook is narrowed, our activity is restricted, our chances of business success largely diminished when our thinking is constrained within the limits of what has been called an either-or situation. We should never allow ourselves to be bullied by an "either-or." There is often the possibility of something better than either of two given alternatives.'

Follett advocated giving greater responsibility to people at a time when the mechanical might of mass production was at its height. She was also an early advocate of management training and the theory that leadership could be taught. Her work was largely neglected in the West, though not in Japan, which even boasts a Follett Society.

Key texts
- Mary Parker Follett. *Freedom and Coordination*. Pitman, 1949
- Mary Parker Follett. *Creative Experience*. Longman, 1924
- Mary Parker Follett. *The New State: Group Organization – The Solution of Popular Government*. Longman, 1918

Key links
- www.onepine.demon.co.uk/pfollett.htm
- http://sunsite.utk.edu/FINS/Mary_Parker_Follett/Fins-MPF-02.txt
- http://www2.h-net.msu.edu/~apsaph/follett2.htm

Force-field analysis

Force-field analysis is a means of analysing the forces for and against a course of action. First, all of the forces for and against a course of action are listed and each is assigned a score relating to the strength of the force. A diagram is then constructed in the form of a vertical line, with the positive forces arranged to the left of the line and the negative forces opposing on the right. This will give an indication of the viability of a course of action and what forces may need to be adjusted.

Ford, Henry

American manufacturer (1863–1947)

Henry Ford was born on his father's farm in Greenfield, near Detroit, Michigan. As a boy, he showed great interest in mechanics and engineering. He delighted in dismantling his friends' watches and then reassembling them. While still a schoolboy, he built an engine from junk. He was always looking for ways to improve things.

Leaving school at 16, Ford went to work as an engineer for James Flower & Co. in Detroit. To supplement his meagre salary of $2.50 a week, he worked at a jewellers in the evenings. Nine months of gruelling hours later, Ford moved to the Dry Dock Engine Works to try his hand at a different type of engineering. By 1896, he was chief engineer at the Edison electric factory in Detroit. Unable to confine his engineering to work, Ford continued to tinker with engineering projects at home. His first prototype car was the Quadricycle that he built in his garden shed.

For eight years, Ford continued to work twelve-hour days and then come home to improve his invention. Yet despite the potential of his car, he couldn't persuade anyone to invest in it. The turning point came when Ford built a car for the Grosse Point races. Although inexperienced, Ford entered the races, drove the car himself and won emphatically. He repeated the feat the following year, in 1902. The victory attracted financiers and, after a couple of corporate false starts, the Ford

Motor Company was up and running. On the way, Ford broke the world land-speed record for a four-cylinder car, driving a mile over the frozen Lake Sinclair in 39 and one-fifth seconds, seven seconds faster than the existing record.

Ford's idea was to produce a car for 'everyday wear and tear' suitable for the masses. Competitors' cars, like Cadillac's, were expensive at many thousands of dollars each and so beyond the reach of the majority of ordinary people. Ford's first commercial car was the Model A Fordmobile, in 1905. Priced at $850, it undercut its rivals and, in its basic but solid design, it appealed to the mass market. It was followed in 1908 by the Model T.

Ford's commitment to lowering prices cannot be doubted. Between 1908 and 1916, he reduced prices by 58 percent – at a time when demand was such that he could easily have raised prices.

The overwhelming demand for the Model T forced Ford to modify the production process and make it more efficient. Initially, the cars moved along the production line on cradles. At each stop, men climbed over the cars attending to different tasks. Ford simplified the process and made it more predictable. First, he delineated tasks so that one man performed one task repeatedly, instead of several. Second, he roped the cars together so that they travelled at a steady speed through the plant. These simple but effective measures resulted in an increase in annual production from some 70,000 vehicles in 1912 to approximately 170,000 in 1913, with a commensurate reduction in the workforce of nearly 1500 men.

Production line work was arduous and monotonous and staff turnover was high. In 1914, Ford reluctantly increased wages for unskilled workers to a minimum of $5, a move that brought in workers from far and wide. Tens of thousands joined the Ford car manufacturing company. So many prospective employees queued up at the factory gates that the fire brigade had to use its hoses to disperse the crowd.

Ford's coercive managerial style grated on the workforce. To sweeten this, Ford introduced profit sharing and an extensive welfare programme. He stopped short of allowing the workers to form a union, however. When President Roosevelt introduced the Wagner Act of 1935, allowing the unionization of the motor companies, Ford resisted the legislation bitterly, refusing to let unions operate at Ford auto plants. It was only after the adverse publicity that resulted from the infamous Battle of the Overpass in May 1937, when several United Auto Workers' officials were badly beaten, allegedly by Ford employees outside the Rouge plant, that Ford was forced to back down and permit union organization at the company.

By 1924, Ford had manufactured 10 million Model Ts and built a new plant at River Rouge with wages raised to $6 a day. Increasingly, he spent less time managing – his son Edsel had become president in 1919 – and more time pursuing his social ideals. Although a pacifist, Ford was drawn into war manufacturing after Pearl Harbor, when the Willow Plant was built to produce B-24 bombers. This gigantic production works, with its mile-long assembly line, produced one plane every hour with a total of 86,865 aircraft between May 1942 and the end of the war. In 1943, Ford returned as **CEO** after his son Edsel died.

More at home on the factory floor addressing engineering problems, Ford lacked the managerial skills and flexibility necessary to keep the company ahead of the competition. Fixated on the Model T, he waited too long to develop the company's next car model, the revamped Model A launched in 1927, and so lost the initiative forever to General Motors. Like many entrepreneurs, Ford was reluctant to give up his company. A poorly managed succession further damaged the company, with Ford finally handing power to his grandson Henry II in 1945. Ford died at the age of 84 on 7 April 1947.

Henry Ford developed mass production not because he blindly believed in the most advanced production methods. Ford believed in mass production because it meant he could make cars that people could afford. And this, with staggering success, is what he achieved.

On a darker note, two recent books examine the ugly face of Ford's deep, lifelong anti-Semitism.

The first, *International Jew*, is based on research Ford commissioned on 'the Jewish question', and the second, *Henry Ford and the Jews*, explores the anti-Semitic climate in which Ford grew up and its impact on his psyche and actions, as well as the response of the Jewish community and broader society to Ford's actions. In reviewing the latter book, *Publishers Weekly* noted, 'Ford, who was raised on a farm, believed that Jews were responsible for the evils of modern cities and America's interventionist foreign policy, even as he remained friends with individual Jews. And as Baldwin disturbingly shows, Ford also put his twisted ideals into action by creating an anti-Semitic newspaper, the *Dearborn Independent*.' In fact, Ford is arguably America's most famous anti-Semite, and downplaying or ignoring the hatred he espoused – in whitewashed or blind biographies of Ford, for example – simply perpetuates the sort of entrenched anti-Semitic climate that spawned Henry Ford.

Key texts
- Neil Baldwin. *Henry Ford and the Jews*. Public Affairs, 2001
- Henry Ford. *International Jew*. Gordon Press Publications, 1998
- Carol Gelderman. *Henry Ford: The Wayward Capitalist*. Dial Press, 1981
- Edmund O'Connor. *Henry Ford*. Greenhaven Press, 1980
- Anne Jardim. *The First Henry Ford: A Study in Personality and Business Leadership*. MIT Press, 1970
- Keith Sward. *The Legend of Henry Ford*. Rinehart, 1948
- Ralph H. Graves. *The Triumph of an Idea: The Story of Henry Ford*. Doubleday, Doran & Co., 1934
- Henry Ford. *My Life and Work*. Doubleday, Page & Co, 1923

Key links
- www.incwell.com/Biographies/Ford.html
- www.edison-ford-estate.com/henry-ford/Fbio.htm

FOREX (foreign exchange)

The FOREX market is the largest financial market in the world, trading billions of dollars worth of currency daily. Types of transactions include spot (cash), forwards, **options** and futures. Unlike many other financial markets, which are centralized in an exchange, the FOREX market is a 24-hour, over-the-counter market conducted by means of telephone, computer and fax across the globe. Participants in the market include corporate banks, institutional investors such as pension funds, investment banks and private traders.

Key link
- www.fxstreet.com

Forward integration

Forward integration is a phenomenon in which one company merges with or buys a company further down the supply chain, such as a wholesaler purchasing a retailer or a brewery buying a chain of pubs. The reasons for forward integration are several. One reason is that forward integration provides the most control possible over the supply chain. This in turn should restrict conflict between different elements of the supply chain. Another reason is denying access to the supply chain for competitors. Also, in theory, with more control over the supply chain, the company can respond more rapidly to changes in demand or competitive threat. A brewery that purchases a chain of pubs, for example, could control what beers were sold in the pub and therefore exercise control over the competition.

Obtaining the benefits of forward integration is not, however, always so straightforward. For example, for reasons of corporate culture and values, integration with organizations further down the supply chain may not be easily accomplished in practice. Lack of competition can give rise to complacency. Also, consumers do not always react positively to one company exerting control of a market in this manner.

Four 'P's of marketing

See Marketing mix.

Franchise

A franchise is the permission given by one company (franchisor) to another (franchisee) to manufacture, distribute or provide its branded products. There are three principal strands to the franchise relationship. First, there is the right to use the franchisor's trademark. Second, there is a degree of control and/or assistance exercised by the franchisor over the franchisee's business. Finally, there is the payment by the franchisee to the franchisor in return for being able to carry out the franchise operation. Franchise operations tend to be regulated by state legislation. For example, in the United States, both the **FTC** and the individual states regulate the operation of franchises. It is usual for the franchisor to impose minimum quality conditions on its franchisees to make sure that customers receive a fair deal from the franchisee and ensure that the brand image is maintained. Famous examples of franchise businesses include McDonald's and The Body Shop.

In the United States in 2000, most analysts estimated that there were more than 320,000 franchised small businesses generating revenues of $1 trillion in retail sales.

Key links
- www.franchise.org
- www.franchise.com
- www.franinfo.co.uk/index.lasso

Freddie Mac

Freddie Mac (Federal Home Loan Mortgage Corporation) is a stockholder-owned corporation chartered by US Congress in 1970. Its aim is to provide a continuous flow of funds to mortgage lenders to support the purchase and rental of homes by low- and middle-income families. Freddie

Mac does not issue mortgages itself, but purchases mortgages from lenders and packages them into securities that are subsequently sold to investors.

Freddie Mac is identical to **Fannie Mae** with respect to charters, Congressional mandates and regulatory structure. The two companies differ, however, in their business strategy. The element of competition between the two ensures home-buyers and renters secure a better deal than they would otherwise.

Key link
- www.freddiemac.com

Free agent

'Free agent' is a term used in business to describe a person who is not under a permanent contract of employment but operates independently. It has been calculated that there are 14 million self-employed Americans. There are also 8.3 million 'independent contractors' and a further 2.3 million who work for temporary agencies. This adds up to around 25 million free agents, who have been described in their bible, *Fast Company*, as 'people who move from project to project and who work on their own, sometimes for months, sometimes for days'. The term 'free agent' encompasses the self-employed, independent contractors and temps employed via agencies.

Research and experience suggests that people who have escaped (and that is how they tend to regard it) the corporate world actually find greater security in self-employment. The dramatic **downsizing** and restructuring of recent years means that being on your own no longer holds the fear it once did. A marketing consultant related how a bank was dubious about giving a loan to someone without a real job. 'If one of my clients goes away, I'm still going to make my payments,' she explained. 'But if I'm employed by Apple and they let me go, I'm out on the street.'

The experiences and views of the free agents represent a considerable challenge to the traditional business world. The corporation has become the great institution of the twentieth century, but there is no reason to assume that this will continue in the new millennium. 'The economics of free agency relate to a basic psychological shift, a tremendous San Andreas Fault between employee and employer,' says futurist **Stan Davis**. The question must be whether the corporate world has the will or the imagination to bridge the gap.

Key text
- Daniel H. Pink. 'Free Agent Nation.' *Fast Company*, December 1997

Frequency distribution

When an event occurs more than once, the frequency of occurrence can be recorded and the data represented in graphical form. The distribution can be represented as a line graph or **histogram**.

Fringe benefits

Fringe benefits (also known as perks) are an incentive given to employees in addition to their pay or salary. Fringe benefits include company cars, health insurance, mortgage subsidies, extra vacation, tuition fees, health club membership, tech equipment and slightly more esoteric rewards such as cases of wine. Fringe benefits are usually taxable on the value of the benefit. However, companies often try to keep one step ahead of the taxman by finding innovative fringe benefits yet to be caught by tax legislation.

Fritz, Robert

Consultant, author, composer and film director

In management-guru terms, Robert Fritz has a lot going for him. His successful books include *The Path of Least Resistance*; the pithily titled *Creating*, which unveils the world of creativity and promises access for all; and *Corporate Tides: The Inescapable Laws of Organizational Structure*.

In the late 1970s, Fritz joined **Peter Senge** (the MIT academic and author of *The Fifth Discipline*) and Charlie Kiefer as founders of the consulting company Innovative Associates. Senge and Fritz remain close.

Fritz's background lies in music. No dilettante, he trained at the Boston Conservatory of Music and was on the faculty of the New England Conservatory of Music and Berklee College of Music. He still composes music for films, television and opera. He has also played with jazz great Dave Brubeck and recorded for various record labels. On top of that, Fritz has his own consulting company – the Fritz Group. The company, among other things, markets STPro, charting software designed by Fritz for strategic planning and project management.

Fritz's big idea is the decidedly unsexy one of structure or, in Fritz-ese, the structural approach. Luckily, this is not structure in any conventional sense of unmoving, dust-gathering hierarchies and the like. This is structural dynamics. The roots of the world, according to Fritz, can be traced back to the 1970s, when he began to train people in creativity and personal effectiveness. He discovered what he called the 'macrostructural pattern', which describes the long-range pattern in people's lives.

We are all unique, but Fritz determined there are two general types of pattern in people's lives: oscillating and resolving or advancing. According to Fritz, advancement means moving from where we are to where we want to be; oscillation means moving from where we are toward where we want to be, but then moving back to the original position.

Fritz argues that structure is key to organizational success and to individuals' personal success within organizations. A small change in structure can yield major benefits. Inevitably, in reality, companies are addicted to making huge structural changes that yield few benefits.

Fritz develops similarities between the creative process in music and the art of management. Music, he says, teaches us a number of important lessons. First, it builds from contrasts. The jazz soloist can be completely at home in a big band. The second element is truth. The artist, whether a painter or a musician, has to live with the truth of his own performance. A bum note is a bum note and can't be covered up. The artist shrugs and hopes to learn enough and to work hard enough to get it right. In contrast, the harried executive is as likely to cover up the truth as reveal it. Truth, in the corporate world, can be construed as weakness.

Fritz's third line of comparison is that of tension. He says that structural tension is 'the basis for great leadership'. The fourth point is the need for discipline. Fritz observes that the great artists are dedicated to their own development. They are addicted to the discipline of experimentation.

Finally, there must be an overall sense of long-term objectives. Being preoccupied with the short term is the route to endlessly tedious solos rather than overall excellence.

Key texts

- Robert Fritz with Peter M. Senge. *The Path of Least Resistance for Managers: Designing Organizations to Succeed*. Publishers Group West, 1999
- Robert Fritz. *Corporate Tides: The Inescapable Laws of Organizational Structure*. Berrett-Koehler, 1996
- Robert Fritz. *The Path of Least Resistance: Learning to Become the Creative Force in Your Own Life*. Fawcett Books, 1989
- Robert Fritz. *Creating*. Fawcett Books, 1989

Key link

- www.robertfritz.com

Front office

The front office is the element of a company's operations visible to the world at large and, more specifically, the consumer. It is the part the consumer interacts with. For an electrical retailer, the front operation would include the retail-outlet staff and customer-service operations. The hidden elements – the warehousing and manufacturing operations – are known as the back office. Similarly, in a bank, the bank tellers are the front office, with much of the rest of operations, including administrative functions, accounts and marketing, in the back office. As companies become more customer-focused, so more of their activities become part of the front-office operation.

FTC (Federal Trade Commission)

The FTC is a US anti-monopoly organization that enforces federal anti-trust and consumer protection laws. In general, the FTC seeks to ensure that America's markets 'function competitively, and are vigorous, efficient, and free of undue restrictions' and that actions that threaten consumers' opportunities to exercise informed choice are eliminated. Its responsibilities fall under three categories: '(a) Statutes relating to both the competition and consumer protection missions; (b) statutes relating principally to the competition mission; and (c) statutes relating principally to the consumer protection mission.'

As part of its responsibilities, the FTC alerts the public to fraudulent, deceptive and unfair business practices, such as those outlined in its *12 Scams Most Likely to Arrive Via Bulk Email* alert (www.ftc.gov/bcp/conline/pubs/alerts/doznalrt.htm).

Key link
• www.ftc.gov/

FTP (file transfer protocol)

The file transfer protocol is a set of rules that governs the transfer of files between computers over the Internet. The use of FTP avoids incompatibility between individual computers. To use FTP over the Internet, a user must have an Internet connection, an FTP client or World Wide Web browser, and an account on the system holding the files. Many commercial and non-commercial systems allow anonymous FTP clients either to distribute new versions of software products or as a public service.

FTP is commonly used to upload Web pages compiled on the user's machine to a Web server, where they can be accessed via the Internet by other users. It can also be used to download files and programs. Although FTP uses **Unix** commands, there are a number of shareware and freeware programs, such as CuteFTP, that offer a graphical user interface and simplify the process.

Key link
• www.cuteftp.com

Fulfilment

Order fulfilment has become one of the critical issues in e-commerce. Fulfilment – the delivery of goods or services to the purchaser once the purchaser has ordered those goods and services – has proved the acid test for many dotcom companies. E-commerce firms found that signing up users and receiving orders was only half the battle. As many e-commerce companies held no inventory and contracted out order fulfilment, they had no control over fulfilment and suffered as a consequence.

Full line forcing

Full line forcing occurs when suppliers force retailers to carry an entire product line rather than an individual product. The practice is also known as tie-in sales. It is a restrictive trade practice that discourages competition. If a powerful supplier 'asks' a retailer to display its entire product range, or none at all, retailers are often forced to agree. If this eats into shelf space, rival brands will suffer. If the practice does substantially lessen competition, then it may well fall foul of anti-competitive practices legislation.

Functional organization

A functional organization is arranged hierarchically, in the form of a pyramid. Authority cascades down through the organization. The **CEO** stands at the top of the pyramid, with functions like finance director and marketing director on the next level, and functions like sales manager and accounts manager beneath their respective directors.

Henri Fayol, French engineer and management theorist, identified 14 principles that create the perfect organization for functional management to thrive in. His 14 principles are division of work, authority and responsibility, discipline, unity of command, unity of direction, subordination of individual interest to the general interest, remuneration, centralization, scalar chain/line of authority, order, equity, stability of tenure, initiative and enthusiasm, and *esprit de corps.*

Funky business

See Nordström, Kjell and Redderstråle, Jonas

Futurist

Academics or commentators who predict future trends, futurists focus on the following areas: forecasting the future, using quantitative and qualitative means, imagining the future intuitively and creating the future. Notable futurists, past and present, include H.G. Wells (English, 1866–1946), Aldous Huxley (English, 1894–1963), Watts Wacker (American), **Alvin Toffler** (American, b. 1928), and **Peter Schwartz** (German, b. 1946).

G

Game theory

Game theory is based on the premise that no matter what the game, no matter what the circumstances, there is a strategy that will enable you to succeed. Whether you are playing poker, negotiating salaries or bidding in an auction, rules are at work, however elusive and intangible they might be.

Game theory was conceived not in the classroom or in the boardroom but in the casino. In the 1930s, when he was a student at Princeton and Harvard, Hungarian-born US mathematician John von Neumann (1903–1957) was an attentive spectator at poker games. Von Neumann was a mathematical genius rather than a gambler and the result was game theory, a unique mathematical insight into the possibilities and probabilities of human behaviour.

Von Neumann went on to apply his genius to the development of the United States' nuclear arsenal and the first computer, while game theory developed its own Zen-like language of dilemmas and riddles. The most famous of these is the prisoner's dilemma.

Invented by Princeton University's Albert Tucker in 1950, the prisoner's dilemma is an imaginary scenario. Two people are arrested and placed in separate cells, where each is offered the following choices: a) you don't confess and neither does your colleague = 3 years in prison; b) you both confess = 4 years; c) you confess and your partner doesn't = 2 years; d) you don't confess and your partner does = 12 years. The best outcome for both of them collectively is not to confess and get 3 years each. However, if one believes the other will not confess, then by confessing he can get 2 years. Alternatively, if he believes the other will confess, he must also confess to avoid getting 12 years. Logic drives both to confess. This situation is used in economics and other situations to show the relative merits of acting in concert or individually.

The prisoner's dilemma has a fundamental flaw. Game theory is rational; reality is not. Companies that have expressed an interest in game theory tend to be from tightly regulated industries, such as power generation, where there is limited competition or cartels (such as **OPEC** in the oil industry). With a limited number of players, playing by accepted rules and behaving in a rational way, game theory can make sense of what the best competitive moves may be.

Broader interest in game theory was reignited in 1994, when the Nobel Prize for economics was awarded to three renowned thinkers – John Nash, John Harsanyi and Reinhard Selten. Harsanyi has shown that even if players in a particular game are not well informed about each other, the game can still be analysed in the same way as other games. The precociously brilliant Nash (brought to life on the big screen by Russell Crowe in *A Beautiful Mind*) has carved the most notable academic furrow and is the creator of Nash's Equilibrium, an idea developed in his PhD thesis.

The Nash Equilibrium is the point at which no player can improve his or her position by changing strategy. Players in a game will change their strategies until they reach equilibrium. (In the prisoner's dilemma, the Nash Equilibrium is reached when both prisoners confess – they can no longer improve their situation by changing their strategy, as this would send them to prison for a longer period.)

In one classic example, an industry includes two competing companies. Each determines the price of its product. If both were to set high prices, they would maximize their profits. Similarly, if both set their prices at lower levels, they would remain profitable. The trouble comes when they choose different price levels. If one sets a high price and the other a low price, the company with the low price makes far more money. The optimal solution is for both to have high prices. The trouble is if one company has a high price, the other will undercut it and vice versa. Eventually, both companies end up with low prices and lesser profits.

The key lesson from this and other scenarios explored by game theory is simply that the actions of companies and other organizations are interdependent. In fact, game theory encompasses some of the fundamental truths of decision making. If a company decides to make an investment, it should consider how others – whether they be competitors, customers or suppliers – will react. Game theory acknowledges that real life is not conducted in a vacuum.

Instead, companies must visualize and anticipate the reactions and responses of their competitors. In the jargon, putting yourself in the shoes of your competitors – considering their future moves and their likely impact – is labelled 'allocentrism'.

Game theory is more than rational rules for an irrational world. Behind its rationality lies a world of daunting irrationality and maddening paradox. It is best seen as a way of thinking about the future, a tool to get people to think. As a rationalist's guide to business paradoxes, Game theory can be a useful business weapon. Instead of seeking out strategies driven by win-lose scenarios, companies begin to explore the merits of other strategies that may be win-win, with mutual benefits for themselves, their customers, suppliers and even their competitors.

This enables escape from the negative-sum games evident in many industries, where promotions and advertising are quickly countered by yet more promotions and advertising. In such scenarios, the costs of doing business increase, profits fall and market share tends to remain distressingly static. Game theory is dismissive of such short-term, knee-jerk reactions. If you are going to play the game, you have to think ahead. You make your move in anticipation of what you have calculated the competition will do.

One potential growth area for game theory's as-yet minimal usage lies in partnerships. Nash's initial work tackled non-cooperative games, where competitors didn't communicate. Now, game theory has spread its tentacles to embrace the growing trend for partnerships, an area where the full range of uncertainties are evident. Game theory offers a means of rationally interpreting the possibilities of cooperation as managers grapple with the myriad of intangibles produced by win-win relationships.

American academics Adam Brandenburger and Barry Nalebuff suggest the new onus should be on **co-opetition**, an inelegant combination of competition and cooperation. They argue that 'looking for win-win strategies has several advantages. First, because the approach is relatively unexplored, there is greater potential for finding new opportunities. Second, because others are not being forced to give up ground, they may offer less resistance to win-win moves, making them easier to implement. Third, because win-win moves don't force other players to retaliate, the new game is more sustainable. And, finally, imitation of a win-win move is beneficial not harmful.'

Key texts
- John H. Holland. *Emergence: From Chaos to Order*. Addison-Wesley, 1998
- Robert Axelroad. *The Complexity of Cooperation*. Princeton University Press, 1997
- Adam Brandenburger and Barry Nalebuff. *Co-opetition*. Doubleday, 1996
- Martin Osbourne and Ariel Rubinstein. *A Course in Game Theory*. MIT Press, 1994

- Norman Macrae. *John von Neumann: The Scientific Genius Who Pioneered the Modern Computer, Game Theory, Nuclear Deterrence and Much More.* Pantheon, 1992

Gantt chart

Gantt charts are used as an aid to project planning where activity is plotted against time. Horizontal bars represent the tasks scheduled during a project. The bars are stacked up on top of each other, one for each activity. Each bar extends from left to right to reflect how much time the task is expected to take. At the extreme left will be the start time and on the extreme right the finish time. As the project progresses, each bar is shaded to reflect the proportion of the task completed. At any one time, by drawing a vertical line from top to bottom, it is possible to see how the project is progressing. Gantt charts are used as graphical aid in **critical-path analysis**.

Gates, William Henry

Co-founder and CEO, Microsoft (b. 1955)

William Henry Gates III was born in Seattle; his parents nicknamed him Trey from the III in his name. He was a precociously brilliant boy. Before his tenth birthday, he had read the family's encyclopaedia from beginning to end. He excelled at mathematics.

Gates acquired computer guru status early in life. At Lakeside, the exclusive private school he attended in Seattle, he developed an obsession with computers. Still only 13 years old, Gates and some of his computer friends formed the Lakeside Programmers Group, dedicated to using their programming skills to make money. At Lakeside, he developed a friendship with another boy two years his senior. The boy, whose obsession with computers matched Gates's, was **Paul Allen**.

The intellectually driven Gates left Lakeside in 1973, to study law at Harvard. To Gates, law was a lot less appealing than computing. He contacted

Allen and the two teamed up to develop a version of an early computer language – BASIC. Enthusiastic about the possibilities offered by computer programming, Gates dropped out of Harvard in 1977 to start up a small computer software company with Allen. They called it Microsoft.

A brilliant strategic decision in 1980 set Microsoft on the road to global dominance. Without it, Microsoft might have been just one of many software companies founded on the success of the personal computer. At the time, IBM dominated the IT industry through its mainframe business. By the late 1970s, Microsoft was licensing its software to a number of customers. But the prevailing wisdom was that hardware was the business to be in and software was merely an adjunct. IBM certainly thought its future lay with its hardware.

At the time, Apple was developing a proprietary in-house operating system that would provide a competitive advantage. Its strategy was to maintain control over what it regarded as its superior hardware running its own software. Gates thought differently. As far as he was concerned, the more people that used Microsoft software on their machines, the better. So when IBM approached Microsoft to develop the operating system for its first PC, Gates recognized the enormity of the opportunity. IBM's dominance of the IT market meant that its PCs were destined to set the standard – both for hardware and for the OS. Gates capitalized on the situation, cannily retaining the right to license its OS to other PC manufacturers.

The decision of IBM to use Microsoft's MS-DOS was a turning point for both Microsoft and IBM. From that point onward the fortunes of IBM, which singularly failed to grasp the significance of the OS, inexorably declined until Lou Gerstner came to its rescue as CEO in 1993. For Microsoft, the only way was up. MS-DOS, as Gates had intended, rapidly became the industry standard.

Once out in front, Gates never looked likely to relinquish his company's lead. The rise of Microsoft was rapid and relentless. Gates demonstrated that he combined bone-deep technical understanding with superb commercial instincts. When ill health forced Allen to leave Microsoft, Gates's position as leader was confirmed. Microsoft's rapid growth soon made it the darling of Wall Street. From a share price of $2 in 1986, Microsoft stock soared to $105 by first half of 1996, making Gates a billionaire and many of his colleagues millionaires.

Gates has always attracted his share of detractors. Criticism has constantly been levelled at Microsoft, alleging that the company abuses its dominant market position. When the Internet revolution took off in the early 1990s, Microsoft was momentarily caught off balance. It seemed the normally prescient Gates was blind to the potential of the global network and the Web.

A company called Netscape sprang up, giving away a nifty piece of software called a browser, and Microsoft found itself desperately trying to catch up. It responded by licensing Mosaic browser technology, tweaking it and repackaging it as the Microsoft browser Internet Explorer. It began to make inroads into the Internet market. To cover all the bases, Microsoft also bought WebTV, eShops, Hotmail and Vermeer (the original developers of the Front Page HTML editing software). Catch-up is a game at which Gates and Microsoft excel.

Critics, however, regularly deride the company for buying technology rather than developing its own solutions. At one time or another, the major players in the software market – Sun Microsystems, RealNetworks, Netscape – have all found themselves on a collision course with the pugnacious Gates, and have been vocal in their complaints about Microsoft's behaviour.

Matters came to a head when the US Justice Department investigated Microsoft to establish whether the company was in breach of anti-trust law. After a lengthy trial – and a mountain of depositions – US District Judge Thomas Penfield Jackson ordered Microsoft to be split into two companies in June 2000, holding that it had violated the nation's anti-trust laws by using monopoly power to push aside potential competitors to the detriment of consumers. Microsoft took the case back to appeals court in February 2001, and

in June 2001 the court decided to overturn part of the original decision, withdrawing the requirement for Microsoft to be broken up.

Ultimately, it may not be the anti-trust ruling that poses the biggest threat to Microsoft's bottom line. Microsoft may still dominate desktop computer operating systems, but the world no longer revolves solely around the desktop PC. Microsoft risks being sidelined by the sheer pace of technological progress. Handhelds and mobile phones may be the PCs of the future, and those markets are not dominated by Microsoft. Even on its home ground of PC operating systems, open-source software such as Linux poses a threat.

Bill Gates is lauded and reviled in almost equal measures. But whatever you think of the dominance of Microsoft or the methods of Gates, it cannot be doubted that when it comes to building and retaining a competitive advantage, Gates has few peers.

Key texts

- Bill Gates with Collins Hemingway. *Business @ the Speed of Thought: Using a Digital Nervous System.* Warner Books, 1999
- Des Dearlove. *Business the Bill Gates Way.* Capstone, 1998
- James Wallace and Jim Erickson. *Hard Drive: Bill Gates and the Making of the Microsoft Empire.* John Wiley, 1992
- Stephen Manes and Paul Andrews. *Gates.* Doubleday, 1992

Key links

- www.microsoft.com/billgates/default.asp
- www.business2.com/webguide/0,1660,6491, FF.html
- www.business2.com/webguide/0,1660,54086, FF.html

GATT (General Agreement on Tariffs and Trade)

First signed shortly after World War II, in 1947, the General Agreement on Tariffs and Trade (GATT) was designed to provide an international forum to encourage regulation of international trade and provide a trade dispute resolution mechanism. Hard on the heels of the agreement came an international organization created to support the agreement. GATT, the international agency, has since been replaced by the **World Trade Organization** (WTO), which was established following the Uruguay Round in 1995. Much of the work associated with GATT has been concerned with trade and the environment. In the original agreement, however, there was no explicit provision for environmental issues. It wasn't until 1991 that a GATT committee on the environment met for the first time. GATT – the legal agreement – still exists, although it was updated in 1994 to reflect a shift from trade in goods to trade in goods, services and intellectual property. The new GATT agreements are administered by the WTO. GATT membership now includes more than 110 countries.

Key link
• www.wto.org

GDP (gross domestic product)

GDP refers to the market value of all final goods and services produced within a country within a given time period. Intermediate goods such as plastic, steel, etc. are not included to avoid double counting, as they are not in their final stage and will eventually be turned into final goods. Household goods are included, as they are intended for consumption or use, rather than to be turned into other goods. GDP (the expenditure method of calculation) consists of four elements: consumption, which includes all prices in the household sector (services, non-durable goods and durable goods); investment, which includes all business expenditure on goods that will be used to produce more goods and services; government expenditure; and net exports, i.e. exports/imports. As total output and/or prices changes, so too does GDP. Thus GDP is an indicator of the state of an economy. A rise in total output means an economy is growing;

two consecutive quarters of decline in total output equals a technical recession. Optimal economic growth with full employment is considered to be in the 2 to 2.5 percent range. As GDP is affected by a change in prices as well as a change in output, it needs to be adjusted to account for inflation. Inflation-adjusted GDP is known as real GDP and is calculated by dividing nominal GDP by the appropriate price index.

Gearing

Gearing is a situation in which control of an asset is acquired for a small upfront cost. The result is that profit or loss percentages are magnified accordingly. This situation can rise in individual markets that trade on a margin, such as the futures market. An individual only puts up a fraction of the cost of the future – the margin – although he is liable in full for any losses or entitled in full to any profits.

In a company, the level of financial gearing is determined by the gearing ratio, also known as the gearing to equity ratio. This shows the relationship between company funding that bears a fixed-interest charge, such as debentures and preference shares, and its equity or ordinary share capital. It is usually defined as borrowings divided by shareholders' funds, expressed as a percentage, although the definition varies from situation to situation. When the proportion of long-term fixed-interest capital is greater, the company is said to be highly geared. Highly geared companies are considered speculative investments for ordinary shareholders, as the fixed interest is paid before funds become available for other purposes, such as paying a dividend.

Geneen, Harold
CEO of ITT; king of conglomerates (1910– 1997)

Son of a Russian Jewish father and an Italian Catholic mother, Harold Geneen was born in Bournemouth. Geneen's family moved to America before his first birthday, but his parents separated soon after they arrived. As a result, Geneen's childhood was spent at boarding schools and summer camps. When Geneen started work as a runner for the New York Stock Exchange, he continued to study at night at New York University. In 1934, his hard work was rewarded with a degree in accounting.

For the next 25 years his career took him to a string of companies, starting with the forerunners of Coopers & Lybrand, followed by Montgomery, an accounting firm, the American Can Co., Bell and Howell Co., Jones and Laughlin Steel Co. and Raytheon. After Raytheon, where Geneen was vice-president, came the biggest challenge of Geneen's career and the job that made him famous – CEO of International Telegraph and Telephone Company, more commonly known as ITT.

When Geneen arrived at ITT in 1959, the corporation was a rag-bag of businesses, loosely focused around telecommunications, with revenues of $800,000. During the 1960s, the predominant organizational trend was one of diversification and conglomeration. CEOs went into a purchasing frenzy, raiding the corporate aisles for any company, no matter what business it was in, so long as it turned a profit. Geneen was no exception.

Over the ensuing decade, Geneen purchased over 300 companies operating in over 60 different countries. There was no rationale to these purchases, no common thread, other than that of profit. Sheraton hotels, Avis car rental and Continental Baking were all tucked away in ITT's roomy locker. 'I never met a business that I didn't find interesting,' said Geneen – and the ITT balance sheet certainly bore him out.

It was a mammoth undertaking to manage so many disparate companies. Fortunately for ITT, Geneen was no slouch. On the contrary, he was a fiercely driven workaholic. His ITT office in New York was equipped with eight telephones and a clock that showed which parts of the world were in daylight and which in darkness. Ten suitcase-sized leather attaché cases crammed full of documents were stacked along the window ledges. Six

of the cases, stuffed with reports, communiqués and memos from more than 400 reporting corporations, followed Geneen around the country and the world.

A typical Geneen story is recounted by an old ITT executive. Dragging a group of executives in for an evening meeting, Geneen worked them late into the night. At 11:45 p.m., the last of the executives made his way out of the office, pausing to wait for Geneen. Instead, the CEO peeled off his jacket, pulled on a sweater and carried on with his work – the last executive in the building.

To keep ITT under control, Geneen employed rigorous financial accounting methods. Each month, 50 or more executives flew to Brussels to spend several days examining the figures. 'I want no surprises,' was one of Geneen's mantras. Full information was paramount, as was the ability to tell real facts from details masquerading as facts. 'The highest art of professional management requires the literal ability to smell a real fact from all others,' asserted Geneen.

His approach seemed to work. From 1959 to 1977, ITT sales rocketed from some $765 million to nearly $28 billion, with earnings up from $29 million to $562 million. It was a success by most standards, not just Geneen's. Yet the more companies Geneen acquired, the harder it was to keep all the plates spinning in the air. In 1974 and 1975, profits fell. Geneen may have been able to keep up a relentless place, but his followers were either unable or unwilling to match it.

Geneen's efforts to support his company's share price sometimes strayed outside the boundaries of acceptable practice. For example, in 1972 the **Securities and Exchange Commission** discovered $8.7 million had been sunk into nefarious and illegal activities around the world. This allegedly included bribery and colluding with the CIA in an attempt to undermine the Allende government in Chile.

Geneen stepped down as chief executive in 1977, as chairman in 1979, and as a director four years later, but such a relentless man could never retire to a life of quiet contemplation and gentle pastimes. In his late 80s, long after he left

ITT, Geneen was still working a ten-hour day at his office in New York's Waldorf-Astoria hotel running a company, Gunther International, that he had bought into in 1992. Geneen carried on working in a number of different companies of his own creation until his death from a heart attack in 1997.

ITT, however, was a different proposition. Without Geneen to support it, the house of cards collapsed. ITT limped on, but eventually, after selling many of the companies acquired by Geneen, it was split up into three separate companies.

Harold Geneen was one of the last of his breed. He came to power at ITT at the height of the mania for conglomerates. Size mattered, and to Geneen it was very, very important. It's doubtful if any other CEO in corporate history has acquired more companies – over 300 – with less rationale. He was the best of his type, the paragon of his age – the king of the conglomerates.

Key texts
- Harold Geneen with Brent Bowers. *The Synergy Myth*. St Martins Press, 1997
- Robert J. Schoenberg. *Geneen*. W.W. Norton, 1985
- Robert J. Schoenberg. *Managing*. Doubleday, 1984
- Anthony Sampson. *The Sovereign State of ITT*. Stein and Day 1973

Key links
- www.thinkexist.com/English/Author/x/Author_3037_1.htm
- www.time.com/time/time100/builder/other/conglomerates.html

Generation X

'Generation X' is the term used to describe the generation of people born from 1961 to 1981. The core strata of Generation X were born during the narrower range, sometimes referred to as the baby bust, of 1965 to 1975. The term was coined by Canadian author Douglas Coupland (b. 1961), who drew on sociological studies of youth rebellion carried out in the 1960s. Coupland has described Generation X as not a chronological age but rather a 'way of looking at the world'. Defining characteristics of Generation Xers include apathy, lack of direction and a cynical outlook on life, but also the strong desire for a settled life and a healthy respect for the benefit of a college education (even if it is driven by the potential for increased financial rewards rather than learning per se). Generation Xers are also referred to as the slacker generation and the MTV generation. However, it might be also be pointed out that it was members of Gen X such as **Michael Dell**, **Jeff Bezos** and **Pierre Omidyar** who were the driving force behind the dotcom boom.

Key text
- Douglas Coupland. *Generation X*. St Martin's, 1991

Generation Y

Generation Y is the US generation produced by the **baby boom** between a period variously described as 1979 to 1994 or 1980 to 1996. Generation Y is three times the size of Generation X, and close to the 72 million of the original baby boomers. Between the years 2010 and 2020, Generation Y will make up 41 percent of the US population. With their current spending power estimated in excess of $250 million, marketers will be following the fortunes of Generation Y very closely. Generation Y is also known as the Millennium Generation and Echo Boomers.

Generic brand

When a brand becomes so closely associated with a product that it becomes synonymous with that product, it is known as a generic brand. Examples include Hoover, Sellotape, Frisbee, Polaroid,

Tampax and Band-Aid. Generic brands are not good news for the original brand, as all notion of brand identity and brand value is lost.

Gerstner, Louis V. Jr

CEO, IBM (b. 1942)

Born in Mineola, New York, Louis V. Gerstner Jr was the second of four sons. His early education was courtesy of the local Catholic school. His higher education is a textbook progression for many of today's top executives. First Gerstner majored in a specialized discipline, in his case engineering science, at Dartmouth, graduating in 1963. After Dartmouth, he went on to obtain an **MBA** from **Harvard Business School**. He then joined management consulting firm **McKinsey & Company** in 1964.

At McKinsey, Gerstner made rapid progress. As a still youthful 28-year-old Gerstner was appointed director after only five years. His early career post-McKinsey was no less impressive. At American Express during the 1980s, he revitalized the company's credit card division and saw net income grow by 66 percent. He then moved on to RJR Nabisco Holdings, where he cut a debt mountain of $26 billion to $14 billion, preparing the company for the largest leveraged buyout in corporate history.

When IBM cast around for an executive to replace CEO John Akers and pull them out of the mire, they chose Gerstner. The surprise was that Gerstner, with a glittering career ahead of him, entertained the offer to chase an apparently lost cause. But to the relief of 'Big Blue' and headhunters Heidrick & Struggles, Gerstner joined IBM as its new CEO in 1993.

When Gerstner arrived at IBM, it was in big trouble. For years, Big Blue had been the dominant company in the information technology industry and reaped massive profits through sales of its mainframe computers. But by the late 1980s the company had become complacent, lazy and slow. Full of its own self-importance, it ceased to innovate and lagged behind a rapidly changing IT market. Although it had introduced an IBM-badged PC, by outsourcing the two key components – the operating system and the processing chip – the company had handed the advantage to the Wintel twins – Microsoft and Intel.

Bogged down in bureaucracy and bloated with top-heavy management, IBM ground to a halt. In 1990, gross profit margins were a healthy 55 percent; by 1993, they had slumped to 38 percent. There was no sign of an end to the downward trend. Gerstner's response was immediate, dramatic and effective. His recovery checklist was to cut costs, get customers on IBM's side again, find strategic direction, and restore employee morale.

Cutting costs was comparatively easy, if painful. Gerstner budgeted for a restructuring cost of $8.9 billion, and set about laying off 35,000 employees before the end of 1995. The figure ended closer to 85,000. Elsewhere, measures such as centralized purchasing, better inventory management and the eradication of duplication in areas such as product development all contributed to improving the balance sheet position. In a move to improve customer relations, Gerstner made a special effort to get out and see the customers in person. The feedback from thousands of customer contacts persuaded him to retrain his generalist workforce to become the product specialists that customers demanded.

As Gerstner got rid of staff, he also took the opportunity to get rid of some of the ingrained corporate culture. Out went the traditional IBM executive look of blue suits and white shirts. Gerstner made a point of wearing a blue shirt.

Innovation is the central plank of Gerstner's strategy. In the year that Gerstner arrived, IBM filed for more patents than any other company in the United States. Thereafter, each year brought new innovative technologies from the supposedly directionless IT giant. Voice-recognition technology, the world's fastest supercomputer, copper-wired semiconductors, promising new technology to replace silicon chips, nanotechnology – the list of IBM innovation under Gerstner runs on.

Much of IBM's creativity is aimed at **e-business**, an area Gerstner believes is vital to the future success of Big Blue. By the beginning of 2001, the fastest growing segment of the roughly $90 billion company was its services business. Gerstner has repositioned the company as a major e-business company while hanging on to core business such as **servers**, storage, **networking** and middleware. It's a neat trick. Cleverly, he has also abandoned IBM's closed proprietary approach to technology and embraced the philosophy of the open-source movement, opening up IBM's technologies to other companies in a flurry of partnering deals.

In 1994, nearly two years after Gerstner's arrival, IBM posted a $3 billion profit on sales of $60 billion. This came after three consecutive years of losses totalling $15 billion. Share price improved to $89 by early 1994. By October 2001, the stock price had broken through the $100 barrier and the company was valued at an incredible $178 billion.

The challenge facing Gerstner and IBM now is to sustain the transformation. For a company of IBM's size, perpetual motion is a necessary but elusive quality. Gerstner seems to have confounded the critics by creating an agile and innovative company from a stagnant behemoth without, as was predicted, splitting it into smaller units. Gerstner's contract is up in 2002, by which time he will be close to 60.

Gerstner's timely arrival saved one of the largest and most famous IT companies in the world from extinction. He rediscovered the tradition of innovation and customer service ingrained in the organization by its founder, **Thomas Watson Sr.** Gerstner was the right leader in the right place at the right time. After a stellar career at companies such as McKinsey, American Express and RJR Nabisco, Gerstner's triumph at IBM was a fitting capstone for one of the finest managers of his generation.

Key texts
- Doug Garr. *IBM Redux: Lou Gerstner and the Business Turnaround of the Decade.* Harper Business, 1999
- Robert Slater. *Saving Big Blue: Leadership Lessons and Turnaround Tactics of IBM's Lou Gerstner.* McGraw-Hill Education Group, 1999

Key links
- www.ibm.com/lvg/bio.phtml
- www.business2.com/webguide/0,1660,6565,FF.html

Getty, John Paul

Founder, Getty Oil Company and J. Paul Getty Museum (1892–1976)

The son of oil businessman and lawyer George Franklin Getty, John Paul Getty was born in Minneapolis, Minnesota, on 15 December 1892. When Getty was 11, his father took him on a tour of his oilfields, teaching the boy about the oil industry. In 1906, Getty moved with his family to California.

A good scholar, Getty's studies took him through the Harvard Military Academy and the Polytechnic High School, both in Los Angeles, and on to the University of Southern California and the University of California at Berkeley. In 1914, Getty completed his studies with two terms at Oxford University, where he took a diploma in politics and economics.

When he returned to the United States after Oxford, he was determined to enter the Diplomatic Corps. Getty's father had other ideas. By this time he had built a multimillion dollar oil business. Getty was his only son, and he was desperate for him to commit to the family business. Getty, persuaded by his father, agreed to try his hand at the oil business. He struck a deal with his father. He would have a free hand to purchase leases on land he suspected might hold oil. His father would finance the operation and Getty could keep 30 percent of any profits.

Getty started in business in September 1914, buying oil leases and prospecting for oil. By June 1916, the 23-year-old had made a million dollars. With his newly acquired riches, Getty gave free rein to the impulses of youth and headed for Los Angeles, where he spent the next few years living the life of a wealthy playboy. Popular with women, he built – and crashed – his own sports car and generally lived life to the full. But in 1919, tiring of his leisurely life, Getty returned to the oil business. He joined his father's company, starting at the bottom as a 'roustabout' on the drilling operations, and earning a meagre $3 a day. It was tough manual labour but Getty thrived on it. The experience taught him a valuable lesson – always supervise the drilling of wells in person.

Although Getty had proved a shrewd businessman while working with his father, it was his father's death in 1930 that set Getty onto the path toward the oil empire he would eventually accumulate. His father, who was not impressed by Getty's frequent marriages and was aware that his personal wealth was considerable, left him only $500,000 of his $10 million fortune. The bulk of his estate he left to Getty's mother.

With less inheritance than he might have bargained for, and with the control of the Getty oil empire vested with his mother, Getty was forced to start over without his father's backing. Getty set out to prove he had as much commercial acumen as his father. Through a series of shrewd deals, Getty acquired the Western Oil Corporation, a controlling interest in his father's company, the Mission Corporation and thereby Tidewater Oil and Skelly Oil Company.

It took Getty 20 years to put the pieces in place that would eventually be controlled by the Getty Oil Company, of which Getty owned 80 percent. It was a long, protracted battle and Getty admitted that had he known that it was **Rockefeller**'s Standard Oil that owned Tidewater Oil, he would never have set out to buy it.

Oil wasn't the only business Getty was interested in. For example, in 1938 he expanded into the hotel business, buying the Pierre at Fifth Avenue and 60th Street for $2,350,000. This was followed by other property deals, such as the Pierre Marques Hotel near Acapulco, Mexico. During World War II, his Spartan Aircraft Company, a subsidiary of Skelly Oil, turned out training planes and aircraft parts for the war effort and, following the war, turned its efforts to mobile home construction.

Getty's approach to business is well illustrated by one of his most celebrated deals. In 1949, back-

ing a hunch, Getty negotiated the rights to a 60-year drilling concession in an area of desert lying between Saudi Arabia and Kuwait, known as the Neutral Zone. No oil had ever been found there, and no surveys had suggested oil would be found there. Nonetheless Getty agreed to pay King Saud $9.5 million in cash plus $1 million a year regardless of whether Getty struck oil or not. 1950 came and went, as did 1951, and no oil in commercial quantities had been discovered. When 1952 drew to a close and there was still no oil, observers began to doubt Getty's legendary knack for finding oil. In 1953, the doubters were silenced when Getty finally struck oil. It was an enormous find, and soon the field was producing more than 16 million barrels a year.

During the 1950s, Getty moved to England, buying through his company one of the country's most celebrated Tudor mansions, Sutton Place, north of Guildford, in Surrey. From there he orchestrated his business interests in Europe and the Middle East. His later life was spent dealing with personal tragedy – the premature death of two of his sons and the kidnapping of his grandson – writing his memoirs, and building his collection of art masterpieces, antiquities and carpets. He died in 1976.

John Paul Getty had the confidence of a millionaire's son and the understanding of money that comes with it. 'If you owe the bank $100, that's your problem. If you owe the bank $100 million, that's the bank's problem,' he once observed.

His business instincts were invariably right, and he was resolute to the point of stubbornness in backing his hunches. He could have cut his losses in the Middle East when no oil had been discovered. Instead he gritted his teeth and stuck it out, and in the end was proved right. Getty's instincts made him a rich man. In October 1957, *Fortune* magazine named Getty the richest man in the world.

Key texts

- Russell Miller. *The House of Getty*. Henry Holt, 1985
- Robert Lenzer. *The Great Getty: The Life and Loves of J. Paul Getty*. Crown, 1985

Key links

- www.getty.edu/museum
- www.cnn.com/TRAVEL/NEWS/9712/16/ getty.opening/getty.man/

Ghoshal, Sumantra

London Business School professor and author (b. 1948)

With his film-star cheekbones, piercing eyes, hawkish intensity and intellectual brilliance, Sumantra Ghoshal is an intimidating figure. Working along with Harvard Business School's **Christopher Bartlett**, he has become one of the most sought-after intellectuals in the business world.

Ghoshal is Robert P. Bauman Professor of Strategic Leadership at London Business School. He joined London Business School in 1994 after holding positions as professor of business policy at INSEAD and visiting professor at MIT's Sloan School. He is also the author of *Transnational Management: Text, Cases, and Readings* (1990); *Organization Theory and the Multinational Corporation* (with Eleanor Westney, 1993); and *The Strategy Process: European Perspective* (with Henry Mintzberg and J.B. Quinn, 1995).

Ghoshal first came to prominence with the book *Managing Across Borders* (with Christopher Bartlett, 1989), which was one of the boldest and most accurate pronouncements of the arrival of a new era of global competition and truly global organizations. Their 1997 book, *The Individualized Corporation*, marked a further step forward in the thinking of Ghoshal and Bartlett.

Ghoshal has mapped and recorded the death of a variety of corporate truisms. He insists that his questions have remained the same, but the answers have changed – 'I am a plain vanilla strategy guy. What does strategy mean is where I started.'

Today's reality, as described by Ghoshal, is harsh: 'You cannot manage third generation strategies through second generation organizations with first generation managers.' Even the perspectives from 'successful' companies appear bleak.

'Talk of transformation and you get the same examples,' he says. 'Toshiba in Asia Pacific, ABB, GE. If you listen to managers of those companies you will detect great scepticism about achieving victory. The battle ahead is far more complex.'

Despite such a damning critique of corporate reality, Ghoshal is not totally discouraged. 'Look at today and compare it to years ago. The quality of the strategic debate and discussion has improved by an order of magnitude,' he says.

The shift in emphasis in Ghoshal's work is from the cool detachment of strategy to the heated complexities of people. While *Managing Across Borders* was concerned with bridging the gap between strategies and organizations, Ghoshal and Bartlett's sequel, *The Individualized Corporation*, moved from the elegance of strategy to the messiness of humanity.

One of the phenomena Ghoshal has examined is the illusion of success that surrounds some organizations like a well-burnished halo. 'Satisfactory underperformance is a far greater problem than a crisis,' he says, pointing to the example of Westinghouse, which is now one-seventh the size of GE in revenue terms. 'Over 20 years, three generations of top management have presided over the massive decline of a top US corporation,' says Ghoshal. 'Yet, 80 percent of the time the company was thought to be doing well. Westinghouse CEOs were very competent and committed. They'd risen through the ranks and did the right things. Yet they presided over massive decline.'

The explanation he gives for this delusion of grandeur is that few companies have the ability for self-renewal. 'You cannot renew a company without revitalizing its people. Top management has always said this. After a decade of restructuring and **downsizing**, top management now believes it. Having come to believe it, what does it really mean?'

Ghoshal contends that revitalizing people is fundamentally about changing people. The trouble is that adults don't change their basic attitudes unless they encounter personal tragedy. Things that happen at work rarely make such an impact. If organizations are to revitalize people, they must change the context of what they create around people.

'The oppressive atmosphere in most large companies resembles downtown Calcutta in summer,' says Ghoshal. 'We intellectualize a lot in management. But if you walk into a factory or a unit, within the first 15 minutes you get a smell of the place.'

The way out of the smog is through purpose ('the company is also a social institution'); process ('the organization as a set of roles and relationships'); and people ('helping individuals to become the best they can be'). Undoubtedly these factors are less hard and robust than the three 'S's of strategy, structure, and systems, but Ghoshal believes they are the way forward.

Key texts

- Sumantra Ghoshal and Christopher A. Bartlett. *The Individualized Corporation: A Fundamentally New Approach to Management*. Harvard Business School Press, 1999
- Christopher A. Bartlett and Sumantra Ghoshal. *Managing Across Borders: The Transnational Solution*. Second edition, Harvard Business School Press, 1998

Ghost sites

Just like previous gold rushes, the Internet has spawned its share of deserted mines. For every successful entrepreneur, there are many more who failed to strike it rich. The hopeful dotcommer would buy a domain name, build the site – in some cases extremely well – and sit back waiting for the orders to roll in. When the in-tray remains ominously empty, the financiers keep their hands in their pockets, which marks the beginning of the end for the Web site. Updates become less frequent and when the founder finally pulls the plug, the site is left to languish usually with only a splash page to inform visitors of its demise. Only a ghost site remains.

So how long do these sites linger on the Net? Often it depends on the renewal of the domain name. When the domain name comes up for renewal, if it hasn't already been sold as part of a liquidation process, the ghost site will finally pass over to the other side. Some ghost sites, however, may continue indefinitely. While ISPs usually reserve the right to remove such sites, they often don't bother.

Key link

- www.disobey.com/ghostsites/

Gilbreth, Frank B. Sr and Lillian E.

Originators of time and motion studies (1868–1924; 1878–1972)

Truth be told, motion study had two authors: Frank Gilbreth and his wife Lillian. If every movement needs its zealots, the Gilbreths were the greatest disciples of **scientific management**.

Frank Bunker Gilbreth, born in Fairfield, Maine, was a bricklayer, building contractor and management engineer. Lillian Evelyn Moller, born in Oakland, California, received a BA and MA from the University of California, and later a PhD in psychology from Brown University. Married in 1904, the Gilbreths raised a dozen children and partnered in their consulting firm Gilbreth, Inc.

The Gilbreths put scientific management to the test. They made an art of measurement and, in doing so, helped further confuse the borders between measurement and management. The angle pursued by the Gilbreths was what they labelled 'motion study'. Most famously, Frank Gilbreth examined bricklayers at work. The bricklayers were inefficient. In response, Gilbreth designed and patented scaffolding that reduced bending and reaching, and increased output by over 100 percent. Gilbreth also invented the process-flow diagram, worked with the typewriter maker, Remington, and helped develop the Dvorak keyboard, a more efficient alternative to the Qwerty layout.

Their analysis of motion – aided by photography – led the Gilbreths to conclude there were 16 units of movement. These units they named **ther-**

bligs – Gilbreth backwards and slightly altered for ease of pronunciation.

When Frank Gilbreth died in 1924, Lillian picked up where he had left off and turned herself into an exemplar of industry. Not only did she bring up their large family; she headed the women's division of President Hoover's Organization on Unemployment Relief (1930–32), gained various degrees and, along the way, became famous. In 1938, Gilbreth was named one of twelve women 'capable of holding the office of president of the United States'. In 1944, the *California Monthly* said Lillian was 'a genius in the art of living'.

In fact, after Frank Gilbreth's death, his consulting clients all refused to use Lillian Gilbreth as a consultant simply because she was a woman. Her response was to use this to her advantage. 'If the only way to enter a man's field was through the kitchen door, that's the way she'd enter,' wrote Frank Jr and Ernestine Gilbreth in their book *Belles on Their Toes*. Lillian simply applied efficiency theories to her and her family's domestic arrangements. The children were brought up using efficiency techniques. Charts recorded if they had brushed their teeth. The children dusted the furniture before being allowed to play. Two stenographers were on hand to record Lillian's insights. (Two of the children, Frank and Ernestine Gilbreth, later shared their comical views of being raised by their efficiency-expert parents in the perennial favourite, *Cheaper by the Dozen*. The book was first published in 1950, made into a film that same year with Clifton Webb and Myrna Loy, and since republished several times.)

Though there was a farcical air to many of their endeavours and their blind enthusiasm took them down some unusual avenues, the Gilbreths had a powerful effect on management thinking. They elevated measurement to an all-embracing credo and helped establish it as one of the central tasks of management.

Key texts
- Frank B. Gilbreth Sr. *Bricklaying System*. Hive Publishing Company, 1974
- Frank B. Gilbreth Sr and Lillian M. Gilbreth. *Applied Motion Study: A Collection of Papers on the Efficient Method to Industrial Preparedness*. Hive Publishing Company, 1973
- Frank B. Gilbreth Jr and Ernestine Gilbreth Carey. *Cheaper by the Dozen*. Reissue edition, Harper Perennial, 2002
- Frank B. Gilbreth Jr and Ernestine Gilbreth Carey. *Belles on Their Toes*. Bantam Books, 1983

Key links
- http://gilbrethnetwork.tripod.com/bio.html
- http://access.tucson.org/~michael/hm_2.html

Gilder, George

Economist; futurist; Senior Fellow at Discovery Institute (b. 1939)

George Gilder's career has plotted an interesting course ever since he left Harvard University, where he majored in government and studied under Henry Kissinger. He wrote speeches for Nelson Rockefeller and Richard Nixon in the 1960s; pioneered supply-side economics as chairman of the Lehrman Institute's economic round table and programme director for the Manhattan Institute; was President Reagan's most frequently quoted living author; and wrote influential books on the causes of property, wealth, and entrepreneurialism.

Arguably, however, Gilder is most famous for his prescient and detailed examination of the semiconductor industry in the bestselling book *Microcosm* (1989), and his contributions to *Forbes ASAP*, which he also founded. *Microcosm* is notable for its coverage of Intel and **Andy Grove**.

Gilder could never be accused of sitting on the fence. Over the years, he has taken a strong line on the potential of many emerging technologies. Those that he has been less than keen on include HDTV interactive television and 3-D game machines. And the ones he liked? The **Java** programming language and optical networks.

Not bad going in an industry that's notoriously difficult to predict from one month to the next, let alone years ahead.

Gilder's next big prediction was that computers and telecommunications would displace broadcast TV's supremacy. He articulated his views on this in *Life After Television*. That book led to *Telecosm*, a Discovery Institute project on the future of telecommunications. If you want to get the latest on the future, sign up for the Gilder Technology Report at www.gildertech.com.

Key texts

- George Gilder. *Telecosm: How Infinite Bandwidth Will Revolutionize Our World*. Free Press, 2000
- George Gilder. *Wealth and Poverty*. ICS Press, 1993
- George Gilder. *Recapturing the Spirit of Enterprise*. ICS Press, 1992
- George Gilder. *Life After Television*. W.W. Norton, 1992
- George Gilder. *Microcosm: The Quantum Revolution in Economics and Technology*. Simon & Schuster Trade Paperbacks, 1990

Key links

- www.discovery.org/gilder/index.html
- www.gildertech.com
- www.pff.org/aspen96/gilder.html

Gillette, King Camp

Inventor and entrepreneur (1855–1932)

King Camp Gillette was born in Fond du Lac, Wisconsin, into a family of innovators. His father was a patent agent and small-time inventor. His mother wrote a cookery book based on a lifetime of culinary experimentation; the book was still in print a century later. When Gillette was four, his family moved to Chicago to start up a hardware business. Unfortunately, the business was ravaged by the Great Fire. In 1871, the family moved once again, this time to New York City.

Gillette took a job as a travelling salesman. Not content with merely selling his products, Gillette couldn't resist improving them. By 1890, he had accumulated four patents. In 1895, Gillette was working for the man who had invented cork-lined bottle caps. He had some simple advice for Gillette: 'Invent something people use and throw away.' Gillette took his words to heart and turned his attention to the safety razor.

Traditionally, men of the time used the straight-handled razor blade to shave. The increasing use of the railway, however, had prompted a rethink in the design of this basic implement. The swaying of the carriages made it downright dangerous to use the traditional cut-throat razor. Safety razors had been invented – a heavy blade fitted at right angles to a short handle – but they still had major shortcomings. Gillette used a Star Safety razor. This required continual sharpening on a leather strap, just as the traditional razor did. Eventually the blade would wear out.

Gillette had an idea. What if it was possible to take a small square of sheet steel and put a permanently sharp edge on it? Such a product would be affordable enough to throw away when it became dull.

To help him in his quest for a new improved safety razor, Gillette turned to metallurgists at the Massachusetts Institute of Technology. They assured Gillette that his idea was impossible. Undaunted, Gillette continued to search for someone who shared his belief and vision. That person was William Emery Nickerson, an inventor who, ironically, was educated at MIT.

Gillette's search had taken six years. His doggedness was rewarded in 1901 when Gillette and Nickerson formed the American Safety Razor Company. In 1903, they began production on the new safety razor, bundling up razor blades and selling them as a package. The razor handle was sold as a onetime purchase. In 1904, the renamed Gillette Safety Razor Company was awarded the patent for the new invention. Initial sales were disappointing. After an intensive advertising campaign in men's magazines and newspapers in the United States and Europe, things improved. By

1906, Gillette had sold 12 million blades, generating revenues of $90,000.

The inevitable patent battles ensued. With a large proportion of the world's population as a potential market, sharp practices were rife. Competitors came to the market with modified versions of Gillette's product. Gillette responded with litigation or, in many cases, by buying the competition. All the while, he continued to tinker with his invention. In 1904, he came up with the double-edged blade, a concept still used to this day. With his face plastered over the wrappers of his razor blades, Gillette became a celebrity.

Although the Gillette razor made King Camp Gillette a millionaire, he remained unfulfilled. Gillette had strong philosophical and political beliefs. With his newly made millions, he was now a powerful figure in American commerce. He had a vision of an idealistic utopian society based on universal cooperation, and he now had the means to attempt to make it a reality.

Gillette had written several books outlining his vision, beginning with *The Human Drift* (1894), which predated the invention of the Gillette razor. In a reaction to the mass pollution and sprawling urban development of the industrial revolution, Gillette planned pollution-free cities contained in giant glass domes. In this new utopia, one company would carry out all production with the citizens as the shareholders. 'Selfishness would be unknown, and war would be a barbarism of the past,' wrote Gillette.

Gillette's attempts at social engineering came to nothing. The Wall Street Crash of 1929, coupled with boardroom machinations and constant patent litigation, put paid to Gillette's personal fortune. He spent much of his final years trying unsuccessfully to extract oil from shale. In the end, Gillette died unfulfilled and frustrated in 1932. The Gillette Safety Razor Company thrived; it carried on its founder's tradition of innovation and remained on the cutting edge of safety razor development. The company introduced foam shaving cream (Foamy), antiperspirant (Right Guard), and continued to do what Gillette had always done – improve the safety razor with the twin-blade pivoting head, disposable and triple-blade razors.

King Camp Gillette will be remembered for creating a product used daily by people the world over. Not only did he pioneer the market for disposable products; he also showed an early and prescient awareness of the power of both celebrity and the brand. Gillette's image on the packaging of his product made him famous and helped reassure the consumer about the product's quality. This in turn boosted sales and helped make the Gillette Safety Razor Company the leader in its market.

Key texts
- J. Mansfield. 'The Razor King.' *American Heritage of Invention and Technology*. Spring 1992
- Russell B. Adams Jr. *King C. Gillette: The Man and His Wonderful Shaving Device*. Little, Brown & Co., 1978
- K.C. Gillette. *The People's Corporation*. Boni and Liveright, 1924
- K.C. Gillette. *The Human Drift*. New Era, 1894

Key links
- www.gillette.com
- www.school-for-champions.com/biographies/gillette.htm
- http://web.mit.edu/invent/www/inventorsA-H/gillette.html

Glass ceiling

The glass ceiling is an artificial invisible barrier to career advancement. The term is used particularly in conjunction with women and minorities. Equal opportunity legislation is intended to address issues such as the glass ceiling and there has been much talk in the media and among governments over the last decade about shattering the glass ceiling. Yet talk is often all it is.

Take women in senior management positions, for example. Despite all the talk about the softer side of management and the need to recruit more women to utilize their soft skills and sensitivity, women are notable by their absence from the world's boardrooms. Research from the Kelly School of Business, for example, shows that the number of women with executive positions in the United States is now lower than it was ten years ago. In 1987, there were eleven female directors at *Fortune* 500 companies, but by 1997, there were just eight. The number of women CEOs was two in 1987 and had only grown to four by 2002.

Global brand

It is not that long since brands were generally, though not exclusively, national in character. Consumer tastes were conveniently assumed to correlate with borders. Thus the British had the steady reliable Morris Minor, Germans had the durable Mercedes, and the French had Citroën's idiosyncratic classic, the Deux Chevaux. Today, brands and businesses know no borders. Products are less likely to be predominantly German or French in character – they may be European, but are more likely to have no fixed place of birth. Increasingly, brands are cosmopolitan pan-nationals.

One of the triggers for this global attitude toward brands was a theory proposed by one of the leading marketing academics and researchers of the post-war period: **Theodore Levitt**.

In his influential *Harvard Business Review* article, 'The Globalization of Markets', Levitt argued that the state of global economic and cultural integration was sufficient to allow the sale of products and services with a consistent marketing and advertising campaign, regardless of the country.

As a result of Levitt's views on globalization, many corporations were persuaded to rein back decision-making powers over their brands from the regional markets. Instead, there was a move toward centralization of marketing planning at corporate headquarters. Global brands offered potential advantages in a number of areas, including research and development, purchasing, production, marketing, distribution and sales.

The rise of globalization was one of the most striking trends in the business world of the 1990s. Brands have, to a large extent, led the way. Their flexibility and increasingly international nature mean that it has been automatically assumed in many quarters that particular brands are ripe for a global approach.

Many are. To prove the point, any major international sporting event will feature an array of global brands, whether they are Mars, Coca-Cola, McDonald's or Hertz. Brands travel well and global brands have now penetrated virtually every country on earth. Research by Gallup into the brand awareness of the Chinese found that Coke was already the second most popular brand, following Hitachi. And although some concessions may be made to local tastes and customs, the emphasis is on standardization. Coca-Cola and McDonald's are examples of global brands.

Globalization, fuelled by technology, international travel and the rise of truly mass media, is a relatively recent phenomenon. The emphasis on scalability that most venture capital firms gave to dotcom ventures has only served to magnify the attention on the potential for branding to be applied on global basis. Some brands, however, recognized the benefits of globalization before it became academically fashionable. Take Hilton Hotels, for example. **Conrad Hilton**, the group's founder, noticed that hotels were used not just by vacationers but by the travelling foot soldiers of the business world, who utilized them as temporary homes and offices. While hotels crumbled through competition from motels, Hilton invented a lucrative business offering high-quality, standardized service regardless of where the hotel was located in the world. The global and standardized brand remains firmly in place – the Hilton in Miami is the same as that in Rome or elsewhere. The company even used advertising featuring a taxi in a city with the caption 'Take me to the Hilton' – the assumption being that any major city has a Hilton, 'where you can be yourself again'. Senior managers still flock to Hiltons.

Key text
- James R. Gregory with Jack G. Wiechmann. *Branding Across Borders: a guide to global brand marketing.* McGraw-Hill, 2002

Global Business Network

The Global Business Network (GBN) is a 'community of individuals and organizations committed to thinking broadly and collaboratively about the future' founded by US futurist and business strategist **Peter Schwartz** and others in 1987. GBN 'associates' include Laurie Anderson, Bill Joy, Brian Eno, Paul Saffo, **Peter Senge**, **Esther Dyson** and **Kevin Kelly**.

Based in Emeryville, California, in a former tractor factory, GBN has approximately 100 clients, including the government of Singapore, as well as big corporations. (Its members are predominantly American. Approximately 60 percent have headquarters in North America, with another 30 percent in Europe and 10 percent in Asia, Africa and Latin America.)

'Basically, GBN does two very different, though related, kinds of things,' explains Peter Schwartz. 'One is to help people get information about leading-edge change. Particularly, what we're interested in are those things that come in from the fringes, from left field, as it were – the things that are likely to cause great surprise and that, by definition, companies are not going to see by looking at the mainstream sources of information. Secondly, we try to give our client companies a process, a tool – namely scenario planning – that offers a more rigorous approach to thinking about the future.'

Corporate membership is not cheap; it costs more than $30,000 annually, and individual members are invited to join only if they can 'contribute remarkable insights, provocative ideas, and deep experience.' GBN also provides consulting services for individual firms. Scenario planning, a concept invented by members of the GBN's staff and Royal/Dutch Shell back in the 1970s, features prominently.

Key link
- www.gbn.org

G-mail

See SMS (short message service).

Godin, Seth

Founder and CEO, Yoyodyne; creator of permission marketing

Seth Godin is a respected **e-commerce** pioneer, specializing in online marketing. He first went online in 1976. He is best known for introducing the idea of **permission marketing**.

After graduating from Tufts University in 1982, Godin went to work as brand manager for Spinnaker Software. His next stop was an **MBA** at Stanford Business School, graduating in 1984.

Godin has written a number of bestselling online business books, including *E-Marketing*, the *Guerilla Marketing* handbook, the *Information Please* almanac and *Permission Marketing: Turning Strangers into Friends and Friends into Customers. Permission Marketing*, among Amazon.com's 100 bestsellers since June 1999, was also selected as one of *Fortune* magazine's best business books. His two most recent creations are *Survival is Not Enough* and *Unleashing the Ideavirus*.

At Yoyodyne Entertainment, the company Godin founded and named after the character in Thomas Pynchon's novel *The Crying of Lot 49*, he set about changing the world of online marketing. His idea was to persuade people to accept product pitches from companies by offering them an incentive. A permission marketing campaign might, for example, involve an airline offering free flights or a chance to win the trip of a lifetime, in return for which the customer would grant permission to the airline to e-mail offers of other products it thought the customer might be interested in. This model has become one of the most popular ways of marketing online.

In late 1998, Yahoo! bought Yoyodyne and Godin became Yahoo!'s VP of direct marketing. Godin left Yahoo! in January 2000, but continues to serve as an external consultant and adviser to the company. He is also a contributing editor to **Fast Company**. His 2001 book, *Unleashing the Ideavirus* (co-authored with Malcolm Gladwell), became arguably the most downloaded e-book in history. Of course, Godin followed his own prescription in marketing *Ideavirus* and unleashed another epidemic of Seth Godin.

Key texts

- Seth Godin. *Survival is Not Enough*. Free Press, 2002
- Seth Godin and Malcolm Gladwell. *Unleashing the Ideavirus: Stop Marketing at People! Turn Your Ideas into Epidemics by Helping Your Customers Do the Marketing for You*. Hyperion, 2001
- Seth Godin. *Permission Marketing: Turning Strangers into Friends and Friends into Customers*. Simon & Schuster, 1995
- Seth Godin. *Wisdom, Inc.: 30 Business Virtues That Turn Ordinary People into Extraordinary Leaders*. Harper Business, 1995
- Jay Conrad Levinson and Seth Godin. *The Guerilla Marketing Handbook*. Houghton Mifflin, 1994

Key links

- www.fastcompany.com/team/sgodin.html
- www.sethgodin.com/sg
- www.business2.com/webguide/0,1660,34665,FF.html

Goizueta, Roberto

Former CEO, Coca-Cola (1932–1997)

Roberto Crispulo Goizueta was born in Havana, Cuba. He was a bright child who had a privileged upbringing. He attended a private school, the Cheshire Academy in Connecticut, where he mastered the English language through an unusual combination of formal tuition and sitting through countless hours of American movies.

After college, he went to Yale University to take a degree in chemical engineering. Goizueta graduated tenth in his class in 1953, returning to Cuba to work at his family's sugar refining business. Goizueta didn't spend long in the family business. He wanted to carve out a career for himself and, on an off chance, answered an ad in a Havana newspaper for a bilingual chemical engineer. Goizueta got the job and started work on 4 July 1954. It was with the Coca-Cola Company.

In 1959, Fidel Castro seized power in Cuba. Eighteen months later, Goizueta, his wife Olga and their three children left for the United States. Apart from his family, a suitcase, $200 in cash and 100 Coca-Cola shares, Goizueta left everything he owned in Cuba. The year was 1960.

Goizueta and his family settled in Miami, where he worked for the Latin American division of Coca-Cola. In 1964, he was moved to the technical research and development department at the company's headquarters in Atlanta.

He was a hard worker known for his tidiness and sharp dress sense. In Atlanta he found himself working closely with a company legend, **Robert Woodruff**. Woodruff had organized the syndicate that in 1923 bought out the Candler family's interests in Coca-Cola. He had overseen the company's global expansion and growth into one of the world's most valuable brands. Woodruff was still a major player. Goizueta clearly made a good impression on Woodruff as, in 1966, he was made company vice-president. Aged just 35, he was the youngest executive ever to have held the post.

His meteoric rise continued; he became senior vice-president in 1974 and a vice-chairman in 1979. Finally, in May 1980, he became CEO and chairman of Coca-Cola. It was a long way from the family sugar refinery in Cuba.

When Goizueta took the helm, Coca-Cola was facing one of the toughest challenges in its history. Rival Pepsi Co. was using a taste test dubbed the 'Pepsi Challenge' to turn soda drinkers into Pepsi purchasers. Worryingly, in a blind taste test, many consumers preferred Pepsi to Coke. Goizueta had promised that, in an effort to revitalize the company, he was prepared to take risks. In April 1985, he proved true to his word when he announced that Coca-Cola was replacing its traditional recipe with New Coke. It was, according to Goizueta, 'the boldest single marketing move in the history of the consumer-goods business'. Unfortunately, it also proved one of the major marketing mistakes of the twentieth century.

Detailed research conducted by Coca-Cola supported the move, indicating that most consumers preferred the new recipe. Yet while Pepsi was a threat, the old version of Coke was still selling in millions of units every day. The move made the Coca-Cola brand look weak. By reacting to the goading of its rival, instead of shrugging off the threat in the manner of the market leader that it was, Coca-Cola appeared worried. Furthermore, by producing a drink named 'New Coke', the company decoupled its brand values of tradition and authenticity from its new product. To call this the marketing disaster of the century would be to understate the effect only slightly. Goizueta was buried under an avalanche of criticism. Coke fans uncharitably said that the new formula tasted like 'furniture polish' and 'sewer water'.

To his credit, Goizueta didn't let pride or stubbornness get in the way of good marketing. Realizing that the introduction of New Coke had been a disaster, he backtracked and, after only 90 days, reintroduced the original recipe as Classic Coke. It has not been tinkered with since.

With the exception of the New Coke debacle, Goizueta's period at the helm of Coke was a huge success. In 1982, Goizueta led Coke in a new direction, agreeing to purchase Columbia Pictures. Though a nightmare to manage, this turned out to be a smart deal. Just a few years later, Coca-Cola sold Columbia to Sony, making a profit of nearly $1 billion. Goizueta also oversaw the successful product launch of Diet Coke.

Goizueta died in 1997 at the age of 65. When he died, the company was valued at $145 billion, compared with a value of $4 billion when he became CEO. Perhaps less well known about Goizueta is his commitment to education and to the Atlanta community. Over the years, he worked to strengthen non-profit organizations in the region and to bring the Olympics to Atlanta for the benefit of the entire city.

Key text
- David Greising. *I'd Like the World to Buy a Coke: The Life and Leadership of Roberto Goizueta.* John Wiley, 1998

Key links
- www.coca-cola.com
- www.nishna.net/501c3/nov97a5.htm

Golden hellos and goodbyes

Golden hellos and goodbyes, in their various forms, are contractual incentives to reward executives for joining a company and compensate them when they leave. Their benefits are usually restricted to high-ranking executives. Run-of-the-mill employees can expect to receive little or nothing of a contract is severed, especially if they are the ones who sever the contract. With senior executives, however, the situation can be very different.

A golden hello acts as an incentive for a prospective employee to join a company. Usually a financial bonus, it may or may not be taxable according to the structure of the payment. Golden handcuffs are another incentive, usually in the form of a financial bonus, used to tie an employee to a company. The aim is to prevent the employee from being poached by another company, thus golden handcuffs are usually structured to last for a period of time, often several years. Stock options are a popular form of golden handcuff.

When it comes to leaving the company, executives may benefit from a golden parachute. This clause provides for financial or other benefits should the executive be sacked or leave as a result of a merger, takeover or buyout. There may be a golden parachute where a severance payout is made to an employee, usually a senior manager or director, who is forced to retire before the end of his employment contract. A golden handshake is usually a substantial sum. The use of some of these clauses can be controversial, especially where the payment is made to executives following poor performance by the company.

Goleman, Daniel

CEO, Emotional Intelligence Services (b. 1946)

Born in Stockton, California, Daniel Goleman is a magna cum laude graduate of Amherst College, where he was an Alfred P. Sloan Scholar. He was a Ford Fellow at Harvard, where he took his MA and PhD in clinical psychology and personality development. At Harvard he studied with David McClelland, who inspired him to write about emotional quotient or EQ.

While at Harvard, Goleman journeyed to India, where he learned to meditate. Meditation has been an integral part of his life ever since. Goleman has been twice nominated for the Pulitzer Prize. For many years, he wrote on the brain and behavioural sciences for *The New York Times* and numerous other publications.

Author of the bestselling *Emotional Intelligence*, Goleman has created an industry, a touchy-feely world in which executives are encouraged to get in touch with their feelings as well as their balance sheets. 'The qualities of leadership and the qualities of the heart ... are largely the same,' Goleman writes, going on to explore the importance of the emotional dimension in determining the effectiveness of leaders.

Goleman argues that human competences such as self-awareness, self-discipline and empathy are more important than qualities such as a high IQ – in life and in business. In demanding jobs where above-average IQ is a given, superior emotional capability gives leaders an edge. At senior levels, emotional, rather than rational, intelligence marks the true leader. This is supported by studies

of outstanding performers that show that about two-thirds of the abilities that set star performers apart are based on emotional intelligence. Against this, only one-third of the skills that matter relate to raw intelligence (as measured by IQ) and technical expertise.

'Our emotions are hardwired into our being,' he explains. 'The very architecture of the brain gives feelings priority over thought.' In reality, it is impossible to entirely separate thought from emotion. 'We can be effective only when the two systems – our emotional brain and our thinking brain – work together,' says Goleman. 'That working relationship, which encompasses most of what we do in life, is the essence of emotional intelligence.'

The good news is that emotional intelligence can be learned. There are five dimensions to this, he says, each of which is the foundation for specific capabilities of leadership. These are:

- **Self-awareness:** We seldom pay attention to what we feel. A stream of moods runs in parallel to our thoughts. Our moods and previous emotional experiences provide a context for our decision making.
- **Managing emotions:** All effective leaders learn to manage their emotions, especially the big three of anger, anxiety and sadness. This, in the self-improvement argot, is a decisive life skill.
- **Motivating others:** According to Goleman, the root meaning of 'motive' is the same as the root of 'emotion': to move.
- **Showing empathy:** The flip side of self-awareness is the ability to read emotions in others.
- **Staying connected:** Emotions are contagious. There is an unseen transaction that passes between us in every interaction that makes us feel either a little better or a little worse. Goleman calls this a 'secret economy'. He, however, has unearthed a far more open economy.

Key texts

- Daniel Goleman, Richard Boyatzis and Annie McKee. *Primal Leadership: Realizing the Power*

of *Emotional Intelligence*. Harvard Business School Press, 2002
- Daniel Goleman. *Working With Emotional Intelligence*. Bantam Doubleday Dell, 2000
- Daniel Goleman. *Emotional Intelligence*. Bantam Books, 1997
- Daniel Goleman and Ram Dass. *The Meditative Mind: Varieties of Meditative Experience*. J.P. Tarcher, 1996

Key links
- www.ncteamericancollection.org/litmap/ goleman_dan_ca.htm
- http://ei.haygroup.com/default.asp

Goodwill

Traditionally, goodwill has been defined as the difference between the purchase price of a company's assets and the book value. This definition, which originated in the 1880s, has since been refined. There are now two possible definitions of the world. One, the residuum approach, states that goodwill is the difference between the purchase price of a company and its fair market value. The other, the excess-profits approach, states that goodwill is the difference between the combined company's profits over normal earnings for a similar business.

Goodwill includes a company's relationship with its customers and other intangibles such as its knowledge pool, intellectual property and location. Goodwill within an organization is not normally reflected as a value in its accounts, unless it is as a result of acquiring another company.

Gosling, James

Vice president and Sun Fellow at Sun Microsystems; creator of the Java programming language (b. 1956)

Canadian-born James Gosling received a BS degree in computer science from the University of Calgary, Canada, in 1977. He took his PhD in computer science from Carnegie Mellon University in 1983.

Gosling worked in IBM's research division before joining Sun in 1984 as a lead engineer for Sun's NeWS window systems. He also authored the EMACS text editor for **UNIX** systems, built satellite data-acquisition systems, a multiprocessor version of UNIX, several compilers, mail systems and a WYSIWYG text editor.

But Gosling made his name with **Java**. In December 1990, Sun Microsystems set up an in-house research project to look at the future of computing. The original members of the team were Patrick Naughton, Mike Sheridan and Jim Gosling. The project was named the Green project. All the members of the team came from product groups within Sun. This was a key factor in the success of the project. The group determined to produce a number of working prototypes and a business plan.

In 1991, the Green project moved offsite to premises on Sand Hill Road in Silicon Valley and recruited additional members. The group worked prolifically, producing a raft of different prototype multimedia products as well as a dynamic programming language to help communicate between the prototypes. The programming language, which was named Oak, was subsequently renamed Java.

It wasn't until 1993, however, when **Marc Andreessen** developed the Mosaic browser for the World Wide Web, that Java really took off. By 1994, the first prototype was up and running, and in 1995 Java was released to the world after the *San Jose Mercury News* leaked its location on the Net.

Java has now become one of the most important programming languages in computing – particularly in e-commerce, networks and Web development.

Key texts
- Ken Arnold, James Gosling and David Holmes. *The Java Programming Language*. Addison Wesley Longman, 2000
- James Gosling, Gilad Bracha and Bill Joy. *The Java Language Specification, Second Edition:*

The Java Series. Addison Wesley Longman, 2000

Key links

- http://java.sun.com/people/jag/
- www-106.ibm.com/developerworks/features/gosling

GIF (Graphics Interchange Format)

The graphics interchange format is a picture-file format developed by CompuServe in 1987, with further features added in 1989 (the two formats are known as GIF89 and GIF 89a). Along with **JPEG**, GIF (pronounced with a hard 'g') is one of the two most commonly used file formats for pictures on the World Wide Web. This is because pictures saved in this format take up a relatively small amount of space. Its principal limitation, however, is that it is restricted to 256 colours, whereas JPEGs can portray many millions. GIF uses LZW compression (the compression of a file data into a smaller file using an algorithm invented by Abraham Lempel, Jacob Ziv and Terry Welch), for which Unisys holds the copyright, and this fact has prompted moves to replace it with alternative formats such as Portable Network Graphics (PNG).

GNP (gross national product)

A country's gross national product is a measure of its total economic activity – an estimate of the value of all final goods and services produced in a given time period by the factors of production owned by a particular country's residents.

GNP is usually assessed quarterly or yearly and equals **GDP** plus income earned by domestic residents from foreign investments minus income earned by foreign investors in the country's domestic market. Like many economic measures, GNP has its faults. For a start, GNP accounts for goods traded in a free market. However, many goods are not traded in this manner. For exam-

ple, the government provides many services and goods to the public, which are paid for by taxation extracted as a compulsory measure. Equally, a significant proportion of the trading in any economy is 'hidden', a part of the black economy. This may be because the nature of the trading is illegal, or merely to avoid taxation. Also, currency fluctuations and inflation from year to year make it difficult to interpret GNP figures. Yet GNP figures are still used as an important indicator of an economy's strength and productivity. Two successive quarters of decline in GNP means that an economy is technically in a recession.

Grassroots leadership

Leadership was once about heroes, indomitable individuals fighting against the odds, leading organizations from the front. Then it all changed. First came the fashion for empowerment. This created a lot of talk about changing leadership roles and skills, but examples of empowering leaders were usually notable by their absence. Second, uncertainty levels increased through industry after industry. Leaders traditionally thrived on creating certainty. If they didn't know where they were going, how was anyone else to know?

Grassroots leadership is an attempt at squaring the leadership circle, an approach used by Royal/ Dutch Shell. This addition to the management vocabulary is attributed to Steve Miller, group managing director of Shell. Miller observed the difficulties the company was experiencing in becoming more creative, innovative and faster moving. It was attempting to transform itself, one layer of management at a time. Change quickly became becalmed.

Miller cut out the middlemen and went straight to employees. In small groups, the people from filling stations and the like were brought in for intensive training. Miller concentrated half of his time on talking to, meeting with and involving 'grassroots' people. 'As people move up in organizations, they get further away from the work that goes on in the field – and as a result, they tend to devalue it,' he says. 'People get caught up in broad strategic issues, legal issues, stakeholder issues. But what really drives a business is the work that goes on down at the coal face. It's reliability, it's producing to specification, it's delivering to the customer.' Grassroots leadership is, in essence, another attempt to put managers in touch with what really happens in their organizations.

Key text
- Richard Pascale. 'Grassroots Leadership.' *Fast Company*, April/May 1998

Green shoe option

A green shoe option gives the underwriter or manager of a new share issue an option to acquire shares from the company after the issue. In an **IPO**, especially when demand is heavy, an investment bank will oversell an issue, selling 110 percent of new stock, for example. Then, if the share price rises in the market above the issue price, the underwriter can go back to the company, exercise the right to buy more shares, and so cover his position. If the price falls, then the company purchases shares on the open market to close the position, which creates demand for the shares and acts as a stabilizing influence on the market.

Greenmail

Greenmail is one of a raft of unusually named terms relating to mergers and acquisitions, such as the **macaroni defence** and the **poison pill**. Greenmail refers to the situation in which a potential predator takes a large shareholding in a company. The whiff of a takeover will usually drive the share price up, forcing the target company to pay a premium to purchase the stock necessary to prevent a takeover. The target company does not know, of course, whether the potential predator is serious or not. It's a sharp practice, but not illegal.

Greyhairs

The term 'greyhairs' refers to senior executives. It became popular during the dotcom boom. The **venture capital** companies providing early-stage finance to dotcom start-ups drafted experienced executives onto the start-ups' boards to lend weight to the management team.

Gross profit

The gross profit figure is the difference between the revenue from sales and the direct cost of production for a business. It does not take account of the overheads of the business. Gross profit is usually shown in the profit-and-loss account of the company. Dividing gross profit by revenue gives the figure for gross margin. This is the figure that indicates what price a company is getting for its product. Falling gross margins suggest the company is unable to obtain such a good price for its products and services.

Group norms

Group norms are modes of acceptable behaviour within a group strong enough to override individual behaviour. The importance of group norms in a work context was discovered during research conducted by Australian-born **Elton Mayo**. Mayo conducted a series of studies at the Western Electric plant at Hawthorne, Illinois in the 1940s. He discovered that groups of individuals in the workplace collectively developed spoken or unspoken rules that governed group behaviour. Individuals who did not conform to the group norms he termed 'deviants'. These people were likely to be ostracized from the group.

These rules or group norms are strong enough to override individual or externally imposed norms. Thus the introduction of a worker who works harder than the accepted group norm level of activity, for example, is likely to demotivate the group and be unpopular.

Key text
- Elton Mayo. *The Social Problems of an Industrial Civilization.* Harvard, 1945

Grove, Andy

Former CEO, Intel; author (b. 1936)

Illness, discrimination, poverty: Andy Grove, born Andras Grof in pre-war Hungary, suffered them all as a child. At the age of four, Grove fell ill with scarlet fever. He recovered, although the illness left him with impaired hearing. Another, more sinister threat cast its shadow. As the Nazis swept to power in Europe, the Jewish Grof family feared for their lives. Grof and his mother were sheltered by friends. They assumed false identities. The young Grof became Andras Malesevics.

Miraculously, he and his family avoided the death camps and survived the war. Their celebrations were short-lived, however, as in 1956 Communist Russia invaded Hungary, and Grof and the rest of his family found themselves on the wrong side of the Iron Curtain. Weighing up his options, Grof, by now used to playing with high stakes, decided to escape.

He fled to Austria and from there to the United States, changing his name to Andrew Grove along the way. Arriving in the United States in 1957, he enrolled at the City College of New York, graduating in 1960 with a degree in chemical engineering. After City College, he studied at the University of California at Berkeley, receiving his PhD in 1963. His first job after graduation was at Fairchild Semiconductors, a company formed by several research scientists, including **Gordon Moore** and Bob Noyce.

Fairchild Semiconductors revolutionized the world of computing through its work on the silicon transistor. Spin-offs from Fairchild included some of the best-known companies in Silicon Valley: Intel (Bob Noyce and Gordon Moore), Advanced Micro Devices (Jerry Sanders) and National Semiconductor (Charlie Sporck).

When Gordon Moore and Bob Noyce left Fairchild in 1968 to set up Intel, they asked Grove to come with them. Grove was Intel's fourth employee. Noyce and Moore's original business plan involved manufacturing a new kind of computer memory using semiconductor technology. In 1970, the first dynamic random access memory (DRAM) for commercial use rolled off Intel's production lines.

Intel had also been approached by a Japanese company, the Nippon Calculating Machine Corporation (NCM), to produce some logic chips. Intel had been working on a smaller single-chip, general-purpose logic device, and now offered its own solution. Instead of the patent rights passing to the Japanese firm, Intel retained the ownership and licensed the right to manufacture and sell the chip. It was this decision by Grove and the management team that paved the way for Intel to become the microprocessor giant that it is today.

Intel's success was founded not only on its innovative skills but also on its skilful repositioning of what had previously been no more than a commodity computer component into a household name brand. TV commercials elevated the mundane microchip to an aspirational product. Encouraged by the 'Intel Inside' campaign, consumers insisted on having an Intel chip inside their PCs. The Intel Pentium processor became as strongly associated with PCs as Microsoft's Windows operating system, another marketing success story.

Andy Grove's vision was instrumental in Intel's success. Grove steered the company from a fledgling producer of memory chips to a giant of the microprocessor industry. He got things done. In the early days, he was the man who organized the office space and manufacturing capacity. He played a key role in the negotiations with IBM in 1981 that saw Intel beat off competition from Motorola to supply the microprocessors for IBM's PCs. In many ways, Grove's childhood experiences in war-torn Europe had prepared him well for business life. Grove was a man who didn't shirk from the tough decisions.

In the 1980s, when microprocessors looked like they might be a better bet than memory manufacturing, Grove made the bold and risky decision to refocus the company's efforts. It was a tough call that meant laying off thousands of employees.

In 1987, Grove became CEO of Intel. The decisions didn't get any easier. Grove averted a potential crisis when a flaw was discovered in the company's flagship Pentium microprocessor. With a technical problem probably only discernible to mathematicians threatening to balloon into a PR disaster of epic proportions, Grove acted decisively. He could have used Intel's muscle to pass on the burden of replacement to the retailers and consumers. Instead, Grove offered to replace the processors. The move may have cost $475 million, but it safeguarded the Intel brand. Profits went up.

Grove was a godsend to the company's shareholders. During his tenure as CEO, the stock increased in value 24-fold. In May 1998, Grove stepped down as CEO. He was replaced by Craig Barrett.

Since Grove took a back seat at Intel, the company has been wrestling with a number of difficult issues, not least a likely decline in microchips in the future. Moore's Law (originated by Intel co-founder Gordon Moore) states that microprocessing power will double every 18 months. It has held true for over a decade, delivering revenue growth to Intel through consumer chip upgrades. Eventually, though, the rate of increase will slow. At least, Moore believes so – and he should know. Grove appears to be prepared for this. He is on record as saying that 'all companies will be Internet companies.' Backing this view, Intel has diversified its operations to embrace the Internet.

Grove, meanwhile, has waged a high-profile battle against prostate cancer. In characteristic fashion, Grove armed himself with all the information he could accumulate about his condition, weighed the options, and then chose the course of action that he thought offered the best outcome. In the case of his particular illness, that option was high-dose radiation. Once again, it was a brave and risky decision. Happily, it appears to have done the trick.

Key texts

- Andrew S. Grove. *Swimming Across: A Memoir.* Warner Books, 2001
- Tim Jackson. *Inside Intel.* Dutton, 1997
- Andrew S. Grove. *Only the Paranoid Survive.* Currency Doubleday, 1996

Key links

- www.intel.com/pressroom/kits/bios/grove/bio2.htm
- www.business2.com/webguide/0,1660,6571,FF.html
- www.myprimetime.com/work/ge/grovebio/index.shtml

Growth strategy

A technique for stock selection, growth strategy, as the name suggests, involves selecting stocks that are expected to grow in value. A fundamental approach, growth selection limits an investor to companies whose earnings and sales are constantly increasing. As well as obvious financial indicators, such as quarter-on-quarter rising revenue, another indicator that is useful for making a judgement about whether a stock is suitable for selection as part of a growth strategy is **earnings per share** – the higher the value, the better suited the stock.

Guerrilla marketing

Guerrilla marketing is marketing using unorthodox methods. 'Guerrilla' was the Spanish word used to describe the irregular troops who fought with Wellington against Napoleon Bonaparte during the Peninsular War (1808–1814). Lacking professional training, the guerrillas resorted to unconventional tactics to achieve their aims. The term 'guerrilla marketing' was coined by

American marketing guru and academic Jay Conrad Levinson to describe an equally unconventional and unorthodox, but nevertheless effective, approach to marketing. One advantage of guerrilla marketing is that it can be highly cost-effective. The Internet is a particularly suitable medium for guerrilla-marketing campaigns. Guerrilla marketing techniques include Web sites, flyers, posters, point-of-purchase materials, stunts and many other innovative strategies.

H

Hacking

'Hacking' refers to the process of gaining unauthorized access to a company's computer systems, usually from a remote location with the aid of another computer. In recognition of the potential cost to business that hacking can cause, many jurisdictions, including the United States, have made hacking illegal. One of most celebrated hacking cases was that of Kevin Mitnick, who was incarcerated in February 1995 for five years after pleading guilty to 25 counts of computer and wire fraud and one charge of cracking. Mitnick had hacked into computers at the University of Southern California and tampered with data. Released in 2000, Mitnick is on parole until 2003. His release conditions severely restrict his access to any computer, although the US government has tapped his knowledge on computer security. He spent two days briefing the US Commission on National Security.

Some hackers call themselves 'ethical' or 'white-hat' hackers. Often poachers turned gamekeepers, ethical hackers probe Web sites for holes in their security systems, and fix them or alert the company in question when they find them. There is some dispute over the correct use of the term 'hacker'. Some believe it should be used to describe people who develop computer software or explore aspects of computer security to satisfy their intellectual curiosity, with the term 'cracker' used for a person who maliciously breaks into a computer system.

Key texts
- Jonathan Littman. *The Fugitive Game – Online with Kevin Mitnick – The Inside Story of the Great Cyberchase*. Little Brown, 1996
- Stuart McClure, Joel Scambray and George Kurtz. *Hacking Exposed: Network Security Secrets and Solutions*. McGraw-Hill Professional, 2001

Key link
- www.hackingexposed.com

Halo effect

The halo effect is the tendency to rate certain people (or objects) in a way that reflects what was previously anticipated, meaning there is bias built into the perception. The halo effect became a popular business term in Internet circles during the dotcom revolution. It was used to describe the aura surrounding a successful **entrepreneur**, particularly an Internet entrepreneur. If an entrepreneur has achieved success, there is a presumption that they know what they're talking about. Proven Internet entrepreneurs find it much easier to attract funding the second time around, whether or not they merit it.

Hamel, Gary

American academic and consultant (b. 1954)

In 1978, Gary Hamel left his job as a hospital administrator and went to the University of

Michigan to study for a PhD in International Business. At Michigan, Hamel met his eventual mentor, **C.K. Prahalad**. Twenty years later, Hamel has established himself at the vanguard of contemporary thinking on strategy. As well as being visiting professor at Harvard Business School and London Business School, California-based Hamel is a consultant to major companies and chairman of Strategos, a worldwide strategic consulting company.

Hamel's reputation has burgeoned as a result of a series of acclaimed articles in the *Harvard Business Review* (ten in 14 years, four of which won the prestigious McKinsey award), in addition to three cover stories for *Fortune* magazine and several bestselling books, including *Competing For the Future*, co-written with C.K. Prahalad, and *Leading the Revolution*. Along the way, Hamel has created a new vocabulary for strategy that includes strategic intent, strategic architecture, industry foresight (rather than vision), and core competencies.

The need for new perspectives on strategy is forcefully put by Hamel. 'We like to believe we can break strategy down to Five Forces or **Seven 'S's.** But you can't. Strategy is extraordinarily emotional and demanding. It is not a ritual or a once-a-year exercise, though that is what it has become. We have set the bar too low,' says Hamel. As a result, managers are bogged down in the nitty-gritty of the present, spending less than 3 percent of their time looking to the future.

Hamel's argument is that complacency and cynicism are endemic. '*Dilbert* is the bestselling business book of all time. It is cynical about management. Never has there been so much cynicism,' Hamel points out. It is only by challenging convention that change will happen. 'Taking risks, breaking the rules, and being a maverick have always been important, but today they are more crucial than ever. We live in a discontinuous world – one where digitalization, deregulation and globalization are profoundly reshaping the industrial landscape,' he says.

Hamel argues that there are three kinds of companies. First are 'the real makers', companies such as British Airways and Xerox. They are the aristocracy; well-managed, consistent high achievers. Second, says Hamel, are the takers, 'peasants who only keep what the Lord doesn't want'. This group typically has around 15 percent market share – such as Kodak in the copier business, or Avis.

Third are the breakers: industrial revolutionaries. These are companies Hamel believes are creating the new wealth, and include the likes of Starbucks in the coffee business. 'Companies should be asking themselves, who is going to capture the new wealth in your industry?' he says.

When Hamel talks of change, he is not considering tinkering at the edges. 'The primary agenda is to be the architect of industry transformation, not simply corporate transformation,' he says. Companies that view change as an internal matter are liable to be left behind. Instead, they need to look outside of their industry boundaries. Hamel calculates that if you want to see the future coming, 80 percent of the learning will take place outside company boundaries. This is not something companies are very good at.

Many will continue to ignore Hamel's call for a revolution. 'There is a lot of talk about creating shareholder wealth. It is not a hard thing to do. Just find a 60-year-old CEO and set a 65-year-old retirement age and then guarantee a salary based on the share price growing.' The trouble is that it is here, at the stock-option-packed top of the organization, that change needs to begin. 'What we need is not visionaries but activists. We need antidotes to Dilbert,' Hamel proclaims.

Key texts

- Gary Hamel. *Leading the Revolution*. Harvard University Press, 2000
- Gary Hamel and Aimé Heene (eds). *Competence-Based Competition*. John Wiley, 1995
- Gary Hamel and C.K. Prahalad. *Competing for the Future*. Harvard University Press, 1994

Key links

- www.strategosnet.com
- www.business2.com/webguide/0,1660,26238, FF.html

Handy, Charles

British academic and commentator (b. 1932)

Charles Handy is a bestselling writer and broadcaster. His work is accessible and popular. Because of this, it is dismissed by some. Yet Handy has brought major questions about the future of work and of society onto corporate and personal agendas.

Irish-born Handy worked for Shell until 1972, when he left to teach at London Business School. He spent time at MIT, where he came into contact with many of the leading lights in the human-relations school of thinking, including **Ed Schein**.

Handy's early academic career was conventional. His first book, *Understanding Organizations* (1976), gives little hint of the wide-ranging social and philosophical nature of his later work.

It was in 1989, with the publication of *The Age of Unreason*, that Handy's thinking made a great leap forward. The age of unreason that Handy predicts is 'a time when what we used to take for granted may no longer hold true, when the future, in so many areas, is there to be shaped, by us and for us; a time when the only prediction that will hold true is that no predictions will hold. A time, therefore, for bold imaginings in private life as well as public, for thinking the unlikely and doing the unreasonable.'

In practice, Handy believes that certain forms of organization will become dominant. These are the type of organizations most readily associated with service industries. First and most famously, there is what he calls the 'shamrock organization': 'a form of organization based around a core of essential executives and workers supported by outside contractors and part-time help'. The consequence of such an organizational form is that organizations in the future are likely to resemble the way consultancy firms, advertising agencies and professional partnerships are currently structured.

The second emergent structure identified by Handy is the federal one. It is not, he points out, another word for decentralization. He provides a blueprint for federal organizations in which the central function coordinates, influences, advises and suggests. It does not dictate terms or short-term decisions. Instead, the centre is concerned with long-term strategy. It is: 'at the middle of things and is not a polite word for the top or even for head office.'

The third type of organization Handy anticipates is what he calls 'the Triple I'. The three 'I's are information, intelligence and ideas. In such organizations, the demands on personnel management are large. Explains Handy: 'The wise organization already knows that its smart people are not to be easily defined as workers or as managers but as individuals, as specialists, as professionals or executives, or as leaders (the older terms of manager and worker are dropping out of use), and that they and it need also to be obsessed with the pursuit of learning if they are going to keep up with the pace of change.'

As organizations change in the age of unreason, Handy predicts, so will other aspects of our lives. Less time will be spent at work: he estimates 50,000 hours in a lifetime rather than the present figure of around 100,000. Handy does not predict, as people did in the 1970s, an enlightened age of leisure. Instead, he challenges people to spend more time thinking about what they want to do. Time will not simply be divided between work and play; there could be 'portfolios', which split time between fee work (where you sell time); gift work (for neighbours or charities); study (keeping up to date with your work); homework; and leisure.

Handy has reached his own conclusions. He says he has made his last speech to a large audience. He now sets a limit of twelve to his audiences, reflecting that 'enough is enough'. Handy has become a one-man case study of the new world of work he so successfully and humanely commentates on. At a personal level, he appears to have the answers. Whether these can be translated into answers for others remains the question and the challenge.

Key texts
- Charles Handy. *The Elephant and the Flea.* Harvard Business School Press, 2002

- Charles Handy. *The Hungry Spirit.* Hutchinson, 1998
- Charles Handy. *Beyond Certainty: The Changing World of Organizations.* Century, 1995
- Charles Handy. *The Empty Raincoat.* Hutchinson, 1994
- Charles Handy. *Waiting for the Mountain to Move and Other Reflections on Life.* Arrow, 1991
- Charles Handy. *Inside Organizations: 21 Ideas for Managers.* BBC Books, 1990
- Charles Handy. *The Age of Unreason.* Business Books, 1989
- Charles Handy and John Constable. *The Making of Managers.* Longman, 1988
- Charles Handy. *Gods of Management.* Business Books, 1986
- Charles Handy. *The Future of Work.* Basil Blackwell, 1984
- Charles Handy. *Understanding Organizations.* Penguin Books, 1976

Key links

- http://my.linkbaton.com/bibliography/handy/charles
- www.pfdf.org/leaderbooks/l2l/summer97/handy.html

Hard currency

A hard currency is one commonly accepted across the world. Hard currencies are usually those of the industrialized nations; US dollars and pounds sterling are two of the most popular. Retailers in countries with soft currencies, such as the old USSR, China and many African states, often prefer to take hard currency instead of their national currency in exchange for goods and services.

Harvard Business School

Harvard Business School is one of the world's leading business schools and the premier brand in business education. It is a brand that allows the business school to charge premium prices for everything it does.

Harvard Business School was founded in 1908, and awarded its first Masters degree in management in 1910. Although other schools – notably the Tuck School at Dartmouth – claim to have had graduate programmes in management before that date, HBS was the first business school to require a university degree for entry to its management programme.

What the school also had that set it apart from many of the other business schools springing up in America at that time was the Harvard brand. The combination of the Ivy League prestige of Harvard University, the serious approach the new school took to the fledgling discipline of management, and its ability to attract gifted professors – some of them from other parts of the university – soon established the school as the top institution of its kind.

Wallace Dohan, dean of Harvard Business School, oversaw the 1922 launch of the *Harvard Business Review.* Early articles, such as 'The Effect of Hedging upon Flour Mill Control', hardly set the pulse racing, but the *Harvard Business Review* was the beginning of a publishing success story and a prestigious addition to the Harvard brand. For more than 75 years, the *Harvard Business Review* has been influential in shaping management thinking around the globe. Today, along with reprints of articles from the *HBR* archive, busy executives can buy audio tapes of articles to listen to in their cars or on long flights.

HBS benefited from the **MBA** boom. While the qualification cemented its place during the 1960s and 1970s, its apotheosis came in the 1980s. Suddenly, it seemed that recruiters couldn't get enough of the newly minted business school graduates. The investment banks and management consultancies, which had always valued the analytical skills provided by the MBA, were joined by blue-chip companies from other sectors.

With a flourish, the MBA seemed to epitomize the free market philosophy that dominated Western democracies during that decade. Margaret Thatcher and Ronald Reagan's children were bottle-fed on the enterprise culture. Suddenly, commerce in all its guises was not just a respectable activity, but a moral imperative.

At the top of the pile was the Harvard-branded MBA. It also appealed to those in search of a branded CV. Management guru **Tom Peters** admits, 'I didn't know what to do after the Navy. I didn't have any better ideas than doing an MBA. I went to business school because that's what people were doing. My half-dozen best friends had decided the MBA was hot. The MBA became a popular phenomenon at the time and two-thirds of my buddies went to Harvard.' The Harvard MBA programme currently has an intake of around 900 students.

The HBS brand is also a big draw in the executive education market. Companies happily fork out $40,500 to send executives on the prestigious nine-week Advanced Management Program at Harvard.

Traditionally, the case study has been one of the educational building blocks of MBA programmes throughout the world. It was established as the primary method of teaching at Harvard Business School as long ago as 1924. Case studies present students with a corporate example. From the narrative, they are expected to reach conclusions about what was the right or wrong thing to do, identify best and worst practice, and learn something about managerial behaviour. Harvard alone has generated 5310 cases. The case study method remains a globally accepted and practised approach.

In recent years, HBS branding has gone high-tech, creating CD-ROM, audio and video formats for many of its products. It is now possible to pay for *HBR* articles online and download them instantly. Even the traditional case study has taken a digital turn. Harvard put its first electronic case to work in 1996 and now boasts that its MBA curriculum is 'virtually paperless', with an expanding number of electronic cases incorporating on-site video sequences and links to real-time information on the Internet.

Harvard's influence stretches around the world. The Indian Institute of Management, for exam-

ple, was established with Harvard's support and remains a devout follower to this day. A number of European business schools also followed the Harvard model, including IESE, the prestigious Spanish school. In Asia, the Manila-based Asian Institute of Management was launched in 1968 and initially used material from Harvard for all of its programmes. Harvard even offers a one-year programme in applied economics with the Ho Chi Minh City Economics University in Vietnam, thus achieving by stealth what the United States failed to achieve through warfare.

Key link
- www.hbs.edu

Harvey-Jones, Sir John

Former chairman of ICI (b. 1924)

Born in Hackney, London, John Harvey-Jones spent his early childhood in India, where his father acted as a guardian to one of the Maharajahs who governed a part of India that did not fall under the control of the British Empire. The early part of Harvey-Jones's childhood was spent in the luxurious surroundings of the Maharajah's palace. His surroundings changed, however, when he was sent to preparatory school at Tormore in Kent, England.

Harvey-Jones did not enjoy his time at prep school. Deal, the local town, was, as he later said, 'the coldest place I have ever lived until I visited the Antarctic.' It was also an emotionally cold experience, as Harvey-Jones was bullied mercilessly. At the age of 13, prep school was succeeded by the Dartmouth Royal Naval College. Here Harvey-Jones spent a happier time preparing for a life in the services.

In 1941, at the age of 16, Harvey-Jones went to war as a midshipman. Luck went with him. Twice he was posted to ships that were sunk; the second time he was lucky to escape with his life. For his next posting, he took up service on a submarine where he saw out the war, serving in the Mediterranean, Ceylon, and Australia.

When the war ended, Harvey-Jones joined Naval Intelligence. Already fluent in German, he added to his language skills by learning Russian in just six months. His career in intelligence was a distinguished one, earning him a Member of the British Empire award after stints in the field and in the Cabinet Office. He resigned from the services in 1959 to spend more time with his family after his daughter contracted polio.

When Harvey-Jones left the Intelligence Service to join chemical company ICI in 1959, he could not have known whether he was cut out for a career in business. His entire working life until then had been spent in the somewhat cloistered existence of the military services. As it turned out, his talents were equally suited to civilian life.

At ICI, he started in the work-study department located in Middlesborough, and swiftly worked his way up through the ranks. One management position followed another: chairman of the Heavy Organic Chemical Division (1970), a seat on the main board (1973), ICI Fibres Products director (1975), and deputy chairman of the company (1978). By 1978, though, it seemed that Harvey-Jones had risen as far as he could. In ICI's history, only one other person had joined the company after enjoying another career and made it to the position of chairman; more significantly, no non-chemist had ever made to the top. But times were changing at ICI. The company had run into difficulties and a new style of leadership was required. In April 1982, beating odds of 15 to 1, Harvey-Jones was appointed chairman of ICI.

There was no honeymoon period. ICI were facing losses of some £200 million. Harvey-Jones applied his idiosyncratic management style and began to turn things around. In the corridors of ICI and in the strait-laced atmosphere of London, he cut a dashing figure, with his flowing locks and flamboyant kipper ties. He favoured an informal style of leadership, leading by example. Employees, he believed, needed an identifiable figure at the head of the organization from whom they could take inspiration and values. He saw three definite strands to his particular role as leader: that vision should come from the top and engage those below; that the management board should act as enablers; and that a values-driven culture should be cultivated and should include principles such as openness and high achievement.

Harvey-Jones took several steps to turn the company around. He used a rule of thumb that a business strand must produce profit, cash or be strategically necessary for it to exist or be worth pursuing. His flamboyant style made him a familiar public figure. By the time he stepped down as chairman in 1987, he had turned ICI's loss into a £1 billion profit. The heroic turnaround secured Harvey-Jones's future as well as ICI's.

Harvey-Jones didn't entirely abandon management after ICI. When he left the Navy, he had stated his intention to find a nine-to-five job. So far, it has eluded him. In 1989, he added the directorship of *The Economist* to a wide career portfolio that includes board positions at a number of non-profit and commercial organizations. In 1986, for example, he was made Chancellor of Bradford University. He has also been a vice-president of the Royal Society of Arts, vice-chairman of the Policies Studies Institute and the Institute of Marketing, a trustee of the Science Museum, and a non-executive director at Guinness Peat Aviation and Grand Metropolitan. He was also chairman of the Wildfowl & Wetlands Trust.

Fêted with awards – including Britain's most impressive industrialist in 1985 and Industrialist of the Year in 1986, 1987 and 1988 – Harvey-Jones has also hosted a successful television series. Between 1990 and 2000, he filmed five series of *Troubleshooter* for the BBC, bringing his own brand of management to a wider audience. In the programme, Harvey-Jones would descend on a small or mid-size company that was ailing or stagnating, and dispense advice with the authority of a man who had turned around a multimillion-dollar business. For the viewer, it was like watching a master giving lessons to a semi-willing pupil. Having assessed the business and said his piece, Harvey-Jones would then leave, only to return some time later to see what changes, if any, had been made and how the company was faring.

John Harvey-Jones marks a transition in the United Kingdom from management by people experienced in a particular industry to management by the people with the best management skills. Harvey-Jones saved a British institution – ICI – that was in severe financial difficulties when he took over as chairman. Blowing away the cobwebs from this fusty member of the United Kingdom's corporate establishment, the flamboyant Harvey-Jones gave the workforce a leader whose example they could follow. He also gave the British media a larger-than-life business personality. But his unorthodox image didn't detract from his chief purpose: turning a potential £200 million loss into a £1 billion profit.

Key texts
- Ron Sewell and John Harvey-Jones. *The Twelve Pillars of Business Success*. Kogan Page, 1997
- John Harvey-Jones. *Getting It Together*. Heinemann, 1991
- John Harvey-Jones. *Making It Happen: Reflections on Leadership*. HarperCollins, 1988

Key links
- www.vnunet.com/Analysis/1102416
- www.cmmol.net/sir_john_harvey_jones.htm
- www.select-speakers.com/____sir_john_harvey-jones.html

Hawthorne effect

Between 1927 and 1932, Harvard Business Professor **Elton Mayo** and colleagues F.J. Roethlisberger and William J. Dickson conducted a series of experiments at the Hawthorne Plant of the Western Electric Company in Cicero, Illinois. They started by looking at the work environment – brightness of lighting, for example – and its influence on the workforce. They then progressed to psychological aspects of work, such as the socio-dynamics of working groups.

One strange finding of their research was that no matter what factor they adjusted, productivity improved. Thus, if lighting was increased or

decreased, or hours increased or decreased, productivity increased regardless. It seemed, therefore, that the improvement in productivity must be due to the attention given to the workforce by the research team. An increase in productivity resulting from observation became known as the Hawthorne effect.

Key text
- F.J. Roethlisberger, W.J. Dickson and H.A. Wright. *Management and the Worker. An Account Of A Research Program Conducted By The Western Electric Company, Hawthorne Works, Chicago*. Harvard University Press, 1949 – reprint

Headhunter

Few senior executives obtain their positions by applying to a job advertisement. Most are headhunted by a firm of headhunters or executive search agencies, as they are also known. A headhunter is a recruitment consultant who adopts a proactive strategy for filling a vacant position at a client company. Unlike conventional recruitment agencies, a headhunter uses his network of contacts to actively search out a candidate. The prospective candidate will invariably be in a position already. Headhunting is an expensive method of tracking down a potential employee, but a practice used to locate most senior executives at large companies, where the position is not filled internally.

Hearst, William Randolph

American media mogul, congressional representative and New York City mayor (1863–1951)

William Randolph Hearst was born in San Francisco to a wealthy industrialist and speculator father and a socialite, philanthropist mother. It was a potent cocktail of wealth, commerce and culture that would have a profound effect on

Hearst. An only child, he spent his early years shuttling between the family's huge estate at San Simeon, California, and their home in New York.

Hearst followed the classical academic route for the privileged: St Paul's Preparatory School in Concord, New Hampshire, a first-class prep school, followed by an Ivy League university, Harvard. At Harvard, Hearst excelled in social activities. He was a member of the Hasty Pudding Theater and, more notably, business manager for the college magazine, the *Harvard Lampoon*. Hearst put a good deal of energy into his social life – so much so that he neglected his academic work to the extent that he was expelled and never received his degree.

Hearst shrugged off his academic failure and instead took a job at the *New York World*. At the time, Joseph Pulitzer's newspaper was one of the leading newspapers in New York. Hearst may not have paid attention in his Harvard classes, but at the *New York World* he received a first-class education in how to run a newspaper. Soon, however, Hearst's father summoned him back to San Francisco.

In contrast to media moguls like **Louis B. Mayer**, who worked his way up from the bottom of the pile, Hearst was handed his first newspaper as a gift. Hearst's father had purchased the *San Francisco Examiner* to provide him with a voice when he was running for the US Senate. With a Senate seat secured, the paper was no longer required. Neglected, its circulation dwindled. The younger Hearst was desperate to take charge of the paper. His father was less keen and offered him a one-million-acre ranch in Chihuahua, the 275,000 acre San Simeon ranch north of San Luis Obispo, Anaconda copper mines in Montana, and the Homestake gold mine in South Dakota as alternative inducements. Hearst refused them all, saying, 'You are very kind, but I would rather have the *Examiner*.' Reluctantly, his father relented.

On 4 March 1887, Hearst took up residence at the *San Francisco Examiner*. He had discovered his *métier*: he was a brilliant newspaper proprietor. Thanks to a radical overhaul, by 1889 the *Examiner* was making a profit. The staid format Hearst had inherited was replaced with hard-hitting investigative reporting, coupled with sensationalistic, attention-grabbing headlines. Increased sports coverage, serialized stories by well-known authors, banner headlines like 'Huge Frantic Flames', biographical sketches and exposés of the seedy underbelly of Californian life all contributed to the heady populist mix.

As circulation and profits rose, Hearst expanded the business. In 1895, he returned to his old hunting ground on the East Coast to save the *New York Morning Journal*. It was a decision that put him in direct competition with his one-time mentor, Joseph Pulitzer. Hearst pulled no punches in the ensuing circulation war. He added the *Evening Journal* to his stable in 1896 and poached some of Pulitzer's top writers. It was a period that gave rise to the term 'yellow journalism', in which the newspaper assumed the role of opinion-former and determiner of morals. In scenes commonplace today, rival newspapers vied for scoops and used their front pages to boast of their achievements.

The most famous example of Hearst's proactive stance to newspaper reporting is the comment attributed to him when illustrator Frederick Remington informed Hearst that he wished to return from an uneventful Havana. Hearst supposedly responded, 'Please remain. You furnish the pictures and I'll furnish the war.'

His methods may have been controversial, but they worked. Hearst was unstoppable. He soon acquired newspapers in major cities throughout America. Following in his father's footsteps, he became involved in politics. In 1902, Congress welcomed Hearst as the Democratic representative for New York. In all, he served two terms in Congress and also became mayor of New York City.

With his newspaper empire firmly established, Hearst expanded into other areas of the media. As a publisher, he produced titles that included *Cosmopolitan*, *Good Housekeeping* and *Harper's Bazaar*. He also moved into the movie business, cutting his teeth with Hearst-Metronome News. Ultimately it was the movie industry, coupled with his infatuation for the actress Marion Davies, that proved to be Hearst's downfall.

He formed W.R. Hearst's Cosmopolitan Productions as a vehicle for Davies, his Brooklyn-born mistress and a former Ziegfeld Folly. Abandoning his political career after failed attempts at the Senate and the presidency, Hearst focused solely on films. Of the 100 films Hearst sanctioned over the next 20 years, half featured his mistress. As well as sinking millions of dollars into making movies, Hearst spent more millions on a Beverly Hills mansion for Davies. Finally, he embarked on the folly that was to prove his undoing: the construction of the Hearst Castle estate at San Simeon. The 25,000 acres of the estate and castle contained rare and priceless works of art, antiquities, a zoo, an airfield and guesthouses that were chateaux dismantled in Europe and flown to California to be reassembled stone by stone.

Hearst might have survived such profligate extravagance had it not been for the Great Depression. During the 1930s, he was forced to consolidate his empire, selling newspapers and works of art to remain afloat. By the end of the decade, Hearst had halved his business interests and plundered the treasures at San Simeon. Marion Davies had herself liquidated her personal assets and pumped a million dollars into Hearst's business. His final years were spent trying to prevent the release of Orson Welles's film *Citizen Kane*, a thinly disguised biopic of Hearst. He failed. In the end, in ill health and bitter at the Welles episode, he retreated to San Simeon, handing over control of his empire to lawyers and managers. He died at the home of Marion Davies on 14 August 1951.

Key texts

- David Nasaw. *The Chief: The Life of William Randolph Hearst*. Houghton Mifflin, 2000
- Ben Proctor. *William Randolph Hearst: The Early Years 1866–1910*. Oxford University Press, 1998
- Marion Davies. *The Times We Had: Life with William Randolph Hearst*. Ballantine Books, 1975

- Fremont Older. *William Randolph Hearst: American*. Books for Libraries Press, 1972
- John Kennedy Winkler. *William Randolph Hearst: A New Appraisal*. Hastings House, 1955
- John Tebbel. *The Life and Good Times of William Randolph Hearst*. E.P. Dutton, 1952
- Ferdinand Lundberg. *Imperial Hearst: A Social Biography*. Equinox Cooperative Press, 1936

Key links

- www.hearstfdn.org
- www.zpub.com/sf/history/willh.html
- www.spanam.simplenet.com/Hearst.htm

Hefner, Hugh

Founder, Playboy Enterprises (b. 1926)

Born in Chicago, Illinois, on 9 April 1926, Hugh Hefner attended Sayre Elementary School and Steinmetz High on the West Side of Chicago. Hefner was no great academic. He was not a dunce – he has an IQ of 152 – but he preferred to direct his energies to other activities. At school, he served as student council president, launched a school newspaper, and spent a lot of time drawing cartoons.

Hefner graduated from high school in 1944 and joined the US Army as an infantry clerk. His job was a little unusual; it entailed drawing cartoons for the Army press. When World War II was over, Hefner was discharged from the army. Wishing to continue his education, he enrolled at the University of Illinois in Champaign/Urbana.

In college, Hefner continued to display a capacity for multitasking that set him apart from his peers. Not only did he get through his degree in two and a half years, he also found time to draw cartoons for the *Daily Illinois* and edit the campus magazine, *Shaft*. In a sign of things to come, Hefner was responsible for the introduction of a new feature in *Shaft*: 'Coed of the Month.'

Hefner left school and embarked on a career as a cartoonist. He joined the Chicago Cartoon Company in 1949 as an assistant personnel manager and later, in 1950, worked as an advertising copywriter for the Carson, Pirie, Scott department store. By 1951, Hefner was working for *Esquire* magazine as promotion copywriter. He looked set for an uneventful ordinary working life when the company announced it was relocating to New York. Hefner was happy in Chicago, so he decided to stay and set up his own magazine.

The days of glamorous offices and lavish mansions were still a long a way off. The first issue of *Playboy* magazine was put together on Hefner's kitchen table in his South Side apartment. The magazine featured a calendar photo of Marilyn Monroe. Unsure about how his revolutionary magazine would be received and whether he would be able to produce another, Hefner left off the cover date. The first issue went on sale in December 1953.

Hefner's publishing instincts were vindicated when the first issue sold 50,000 copies. The revenue from this edition alone allowed him to cover his costs and produce another edition. The magazine that would bring the world the Playboy bunny was up and running.

Part of the reason for the magazine's phenomenal success during the 1950s and 1960s were the ideals espoused by Hefner and reflected in his magazine. *Playboy*, Hefner insisted, was never intended to be a smutty publication. Instead, it aimed to bring pictures of naked women out from under the bed and onto the coffee tables.

With a mixture of photo sets featuring perfect looking, scantily dressed women and articles addressing issues of the time, Hefner tapped into the flight from the prudish mentality of the 1950s. The heady mixture of liberal journalism and eroticism brought sales of more than 6 million in the 1970s. It also bought Hefner a Playboy jet and a hedonistic lifestyle that was the envy of many a red-blooded male.

In just seven years, Hefner amassed enough wealth to fund the purchase of the 70-room Playboy Mansion on Chicago's Gold Coast. Not long afterward, he moved out of the Playboy headquarters and into the mansion, where he lived and worked for the best part of a decade.

In 1971, Hefner moved once again – this time to the Mansion West in Holmby Hills, California. The old Playboy mansion was donated to the Art Institute of Chicago and subsequently converted into apartments.

During his years at the helm of the Playboy business, Hefner gained a reputation for eccentricity. His dress sense is a little unconventional. Way ahead of his time, Hefner anticipated dress-down Fridays with his own version of casual dress every day. Unless venturing outside the substantial gates of his mansion, Hefner likes to spend the day dressed in his pyjamas. This sartorial quirkiness dates back to the early days of *Playboy*, when Hefner, working long hours, just never got around to getting dressed. Once behind closed doors, in the Chicago Playboy mansion, he didn't see any need to change and so continues to wear a fresh pair of pyjamas every day – and change into a different pair for the evening. If he has company, he just dons a smoking jacket.

To some, Hugh Hefner is one of the twentieth century's greatest pornographers, but a pornographer nonetheless. To others, he is a business icon, a man who, in the spirit of the greatest entrepreneurs, saw an opportunity and exploited it. It takes tremendous skill to expand a business rapidly, retain control over it, continue to manage it effectively, and protect the brand. Hefner succeeded in building a multimillion-dollar empire and brand recognized the world over. Unlike many founders of big businesses, he even managed a painless succession handing over control to his daughter, Christie.

Regardless of the morals of the business on which *Playboy* is founded – Hefner is on record as saying that he is merely combating hypocrisy over attitudes toward sex in society, bridging 'the gap between what we said and what we actually did' – there is no denying Hefner's genius for business.

Key texts
- Russell Miller. *Bunny: The Real Story of Playboy*. Holt, Rinehart and Winston, 1985
- Frank Brady. *Hefner*. Macmillan, 1974

- Stephen Byer. *Hefner's Gonna Kill Me When He Reads This … .* Allen-Bennett, 1972

Key link
- www.playboyenterprises.com

Henderson, Bruce D.

Australian consultant; founder, Boston Consulting Group (1915–1992)

While managers may rely on experience to predict how their businesses will respond to their actions, strategists and economists rely on their models, which are amalgams of many different experiences. The man who brought business models into the mainstream was Bruce Henderson. Henderson was an engineer who worked as a strategic planner for General Electric. He then joined the management consultancy Arthur D. Little before leaving in 1963 to set up his own consultancy, the Boston Consulting Group (BCG).

BCG is regarded by some as the first pure strategy consultancy. It quickly became a great success. Within five years, BCG was in the top group of consulting firms, where it has largely remained. It has been called 'the most idea-driven major consultancy in the world'.

The first model Henderson discovered – or rediscovered, in this case – was something of an antique. In the 1920s, an obscure company called Curtiss Aircraft came up with the concept of the 'learning curve', which also became known as the 'experience curve'. This posited that unit costs declined as cumulative production increased because of the acquisition of experience. This had been applied solely to manufacturing. Henderson applied it to strategy rather than production and found that it still worked and provided a useful practical tool.

The model for which Henderson and BCG are best known is the Growth/Share Matrix. It measures market growth and relative market share for all of the businesses in a particular firm. The hypothesis of this particular framework is that companies with higher market share and growth are more profitable.

BCG then superimposed a theory of cash management on the matrix. It included a hierarchy of uses of cash, numbered from 1 to 4 in order of their priority. Richard Koch, in his *Financial Times Guide to Strategy*, says, 'Bruce weaved it all together in a coherent philosophy of business that highlighted more clearly than ever before the compelling importance of market leadership, a low cost position, selectivity in business, and looking at cash flows.'

Key texts
- Bruce D. Henderson. *The Logic of Business Strategy*. Harper Business, 1985
- Bruce D. Henderson. *Henderson on Corporate Strategy*. ABT Books, 1979

Key link
- www.bcg.com/this_is_bcg/mission/experience_curve.asp

Hershey, Milton Snavely

Founder, Hershey Chocolate (1857–1945)

Milton Snavely Hershey was brought up in Hockersville, Pennsylvania. It was a small rural town and Hershey was educated in a one-room schoolhouse. His parents were farmers and, from a very early age, Hershey was expected to help out on the farm, tending the livestock.

After a string of schools, including an unsuccessful period at a private high school, the Village Academy of Green Tree, Hershey gave up on school and took a position as an apprentice with a German-language newspaper based in Gap, Lancaster County. It was soon clear that Hershey's talents did not lie with either journalism or publishing. Hershey left the paper and joined Joseph H. Royer of Lancaster as an apprentice confectioner.

He was an ambitious young man. At the age of 19, he founded his own company: M.S. Hershey, Wholesale and Retail Confectioner. The business failed and was sold in 1882. Over the following few years, Hershey travelled the country, trying to set himself up in the candy business. In Denver, Colorado, he learnt how to make caramels. In New York City, he sold his candy on the street.

None of these ventures prospered, so Hershey headed back to Lancaster. It was in Lancaster, the scene of his first business failure, that Hershey finally met with some success.

Hershey put his caramel-making skills to work. From the outset, his business was based on the quality of his product. 'Give them the quality; that's the best kind of advertising in the world,' was his motto. The business took off when Hershey's caramels came to the attention of a candy importer, who bought some to sell in England.

In 1893, while visiting the World Exposition in Chicago, Hershey met the manufacturer of a German-made chocolate-making machine. Hershey ordered one of the machines and had it shipped to Lancaster. The result was Hershey Chocolate.

Hershey decided to focus on chocolate. In 1900, he sold his caramel business for $1 million to the American Caramel Company of Philadelphia. With the proceeds, he invested in a new chocolate factory near his family home in Derry Church. With the caramel business, Hershey had excelled in creating a diverse range of candy products. Now he concentrated on perfecting a single product: chocolate.

Hershey had no recipe book to rely on, no magic formula for making chocolate. Together with a few trusted colleagues, he locked himself away and laboured over the perfect milk chocolate recipe. 'Nobody told Mr Hershey how to make milk chocolate. He just found out the hard way,' recalled one of his employees. Hard work though it was, Hershey struck chocolate gold. The result of his research – the Hershey chocolate bar – soon became a byword for quality in the United States.

Hershey continued to consolidate his chocolate business. He produced variations on the standard bar, including Mr Goodbar, a milk chocolate and peanut candy bar, in 1925; Krackel, a chocolate bar filled with crisped rice, in 1938; and Hershey's Miniatures, small versions of all of Hershey's chocolate bars, in 1939. To secure his sugar supply and ensure its quality, he built a sugar mill and small town in Cuba.

In 1920, Hershey experienced a setback when he lost $2.5 million on the sugar futures market. He was forced to borrow from the bank and, as a condition of the loan, the bank put a representative in Hershey's factory. It took him two years to pay the loan off and eject the overseers.

As Hershey's business grew, so too did the town surrounding the factory. Hershey wanted to build a town in keeping with his social philosophy in the same way that other chocolate philanthropists, like Joseph Rowntree and George Cadbury, had done in England. Hershey drew up plans for an idyllic community that would not only house its inhabitants but provide for their every need, including employment at the Hershey chocolate factory. When the town was completed, it contained parks, churches, a school, a hotel, churches, a golf course and even a zoo. Townfolk would walk along streets called Areba, Caracus and Para, all named after cocoa-bean producing countries. Hershey held a competition to name the new town. The US Post Office vetoed the winning entry, Hersheyoko, so Hershey settled for plain old Hershey Town. Hershey also constructed a mansion, High Point, overlooking the chocolate factory to house his family.

Shortly before his death, one last act by Hershey assured the Hershey name a place in business history. When America entered World War II, the US military instructed Hershey to develop a chocolate bar for the troops – one that wouldn't melt. Hershey once again set about chocolate innovation. The resulting Field Ration D Chocolate Bar formed an essential part of the US army's personal kit. Not only was it a great favourite of US personnel, but with the stationing of American troops in England and the subsequent D-Day invasion of Europe, the Hershey bar became part of World War II folklore. Hershey died on 13 October 1945, at the age of 88.

Key texts
- Joël Glenn Brenner. *The Emperors of Chocolate: Inside the Secret World of Hershey and Mars*. Random House, 1999
- James D. McMahon. *Built on Chocolate: The Story of the Hershey Chocolate Company*. General Publishing Group, 1998

Key links
- www.hersheys.com/about/milton.shtml
- http://miltonhershey.com

Herzberg, Frederick

American educator (b. 1923)

Frederick Herzberg served in the World War II and was posted to Dachau concentration camp after its liberation. This proved a powerful experience. On his return to the United States, Herzberg studied at the University of Pittsburgh and worked for the US Public Health Service in his area of expertise, clinical psychology.

Along with **Abraham Maslow** and **Douglas McGregor**, he was identified with members of the human-relations school during the 1950s. Herzberg coined the now popular phrase 'job enrichment'. He believes that business organizations can be an enormous force for good, provided that they liberate both themselves and their people from the thrall of numbers and get on with creative expansion of individuals' roles within the organization. Herzberg eventually became a professor of management at the University of Utah.

It is astonishing how little time is spent by management researchers actually talking to people in real situations. The strategist **Henry Mintzberg** is a notable exception to this; so, too, is Frederick Herzberg. In the late 1950s, as part of their research, Herzberg and his colleagues asked 203 Pittsburgh engineers and accountants about their jobs and what pleased and displeased them.

This was hardly an original approach. But Herzberg's conclusions were. He separated the motivational elements of work into two categories – those serving people's animal needs (hygiene factors) and those meeting uniquely human needs (motivation factors).

Hygiene factors – also labelled maintenance factors – were determined to include supervision, interpersonal relations, physical working conditions, salary, company policies and administrative practices, benefits and job security. 'When these factors deteriorate to a level below that which the employee considers acceptable, then job dissatisfaction ensues,' observed Herzberg. Hygiene alone is insufficient to provide the 'motivation to work'. Indeed, Herzberg argued that the factors that provide satisfaction are quite different from those leading to dissatisfaction.

True motivation, said Herzberg, comes from achievement, personal development, job satisfaction and recognition. The aim should be to motivate people through the job itself rather than through rewards or pressure.

After the success of his 1956 book, *The Motivation to Work*, there was a hiatus until Herzberg returned to the fray with an influential article in the *Harvard Business Review* in 1968. The article, 'One More Time: How Do You Motivate Employees?' has sold over a million copies in reprints, making it *HBR*'s most popular article ever. The article introduced the helpful motivational acronym KITA (kick in the ass) and argued: 'If you have someone on a job, use him. If you can't use him, get rid of him.' Herzberg said that KITA came in three categories: negative physical, negative psychological and positive. The latter was the preferred method for genuine motivation.

Herzberg's work has had a considerable effect on the rewards and remuneration packages offered by corporations. Increasingly, there is a trend toward 'cafeteria' benefits, in which people can choose from a range of options. In effect, they can select the elements that they recognize as providing their own motivation to work. Similarly, the current emphasis on self-development, career management and self-managed learning can be seen as having evolved from Herzberg's insights.

Key text

- Frederick Herzberg, Bernard Mausner and Barbara Bloch Snyderman. *The Motivation to Work*. John Wiley, 1959

Key links

- www.accel-team.com/human_relations/hrels_05_herzberg.html
- www.lib.uwo.ca/business/herzberg.html

Hierarchy of needs

American behavioural psychologist **Abraham Maslow** studied law at the City College of New York and Cornell before studying psychology at the University of Wisconsin. It was there that he met and worked with Harry Harlow, who was known for his experiments on attachment behaviour with rhesus monkeys. It was Maslow's observations of the monkeys that sowed the germs of his theory of needs.

Maslow's hierarchy of needs sets out a classification of needs in a hierarchy from basic physical needs through social needs to psychological needs. Maslow's hierarchy is represented in graphical form by a pyramid with five levels, each representing a different need. The needs at the lower levels must be fulfilled before progressing to the higher levels. At the base of the pyramid are physical needs: eating, drinking and sleeping. Above this are safety needs: the need to be safe. Next come social needs: relationships, love and human interaction. After this are the esteem needs: the desire for respect from others and self-respect. And last, at the pinnacle of the pyramid, is self-actualization (Maslow used several names for this need, including growth motivation and being needs): self-fulfilment through action and achievement. Maslow believed that people strived for self-actualization without ever achieving it.

Key text

- Abraham H. Maslow. *Toward A Psychology Of Being*. Van Nostrand Co., 1968

Hill, James Jerome

Founder, Great Northern Railway (1838– 1916)

Born plain James Hill in Rockwood, Ontario, Hill adopted the middle name Jerome after Napoleon's brother. At the age of 9, he lost his sight in one eye when he was accidentally shot with an arrow. At 18, Hill left Canada with a head full of ideas about a life of adventure. He headed West, hoping to take a job as a trapper. He arrived in St Paul, Minnesota, a few weeks after the last trappers had left for the wilds. The trappers wouldn't be back until the following year, so Hill looked for work.

He found a job with a wholesaling operation handling freight transfers between the warehouse and the trains and steamboats. When the Mississippi River was frozen in the winter, he worked for himself, supplying wood to the local railways and steamboats. Buoyed by his experience working on his own, Hill started his own business in 1866 as an independent freight agent for the First Division of the St Paul & Pacific Railroad. Showing a presence of mind beyond his years, Hill built a large warehouse by the river and ran the train tracks right through it to save on transportation costs.

Throughout his career, Hill correctly predicted economic trends. He anticipated the demise of the independent freight agent, understanding that in a conflict of interests between the agent and the railroad, the railroad would always win. Hill diversified into the steamboat business. In 1872, he merged his small business on the Red River with that of another businessman, Norman Kittson, thereby securing a monopoly. At the same time, he moved into the coal business. This was based on a hunch that in the long run, wood wasn't going to be a viable fuel in such a thinly wooded region.

By 1874, Hill was dealing in coal extensively. Hill used the synergies in his business to his advantage. He brought coal into the area by steamer and stored vast quantities of it in his yards. In 1877, he founded Northwestern Fuel Co., an organization that combined rival coal merchants in an alliance.

Before long, Hill was one of the most important coal merchants in the United States, and the Twin Cities of Minneapolis and St Paul were main distribution points for fuel. By the late 1870s, Hill had expanded his business interests to include transportation, fuel and banking.

In his usual style, Hill approached his foray into the railways with caution. His *modus operandi* was first to study everything he could lay his hands on about his intended business, then bide his time for an opportunity. The opportunity first presented itself in 1873, when the St Paul & Pacific Railroad went into receivership. Following three years of examining the business and all of the options, Hill put together a complex deal to buy the railroad. The deal was predicated on the fact that although it would cost more than $250,000, land rights worth many millions were available as a potential reward. Hill figured he could increase operating profits. He formed a syndicate and bought the railway in 1878. With three partners, he formed the St Paul, Minneapolis & Manitoba Railway Co. in 1879, with himself as manager.

The way Hill turned a bankrupt line into a profitable one is a lesson to all businesspeople. He upgraded infrastructure, selling old iron rails when the price was right on the scrap market and replacing them with steel rails, and upgraded rolling stock by switching to coal-powered engines. He created a need for the railways by encouraging people to settle alongside them. He offered low fares for the immigrant population and even imported hardy varieties of wheat to help them farm. He built a bridge over the Mississippi River to increase trade and communications between Minneapolis and St Paul. The profitable running of the railway was so important to him that he personally checked out new railway routes on horseback. Such innovative and attentive management increased the value of his association of partners from $278,000 in 1880 to $25,000,000 in 1885. Instead of taking the money out to pursue an extravagant lifestyle, Hill ploughed it back in to the business.

As Hill extended his railway to the north, he grew more ambitious. He decided that in order to control his own destiny and not have to rely on other railroad companies, he would extend his railway all the way to the Pacific Ocean. Hill would connect the Great Lakes with the sea, and thereby facilitate and control transcontinental freight in the north of America. It was an ambitious undertaking.

Hill's Great Northern Railway was a phenomenal achievement. It required finding the lost pass across the Rockies, building bridges and laying hundreds of miles of track in the most adverse of conditions. It took 3300 horse teams and 8000 men to build it. The line reached Seattle, Washington, in January 1893. But possibly the most prodigious achievement of all was the fact that it was completed without the assistance of any public money or land grants – unlike all of the other transcontinental railways. Unencumbered by the burden of public money, Hill could run the railway as he saw fit.

The line was finished, but Hill still faced threats to his business. In 1893, there was a financial panic followed by a depression. Hill survived by helping his customers survive. He intervened personally to ensure wages were paid and that farmers got good prices for their crops. At the same time, he improved efficiency and cut costs. Between 1893 and 1895, all of the other transcontinental railways went bankrupt. Hill and the Great Northern prospered. By 1901, his net worth had increased to $19.4 million from $9.6 million in 1895.

The remaining years of Hill's life were spent trying to secure his railroad, extend it, and protect it from competitors and the government. He locked horns with rival Edward H. Harriman, financier and railroad man, over control of the Northern Pacific railway. He also incurred the wrath of US President Theodore Roosevelt and his trustbusters, who dissolved one of his companies, the Northern Securities Company, in 1904. The last few years of his life were spent campaigning tirelessly to improve the lot of farmers through more scientific farming methods. He died in 1916.

Key texts

- Stuart Bruchey (ed). *Memoirs of Three Railroad Pioneers*. Arno Press, 1987
- Mildred Houghton Comfort. *James J. Hill: Young Empire Builder*. Bobbs-Merrill, 1968
- Joseph Gilpin Pyle. *The Life of James J. Hill*. Doubleday, Page & Co., 1917

Key links

- www.railserve.com/JJHill.html
- www.jjhill.org/Man_Services/james_hillcol.html

Hilton, Conrad Nicholson

Founder, Hilton Hotels (1887–1979)

The son of a Norwegian immigrant father and a German-American mother, Conrad Nicholson Hilton was born in San Antonio, New Mexico, on Christmas Day in 1887. He was educated at the Goss Military Institute in Albuquerque, the New Mexico Military Institute at Roswell, and St Michael's College in Santa Fe.

Hilton's first taste of the hotel business came in 1907. During the 'panic' of 1907, money was scarce for the Hilton family. At Hilton's suggestion, they converted part of the family's general store into a small hotel. To drum up trade, Hilton went to the local train station and offered travellers a room for a dollar.

Hilton's early skirmish with the hotel industry ended when he was dispatched to the New Mexico Institute of Mining at Socorro and then became a partner in a business venture. He made quick progress in business – and politics. In 1912, he was elected to serve a term in the first New Mexico state legislature. Still in his early twenties, he founded the New Mexico State Bank, but was considered too young to serve as CEO. When World War I came, he enlisted and served as a lieutenant in the Quartermaster Corps of the American Expeditionary Force.

When Hilton was discharged from the army in 1919, he made a more serious start in the hotel business. In June of that year, he visited the town of Cisco, Texas. The small town was close to the Ranger oilfields, and Hilton intended to buy a bank in the town. Instead, he bought the Mobley Hotel, hoping to capitalize on his brief experience in the hotel business. It was a good decision. In the Great Depression of the late 1920s and 1930s, 11 of the region's 13 banks failed. Hilton's fledgling hotel business survived thanks to a smart tactical move: he rented out his rooms in eight-hour shifts to match the working patterns of the oilmen. It was the beginning of Hilton's hotel empire.

Hilton bought a hotel in Fort Worth, Texas, in 1919, then two smaller hotels in 1920. In 1925, he constructed his first hotel: the Dallas Hilton. In the five years from 1925 to 1930, Hilton opened a new hotel every year. In 1929, the Wall Street crash and the Great Depression that followed hit Hilton's business badly. By this time, he had eight hotels. Advertising in national magazines helped, but by 1931 travel had dipped throughout the United States, bringing him close to bankruptcy. In 1933, he was forced to sell his hotel in El Paso.

Help arrived in the guise of William L. Moody Jr of Galveston, Texas. Moody was the son of Texan millionaire who had made a fortune primarily through the cotton business. To survive, Hilton joined forces with Moody to form the National Hotel Company. Hilton was general manager. But Moody and Hilton disagreed on how to run the business. In 1934, Hilton left the National Hotel Company and started on his own again, this time with five hotels.

By 1939, Hilton had paid off his debts and started to expand his business. He took advantage of the weakness of the economy to buy a string of hotels. These included prestigious names such as the Plaza and the Waldorf-Astoria in New York City, the Palmer House in Chicago and the Sir Francis Drake in San Francisco.

Hilton tailored service to customers' needs, which distinguished his hotels from the competition. As well as excellent customer service, Hilton used techniques to make his business more efficient than his rivals. He was a master of squeezing profits out of his hotels. Take the landmark Hilton hotels, for example. Hilton bought the Plaza Hotel in 1943, carried out decorative improvements, and boosted revenues by 8 percent. This in turn allowed Hilton to spend $500,000 on improving facilities.

Hilton called this tactic 'mining for gold'. He used it in all of his flagship hotels. In its first year, the Waldorf-Astoria increased revenues by more than $1,500,000 with 95 fewer employees. In the Mayflower Hotel, profits on food increased from 7 percent to 19 percent. Between 1948 and 1950, Hilton increased profits from 18 percent to 26 percent. In the same period, the payroll came down by 4.5 percent, with other expenses down by 3 percent. Hilton's 'magic formula' meant that hotels were profitable even in times of low occupancy.

Hilton Hotels was incorporated on 29 May 1946. Hilton became chairman. After World War II, Hilton travelled to Europe to assess the commercial opportunities. He wanted to operate hotels outside of the United States. His board of directors was not convinced, and advised him against it. Nevertheless, he went ahead and incorporated Hilton Hotels International in 1948.

Hilton opened his first hotel abroad in December 1949. The 300-room Caribe Hilton hotel was built in Puerto Rico at a cost of $5.5 million. In its first year, it made a profit of $100,000, and went on to be very profitable venture for Hilton. But, as importantly, it paved the way for Hilton's international ambitions. He expanded extensively, with hotels in cities across the globe, including Berlin, Cairo and Istanbul. By the late 1950s, Hilton owned 188 hotels in 38 US cities, as well as 54 abroad. On October 27, 1954, Hilton paid $111 million for the Statler hotel chain. At the time, it was the largest commercial property deal in history.

Between 1960 and his death in 1979, Hilton increasingly devoted his time to the Conrad N. Hilton Foundation, which he had founded in 1944. The Foundation was instrumental in building the famous Mayo Clinic as well as setting up the Conrad N. Hilton College of Hotel and Restaurant Management at the University of Houston.

Hilton Hotel's corporate motto was 'World Peace through International Trade and Travel'. It was also Hilton's personal belief. He reasoned that through his business, he could contribute to global economic stability. When he died in 1979, the administrators of his estate, once they had sorted through his 35 separate wills, discovered that he had left the bulk of his estate to his foundation.

Key texts
- Rufus Jarman. *A Bed for the Night: The Story of the Wheeling Bellboy E.M. Statler and His Remarkable Hotels.* Harper and Brothers, 1952
- Conrad Hilton. *Be My Guest.* Prentice Hall, 1957

Key links
- www.hilton.com
- www.hrm.uh.edu

Histogram

A histogram is constructed from a frequency table. It is a graph showing frequency of data, in which the horizontal X-axis details discrete units or class boundaries, and the vertical Y-axis represents the frequency. Blocks are drawn such that their areas are proportional to the frequencies within a class or across several class boundaries. There are no spaces between blocks.

Historic cost

Historic cost is an accounting valuation method that uses the original cost of an asset as its valuation for the purpose of the accounts. Therefore, entries in historical cost accounting reflect the original cost of the asset to the organization, minus – in the case of fixed assets – depreciation.

Hockey stick graph

A plotted graph that at first rises slowly but then steeply is known as a hockey stick graph because of its resemblance to the aforesaid sporting implement. Although the term is well established, it was particularly prevalent during the dotcom boom as the kind of projected growth curve venture capitalists liked to see in start-up companies' business plans.

Hofstede, Geert

Dutch educator (b. 1928)

Born in Haarlem, Netherlands, Geert Hofstede received his MSc from the Delft Institute of Technology in 1953 and his PhD (cum laude) from Groningen University in 1967. Hofstede is professor of organizational anthropology and international management in the Department of Economics and Business Administration at the University of Limburg at Maastricht, as well as director of IRIC, the Institute for Research on Intercultural Cooperation, at Tilburg University. Prior to his academic career, Hofstede worked as a sailor, factory worker, industrial engineer, plant manager and personnel director; he also held the position of chief psychologist on the international staff of IBM. He has since taught and conducted research at many of Europe's top schools, including IMD, INSEAD, EIASM and IIASA. He has also consulted for a wide range of public and private organizations throughout Europe and beyond.

According to *The Economist*, Geert Hofstede 'more or less invented [cultural diversity] as a management subject'. Few would deny that this is the case. The Dutch academic has exerted considerable influence over thinking on the human and cultural implications of globalization.

In Hofstede's hands, culture becomes the crux of business. He defines it as 'the collective programming of the mind, which distinguishes the members of one group or category of people from another.' Hofstede's conclusions are based on huge amounts of research. His seminal work on cross-cultural management, *Culture's Consequences*, involved over 100,000 surveys from more than 60 countries. The sheer size of Hofstede's research base leads to perennial questions about how manageable and useful it can be.

Each society faces some similar problems, but solutions differ from one society to another. Hofstede identified five basic characteristics that distinguish national cultures. These dimensions are:

- **Power distance:** the extent to which the less powerful members of institutions and organizations expect and accept that power is unequally distributed.
- **Individualism:** the strength of ties between individuals, ranging from loose in some societies to involving greater collectivism and strong cohesive groups in others.
- **Masculinity:** the markedness of distinction between social gender roles.
- **Uncertainty avoidance:** the extent to which society members feel threatened by uncertain or unknown situations.
- **Long-term orientation:** the extent to which a society exhibits a pragmatic, future-oriented perspective.

Key texts

- Geert Hofstede. *Culture's Consequences: Comparing Values, Behaviors, Institutions, and Organizations Across Nations*. Second edition, Sage Publications, 2001
- Geert Hofstede. *Uncommon Sense About Organizations*. Sage, 1997
- Geert Hofstede. *Cultures and Organizations*. McGraw-Hill, 1995

Key link

- www.business.com/directory/management/ management_theory/organization_behavior_ and_culture/hofstede,_geert/

Holding company

A holding company is one in which the principal business is holding shares and securities in either another holding company or a trading company. The nature of the interest that the supposed holding company has in its subsidiaries is important for the purposes of deciding whether the company is in fact a holding company or not. In the case of another holding company, the required interest is usually 90 percent. In the case of a trading company, a controlling interest (51 percent) is required. Determining if a company is a holding company or not is often important for tax purposes.

Homeworking

Like part-time work, homeworking was once the province of poorly paid piece workers carrying out low-paid employment such as stuffing envelopes or sewing. With the advances in information and communications technology over the last 15 years, homeworking – or teleworking, as it is also known – has gradually become accepted practice for more senior, better-paid workers and a more feasible and attractive option for many companies. Whether the individual occasionally works from home or is based at home and occasionally comes into the company's offices, many jobs offer the opportunity to work at home for some of the time. Homeworking is not for everyone. It may sound like an ideal situation, but for the wrong person, it can turn out to be a nightmare. Homeworking requires the ability to work despite distractions and to separate personal from working life.

Honda, Soichiro

Founder, Honda (1906–1992)

Born in the small Japanese town of Komyo in 1906, Soichiro Honda spent his early childhood helping his father with his bicycle-repair business. At 15, without the benefit of a formal education, Honda travelled to Tokyo to look for work. He obtained an apprenticeship at a garage but ended up babysitting for the garage owner. Frustrated and dispirited, he returned home, only to be called back within six months. This time, he stayed for six years working as a car mechanic before returning home once more to start his own mechanic business. He was 22.

His love of cars extended to racing them. He set a new average speed record in 1936. Unfortunately, he suffered a bad crash, breaking several bones, including both wrists. His wife, fearing for Honda's health, persuaded him to give up his hobby. With the distraction of racing gone, Honda concentrated his energies on his business and in 1937, he expanded into piston ring manufacturing, setting up Tokai Seiki Heavy Industry (TSHI). Honda was still conscious of his lack of education, however, and finally decided to address the situation, enrolling at the Hamamatsu School of Technology. As it turned out, he needn't have bothered.

Honda made a poor student. The demands of his business meant he found it difficult to keep up with his class work. He was reluctant to pay attention to engineering lectures that didn't involve piston rings and refused to take notes or attend written examinations. When the school's principal warned Honda that if he did not submit to examination he would not receive his diploma, Honda was unrepentant. 'I am not impressed by diplomas. They don't do the work,' he later said. Giving up on the diploma and therefore shunning the *gakubatsa*, the Japanese old-boy networking system, the maverick Honda set out to make his fortune on his own terms.

Honda had tried to retire, but he couldn't resist the lure of engineering; in 1946, he established the Honda Technical Research Institute. By 1948, Honda had sold TSHI to Toyota for 450,000 yen (worth about $1 million today). That year, Honda met a kindred spirit in financier Takeo Fujisawa. The two men had similar opinions on Japan's post-war industrial strategy. Both believed in long-term investment. Fujisawa agreed to invest his money in Honda's company. Honda retained responsibility for engineering while Fujisawa dealt with marketing and sales.

Honda was now in the engine manufacturing business. By the 1950s, Honda had signed a contract to sell the company's entire output of motorcycle engines to a company called Kitagawa. This wasn't as good a deal for Honda as it first appeared. Honda was geared up to produce 100 engines per month while Kitagawa only produced 80 motor-cycles, at the most, during the same period. This caused cash flow problems for its engine supplier. Honda tore up its contract with Kitagawa. In its place, Honda signed deals with distributors that provided for Honda to deliver a complete motor-cycle rather than just an engine.

The company's first big hit was the Cub. Cus-tomers could either buy the engine to fit to their bicycles or buy the complete machine. In less than a year, the Cub was selling 6500 units a month and had captured over 70 percent of the Japanese domestic motorcycle market.

While Honda's reluctance to play by the rules caused problems in some areas, particularly with the Japanese Ministry of International Trade and Industry (MITI), it served the company well in others. Honda adopted a refreshingly open recruitment policy. Although the company had problems recruiting graduate students because of Honda's unwillingness to play the *gakubatsu* game, it attracted many ultimately high-calibre employees who were rejected by other Japanese corporations.

When it came to product design, Honda was a perfectionist. He travelled the world conducting market research in person. He would also attend motorcycle races, taking notes on the competition. By using the best of the competition as a bench-mark, Honda managed to turn Honda motorcy-cles from an average product into the best racing motorcycles in the world. Success in motorcycle racing was important because it raised the public profile of the company, added to the brand value and allowed racing technology to filter down to the standard production model.

1959 was a big year for Honda. The company went into large-scale production on a new model that would sweep all before it – the Super Cub. To build it, Honda built a new plant in Suzuka City. The world's largest motorcycle plant, it turned out 30,000 machines a month. 1959 was also the year the Honda motorcycle racing team, launched in 1954, won first prize at the Isle of Man motorcycle races. Success on the track translated into sales. In the same year, Honda Motorcycles opened its first

dealership in the United States. Rather than sell through the existing US motorbike distributors, Honda went for a more unconventional approach. He sold the small Honda motorcycles wherever he though he might attract the customers.

At the time, total motorcycle sales in the United States were less than 5000 per year. But by 1963, the company was selling 7800 units; by 1984, it had sold some 10 million Honda 50s. The remark-able success was due to the quality of the product and the brilliant advertising campaign. Instead of targeting its product at conventional motor-cycle enthusiasts, Honda authorized a campaign with the slogan, 'You meet the nicest people on a Honda'. The campaign targeted the family market and was a huge success.

The company that Honda built went on to dominate the motorcycle market and make a big impact in the car market. At the end of the twen-tieth century, the company was still the world's number-one motorcycle manufacturer. Honda retired in October 1973 and took an office in Tokyo, where he busied himself with work con-nected with the Honda Foundation. He died in 1991.

Key texts

- Dave Nelson, Patricia E. Moody and Rick Mayo. *Powered by Honda: Developing Excel-lence in the Global Enterprise.* John Wiley, 1998
- Otsuki Satoru, Sakurai Yoko and Tanaka Fumiya. *Good Mileage: The High-Performance Business Philosophy of Soichiro Honda.* Japan Broadcast Publishing Co., 1995

Key links

- www.hondamotorcycle.com/milestonemodels/mrhonda
- www.hondacorporate.com/index.html
- www.honda305.com/cb77_600/cb77–603.htm

Horizontal integration

The takeover of, or merger with, one company

by another company where both are in the same industry and operating at a similar stage in the production chain is known as horizontal integration. The production and supply chain run from the sourcing of the raw material through to the sale to the consumer. In the production of motor vehicles, for example, one auto manufacturer might horizontally integrate with another. Further down the supply chain, two auto dealers might merge. The benefits of this type of integration come from power in the market place and economies of scale. But if the resulting company exerts too much control over the market it operates in, it may fall foul of legislation designed to prevent companies from obtaining a monopoly advantage.

Hostile takeover

When one company – a predator – wishes to purchase another – the target – against the wishes of the target company, then the approach is termed a hostile takeover. Even if the target company does not wish to be acquired, the predator can install its own directors if it can purchase enough shares in the target company to gain control.

Once a predator has made its intentions clear, it must succeed in persuading the company's shareholders to back the bid within a time period specified by the relevant takeover legislation. A target company can employ a range of strategies to defend itself, including finding a **white knight** to rescue it. Hostile takeover bids are often criticized for being an unnecessary drain on the resources of the predator and the target company, as both will spend large sums on persuading the public and shareholders of the merits of their positions. Predators will usually counter that they are unlocking shareholder value.

Hughes, Howard Robard Jr

Founder, Hughes Aircraft and TWA (1905–1975)

There is much disagreement about the facts surrounding the life of Howard Robard Hughes Jr. The disagreement even extends to his birthplace, which was either the city of Houston or the oil town of Humble, Texas. Hughes's father, Howard Sr, was a wealthy man, with a business degree from Harvard and a law degree from Iowa State University. In 1909, Howard Sr formed the Sharp-Hughes Tool Company, manufacturing drill bits for the oil industry. It was his invention of a new oil drill bit that, despite the profligacy of Howard Sr, propelled the Hughes family to wealth.

As a boy, Howard Jr was especially interested in engineering. He showed an impressive knack for building machines, constructing his own radio set as well as a motorcycle. Away from engineering, Hughes's Uncle Rupert, a novelist and playwright, would take the boy to visit the Goldwyn studio, where he developed a fascination for the movies.

Both of Hughes's parents died before he was 20. On the death of his father, he somehow persuaded his relatives to sell him the Hughes Tool Company. Then, in 1925, Hughes married a wealthy woman, Ella Rice, and moved to Hollywood, California. In Hollywood, Hughes began to exhibit the almost maniacal energy and drive that sustained him throughout his varied career.

By 1925, Hughes had created the Caddo Rock Drill Bit Company, bought a controlling interest in Multi-Color Inc., moved into a house on Muirfield Road in Los Angeles, and hired Noah Dietrich, ostensibly as an assistant. Dietrich was the 'fixer' for Hughes's empire in the coming years. Hughes also purchased more than 100 movie theatres to assist him in his latest venture – filmmaking.

Hughes's first film, *Swell Hogan*, was a flop; his third, *Two Arabian Knights*, made money and won the 1927 Academy Award for comedy. Hughes had another hit with *Scarface*, followed by *Front Page*. The difficulty of making *Scarface*, stemming partly from antagonism toward Hughes's anti-Semitic beliefs, took its toll on Hughes and he temporarily abandoned filmmaking. For a time, he restricted his film interests to dating some of the most beautiful women of the time, including Ida Lupino, Katharine Hepburn, Ginger Rogers, Ava Gardner and Lana Turner. Instead of making movies, he turned his attention to the aviation business.

Hughes decided to form an aircraft company, hired a brilliant aeronautical engineer, Glen Odekirk, and set up business in a hangar in California. In the period between filming *Front Page* and setting up the Hughes Aircraft Company in 1934, he disappeared from sight. Appearing at about the same time was a tall, gangly employee of American Airways, Charles Howard, who irritatingly asked endless questions about the airline's operations. Charles Howard, it transpired, was none other than Howard Hughes. Hughes also spent some of this 'missing' period travelling as a hobo and as a society photographer, a business he started from scratch in Huntsville, Texas, under the name R. Wayne Rector.

In 1939, Hughes helped finance Transcontinental & West Airline, obtaining a majority share in the process. The airline was later named Trans World Airlines (TWA). By 1940, a dynamic Hughes was simultaneously running several businesses in different fields. He still owned the tool-manufacturing company he had bought from his father's estate, which brought him $2 million a month. In addition, he was back in the movie business, running an airline, and gearing up for wartime manufacturing.

In the first half of the 1940s, Hughes ordered commercial aircraft from Lockheed, made and released the film *The Outlaw*, created a new starlet in Jane Russell, opened a manufacturing plant in Los Angeles to assist the US war effort, and crashed yet another aircraft – he had crashed two planes previously – killing two passengers.

In 1946, after another period of absence, Hughes reappeared to test his experimental reconnaissance aircraft, the XF-11. At 400 mph, the plane became unstable. To the consternation of the members, Hughes tried to land on the Los Angeles Country Club golf course. Luckily for the club, but unluckily for Hughes, he didn't make it, ploughing into a house on the way down. Admitted to Cedars of Lebanon Hospital, doctors predicted Hughes wouldn't last through the night. His injuries were extensive: crushed chest, twelve broken ribs, collapsed left lung, fractured shoulder and crushed vertebrae. Worse, a large proportion of his body from the waist down was covered in third-degree burns. Remarkably, the apparently indestructible Hughes eventually made a good recovery. He was left with burn scars and a deformed left hand, but very much alive.

Discharged from the hospital, Hughes set about turning TWA around. Hughes saved the ailing airline by obtaining a subsidy from the Civil Aeronautics Board in 1948, and a $10 million loan from the Reconstruction Finance Corporation. He also bolstered his movie business, buying the struggling RKO studio for $9 million. In 1954, Hughes sold most of RKO to concentrate on TWA. In 1955, he established the Howard Hughes Medical Institute in Miami, Florida, in an attempt to reduce his tax liabilities. On 3 May 1966, Hughes sold 78 percent of his TWA stock for $546,549,771, making him, temporarily, the richest man in the world.

The remainder of Hughes's career, until his death in 1975, was characterized by his obsessive, neurotic behaviour and his flight from the IRS. Yet despite his continual dislocation, moving from one hotel to another and one country to another, his increasingly bizarre behaviour, and his dependence on pain-killing drugs, Hughes somehow managed to control his businesses over the phone. He even expanded into hotels and gaming, buying the Desert Inn, Sands, Castaways, New Frontier and Silver Slipper on the Strip in Las Vegas, as well as thousands of acres of land and more than 500 mining concessions, in an incredible spending spree.

The fact that Hughes's disparate collection of companies fell apart within twelve years of his death is evidence, if any were needed, that Hughes's bizarre personality was the glue that bound his business empire together.

Key texts
- Peter Harry Brown and Pat H. Broeske. *Howard Hughes: The Untold Story*. Dutton, 1996

- Charles Higham. *Howard Hughes: The Secret Life*. Putnam's, 1993
- Robert Maheu and Richard Hack. *Next to Hughes: Behind the Power and Tragic Downfall of Howard Hughes*. HarperCollins, 1992
- Robert W. Rummel. *Howard Hughes and TWA*. Smithsonian Institution Press, 1991
- Tony Thomas. *Howard Hughes in Hollywood*. Citadel, 1985
- James Phelan. *Howard Hughes: The Hidden Years*. Random House, 1976
- Blythe Foote Finke. *Howard R. Hughes: Twentieth-Century Multi-Millionaire and Recluse*. Sam-Har Press, 1974
- John Keats. *Howard Hughes*. Random House, 1972

Key links

- http://users.erols.com/dbarrese
- www.wsone.com/fecha/hughes.htm

Human capital

The concept of human capital was introduced during the 1960s by Gary Becker, an economist and professor of economics and sociology at the University of Chicago. A regular columnist in *BusinessWeek* magazine, Nobel laureate winner Becker wrote in that same publication that wealth 'in the form of human capital consists of present and future earnings because of education, training, knowledge, skills, and health. Since wages and salaries account for over 75 percent of the national incomes of developed countries, it should be no surprise that human capital is estimated to be three to four times the value of stocks, bonds, housing, and other assets.' In fact, while Becker has estimated that human capital may represent some 80 percent of the world's wealth, others put the figure even higher. Human capital can be increased by investment in training and education, yet it can be risky for anyone but the recipient of such training or education to make such an investment. This is because there is no guarantee that the purchaser of the training and education, such as a corporation, will reap the benefits.

Key text

- Gary Becker. *The Economic Approach to Human Behavior*. Chicago, University Press, 1976
- Gary Becker. *Human Capital: A Theoretical and Empirical Analysis, with Special Reference to Education*. University of Chicago Press, 1983 – Second Edition

Human-relations school

Australian **Elton Mayo** was a leading member (along with Fritz Roethlisberger, 1898–1974) of the human-relations school, founded in the 1930s. The human-relations school or movement consisted of a number of management theorists who supported the idea that social factors in the workplace determined productivity. The movement was important at the time as the US economy was struggling to accommodate new forms of mass manufacturing with an increasingly dissatisfied, dehumanized workforce.

Mayo and his associates moved away from the scientific management view of employees as isolated factors of production. Mayo studied workers in small groups at the Western Electric Co. from 1927 to 1932. He discovered a range of factors that influenced the workers' productivity, including morale and group norms. He concluded that employees profited from working in groups and needed supportive social structures in the workplace. Social bonds within working groups were so strong that group interests were sometimes placed above individual financial rewards. Mayo's findings ushered in a more enlightened approach to working conditions, including increased communications between employees and management, better social facilities and the infrastructure to support them.

Key text
- F.J. Roethlisberger, W.J. Dickson and H.A. Wright. *Management and the Worker. An Account Of A Research Program Conducted By The Western Electric Company, Hawthorne Works, Chicago.* Harvard University Press, 1949 –reprint.

Hurdle rate

The hurdle rate is the minimum rate of return an investor requires before he is prepared to make that investment. The hurdle rate will be a measure of the investor's risk aversion. Hurdle rates vary from organization to organization and from project to project. Risk, costs of capital and projected investment returns are all factors to be considered in setting a hurdle rate.

The term is also used in fields other than finance. For example, it is used in relationship marketing to indicate the percentage of customers exhibiting a certain level of a particular behaviour being studied.

Hygiene factors

See Herzberg, Frederick.

Hypertext

The term 'hypertext' was coined by US academic and visionary writer Theodor Homm Nelson in his book *Literary Machines* (1982). He explained: 'By "hypertext" I mean non-sequential writing – text that branches and allows choice to the reader, best read at an interactive screen. As popularly conceived, this is a series of text chunks connected by links that offer the reader different pathways.' Hypertext, then, is the presentation of information in a non-linear manner as a series of interconnected nodes, which the reader is free to navigate however they want.

The idea was adopted in 1990 by **Tim Berners-Lee**, inventor of the **World Wide Web**, who used the interlinked nature of the hypertext concept to link from one Web page to another through text links. Using hypertext linking on the Web allows the user to reach related items of information easily. For example, the program might display a map of a country; if the user clicks (with a mouse) on a particular city, the program will display information about that city, or take the viewer to another Web site about that city.

HTML (hypertext mark-up language)

HTML is the standard for structuring, describing, and publishing a document on the **World Wide Web**. The HTML standard provides labels for the different elements of a document (for example, headings and paragraphs) and permits the inclusion of images, sounds and 'hyperlinks' to other documents. A browser program is then used to convert this information into a graphical document onscreen. HTML can be created the help of the proprietary WYSIWYG software, such as Macromedia's Dreamweaver, or typed in from scratch using a simple plain text editor. The specifications for the latest HTML version can be obtained at the W3C Web site.

Key link
- www.w3.org

HTTP (hypertext transfer protocol)

Behind the browser that the user sees when surfing the **World Wide Web** is the network that connects the users to the Web servers containing Web sites and the Internet protocol – the set of rules that governs communications between the client (the Web browser) and the server. The protocol of the Web is HTTP or hypertext transfer protocol, first implemented by **Tim Berners-Lee**, inventor of the

Web, while he was working at the CERN particle physics laboratory in Geneva, Switzerland.

Key link

- www.w3.org

Key texts

- Theodor H. Nelson. *Computer Lib/Dream Machines*. 1974
- Theodor H. Nelson. *Literary Machines 93.1*. Mindful Press, 1991
- Tim Berners-Lee. *Weaving the Web*. Orion, 1999

Iacocca, Lee

Former Chairman and CEO, Chrysler Corporation (b. 1924)

The automotive industry has produced more than its share of great leaders. Brilliant businessman such as **Henry Ford**, **Walter Chrysler** and **William Crapo Durant** long ago earned their place in the auto hall of fame. But among the post-war generation, few deserve to sit alongside the founding fathers of the car industry. Lee Iacocca is one of those who does.

Iacocca was born on 15 October 1924, in Allentown, Pennsylvania. He came from a family of Italian immigrants who hailed from a small town, San Marco, just north of Naples. Iacocca's father ran a small hot dog business. As with many other families during the 1920s, times were hard. Iacocca won a scholarship to Princeton, where he completed a thesis in two semesters before joining Ford as a trainee engineer in 1946. Graduating from his trainee course, Iacocca decided against engineering and instead went to work in the Ford sales office in Chester, Pennsylvania. From being a bashful, stammering sales clerk, he became sales manager in 1949.

The 1950s were good years for Iacocca. He survived the wholesale staff cutbacks at Ford during the early 1950s, and by 1953 was assistant sales manager of the Philadelphia district. In 1956, to combat poor sales of Ford cars, he introduced a new finance scheme called '56 for "56"', which allowed the cash-strapped purchaser to put down a modest down payment of 20 percent with three further payments of $56. Credit financing was just beginning to take hold as a way to purchase cars, and Iacocca's plan was a success; it was adopted company-wide. Robert S. McNamara, Ford's vice-president, later estimated that 75,000 extra cars were sold as a result of Iacocca's financing scheme. The scheme's success made Iacocca an overnight star within the Ford ranks. One promotion quickly followed another. By 1960, he was head of the Ford division. At the age of 36, Iacocca was general manager of the largest division in the world's second-biggest car company.

In charge of the Ford division, he soon stamped his authority on the company. He played an influential role in the decision to abandon the proposed new model, the Cardinal, which was dropped even though it incurred a $35 million loss. The first Ford Mustang rolled off the assembly line in its place on 9 March 1964. The new car had been designed from scratch and was priced at an affordable level. Its launch created a wave of publicity, simultaneously featuring on the covers of *Time* and *Newsweek* magazines. The Mustang was the car the market had been waiting for. In its first year, it sold a record 418,812, making a profit of $1.1 billion. Iacocca had much to thank the Mustang for. In January 1965, he was promoted to vice-president of the corporate car truck group, and on 10 December 1970 he became president of the Ford empire.

President he may have been, but Iacocca was not the most powerful person at Ford. That honour was reserved for the founder's grandson, Henry Ford II. In 1977, Ford turned to the management consulting firm **McKinsey & Co.**, calling them into reorganize the company's management structure. McKinsey recommended a new management structure with the chairman/CEO, the vice-chairman and the president at the top. Iacocca became number three in the ruling triumvirate. Then, in 1978, Ford fired Iacocca. The reason, in Ford's own words, was, 'Sometimes you just don't like somebody.' The fact that Iacocca had made millions of dollars for Ford and introduced the Mustang, the Mark 3 Lincoln and the Fiesta, some of the company's most popular car models, didn't matter.

Iacocca was 54; he could have retired. But a few months later, he joined Chrysler Motor Corporation, becoming chairman and CEO in September 1979. During Iacocca's time at Chrysler, he executed one of the most impressive turnarounds in car manufacturing history. When he arrived, the Detroit press was full of gloomy headlines, such as 'Chrysler Losses Are Worst Ever'. The company was struggling, but Iacocca had not realized how serious its problems were when he joined. He soon found out: Chrysler was running out of money, and fast. Iacocca took swift remedial action, eradicating excess inventory, renegotiating contracts with car-rental companies Hertz and Avis, recruiting a slew of top talent and making substantial layoffs. Most important of all, Iacocca went, cap in hand, to the government and applied for a loan guarantee for $1.2 billion. It required new legislation. To secure government support, Iacocca had to give testimony before the House of Representatives and Senate hearings in Washington. But the request was granted.

As Iacocca cut costs at Chrysler (he cut his own salary to $1) and the car market picked up, Chrysler's flagging fortunes revived. In 1983, Chrysler made a profit of $925 million. Iacocca was fêted as the saviour of the company. In 1983, not long after a new stock offering, Iacocca wrote out a historic cheque for $813,487,500 to clear the balance of the company's debt outstanding on the government loan.

Iacocca went on to steer Chrysler to greater success. He engineered the company's $1.5 billion acquisition of American Motors and incorporated Jeep into Chrysler's product offering. He also successfully promoted the fuel-efficient K-car. Iacocca retired from Chrysler in 1992, but his enthusiasm for business remained undiminished. Leaving the motor giants behind him, he founded a small start-up company, EV Global Motors, selling electric-powered bicycles.

Key texts

- Lee Iacocca with Sonny Kleinfield. *Talking Straight.* Bantam Books, 1988
- Peter Wyden. *The Unknown Iacocca.* Morrow, 1987
- Lee Iacocca with William Novak. *IACOCCA: An Autobiography.* Bantam Books, 1984

ICANN (Internet Corporation for Assigned Names and Numbers)

ICANN is the non-profit, private-sector organization that oversees the management of the Internet's domain-name system. It is comprised of a powerful coalition of parties from across the Internet industry that includes the Internet's business, academic, and user communities.

ICANN doesn't 'run the Internet'; at least, that's not part of its official mandate. Instead, it coordinates and manages key area such as the domain name system (**DNS**), the allocation of IP (Internet provider) address space, the management of the root server system and the coordination of protocol number assignment.

This is all essential to the smooth running and growth of the Internet. The most obvious manifestation of ICANN's role to the average Internet user is the introduction of new top-level domains. ICANN has broken up the monopoly that Network Solutions enjoyed over the registration of .com names. With the availability of good .com names, and even .org names, diminishing daily, ICANN will approve the introduction of new top-level domains, such as .web and .store.

Key link

- www.icann.org

IDE (integrated development environment)

An integrated development environment is the environment in which computer code is written, compiled and debugged. As the tools in the environment are all constructed to deal with the programming language being used – **Java** for example – the environment is referred to as integrated.

Idle time

Idle time is the amount of time, measured in man or machine hours, that a workstation or production facility is unavailable for use. Reasons for idle time include faulty machinery and lack of skilled operators. The concept is also used in **queuing theory**. In many production processes, one stage of production is dependent on another. Not all stages of a production process are always able to run at the same speed. This means that if the stages run at their full capacity, at some point the faster stages will need to stop to allow the slower stages to catch up. This period of downtime is known as idle time.

Inc.com

The online extension of *Inc.* magazine, Inc.com proclaims itself as the Web site for business builders who are 'long on work and short on time'. The site offers advice, information products and online tools aggregated from many different sources. It is one of the most useful Web sites on the Internet for **small to midsize businesses** and **entrepreneurs**.

One of the best sections on the site is the advice section, divided into two principal areas: 'Getting Started' and 'Growing Your Business'. 'Getting Started' provides articles, case studies, research reports and tips on the best way to go about starting up your own business. The business plan is a key element in any start-up's strategy to raise finance, but it is difficult to find good information on the Internet about what exactly is required in a business plan without having to pay for it. Inc.com, however, in the 'Writing a Business Plan' subsection, supplies links to online sources where information about business plans is freely available, including comprehensive templates.

'Growing Your Business' covers a comprehensive range of subjects. These include those that you would expect to find such as marketing, **e-commerce**, sales, finance and law, plus more surprising but no less interesting categories, like the section on business ethics.

Key link
- www.inc.com

Incorporation

Incorporation is the formation of an association that has corporate personality and is, therefore, distinct from its individual members, who have no liability for its debts. Corporations, such as companies, can own property and have their rights and liabilities in law. In the United Kingdom, the two main forms of incorporation are the limited company and the public limited company.

A limited company (ltd) is a registered company that has limited liability, which means the shareholders cannot lose more than their original shareholdings; it has a minimum of two shareholders and a maximum of 50. It cannot offer its shares or debentures to the public, and their transfer is restricted. To form a limited company, two documents are required: the company memorandum and the articles of association. A limited company must also have a director and a company secretary. It is treated as a legal entity.

A public limited company (plc) is a company registered as a plc under the provisions of the Companies Act 1980. A plc must have the letters 'plc' after its name and have authorized share capital of more than £50,000, with more than £12,500 paid to the company by the shareholders. Plcs may offer shares to the public and are more tightly regulated than limited companies. Converting a private limited company into a public one has advantages, such as the ability to raise share capital. It does, however, have potential disadvantages, such as being subject to the scrutiny of the financial media and city analysts. If the founder of a plc believes the company's share price undervalues the company, he may seek to take the company private once more, as **Richard Branson** did with Virgin in 1989.

In the United States, those starting up a small business have a number of corporate forms to choose from. A 'C Corporation', so named because it is taxed under Sub-chapter C of the Internal Revenue Code, is treated as a separate legal entity from stockholders, i.e. the owners of the corporation, as long as the correct company procedures are maintained. The founder will have to file documents including Articles of Incorporation and Corporate Bylaws; he will also have to make a decision about which state to incorporate in, as incorporation in some states has different tax implications.

It is also possible to incorporate as an S Corporation. With this type of corporate form, the small business is taxed as if it were a partnership or sole trader. This avoids one of the main drawbacks of the C Corporation, double taxation, where the company profits are taxed before being distributed to the stockholders as dividends, which are also taxed.

To qualify as an S Corporation, the company must have a limited number of stockholders and receive the appropriate approval from the IRS. Another alternative is the limited liability company (LLC), a hybrid of a corporation and a partnership.

Increasing returns

Santa Fe Institute economist **W. Brian Arthur** is among those who has argued that the classic economic law of diminishing returns has been turned on its head to produce the law of increasing returns. This means that under certain circumstances, companies can quickly come to totally dominate a market. Such is the power of increasing returns that the power of market forces appears negated – indeed, for a while it is. The invisible hand of market forces is 'a little bit arthritic', notes Arthur.

'High technology operates under increasing returns, and to the degree modern economies are shifting toward high technology, the different economics of increasing returns alters the character of competition, business culture, and appropriate government policy in these economies,' Arthur says.

Stan Davis and **Chris Meyer** also weigh in on increasing returns in their 1999 book *Blur*, writing, 'The blur of businesses has created a new economic model in which returns increase rather than diminish; supermarkets mimic stock markets; and you want the market – not your strategy – to price, market, and manage your offer.'

Key text
- W. Brian Arthur. *Increasing Returns & Path Dependence in the Economy*. University of Michigan Press, 1994

Incubator

An incubator is an organization that provides funding to start-up ventures and acts as a catalyst for entrepreneurial activity. A key difference between incubators and other kinds of financing for start-ups is the extent of assistance provided; the average incubator offers services including office space, technological know-how, legal and financial advice and Web design. In return, incubators take a slice of the equity.

Although incubators are associated with Internet start-ups, they are not a new phenomenon. In the United States, they date back to the 1950s, when local governments created them to stimulate regional business activity. The growth of incubators worldwide has been spectacular, rising from just 14 in 1995 to 348 by May 2000, with the numbers doubling in the seven months from November 1999.

Increasingly, incubators on both sides of the Atlantic are changing their emphasis from developing companies purely to profit from their IPOs to establishing a symbiotic network of companies similar to the Japanese *keiretsu*. These networks are known as econets or economic networks.

Well-known incubators include Idealab in the United States and Brainspark in the United Kingdom. Some business schools, such as the Haas School of Business at Berkeley in the United States and Cranfield School of Management in the United Kingdom, also offer an incubator-like environment for their **MBA** students. Traditional consulting powerhouses have also embraced venture consulting. Take Bain & Co., for example, which set up Bainlabs: incubator units set up to nurture fledgling Internet businesses. The first two Bainlabs were established in 1999 in San Francisco and London. Others followed in Paris, Milan, Munich, Singapore, Hong Kong and Boston. The idea was that at the end of each year, the rank-and-file consultants receive a share of the action as part of their annual bonus.

Induction

The employee induction, or orientation in the US, is an initial period of training, during which a new worker is likely to learn about a company and how it operates, as well as, perhaps, more job-specific skills. Inductions are usually given at the beginning of the period of employment and may last for many weeks, even months. The aim in the induction is to integrate the employee into the new operation as swiftly as possible. As a result, induction will normally include basic details about the company, such as geographical locations, number of employees, organizational structure and company culture. It will also include details such as dress code and disciplinary procedures. It is also the period during which the new employee will receive any equipment needed to carry out the job and possibly a detailed job description, as well as the induction manual. Induction also provides the opportunity for the new employee to ask any questions about the new job that they failed to ask earlier.

Industrial democracy

Industrial democracy is the idea that ownership and control of a company or organization should be wholly or partly in the hands of the employees, who therefore take their share of responsibility for the company's success or failure. Although it might be supposed that industrial democracy is solely associated with socialist politics, a wide range of political systems have embraced the idea of the worker cooperative, from the free market United States through the social democrats of Sweden to socialist Russia. In the United States, for example, the passing of the National Labor Relations Act in 1935 was intended to improve a general malaise in industrial relations as well as encourage democracy in the workplace. The NRLA provided for 'free collective bargaining' by employees and encouraged the formation of unions and their role in championing the rights of workers. Unfortunately for advocates of industrial democracy, the forward-thinking legislation didn't lead to wholesale changes in working practices and organizational structure. Instead, the power of unions has been constantly eroded and collective bargaining has been nearly abandoned. A good example of an industrial democracy in practice today is the pioneering Semco Corporation in Brazil, run by **Ricardo Semler**.

Key text

* Ricardo Semler. *Maverick: The Success Story Behind the World's Most Unusual Workplace.* Warner Books, 1993

Industrial inertia

Industrial inertia is the situation in which an industry or group of industries remains in one geographical location, continuing to invest in that region even though it is no longer the best location for the industry. For example, iron and steel are still produced in Sheffield, even though the local supplies of iron ore ran out some time ago. The cost of moving is one reason that industries may stay in a particular place. The concept's origins may lie in an investigation into the US steel industry by Allan Rogers in 1952 entitled 'Industrial Inertia: A Major Factor in the Location of the Steel Industry in the United States', published in *Geographical Review*.

Industrialization

Industrialization is the process by which an increasing proportion of a country's economic activity is involved in industry. It is essential for economic development and largely responsible for the growth of cities. Industrialization in the form of the Industrial Revolution began in Europe in the late 1700s following the mechanization of the textile industry. Britain imported just over 1000 tons of raw cotton in 1760; by 1850, that figure had risen to 222,000, creating large areas of industrial urbanization across the Midlands and North of England. The amount of raw cotton Britain imported between 1760 and 1850 illustrates the huge increase in productivity made possible by the use of machines.

In the United States, wholesale industrialization occurred from the mid- and late 1800s onward, sparked by technological advances, in particular the railway, the discovery of large deposits of natural resources, and the development of mass production.

Key text
• W.O. Henderson. *The Industrialization of Europe: 1780–1914*. Thames and Hudson, 1969

Industry analysis

As part of a business plan, the industry analysis concentrates on the industry sector within which the proposed company will operate. The summary of the industry needs to include information such as the size of the industry, both in revenue and company terms; significant industry trends; government regulations affecting the industry; barriers to entry; predicted growth (or contraction) of the industry; and technological advancements. By addressing these issues, it is possible to provide a clear picture of the target market and competition.

Inertia selling

Also known as negative option selling, inertia selling is a sales technique in which goods are sent to potential consumers on an unsolicited basis. The selling company may then follow up by billing the consumer, on the basis that if the consumer does not return the goods within a certain time, he will be liable for the cost of those goods. The type of inertia selling that holds the recipient liable if he does not return the goods is illegal in many countries. However, the type of inertia selling that does not place an obligation on the recipient of the goods when the goods are delivered on a sale-or-return basis is widely practised. It is popular with book and record clubs, for example.

Inferior good

Unlike a normal good, an inferior good is one for which demand falls as the income of consumers rises. It therefore exhibits a negative income elasticity of demand. Examples of inferior goods often given include bread, bus journeys, and margarine. Take bus journeys, for example. As a person's income rises, he will rely less on public transportation and bus journeys, instead taking taxis or buying his own car.

In contrast, a 'Giffen good' is, curiously, one for which demand increases as the price increases.

Inflation

The most common definition of inflation is a sustained rise in the general level of prices. The many causes include cost-push inflation, which results from rising production costs, thus forcing up the costs of products and services; demand-pull inflation, which occurs when overall demand exceeds supply and too much money chases too few goods; suppressed inflation, which occurs in controlled economies and is reflected in rationing, shortages and black-market prices; and hyperinflation, which occurs when public confidence in the value of money is poor and the public subsequently decides to spend its money as quickly as possible to obtain maximum possible value from it, leading to inflation often exceeding 100 percent in one month. Inflation is usually measured using a weighted index of prices from a large sample of popular goods and services. **Deflation**, a fall in the general level of prices, is the reverse of inflation.

Information overload

'Information overload' is the term used to describe the modern phenomenon of workers deluged by a flood of information that impairs their ability to perform their jobs. Technological advances including e-mail, the Internet and the mobile phone have exacerbated the situation. The problem of information overload should not be underestimated, as it can cause workplace stress.

In 1996, British psychologist David Lewis produced the report *Dying for Information?*, commissioned by London-based Reuters Business Information. In the report, Lewis coined the term Information Fatigue Syndrome to describe a condition that includes symptoms such as 'a hyper-aroused psychological condition', 'paralysis of analytical capacity' and 'anxiety and self-doubt'. The result of these symptoms is poor decision-making and, worse, moderate to major ill health. The report maintains that Information Fatigue Syndrome is particularly bad among so-called knowledge workers. Likely solutions include delegation to subordinates and learning to recognize the optimum amount of information required to make a decision.

Key text
- David Lewis. *Dying for Information? An Investigation Into the Effects of Information Overload in the USA and Worldwide.* Reuters Limited, 1996

Information superhighway

A popular collective name for the Internet and other related large-scale computer networks, the phrase 'information superhighway' is used to suggest a large network of integrated interactive private and public electronic networks. It has also been used synonymously with the term National Information Infrastructure (NII).

The term 'information superhighway' is attributed by some to former US vice-president Al Gore, who said in a 1999 speech: 'Three years ago, on the 30th anniversary of the interstate highway system, I sponsored the Supercomputer Network Study Act to explore a fibreoptic network to link the nation's supercomputers into one system. High-capacity fibreoptic networks will be the *information superhighways* of tomorrow.' Although Gore has been ridiculed for a statement that was interpreted by many as claiming invention of the Internet, no less a person than **Vinton Cerf** has acknowledged the contribution of Gore to the development of the Internet in modern society.

Key link
- www.ipo.com

Innovation

Innovation, the creation of something new, is an essential element of economic development. Innovation may entail the creation of a new product or product modification, both of which are considered product innovation, or a new way of doing something, such process innovation. Product innovation will often give a company competitive advantage in a product market that is relatively static. When Nike introduced the 'Air' training shoe, for example, it transformed the training shoe from a sports accessory to mainstream street fashion. Process innovation, such as the development of production line manufacturing, can lead to significant cost reductions and licensing opportunities.

For it to have an economic value, innovation must be capable of being protected. This is done by obtaining a patent or, usually, several patents. A patent allows the holder to defend his invention against those who would copy it and effectively steal the economic benefit. One way around a patent, however, is the practice of reverse engineering. This involves taking an existing product and deconstructing it to learn how to build a similar but suitably different product. Reverse engineering has reduced the timescale over which the benefits of innovation can be enjoyed.

Insider dealing

The trading of securities takes place in what is supposed to be a free and fair market, where all participants are presumed to have equal knowledge available to them – not that they possess equal knowledge, but that they should be able to obtain that information if they wish and know how to. On occasion, however, the trading of securities takes place with the benefit of price-sensitive information not generally known to those persons who are accustomed or would be likely to deal in the securities of the company.

Such information is known as 'insider information' – that is, specific information about a corporation that is not generally known to those persons who are accustomed or would be likely to deal in the listed securities of that corporation, but that would, if it were generally known to them, be likely to affect materially the price of those securities.

Insider dealing is illegal in most jurisdictions and has been a criminal offence in the United States since 1993, where the practice is known as 'insider trading', and in the United Kingdom since the 1980s. In the United Kingdom, there is a raft of legislation covering insider dealing, including the Companies Act 1980, the Criminal Justice Act 1993 and the Financial Services and Markets Act 2000.

Although some economists argue that insider dealing may be beneficial rather than harmful to markets, most academics agree that the damage it does to market confidence by shattering the impression of a level playing field is justification for its criminalization.

Defences to the charge of insider dealing include proving that the alleged inside information is in fact market information or that the alleged insider dealer would have acted in the same way had he not been privy to the inside information.

Insolvency

Insolvency occurs when a company or individual is unable to pay debts when they are due or, in the case of a company, when its liabilities exceed its assets (technical insolvency). Individuals who are insolvent may become bankrupt; companies may go into liquidation. In the United Kingdom, companies do not become bankrupt. Instead, they usually go into administration or receivership. This is a measure taken by a court acting under insolvency legislation to place an administrator in charge of a company in financial difficulty. This action is taken to protect the shareholders' interests and keep the company trading as a going concern. Alternatively, the company may be wound up or enter a Company Voluntary Arrangement. In the case of liquidation, an insolvency practitioner is likely to be appointed as a trustee in **bankruptcy** or liquidation to salvage assets for the creditors. With a strict pecking order for creditors, ordinary shareholders have little, if any, hope of recovering their investment.

In the United States, the terminology is slightly different. Companies will usually go into **Chapter**

11 bankruptcy when in severe financial difficulty. This option allows them to restructure and, if possible, emerge from bankruptcy as a solvent trading company once more. There has been a suggestion that European companies may move toward the American model. France already has an option that is similar to the US Chapter 11 bankruptcy provision.

As far as the directors' liability is concerned, in the United Kingdom, they can be held personally liable if they continue to trade when their company is technically insolvent. In the United States, however, the directors are rarely, if ever, held personally liable.

Key link
- www.abiworld.org/

Institutional investor

Institutional investors are organizations that invest large sums in the financial markets, in both gilts (government-issued debt) and equities. Institutional investors include organizations such as pension funds, trade unions, and insurance companies. They usually have an in-house investment department employing financial industry specialists, such as fund managers and analysts, to manage their investments. Because institutional investors invest such large sums in the financial markets, they have considerable power to both influence corporate policy and affect market sentiment. This power is often exercised during takeover bids or to express dissatisfaction at the performance of company directors. **IPOs (initial public offerings)**, rights issues and other share placings are frequently offered to institutional markets on preferential terms before they are offered to the public.

Insurance

An insurance policy is a contract guaranteeing compensation to the payer of a premium against loss by fire, death, accident and so on, which is known as 'assurance' in the case of a fixed sum and 'insurance' where the payment is proportionate to the loss. The party to the contract benefiting from the insurance is known as the insured. The insured, which can be an individual or an organization, has certain obligations under the insurance contract. These include making a full declaration of all material facts on the insurance proposal and minimizing any losses that may occur.

The party granting the insurance is known as the insurer. The insurer agrees to pay claims on a policy, subject to the terms of that policy. Common terms for the insurer include payment of an insurance premium, an agreement to permit a survey and be bound by any recommendations (in the case of a property risk), and an obligation to minimize any losses. Insurance contracts are normally renewed on an annual basis, when the risk will be reassessed in the light of any material changes and the claims history.

Insurance contracts are governed not by the doctrine of **caveat emptor** or buyer beware but by the doctrine of **uberrima fides** or utmost good faith. This means that all parties to the insurance contract must deal in good faith, i.e. making a full declaration of all material facts in the insurance proposal.

The world's largest insurance market used to be Lloyd's of London. A unique organization, it was comprised of a number of insurance syndicates. An insurance syndicate was a professional underwriter or underwriters who wrote business backed by the funds from private individuals, which would be used to meet future and present claims. The private individuals or 'names', as they were known, had unlimited liability. It was the Lloyd's insurance market that was largely responsible for developing and refining the nature of commercial insurance contracts from the 1680s until the early 1900s. The Lloyd's insurance market underwent considerable upheaval, however, in the wake of a number of heavy reinsurance claims, many related to asbestosis, which resulted in the bankruptcy of a number of names. Many syndicates were subsequently restructured as limited liability companies.

Intangible assets

Intangible assets are those that do not exist in a physical form and so cannot be touched or seen. A major class of intangible assets is intellectual property, such as **copyright**, **trademarks** and **patents**. Copyright is the exclusive right given to the author of a work – whether words, music, video, sound, picture, architecture, etc. – to reproduce, distribute, display, license or perform that work. A trademark is a distinctive word, picture or symbol that is used to distinguish and identify the origin of a product. A patent allows the inventor of a piece of intellectual property to prevent others from using the patented design for a limited period. This covers hardware and software. The problem with patents is that it may only take minor differences in design to negate the protection afforded by the patent. Another example of an intangible asset is **goodwill**.

Intangible assets create a problem for accounting purposes. While they often have a significant financial value, as in the case of a brand, quantifying that value for accounting purposes is often impossible or highly problematical.

Intellectual capital

Capital was once viewed in purely financial terms. The answer to all questions seemed to lie in the corporate balance sheets. During the 1990s, however, there was a drive to reflect intangible corporate assets in the balance sheet. The value of brands, for example, has been lengthily debated and intricate valuation systems championed. In their annual reports, British football clubs state the theoretical transfer value of their players as well as pure financial facts. Now, there is a move toward greater understanding – and perhaps valuation – of the most intangible, elusive, mobile and important asset of all: intellectual capital.

Intellectual capital can be crudely described as the collective brainpower of the organization or, alternatively, as intellectual material such as knowledge, intellectual property and information that can be used to create wealth. The concept is irrevocably bound up with the notion of the **knowledge worker** and knowledge management. In some hands, the terms are used virtually synonymously.

Intellectual capital is often divided into three categories: human capital, customer capital and structural capital. Human capital is implicit knowledge – the knowledge in employees' heads. Customer capital involves recognizing the value of relationships between companies and their customers. Structural capital is knowledge retained within the organization and can be passed onto new employees.

The root of the concept, as with so many other ideas, lies in the work of **Peter Drucker**. His 1969 book, *The Age of Discontinuity*, introduced the term 'knowledge worker' to describe the highly trained, intelligent managerial professional who realizes his own worth and contribution to the organization. The knowledge worker was the antidote to the previous model of the corporate individual.

'The knowledge worker sees himself just as another *professional*, no different from the lawyer, the teacher, the preacher, the doctor, or the government servant of yesterday,' wrote Drucker in *The Age of Discontinuity*. 'He has the same education. He has more income; he has probably greater opportunities as well. He may well realize that he depends on the organization for access to income and opportunity, and that without the investment the organization has made – and a high investment at that – there would be no job for him, but he also realizes, and rightly so, that the organization equally depends on him.'

Drucker recognized the new breed, but key to his contribution was the realization that knowledge is both power *and* ownership. Intellectual capital is power. If knowledge, rather than labour, is the new measure of economic society, then the fabric of capitalist society must change: 'The knowledge worker is both the true "capitalist" in the knowledge society and dependent on his job. Collectively the knowledge workers, the employed educated middle-class of today's society, own the means of production through pension funds, investment trusts, and so on.'

In his 1992 book, *Managing for the Future*, Drucker observes: 'From now on the key is knowledge. The world is becoming not labor intensive, not materials intensive, not energy intensive, but knowledge intensive.'

The information age places a premium on intellectual work. There is a growing realization that recruiting, retaining, and nurturing talented people are crucial to competitiveness. The challenge is that talent or intellectual capital is a scarce and therefore highly prized resource (one explanation for booming executive pay). Intellectual capital is, in many ways, simply concerned with fully utilizing the intellects of those employed by an organization. 'If Hewlett-Packard knew what it knows we'd be three times more productive,' reflected Hewlett-Packard CEO Lew Platt.

Having identified intellectual capital as important, the next question is inevitable: how can it be measured? After all, what gets measured gets done. Intellectual capital is increasingly codified as part of corporate life. The Swedish company Skandia has a 'director of intellectual capital' and others are following suit – with job titles, at least. Skandia's Leif Edvinsson is one of the thought leaders in this field: he has developed a model for reporting on intellectual capital based around customers, processes, renewal and development, human factors and finance.

The trouble is that turning bland statements about knowledge and intellectual capital into reality is a substantial challenge. Intellectual capital is good, but how do you create it? Here, companies can hit a wall. Research by Booz Allen & Hamilton consultants Charles Lucier and Janet Torsilieri found that most knowledge management programmes have limited results. Indeed, they estimate that 'about one-sixth of these programs achieve very significant impact within the first two years; half achieve small but important benefits;

and the remaining third – the failures – have little business impact.' For all the talk, successfully harnessing intellectual capital remains a formidable challenge that few corporations can claim to have overcome.

Key texts

- Leif Edvinsson and Michael Malone. *Intellectual Capital*. Harper Business, 1997
- David A. Klein (ed). *The Strategic Management of Intellectual Capital*. Butterworth-Heinemann, 1997
- Thomas A. Stewart. *Intellectual Capital*. Doubleday, 1997

Intelligent agent

Also known as a **bot**, an intelligent agent is a software program written to act independently of, but on the behalf of, its user. Research into intelligent agents at organizations such as Xerox PARC and the Massachusetts Institute of Technology suggests intelligent agents will play a big part in the future of the Internet. Intelligent agents will, for example, be able to carry out shopping tasks remotely. An intelligent agent called a shopping bot will carry out shopping transactions over the Internet on the behalf of a user. Once instructed, they will seek out the best deal for a good or service, perform price comparisons, complete the order and arrange for delivery – all without the intervention of the user, other than for the initial instruction.

Key link

- www.botspot.com

Interest rate

The interest rate is the cost of borrowing money for a specified period, and is usually expressed as a percentage of the amount borrowed a year. Thus, borrowing £100,000 for one year at a cost of £10,000 would be expressed as an interest rate of 10 percent on the principal (the amount borrowed). This would make the total amount payable £110,000. As loans are not normally as straightforward as this example, interest rates are normally defined as part of the complex contract between lender and borrower.

Demand for loans in comes from a variety of sources, including households – which require them for the purchase of large items such as houses, vacations and cars – and companies, which need to borrow money for expansion purposes and other forms of investment. Similarly, governments borrow money in order to meet the shortfall between taxation and expenditure.

Loans are supplied with funds that come from households and companies through money deposited with financial intermediaries such as banks. Alternatively, they may come directly from the lender through financial instruments such as bonds.

The cost of borrowing is determined by the relationship between the supply and demand of the funds from the above sources. There is, of course, no single interest rate; instead, there is a range of interest rates governing a myriad of loans.

Interest rates play a very important role at a macroeconomic level, both on the supply side and the demand side of the economy. They can be used to stimulate or put a break on demand and so have a major impact on inflation, currency rates and economic growth.

For example, if interest rates rise, consumers will be rewarded for saving and penalized for borrowing. If consumers save, then they are less likely to spend. Less consumer spending, if it continues, will lead to an easing of prices and a break on inflationary pressures. Conversely, low interest rates make it easier for companies to borrow and expand and easier for consumers to borrow and spend. This tends to stimulate the economy and increase inflationary pressures.

As interest rates are such a powerful economic tool, governments have a tendency to interfere and manipulate interest rates to suit their political ends, if they are allowed to. Consequently, there has been a move to hand control of setting of base interest rates to independent banks. Thus, in the United Kingdom, interest rates are set by the **Bank of England**, and in the United States, interest rates are set by the **Federal Reserve** Bank – both theoretically free from political influence.

Interim management

Interim management is seen as one solution to corporate crises and other managerial resourcing issues. It involves hiring highly qualified and experienced freelance executives and dropping them into a business dilemma, with a specific mission and a limited length of time to implement it.

It is hard to pinpoint exactly when the first interim manager emerged, but most commentators agree that the practice started in the Netherlands in the mid- to late-1970s. At that time, it was seen as a way to get around strict Dutch labour laws, which meant that companies taking on full-time managers incurred substantial additional fixed costs. The opportunity to take on executives on a temporary basis was seen an ideal way to add additional executive resources without the negative effects. Since then, the practice has spread to other countries.

The appointment of an interim manager can actually reassure investors. In September 1996, for example, PepsiCo Inc. appointed Karl von der Heyden to be chief financial officer (CFO) and vice-chairman for a year. A former chief of RJR Nabisco, von der Heyden's main role at Pepsi was to help chart strategy in the wake of a string of operational problems that had plagued the company and to find a 'world-class' CFO to succeed him. Wall Street clearly approved of the idea; when the announcement was made, Pepsi shares promptly jumped 50 cents to $29.50.

Today, the use of interim managers – also known as 'transition managers', 'flexi-executives', 'impact managers', 'portfolio executives' and 'Handymen' (after UK management guru **Charles Handy**, who was one of the first to advocate flexible working patterns) – is establishing itself as key strategic resource for companies.

In her book *Strike a New Career Deal*, Carole Pemberton explains the rise of interim management as follows: 'An organization seeks help because there are major projects where it does not have sufficient in-house expertise, but where once the change has been introduced, the job can be managed internally. They (the top management team) know that they are getting an individual who has not only done the job before, but will probably have done it for a far larger enterprise.'

Scenarios in which an interim manager might be considered could include any of the following:

- implementation of systems, particularly new or updated high-tech installations
- helping companies to take advantage of expansion or new opportunities
- the preparation a subsidiary for sale, especially in an underperforming company in dire need of reorganization
- the sudden or unexpected departure or illness of a senior executive.

The wider strategic significance of the interim management concept is becoming apparent. It is very much in tune with other employment trends. According to *Fortune* magazine, for example, one in four Americans is now a member of the contingent workforce – people who are hired for specific purposes on a part-time basis.

There is little doubt that interim management is a timely addition to the corporate resourcing armoury. Interim managers are ideally matched to the changing business environment companies now face.

Key texts

- Des Dearlove and David Clutterbuck. *The Interim Manager*. Financial Times Management, 1998
- Godfrey Golzen. *Interim Management*. Kogan Page, 1992

Interim report

A report on a company's financial position is known as an interim report when the period covered is of less than a year. In the United Kingdom there is no legal requirement to produce regular interim reports. However, the **London Stock Exchange** requires listed companies to produce half-yearly profit and loss statements. Even where there is no legal requirement, many large corporations choose to produce interim reports. In the United States, the practice is to produce quarterly financial reports showing profit and loss and cash flow, and this is the model most large UK corporations tend to follow. This is partly for the benefit of the shareholders and partly as a public-relations exercise for investment analysts and the media.

Internet

The Internet is a global public computer network that provides the communication infrastructure for applications such as e-mail, the **World Wide Web** and file transfer protocol (**FTP**). Rather than being just one network, the Internet is an interconnected system of smaller networks that use common protocols to pass packets of information from one computer to another.

The origins of the Internet go back to the 1960s, when computer gurus Leonard Kleinrock (b. 1934) and J.C.R. Licklider (1915–1990), then at the Massachusetts Institute of Technology, wrote academic papers on, respectively, packet-switched networks and globally connected computers. This was followed by the work of Larry Roberts on the ARPANET, Bob Kahn (b. 1938) and **Vint Cerf** on Internet Protocol, and Bob Metcalfe (b. 1946) on the Ethernet. It was on 1 January 1983, that the TCP/IP protocol became the only protocol to be used on the ARPANET network. Arguably, this is the birthday of the modern Internet, which, with the invention of the World Wide Web by **Tim Berners-Lee** in 1991 and the Mosaic browser by **Mark Andreessen** in 1993, has become a global civilian communication tool used for commerce and pleasure, rather than just as a tool for the US government.

Key text
- John Naughton. *A Brief History of the Future: The Origins of the Internet.* Weidenfeld & Nicolson, 1999

Internet business models

With the invention of the graphical browser in the early 1990s, the Internet suddenly became accessible to the masses rather than just to those with the requisite technological know-how. It wasn't long before businesses were clamouring to get onto the Internet. Soon the media were debating the merits of B2B, B2C and a variety of other acronyms describing business models touted for success on Internet.

One of the most frequently described models was B2B (business-to-business), which describes a business predicated on the exchange of information, such as purchase orders, invoices and stock levels, and goods, such as stock and equipment, between one business and another rather than between business and consumers, using the Internet. The supposed advantages include increased speed and reduced cost, although because the Internet is a public network, security remains a major concern for B2B systems developers. Two common examples of B2B Web sites are procurement exchanges for sourcing equipment and goods and industry-specific vertical portals, or **vortals.**

B2B can be contrasted with B2C – business-to-consumer transactions – also known as e-tailing. B2C describes any e-commerce system that sells products or services direct to the consumer, especially over the Internet. Most B2C systems are extensions of businesses that still maintain conventional sales and service outlets.

Another business model is the consumer-driven business model, **C2B** (consumer-to-business). This refers to the situation in which the consumer drives the transaction, determining

factors normally determined by the business, such as price. An example of the C2B business model is the consumer-driven Internet business priceline.com, where the customer sets the criteria for a flight, including price, and priceline.com attempts to deliver a suitable product.

Alternatively, there is **C2C** (consumer-to-consumer), in which Internet transactions are conducted between one consumer and another. Online auctions such as eBay are effectively C2C Web sites, as the majority of transactions taking place are between private individuals. P2P (**peer-to-peer**) networking, in which individuals access each other's hard drives for information, is another example.

Another term used with reference to Internet business models is clicks-and-mortar. This is the term used to describe companies that have combined an online business strategy (clicks) with a traditional offline strategy (mortar). This is in contrast to Internet **pure plays**, such as Yahoo!, that operate online only and bricks-and-mortar companies that do not operate online. Many clicks-and-mortar companies, including major companies such as eBay, started as pure plays but diversified either by starting up their own physical operations, often for order fulfilment, or by acquiring well-established traditional businesses.

Interstitials

A form of interruption marketing, interstitials are a form of Web advertising that pop up in-between two pages of Web content. Traditional interstitials start streaming to the browser at the same time as the next page downloads. This usually results in delayed access to the page and a disjointed viewing experience, and can be very intrusive. This has resulted in a common dislike of the 'pop-up' interstitial, usually a smaller ad that literally pops up and can be hard to get rid of. Technological advances reworked the interstitial format to download to the viewer's browser only when there is no content downloading. As the format supports Flash, **HTML**, audio and **Java**, advertisers are able to create full- or half-page, eye-catching animated advertising.

Intranet

An intranet is effectively an internal **Internet** for a corporation. It allows file sharing and file transfer over an internal computer network based on the same TCP/IP protocols as the Internet. To the user, the intranet will resemble an external Internet Web site. The major difference between the Internet and an intranet is that the only access permitted to the intranet is that authorized by the organization. This usually extends to all employees. A firewall and other security precautions will prevent unwanted external access. A hybrid version of the intranet and Internet, sharing characteristics of both and allowing some external access as well as internal networking, is known as an **extranet**.

Intrapreneur

If the idea of starting your own business is appealing but you don't feel confident enough to make the commitment, some employers offer an opportunity to sample the entrepreneurial life without all of the associated risk. Occasionally, companies will allow employees to start up their own ventures within the company. This halfway house is known as intrapreneuring, with the individual operating within the organization as an **entrepreneur** would in a separate company.

Gifford and Elizabeth Pinchot were perhaps the first to herald the arrival of the 'intra-corporate entrepreneur' back in 1978, and Gifford is credited with coining the term 'intrapreneur'. His book *Intrapreneuring: Why You Don't Have to Leave the Corporation to Become an Entrepreneur* came out in 1985; the *American Heritage Dictionary* added the term 'intrapreneur' in 1992, and the rest, as they say, is history.

History has moved on. Intrapreneuring has grown up and become subsumed within the broader realm of 'corporate venturing'. The Center for Business Incubation in the United Kingdom defines corporate venturing as 'a formal, direct relationship, usually between a larger and an independent smaller company, in which both contribute financial, management, or technical resources, sharing risks and rewards equally for mutual growth'. These relationships may take the form of intrapreneurial ventures, as when large companies spin off new businesses and/or technologies. However, they may also involve the provision of equity and/or non-equity investment to small, independent ventures.

An intrapreneur has some advantages over the go-it-alone entrepreneur. They benefit, for example, from the reputation of the corporate parent, which may help foster trust in the new corporate venture. That heightened trust, rooted in the history and legitimacy of the parent organization, may make it easier for the venture to obtain financing from both internal and external sources. In addition, the longer developmental timeframe associated with corporate ventures provides an extended opportunity for the intrapreneur to develop social capital networks, thereby increasing his access to financial, technical and other resources.

Unlike the independent entrepreneur, the intrapreneur has a bank of organizational policies, procedures, systems and culture to draw upon, thereby freeing up time that may be more profitably devoted to core venture activities. The benefits may come at a cost, however. They may prove disadvantageous, for example, if they inhibit the new venture's flexibility and responsiveness.

Key text
- Gifford Pinchot. *Intrapreneuring: Why You Don't Have to Leave the Corporation to Become an Entrepreneur*. HarperTrade, 1985

Key links
- www.intrapreneur.com
- www.ukbi.co.uk

Intrinsic motivation

Intrinsic motivation is motivation that comes from within. It is a person's internal drive for achievement. Intrinsic motivation may arise from many factors: pride, self-fulfilment, competitiveness, or other psychological factors. The opposite of intrinsic motivation is extrinsic motivation. This is motivation that arises from the effects of external factors, such as pay, working conditions, bonuses and other incentives.

IP address

An IP address is the numbered address assigned to an **Internet** host, which underpins the alphanumerical domain name in the form of www.myname.com. Traditionally, IP addresses are 32-bit, which means that numbered addresses have four sections separated by dots, each a decimal number between 0 and 255. IP is an abbreviation for Internet protocol.

IPO (initial public offering)

When a private company issues its ordinary shares to the public for the first time, it is known as an 'initial public offering'. This happens when a company wishes to list on a stock exchange or raise capital. The issue of shares is generally managed by a financial institution, such as a merchant bank. It acts as an underwriter – organizing the issue, promoting it with the aid of an offer document or prospectus and agreeing to purchase any unplaced shares.

Shares are first sold at the set issue price in the primary market, usually to **institutional investors** and the like. If the issue is a popular one, it is unlikely that private investors will be able to participate at this point. Following this financing, the shares are then traded in a secondary market, also known as the aftermarket. Only then will the general public be able to buy the shares.

Key text
- Stephen Blowers. *The Ernst & Young Guide to the IPO Value Journey.* Wiley, 1999

IPV6 (Internet Protocol Version 6)

Sometimes referred to as Ipng or next-generation Internet, IPV6 is the version of Internet Protocol destined to replace the current Internet Protocol Version 4 (also known as Ipv4), which is now over 20 years old. IP refers to Internet protocol – that is, the accepted standards for transmitting data from one computer, known as a host, to another over the Internet. When IPv4 was first developed, no one could have imagined how vast and popular the Internet would become. As a result, IPv4 is fast running short of addresses as new machines are continually added to the Internet. IPV6, drawn up by the Internet Engineering Task Force (IETF), is effectively an upgrade to Ipv4 rather than a radical change, although it will introduce a number of improvements and increase the number of addresses available. It will coexist with Ipv4 for some time.

Key link
- www.ipv6.org

IRC (Internet Relay Chat)

IRC is a multi-user chat system that allows many users to 'chat' with each other in real time. In this case, 'chat' means type quickly, as users have to do if they wish to keep up with the conversation. IRC was developed by Jarkko Oikarinen in Finland in 1988. It works via a number of dedicated IRC servers around the world. IRC is multichannel and anything written in one channel can be seen by all other users of that channel. Private channels can be used for private conference calls. To use IRC, the user must run a 'client' program – normally called IRC – to connect the user to the IRC network and to another user via a server. IRC is popular with hackers as a vehicle for propagating computer viruses as well as with people who like to chat with one another.

ISDN (integrated services digital network)

An integrated services digital network is a telecommunications network that allows faster data transfer rates than the older analogue telephone circuits. Theoretically, speeds of roughly 128,000 bits per second are possible using existing traditional copper wire telephone lines. ISDN services come in two basic types: Basic Rate Interface (BRI) and Primary Rate Interface (PRI). BRI consists of two 64 kbps B channels and one 16 kbps D channel for a total of 144 kbps. 'Integrated services' refers to the ability of ISDN to make two connections simultaneously, in any combination of data – voice, video, fax – over a single line. 'Digital' refers to the nature of the data transmission. And 'network' refers to the fact that ISDN is delivered over the telecommunications network to the remote user. In the United States, implementation of ISDN was slow. One reason for this was that two of the major switch manufacturers, Nortel and AT&T, chose to implement the standards governing ISDN in different ways. Although the industry agreed to create a national ISDN standard – NI-1 – there were still many problems gaining consensus for the standard.

Ishakawa diagram

Also known as a **fishbone diagram** (due to its shape) or a cause-effect diagram, the Ishikawa diagram is named after its inventor, Japanese engineer Kaoru Ishikawa (1915–1989). The technique, which is used to discuss the causes of problems in a **quality circle**, was taken up and popularized by **W. Edwards Deming** and the **Total Quality Management** school. The idea is to draw a diagram working back from the problem to identify the possible causes of the problem. A horizontal line is drawn; branching off from this, both above and below, are other lines that represent main causes. Branching off from these are more lines, representing subcauses. The causes fall within four main categories – the four Ms – men, methods, machines and materials. There are four steps to the process: identifying the problem, identifying the possible causes within the main categories, identifying possible detailed causes and drawing the causes on the diagram for the discussion.

Key text
- Kaoru Ishikawa. *What Is Total Quality Control? The Japanese Way*. Prentice-Hall, 1985

ISP (Internet Service Provider)

Short for Internet Service Provider, an ISP is an organization that provides Internet services, including access to the Internet. ISPs provide Internet services to individuals as well as companies, and act as gatekeepers to the Internet. ISPs connect to other ISPs via Network Access Points (NAPs), which are major Internet connection points. These enable a user with one ISP to view a Web site hosted by another ISP on the other side of the world. With more than 25 million subscribers, AOL is the largest dial-up ISP in the world by far, with Microsoft's MSN a distant second.

ISPs charge for services in several different ways. Some charge a flat monthly or quarterly fee; others do not charge for Internet provision but instead aim to generate revenue from advertising and e-commerce; still others obtain revenue through a complex arrangement with the companies that provide physical delivery, such as telecoms and cable companies.

Key link
- www.isp-planet.com/

ISO (International Organization for Standardization)

A non-governmental organization established in 1947, the International Organization for Standardization is a global federation of national standards bodies from over 140 countries, one from each country. The mission of the ISO is to promote the development of standardization and other related activities in the world. The work of the ISO results in international agreements that are published as International Standards. ISO is derived from the Greek *isos*, which means equal. It is not (obviously) an acronym.

Key link
- www.iso.ch

J

Jaques, Elliott

Canadian educator (b. 1917)
Creator of a theory of the value of work, Elliott Jaques is a Canadian-born psychologist who has ploughed an idiosyncratic furrow throughout his career. He is best known as an advocate for and examiner of a long-term industrial democracy experiment. His work is based on exhaustive research and has generally been ignored by the mass managerial market.

Jaques was involved in an extensive study of industrial democracy in practice at the Glacier Metal Company in the United Kingdom between 1948 and 1965. Glacier introduced a number of highly progressive changes in working practices: a works council was introduced and no change of company policy was allowed unless all members of the works council agreed. 'Clocking on', the traditional means of recording whether someone had turned up for work, was abolished.

The emphasis was on granting people responsibility and understanding the dynamics of group working. 'I'm completely convinced of the necessity of encouraging everybody to accept the maximum amount of personal responsibility, and allowing them to have a say in every problem in which they can help,' said Jaques. The Glacier research led to Jaques's 1951 book, *The Changing Culture of a Factory*.

In 1976, in *The General Theory of Bureaucracy*, Jaques presented his theory of the value of work. This was ornate, but aimed to clarify something Jaques had observed during his research: 'The manifest picture of bureaucratic organization is a confusing one. There appears to be no rhyme or reason for the structures that are developed, in number of levels, in titling, or even in the meaning to be attached to the manager-subordinate linkage.' His solution was labelled the *time span of discretion*, which contended that levels of management should be based on how long it was before their decisions could be checked, and that people should be paid in accordance with that time. This meant that managers were measured by the long-term impact of their decisions.

Key texts
- Elliott Jaques. *A General Theory of Bureaucracy*. John Wiley, 1976
- Elliott Jaques. *The Changing Culture of a Factory*. Tavistock, 1951

Java

Java is a multipurpose, cross-platform programming language for the **World Wide Web**, developed by Canadian **James Gosling** at Sun Microsystems in 1995. It is widely used for network computing. When users connect to a **server** that uses Java, they download a small program called an **applet** onto their computers. The applet then runs on the computer's own processor via a Java Virtual Machine program or JVM. Java comes in three flavours: Java 2 Platform, Standard Edition, for standard Java applications; Java 2 Platform, Micro Edition, for small devices such as handhelds, pagers and mobile phones; and Java

2 Platform, Enterprise Edition, which is aimed at enterprise solutions and is available in modules called Enterprise JavaBeans.

Key link
- http://java.sun.com/

Job evaluation

Job evaluation is the process of comparing, ranking and evaluating jobs to determine their relative worth. The comparison is accomplished using specific qualitative or quantitative factors, such as complexity of the work, mental and physical skills, degrees of responsibility and working conditions. It is important to note that it is the qualities and skills necessary to perform the job that are being measured, not the ability or skills of the person performing the job.

The result of a job evaluation will be a list of jobs that are graded and can then be ranked and compared with other jobs in the same organization. Job evaluation is usually carried out so that salaries can be determined for the various jobs within an organization.

Job satisfaction

Difficult to define or measure, job satisfaction is the pleasure an individual derives from his work. Organizational psychologists have studied the relationship between job satisfaction and performance, as well as the factors that constitute job satisfaction. However, the link between satisfaction and performance remains elusive. As far back as 1974, it was argued that companies need to provide a combination of wages and non-pecuniary factors to avoid worker discontent, that the best combination changes from worker to worker, and that it is likely to change as a worker's salary increases.

Factors that affect job satisfaction include pay, working hours, complexity and difficulty of job, promotion prospects and personal relationships with co-workers. Research into job satisfaction suggests that pay is a more important factor with men and hours worked more important with women. The research also suggests pay becomes more important with age, and promotion prospects less so. Lack of job satisfaction may lead to a demotivated workforce, **absenteeism**, and high staff turnover.

Key text
- R.J. Flanagan, G. Strauss and L. Ulman. 'Worker Discontent and Work Place Behavior.' *Industrial Relations*, 13, pp.101–23 (1974)

Job title

Job titles used to be straightforward. A job title was (and still is, in many cases) the title given to an individual in relation to his function, especially in organizations structured along functional or hierarchical lines. In an insurance underwriting company, for example, job titles may start at the lower level with junior underwriter and rise up through section leader, senior underwriter, chief branch underwriter, area underwriter, head of underwriting and then to the directors responsible for underwriting within the company. In addition, underwriting job titles may be divided between classes of underwriting, such as property and liability.

In the modern world of work, however, the issue of job titles has grown a little more confusing. One would have thought in the hierarchy-free age of **Generation X**, **Generation Y** and virtual organizations, job titles would have slipped off the executive agenda. Far from it. *Fast Company* magazine has a regular feature on job titles, and they seem as loaded and important as ever.

Two approaches to job titles are popular. First, there are companies who have, at some point in their history at least, moved to eliminate job titles. Disney, Harley-Davidson, Bloomberg, Microsoft and Silicon Graphics are among those who have been reported as dropping job titles. (Bloomberg had names only; Harley-Davidson abolished executive vice-presidents, as well as machine operators and machine inspectors.) At the other end of the naming scale are the organizations that have allowed their imaginations to run riot with job titles: chief of strategic sourcing, chief quality officer, leader of change, chief learning officer. All of these job titles share one thing: you have no idea what they might involve.

'Technological developments and dynamic business processes certainly are the driving forces,' said Louisa Wah of *Management Review*. 'A new generation of workers, a new workplace culture, and a break from tradition all call for a rethinking of job functions and the titles that reflect them.'

Job titles do have a serious role: They are signposts to corporate culture. They signal what the organization considers to be important. Appointing a vice-president of diversity makes it clear that the company is dedicated to fair employment opportunities. Similarly, chief knowledge officer is a statement of intent as much as a new job. After all, companies have been gathering and utilizing knowledge since time immemorial. The job title sends a message.

'There has got to be a change in the titles to show that employees do not belong to the old paradigm, but to a new paradigm,' says one executive. 'The important thing is that these titles must convey the true meaning they are used for. It's very important to make them compatible with the level of knowledge and the type of culture of the organization.' To work, job titles must describe the job. They must be meaningful to communicate.

Jobs, Steve

Co-founder, Apple Computer (b. 1955)

Steve Jobs, co-founder of Apple Computer and one of the folk-hero CEOs of the twentieth (and possibly the twenty-first) century is one of a select group of IT whizz-kids that includes **Bill Gates**, **Larry Ellison**, and **Scott McNealy**.

In February 1955, Paul and Clara Jobs of Mountain View, California, adopted an orphan – Stephen Paul Jobs. Because Jobs was unhappy at school, his parents moved to Los Altos, California, where Jobs attended Homestead High School.

Once out of school, Jobs attended lectures at the Hewlett-Packard electronics company, and it was while working at Hewlett-Packard one summer that he met Stephen Wozniak, engineering whizz-kid and UCLA Berkeley dropout.

After a brief flirtation with Atari, as a video game designer, and travel in India as a young man in search of spiritual enlightenment, Jobs once again hooked up with Wozniak, attending meetings of the 'Homebrew Computer Club'. Jobs's talent was not as much for electronic gadgets as for style, utility and marketability. He persuaded Wozniak to work with him to build a personal computer. The result was the Apple I computer, which was designed in Jobs's bedroom and constructed in his garage.

To start their own company, they sold their most treasured possessions: Jobs sold his Volkswagen microbus, and Wozniak sold his prized Hewlett-Packard calculator. With the $1300 they raised, the two started a new company: Apple.

The company's first product, the Apple I, was marketed in 1976, priced at $666. Sales of the Apple I brought in $774,000, and soon the two entrepreneurs were working on the Apple II. Jobs's marketing savvy led him to engage Mike Markkula, who bought shares in the company and became chairman in May 1977, the year the company was incorporated, and Regis McKenna, the best public relations man in Silicon Valley, who went on to popularize relationship marketing.

Markkula brought in investment money for the likes of legendary venture capitalist Arthur Rock; McKenna brought marketing genius. Within three years, revenues from the Apple II reached $139 million.

Apple went public in 1980. The stock price rose to $29 on the first day, capitalizing the company at $1.2 billion. Between 1978 and 1983, in the absence of any real competition, Apple forged ahead in the personal computer market; the company's compound growth rate was in excess of 150 percent per annum. Then, in 1981, IBM introduced its first PC, using an operating system called MS-DOS, licensed from a small software company called Microsoft. Within two years, IBM had exceeded Apple's dollar sales of PCs. Jobs realized that if IBM and Microsoft were allowed to dominate the market, then Apple would become marginalized.

To restore Apple's fortunes, Jobs turned to Pepsi CEO John Sculley. He issued Sculley a challenge: 'If you stay at Pepsi, five years from now all you will have accomplished is selling a lot more sugar water to kids. If you come to Apple, you can change the world.' Sculley came to Apple. The result of this unlikely alliance between the corporate suit Sculley and the counterculture kid Jobs was the Apple Macintosh: the personal computer that cemented Apple Computer's status as the computer enthusiasts' favourite computer company.

Yet while Apple became the darling of the creative world, Microsoft continued to dominate the PC software industry, commanding 80 percent market share to Apple's 20 percent. In the end, that proved critical. In 1985, Sculley did the unthinkable and removed Jobs from Apple. Jobs moved on – first to start-up NeXT Computer, then to Pixar Animation Studios, in which he invested $60 million of his own fortune. That investment paid off on the back of computer-animated blockbusters *Toy Story* and *A Bug's Life*. Sculley was booted out of Apple in 1993 after a disastrous period that saw Apple's market share plummet from 20 percent to just 8 percent. He was replaced by Michael Spindler, who lasted until 1996, by which time market share had fallen to just over 5 percent. Spindler was shown the door, and Gil Amelio stepped into the hot seat. After 500 days in the post, Apple's market share remained unmoved and Amelio invited Jobs back to help in a consulting role. Soon Amelio was on his way out and Jobs, now Apple's self-styled interim CEO, was back where he started.

Jobs breathed new life into Apple. He dumped the NeXT operating system that he had sold to Apple, ditched loss-making licensing contracts, and, most significantly, launched the new iMac. With eye-catching design, simple operation and no floppy disk drive, the stylish Internet-ready computer that Jobs hoped would restore the company's fading fortunes was launched with the slogan 'Chic Not Geek' blazed across advertising posters. The iMac, a vision in translucent blue, sold 278,000 units in the first six weeks, an achievement that had *Fortune* magazine describing it as 'one of the hottest computer launches ever'. Wall Street, too, recovered its confidence in Apple; the company's share price doubled in less than a year. Apple's share price may have been caught up in the same vortex as other technology companies' and the future may be unclear, but without the help of Jobs, Apple might well have been another company in Chapter 11 by now.

Key texts

- Alan Deutschman. *The Second Coming of Steve Jobs*. Broadway Books, 2000
- Jim Carlton. *Apple: The Inside Story of Intrigue, Egomania, and Business Blunders*. Random House, 1997
- Jeffrey S. Young. *Steve Jobs: The Journey Is the Reward*. Lynx Books, 1988

Key link

- www.apple.com

JPEG (Joint Photographic Experts Group)

JPEG is short for the Joint Photographic Experts Group, a group of experts selected by national standards bodies and corporations to produce standards for continuous-tone image coding. The group acts as a committee working on **ISO** standards; its official name is ISO/IEC JTC1 SC29 Working Group 1.

Most people associate JPEG with the implementation of the image compression format in association with a file format developed by C-Cube Microsystems – JFIF – that has been in the public domain since the 1990s. That is, to most people JPEG is a type of image used on the Web.

Progressive JPEG is another common type of JPEG used on the Web. It allows images to be downloaded progressively, with an image of lower resolution appearing in the browser before the full-resolution image is downloaded.

Junk bonds

A junk bond is a fixed-interest loan paying an above-average level of interest, with an above-average level of risk attached to it. The invention of junk bonds is credited to American corporate raider and bond trader Michael Milken (b. 1946).

Milken worked for brokerage Drexel Burnham Lambert on corporate takeovers during the 1980s. He developed junk bonds to help finance leveraged buyouts. A company could issue large quantities of junk bonds and raise sufficient capital to take over a target that would normally be beyond its reach. The company would then break up or sell large portions of the target company to finance the debt. A good example of this was the $20 billion takeover of RJR Nabisco. The problem with this strategy as it was used during the 1980s was that following the takeover, the resulting company was so highly geared that its debt repayments eroded any potential profits.

Milken became phenomenally wealthy as a result of his work. According to the US government, Milken was paid $296 million by Drexel in 1986 and $550 million in 1987. Unfortunately for Milken, he was indicted by a federal grand jury for violations of federal securities and racketeering laws. He pleaded guilty to some charges and escaped others as part of a plea bargain that saw him fined and sentenced to ten years' imprisonment, subsequently reduced to two years plus three years' probation. Junk bonds, meanwhile, have established themselves as an acceptable and useful, if risky, financial instrument.

Key texts
- Mary Zey. *Banking on Fraud: Drexel, Junk Bonds & Buyouts* (Social Institutions and Social Change Ser.). Aldine de Gruyter, 1993
- Glenn Yago. *Junk bonds how high yield securities restructured corporate America*. Oxford University Press, 1991

Jupiter Media Metrix

Internet consultancy Jupiter Media Metrix was founded in September 2000 as a result of the merger of Jupiter Communications and Media Metrix. Founded in 1986, Jupiter Communications was one of the first companies to provide research on the Internet. Media Metrix, founded in the 1990s, pioneered the measurement of Internet metrics. The result of the merger is a company that is one of the leading worldwide authorities on e-commerce. It provides analysis and insight to help its clients gain a competitive advantage in the complex world of the Internet economy. Clients receive information on industry trends, forecasts and current best practice, backed by JMM's own expert analysis.

Key link
- www.jmm.com

Juran, Joseph M.
American engineer, statistician and consultant (b. 1904)

Along with **W. Edwards Deming**, Joseph M. Juran introduced Japanese industry to quality control techniques that formed the basis for its managerial ascendancy. Trained as an electrical engineer, Juran worked for Western Electric in the 1920s and then AT&T. His weighty *Quality Control Handbook* was published in 1951. In 1953, he made his first visit to Japan. For two months, Juran observed Japanese practices and trained managers and engineers in what he called 'managing for quality'.

For the next quarter of a century, the Romanian-born Juran continued to give seminars on the subject of quality throughout the world. Western companies continued to assume that the Japanese were low-quality imitators. Then, at the beginning of the 1980s, the world woke up to quality. From being peripheral, Juran and his Juran Institute found themselves near the epicentre of an explosion of interest.

Juran's quality philosophy is built around a trilogy: quality planning, quality management and quality implementation. 'In broad terms, quality planning consists of developing the products and processes required to meet the customers' needs,' he says. While Juran is critical of W. Edwards Deming as being overly reliant on statistics, his own approach is based on the forbiddingly titled Company-Wide Quality Management (CWQM), which aims to create a means of disseminating quality to all.

Juran is innovative in his belief that there is more to quality than specification and rigorous testing for defects; he believes that the human side of quality is critical. He was an early exponent of what has come to be known as empowerment. For him, quality has to be the goal of each employee, individually and in teams, through self-supervision.

Juran's message – most accessibly encapsulated in his book *Planning for Quality* – is that quality is nothing new. If quality is so elemental and elementary, why had it become ignored in the West? Juran's unwillingness to gild his straightforward message is attractive to some, but has made the communication of his ideas less successful than he would have liked.

Key texts

- Joseph M. Juran. *Juran on Planning for Quality*. Free Press, 1988
- Joseph M. Juran. *Managerial Breakthrough*. McGraw-Hill, 1964

Key links

- www.juran.com
- www.juran.com/drjuran/bio_jmj.html
- www.hq.nasa.gov/office/hqlibrary/ppm/ppm20.htm

Just-in-time (JIT)

Just-in-time or *kanban* is an approach to inventory management based on the efficient delivery of components to the production line at the time they are required. A management technique associated with the Japanese economic miracle after World War II, it is one of a range of quality approaches introduced by, among others, Toyota and Kawasaki, and is an essential part of the **lean production** process.

The goal of *kanban* was zero inventory. It aimed at a system whereby components for final assembly should arrive just when they were needed, reducing the inventory carrying costs. Early production management emphasized ordering materials in economic lot sizes, but the JIT model utilized computer technology to emphasize timing rather than the amount of inventory.

Since the 1980s, international competition and lessons from Japanese practice have encouraged the adoption of JIT methods and quality management methods throughout the western world. Technological advances, too, have had a major impact on inventory management.

New mechanical and automated equipment have made stock movement more efficient, with better use of warehousing and major improvements in distribution and logistics management. In particular, IT-based stock control systems with barcoding are integrated with other systems to give better control over order assembly, stock availability, and monitoring.

By creating a system that pulls in parts as and when they are needed, JIT dramatically reduces the amount of capital tied up in idle inventory, thereby increasing efficiency and reducing costs. Under JIT, a company must manage the overall supply chain efficiently and effectively. Reducing levels of stock in manufacturing is seen as both an internal and external matter, involving relationships between workers at different stages in the production process and with external suppliers.

JIT, however, is not an easy concept to apply. In the past, a number of Western companies attempted to introduce the JIT in isolation from other total quality techniques without understanding the wider implications and without instigating the necessary changes in production management.

The human aspects of quality management are sometimes overlooked. Quality management systems that emphasize a 'right first time' philosophy also promote the 'empowerment' of employees via team development, **quality circles** and training. In particular, plant maintenance improvements to reduce downtime and secure better reliability of machinery are integral to the successful application of JIT. This is coupled with improved 'housekeeping' to maintain clean, tidy, orderly facilities. Typically, this is part of a team's or cell's discipline, with staff making a vital contribution to the overall efficiency of the approach.

In recent years, many firms have implemented ISO 9000 systems to define quality standards, processes and control systems with documentation of action taken to ensure quality. Introducing such systems involves close examination of existing production and operational and support processes (including inventory standards and flows). Standards and systems are improved as a consequence.

If change is piecemeal and management attention wanes, then JIT is unlikely to produce the desired improvements. An integrated perspective is needed with coherent strategic direction to secure improvements in productivity/effectiveness at each operational level so that the whole supply chain has a competitive edge. JIT is only as good as the weakest link in the production chain.

Key texts

- Taiichi Ohno. *Toyota Production System: Beyond Large-Scale Production.* Productivity Press, 1988
- Yasuhiro Monden. *Applying Just in Time: The American–Japanese Experience.* Engineering & Management Press, 1986
- W. Edwards Deming. *Out of the Crisis.* MIT, 1992

K

Kaizen

As much a social system as an industrial process, *kaizen* is at the heart of the quality philosophy and involves the use of **quality circles**, or small teams of workers, to analyse and make suggestions for improving their own work tasks.

In his book *Kaizen*, translated into English in the early 1980s, Masaaki Imai describes the continuous improvement concepts that underpin the quality approach.

American quality pioneer **W. Edwards Deming** is credited with introducing the continuous improvement philosophy in Japan. Deming's work inspired small, problem-solving teams of workers, supervisors and experts with the aim of improving the efficiency and quality of their work. Japanese companies, notably Toyota, developed the idea, and quality circles became an instrumental part of the Japanese economic miracle.

While many Western concepts are based on the notion of a step-change improvement, *kaizen* is precisely the opposite. The word literally means 'gradual progress' or 'incremental change'. Through continuous gradual improvements, *kaizen* aims to achieve continuous evolutionary rather than revolutionary change – hence the term continuous improvement.

Kaizen-consciousness is based on a group of shared values rooted in the Japanese culture. These include self-realization, recognition of diverse abilities and mutual trust. These values lead to a strong belief that individual workers are the experts at their jobs and therefore know better than anyone else how to analyse and improve their work. Integral to the system is an understanding that managers will consider and, where possible, support their efforts to improve the work processes.

Interestingly, the pendulum may now be swinging back toward the Western style of thinking and the notion of a 'leap forward'. The pace of change in business has caused many of the high-tech companies that have emerged in recent years to take a much more revolutionary approach to innovation, favouring 'discontinuous change' over 'incremental improvement'.

Quality circles are not a panacea for quality improvement, but – given the right top-management commitment, employee motivation and resourcing – they can support continuous quality improvement at the shop-floor level.

Key texts

- Masaaki Imai. *Kaizen: The Key to Japan's Competitive Success*. Random House, 1986
- W. Edwards Deming. *Out of the Crisis*. Cambridge University Press, 1988

Kakabadse, Andrew

British professor, researcher and writer

Based at Cranfield School of Management in the United Kingdom, Andrew Kakabadse is one of Europe's leading experts on leadership and executive performance. A prolific researcher, writer, and speaker, Kakabadse remains one of the most insightful commentators on boardroom behaviour and other executive-performance-related issues.

He is best known for his work on the performance of top teams, which includes a database covering more than 10,000 private and public sector organizations from 14 countries. In recent years, his study of the strategic skills of top teams has been extended to Japan, China, Hong Kong and the United States. He is also the author of 21 books, including the bestselling *Essence of Leadership, Politics of Management* and *The Wealth Creators.*

With his wife, Dr Nada Kakabadse, a senior research fellow at Cranfield, Kakabadse's current research interests include the impact of boardroom dynamics on corporate governance. The Kakabadses bring an intriguing geopolitical dimension to the governance debate, highlighting the differences between, especially, the Anglo-Saxon governance model and that of Continental Europe.

'There is an inherent tension between the US governance philosophy, which is based on shareholder value, and the Continental European philosophy, which is based on stakeholders,' says Kakabadse. 'That is often a root cause of problems with mergers between US and European companies.'

The shareholder-versus-stakeholder thinking later was published as a book entitled *The Geopolitics of Governance.* The Kakabadses' research on **outsourcing** was published as a book entitled *Smart Sourcing: International Best Practice.*

Other projects in the pipeline include a major international study of corporate reputation. The research is ongoing. Together with partner institutions in the United Kingdom, the United States, Japan and Germany, Kakabadse embarked on an in-depth international comparison of how top teams and executive and non-executive directors are able to enhance the reputation of their corporations to the point where corporate reputation improves shareholder value through exemplary leadership and boardroom behaviour. The study hopefully will be completed by the end of 2002.

Key texts
- Andrew Kakabadse and Nada Kakabadse. *Smart Sourcing: International Best Practice.* St Martin's Press, 2002
- Andrew Kakabadse and Nada Kakabadse. *The Geopolitics of Governance: The Impact of Contrasting Philosophies.* St Martin's Press, 2001

Kamprad, Ingvar

Founder, IKEA Group (b. 1926)

A brilliant if unorthodox businessman, Ingvar Kamprad has taken his values, carved in the harsh terrain of Småland, Sweden, and assembled them into the international furniture company IKEA.

Ingvar Kamprad was born on the family farm, Elmtaryd, in 1926. His was a tough upbringing: Sweden in the late 1920s and early 1930s was a difficult place in which to grow up. Outside of the Swedish cities, the cold, unforgiving landscape of the country offered few opportunities for advancement. Yet Kamprad was resourceful and full of the enthusiasm of youth. 'I suppose I was slightly peculiar,' says Kamprad in his biography, 'in that I started tremendously early doing business deals.'

He was only 17 when, in 1943, he started his own company. He called it Ikéa (later dropping the accent and changing the letters to capitals): IK from his initials, E for Elmtaryd, and A for Agunnaryd, his home village. By 1945, Kamprad was selling a hotchpotch of products. His business had outgrown local delivery and he began to sell by mail order. Newspaper advertisements stimulated demand, and the local milk cart and train network solved his distribution problems. Soon pens, pencils, picture frames, wallets, watches and other assorted goods were wending their way across Sweden, courtesy of IKEA.

Kamprad advertised furniture for the first time in 1948. His decision to sell furniture was initially a result of matching his main competitor. The furniture was sourced from local manufacturers, it was cheap, and sales were promising – so promising that four years later, he abandoned his other products to concentrate on affordably priced furniture and domestic articles. Kamprad bought a local joinery in Älmhult that was about to close and informed his customers that IKEA was now a furniture company. If the customers wished to see the products in the catalogue close up, then they could visit IKEA's furniture exhibition when it opened on 18 March 1953. It was a gamble. On the opening day, a nervous Kamprad threw back the doors of his new display store-cum-furniture factory. At least 1000 people were waiting patiently outside.

The principles that underpin IKEA's business today were developed in those early days. Cost awareness was one fundamental principle. Kamprad saved on string, boxes, paper – whatever he could. Another feature was the provision of food. For Kamprad, it was always a practical decision to provide food. As he says, 'No good business is done on an empty stomach.' As people were travelling long distances to reach the Ämhult factory, it was only reasonable to offer food for sale. This developed into the concept of the IKEA experience, where the customer turns a visit to IKEA into a day trip.

IKEA milestones followed swiftly, one after another. Flat packaging was introduced in 1956, so that customers could get the furniture into their cars more easily. A 6700 square-metre IKEA store was opened in Älmhult in 1958, and the company signed on its 100th employee. Self-service was introduced in 1965. By the 1970s, IKEA was an international company with stores across Europe. By 1999, the company had 150 stores in 30 countries, employing 44,000 people. Revenues were in excess of $7 billion and the IKEA catalogue's circulation was a staggering 100 million.

Although Kamprad is officially retired from day-to-day management, he remains the company's totemic leader in the minds of many. Despite his phenomenal wealth – taxation and legal issues mean that he resides in Switzerland – Kamprad appears to be fundamentally the same person who started out selling matches all those years ago. 'I

see my task as serving the majority of people,' he says. 'The question is, how do you find out what they want, how best to serve them? My answer is to stay close to ordinary people, because at heart I am one of them.'

Key text
- Bertil Torekull. *Leading by Design: The IKEA Story.* HarperBusiness, 1999

Kanban

See Just-in-time.

Kanter, Rosabeth Moss

American educator and consultant (b. 1943)

Though she is now the Class of 1960 Professor of Business Administration at **Harvard Business School**, Rosabeth Moss Kanter began her career as a sociologist before her transformation into an international business guru. Her first book, *Men and Women of the Corporation* (1977), looked at the innermost working of an organization. It was a premature epitaph for corporate man and corporate America before **downsizing** and technology hit home.

Kanter has mapped out the potential for a more people-based corporate world, driven by smaller organizations, or at least less monolithic organizations. She introduced the concept of the post-entrepreneurial firm, which manages to combine the traditional strengths of a large organization with the flexible speed of a smaller organization.

Key to this is the idea of innovation. This has been a recurrent theme of Kanter's since her first really successful book, *Change Masters*. In the book, she defines 'change masters' as 'those people and organizations adept at the art of anticipating the need for, and of leading, productive change'. The opposite of the change masters are the 'change resisters', intent on reining in innovation.

Change is fundamentally concerned with innovation (or 'newstreams' in Kanter-speak). The key to developing and sustaining innovation is, says Kanter, an 'integrative' approach rather than a 'segmentalist' one. (This has distinct echoes of the theories of that other female management theorist, **Mary Parker Follett**, whose work Kanter admires.) American woes are firmly placed at the door of 'the quiet suffocation of the entrepreneurial spirit in segmentalist companies'.

Kanter was partly responsible for the rise in interest – if not the practice – of empowerment. 'The degree to which the opportunity to use power effectively is granted to or withheld from individuals is one operative difference between those companies that stagnate and those that innovate,' she says.

Key texts

- Rosabeth Moss Kanter. *Evolve!: Succeeding in the Digital Culture of Tomorrow*. Harvard Business School Press, 2001
- Rosabeth Moss Kanter. *World Class: Thriving Locally in the Global Economy*. Simon & Schuster, 1995
- Rosabeth Moss Kanter, Barry Stein and Todd Jick. *The Challenge of Organizational Change: How Companies Experience It and Leaders Guide It*. Free Press, 1992
- Rosabeth Moss Kanter. *When Giants Learn to Dance*. Simon & Schuster, 1989
- Rosabeth Moss Kanter. *The Change Masters: Innovation and Entrepreneurship in the American Corporation*. Simon & Schuster, 1983
- Rosabeth Moss Kanter. *Men and Women of the Corporation*. Basic Books, 1977

Kaplan, Robert

Author and Harvard Business School professor

Robert Kaplan, Marvin Bower Professor of Leadership Development at **Harvard Business School**, is responsible for a landmark in the history of organizational management. Together with his colleague David Norton, Kaplan the created the concept of the **balanced scorecard**: a means of linking a company's current actions to its long-term goals. The method has been endorsed by corporate heavyweights such as Mobil and Sears. Kaplan is also co-developer of **activity-based costing** (ABC), a technique for determining the underlying economics of a business.

In Kaplan and Norton's recent book *The Strategy-Focused Organization*, the authors use their extensive research of companies that implement the balanced scorecard to suggest a new performance-management framework centred on strategy.

Key texts

- Robert S. Kaplan and David P. Norton. *The Balanced Scorecard: Translating Strategy into Action*. Harvard Business School Press, 1997
- Robert S. Kaplan. *Strategy-Focused Organization: How Balanced Scorecard Companies Thrive in the New Business Environment*. Harvard Business School Publishing, 2001

Kay, John

British professor and economist

John Kay is one of Britain's leading economists. He began his academic career when he was elected a fellow of St John's College, Oxford, at the age of 21, a position he still holds. He went on to become research director and director of the Institute for Fiscal Studies, a think-tank, and a professor at London Business School and the University of Oxford. He was the first director of Oxford University's Said Business School. In 1986, he founded London Economics, which grew to become the United Kingdom's largest independent consultancy, with a turnover of £10 million and offices in London, Boston and Melbourne. He has been a director of Halifax plc, a UK bank, and remains a director of several investment companies. He now writes a fortnightly column for the *Financial Times*. In 1999, he resigned from Said Business

School and now devotes most of his time to writing. His books include *Foundations of Corporate Success* and *The Business of Economics*.

Key texts
- John Kay. *The Business of Economics*. Oxford University Press, 1996
- John Kay. *Foundations of Corporate Success: How Business Strategies Add Value*. Oxford University Press, 1993

Key link
- www.johnkay.com

Keiretsu

Following World War II, the Allies felt that Japan's large companies should be dismantled to reduce their economic power. However, it soon became apparent that rather than a weak Japan, an industrially strong Japan was required. This was especially so as the Korean War loomed large. In a policy turnaround, the West pumped money into the Japanese economy and the partially dismantled companies reformed around the major banks, which in turn took a financial stake in those companies. The resulting network of companies was called a *keiretsu*.

The *keiretsu* is a typical organizational structure in Japan. One of its chief benefits is that it encourages the companies within the network to transact business with each other, thus promoting the interests of the *keiretsu* as a whole. Notable examples of *keiretsu* organizations include Mitsubishi and Yamaha. In the United States, the term was used to describe the network of associated companies that some **incubators** or **venture capital** firms built up through start-up investment. Leading venture capital firm Kleiner, Perkins, Caufield & Byers are a good example.

Key text
- Kenichi Miyashita and David W. Russell. *Keiretsu*. McGraw-Hill, 1994

Kelleher, Herb

Former CEO, Southwest Airlines (b. 1932)

Southwest Airlines took a risk when it named one of its founders, Herb Kelleher – a lawyer with no practical airline experience – as president and then CEO. It paid off. With his personal brand of madcap management, Kelleher created a company with $5 billion in annual revenues and a record of more than 25 years of profitability

Born on 12 March 1932, in New Jersey, Herb Kelleher was an exceptional scholar, one of those lucky students who excel at both sports and academics. He racked up an impressive list of achievements, including student president and literary editor of the yearbook, as well as awards as an outstanding student and athlete. He studied law at New York University, graduating in 1956. After law school, Kelleher built up a successful law practice in San Antonio, Texas. Then, in 1966, a chance conversation with one of his clients set him on an entirely new career path.

In a downtown bar, the St Anthony's Club, Kelleher's client Rollin King explained his idea for a budget airline service to connect three of Texas's main cities: Dallas, Houston and San Antonio. The two of them drew up a business plan and jotted down the flight pattern on the back of a paper napkin. It was the outline for Southwest Airlines. Kelleher put in $10,000 (for a stake worth more than $200 million by 2001), and the company was incorporated in March 1967.

Over the next four years, Kelleher and Southwest Airlines sunk more than a million dollars into fighting moves to block the company's application for airline certification. It was a bitter fight. One newspaper reported: 'Don't bother spending your money on a movie or going to see a play or attending a concert. Just come over and watch Herb Kelleher and the lawyers for Braniff and Texas International cut each other into little bits and pieces.' A dogged Kelleher won on a final appeal to the Texas Supreme Court.

Southwest Airlines opened for business in 1971. Under intense pressure from the competition, Southwest toughed out the early years. It wasn't until the company's third year in business that it turned a profit. But in 1978, Southwest Airlines flew into more turbulence when CEO Lamar Muse, an industry veteran, resigned. Enter Kelleher, as president. In 1982, he became CEO. He was to prove one of the most unorthodox, innovative, and successful CEOs of any major US corporation.

Kelleher had two principal aims: keeping the customer happy and keeping costs down. He introduced a range of cost-cutting measures: seats were allocated on a first come, first served basis, and those hoping for a meal discovered there were no in-flight meals, only peanuts, which saved time and speeded up turnaround.

Kelleher's backed up the no-frills service with excellent customer care, driven by even better employee care. Kelleher inspired a unique corporate culture at Southwest: he decided that working for Southwest Airlines should be fun. At Southwest headquarters, casual dress is the norm, practical jokes are encouraged, employee birthdays are celebrated, and any excuse to have a party is a good one. It is no different on the planes. Passengers are likely to be greeted by flight attendants dressed as leprechauns on St Patrick's Day, have their safety instructions delivered in a Southwest Airlines version of stand-up comedy, or jump out of their skins when the flight attendants pop out of the overhead luggage compartments.

Kelleher is no stranger to bizarre pranks, either. How many CEOs of major American companies can admit to settling a high-level dispute with another corporation by arm-wrestling their opponent? Kelleher arm-wrestled Kurt Herwald, chairman of Stevens Aviation, instead of going to court over an ad (he lost). Or who, when faced with a complaining customer who is clearly in the wrong, authorized a letter to the offending party advising them to fly with another airline? Who else would have dressed up as Elvis for a recruitment ad that helpfully suggests CVs should be marked 'Attention Elvis'?

There is method to Kelleher's madness. The staff turnover rate at Southwest, which is below 7 percent, is one of lowest in the industry. The airline has never lost time to union disputes. When Kelleher took over as CEO in 1982, revenues were $270 million; there were 2000 employees and 27 planes. By 2001, revenues had soared to more than $5 billion, with 30,000 employees and 344 planes.

In 2001, Kelleher retired as CEO. When asked what he would be doing with his new-found free time, he replied in his characteristic indomitable but offbeat style, 'I might write about science. I might write about astronomy.'

Key texts

- Larry Goddard and David Brown. *The Turbo Charged Company: Igniting Your Business To Soar Ahead of the Competition.* The Parkland Group, 1995
- Kevin Freiberg and Jackie Freiberg. *NUTS! Southwest Airlines' Crazy Recipe for Business and Personal Success.* Bard Press, 1996

Kelly, Kevin

Editor, Wired *magazine (b. 1943)*

Kevin Kelly is editor-at-large for *Wired* magazine, the magazine that chronicles the impact of technology on society. In his book *New Rules for the New Economy*, Kelly analyses the strategies business needs to implement in order to prosper in the wired world.

Kelly is rooted in the digital culture. He is a founding board member of the pioneering online service WELL and co-founder of the annual Hackers' Conference. In the late 1980s, he was publisher and editor of the *Whole Earth Review*, one of the first publications to look at technology from a non-industry perspective. Kelly is also a member of the influential consulting group/think-tank/intellectual club the Global Business Network.

Key texts

- Kevin Kelly. *Signal communication tools for the information age: A Whole Earth Catalog.* Harmony Books, 1988

- Kevin Kelly. *New Rules for the New Economy: 10 Radical Strategies for a Connected World*. Viking Penguin, 1999

Kepner-Tregoe

In the 1960s, Charles H. Kepner (b. 1922) and Benjamin Tregoe identified three components of effective decision making: quality of the decision factors to be satisfied; quality of the evaluation of the alternatives; and quality of understanding of what alternatives can produce. This analysis was used to develop a decision-analysis methodology, the Kepner-Tregoe model. The model involves constructing a decision statement in a group environment; identifying the objectives by listing criteria that can be considered as 'musts' or 'wants'; identifying the alternatives; and evaluating the consequences of the choice of outcome.

Key text
- Charles Kepner and Benjamin Tregoe. *The Rational Manager*. McGraw Hill, 1965

Killer application

Originally, the term 'killer application' ('killer app') was coined to describe a computer program that was so compelling to certain potential users that they would buy a personal computer just so that they were able to use the program. The term's meaning has since been widened to refer to something, an idea or a product for example, that is powerful and compelling.

Kim, W. Chan

INSEAD professor

Korean W. Chan Kim is Professor of International Management at the top French business school, INSEAD. Kim was formerly at Michigan Business School and also studied at the Asian Institute of Management and Seoul National University. He is currently one of those select academics whose intellectual star is in the ascendant. This can be accredited to Kim's work with Renée Mauborgne, which has produced a series of articles and a book on managing in the knowledge economy.

With diligent academic work, Kim and Mauborgne inject an air of common sense into the frenzied debate concerning knowledge. Among the concepts they champion is that of 'fair process', which contends that 'people care as much about the fairness of the process through which an outcome is produced as they do about the outcome itself'. Fairness should permeate managerial systems. In a study of 19 companies, Kim found that there was a direct link between processes, attitudes and behaviour. He explains, 'Managers who believed the company's processes were fair displayed a high level of trust and commitment which, in turn, engendered active cooperation.'

Elsewhere, Kim and Mauborgne argue that successful companies are differentiated from the pack by 'the way managers make sense of how they do business'. Outsmarting the competition involves challenging industry conditions; not benchmarking against competitors; focusing on what customers value; thinking like a start-up business; and thinking 'in terms of the total solution buyers seek.'

Key link
- www.insead.fr

KISS

KISS, short for 'Keep It Simple, Stupid', is a quick way of expressing the opinion that the simple way of doing something is often the best. While the precise origins of the acronym are unknown, the concept is a familiar one among the scientific community, where it is known as 'Ockham's (or Occam's) Razor' after William of Ockham (1285–1347/49), an English-born Franciscan who studied at the University of Oxford. Ockham was a keen fourteenth-century advocate of simplicity. He applied the principle of economy – 'entities are not to be multiplied beyond necessity' – to the study of formal logic and other subjects so often that it became known as 'Ockham's Razor' – a medieval version of Keep It Simple, Stupid.

Key text

- Arthur Stephen McGrade. *Political Thought of William of Ockham: Personal and Institutional Principles.* Cambridge, 1974

Kiting

'Kiting' is a US term that refers to fraudulent practices, which vary depending on which field of finance is involved. In accounting, it refers to the practice of artificially boosting a company's value in its accounts. On the last day of the accounting period, cash is paid into one current account from another. The account transferring the money out will not be debited in the accounting period, but the new account will be credited.

Cheque kiting is a banking fraud where someone draws a cheque from empty account A at Bank A and then pays it into account B at Bank B to cover funds withdrawn from account B. The fraud is possible because it takes a few days for Bank B to discover the cheque from Bank A is a dud.

In securities trading, kiting refers to practices that artificially inflate a stock price.

Kleiner, Art

American researcher, writer and educator

Art Kleiner, who teaches in New York University's Interactive Telecommunications Program, is best known as the ghostwriter behind a string of successful business books. He worked as 'a consulting editor' on *The Fifth Discipline* by **Peter Senge**, *The Art of the Long View* by **Peter Schwartz**, *Control Your Destiny* by Noel Tichy, *The Last Word on Power* by Tracy Goss, *The Living Company* by **Arie de Geus**, and other, less prominent volumes.

'Many business people don't know how to convert their speaking insights to the printed page,' says Kleiner, who began ghostwriting in 1989. It wasn't easy – 'I felt tainted, like an honest trucker who drifted into contraband' – but it paid well.

Kleiner's own work includes *The Age of Heretics* and *The Dance of Change* (with Peter Senge and others). He has also worked with MIT's George Roth in research, examining the phenomena of workplace experience – one of the great mysteries of organizational life. Kleiner and Roth believe that there are means by which companies can actively harness their own experience.

Kleiner and Roth say that, 'managers have few tools with which to capture institutional experience, disseminate its lessons, and translate them into effective action.' To do so, they suggest using a tool called the *learning history* – 'a narrative of a company's recent set of critical episodes, a corporate change event, a new initiative, a widespread innovation, a successful product launch, or even a traumatic event like a downsizing.' The histories can be anywhere from 25 to 100 pages in length and are arranged in two columns. In one column, the people involved in the events describe what happened. In the opposite column are comments and observations from grandly titled 'learning historians'. These are consultants and academics from outside the organization, though people from inside the corporation may also comment. The commentary draws out the lessons, trends and conclusions that can be drawn from the narrative. The history can then be discussed by groups.

While this may all sound remarkably flaky – Kleiner and Roth believe it is related to ancient community story-telling – the observed benefits are worthy of consideration. The method, say the authors, builds trust. People are asked about their version of events. They can speak out without fear on subjects that may have concerned them for years, since the contributions are anonymous. Most importantly, learning histories can allow an organization to transfer experience from one division to another. The end result could be organizations that genuinely learn from experience and 'a body of generalizable knowledge about management'.

Key text

- Art Kleiner. *The Age of Heretics: Heroes, Outlaws, and the Forerunners of Corporate Change.* Bantam Doubleday Dell, 1996

Knight, Philip H.

CEO, president and chairman, Nike Inc. (b. 1938)

The story of Phil Knight and the sports shoe company he founded is one of the great marketing stories of the twentieth century. The company is Nike, and the masterstroke of marketing genius (one of them, at least) was turning the humble training shoe into a must-have street fashion item. It was a masterstroke that allowed Knight to take Nike from a niche manufacturer of sporting footwear to a clothing and footwear giant and internationally recognized brand.

Knight was born in Portland, Oregon. At Oregon University, where he earned a BS in business administration, Knight joined the University track team under coach Bill Bowerman. As well as conducting the training, Bowerman would experiment with his athletes' equipment to try and reduce times. He constructed prototype running shoes made of lightweight leather, and later nylon, uppers.

After Oregon University, Knight went to Stanford Graduate Business School to study for an **MBA**. He wrote a marketing paper as part of his degree, arguing that cheaper labour coupled with efficient manufacturing processes could threaten the dominance of German companies, such as Adidas and Puma, in the athletic-shoe market. Knight graduated from Stanford and, deciding to back his hunch, travelled to Japan in search of a track-shoe manufacturer. He found a small factory run by the Onitsuki Tiger Company and convinced them to supply him with shoes to import to the United States.

Back in America, Knight teamed up with his old track coach Bowerman to form Blue Ribbons Sports in 1964. Knight and Bowerman invested $500 each in the new company. Knight's first retail outlet for the shoes was the back of his car, from which he would sell track shoes at high school track meets.

To supplement his income from his shoe enterprise, Knight took a job teaching accounting at Portland State University. In 1971, Knight and Bowerman decided to rename the company's brand. They chose Nike as the new name.

Bowerman's bizarre experimentation with shoe design paid off when he made an outsole by pouring rubber into a waffle iron. Later that year, Knight commissioned graphic design student Carolyn Davidson to produce some work for his company. Pleased with the results, he asked her if she could design a logo for the company. The brief was simply that the logo should suggest movement. From a selection of designs, Knight chose the 'swoosh' sign, adopting it as the brand logo in 1972. Today, the swoosh logo is synonymous with Nike and recognized throughout the world. (The Nike brand was number 30 in the Interbrand Most Valuable Brands 2000 survey, valued at $3015 million.)

By 1978, the Blue Ribbon Sports company had been officially renamed Nike Inc. In the same year, Nike's revenues were $71 million. The company went public in 1980. In 1983, revenues were $149 million and by 1986, a massive $1 billion.

When Chicago Bulls superstar Michael Jordan succeeded runner Steve Prefontaine as the Nike sports star (Fontaine tragically died in an road accident) Jordan became a US sport icon and Nike sports shoes became everyday wear for hip and happening youth culture. Knight continued to push technical innovation in the Nike products with the launch of the Air Jordan in 1985. Whether the revolutionary product's air cushioning was a gimmick or actually increased performance didn't appear to matter as the trendy trainer outstripped the competition, becoming Nike's bestselling shoe.

When the company's fortunes flagged in the early 1990s, Knight decided to broaden the company's appeal. 'We decided we're a sports company, not just a shoe company,' Knight observed. He broadened the appeal of Nike across a greater breadth of sports. More stars, such as golfer Tiger Woods and tennis star Andre Agassi; more sports, like soccer and tennis; and more innovations, including the Predator soccer boot, have kept Nike at the front of the pack.

The biggest threat to Nike's wellbeing in the late 1990s was the issue of worker exploitation and child labour. Knight headed off the protests. In a statement to the National Press Club in May 1998, Knight said that 'the Nike product had become synonymous with slave wages, forced overtime, and arbitrary abuse,' and pledged to change things. He implemented a series of high-profile initiatives at the company that attempted to address the issue of exploitation of foreign workers. A willingness to face ethical issues has seen Nike emerge in a better shape than some other multinationals and while the controversy may continue to rumble, Knight and Nike march on.

Key texts

- Robert Goldman and Stephen Papson. *Nike Culture: The Sign of the Swoosh*. Sage Publications, 1998
- Donald Katz. *Just Do It: The Nike Spirit in the Corporate World*. Random House, 1994
- J.B. Strasser and Laurie Becklund. *Swoosh: The Unauthorized Story of Nike and the Men Who Played There*. Harcourt Brace Jovanovich, 1991

Key link

- www.nike.com

Knowledge management

Knowledge management (KM) is one of the most influential new concepts in business today. A logical follow-up to the concept of **intellectual capital**, knowledge management is based on the idea that companies should make better use of their existing knowledge – everything from licences and patents to internal processes and information about customers. The concept has been steadily gaining ground since the early 1990s.

Lew Platt, the former CEO of Hewlett-Packard, is attributed with famously saying: 'If H-P knew what it knows, we'd be three times as profitable.' This statement sums up the challenge facing firms that want to create value from the knowledge that exists, in fragmented forms, inside their organizations. The logic is that in an accelerated business world, a company's knowledge base is really its only sustainable competitive advantage.

In their efforts to corral know-how and expertise, some companies have even created the new post of chief knowledge officer (CKO). Those attempting to capture and exploit their hitherto hidden know-how include Unilever, BP, Xerox, General Electric and Motorola. Behind their efforts is the idea that they are sitting on a treasure trove of knowledge that could improve their business operations if only it was captured and made available to everyone in the organization.

'To make knowledge work productive is the great management task of this century, just as to make manual work productive was the great management task of the last century,' **Peter Drucker** has observed. Managing something as ethereal as knowledge, however, is problematic.

Research suggests that many knowledge management initiatives have failed to make a significant contribution to corporate effectiveness. In part, the problem seems to lie with the corporate mindset and, more specifically, with overzealous IT departments. Technology has its uses, of course, but it is diverting attention from the human dimension of knowledge creation.

In particular, there seems to be some confusion about what constitutes knowledge and what is merely data. Many knowledge management initiatives have involved the creation of large-scale repositories of information in databases or **intranet** sites. To some extent, this misses the point by simply collecting data without understanding its significance or usefulness.

Knowledge is not simply an agglomeration of information; it is the ability of the individual or the company to act meaningfully on the basis of that information. Information is not knowledge until it has been processed by the human mind. Technology may be the conduit, but the rubber hits the tarmac at the point where the human brain and the technology meet.

Modern technology makes transmitting information easy, but companies have to create the right environment and incentives to persuade individuals to share what they know. The trouble is that knowledge, as the old adage tells us, is power. One of the greatest barriers to effective knowledge management lies in the basic insecurity and fear that prevails in many companies.

The real issue for companies is how they persuade individuals to hand over their know-how when it is the source of their power – and the only guarantee of their continuing employment. Until companies address this, knowledge management will remain a pipe dream for most.

Key texts

- Frances Horibe. *Managing Knowledge Workers: New Skills and Attitudes to Unlock the Intellectual Capital in Your Organization.* John Wiley, 1999
- David A. Klein (ed). *The Strategic Management of Intellectual Capital.* Butterworth-Heinemann, 1997
- Leif Edvinsson and Michael Malone. *Intellectual Capital: Realizing Your Company's True Value by Finding Its Hidden Brainpower.* Harper Business, 1997

Knowledge worker

A knowledge worker is one who relies on information to carry out his job. This is in contrast to traditional manual workers, who acquired a single skill and used that skill continually to carry out their work. Knowledge workers often have jobs that are closely involved with information technology; they may work in virtual or local teams,

with information that provides a competitive advantage.

Kondratieff cycle

At the beginning of the twentieth century, Russian economist Nikolai Kondratieff (1892–1938) proposed an alternative to the commonly accepted idea of the five-to-ten-year trade cycle. Kondratieff suggested another trade cycle, a much longer 50-year cycle of economic upturn and downturn, existed in addition to the commonly accepted one. Kondratieff's ideas, dismissed at the time, have since been re-evaluated. With the benefit of greater historical perspective, the depressions in the 1880s and 1930s depressions and the recessions that occurred between 1970 and the mid-1990s all support Kondratieff's ideas. It is thought that these longer cycles, if they do exist, are related to major technological change and the turmoil that follows.

Kotler, Philip

American educator (b. 1931)

Philip Kotler has a penchant for useful definitions. 'When I am asked to define marketing in the briefest possible way, I say marketing is meeting needs profitably. A lot of us meet needs – but businesses are set up to do it profitably,' he says. 'Marketing is the homework that you do to hit the mark that satisfies those needs exactly. When you do that job, there isn't much selling work to do because the word gets out from delighted customers that this is a wonderful solution to our problems.'

Kotler also provides a useful definition of a product as 'anything that can be offered to a market for attention, acquisition, use, or consumption that might satisfy a want or need'. He says that a product has five levels: the core benefit ('Marketers must see themselves as benefit providers'); the generic product; the expected product (the normal expectations the customer has of the product); the augmented product (the additional services or benefits added to the product); and, finally, the potential product ('all of the augmentations and transformations that this product might ultimately undergo in the future').

Now nearing 70, Kotler's lengthy academic career – based at Northwestern University in Chicago – has charted the shift from 'transaction-oriented' marketing to 'relationship marketing'. He explains, 'Good customers are an asset which, when well managed and served, will return a handsome lifetime income stream to the company. In the intensely competitive marketplace, the company's first order of business is to retain customer loyalty through continually satisfying their needs in a superior way.'

Kotler regards marketing as the essence of business and more. 'Good companies will meet needs; great companies will create markets,' he writes. 'Market leadership is gained by envisioning new products, services, lifestyles, and ways to raise living standards. There is a vast difference between companies that offer **me-too products** and those that create new product and service values not even imagined by the marketplace. Ultimately, marketing at its best is about value creation and raising the world's living standards.'

A restless researcher, Kotler has written books about the marketing of places (*Marketing of Places*), the marketing of ideas (*Social Marketing*) and the marketing of persons (*High Visibility*). He has, more recently, turned his attention to e-marketing and holistic marketing, the latter of which Kotler defines as being 'where a company develops its target customer focus, defines its core competences, and outsources other functions to a collaborative network of business partners. Central to holistic marketing is the use of the Internet, company Intranet, and various Extranets to guide the company's drive toward profitable growth.'

Key texts
- Philip Kotler. *Kotler on Marketing*. Free Press, 1999

- Philip Kotler. *Marketing Management: Analysis, Planning and Control*. Eighth edition, Prentice Hall, 1994

Key link
- www.kotlermarketing.com

Kroc, Raymond Albert
Former CEO, McDonald's (1902–1984)

Ray Kroc changed the way the world eats. He turned his back on a comfortable retirement and embarked on a new business opportunity at the age of 52. Kroc single-handedly invented the modern concept of fast food. He also pioneered the global brand, serving up a McDonald's-style food revolution across the world.

Born in Oak Park, Illinois, on 5 October 1902, Kroc's life and career can be divided into two periods: pre-McDonald's and post-McDonald's. In his life pre-McDonald's, Kroc tried a variety of jobs before carving out a role as a milkshake-mixer salesman. In 1922, after some time spent playing the piano for a living, he landed a job selling paper cups for the Lily Tulip Cup Company. A good salesman, he had an eye for business and when one of his customers, patron of Prince Multimixers Earl Prince, showed Kroc the five-spindle mixer he had invented, Kroc switched companies. He spent the next 17 years selling mixers. At 52, Kroc was comfortably settled, and like most of men of that age, he was thinking about his retirement – until, that is, the day in 1954 when he walked into the small burger restaurant in San Bernardino run by the McDonald brothers.

Kroc was impressed by the way brothers Dick and Mac McDonald ran the burger restaurant. It was Henry Ford-style mass production applied to the food business. There were eight five-milkshake mixers churning out 40 milkshakes at a time. To speed the cleaning up, the brothers dispensed plastic utensils and paper napkins. The McDonald's operation was so efficient customers received their meal within 60 seconds. For Kroc, it was commercial love at first sight. 'I felt like some latter-day Newton who'd just had an Idaho potato caromed off his skull,' he said later.

Kroc, convinced that fast food McDonald's-style could be the next restaurant revolution, sold himself to the McDonald brothers, persuading them to license their name to him. In return, they would receive a percentage of the sales for each franchise he created. Kroc brought dynamism and a homespun business philosophy to the McDonald's model. 'Luck is a dividend of sweat,' he once observed. 'The more you sweat, the luckier you get.'

The four pillars on which Kroc built the McDonald's empire were quality, service, cleanliness and value. He introduced some of his own ideas, such as standardizing the size of the burger and the amount of onions served with each one. He even built a laboratory in Chicago to research the ultimate French fry. Kroc's obsession with perfecting the McDonald's business formula cost him his marriage.

In 1955, Kroc's first restaurant opened in Des Plaines, Illinois. Several others quickly followed. Kroc insisted that franchisees run their restaurants according to his strict guidelines. In 1961, he bought out the McDonald brothers for just $2.7 million. It was one of the best deals in business history – for Kroc, at least. He then embarked on a massive advertising campaign. The McDonald's landmarks kept coming: a billion hamburgers by 1963, the 500th restaurant, and the brilliant conception of the burger clown Ronald McDonald to appeal to the children of America. So popular was Ronald McDonald that not long after his first national ad appearance in 1965, more children knew his name than that of the US President.

The company went public in 1965, leaving Kroc $3 million richer. His fortune grew to $500 million by the mid-1970s as McDonald's franchises sprang up everywhere. With the company firmly established in the United States, Kroc expanded overseas. In 1967, he exported the golden arches to Canada, followed by Europe, Asia and the rest of the world. By the time of his death in 1984, at the age of 81, the McDonald's golden arches were recognized the world over as a symbol for convenient and cheap fast food.

Key texts
- John Love. *McDonald's: Behind the Arches.* Bantam Books, 1986
- Ray Kroc with Robert Anderson. *Grinding It Out: The Making of McDonald's.* Henry Regnery Co., 1977
- Max Boas and Steve Chain. *Big Mac: The Unauthorized Story Of McDonald's.* A Mentor Book/New American Library, 1977

Kunde, Jesper
Danish branding expert

Danish branding expert Jesper Kunde follows in a long line of original thinkers from Scandinavia. In his recent book *Corporate Religion*, Kunde asserts that branding is not just about the marketing of a company's products and services, but is the key to the strategic positioning of the entire business.

Indeed, he goes further, claiming that creating and sustaining the **brand** is the future role of management. Brand power in the 'outside' market, he says, is a direct by-product of the internal soul and personality of the firm. What a company does/makes/sells is inseparable from what it is. Authenticity is everything.

Corporate Religion is a provocatively titled book with a serious message. Kunde offers not just a new perspective on branding, but a radical reframing of the bonds between customer, employer and employee. He claims that in the future, branding will have to go much deeper, embodying the personality and corporate soul of the company. Defining the brand will be the primary task of senior managers.

To be successful, he argues, companies have to create their own brand religion: a religion that brings together the internal company culture and the external market position through a mutual set of beliefs. (The word 'religion' derives from the

Latin *religare* – to bind something together in a common expression.)

Based in Copenhagen, Kunde worked at Carlsberg and the electronics company LK before starting his own advertising agency, Kunde & Co., with partner Gaute Hogh in 1988. The company also has a UK arm run by B.J. Cunningham. No stranger to controversy, Cunningham was the man behind the Enlightened Tobacco Company, which marketed DEATH cigarettes in the early 1990s.

Key text

- Jesper Kunde. *Corporate Religion*. Pearson Professional Education, 1999

L

Labour flexibility

Labour flexibility refers to the ability of a workforce to undertake different tasks, thereby creating competitive advantage. A company with high labour flexibility will be able to respond to changes in the market more quickly than less flexible competitors. There are a number of factors that affect labour flexibility, including the nature of the training undertaken by the workforce (the more general the training, the more easily employees will be able to switch); the structure of the company (if the organization is structured tightly along functional lines, this may restrict labour flexibility); and whether or not the workforce is resistant to change.

Labour mobility

Labour mobility is the degree to which labour is willing to move in order to obtain employment. Movement from one type of employment to another is known as 'occupational mobility'. Moving from one part of the country to another or from one country to another is known is geographical mobility. Factors that affect geographical mobility include regional property price, local ties and communications infrastructure.

Labour mobility may be restricted by national restrictions on immigration; economic migrants are unwelcome in many Western countries. The United States, for example, has tight restrictions in place to prevent economic migrants from settling and fights an active campaign to repel illegal immigrants who attempt to cross the border from Mexico. Similarly, while the European Union allows free movement within the member states, entry to the EU from economic migrants outside the EU is tightly restricted.

It has not always been this way. Currently, approximately 2 percent of the world's population lives in countries to which they have emigrated; 100 years ago, that figure was closer to 10 percent. In the 40 years prior to 1910, the United States let in some 20 million people. It wasn't until the Great Depression that the government began to severely restrict entry. The trend for restrictions to entry for economic migrants may change in the forthcoming decades as demographics have a big impact on the percentage of the population in the developed world that is of working age. As the **baby boomers** retire in ever-increasing numbers, the ratio of workers to retirees will steadily decline and countries in the developed world may be forced to relax their immigration laws, paving the way for greater geographical labour flexibility.

LAN (local area network)

A local area network is a group of hardware, usually computers and printers, that is connected to each other. The equipment is usually close together – in the same room or building. Local area networks enable around 500 devices, usually microcomputers acting as workstations, as well as peripheral devices, such as printers, to be connected together. A LAN may be connected to other LANs to form a wide area network or WAN. The point of LANs is to allow users to share information from different locations, using different machines. The applications and files accessed over the LAN are usually kept in a single location on a computer known as a **server**. The individual machines on the LANs – or nodes – will usually have their own microchips and will be able to run applications themselves or run them from a server.

The origins of LANs date back to the work of Robert M. Metcalfe at Xerox PARC during the 1970s. Attempting to construct a network that would allow the Alto computers at PARC to communicate with each other, Metcalfe started with two computers named Michelson and Morley, after the physicists who disproved the theory that an invisible 'ether' filled the universe. When Metcalfe and his colleagues successfully networked the two machines, they named the network protocol Ethernet. Metcalfe went on to commercially develop his idea at the company he founded, 3Com, which stands for Computer, Communication and Compatibility.

Land, Edwin Herbert

Inventor; pioneer of instant photography for the masses (1909–1991)

Best known for the invention of the Polaroid camera, Edwin Herbert Land was born in Bridgeport, Connecticut, on 7 May 1909. A keen scholar, he is said to have slept with a copy of R.W. Wood's *Physical Optics* beneath his pillow and was cited as a 'star in his studies' in his high school yearbook.

He graduated with honours from Norwich Free Academy. He then attended Harvard University, where he developed a cheap, effective polarizer of light that he called Polaroid. He dropped out after his freshman year in 1926 to concentrate on his advances in the field of light polarization.

When Land began to apply his mind to the subject, the main tool in use was the Nicol Prism, a bulky and expensive piece of equipment used to study light polarization. Following observations based on his studies in the New York Library,

Land placed a large number of aligned crystals in transparent plastic. The plastic was set, fixing the position of the crystals. After a few preliminary experiments, Land gave a lecture at Harvard on his idea.

Land patented his new invention in 1929 and then set up companies to develop and exploit it: first the Land-Wheelwright Laboratories in 1932, which Land set up with his Harvard physics instructor George Wheelwright III, and then the Polaroid Corporation in Boston in 1937. Next Land sought to find commercial applications for his invention.

The first idea was to use the technology to reduce glare in car headlights. Land found, however, that implementation led to increased fuel consumption. Unable to sell his idea to the car manufacturers, he proceeded to develop a variety of products that used the new technology. Many were inspired by chance discoveries.

Take Polaroid sunglasses. When one of Land's colleagues took a Polaroid strip with him when he went fishing, he returned to tell Land that looking through the Polaroid reduced the surface glare from the water and enabled him to spot the fish. This discovery led to the manufacture of Polaroid sunglasses, which were initially sold in specialist hunting and fishing shops but eventually reached a wider market. The sunglasses led to other product developments, such as camera filters and antiglare screens.

The success of Polaroid sunglasses spurred on Land. He assembled a team of brilliant minds at his research labs in Boston. They contributed to the US war effort in the 1940s with inventions such as a new method of 3-D photography used extensively for reconnaissance, night goggles and the polarizing ring sight. Land also contributed to the technology used during the Cold War, including the surveillance equipment employed in the high-altitude U2 spy planes and spy satellites.

Land is probably best known for the invention of instant photography and the Polaroid camera. The invention was prompted by a question from his three-year-old daughter in 1944. On a sunny day in Santa Fe, New Mexico, when Land took a snapshot, his daughter asked why she couldn't see the picture immediately. This set Land thinking and after pacing the town for an hour, he had arrived at a solution.

Land's revolutionary new instant camera was demonstrated in February 1947 at a meeting of the Optical Society of America. The commercial model was on sale within two years. It was priced for the mass market at $89.50.

Land retired as president of Polaroid in 1982, but continued his research. He built a research institute, the Rowland Institute for Science in Cambridge Massachusetts, alongside the Charles River, and continued to experiment along with a group of fellow researchers until his death at the age of 81, in 1991. With Land gone, the company he founded has struggled. By 2001, with debts of $950 million, the company **downsized** approximately 25 percent of the workforce and was fighting to avoid bankruptcy.

Key texts
- Victor K. McElheny. *Insisting on the Impossible: The Life of Edwin Land*. Perseus, 1998
- Mark Olshaker. *The Polaroid Story: Edwin Land and the Polaroid Experience*. Stein and Day, 1982

Lane, Allen

Publishing radical and pioneer (1902–1970)

The eldest of four children, Allen Lane was born in Bristol on 21 September 1902. In 1919, at the age of 17, after an undistinguished passage through Bristol Grammar School, Lane went to work for The Bodley Head publishing house. Owned by Lane's uncle, John Lane, the once-prosperous firm of publishers had run into financial difficulties.

Lane started as a lowly office boy, but was soon finding new authors, discussing contracts and acting as if he was director. Lane was promoted to the board in 1924. His uncle died soon after.

Sometime in 1934, Lane spent a weekend with crime author Agatha Christie and her husband in Devon. Returning by train to London, Lane neglected to take any reading matter and lamented the lack of reasonably priced, portable, well-presented literature. Back in London, he persuaded his brothers Richard and John, who also worked at The Bodley Head, that the principles of a mass-market, mass-production, mass-distribution retail operation could be applied to publishing.

Lane pressed ahead with a new imprint for the mass market, despite resistance from other Bodley Head directors. He chose a name from a short list of Dolphin, Porpoise and Penguin, eventually settling on Penguin. The new 'Penguins' were small, lightweight paperbacks with an eye-catching design, priced at sixpence each. An order of 63,000 copies from retailers Woolworth secured the future of the Penguin imprint.

The first books came off of the Penguin presses in July 1935. The first batch of ten titles began with *Ariel*, a biography of Percy Bysshe Shelley, by Andre Maurois, as well as *The Mysterious Affair at Styles* by Agatha Christie and Ernest Hemingway's *A Farewell to Arms*. The books were colour-coded to indicate their type: orange for general literature; green for crime; pink for travel; and blue for biography. They were also numbered (up to number 3224, published in 1974), and on the spine and the front cover was the distinctive Penguin logo, designed by Edward Young, an amateur artist who worked for The Bodley Head.

Resigning from The Bodley Head in 1936, Lane founded Penguin Books Ltd with just £100 in capital, taking offices in the crypt of Holy Trinity Church, Marylebone Road. In 1937, The Bodley Head went into voluntary liquidation, the same year that Penguin moved to a three-and-a-half-acre plot at Harmondsworth, Middlesex. The property cost £2000, plus an additional £200 for the crop of cabbages already planted on the land.

Penguin paperbacks were an immediate hit with the public. Within six months, they had sold over a million copies. By the end of 1936, there were 70 titles on the Penguin list. 1937 saw the first of a number of new series: the Pelicans, focusing on non-fiction. Penguin Specials, which focused on current affairs, were designed to feed the increasing appetite for public affairs during the Depression and in the run-up to World War II. They sold a quarter of a million copies in just a few weeks.

Although paper was rationed severely during World War II, Lane was friendly with the director of Army Warfare and managed to secure a monopoly for supplying service personnel with books, as well as an adequate supply of raw materials. Ironically, the war turned out to be a boon to the rapidly growing publishing company. The name of Penguin books and its famous logo became familiar to armed forces across the world.

Penguin Books Ltd became a publicly listed company on 20 April 1961. Lane signed a seven-year contract to serve as chairman and managing director of the new company. He spent his final years planning his succession, working on a hardback imprint – The Penguin Press – and fighting a guerrilla war against an increasingly vocal board of directors. In 1968, Lane entered into merger negotiations with publisher Longman, hoping to inject some badly needed capital into Penguin. During the negotiations, Longman was swallowed by S. Pearson & Co. to form Pearson Longman. It was Pearson Longman that finally bought Penguin for £15 million in 1970. By then Lane was dead: he died of cancer on 7 July 1970.

Key texts

- Jack E. Morpurgo. *Allen Lane, King Penguin.* Hutchinson, 1979
- W.E. Williams. *Allen Lane: A Personal Portrait.* The Bodley Head, 1973

Last-Mover Advantage

See First-mover advantage.

Lateral thinking

See De Bono, Edward.

Lauder, Estée

Cosmetics retailer and marketing innovator (b. 1908)

Much of the American cosmetic queen Estée Lauder's early life is shrouded in mystery. It is usually accepted that Estée Lauder was born Josephine Esther Mentzer in Queens, New York, in 1908. As a girl, she was introduced to the cosmetics business by her uncle, Dr Schotz, a chemist. His business, New Way Laboratories, was founded in 1924. As well as poultry lice killer, paint stripper, varnish and embalming fluid, Schotz produced several beauty treatments, such as Six-in-One Cold Cream and Dr Schotz Viennese Cream. Lauder helped out by selling these products.

By 1939, Lauder had married, separated from, and remarried one Joe Lauder and focused all of her energies on selling cosmetics products. She set up her own office at 39 East Sixtieth Street in February 1944. Lauder had a sales concession in the Bonwit department store, but coveted a concession in the famous Saks department store on Fifth Avenue. Lauder told the cosmetics buyer at Saks, Bob Fiske, that she deserved a concession. Fiske declined, citing lack of demand for Lauder's products. A canny Lauder created demand by handing out her products at a talk in the Waldorf-Astoria Hotel. Fiske gave her a concession.

In the late 1940s, Lauder's business thrived, using innovative marketing methods such as handing out samplers and gifts as an enticement for customers to visit her store concessions. Lauder's first fragrance was the bath oil Youth-Dew. Introduced at Bonwit's department store, it was an instant success. For $8.50, customers got a perfume that lasted a whole day. Shrewdly, Lauder used the demand for the new perfume to sell her other cosmetics. She extended the Youth-Dew brand to a range of cosmetics. With Lauder promoting the company at every opportunity, it wasn't long before Estée Lauder was the third largest cosmetics business in the United States, behind Arden and Rubenstein.

Lauder's marketing acumen was again evident when a spate of skincare products making dubious scientific claims began to spread from Europe to the United States. The Food and Drug Administration in the United States imposed tough regulations on products making any such claims and a number of skincare products were withdrawn. Instead of making scientific claims for her new skin product, Lauder simply named it Re-Nutriv, conjuring up an image of health-enhancing attributes. Advertising focused on the high price of the product, and how a price of $115 per pound was justified by inclusion of the 'costliest' ingredients.

By the 1970s, Estée Lauder had added the Clinique brand to its beautifying armoury and moved to new headquarters in the General Motors Building. Lauder herself had outlasted her personal rivals Elizabeth Arden and Helena Rubenstein, who died within a year of each other in the 1960s. Her son Leonard became president of the company in 1972, with Lauder remaining as chairman.

Estée Lauder remained an entirely private company until its **IPO** in 1995. The Lauder family still holds a significant proportion of the shares. Although Lauder has progressively taken a back seat since the 1980s, her sons Leonard and Ronald, daughter-in-law Evelyn, grandson William and great-granddaughter Aerin remain actively involved in the company.

By 2000, the 'little business' that Leonard Lauder once said his mother was growing controlled over 40 percent of the cosmetics market in US department stores. Available in 118 countries, Estée Lauder products earned over $3 billion in revenue that year.

Key texts

- Estée Lauder. *Estée: A Success Story*. Random House, 1985
- Lee Israel. *Estée Lauder: Beyond the Magic*. Macmillan, 1985

Key link

- www.esteelauder.com

Lauren, Ralph

Fashion icon; founder, Polo Ralph Lauren Corp. (b. 1939)

Today, the great cities of the world are festooned with designer stores; designer brands sell everything from sunglasses to perfume. It wasn't always this way. In life before DKNY, Calvin Klein and Armani, there was Polo, fashioned by the American designer Ralph Lauren.

Lauren has built Polo's quintessential clean-cut, preppy look into a global brand, selling not just clothes but a way of life, a glimpse of which is revealed in its stylized advertising. Lauren says, 'I don't design clothes, I design dreams.' There are more than 130 Polo/Ralph Lauren stores around the world, selling a range of products from fragrances to footwear, fabric to furniture, and the classic menswear with which Lauren made his name. The company's brand names include Polo, Polo by Ralph Lauren, Polo Sport, Ralph Lauren, Lauren, RALPH, Ralph Lauren Purple Label, Polo Jeans Co. and many others. If you have $150,000 to spare, you can even buy a Ralph Lauren caravan: a gleaming silver Airstream with a choice of four differently themed interiors.

Born in New York City in 1939, Lauren always had an eye for fashion. His father was a mural painter and Lauren inherited an eye for shape and colour. Although Lauren was always a snappy dresser, it was only receiving a business degree at City College in Manhattan that Lauren turned his attention to the fashion business.

Lauren took a job as a salesman at a glove company, followed by a similar job at a tie manufacturer. While at the tie firm, A. Rivetz & Co., Lauren took the first tentative steps toward building his fashion empire by creating his own tie designs. In 1968, Lauren left Rivetz with $50,000 and his tie designs and, together with his elder brother, formed his own company, Polo.

The name Polo was chosen because of its preppy connotations. Polo began life as a tie store. Distinctively wide for the fashion of the time, Lauren's ties were popular with the customers but less so with other department stores, who were reluctant to stock the designs. Initially Bloomingdale's, the famous US store, asked Lauren to modify his designs and make the ties narrower. It also insisted he remove his brand label. Lauren refused. Before long, Bloomingdale's was back, agreeing to stock Polo designer ties on Lauren's terms.

One of the first men's fashion designers to open a store in his own name, Lauren's first store opened in 1971. With the help of his brother Jerry, he continued to establish the brand. As more stores opened, Lauren extended his range to women's wear, and then to his 'home collection' line with linen, towels, furniture and similar products. The flagship store in Rhinelander Mansion on Madison Avenue opened in 1986. The Polo Sport store opened across the street in 1993.

The 1980s saw an extension of the Polo brand into new areas. It also brought new competition with the emergence of the Giorgio Armani power suit, very much part of the 1980s Zeitgeist. Lauren modified his designs to produce crisp-looking, sophisticated suits, but refused to abandon the ethos of the Polo brand for short-term gain. 'I'm a long-term person,' he said. 'I'm long-term about my work. I'm a builder. Everything I do is an extension of my life.' It was an astute move. What was considered fashionable at the height of the 1980s seemed showy in a more reserved 1990s.

Without his innate sense of style and an innovative eye for fashion, Lauren would never have succeeded. But equally important is Lauren's adept handling of the brand-building exercise. In Lauren's capable hands, Polo and associated brands became a lifestyle choice as well as a design choice. Throughout the 1980s, the Polo brand was backed by a procession of distinctive advertising, conjuring a range of associations from safaris to the English aristocracy.

In June 1997, the company went public with an **IPO** that raised $767 million for Polo Ralph Lauren, making Lauren a very wealthy man. As befits the man behind one of the hottest fashion properties of the twentieth century, Lauren lives a stylish life. His fashion house has bought him all the trappings of the mega-wealthy: properties in Jamaica, Long Island and Fifth Avenue as well as an estate in Bedford, New York, and a ranch in Colorado. He also owns a collection of prestigious cars that includes a 1937 Alfa Romeo and a 1938 Bugatti.

Key text
- Jeffrey A. Trachtenberg. *Ralph Lauren: The Man Behind the Mystique*. Little, Brown & Co., 1988

Key link
- www.polo.com

Leadbeater, Charles

Author and consultant

An Oxford graduate, Charles Leadbeater is a freelance writer, Demos think-tank research associate, and consultant to a number of companies, including the **venture capital** firm Atlas Venture in London. After graduating from college, Leadbeater had stints in television at TV-AM and in journalism at the UK broadsheet *The Independent* and at the *Financial Times*, where he worked as Industrial Editor and Tokyo Bureau Chief.

In his 1999 book *Living on Thin Air*, Leadbeater sets out a New Constitution for the **New Economy**. He argues for a restructuring of business and society to harness the power of the knowledge economy and create an innovative and inclusive environment in which the New Economy can flourish. 'I'm struck by the number of large organizations, both public and private, that are realizing that leadership involves stewardship, looking after people and assets, as well as entrepreneurship, looking at new opportunities,' he says.

Key text
- Charles Leadbeater. *Living on Thin Air: The New Economy*. Viking, 1999

Leadership

Leadership was once about hard skills, such as

planning, finance and business analysis. When command and control ruled the corporate world, leaders were heroic rationalists who moved people around like pawns. They spoke and the company jumped. Now, if the gurus and experts are right, leadership is increasingly concerned with soft skills, including teamwork, communication and motivation. The trouble is that for many executives, the soft skills remain the hardest to understand, let alone master.

After all, hard skills have traditionally been the ones to get you to the top of the corporate ladder. 'The entire career system in some organizations is based on using hard functional skills to progress,' says Philip Hodgson of Ashridge Management College. 'But when executives reach the top of the organization, many different skills are required. Corporate leaders may find that though they can do the financial analysis and the strategic planning, they are poor at communicating ideas to employees or colleagues, or have little insight into how to motivate people. The modern chief executive requires an array of skills.'

Indeed, some suggest that we are expecting too much. 'Leadership in a modern organization is highly complex and it is increasingly difficult – sometimes impossible – to find all the necessary traits in a single person,' says Jonas Ridderstråle of the Stockholm School of Economics. 'Among the most crucial skills will be the ability to capture the attention of your audience – you will be competing with lots of other people for their attention. The leaders of the future will also have to be emotionally efficient. They will promote variation rather than promoting people in their own likeness; they will encourage experimentation and enable people to learn from failure; they will build and develop people.' Is this too much for one person to do? Ridderstråle thinks so and predicts, 'In the future, we will see leadership groups rather than individual leaders.'

This change in emphasis from individuals toward groups and teams has been charted by leadership guru **Warren Bennis**. His recent work concentrates on the power of famous groundbreaking groups rather than individual leaders.

His book *Organizing Genius* tells the stories of exceptional groups, including Xerox's Palo Alto Research Center (PARC), the group behind the 1992 Clinton campaign, Lockheed's Skunk Works and the Manhattan Project, which invented the atomic bomb. 'None of us is as smart as all of us,' says Bennis. 'The Lone Ranger is dead. Instead of the individual problem solver, we have a new model for creative achievement. People like Steve Jobs or Walt Disney headed groups and found their own greatness in them.'

Bennis provides a blueprint for the new model leader. 'He or she is a pragmatic dreamer, a person with an original but attainable vision,' he says. 'Inevitably, the leader has to invent a leadership style that suits the group. The standard models, especially command and control, simply don't work. The heads of groups have to act decisively, but never arbitrarily. They have to make decisions without limiting the perceived autonomy of the other participants. Devising and maintaining an atmosphere in which others can put a dent in the universe is the leader's creative act.'

As Bennis's comments suggest, the role of the new model leader is riddled with paradox. For example, the leader has to be decisive and yet empower others to make decisions. 'Paradox and uncertainty are increasingly at the heart of leading organizations,' observes Robert Sharrock of the business psychologists' organization YSC. 'A lot of leaders don't like ambiguity so they try to shape the environment to resolve the ambiguity. This might involve collecting more data or narrowing thing down. These may not be the best things to do. The most effective leaders are flexible, responsive to new and emerging situations. If they are particularly adept at hard skills, they surround themselves with people who are proficient with soft skills. They strike a balance.'

While flexibility is clearly important in this new leadership model, it should not be interpreted as weakness. The two most lauded corporate chiefs of the last decade have been **Percy Barnevik** of Asea Brown Boveri (ABB) and **Jack Welch** of General Electric. Somewhat surprisingly, perhaps, they share a number of characteristics. Both are incessant communicators with the capacity to endlessly repeat the same message to different audiences. Barnevik estimates that he spends one-tenth of his time deciding on the strategy and the rest communicating it.

Both Barnevik and Welch also dismantled traditional bureaucratic structures filled with strategists and overseers. Adept at soft and hard skills. they continually coached and cajoled as well as commanded and controlled.

The leader as coach is yet another of those phrases more readily seen in business books than in reality. Acting as a coach to a colleague is not something that comes easily to many executives. Indeed, there appears to be growing demand for support for corporate leaders. Sharrock says, 'It is increasingly common for senior executives to need one-to-one coaching and **mentoring**. They need a sounding board to talk through particular decisions – particularly people-related decisions – and to think through the impact of their behaviour on others in the organization.'

In the past, such support may have been construed as weakness. In the era of macho, heroic leadership, support was for failures. Now, there appears growing realization that leaders are human after all and that leadership is as much a human art as a rational science. 'Today's leaders don't follow rigid or orthodox role models, but prefer to nurture their own unique leadership style. They don't do people's jobs for them or put their faith in developing a personality cult,' concludes Ashridge's Philip Hodgson. 'They regard leadership as drawing people and disparate parts of the organization together in ways that makes individuals and the organization more effective.'

Key texts
- Warren Bennis. *Why Leaders Can't Lead The Unconscious Conspiracy Continues*. Jossey-Bass, 1989
- General H. Norman Schwarzkopf written with Peter Petre. *It Doesn't Take a Hero: The Autobiography*. Bantam Books, 1992

- Warren Bennis. *An Invented Life: Reflections on Leadership and Change*. Addison-Wesley Publishing Company 1993

Lean production

During the last 40 years, Western auto manufacturers have lurched from one crisis to another, always a step behind. The company they have been following is Japanese automotive giant Toyota.

If you go into the Toyota headquarters in Japan, you will find three portraits. One is of the company's founder; the next is of the company's current president; and the final one is a portrait of American quality guru **W. Edwards Deming**. While Western companies produced gas-guzzling cars with costly, large and unhappy workforces in the 1970s, Toyota was forging ahead with implementation of Deming's ideas. In the early 1980s, Western companies finally woke up and began to implement Deming's quality gospel. By then it was too late. Toyota had moved on.

Toyota progressed to what has been labelled 'lean production', or the Toyota Production System. The architect of the Toyota Production System is usually acknowledged as being Taiichi Ohno, who wrote a short book on the Toyota approach and later became a consultant. From Toyota's point of view, there was nothing revolutionary in lean production. In fact, lean production was an integral part of Toyota's commitment to quality and its roots can be traced back to the 1950s. In 1984, when Toyota opened up a joint venture with General Motors in California, the West began to wake up and the word began to spread.

The Toyota Production System was based on three simple principles. The first was that of **just-in-time** production. There is no point in producing cars, or anything else, in blind anticipation of someone buying them. Waste (*muda*) is bad. Production must be closely tied to the market's requirements. Second, responsibility for quality rests with everyone and any quality defects need to be rectified as soon as they are identified. The third, more elusive, concept was the 'value stream.' Instead of seeing the company as a series of unrelated products and processes, it should be seen as a continuous and uniform whole, a stream including suppliers as well as customers.

The concepts were brought to mass Western audiences thanks to work carried out at the Massachusetts Institute of Technology as part of its International Motor Vehicle Program. The MIT research took five years, covered 14 countries, and looked exclusively at the worldwide car industry. The research concluded that while American car makers remained fixed in the mass production techniques of the past, Japanese car makers managed to square the manufacturing circle: management, workers and suppliers worked toward the same goals, resulting in increased production, high quality, happy customers and lower costs. The research spawned the 1990 bestseller by James Womack, Daniel Jones and Daniel Roos, *The Machine That Changed the World*. (Womack and Roos were from MIT while Jones was from Cardiff Business School.)

Lean production became fashionable. As with most management fads, it was wilfully misinterpreted. It became linked to reengineering and, more worryingly, to **downsizing**. The reality is that lean production is a highly effective concept. 'Lean production is a superior way for humans to make things,' Womack, Jones and Roos argue. They are right. If, as Toyota has largely done, you get it right, lean production gives the best of every world: the economies of scale of mass production; the sensitivity to market and customer needs usually associated with smaller companies; and job enrichment for employees.

The trouble is that getting it right has proved difficult. In many cases, Western organizations were so committed to their very different ways of working that the changes required were impossibly all-embracing. But it is not only that lean production requires large-scale changes in practice and attitude. The West continues to equate leanness with numbers. Lean production is seen as a means of squeezing more production from fewer people. This is a fundamental misunderstanding. Reduced numbers of employees is the end goal, rather than the means. Western companies have tended to reduce numbers and then declare themselves lean organizations. This overlooks all three of the concepts that underlie genuine lean production (just-in-time manufacturing; responsibility for quality; and the company as value stream). Womack argues that while lean production requires fewer people, the organization should then accelerate product development to tap new markets to keep the people at work.

Lean production has moved the debate about quality forward. It has raised awareness, provided a new benchmark, and brought operational efficiency to a wider audience. 'Organizations did well to employ the most up-to-date equipment, information technology, and management techniques to eliminate waste, defects, and delays,' says Harvard Business School's **Michael Porter**. 'They did well to operate as close as they could to the productivity frontier. But while improving operational effectiveness is necessary to achieving superior profitability, it is not sufficient.'

Key texts
- James Womack and Daniel T. Jones. *Lean Thinking*. Simon & Schuster, 1996
- James Womack, Daniel T. Jones and Daniel Roos. *The Machine That Changed the World*. Rawson Associates/Macmillan, 1990
- Yasuhiro Monden. *Toyota Production System*. Institute of Industrial Engineers, 1988
- Taiichi Ohno. *Toyota Production System*. Productivity Press, 1988

Learning organization

The term 'learning organization' was first used by Harvard Business School's **Chris Argyris** in the 1970s to mean a firm that learns as it goes along, responsively adjusting its way of doing business.

Closely involved and greatly influenced by the human-relations school of the late 1950s, Argyris has examined learning processes, both in individual and corporate terms, in depth. 'Most people define learning too narrowly as mere *problem solving*, so they focus on identifying and correcting errors in the external environment. Solving problems is important, but if learning is to persist, managers and employees must also look inward. They need to reflect critically on their own behaviour,' he says.

Problems with learning, as Argyris has revealed, are not restricted to a particular social or professional group. Indeed, it is the very people we expect to be good at learning – teachers, consultants and other 'professionals' – who often prove the most inadequate at actually doing so.

The entire concept of learning was brought back onto the agenda with the publication and success of the 1990 book *The Fifth Discipline*. Written by **Peter Senge** of the MIT Sloan School of Management, it was released to immediate acclaim. 'Forget your old, tired ideas about leadership,' *Fortune* magazine advised its readers. 'The most successful corporation of the 1990s will be something called a learning organization.'

The Fifth Discipline brought the learning organization concept to a mass audience. It was the result of extensive research by Senge and his team at the Center for Organizational Learning at MIT's Sloan School. In it, Senge argued that learning from the past is vital for success in the future.

'In the simplest sense, a learning organization is a group of people who are continually enhancing their capability to create their future,' he said. 'The traditional meaning of the word *learning* is much deeper than just *taking information in*. It is about changing individuals so that they produce results they care about, accomplishing things that are important to them.'

The organizations that would thrive, Senge claimed, would be those that discovered how to tap their people's commitment and capacity to learn at every level in the company. This involved encouraging managers and other employees to experiment with new ideas and feed back the results to the wider organization.

The book looked at how firms and other organizations can develop adaptive capabilities

in a world of increasing complexity and rapid change. Senge argues that vision, purpose, alignment and systems thinking are essential for organizations. He gave managers tools and conceptual archetypes to help them to understand the structures and dynamics underlying their organizations' problems. 'As the world becomes more interconnected and business becomes more complex and dynamic, work must become more *learningful*,' he wrote.

For the traditional company, the shift to becoming a learning organization poses huge challenges. In the learning organization, managers are researchers and designers rather than controllers and overseers. Senge argues that managers should encourage employees to be open to new ideas, communicate frankly with each other, understand thoroughly how their companies operate, form a collective vision and work together to achieve their goal.

One of the clearest indications of the decision-making culture of an organization is how tolerant it is of mistakes. To a large extent, this will determine how willing managers are to take risks: managers are unlikely to voluntarily shoulder additional responsibilities if the message from the organization's culture is that they are likely to get shot if they put their heads above the parapet. An organizational willingness to make mistakes is also an important factor in whether the organization has the ability to learn.

Yet despite current thinking, which suggests that experimentation is vital for companies to remain vigorous, in many corporate cultures there is a very low tolerance for mistakes, and individuals' career prospects can be severely damaged if a creative decision goes wrong. Creating learning organizations has proved difficult in practice, not least because companies are set in their ways.

Key text
• Peter Senge. *The Fifth Discipline*. Doubleday, 1990

Legacy systems

Legacy systems are old in-house, back-room computing systems. They are a hangover from the pre-Internet business world that must be overhauled for a company's front- and back-room operations to seamlessly integrate with the Internet and Internet applications.

Companies have proved reluctant to ditch their old systems, and it's not difficult to understand why. Some estimates have put the investment in legacy systems at over $4 trillion worldwide. Couple this with the fact that some three-quarters of businesses still process data on these systems, and the reasons for resisting overhaul become clearer.

There are options other than abandoning a legacy system entirely. Organizations such as Oracle supply integration solutions that attempt to translate data from the old system to new, e-commerce-oriented technology. They do this, for example, by intercepting data and converting it to XML. These 'middleware' applications should work well on simple legacy systems such as IBM 390s. More complex legacy systems present a greater challenge. There are also added problems inherent in the older systems, such as batch processing, in which data is 'saved up' to be processed in batches. This is anathema to the seamless progressive nature of the most up-to-date, e-commerce solutions. Application Service Providers are a possible interim solution. With **ASP**s, companies can offload their software applications to the ASP's servers while they transfer from the legacy systems to new technology.

Level output strategy

See Managing demand.

Leveraged buyout

A leveraged buyout (LBO) is the purchase of a controlling proportion of the shares of a company financed almost exclusively by borrowing. It is so called because the ratio of a company's long-term debt to its equity (capital assets) is known as its 'leverage'. The idea is that by funding the deal with high-risk debt, such as **junk bonds**, a purchaser can take over a company cheaply if he can fund the interest on the debt from revenues of the target company. Thus the company is acquired at little or no risk on the purchaser's part. The security for the debt is effectively the target company's assets. If the revenue proves insufficient to meet interest payments, the acquirer can sell off all or part of the target company to meet the debt and still make a profit from whatever is left. The difficult part of the LBO is persuading the shareholders there is enough value in the deal for them.

The leveraged buyout became popular during the 1970s and 1980s. The market was started by Henry R. Kravis and his firm of Kohlberg Kravis Roberts and Theodore J. Forstmann, founder of Forstmann Little & Co. In the 1970s, these were probably the only two serious contenders in the LBO market. Today there are more than 800 firms chasing LBO business.

The nature of the LBO has also changed. In the 1980s, the key was debt. Most big LBO deals were 95 percent financed by debt, often junk bonds. However, with the collapse of the junk-bond market and the lack of confidence following the dotcom slump, the leverage in most modern LBOs is much reduced. Most LBOs have debt levels of less than 75 percent. But as the equity element of the deal goes up, the investment return comes down. Returns are down from an annualized 35 percent in the mid-1980s to 20 percent in early 2000. Yet Kohlberg Kravis Roberts is still in the market and, as the new millennium dawned, was compiling its biggest war chest ever – a $6 billion LBO fund.

Levitt, Theodore

American educator (b. 1925)

Theodore Levitt reignited the serious study of marketing in the early 1960s and later was the first to explore some of the marketing implications of globalization. The July–August 1960 issue of the *Harvard Business Review* launched his career with his article 'Marketing Myopia', which, totally unexpectedly, brought marketing back onto the corporate agenda. 'Marketing Myopia' has sold more than 500,000 reprints and belongs to a select group of articles that have genuinely changed perceptions.

In '**Marketing Myopia**', Levitt argued that the central preoccupation of corporations should be with satisfying customers rather than simply producing goods. Companies should be marketing-led rather than production-led, and the lead must come from the chief executive and senior management. 'Management must think of itself not as producing products but as providing customer-creating value satisfactions,' Levitt writes. In his ability to coin new management jargon, as well as his thinking, Levitt was ahead of his time.

At the time of Levitt's article, the fact that companies were production-led was not open to question. **Henry Ford**'s success in mass production had fuelled the belief that low-cost production was the key to business success.

Levitt observed that production-led thinking inevitably led to narrow perspectives. He argued that companies must broaden their view of the nature of their business, or their customers will soon be forgotten. 'The railroads are in trouble today not because the need was filled by others … but because it was not filled by the railroads themselves,' wrote Levitt. 'They let others take customers away from them because they assumed themselves to be in the railroad business rather than in the transportation business. The reason they defined their industry wrong was because they were railroad-oriented instead of transportation-oriented; they were product-oriented instead of customer-oriented.' The railroad business was constrained, in Levitt's view, by a lack of willingness to expand its horizons.

In 'Marketing Myopia', Levitt also made a telling distinction between the tasks of selling and marketing. 'Selling concerns itself with the tricks and techniques of getting people to exchange their cash for your product. It is not concerned with the values that the exchange is all about. And it does not, as marketing invariably does, view the entire business process as consisting of a tightly integrated effort to discover, create, arouse, and satisfy customer needs,' he writes.

Levitt's other major insight was on the emergence of globalization. In the same way as he had done with 'Marketing Myopia', Levitt signalled the emergence of a major movement and then withdrew to watch it ignite. 'The world is becoming a common market place in which people – no matter where they live – desire the same products and lifestyles. Global companies must forget the idiosyncratic differences between countries and cultures and instead concentrate on satisfying universal drives,' he says.

Key texts
- Theodore Levitt. *Thinking About Management*. Free Press, 1991
- Theodore Levitt. *The Marketing Imagination*. Free Press, 1983
- Theodore Levitt. *The Marketing Mode*. McGraw-Hill, 1969
- Theodore Levitt. *Innovation in Marketing*. McGraw-Hill, 1962

Levitt, William
Property developer (1906–1993)

Born on 9 January 1906, the son of a New York-based lawyer, William Levitt got into the real estate business after an education at the Boys High School at Bedford-Stuyvesant and New York University, where he studied math and English.

It was a bad business deal that got Levitt started, when his father bought 100 building plots from a bankrupt client and roped in Levitt to help complete them. The houses were finished and Levitt's father, encouraged by the efforts of his sons, formed Levitt & Sons. At 22, Levitt became president of the newly formed building firm. He was responsible for marketing, sales and financing.

Even during the Great Depression, Levitt's flamboyant sales patter managed to persuade the upper middle classes to part with their dollars. After Levitt sold 18 houses from the original development, the firm committed to build another 600 over a four-year period.

Despite Levitt's incredible success – two developments in Manhasset, Long Island that totalled more than 2000 houses – some dubious ethical practices regarding sales would return to haunt him. The grandson of a rabbi, Levitt restricted who could purchase his new houses: no Jews, no blacks. It was a practice that stained Levitt's reputation.

In the 1940s, Levitt & Sons switched its strategy from building housing for the well-off to the construction of mass-market housing. Traditionally, builders in the United States built three to four houses a year. Levitt planned to build up to 40 a day. Construction was based on assembly-line production, broken down into its constituent parts – 27 of them. A specialist team was assigned to each process. There was a team for carpentry, for tiling, for roofing. There was even a team for red paint and one for white paint.

In 1944, Levitt was called up to serve with the Navy construction unit in Oahu, Hawaii. While Levitt was in the military, his brother and father were buying tracts of potato farmers' land on the Hempstead Plains in Nassau County, Long Island, New York. The plan was to build a self-contained community of 6000 homes to meet the huge pent-up demand for low-cost housing in post-war America. In creating what was by far the largest-ever planned housing development in the United States, Levitt's brother and father bought the land and planned the houses while Levitt schmoozed the politicians and persuaded them to rewrite the planning laws.

Construction started in 1947 on 7.3 square miles of land in Nassau County, and became the most celebrated (and at times criticized) development in the United States. By 1951, there were over 17,400 homes.

In 1954, the brothers agreed to go their separate ways. It was an inevitable parting. Levitt was a flamboyant roisterer with a stylish Manhattan apartment and celebrity friends. *Time* magazine called him a 'cocky rambunctious hustler'. His brother Alfred was quiet and retiring and embarrassed about his brother's taste for the limelight.

It was a difficult time for Levitt's company, which went public in 1960, but posted a loss of $1.4 million in 1961. Demand for housing was falling and land suitable for building was becoming scarce. Levitt spread out his projects, undertaking small developments both in the United States and abroad. In Puerto Rico, he successfully completed a development with 12,000 homes. By the end of the 1960s, the business was back on track and making profits.

In 1967, Levitt pulled off the biggest deal of his career, negotiating the sale of his building firm to **Harold Geneen's** International Telephone & Telegraph Corporation (ITT). With a price tag of $92 million, it seemed like tremendous deal for Levitt, who ostensibly became a multimillionaire with $62 million worth of ITT stock.

The downside was that Levitt lost the thing that defined him as a person; he gave up the right to build housing in the United States for ten years. As a tax planning measure, Levitt held on to his ITT shares, borrowing against them to raise cash. When the shares slumped to 10 percent of their original value, Chase Manhattan bank stepped in and seized the stock as security.

In the 1980s, Levitt attempted a comeback but had lost the magic touch. He became involved in suspect financial practices and diverted funds from his business to feed his extravagant lifestyle. As a result, he was barred from doing business in New York and accused of siphoning $70 million from his family's charities. Optimistic to the end, he died in 1993 still talking about his imminent comeback. 'I have a regular organization ready to punch in full time. I need another six months,' he said in his last interview. He died three months later.

Key texts
- Margaret Lundrigan Ferrer and Tova Navarra. *Levittown: The First 50 Years*. Arcadia, 1997

- Herbert J. Gans. *The Levittowners: Ways of Life and Politics in a New Suburban Community.* Pantheon, 1967

LFT (latest finish time)

See Critical-path analysis.

Lewin, Kurt

German-American psychologist (1890–1947)

Kurt Lewin fled from the Nazis to America in 1933, where he worked at MIT founding a research centre for group dynamics. His work was at the forefront of the research into group dynamics, which formed the basis for much of the theorizing of the human-resource school of the 1950s.

In 1946, Lewin was called into a troubled area of Connecticut to help create better relations between the black and Jewish communities. He found there that bringing together groups of people was a very powerful means of exposing areas of conflict. The groups were christened T-Groups, with the T standing for training.

The theory underlying T-Groups and the Lewin model of change was that behaviour patterns need to be 'unfrozen' before they can be changed and then 'refrozen.' T-Groups were a means of making this happen.

Keen to take the idea forward, Lewin began making plans to establish a 'cultural island' where T-Groups could be examined more closely. A suitable location was identified shortly before Lewin's premature death, which robbed the human-relations movement of its central figure. The National Training Laboratories for Group Dynamics were established in Bethel, Maine, and proved highly influential to an entire generation of human-relations specialists, including **Warren Bennis**, **Douglas McGregor**, **Robert Blake**, **Chris Argyris** and **Ed Schein**.

Key text

- Kurt Lewin. *A Dynamic Theory of Personality.* McGraw-Hill, 1935

Likert, Rensis

American psychologist (1903–1981)

Psychologist Rensis Likert was a pioneer of attitude surveys and poll design, as well as social research as a whole. Originally from Cheyenne, Wyoming, Likert studied civil engineering at the University of Michigan. He then changed tack to major in sociology and economics. He completed a doctorate in psychology at Columbia University.

Likert then joined the psychology faculty at New York University before leaving academia to become director for research at the Life Insurance Sales Research Bureau in Hartford, Connecticut. Likert moved on to work on statistics at the US Department of Agriculture before returning to academia to form the Survey Research Center at the University of Michigan in Ann Arbor. This developed into the Institute for Social Research. Likert was also professor of psychology and sociology at the university.

While Likert was a doctoral student at Columbia University, his 1932 doctoral thesis was entitled 'A Technique for the Measurement of Attitudes'. This introduced a straightforward five-point scale by which attitudes could be measured. The now well-known scale ranges from strongly agree to strongly disagree. This became known as the Likert Scale. Later, Likert examined supervision styles in the insurance industry and interviewed farmers to discover their attitudes toward government programmes.

During the World War II, Likert was highly active in studies related to the war effort. Most notably, Likert was involved in the Strategic Bombing Survey, in which he examined the effect of bombing campaigns on the morale of the populace. The conclusions had a major effect on government policy in the post-war years. Likert's groups found that light bombing decreased morale, while heavy bombing was likely to have little effect on morale. This conclusion has provided justification for such campaigns as that waged in Kosovo in 1999.

Likert's business research focused on the ways in which participative groups could improve management and performance, and on the human systems that exist in organizations. 'The greater the loyalty of a group toward the group, the greater is the motivation among the members to achieve the goals of the group, and the greater the probability that the group will achieve its goals,' he wrote. Likert identified four types – Systems 1 to 4 – of management style. The first is exploitative and authoritarian; the second, 'benevolent autocracy'; the third, 'consultative'; and the fourth, 'participative'. The latter was seen by Likert as the best option, both in a business and a personal sense. He also proposed System 5, in which there was no formal authority. 'Each system tends to mold people in its own image. Authoritarian organizations tend to develop dependent people and few leaders. Participative organizations tend to develop emotionally and socially mature persons capable of effective interaction, initiative, and leadership,' wrote Likert in his key book, *New Patterns of Management*.

In *New Patterns of Management*, Likert provides a blueprint of the ideal organization that has largely stood the test of time – though it has not, except in a few cases, become reality. Likert's description of the organizational ideal would be at home in an issue of ***Fast Company*** magazine: 'An organization should be outstanding in its performance if it has competent personnel, if it has leadership which develops highly effective groups and uses the overlapping group form of structure, and if it achieves effective communication and influence, decentralized and coordinated decision-making, and high performance goals coupled with high motivation,' he wrote.

Key texts
- Rensis Likert. *New Patterns of Management*. McGraw-Hill, 1961

- Rensis Likert. *The Human Organization, Its Management & Value*. McGraw-Hill, 1967
- Rensis Likert. *New Ways Of Managing Conflict*. McGraw-Hill, 1976

Line extension

When an existing product line or brand is expanded through the addition of a new flavour, for example, or other modification, the practice is called 'line extension'. An example might be the addition of a dark-chocolate version of a chocolate bar to the existing product line, or the introduction of an ice-cream version of a branded chocolate bar.

One advantage of line extension is that it protects a product line from competition by anticipating a rival's product development and preventing the rival from filling a gap in the market. A possible disadvantage, however, is that rather than adding additional customers, it merely spreads the existing customers over a wider product range. When a company extends its product line, there is always a risk that without sufficient product differentiation, the new product will cannibalize the brand; i.e. it will draw customers from other products in the same line rather than new customers.

Liquidity ratio

The liquidity ratio, also known as the **acid test ratio** and the quick ratio, is the proportion of a company's assets in a readily cashable form. It is a commonly used measurement of a company's ability to meet short-term debts. The liquidity ratio is calculated by dividing current assets minus stock by current liabilities. If a company has assets of $10,000 and liabilities of $20,000, the liquidity ratio is 0.5, or 50 cents on the dollar. If the company was forced by its creditors to pay its debts, it would be unable to pay them and, therefore, be insolvent. A liquidity ratio of any figure less than 0.7 may indicate that the company is in potential difficulties. However, in some industries, liquidity ratios are traditionally low.

Listed stock

A listed security is one listed on a stock exchange, such as the **New York Stock Exchange** or **London Stock Exchange**, and capable of being bought and sold on the open market.

Loan

A loan is a sum of money lent at a rate of interest. The loan will usually be at a fixed rate of interest for a specified time. Assets belonging to the borrower are usually required as security for loans advanced by banks. With a loan to a small company, a bank will usually request that a director personally guarantee the loan with assets of his own, to prevent the borrower from defaulting on the loan and sheltering behind the restricted liability of a limited company. Historically, the loan industry took some time to develop because of biblical prohibitions on the charging of usury.

Medieval philosopher St Thomas Aquinas summed up the position in his *Summa Theologica*: 'Hence it is by its very nature unlawful to take payment for the use of money lent, which payment is known as usury: and just as man is bound to restore ill-gotten goods, so is he bound to restore the money which he has taken in usury.' The biblical source is Deuteronomy 23:19: 'You shall not lend upon interest to your brother, interest on money, interest on victuals, interest on anything that is lent for interest.'

When Henry VIII concluded his separation from the Roman church in 1534 with the British Act of Supremacy, he also took the opportunity, in 1545, to legalize the payment of interest to a maximum of 10 percent per annum. It took several hundred more years for a limit on the rate of interest chargeable to be removed. As late as 1787, philosopher Jeremy Bentham was writing *Defence of Usury*. In Canada, interest rate caps were only removed from the statutes in 1967.

Key text
- Benjamin N. Nelson. *The Idea of Usury: From Tribal Brotherhood to Universal Otherhood*. Princeton University Press, 1949

Locke, Christopher

Author and marketing expert (b. 1947)

'Markets are conversations and those conversations are getting smarter and faster than most companies,' says Christopher Locke. At personalization.com, editor and publisher Locke stimulates debate among the **e-business** industry about how personalization techniques will shape the nature of e-commerce and e-marketing strategies.

It is a theme echoed in the book *The Cluetrain Manifesto*, co-authored by Locke, in which he challenges assumptions about transacting business in a digital world. The book highlights how customers and employees have found a voice on bulletin boards and in chat rooms, e-groups and Web sites – a voice companies would do well to listen to.

In his follow-up book, *Gonzo Marketing*, Locke – a contributor to publications such as *Internet World*, *Byte* and *The Industry Standard* – examined the shift from mass-market broadcast advertising to narrowcast Web-based Internet advertising and the challenges it presents.

Key texts
- Christopher Locke. *Gonzo Marketing: Winning Through Worst Practices*. Perseus, 2001
- Rick Levine, Christopher Locke, Doc Searls and David Weinberger. *The Cluetrain Manifesto: The End of Business as Usual*. Perseus, 2000

Key links
- www.personalization.com
- www.cluetrain.com

Lockup clause

The underwriters of a new share issue may prevent the management and other employees of the company from selling their stock for a minimum period of time following the IPO. The stock is not transferable during the lockup period. This type of clause is known as a lockup clause. It is often used to tie in **entrepreneurs** and other key personnel after an **IPO** or **MBO**.

Logo

A logo is a symbol representing a business, often linked to a brand name or trademark. It may be the name of a company in special type, or a drawing, or a combination of letters and pictures. The logo should be designed to present a positive image of the company to others and be part of the marketing strategy of the organization. Well-known logos include the Nike swoosh and the Chrysler star. Writer Naomi Klein took an interesting and alternative look at the rise and merit of the logo and what it stands for in her book *No Logo*.

Key text
- Naomi Klein. *No Logo: Taking Aim at the Brand Bullies*. Picador, 2000

Key link
- www.nologo.org

London Stock Exchange

The London Stock Exchange (LSE) is London's principal stock exchange. It was founded in 1773, when 150 brokers who had been thrown out of Royal Exchange for bad behaviour convened at Jonathan's Coffee House 13 years later. In 1801, it became a regulated Exchange. The market underwent its biggest reorganization 150 years later. In 1986, a reorganization dubbed 'the big bang' introduced a number of changes. It allowed ownership of member firms by outside corporations, and firms were able to operate as both brokers and dealers, a function previously separated. At the same time, the LSE became a private limited company. In July 2001, the London Stock Exchange received a listing itself. Its shares are tradable on the Exchange's main market.

The LSE provides services in three principal areas. It provides markets for companies to raise capital; it provides trading services for those wishing to buy and sell shares in listed companies; and it provides both real-time and historical information to market users worldwide.

Key text
- Ranald C. Michie. *The London Stock Exchange – A History*. Oxford University Press, 1999

Key link
- www.londonstockexchange.com

Loss leader

A loss leader is a good or service deliberately offered to the consumer at a price that is less than the cost of production. This may be to persuade customers to buy other products: for example, a supermarket may sell baked beans or bread at below cost in order to attract customers into the supermarket. Loss leading may also be a promotional device to persuade consumers to try out a product or service in the hope that they will buy more at full price in the future.

Loyalty

During the more stable times of the 1950s and 1960s, corporate executives enjoyed careers built on solid foundations. This was the era of corporate man (there was no such thing as corporate woman at this time). Grey-suited and obedient, corporate man was unstintingly loyal to his employer. He spent his life with a single company and rose slowly, but quietly, up the hierarchy.

Implicit to such careers was the understanding that loyalty and solid performance brought job security. This was mutually beneficial. The executive gained a respectable income and a high degree of security. The company gained loyal, hardworking executives.

This unspoken pact became known as the psychological contract, a kind of corporate loyalty bond. The originator of the phrase was the social psychologist **Ed Schein** of MIT. While the phrase is comparatively recent, blind corporate loyalty is longstanding. 'The most important single contribution required of an executive, certainly the most universal qualification, is loyalty [allowing] domination by the organization personality,' noted **Chester Barnard** in *The Functions of the Executive* (1938). (The word 'domination' suggests which way Barnard saw the balance of power falling.) While loyalty is a positive quality, it can easily become blinkered. What if the corporate strategy is wrong or the company is engaged in unlawful or immoral acts? Also, there is the question of loyal to what? Thirty years ago, corporate values were assumed rather than explored.

Loyalty meant that executives were hardly encouraged to look over the corporate parapets to seek out broader viewpoints. The corporation became a self-contained and self-perpetuating world, supported by a complex array of checks, systems and hierarchies. The company was right. Customers, who existed in the ethereal world outside the organization, were often regarded as peripheral.

Clearly, such an environment was hardly conducive to the fostering of dynamic risk-takers. The psychological contract rewarded the steady foot soldier, the safe pair of hands. It was hardly surprising, therefore, that when she came to examine corporate life for the first time in her 1977 book, *Men and Women of the Corporation*, **Rosabeth Moss Kanter** found that the central characteristic expected of a manager was 'dependability'.

The reality was that the psychological contract placed a premium on loyalty rather than ability and allowed a great many poor performers to seek out corporate havens. It was also significant that the psychological contract was regarded as the preserve of management. Lower down the hierarchy, people were hired and fired with abandon. Their loyalty counted for little.

As the use of the past tense suggests, recent years have seen radical changes to the psychological contract between employers and employees. The rash of **downsizing** in the 1980s and 1990s marked the end of the psychological contract.

Expectations have now changed on both sides. Employers no longer wish to make commitments – even implicit ones – to long-term employment. The emphasis is on flexibility. On the other side, employees are keen to develop their skills and take charge of their own careers. **Employability** is the height of fashion.

As a result, the new psychological contract is more likely to be built on developing skills than blind loyalty. The logic is that if a company invests in an individual's development, the employee will become more loyal. The trouble is that the employee also becomes more employable by other companies.

In the age of flexible employment, downsizing and **career** management, conventional loyalty is increasingly elusive as managers flit from job to job, company to company. Yet, at the same time, some research suggests that free agents, the managers who take control of and responsibility for their own careers, tend to be more loyal to their new employers than their previous employers. The logic behind this is that those who have remained with their employer since 1989 have usually seen a decrease in opportunities and their view of the company has probably suffered a buffeting. Those who left tend, therefore, to feel that their decision was the right one and feel more benevolent toward their current employer.

Key texts

- Edgar G. Schein. *Organizational Culture and Leadership*. Jossey-Bass, 1997
- Edgar G. Schein. *Organizational Psychology*. Third edition, Prentice Hall, 1980

LST (latest start time)

See Critical-path analysis.

Ltd

See Incorporation.

Luce, Henry Robinson

Publishing magnate; founder, Time Inc. (1898–1967)

Born on 3 April 1898, in Tengchow, China, Henry Robinson Luce's upbringing was an austere one. His daily schedule began at six in the morning with a cold bath, followed by a half-hour of Bible study plus six hours of Chinese lessons a day. A precocious scholar, Luce remained in China until he was 14. He attended the British-run boarding school in Chefoo.

After Chefoo, Luce continued his outstanding scholastic record at the Hotchkiss School in Connecticut. He received the highest marks in the country in his Greek exams, was included on the honour roll, and was the leader of his class in most subjects. Extracurricular activities included a role as editor-in-chief of the *Hotchkiss Literary Monthly* as well as assistant managing editor of the weekly school newspaper *The Record*. Luce had found his vocation.

At Yale, Luce started his career publishing in earnest. With fellow student and ex-Hotchkiss pupil Briton Hadden, Luce radically overhauled the Yale newspaper, the *Daily News*. On graduation in 1920, Luce was voted 'most brilliant' and Hadden 'most likely to succeed'. After Yale, Luce headed for Oxford, England, where he studied history. When he returned to the United States, he worked on the *Chicago Daily News* and then the *Baltimore News*. In Baltimore, Luce joined his old friend Hadden. Together they developed a plan to launch a new weekly news magazine called *Facts*. When the magazine was launched, it was called *Time: The Weekly-News Magazine*.

In February 1922, the pair left Baltimore for New York. They managed to raise launch funds (partly through a share issue), and incorporated the business on 28 November 1922. To decide who would edit the magazine and who would manage the business side of things, Hadden and Luce tossed a coin. Luce lost and became the business manager. The first issue of *Time* hit the newsstands in March 1923, with a cover price of 15 cents. With the law stating that any news more than 24 hours old belonged in the public domain, news elements of the magazine came almost entirely from *The New York Times*.

Distribution of the first issue was farcical, with a major subscribing mix-up meaning many subscribers failed to receive their issue. But from that inauspicious start, circulation grew steadily. By the third year, it had reached 110,000, with advertising revenue of $283,000, and in 1927, the new magazine made a profit of $3860. By 1928, that figure had increased to $126,000 and from that point onward, figures improved rapidly.

By 1927, *Time* had moved again, coming to rest eventually in Manhattan, just off of Fifth Avenue. Luce's lifelong friend Hadden died from a streptococcus infection in February 1929. Luce was left in sole charge of the magazine.

As editor, Luce assaulted his readers with an array of innovative literary devices: compound words such as 'sexational' and the more successful 'socialite' made their debut on the pages of *Time*. Foreign words such as tycoon – from the Japanese *taikun*, meaning prince – and pundit – from the Hindu *pandit*, meaning sage – were popularized by Luce. He also made common the use of euphemisms such as 'great and good friend' for mistress, to skirt potentially libellous issues.

Luce's next publication was *Fortune* magazine, based on his instinct that 'business is obviously the greatest single, common denominator of interest among the active leading citizens of the United States – our best men are in business'. Founded in 1929, *Fortune* was two years in the planning.

Although the first issue of *Fortune*, 30,000 copies in all, rolled off the presses just three months after the spectacular stock market crash of October 1929, the first issue was well received, and the magazine survived the economic depression that followed. By 1937, revenues were up to $500,000 and circulation in excess of 460,000. Through the ensuing decades, *Fortune* catalogued the ups and downs of US business life.

Over the next 30 years, Luce built a publishing business with a worldwide circulation of over 13 million. *Time* and *Fortune* were joined by *Life* magazine in 1936 and *Sports Illustrated* in 1954.

In 1967, the circulation of Luce's flagship magazine was some 7,500,000. Advertising, which was twice as much as for any other magazine, brought in $170 million to Time Inc. *Time* magazine itself sold some 3,500,000, yielding $86 million in advertising revenue. The company that Luce founded on a budget of $86,000 had total revenues in excess of $500 million, with profits of $37 million.

Luce suffered a heart attack in 1958 but carried on working. In February 1967, he was still at the helm of his empire when he suffered a fatal heart attack.

Key texts

- David Cort. *The Sin of Henry R. Luce: An Anatomy of Journalism*. Carol Publishing Group, 1974
- W.A. Swanberg. *Luce and His Empire*. Scribner, 1972

M

Macaroni defence

The macaroni defence is employed by companies to avoid a takeover. The target company issues a substantial number of bonds, which are redeemable on the condition that the company is taken over. The redemption price is fixed at a high level, thus making the company an unattractive takeover target. This tactic is similar to the **poison pill,** except that the poison pill uses equity instead of bonds.

Machiavelli, Niccolò

Florentine diplomat (1469–1527)

Power is a fact of corporate life, and there's no doubt as to its patron saint: the Florentine diplomat and author Niccolò Machiavelli. Machiavelli's bible on power is *The Prince*. Within it, embedded beneath details of Alexander VI's tribulations, lie a ready supply of aphorisms and insights which are, perhaps sadly, as appropriate to many of today's managers and organizations as they were half a millennium ago.

Machiavelli portrayed a world of cunning and brutal opportunism. 'I believe also that he will be successful who directs his actions according to the spirit of the time, and that he whose actions do not accord with the time will not be successful,' he wrote.

Machiavelli gave advice on managing change and sustaining motivation, and even had advice for executives acquiring companies in other countries: 'But when states are acquired in a country differing in language, customs, or laws, there are difficulties, and good fortune and great energy are needed to hold them, and one of the greatest and most real helps would be that he who has acquired them should go and reside there … Because if one is on the spot, disorders are seen as they spring up, and one can quickly remedy them; but if one is not at hand, they are heard of only when they are great, and then one can no longer remedy them.' Executives throughout the world will be able to identify with Machiavelli's analysis.

Above all, Machiavelli was the champion of leadership through cunning and intrigue, the triumph of force over reason. An admirer of Borgia, Machiavelli had a dismal view of human nature. Unfortunately, as he sagely pointed out, history has repeatedly proved that a combination of being armed to the teeth and devious is more likely to allow you to achieve your objectives. It is all very well being good, said Machiavelli, but the leader 'should know how to enter into evil when necessity commands'.

Key text
- Niccolò Machiavelli. *The Prince*. Bantam Classics, 1984

Macroeconomics

Macroeconomics is the study of economics – the big picture. It is the branch of economics that is concerned with the study of whole economies or systems. It may include aspects such as balance of payments, fiscal policy, government income and expenditure, investment, inflation and unemployment. It aims to obtain an understanding of the influence of all economic factors on each other and quantify and predict aggregate national income. Macroeconomics deals with such questions as: What impact does government policy have on the economy? What effect does international trade have on the economy? Why do business cycles exist? It is to be contrasted with **microeconomics**, which looks at economics at the level of companies or constituent parts of an economy.

Management by objectives

Management by objectives motivates the workforce within an organization by providing each level of management, and often employees as well, with specific objectives to be achieved during a specific period of time. These objectives are determined by both the subordinates and their superiors. Performance is then periodically measured against the objectives selected. The Austrian management guru **Peter Drucker**, in his book *The Practice of Management*, claimed that management by objectives was the best way of delegating authority in a large organization.

Key text
- Peter F. Drucker. *The Practice of Management*. Harper & Row, 1954

Management by wandering around (MBWA)

Management by wandering around, or management by walking about, is the practice of senior managers interacting with the workforce by visiting the shop floor or offices where the general staff work. The concept was developed and pioneered by Dave Packard and Bill Hewlett at Hewlett-Packard during the 1970s. It was then popularized in the book *In Search of Excellence: Lessons From America's Best Run Companies*, by Tom Peters and Robert Waterman, who called the practice ' the technology of the obvious'. Their research

showed that those companies where managers actively engaged with employees and customers were more successful than those where the management was isolated. Not only does MBWA cut through the vertical lines of communication in a hierarchical organization structure; it also motivates the workforce by suggesting that senior management takes an active interest in them.

Key text
- Thomas J. Peters and Robert Waterman. *In Search of Excellence: Lessons From America's Best Run Companies*. HarperCollins, 1982

Management plan

In a start-up business, the strength of the management team is a key factor in most investors' decision-making. Start-ups need to show that they have people who have strong skills in the key areas of management. The management plan is the section of the business plan that demonstrates the strength of management to investors.

Elements covered in the management section include:

- **Key team members:** Their duties, experience and expertise.
- **The board of directors:** Who is on it and what role they play.
- **Advisers:** Details of the people, normally with extensive industry experience, who advise the start-up.
- **External consultants:** Experts who give the start-up advice.

Non-executive directors can be useful to add ballast to the management team. A special mention and background details are usually included for the founder or founders.

Managerial grid

See Robert Blake.

Managing demand

In an organization, demand must be managed in relation to capacity. There are three main methods of doing this: level-output production, chase-demand production and a mixture of the two.

Chase-demand strategy involves matching supply with demand as demand varies. This strategy is suitable for the end suppliers of a product or service that can closely match supply and demand. Dell, for example, as a computer manufacturer and retailer, can build computers to order. One problem with chase-demand strategy is that in periods of low demand, the company is working below maximum capacity and may have to lay off workers. Methods of chasing demand include employing staff on overtime when necessary; employing flexible and casual labour; buying components that are usually made in-house; and outsourcing elements of the production process.

An alternative to chase demand is level-output strategy, which, as the name implies, involves working to a level capacity. Level output adopts the approach of ignoring demand variations and setting production levels at the level of average demand with steady output. Thus, surplus stock produced in slack times can be used to meet consumer demand in busy times. Clearly this is not suitable for perishable stock.

Managing director

The managing director of a company is the company's most senior manager. He may also be known as the chief executive, or as **CEO** in the United States. The managing director is responsible for the day-to-day running of the company and has a seat on the board of the company. The managing director may also be the chairman of the company. In the United Kingdom, however, especially in large companies and particularly after the Cadbury Report (see **corporate governance**) corporate governance rules suggest that the role of chairman should be separate from that of managing director.

Margin of safety

An investing principle, the margin of safety is the difference between the independently assessed value of a company's stock by the investor and the market price, where the assessed value is in excess of the market price. Many factors go into the pricing of a stock on a stock market, and not all of them relate to the intrinsic value of the company. Rather, they may reflect on such things as market sentiment about a particular industry sector or market sentiment regarding the general economic situation. Margin of safety only looks at the price of the stock and the value of the company as an independent owner of the company would look at it. The concept was introduced by Benjamin Graham and David L. Dodd in their seminal book about investment, *Security Analysis* (1934). It is used by value investors to determine whether a stock is undervalued relative to its intrinsic price.

Key text
- Benjamin Graham and David L. Dodd. *Security Analysis.* Whittlesey House (McGraw-Hill), 1934

Market capitalization

A company's market capitalization is calculated by taking the number of shares issued by a company and multiplying by the price of the shares, to give the total market value of a company's issued share capital. The long-term debt and preferred shares issued by the company should also be included. Investors often use the ratio of working capital to market capitalization as an indicator of a company's financial health.

Market penetration

Market penetration is an aggressive pricing strategy used to gain a foothold in a new market. The company adopting the strategy prices goods or services at a low gross profit margin and relies on high turnover to cover overheads. The aim is to quickly penetrate the market with the new product and capture a large market share. After market penetration is achieved, prices can be raised if there is sufficient **brand loyalty**. One risk associated with the strategy is that the product may be permanently associated with low prices by consumers.

Market research

Market research is the process of gaining information about customers in a market through field research or desk research. Field research involves collecting primary data through such methods as interviewing customers, issuing questionnaires and holding panel discussions with small groups of people who meet on a regular basis to discuss a specific subject, led by a moderator. Desk research involves collecting secondary data by looking at information and statistics collected by others and published, for example, by the government. Market research was born, at least in North America, as far back as 1911, when the Curtis Publishing Company founded the first marketing research department. This was quickly followed by one of the first if not the first comprehensive readership survey conducted by R.O. Eastman, Advertising Manager for the *Kellogg Company*.

During the 1920s, George Gallup conducted the first newspaper public opinion poll, and the American Market Research Council was founded. The first focused interview is said to have been conducted by sociologist Robert Merton and Columbia University in 1941. The British professional body, the Market Research Society, was also formed during the 1940s. The second half of the twentieth century saw market research become ever more sophisticated as a variety of complex statistical and psychological techniques were introduced.

Market saturation

When a market becomes saturated, it means that all of the consumers who wish to purchase a product have done so. Therefore, a saturated market is usually a stable market. Once a market is saturated, the majority of sales, in the case of consumer durables, will come from replacement of items. The market for sports shoes worn for leisure purposes (i.e. trainers) is an example of a market that became saturated during the 1990s, as Nike found out to its cost when revenues stagnated after a long period of growth.

Market segmentation

Marketers believe that it is possible to identify unfulfilled market niches and prepare more effectively targeted advertising by segmenting a market for a product or service according to consumer needs. Markets can be segmented in several ways, including psychographically (according to attitudes, tastes and personality traits, such as aspirational, homely or image-conscious); geographically (by location – national, regional or local); and demographically (by age, sex or class, such as **baby boomers**, **Generation X** or **Generation Y**).

Market share

Market share is the percentage of a market taken by one company or a group of companies. It is measured in three main ways. First, it can be measured in terms of volume of sales: for example, Company A sold 60 percent of all cars sold last year in the US market. Second, it can be measured as the value of sales: for example, Company B sold 60 percent of the total value of all cars sold in the US market last year. Finally, it can be measured in terms of output by volume or value: for example, Company C could have produced 50 percent of all the cars made in the United States last year, even though its market share was only 30 percent because it exported cars to other markets, while some cars sold in the United States were produced in other countries.

In order to measure market share, it is necessary first to know the total size of the market, or market size as defined by the total sales of all companies operating in the industry, or, alternatively, the total number of units sold in the market.

Marketing mix

The concept of the marketing mix was conceived by US marketing guru **Philip Kotler**. It refers to the wide range of factors used to help market a company's products. Kotler's idea was further developed by American academic Jerome McCarthy in 1960, when he introduced the four Ps of marketing. McCarthy identified four critical ingredients of the marketing mix: product (branding, packaging and other features); price (retail price, discounted price and credit terms); place (where to sell the product); and promotion (free samples, competitions and other forms of promotion). The concept of the marketing mix has since been adopted and expanded by others, such as in Neil H. Borden's Borden mix and Frank Jefkins's 20-element marketing mix.

Key text
• Philip Kotler. *Kotler on Marketing*. Simon and Schuster, 1999

Marketing myopia

In his acclaimed article 'Marketing Myopia', written for the *Harvard Business Review* in 1960, American marketing academic **Theodore Levitt** suggested that many companies were handicapped by adopting a shortsighted approach to marketing, viewing it only from the company's perspective as a tool for selling the company's goods. Instead, he asserted, companies should look at marketing from the customer's point of view. Therefore, a company that sells sports shoes should not define its marketing in terms of the sales of sports shoes, but rather see itself as a company concerned with sports and the experience of sports.

Key text
• Theodore Levitt. 'Marketing Myopia.' *Harvard Business Review*, July/August 1960

Marketing plan

The marketing plan is an essential element in every start-up's business plan. It is there to explain to potential investors how the new business intends to attract customers. The marketing costs for a start-up can be huge. Therefore, the plan needs to be well thought out and budgeted. It must define the target market and consider factors such as demographics, age, income, spending habits and location. The investor will want all of this information.

Second, the marketing plan should explain how the new business intends to reach the customer. What advertising medium will it use? What will it cost? What expertise will be required? Will the company use a public relations firm? The marketing plan should demonstrate to the investor that the **entrepreneur** has thought carefully about marketing the product or service effectively.

Marketspace

W. Chan Kim and Renée Mauborgne, of the French business school INSEAD, have produced some of the most interesting work in the area of strategy in recent years. Companies, say Kim and Mauborgne, become mired in taking on their competitors in macho, head-to-head battles. If one company jumps ahead, the others follow by doing the same thing. Competitive advantage is short-lived and insubstantial – an incremental improvement here and there. Breaking free of the competition should be every company's objective. Only by creating its own 'marketspace' can a company achieve significant competitive advantage.

Kim and Mauborgne suggest that only by looking across industries rather than within industries can companies develop the necessary insights to break free. They point to the example of Home Depot, which looked more broadly at the home improvement needs of its consumers and recognized that different consumers have different needs.

Kim and Mauborgne suggest that companies look at buyers within their industry, similar and complementary products, as well as 'across the functional-emotional orientation of an industry'. By looking at old data in new ways, inspirations and insights may arise.

Key text
- W. Chan Kim and Renée Mauborgne. 'Creating New Marketspace.' *Harvard Business Review*, January/February 1999

Mark-up

A good's mark-up is calculated by taking the selling price and subtracting the direct or variable cost of producing the good. For example, a 50 percent mark-up on a good with a direct cost of $5 would mean that the company would sell the good for $7.50. The mark-up has to cover indirect and overhead costs as well as produce a profit.

Maslow, Abraham

American behavioural psychologist (1908–1970)

Born in Brooklyn, Abraham Maslow studied at the University of Wisconsin. His career involved spells in management and academia. In two spells in industry, he worked as a plant manager at the Maslow Cooperage Corporation in Pleasanton, California, in the late 1940s, and with an electronics company in southern California. As an academic, he was initially interested in the social behaviour of primates and worked at Columbia University as a research fellow, Brooklyn College as an associate professor, the Western Behavioral Sciences Institute, and Brandeis University in Massachusetts. It was while working at Brandeis that he wrote *Motivation and Personality*. His other books included *Toward a Psychology of Being*

(1962), *Eupsychian Management* (1965), *The Psychology of Science* (1967) and *The Farther Reaches of Human Nature* (1971).

Maslow was a member of the human-relations school of the late 1950s. *Motivation and Personality* is his best-known work. It contains the exposition of his theory of a **'hierarchy of needs'** – a concept that was first introduced by Maslow in 1943. In the book, Maslow argues that there is an ascending scale of needs that need to be understood if people are to be motivated.

First are the fundamental physiological needs of warmth, shelter and food. 'It is quite true that man lives by bread alone – when there is no bread. But what happens to man's desires when there is plenty of bread and when his belly is chronically filled?' Maslow asks.

Once basic physiological needs are met, others emerge to dominate. 'If the physiological needs are relatively well gratified, there then emerges a new set of needs, which we may categorize roughly as the safety needs,' writes Maslow. 'A man, in this state, if it is extreme enough and chronic enough, may be characterized as living almost for safety alone.'

Next on the hierarchy are social or love needs, and ego or self-esteem needs. Ultimately, as man moves up the scale, with each need being satisfied, he will reach what Maslow labels 'self-actualization': the individual's own personal potential. (Later, Maslow created the word 'Eupsychian' to describe 'the culture that would be generated by 1000 self-actualizing people on some sheltered island where they would not be interfered with'.)

Maslow's hierarchy of needs contributed to the emergence of human relations as a discipline and to a sea change in how motivation was perceived. Instead of being simplistically regarded as driven by punishment and deprivation, motivation became intrinsically linked to rewards. Maslow's concept of 'self-actualization' is increasingly the subject of ~~managerial~~ texts.

Key texts
- Abraham H. Maslow. *Motivation and Personality*. Harper & Row, 1954

- Abraham H. Maslow. *Towards a Psychology of Being.* Van Nostrand, 1968 (reprint)
- Abraham H. Maslow. *Eupsychian Management.* Irwin, 1965
- Abraham H. Maslow. *The Psychology of Science.* Harper, 1966
- Abraham H. Maslow. *Farther Reaches of Human Nature.* Viking, 1971

Mass production

Mass production is the large-scale manufacturing of goods, aiming for low unit cost and high output. In factories, mass production is achieved by a variety of means, such as division and specialization of labour and mechanization. These speed up production and allow the manufacture of near-identical, interchangeable parts. Such parts can then be assembled quickly into a finished product on an assembly line. The technique was first implemented by American car manufacturing pioneer **Henry Ford** in 1908, for the manufacture of the Model T Ford car.

Mass production usually involves manufacturing goods for a mass market. A mass market is the market for a product or service used by a high percentage of the population. Cars, refrigerators and training shoes are all products aimed at mass markets. Marketing a product or service to a large proportion of the population is, not surprisingly, termed mass marketing, as opposed to niche marketing, which targets a small, selective market segment.

Key text
- Elmer Loemker. *100 Million Motor Vehicles. A Story of Mass Production and its Effect on the United States.* Detroit, Automobile Manufacturers Association, 1948

Master of Business Administration (MBA)

A Master of Business Administration is a popular post-graduate degree studying business and management. In Europe, most MBAs, with a few notable exceptions such as the London School of Business, are earned over the course of a single academic year. In the United States, however, courses tend to run for two years. In two-year courses, the first year is taken up by core curriculum in essential business disciplines, such as finance, economics and organizational structure. In the second year, the student takes electives – specialist courses – and can tailor his degree to his own interests.

The MBA has always been a passport to higher earnings, often a six-figure salary, although the increasing number of students taking the qualification has reduced its value slightly in the eyes of employers. Nonetheless, despite the expense and difficulty of getting into the top programmes – including Harvard, Stanford, Wharton and Sloan – MBAs are still a good means of obtaining a senior position with an excellent salary.

Key link
- www.businessweek.com/bschools

Matrix management model

In the beginning, management was concerned with command and control. Organizations were neat, hierarchical and linear, with simple chains of command: worker A reported to manager B who reported to senior manager C who reported to board member D who reported to the managing director.

As companies became larger, they began to organize themselves differently. In the 1920s, the American company Dupont championed the idea of what became known as federal decentralization. This gave the headquarters responsibility for core central functions such as finance and marketing. Business units were granted greater autonomy and responsibility for their own performance. This approach was championed by **Alfred P. Sloan** at General Motors and later emulated by the likes of General Electric and Shell.

Federal decentralization brought professional rigour to management. However, its fundamental flaws were that one central function tended to emerge as the dominant one (in General Motors' case, finance became the behemoth); it did little to share value, information and knowledge between units; and it helped create an entire layer of head-quarters-based middle managers whose value-adding role was increasingly difficult to determine.

The backlash to decentralization was centralization – taking power back to the corporate centre. Perhaps the greatest example is that of **Harold Geneen**, who managed ITT with obsessional vigour during the 1960s. He centralized information in his own formidable brain. Geneen got results, but the company unravelled after his departure.

There is a middle ground: matrix management. A hybrid of decentralization and centralization, matrix organization is organized in such a way that each unit has at least two bosses. Instead of being based around a linear chain of command, the matrix is multidimensional, depending on how many dimensions are deemed to be useful or practically possible. An organization may include regional managers, functional managers, country or continental managers and business sector managers. Thus a manager in a Venezuelan business unit of a multinational widget maker may be answerable – at different times – to the manager of the business unit; the country manager for Venezuela; the South American manager; the marketing chief; and the widget industry chief.

This lateral reporting can be a problem. Matrix management is complex, ambiguous and confusing. It's little wonder that it has generally had a bad – and somewhat bemused – press. In *In Search of Excellence*, **Tom Peters** and Robert Waterman were dismissive of matrix organization as 'a logistical mess', arguing that 'it automatically dilutes priorities' and that structure should be kept as simple as possible.

The criticisms may be justified but the matrix organization is, in fact, a more realistic delineation and description of responsibilities and hierarchies. In any healthy organization, different units must share information, resources and experiences. There are a great many overlapping areas of expertise and activity. Federal decentralization sought to deny them, actively working against such corporate teamwork.

The matrix organization is basically built around a network of responsibilities. It fosters broader perspectives. Managers don't view things within the narrow perspectives of their unit, their function or their fiefdom. Instead, they have to view things from a variety of perspectives – local, corporate, national, international, global and functional.

It is notable that the companies that have made matrix management work successfully are large European multinationals. Philips developed the concept after the World War II, but found that national management structures came to dominate – something it spotted and changed. Royal Dutch Shell also used matrix management.

The most notable contemporary exponent of the concept has been Asea Brown Boveri (ABB), the Swiss-Swedish industrial giant. Under **Percy Barnevik**, the company erected a highly complex matrix system with a group of 250 handpicked 'global' executives (including 136 country managers and 50 business area managers) leading 210,000 employees in 1300 companies, divided into 5000 profit centres located in almost 150 countries, and in four product segments and one financial-services segment.

The ABB system displays the full complexity of matrix management. Business segments – run by a senior manager – were divided into business areas that were treated as worldwide businesses. On the other axis of the matrix, ABB was organized by regions (the Americas, Asia, Europe) or groupings of countries.

The key to actually making this labyrinth work was Barnevik's passionate belief in communication. Matrix management was a means of ensuring that information and resources found their optimum place. This could only be achieved through incessant communication between managers – the kind of communication that matrix management necessitates.

While matrix management clearly worked for ABB, it was also heavily reliant on the dynamic brilliance of Percy Barnevik. He effectively made sense of the manifest ambiguity and confusion caused by the system. He made it work. It is significant that his successor, Goran Lindahl, partly dismantled the matrix structure.

Key texts
- Kevin Barham and Claudia Heimer. *ABB: The Dancing Giant*. FT/Pitman, 1998
- Michael Goold, Andrew Campbell and Marcus Alexander. *Corporate-Level Strategy: Creating Value in the Multibusiness Company*. John Wiley, 1994
- Alfred P. Sloan. *My Years with General Motors*. Doubleday, 1963

Management buyout (MBO)

See Leveraged buyout.

Matsushita, Konosuke

Industrial giant and management guru (1894–1989)

Konosuke Matsushita was born in 1894 in the Wakayama Prefecture in Japan. Though Matsushita was born into a prosperous family, his life became difficult when his father was ruined financially by an unsuccessful rice deal. At the tender age of 9, Matsushita was forced to take work in a charcoal brazier shop in Osaka, followed by an apprenticeship in a bicycle shop.

In 1910, Matsushita was taken on as a wiring assistant at the Osaka Electrical Light Company (OELC). He was a quick learner, and his skill at wiring earned him rapid promotion. However, he left OELC in 1917 because of a debilitating lung condition, figuring that if he could start his own business, he would be able to work around his poor health.

With three employees, the equivalent of $50, and a prototype for a new type of electrical socket, Matsushita founded Matsushita Electrical Appliances on 15 June 1917, at the age of 23. The company became Matsushita Electrical Industrial Company Ltd. – MEI – in 1935. Business was tough until Matsushita developed the company's first mass-market product – a battery-powered bicycle lamp shaped like a bullet. The lamp was unique because it could run for up to 40 hours. Some customers even used it to light their houses.

A good engineer and a better marketer, Matsushita used demand for his bicycle lamp to construct a network of salesmen throughout Japan. Once he had established countrywide distribution, he put the trademark 'National' on Matsushita products and lowered prices to make the lamp a mass-market product. He also pioneered the use of national newspaper advertising, a relatively rare sight in Japan in the 1920s.

Matsushita was an extremely enlightened manager for his time. For example, he adopted the company slogan 'Harmony between corporate profit and social justice'. In 1933, long before corporate missions and corporate values were fashionable in management circles, Matsushita formulated his 'five guiding principles' (to which two more were added in 1937), to shape the conduct of the company. The principles, which are still adhered to today, were service to the public; fairness and honesty; teamwork for the common cause; untiring effort for improvement; courtesy and humility; accord with natural laws; and gratitude with blessings.

A number of decisions that Matsushita made during the 1930s highlighted the leadership style that was to earn him the nickname the 'god of management'. Despite the recession of 1930, Matsushita recruited underemployed factory workers to go out and sell the stockpiled unsold inventory instead of making wholesale layoffs. In 1931, he bought the rights to a radio patent, which he then made freely available to the market. This was an expensive ploy by Matsushita, but it had the effect of stimulating the market and so ultimately benefited the company. In 1932, Matsushita declared that entrepreneurs and manufacturers should aim 'to make all products as inexhaustible and as cheap as tap water'.

In post-World War II Japan, MEI was subject to the severe restrictions imposed on certain Japanese companies by the Allies. Matsushita only avoided being deposed as president through a petition from 15,000 employees in his support. In 1946, he founded the PHP Institute (Peace and Happiness through Prosperity Institute), devoting most of his time to it. On his return to company duties in 1950, he reinvigorated the company, reorganizing it along divisional lines. He also reassessed business processes to make them more efficient and refocused the company on the core values he had expressed in the 1930s.

Over the next 23 years, Matsushita oversaw a huge expansion of the company as it exported its 'three treasures' – washing machines, refrigerators and televisions – as well as other electrical goods around the world. With brand names such as Panasonic and Technics, the company grew to become one of the largest manufacturers of electrical goods in the world.

In his later life, especially after retiring as chairman in 1973, Matsushita concentrated much of his time on developing and explaining his social and commercial philosophies. During his lifetime, he wrote 44 books. The most popular was *Developing a Road to Peace and Happiness Through Prosperity*, which sold more than 4 million copies. He continued to teach his unique concept of management until his death of pneumonia on 27 April 1989. He was 94.

Key texts
- John P. Kotter. *Matsushita Leadership: Lessons from the 20th Century's Most Remarkable Entrepreneur*. Free Press, 1997
- Konosuke Matsushita. *Quest for Prosperity: The Life of a Japanese Industrialist*. PHP Institute, Inc., 1988
- Rowland Gould. *The Matsushita Phenomenon*. Diamond Sha, 1970

Mauborgne, Renée

Winner of the Eldridge Haynes Prize, awarded by the Academy of International Business and the Eldridge Haynes Memorial Trust of Business International, for the best original paper in the field of international business Renée Mauborgne is the INSEAD Distinguished Fellow and a professor of Strategy and Management at INSEAD in Fontainebleau, France and Fellow of the World Economic Forum. She has served as an advisor for a number of multinational corporations in Europe, the US and Pacific Asia.

Over fifteen years Professor Mauborgne has worked as a team with INSEAD colleague W. Chan Kim. Together they have co-authored more than 50 academic and managerial articles. In conducting their research and testing their ideas in companies, their collaboration has occurred across the three continents of the US, Europe, and Asia. They are the co-founders of the Value Innovation Network, a global group of academics, consultants, and business practitioners that spans the three continents developing and practicing the Value Innovation family of concepts. -+

Professor Mauborgne's current research focuses on strategy, innovation and wealth creation in the knowledge economy. Her recent work, with W. Chan Kim, includes the newly released article, 'Charting your Company's Future' (*Harvard Business Review*, June, 2002), as well as the worldwide best-selling articles 'Knowing a Winning Business Idea When You See One' (*Harvard Business Review*, September–October, 2000), 'Creating New Market Space' (*Harvard Business Review*, January–February, 1999), 'Value Innovation: The Strategic Logic of High Growth' (*Harvard Business Review*, January–February, 1997) and 'Fair Process: Managing in the Knowledge Economy' (*Harvard Business Review*, July–August 1997).

Key link
- www.insead.edu

Mayer, Louis B.

Hollywood mogul; co-founder, Metro-Goldwyn-Mayer (1885–1957)

The real-life story of Louis B. Mayer, the American film tycoon, reads like a script from one of his movies. Mayer hauled himself up from his humble beginnings as the son of an immigrant scrap-metal dealer to become a Hollywood legend.

Born Eliezar Mayer on 4 July 1885 in Minsk, Russia (now in Belarus), Mayer emigrated with his family to New Brunswick, Canada, in 1888. There Mayer's father built a small scrap metal concern into a profitable business, which Mayer joined fresh out of elementary school. Soon he had his own scrap business in Boston.

But Mayer had bigger plans. In 1907, he left the family business and bought a small, dilapidated movie theatre in Haverhill, Massachusetts. Soon he was the owner of the largest theatre chain in New England. The huge profits he raked in from showing one of the most popular films of its time, D.W. Griffith's *Birth of a Nation*, enabled Mayer to finance a movie career in Hollywood.

Louis B. Mayer Pictures was the movie-production company Mayer set up in Los Angeles. Initially, productions were funded by the proceeds of the movie chain business. Hollywood was still in its infancy. Though wealthy because of his movie theatre business, Mayer's fortune was small change in an industry dominated by fabulously wealthy powerbrokers. Marcus Loew was the mogul of all moguls. When Loew decided that he wanted to merge his own studio, Metro, with Louis B. Mayer Productions and the Samuel Goldwyn Company, Mayer's position in Hollywood was secure. In 1924, Metro-Goldwyn-Mayer – MGM – as formed with Mayer as vice-president.

Suddenly one of the most powerful men in Hollywood, with a stable of film stars at his disposal, Mayer settled into his role as an autocratic manipulative despot who ruled MGM through arch cunning. The late film scholar Ephraim Katz, author of *The Film Encyclopedia*, describes Mayer as 'a ruthless, quick-tempered, paternalistically tyrannical executive', a man who ruled MGM 'as one big family, rewarding obedience, punishing insubordination, and regarding opposition as personal betrayal'.

At the studio's own town, Culver City, movies were churned out the rate of one a week. Off-screen, Mayer was as ruthless as ever. He used the rise of the talkies as an excuse for a purge of the studio stars. Mayer cast stars that he had helped to make and that had made MGM successful from the lot: Buster Keaton, Erich von Stroheim and even Greta Garbo were dispensed with as Mayer and MGM marched on through the 1930s and 1940s.

Objections to MGM's increasing dominance of the movie industry were thwarted by the construction of an alliance under the banner of the Academy of Motion Pictures Arts and Sciences. Mayer, along with Douglas Fairbanks Sr, was a prime mover behind the Academy's creation in 1927.

In the 1950s, Mayer's ruthlessness eventually caught up with him when he was outmanoeuvered by the scheming of a new generation of studio executives. Ejected from MGM in 1951, he was replaced by Dore Schary. Mayer spent his remaining years trying to persuade the shareholders of MGM's parent company to reinstate him and dump Schary – to no avail. Mayer died of leukaemia in 1957. It was said at the time of his death that the reason that half of Hollywood attended Mayer's funeral was to check that the great man was indeed dead.

At MGM, Mayer presided over a golden age of film-making. He was responsible for a host of hits like *Ben Hur* (1926) and *Dinner at Eight* (1933). At his zenith, he commanded the highest salary in the world – more than a million dollars a year. Bob Hope said of Mayer that he 'came out west with twenty-eight dollars, a box camera and an old lion. He built a monument to himself – the Bank of America.'

Key texts

- Charles Higham. *Merchant of Dreams: Louis B. Mayer, M-G-M, and the Secret Hollywood*. Donald I. Fine Inc., 1993
- Diana Altman. *Hollywood East: Louis B. Mayer and the Origins of the Studio System*. Carol Publishing Group, 1992
- Neal Gabler. *An Empire of Their Own: How the Jews Invented Hollywood*. Doubleday, 1988
- Budd Schulberg. *Moving Pictures*. Stein and Day, 1982
- Gary Carey. *All the Stars in Heaven: Louis B. Mayer's MGM*. Dutton, 1981

- Samuel Marx. *Mayer and Thalberg: The Make-Believe Saints.* Random House, 1975
- Norman Zierold. *The Moguls.* Avon Books, 1972
- Bosley Crowther. *Hollywood Rajah: The Life and Times of Louis B. Mayer.* Holt, 1960

Key link
- www.mgm.com

Mayo, Elton

Australian psychologist (1880–1949)

Elton Mayo had an interestingly diverse career, though he remains best known for his contribution to the famous **Hawthorne** experiments in motivation. The Hawthorne Studies were carried out at Western Electric's Chicago plant between 1927 and 1932. Their significance lay not so much in their results and discoveries, though these were clearly important, but in the statement they made – that whatever the dictates of **mass production** and **scientific management**, people and their motivation were critical to the success of any business. The experiments also left an important legacy: the human-relations school of thinkers that emerged in the 1940s and 1950s.

Mayo's belief that humanity needed to be restored to the workplace struck a chord at a time when the dehumanizing side of mass production was beginning to be more fully recognized. 'So long as commerce specializes in business methods which take no account of human nature and social motives, so long may we expect strikes and sabotage to be the ordinary accompaniment of industry,' Mayo noted. He championed the case for teamworking and for improved communications between management and the workforce. The Hawthorne research revealed informal organizations between groups as a potentially powerful force that companies could utilize or ignore.

Mayo's work, and that of his fellow Hawthorne researchers, redressed the balance in management theorizing. The scientific bias of earlier researchers was put into a new perspective. Mayo's work served as a foundation for all who followed on the humanist side of the divide.

Key texts
- Elton Mayo. *The Social Problems of an Industrial Civilization.* Harvard University Press, 1945
- Elton Mayo. *The Human Problems of an Industrial Civilization.* Macmillan, 1933

McCormack, Mark

Sports management pioneer (b. 1930)

One of the most powerful people in sports, Mark McCormack was born on 6 November 1930. He had a privileged education, attending William and Mary College in Williamsburg, Virginia, the second-oldest educational institution in the United States, from which he graduated in 1951. But it was McCormack's extracurricular activities that led to his business success. A keen golfer from his early childhood, he played with his father on the local links and continued to play while at Yale Law School. A good rather than brilliant golfer, McCormack tried to make it as a pro. He qualified for the US Open as well as several US and British amateur championships, yet recognized his own limitations. Recalling his performance at the 1958 US Open, he said with brutal self-assessment: 'I had no chance, I didn't have a very good swing, and I wasn't very good.'

It was while on the intercollegiate golf tournament rounds in the 1950s that he ran into a promising player by the name of Arnold Palmer. While McCormack began to practise law with the firm of Arter and Hadden in Cleveland in 1960, Palmer, who won the 1958 US Masters, was threatening to unsettle the established golfing hierarchy.

McCormack, moonlighting from his law practice, set up a small sports services company, National Sports Management (NSM), with colleague Dick Taylor. The company booked exhibitions for a number of top golf players, including Arnold Palmer. When Palmer won the 1958 Masters, the administrative work began to be burdensome for him. 'You should have somebody take care of getting you the right insurance and helping you with your taxes and your estate planning and helping you with your contracts and fan mail and bill paying and you just play golf,' said McCormack to Palmer. Palmer agreed on a handshake and McCormack left NSM to deal with Palmer's business affairs exclusively. It was the business that was eventually to become the International Management Group.

'There wasn't much at all going on in the way of corporate sponsorship in golf when Arnold and I got together,' said McCormack, 'but I thought we might have a chance to do something special. Golf was already a popular sport, and it was around that time that television was becoming a more common medium. There was more and more sports on TV, and TV brought golf into the living room. Arnold had his charisma, and it was pretty apparent that he was this exciting and interesting personality who could make things happen.' This led to the first corporate golf outing in 1960, at a resort near Mt Fuji in Japan, for executives with the Asian edition of *Life* magazine. McCormack organized a similar event for *Newsweek*, and corporate golf events began to roll in.

McCormack expanded slowly. By luck or judgement, McCormack signed two other golfers: Jack Nicklaus and Gary Player. He was now the agent for the three greatest players of their era. For his next move, McCormack decided to branch into sports where he could sign up individual sportsmen and women. From 1966 onward, he assembled a stable of stars, starting with the tennis player Rod Laver and skier Jean-Claude Killy. In the 1970s, McCormack moved on to team players, and added an international dimension to the business with offices in Hong Kong and Sydney.

McCormack continued to innovate. He introduced the concept of the corporate hospitality tent at venues such as the Wimbledon tennis tournament. McCormack's logic when selling the idea to corporate executives was impeccable: 'The beauty with an event is that it will never break a leg, it will never retire, and it will never fall apart in the first round,' McCormack noted.

Today, the business includes a television division that produces and distributes more than 6000 hours of sports programming per year; an event-manage-

ment group that is involved with more than 1000 sporting events per year worldwide; management of the Web sites for Wimbledon and the PGA European Tour; negotiation of the television rights for all four tennis Grand Slam tournaments; and representation of sports stars, classical musicians and less obvious clients, such as the Nobel Foundation. Testimony to the power that McCormack wields is the 10-year, $189 million contract he secured for a client named Derek Jeter, a man who hits a ball with a wooden bat for a living.

McCormack seems to have lost none of his enthusiasm for the business. He marches relentlessly on. Senior international vice-president Andy Pierce observed: 'You look at the calls he makes at 4 a.m. his time and at 11 p.m. his time and you know he's working harder than you are. He sleeps, but I don't know how much.'

Key texts
- Mark McCormack. *Never Wrestle with a Pig and Ninety Other Ideas to Build Your Business and Career*. Penguin, 2002
- Mark McCormack. *Staying Street Smart in the Internet Age*. Viking, 2000
- Mark McCormack. *On Managing*. Newstar, 1996
- Mark McCormack. *What They Don't Teach You at Harvard Business School*. Collins, 1994

McCormick, Cyrus Hall

Inventor and mechanization pioneer (1809–1884)

A millionaire by the age of 50, Cyrus Hall McCormick paved the way for an agrarian revolution through the invention of his reaping machine and the innovation of a host of marketing techniques, from the instalment plan to the money-back guarantee.

Son of a farmer and inventor, McCormick was born on 15 February 1809, in Walnut Grove, Virginia. McCormick grew up on the 532 rolling acres of farmland belonging to the family.

In addition to running the family farm in the quiet Virginia Valley, his father Robert spent time tinkering with inventions aimed at easing the burden of the farmer. One such invention was a horse-drawn reaping device, abandoned by McCormick Sr when he failed to perfect it. He handed over ownership of this reaper invention to his son when McCormick Jr was only 21. McCormick worked non-stop for six weeks to perfect the invention and produce a viable working machine.

To turn the reaper into a viable commercial product, McCormick needed to address two issues – quality and marketing. To market the invention, he introduced a series of public demonstrations. In the summer of 1831, in front of a sizeable crowd, the 22-year-old McCormick used his horse-drawn reaper to mow down the field of wheat at John Steele's farm in Rockbridge County, Virginia. It was the beginning of the mechanization of agriculture. Quality control would come later.

Yet despite the obvious advantages of the reaper, developing a business based around it proved difficult. This was partly because of formidable competition from rival inventor Obed Hussey; partly because the product was manufactured too far from its market; partly because the operator of the machine was required to walk alongside it; and also because demand was beginning to outstrip McCormick's ability to manufacture his invention.

McCormick eliminated the competition by arranging a head-to-head showdown with his rival in 1843. The McCormick reaper cut down 17 acres in the time it took Obed Hussey to clear just two.

To help boost sales, McCormick developed a licensing system. Manufacturers close to market were granted a licence to produce the McCormick reaping machine. The agreement could be framed like a franchise, demarcating area in return for a franchise fee, or as a straight commission paying McCormick $20 for each reaper produced and sold.

Next McCormick designed a seat so the operator could sit above the reaper rather than walking alongside it. This design, known as the 'old reliable', became the standard model.

In 1840, from his Walnut Grove base, McCormick sold two machines – they both broke down

– in the first year and seven in the following year. By 1844, still in the Virginia Valley, production had risen to 75 machines, 25 of which were manufactured by licensees. In 1847, bowing to the inevitable, McCormick uprooted his operation and moved to Chicago, where he built a manufacturing plant on the banks of the Chicago River. With 7500 square feet of factory space and river frontage that allowed machines be loaded onto river transport, McCormick rapidly expanded production.

In 1849, before the factory in Chicago was completed, McCormick's company produced 1500 reapers. By 1859, in a new factory premises, production had rocketed to 4119 machines per year. This figure rose to a staggering 10,000 machines per year by 1870. McCormick came up with a number of innovative marketing techniques to boost sales. To make the product more affordable, he introduced an instalment plan that spread payments between harvests. He was also one of the first to provide a money-back guarantee for dissatisfied customers. In another first, he constructed a regional sales force, with commission sales agents placed in charge of sales areas that consisted of one or a number of states.

By 1860, some 70 percent of the country's wheat harvest was gathered using McCormick's reaper. Where it once took a man 40 hours to harvest an acre of wheat, with the McCormick reaper, two people could harvest an acre of wheat in a day. He had single-handedly changed the face of farming in America. McCormick became a millionaire and worldwide celebrity as the machine garnered sales and awards across the globe.

The business suffered a major setback in 1871 when the Great Fire of Chicago destroyed $188 million worth of property at McCormick's manufacturing plant. Ever resilient, McCormick built an even bigger factory and production complex that sprawled over 160 acres. It opened in 1873.

McCormick continued to manage his business well into his 70s. In the final years of his life, McCormick successfully promoted his business abroad, taking the reaper to both the Pacific and South America. He died in 1884, with the business safely in the hands of his son Cyrus McCormick

Jr. In the same year, the McCormick Harvesting Machine Company sold 54,841 harvesting machines produced at its Chicago plant to farmers from the United States to Australia.

Key texts

- Lavinia Dobler. *Cyrus McCormick, Farm Boy*. The Bobbs- Merrill Co., 1961
- Cyrus McCormick. *The Century of the Reaper: Cyrus Hall McCormick & Business*. Houghton Mifflin, 1931
- Herbert N. Casson. *Cyrus Hall McCormick: His Life and Work*. A.C. McClure & Co., 1909

McGregor, Douglas

American social psychologist (1906–1964)

Trained at the City College of Detroit and at Harvard, Douglas McGregor was a social psychologist who spent his career as president of Antioch College (1948–1954) and as a professor of management at MIT. Despite producing a limited number of publications in his short life, McGregor's work remains highly significant. He was a central figure in the human-relations school that emerged at the end of the 1950s, which included **Abraham Maslow** and **Frederick Herzberg** among its other luminaries.

McGregor's best known work is *The Human Side of Enterprise*. He writes in the preface, 'This volume is an attempt to substantiate the thesis that the human side of enterprise is "all of a piece" – that the theoretical assumptions management holds about controlling its human resources determine the whole character of the enterprise.'

The Human Side of Enterprise remains a classic text of its time and of the human-relations school. McGregor's study of work and motivation fit in with the concerns of the middle and late 1960s, when the large monolithic corporation was at its most dominant, and the world at its most questioning. The book sold 30,000 copies in its peak year of 1965, at that time an unprecedented figure.

In *The Human Side of Enterprise*, McGregor presents two ways of describing managers' thinking: Theory X and Theory Y. Theory X is tradi-

tional carrot-and-stick thinking, built on 'the assumption of the mediocrity of the masses'. This assumes that workers are inherently lazy, need to be supervised and motivated, and regard work as a necessary evil to provide money. The premises of Theory X, writes McGregor, are '(1) that the average human has an inherent dislike of work and will avoid it if he can, (2) that people, therefore, need to be coerced, controlled, directed, and threatened with punishment to get them to put forward adequate effort toward the organization's ends and (3) that the typical human prefers to be directed, wants to avoid responsibility, has relatively little ambition, and wants security above all.'

McGregor lamented that Theory X 'materially influences managerial strategy in a wide sector of American industry,' and observed 'if there is a single assumption that pervades conventional organizational theory it is that authority is the central, indispensable means of managerial control.'

'The human side of enterprise today is fashioned from propositions and beliefs such as these,' writes McGregor, before going on to conclude that 'this behavior is not a consequence of man's inherent nature. It is a consequence rather of the nature of industrial organizations, of management philosophy, policy, and practice.' It is not people who have made organizations, but organizations that have transformed the perspectives, aspirations, and behaviour of people.

The other extreme is described by McGregor as Theory Y, which is based on the principle that people want and need to work. If this is the case, then organizations need to develop the individual's commitment to its objectives, and then to liberate his abilities on behalf of those objectives. McGregor described the assumptions behind Theory Y: '(1) that the expenditure of physical and mental effort in work is as natural as in play or rest – the typical human doesn't inherently dislike work; (2) external control and threat of punishment are not the only means for bringing about effort toward a company's ends; (3) commitment to objectives is a function of the rewards associated with their achievement – the most important of such rewards is the satisfaction of ego and can be the direct product of effort directed toward an organization's purposes; (4) the average human being learns, under the right conditions, not only to accept but to seek responsibility; and (5) the capacity to exercise a relatively high degree of imagination, ingenuity, and creativity in the solution of organizational problems is widely, not narrowly, distributed in the population.'

Theories X and Y are not simplistic stereotypes. McGregor is realistic: 'It is no more possible to create an organization today which will be a full, effective application of this theory than it was to build an atomic power plant in 1945. There are many formidable obstacles to overcome.'

It is worth noting that Theory Y was more than mere theorizing. In the early 1950s, McGregor helped design a Procter & Gamble plant in Georgia. Built on the Theory Y model with self-managing teams, its performance soon surpassed other P&G plants. This suggests that Theory Y works, though it has largely remained consigned to textbooks rather than being put into practice on the factory floor.

Key text
- Douglas McGregor. *The Human Side of Enterprise*. McGraw-Hill, 1960

McKinsey & Co.

Conservative, a little on the staid side, but incredibly successful, McKinsey & Co. remains the thought leader among consulting firms. It has been doing for years what other firms are only now discovering. In particular, it has nurtured its brand with care ever since Marvin Bower and A.T. Kearney split the company between them in the 1930s and Bower, sagely, took the McKinsey name rather than attaching his own name to the business. The McKinsey brand remains the touchstone for consulting firm brand wannabes. McKinsey has long been the number-one choice of employer among top business school graduates. The brand makes it much easier for McKinsey to attract the best people and the most prestigious clients.

'McKinsey's level of brand recognition and quality means that it is an automatic port of call for any company seeking high-level strategic consultancy services,' says London Business School Dean John Quelch. 'It achieved this positioning without any significant advertising. Instead, a distinct aim from the outset was to recruit top intellectual talent to be brought to bear on consultancy assignments. That intellectual talent is very important to the brand positioning. There is a strong tradition at McKinsey of encouraging people to write. This helped disseminate the idea of new thinking, which is part of the brand positioning. There is also what can be called the IBM effect – no manager ever got fired for hiring McKinsey. The strength of the brand can help cushion management decision making, or even on occasion rubber stamp a management decision that has already been made.'

One of McKinsey's notable successes is that of its consultancy tool, the McKinsey **Seven S framework**. Devised by McKinsey & Co., in association with American academics **Richard Pascale** and Anthony Athos, the Seven S framework is a distillation of the key elements that make up an organization's personality. A useful checklist for thinking about what makes a business tick, the Seven S framework suggests an examination of seven areas: strategy, structure, systems, style, skills, staff and shared values. The framework has proved a surprisingly robust tool and been linked to two highly influential management books: *The Art of Japanese Management* by Richard Pascale and Anthony Athos, and *In Search of Excellence* by **Thomas Peters** and Robert Waterman.

Key texts
- Thomas J. Peters and Robert Waterman. *In Search of Excellence: Lessons From America's Best Run Companies*. HarperCollins, 1982
- Richard Pascale and Anthony Athos. *The Art of Japanese Management*. Simon and Schuster, 1981

Key link
- www.mckinsey.com

McNealy, Scott

Founder, Sun Microsystems (b. 1954)

An amateur ice-hockey player and 3.3 handicap golfer, Scott McNealy combines the charm and easygoing affability of a best buddy, with the competitive drive required to be a successful sportsman or businessman. Born on 13 November 1954, in Columbus, Indiana, McNealy was educated at Cranbrook, a private preparatory school, and Harvard University, where he studied for a degree in economics. Social popularity and academic achievement came easily to McNealy. An excellent golfer (*Golf Digest* magazine ranked him number one among *Fortune* 500 CEOs in 1999), he captained the university golf team. Interestingly, he was at Harvard at the same time as his longtime business adversary, **Bill Gates**, although neither recalls meeting the other.

After Harvard, McNealy opted for a career in manufacturing at a tractor body-panel factory in Illinois. However, before long, he was packing his bags and heading for Stanford University Business School in California to study for an **MBA**. Graduating in 1980, McNealy went to work for FMC Corporation building military vehicles.

His big business break came in 1982, when Stanford alum Vinod Khosla contacted McNealy about a possible job. Khosla and graduate student Andy Bechtolsheim had developed a workstation for networks. Bechtolsheim had been working on the Stanford University Network project and so the two took the initials – SUN – for the name of their new start-up.

McNealy, by then working for hardware company Onyx, was brought in to provide manufacturing expertise. He joined as VP of manufacturing and operations. The company enjoyed early success, winning a three-year, $40 million deal in 1984 to supply Sun-2 workstations to a company called Computervision.

This commercial success masked internal conflict over how the company should be run. Khosla, who had been the catalyst for starting Sun, found that the skills that had proved essential for getting the start-up off the ground were not necessarily the same skills that a CEO needed to lead the company through the next phase of expansion and consolidation. The uneasiness over Khosla's stewardship of Sun placed McNealy in an awkward position. He had only joined the company at he request of Khosla, who was a personal friend. Nevertheless, he joined co-founders Bechtolsheim and Bill Joy in persuading Khosla to step down and assumed the position of CEO.

McNealy's operational know-how and his improbable combination of easygoing bonhomie and relentless drive kept the workforce engaged while pushing the company through a phase of rapid expansion. 'We wanted to make a Ferrari out of spare parts,' McNealy told *The New York Times*. 'We were either going to be incredibly successful or we were going to empty the pool out with a belly flop.' The company went public in 1986. Sales accelerated from $1 billion to more than $3 billion between 1988 and 1992.

McNealy also took on the Microsoft hegemony and the Wintel alliance (Windows operating system and Intel chips). He embarked on a campaign of antagonism directed at Microsoft CEO Bill Gates that attracted the attention of the media and created a buzz around Sun. McNealy's position was diametrically opposed to Gates's. 'The network is the computer,' preached McNealy, the network evangelist. He even named his 135-pound Greater Swiss Mountain dog Network and gave it its own page on the Sun corporate Web site.

In 1994, a team of Sun programmers led by **James Gosling** developed a new computer language: **Java**. Java was a cross-platform, write-once-run-anywhere language. Here, thought McNealy, was the stick with which to beat Microsoft. McNealy put the full might of the company behind the new language.

McNealy was right. With strong branding and open standards, Java became a commonly accepted language. If anyone could persuade the world of the merits of Java and Sun's business strategy, it was McNealy. *Forbes ASAP* described him as one of the top 10 speakers in the technology industry; *60 Minutes* dubbed him 'one of the most influential businessmen in America'. McNealy's enthusiasm for selling Sun systems extends to some high-profile networking. Famously, he challenged **Jack Welch**, General Electric's celebrated CEO, to a round of golf. McNealy lost, but so impressed Welch that he received a place on the GE board.

With McNealy in charge, Sun has blazed a trail of innovation through the technology industry. In 2000, the company's annual revenues were more than $12 billion. In 2001, they were $17 billion and rising. Still driven by McNealy's war cry of 'the network is the computer', the company continues to provide 'industrial-strength hardware, software, and services that power the Internet and allow companies worldwide to dotcom their businesses'.

Key texts

- Karen Southwick. *High Noon: The Inside Story of Scott McNealy and the Rise of Sun Microsystems*. John Wiley, 1999
- Midori Chan (ed). *Open Minds: Sun Microsystems, Inc. 1982–1992*. Sun Microsystems, 1992

Key link

- www.sun.com

Mean, median, mode

The mean, median and mode are the three most commonly used forms of average.

The mean is the average of a number of terms or quantities. The simple arithmetic mean is the average value of the quantities – the sum of the quantities divided by their number. The weighted mean accounts for the frequency of the terms that are added; it is calculated by multiplying each term by the number of times it occurs, adding the results, and dividing this total by the total number of occurrences. The geometric mean of n quantities is the nth root of their product. The geometric mean is used in statistics as a measure of central tendency of a set of data; that is, one measure used to express the frequency distribution of a number of recorded events.

The median is simply the middle number in an ordered group of numbers. If there is no middle number (there is an even number of terms), the median is the mean of the two middle terms. For example, the median of the group 2, 3, 7, 11, 12 is 7; that of 3, 4, 7, 9, 11, 13 is 8 (the average of 7 and 9). The mode is the most frequently appearing item in a given set of data. For example, the mode for the data 0, 0, 9, 9, 9, 12, 87, 87 is 9.

The median together with the mode and arithmetic mean make up the average of a set of data. In addition, it is useful to know the range or spread of the data.

These different averages can be demonstrated graphically on a normal curve. This is the bell-shaped curve of a normal distribution. It shows that extreme values are infrequent. Most of the values lie toward the centre of the normal curve with the arithmetic mean, median and mode lying at its very centre.

Mechanistic organization

English sociologist Tom Burns and psychologist G.M. Stalker coined the term 'mechanistic organization'. Such an organization is characterized by a high degree of job specialization, clearly demarcated vertical hierarchies and centralized decision making. It stands in contrast to an organic organization, which has decentralized decision-making processes, low job specialization and horizontal communication channels, all of which tend to empower employees.

Mentor

When Odysseus, King of Ithaca, left for the Trojan Wars around 800 BC, he was faced with a problem: who would look after the royal household and groom his son, Telemachus, for the throne in his absence? Odysseus turned to Mentor, his trusted companion, and instructed him to assume the role of father figure, adviser, counsellor, tutor and role model to Telemachus while he was away. Greek mythology also tells us that the goddess Athena would speak to Telemachus in the guise of Mentor. Jump from the writings of Homer to the present day, when the word 'mentor' has become part of our language, signifying a wise and trusted counsellor, a sagacious adviser, a tutor.

Modern definitions of the term include that of Linda Phillips-Jones, one of the leading experts on mentoring, who describes mentors as 'skilled people who go out of their way to help you clarify your personal goals and take steps toward reaching them'. In her book *Mentors and Protégés*, she describes some characteristics of mentors and the mentoring relationship:

- Mentors are usually older than their protégés.
- Mentors frequently – but not always – initiate the relationship.
- Mentor-protégé relationships do not need to be particularly close.
- It is possible to have more than one mentor at a time.
- There are patterns and cycles in mentor-protégé relationships.
- Mentoring should benefit both partners equally.

In an organizational setting, mentoring may cover the following areas: appropriate dress, conflict resolution, communication, company protocol and culture, ethical practice, leadership, networking, office politics, presentation, project management, time management and work/life balance.

Mentoring can be an extremely effective way of assimilating a new employee into an organization, but that depends on the quality and dedication of the mentor. Mentors do not necessarily have to come from within the organization. There are many human-resource consultancies that offer mentoring and coaching services. In these cases, the mentor may be providing his services to many executives at the same time.

Key texts
- David Clutterbuck. *Mentoring Executives and Directors*. Butterworth-Heinemann, 1999
- Linda Phillips-Jones. *Mentors and protégés*. Arbor House, 1982

Merchandising

Merchandising is the term used to describe the many different ways that organizations persuade customers to buy their products in the short term, excluding that of **advertising**. Merchandising includes special offers such as free gifts, discounts, money-off coupons, two-for-the-price-of-one offers, competitions, better-value offers (for example, 500 grams for the price of 400 grams) and trade-ins.

Merrill, Charles

Popularized share buying; co-founder, Merrill Lynch (1885–1956)

Charles Merrill, the son of a shopkeeper and a doctor, was born in 1885 in the small village of Green Cove Springs, Florida. Merrill's academic career was cut short when he was forced to drop out of Amherst College before completing his degree due to financial difficulties. He later abandoned law school, doing a stint as a semi-professional baseball player in Mississippi and then taking a reporting job on a newspaper in West Palm Beach, Florida.

In 1907, Merrill moved to New York and started on the long road to the top when his girlfriend's father got him a job at textile company Patchogue-Plymouth Mills. During the financial crisis of the same year, Merrill was offered an opportunity to make a name for himself. He was dispatched to the National Copper Bank to obtain a loan that would save the company he worked for.

Somehow, a persuasive Merrill managed to obtain a $300,000 loan from the bank president. When Merrill's romance with the boss's daughter fizzled out, Merrill took a job at the newly created bond department of George H. Burr & Co. on Wall Street.

While Merrill was at Burr, he realized that it was possible to sell stocks and bonds to the public rather than just to powerful institutional investors. Merrill wrote down his ideas in a 1911 article, 'Mr Average Investor', published in *Leslie's Weekly*.

Merrill also became involved in a financing deal for a new business phenomenon: a chain of retail stores. He was impressed by the economics.

In 1914, Merrill and colleague Edmund Lynch left Burr to form Merrill, Lynch & Co. At first, Merrill specialized in financing chain store developments throughout the country. His first deal was a contract to underwrite a $6 million chain store financing. The chain store was successfully brought to market in May 1915, earning Merrill $300,000. Merrill retained stock from each deal. This made him a wealthy man and gave the firm a decision-making role in the management of the companies it helped to finance.

A prescient Merrill was one of the few financiers who advocated caution during the rampant speculation of the 1920s. To his partner Lynch he wrote, 'The financial skies are not clear. I do not like the outlook and I do not like the amount of money we owe.' Merrill also wrote to his clients in 1928, advising them that is was a good time to get out of debt. When the financial storm finally arrived in 1929, Merrill Lynch was one of the few financial institutions to remain afloat. Anticipating a lengthy downturn, Merrill transferred his clients' accounts to another brokerage and devoted his time to managing a retail chain and looking after his own personal investments.

When Merrill returned to Wall Street, it was via the brokerage firm EA Pierce & Co., which merged with Merrill Lynch in January 1940. With the new firm Merrill Lynch, EA Pierce and Cassatt, Merrill set about realizing his dream of mass-market stockbroking.

Merrill introduced the chain-store approach to the elite world of stockbroking, ruthlessly driving down costs. A business conducted predominantly by phone didn't need a large, expensive building as headquarters: Merrill moved the firm to a cheaper, less prestigious location at 70 Pine Street. He also created a more broadminded sales force, unencumbered by Wall Street traditions. The newcomers were trained in a specially established school for trainee brokers.

Having marshalled his forces, Merrill took his operation to the US public, building a chain of branch offices throughout the United States. New brokers were salaried rather than rewarded on a commission-only basis. This overcame public concerns that brokers would sell any stock, regardless of merit, merely to line their own pockets with commissions. Merrill backed up his campaign to broaden the appeal of stock-buying by investing large amounts of money on advertising the firm's services. By 1947, Merrill Lynch was the largest retailer of stocks in United States, with $6.2 million in sales and an advertising budget of approximately $400,000.

Following World War II, economic conditions in the United States were favourable for Merrill's business. America began to reinforce its economic superpower status. During the Cold War, much was made of the power of the free market economy in the United States. Individuals were actively encouraged to buy stock in American companies through initiatives such as the Monthly Investment Plan, introduced in 1954, which allowed the purchase of stock by instalment.

The long hours involved in building up this new style of stockbroking business took its toll on Merrill. During 1944, he suffered multiple heart attacks and was forced to enjoy the company's success from the sidelines. He continued to run and organize the business by phone from a variety of destinations, including Palm Beach and Barbados. By the time of Merrill's death in 1956, he had succeeded in broadening the base of stock ownership to include more than 2 million ordinary Americans.

Key link
- www.ml.com/

Messaging

See SMS.

Me-too product

A me-too product follows other similar successful products into a market rather than setting a trend. Me-too products avoid risk and R&D costs by emulating other products that are successful in a market. They also confuse markets by reducing both product differentiation and the impact of strong brands.

Meyer, Christopher

American author and consultant

Economist and Harvard MBA Chris Meyer has transformed himself into a high-tech consultant and author. While at Mercer Management Consulting, Meyer founded the company's practice in IT industries. His eyes were soon opened. 'Around 1980 I started getting interested in telecom and IT and worked with NASA and ITT on the new generation of telecom technology, fibreoptics, digital switching and so on,' he says. 'It was a seminal project from my point of view. It taught me how telecom systems of the world were set to change.'

Meyer has been seeking to understand more about the emerging information economy ever since. He joined Ernst & Young in 1995 and heads the firm's Center for Business Innovation, an R&D shop that aims to identify the issues that will be challenging business in the future and defining responses to them.

Meyer also established the Bios Group, Ernst & Young's initiative to develop complexity-based solutions for management. The entire challenge of making complexity theory understood and practical lies at the heart of Meyer's current work. Forget metaphorical butterflies; Meyer says, 'I am interested in moving between the theoretical and the practical. I enjoy ideas but I also enjoy seeing the business world change. At the moment this is an area of huge opportunity because practice is up for grabs. Complexity, for example, can be applied to operational situations. People understand about the interaction of parts. You don't start with the factory, you start with the machinery. Big things are made up of small things – that's the way the world is.'

Meyer is co-author, with **Stan Davis**, of *Blur*. At the heart of *Blur* are three forces: connectivity, speed and intangibles ('the derivatives of time, space, and mass'). According to Davis and Meyer, these three things 'are blurring the rules and redefining our businesses and our lives. They are destroying solutions, such as mass production, segmented pricing, and standardized jobs, that worked for the relatively slow, unconnected industrial world.' The three forces are shaping the behaviour of the new economy. They are affecting what Davis and Meyer label 'the blur of desires; the blur of fulfilment; and the blur of resources'.

The 'blur of desires' has two central elements: the offer and the exchange. These were once clear-cut. In the product-dominated age, a company offered a product for sale. Money was exchanged and the customer disappeared into the distance. Now, products and services are often indistinguishable from each other and buyers and sellers are in a constantly evolving relationship ('mutual exchange') that is driven by information and emotion as well as by money.

The second aspect of the new economic reality is 'the blur of fulfilment'. As organizations change to meet changing demands so, too, must the entire theory and practice of competitive strategy. Connectivity produces different forms of organization, operating according to different first principles.

The third leg to the economic stool is that of resources and the emergence of intellectual capital as the key resource. Hard assets have become intangibles; intangibles have become the only real assets.

Key text

• Stan M. Davis and Chris Meyer. *Blur: The Speed of Change in the Connected Economy*. Warner Books, 1999

Microeconomics

Microeconomics is the study of individual decision-making units within an economy; i.e. a consumer, firm or industry. Unlike **macroeconomics**, it looks at how individual markets work and how individual producers and consumers make their choices and with what consequences. This is done by analysing how relevant prices of goods are determined and the quantities that will be bought and sold.

Mind mapping

US academic Tony Buzan developed the mind mapping technique in the 1960s, following his research on students' note-taking techniques. The technique involves harnessing words, images, numbers, colours and spatial awareness to represent thoughts. Mind maps resemble unstructured, brightly coloured flow diagrams with pictures. Guiding principles to creating a mind map include: start in the centre of the sheet of paper; use at least three colours; use images, symbols, codes and dimensions throughout; each word/image must be alone and sitting on its own line; lines must be connected, starting as thick lines at the centre and becoming thinner as they radiate outward; use emphasis and show associations. A mind map can be used to give an overview of a large subject, enable route planning of concepts and promote creative thinking by highlighting new creative pathways.

Key link
- www.mind-map.com

Key text
- Tony Buzan. *The Mind Map Book*. BBC Books, 1993

Mintzberg, Henry

Canadian educator (b. 1939)

Henry Mintzberg is professor of management at McGill University in Montreal and professor of organization at INSEAD in Fontainebleau, France. His first book, *The Nature of Managerial Work*, examined how managers worked. Not surprisingly, managers did not do what they liked to think they did. Mintzberg found that instead of spending time contemplating the long term, man-

agers were slaves to the moment, moving from task to task with every move dogged by another diversion. The median time spent on any one issue was a mere nine minutes.

From his observations, Mintzberg broke down the manager's work roles into the following categories:

- Interpersonal roles:
  - **figurehead:** representing the organization/unit to outsiders
  - **leader:** motivating subordinates, unifying effort
  - **liaiser:** maintaining lateral contacts.
- Informational roles:
  - **monitor:** of information flows
  - **disseminator:** of information to subordinates
  - **spokesman:** transmission of information to outsiders.
- Decisional roles:
  - **entrepreneur:** initiator and designer of change
  - **disturbance handler:** handling non-routine events
  - **resource allocator:** deciding who gets what and who will do what
  - **negotiator:** negotiating different elements of decision making.

Mintzberg's work on strategy has been highly influential. In particular, he has long been a critic of formulae and analysis-driven strategic planning. He defines planning as 'a formalized system for codifying, elaborating, and operationalizing the strategies that companies already have'.

Mintzberg identifies three central pitfalls to today's strategy planning practices: first, the assumption that discontinuities can be predicated. Forecasting techniques are limited by the fact that they tend to assume that the future will resemble the past.

The second problem is that planners are detached from the reality of the organization. Planners have traditionally been obsessed with gathering hard data on their industry, markets and competitors. Soft data – networks of contacts; talking with customers, suppliers and employees; using intuition; and using the grapevine – have been all but ignored.

To gain real understanding of an organization's competitive situation, soft data needs to be dynamically integrated into the planning process. Mintzberg writes, 'While hard data may inform the intellect, it is largely soft data that generate wisdom. They may be difficult to "analyse," but they are indispensable for synthesis – the key to strategy making.'

The third and final flaw identified by Mintzberg is the assumption that strategy making can be formalized. The left side of the brain has dominated strategy formulation with its emphasis on logic and analysis. Alternatives that do not fit into the predetermined structure are ignored. The right side of the brain, with its emphasis on intuition and creativity, needs to become part of the process. 'Planning by its very nature,' concludes Mintzberg, 'defines and preserves categories. Creativity, by its very nature, creates categories or rearranges established ones. This is why strategic planning can neither provide creativity, nor deal with it when it emerges by other means.'

By championing the role of creativity in strategy creation and in providing carefully researched rebuttals of formulaic approaches to management, Mintzberg has provided new insights into strategy. 'The real challenge in crafting strategy lies in detecting the subtle discontinuities that may undermine a business in the future,' he says. 'And for that there is no technique, no program, just a sharp mind in touch with the situation.'

Key texts
- Henry Mintzberg. *The Rise and Fall of Strategic Planning*. Prentice Hall, 1994
- Henry Mintzberg. *Mintzberg on Management: Inside Our Strange World of Organizations*. Free Press, 1989
- Henry Mintzberg. *Power In and Around Organizations*. Prentice Hall, 1983
- Henry Mintzberg. *The Nature of Managerial Work*. Harper & Row, 1973

Mission statement

A mission statement is a statement made by an organization that encapsulates the organization's objectives and aims. The mission statement communicates a company's intent to its stakeholders, including its customers, suppliers, and employees. For the employees, the mission statement can act as guidance and provide a sense of common purpose. The corporate mission, while demanding, will be an achievable target – what a company intends to accomplish. It should be powerful, compelling, and brief.

MIT Media Laboratory

Formed in 1980 by **Nicholas Negroponte** and Jerome Wiesner, the Massachusetts Institute of Technology's Media Laboratory carries out advanced research into a broad range of information technologies. It carries out pioneering work in the world of digital television and is at the forefront of research into holographic imaging, electronic publishing, and education.

Only a select few work and/or study there. There are only 30 members of the senior research staff and graduate enrolment totals a little over 150. The Media Laboratory's annual budget is in the region of $25 million per year, and more than 90 percent of its funding comes from approximately 150 corporate sponsors. Cash is allocated to four self-explanatory areas: Digital Life; News in the Future; Things that Think; and Toys of Tomorrow. About half of the sponsors are from America, with a quarter each from Europe and Asia.

This focus on corporate support has helped transfer the technology of the Media Laboratory's projects into worldwide, everyday use.

Key link
- www.media.mit.edu

Mixed economy

A mixed economy combines elements of both the **command economy** and the free market economy. It has a degree of state monopoly blended with the private enterprise of capitalism. In mixed economies, governments seek to control the public services, the basic industries, and those industries that cannot raise sufficient capital investment from private sources. Thus, a measure of economic planning can be combined with a measure of free enterprise.

Mobile commerce

Mobile commerce, or m-commerce, is one of the faster-growing sectors of electronic commerce. It involves the transaction of commerce on the move, using wireless mobile devices such as mobile phones and PDAs (personal digital assistants). As miniaturization, network, wireless and display technologies improve, m-commerce is expected to grow rapidly. Consultancy **Jupiter Media Metrix** anticipates steady growth until 2006, when revenues will be approximately $4 billion.

Mobile information

Back in early computing history, there was the mainframe, which filled an entire room. Now, mainframes fill museums. Mainframes were superseded by the PC revolution. Next comes life – and working life – beyond the PC. In this new business revolution, data constantly shifts, accessible and utilized by far more people than ever before. From being the preserve of the corporate few, data has become the lifeblood of the many.

Computing has moved from being dominated by hardware to a world in which hardware and operating systems matter less and less. 'All of our software is made available across every device, every operating system,' says Jacob Christfort, director of Product Management and Market-

ing for Oracle's Mobile and Embedded Products Group. Now, access to the **Internet** has extended the boundaries of reach and utilization in much the same way as PCs did 20 years ago.

Greater access means more and more information. A trickle has become a deluge and, as executives swamped by the daily flood of e-mails will tell you, more is not always good. In the information business, quantity and quality are rarely synonymous. This has prompted **Larry Ellison** to bemoan the 'irrational distribution of data and complexity'. 'We're putting databases in hamburger stands, branch offices, and banks – it's all a mistake. A colossal mistake, this irrational distribution of information,' warns Ellison.

The message is not that we are in danger of being swamped, but that how you manage the information is, increasingly, the key to competitiveness. How companies manage information can be a vital differentiating factor. A well-managed loyalty programme that maximizes data about customers is a potent commercial weapon. The more you know, the more you can customize products and services for individual customers, delivering exactly what you know they want. The opposite is also true: a poorly managed loyalty programme is as likely to undermine loyalty as to build it.

Clearly, it is not only the amount of information that is crucial, but its timeliness and accuracy. If information has to be inputted by someone when they get back to the office or deciphered from notes made when they talked to the customer, it runs the risk of being slow and inaccurate.

The trouble is that for many years data has been housed in the room with the mainframe or the office with a PC. Companies have made history – but not in the way they would have liked. They have created instant relics. A salesman would visit a customer and dutifully record an order before going back to the office to enter it into the company database; a service engineer would arrive, identify the problem, and then depart to order the necessary parts, only returning a few days later when the parts arrived. Once out of the office, factory, warehouse or depot, the humble employee was basically out of touch. Data was often already old when it was recorded.

The case for enabling data to be put into a database speedily and accurately while people are out of their usual place of work is easily made. Allowing people to gain access to corporate data while on the move enables better decisions in the field – no need for that call to HQ to check the figures – and improved customer relations – a customer's needs can be instantly put into the system. The lift engineer can order the parts immediately and receive them within the hour, with no need for a cost-consuming and customer-annoying second visit. The salesman can place a customer's order on the spot – no need for reams of paperwork.

Technology means that the business case can now be made into reality. Armed with small handheld computers, people can access corporate and public information no matter where they are. Mobile information is the new reality. In the United States, it is estimated that well over 25 percent of the workforce is mobile. Mobile workers defined as those who spend 20 percent or more of their time away from their desk or make use of mobile communications.

Mooney, James D.

Engineer, senior executive and business author (1884–1957)

James D. Mooney was trained as an engineer and then became a senior executive with General Motors. He was a graduate at the Case School of Applied Sciences in Mining and Metallurgy and then spent some time gold mining. He then found more lucrative, though duller, positions at Westinghouse, BF Goodrich and the Hyatt Roller Bearing Company. Next, he became president and general manager of a General Motors subsidiary, the Remy Electric Company. In 1922, he was appointed a vice-president of GM and president of GM Overseas. After becoming heavily involved in wartime activities – including meetings with German leaders to seek out peace – Mooney

became chairman and president of Willys-Overland Motors.

Mooney's most famous work was *The Principles of Organization*, co-authored with Alan Reiley. *The Principles of Organization* provides an organization model that brings the reasoned science of **Frederick Taylor** to the broader organizational canvas.

Mooney and Reiley's book argues that organization is a universal phenomenon. 'Organization is as old as human society itself,' they write. Mooney and Reiley consider the scalar organization of the Catholic Church, governmental organization and the evolution of different forms of organization from Roman times to medieval times through to the company of the early twentieth century. Their conclusion is simply put by the title of the book's first chapter: 'Men Love to Organize'.

The second important strand to Mooney and Reiley's argument is that the organization of businesses is crucial to overall standards of living. They make a direct link between industrial prosperity, built on modern management techniques, and the affluence of society as a whole. 'The highest development of the techniques both of production and distribution will be futile to supply the material wants of those who, because of poverty, are unable to acquire through purchase,' they write. 'The final task of industry, therefore, is to organize participation in these activities, even in the most backward communities and countries, through which alone can purchasing capacity be created and extended.'

A third element in Mooney and Reiley's argument is that production without distribution is worthless. This marks something of a watershed. Prior to the 1930s, production was the overarching driving force; from World War II onward, the emphasis shifted to finding new markets and enhancing and expanding distribution to make inroads into these markets. Size, note Mooney and Riley, isn't everything. 'Modern business leadership has been generally characterized by the capacity to create large organizations, but by failure in knowing exactly what to do with them,' they write.

Table 2 Mooney and Reiley's central organizational principles

	Principle	Process	Effect
The coordinative principle	Authority or coordination *per se*	Processive coordination	Effective coordination
The scalar process	Leadership	Delegation	Functional definition
The functional effect	Determinative functionalism (legislative)	Applicative functionalism (executive)	Interpretative functionalism (judicial)

Mooney and Reiley's theory of organizations identified three central organizational principles: the coordinative principle, the scalar process, and the functional effect.

Key text
- James D. Mooney and Alan Reiley. *The Principles of Organization*. Harper, 1939

Moore, Geoffrey

Consultant and venture capitalist (b. 1946)

'Corporations need to find points of balance that can absorb and survive shocking changes in market dynamics. That balance is to be found in culture,' says Geoffrey Moore. Moore is founder of the consultancy firm the Chasm Group and a partner at **venture capital** firm Mohr Davidow Ventures. After spells at a number of software firms, two of which failed, he joined consulting firm Regis McKenna in 1987. Drawing on his working experiences, Moore wrote *Crossing the Chasm* (1999), outlining how techies need to be able to think mainstream in order to be successful.

Building on the success of the book, Moore founded the Chasm Group. Moore often uses literary references in his writing and consultancy to explore management issues. His academic background is in literature, with a bachelor's degree from Stanford University and a PhD from the University of Washington in literature.

Key text
- Geoffrey A. Moore. *Crossing the Chasm: Marketing & Selling High-Tech Products to Mainstream Customers*. HarperInformation, 1991

Moore, Gordon

IT pioneer; co-founder, Intel Corp. (b. 1929)

In 1965, while working at Fairchild Semiconductor as R&D director, Gordon Moore made a prediction in an obscure magazine. Computer processing power would, according to Moore, double every 18 months over the following ten years. The idea took root in the consciousness of Silicon Valley and became Moore's Law.

The uncannily prescient Moore moved on to co-found the microprocessor giant Intel. Over the next 30 or so years, the industry watched as Moore's words became axiomatic. Moore now serves as Intel's board chair emeritus. The validity of his law, however, is under threat. Moore acknowledges this. In an interview with *Wired*, he admitted that as processing power slows down within the next 15 years, the 18-month period is likely to be stretched.

But with the continual commercial pressures to produce faster and faster chip speeds, the next technological breakthrough, be it quantum computing or organic semiconductors, may yet come to the rescue of Moore's Law.

Key link
- www.intel.com

John Pierpont Morgan

Financier, titan and robber baron (1837–1913)

Proud, vain, arrogant and greedy, yet a remarkable businessman, John Pierpont Morgan's success owed much to his self-belief and opportunism, and a little to his wealthy and well-connected father. Plagued by ill health throughout his life, he suffered the periodic embarrassment of a bulbous red nose, the product of eczema, the appearance of which would inevitably send him into a deep melancholia. Yet despite frequent periods of ill-ness-induced rest and recuperation, Morgan managed to build a string of business interests in the fashionable industries of the day: railroads, shipping, and electricity. He also, on more than one occasion, financed the US government out of a mess.

Morgan was born in Hartford, Connecticut, on 17 April 1837, a year of financial gloom in the United States. Morgan's father was a wealthy commodity broker who, while Morgan was still a boy, moved the family to Boston, where he became involved in the cotton trade.

Morgan's education was conducted at a private school in Switzerland and at the University of Göttingen, where he so impressed his tutors that he was asked to stay on as an assistant to one of the professors. Morgan declined, insisting that it was time to start out in business.

Morgan returned to America in 1857 and joined the firm of Duncan, Sherman and Co. He profited greatly from the American Civil War, which broke out in 1861. He avoided enlistment through the accepted practice among the wealthy of paying a 'substitute' to take his place. (The going rate was $300.) He left Duncan Sherman in 1862 to found his own company, Dabrey Morgan and Co. While the war raged, Morgan piled up profits, amassing more than $50,000 dollars by 1864. By 1871, he had teamed up with the firm of financiers Drexel, based in Philadelphia, to form Drexel, Morgan & Co., which was based on the corner of Wall Street and Broad Street in New York City.

Morgan was soon one of the leading financiers in America, with a salary of more than $500,000 – an astronomical amount at the time. During the 1870s, he began his association with the railroads, which was to lead to his reputation as a robber baron. Financing the railways required signifi-cant private capital – something that Morgan was only too happy to arrange. Acting as a conduit for money from investors both in Europe and the United States, he stitched together deals under-pinning the financing of the US railways. In 1879, for example, he arranged a stock offering of $18 million for the New York Central Railroad, which was owned by William Vanderbilt.

In 1893, the withdrawal of funds from the United States by British investors sparked a finan-cial crisis. Banks failed, the stock market collapsed and the US government resorted to shoring up the financial system with the gold reserves. Statute dictated that the value of the reserves could not fall below $100 million in gold. In January 1895, gold reserves collapsed to $58 million and Secretary of the Treasury John Carlisle turned to Morgan to save the day. Morgan organized a syndicate of investors to sell gold coin to the US Treasury, paid for with newly issued bonds. A brilliant solution, it provided an economic and politically expedient way out. Morgan further guaranteed the scheme to President Grover Cleveland. The Morgan syn-dicate intervention stopped the financial slide and made Morgan a considerable profit, estimated at between $250,000 and $16 million.

He followed up his rescue of the US financial system with a series of breathtaking deals, such as the financing of US Steel, the largest steel company in the world. The early 1900s were devoted to consolidating the railroad companies through Morgan's concern, the Northern Securi-ties Corporation, and to building a shipping trust. Theodore Roosevelt had, however, decided that he could gain a political advantage by cracking down on the so-called trusts, the massive monopolistic corporations that had snuffed out all competition. With the well-known and little-loved figure of Morgan behind the Northern Securities Corpora-tion, Roosevelt decided to make an example of the company. Morgan had met his match. Apart from a brief respite in 1907 when a US President turned to him for salvation during a financial crisis, Mor-gan's power waned from that point onward.

In later life Morgan, devoted more time to his private life and his hobby of collecting art. In

1913, he left America for the last time, travelling to Europe on his doctor's advice for some rest and recuperation. He died in Rome at the age of 76.

Key texts

- John Winkler. *Morgan the Magnificent: The Life of J. Pierpont Morgan.* Vanguard, 1930
- George Wheeler. *Pierpont Morgan and Friends: The Anatomy of a Myth.* Prentice Hall, 1973

Morita, Akio

Electronics pioneer and globalization champion; founder, Sony Corp. (1921–1999)

Akio Morita, along with entrepreneurs like **Eiji Toyoda** and **Soichiro Honda**, ranks as one of Japan's greatest businessmen. Born on 26 January 1921 into an affluent middle-class family in the industrial city of Nagoya, Morita was heir to the family rice-wine brewing business. Morita, however, preferred electronics equipment to rice wine. He was a keen amateur electronics enthusiast, neglecting his studies to build electronic gadgets, including a radio and a record player.

At college, Morita studied physics. During World War II, he joined the Japanese Navy, rising to the rank of lieutenant. With the war over, Morita travelled to Tokyo in 1946, joining navy colleague Masaru Ibuka. With just $530, the two started a new company, Tokyo Tshushin Kyogu (TTK), in a bombed-out department store.

The first product prototype from the man who would build Sony into one of the greatest companies in the world was a distinctly unglamorous specialized rice cooker. In the 1950s, Morita produced his first major product: Japan's first tape recorder.

In October 1954, a joint venture between Texas Instruments and Regency Electronics produced the first commercial transistor radio: the Regency TR-1. The transistor was an American invention, but Morita had travelled to the United States in 1953 to license the technology from Bell Laboratories. In August 1955, Sony produced its first transistor model – the TR-55. Its production was

restricted to Japan. Sony's first radio for export was the TR-63, produced in 1957.

The TR-63 was a huge hit. It was a truly innovative design, sold in a presentation box complete with a soft leather case, anti-static cloth and earphone.

Morita was doggedly persistent in his promotion of his new product. Taking the product direct to the distributors, Morita trekked around New York convincing electronic-store owners to stock the TTK radio. He returned to Japan with a full order book.

In 1958, Morita took the Latin for sound – *sonus* – and a popular colloquial US term, 'sonny', and combined them to arrive at a more catchy name for the company than Tokyo Tsushin Kogyo – Sony. 'We wanted a new name that could be recognized anywhere in the world, one that could be pronounced the same in any language,' Morita said. Morita's strategy worked. In a survey of American radio dealers, the dealers were asked, 'Have you ever handled Japanese radios?' Most of them answered 'no'. However, when asked if they had ever dealt with Sony radios, they gave an unequivocal 'yes'.

Many innovative electronics products followed: the cassette tape recorder and magnetic recording tape in 1950; the pocket radio in 1957; the world's first all-transistor television in 1960; and the first home videotape recorder in 1968.

In 1963, Morita moved to the United States with his family and set up the Sony Corporation of America. It was a bold move for a man from a country whose businessman were traditionally isolationist and protectionist in outlook. Morita pushed Sony's products in America, positioning the brand not as a discount offering but as a premium-quality brand. Soon the company's products were available from the East to the West Coast.

'The public does not know what is possible. We do,' said Morita, insisting that there was a huge market for a portable tape cassette player developed by the company. Morita's colleagues were unconvinced that there would be a market for a cassette recorder (of any size) without a recording facility. But Morita persuaded his colleagues, and in 1980 the Walkman was born.

Another Sony innovation was video technology. Sony's Betamax technology lost out to VHS in the video standards war, but the company was instrumental in making home video recording a mainstream technology. Morita relentlessly pursued his vision of globalization. 'Think globally, act locally' was the phrase Morita coined to describe his philosophy of corporate values that transcended national boundaries.

In later life, Morita kept up a relentless pace. In his 50s, he took up pastimes such as scuba diving, skiing and tennis. He was forced to resign as president of Sony when he suffered a stroke while playing tennis in 1993. He died in October 1999.

Key texts

- John Nathan. *Sony: The Private Life*. Houghton Mifflin, 1999
- Akio Morita with Edwin M. Reingold and Mitsuko Shimomura. *Made in Japan: Akio Morita and Sony*. Dutton, 1986

Key link

- www.sony.com

Motivational speakers

A handful of individuals have created substantial businesses based on their talent to energize the corporate troops. Ken Blanchard, author of *The One-Minute Manager*, runs Blanchard Training & Development from San Diego. It has estimated annual revenues of $15 million. The king of them all, business-wise at least, is **Stephen Covey**, with his Covey Leadership Institute in Provo, Utah. Covey has turned himself into a one-man industry. His books include *The Seven Habits of Highly Effective People* (which has sold 6 million copies in 32 languages), *Principle-Centered Leadership* and *The Seven Habits of Highly Effective Families*. The business also includes a profitable newsletter called *Executive Excellence*, consulting services and Covey's seminars.

The market in motivational speakers is nothing new. **Dale Carnegie**, author of *How to Win Friends and Influence People* (over 15 million copies and still selling) can probably be credited with its invention. More than 40 years after his death, Carnegie's brand of self-help is still big business. The company bearing his name prospers and his book even reached the German bestseller lists when it was re-released. It is surely no coincidence that Covey studied American 'success literature', of which Carnegie is a prime example, before coming up with *The Seven Habits of Highly Effective People*.

The man who really created the modern motivational-speaker business is **Tom Peters**. From being a staid **McKinsey** consultant during the 1980s, Peters transformed himself into a business equivalent of Billy Graham. His seminars became bigger and bigger events. Sweating profusely and stalking the auditorium, he holds audiences in a spell. He shouts. He implores. He laughs. Like any natural performer, Peters knows exactly what he is doing. 'I do pretty good seminars because I know when to screw with people's minds. You can take them to the brink and pull them back,' he admits. With no need to work again, Peters a hectic schedule of seminars, perennially globetrotting armed with a pack of ever-changing slides.

The motivation industry remains thoroughly American. People like Zig Ziglar, 'the world-famous motivator', are barely known in Europe. Yet although it is an American-based industry, motivation is a universal issue. This suggests that the market for motivational speakers is here to stay.

MPEG

An acronym for Moving Picture Experts Group, MPEG (pronounced 'empeg') is a committee of the International Standards Organization formed in 1988 that sets standards for digital audio and video compression. Most people will associate MPEG with video and audio files compressed using those standards. MPEG-1 is the standard for the digital coding of video pictures for CD recording; MPEG-2 is a common standard for broadcast-quality video; and MPEG-4 is for Internet telephony. MPEG-3 no longer exists, as it was absorbed into MPEG-2.

Mui, Chunka

Technology guru

'Technology isn't just the solution. It's also the problem,' suggests Chunka Mui, co-author of the bestselling e-commerce book *Unleashing the Killer App*. Mui is a partner with Diamond Technology Partners, executive director of the Diamond Exchange and executive editor of *Context*, the business magazine that covers 'business strategies for the digital age'. At Diamond, his work includes helping to design digital strategies for clients to help them carve out new competitive opportunities in the digital marketplace.

Mui graduated from the Massachusetts Institute of Technology with a BS in computer science and engineering. At MIT, he specialized in advanced computing and artificial intelligence and participated in research at the Institute's prestigious Artificial Intelligence Laboratory.

Key text
• Larry Downes and Chunka Mui. *Unleashing the Killer App.* Harvard Business School, 1998

Murdoch, Rupert

Media titan; founder, News Corp. (b. 1931)

An astute pragmatist and brilliant **entrepreneur**, with an innate sense of what the public wants, Rupert Murdoch has built a global media empire through instinct, talent and hard work.

Although an American citizen, Murdoch was born in Australia on 11 March 1931. Educated at Geelong Grammar School in Geelong, Victoria, Murdoch was not an impressive student (he admits to being 'bone lazy' at school) other than in English, where his marks were above average.

His conventional education was completed at Worcester College, Oxford University, where he studied economics. His real education, however, took place at the *Daily Express* newspaper in Fleet Street, where he worked before returning home to Australia in 1952.

On the death of his father, Sir Keith Murdoch, a Melbourne publisher, Murdoch inherited the *Adelaide News*. It was the start of Murdoch's mercurial career as a news proprietor and media mogul. The board was reluctant to hand over complete control of the newspaper to the young tyro. But Murdoch had other ideas. With headlines like the sensationalist 'Queen Eats a Rat', Murdoch steered the newspaper in an avowedly populist direction, boosting its circulation and giving it a new lease on life.

Encouraged by his success with the *Adelaide News*, Murdoch bought the *Daily Mirror* in Sydney and dabbled in television. In 1964, he made his boldest move yet, founding *The Australian* – a national broadsheet. *The Australian* gave Murdoch political clout and influence and made him a national figure.

Murdoch moved on to expand his media empire through a spate of acquisitions across the globe. In England, he saved *The News of the World*, a downmarket and populist paper, in 1969. It was the deal that gave Murdoch a toehold in the United Kingdom. Later that year, he bought tabloid newspaper *The Sun* for £500,000. In 1976, he added the *New York Post* to his growing empire. All of the newspapers he acquired received the Murdoch treatment, adopting a populist tone.

In 1981, in the face of fierce competition, Murdoch expanded his British portfolio by buying *The Times*. A serious broadsheet, it was a shrewd purchase. Coupled with *The Sun* and *The News of the World*, it allowed Murdoch to reach a broad cross-section of the British public. Murdoch then took on the powerful UK print unions, challenging their inefficient working practices. He built a new printing plant at Wapping, away from the traditional home of newspapers, Fleet Street; he introduced computerization; and he cut out the unions. For most of 1986, the plant was under virtual siege, becoming the site for a pitched battle between the progressive Murdoch troops and the traditionalist unions. The unions decided to make Wapping their Waterloo. Unfortunately for the unions, it turned into more of a Thermopylae. The outcome: victory for Murdoch and his no-nonsense approach to business.

He emerged from the Wapping episode with the image of a tough, ruthless businessman who would go to almost any length to achieve his aims. The truth was a little more prosaic. Margaret Thatcher's Conservative government and the introduction of tough new anti-strike legislation provided a political environment conducive for such a battle. If Murdoch hadn't challenged the unions, someone else would have. The march of technological progress is relentless, even in the printing industry.

During the remainder of the 1980s, Murdoch branched into film and television, acquiring Fox studios in the United States in 1985 and seven Metromedia TV stations in 1986. The late 1980s saw Murdoch stop and retrench in a massive debt-rescheduling exercise. His empire shored up, Murdoch marched on through the 1990s with one deal hard on the heels of another. Today, Murdoch heads a truly global media empire, with more than 750 businesses in over 50 countries. At the end of 2000, the holding company, News Corporation, was worth some US$38 billion with revenues of US$14 billion. Companies in the News Corp. empire include BSkyB, News International, the Los Angeles Dodgers, Fox TV and Star TV.

Mega-billionaire Murdoch continues to work long days at a fast pace and shows little signs of slowing down. There is much talk in the media of succession, yet Murdoch retains an iron grip on his empire, as demonstrated by his attempts to merge GM-owned DirecTV with his own Sky TV.

Key texts

- Simon Regan. *Rupert Murdoch: A Business Biography*. Angus & Robertson, 1976
- Stuart Crainer. *Business the Rupert Murdoch Way*. Capstone, 1998

Myers-Briggs Type Indicator

The Myers-Briggs Type Indicator (MBTI) is probably the most frequently used personality inventory in the United States alone. Over 3 million MBTIs are administered each year. The MBTI is designed to give people information about their psychological type according to Jungian philosophy. It was developed by Isabel Briggs Myers (1897–1979) and her mother, Katherine Cook Briggs (1875–1968) in the early 1940s to make Carl Jung's theory of human personality understandable, useful and accessible. The MBTI results divide respondent's preferences into four areas: Extroversion (E) or Introversion (I); Sensing (S) or Intuition (N); Thinking (T) or Feeling (F); and Judging (J) or Perceiving (P). Results are usually expressed as four letters indicating the alternate preferences, such as ENTP. The MBTI is used for a variety of purposes, including team-building, management training, organizational development, career development, and self-development. The MBTI instrument is regularly updated to reflect the latest research in type theory. Data from more than 4000 research studies provide a robust empirical foundation for the test.

Key link

- www.cpp-db.com

N

NAFTA (North American Free Trade Agreement)

The North American Free Trade Agreement, which came into force on 1 January 1994, is a trilateral trade agreement between the United States, Canada and Mexico. It is administered from the NAFTA Center, located in Dallas, Texas. NAFTA is intended to promote trade and investment between the signatories. The agreement aims to eliminate tariffs on trade between the three countries, as well as making provisions on transacting business in the free-trade area. Tariffs on trade in goods originating in Mexico and Canada are to be eliminated by 2008.

Key link
- www.nafta-sec-alena.org/english/index.htm

Key texts
- Hermann von Bertrab. *Negotiating NAFTA: A Mexican Envoy's Account*. Praeger, 1997
- Maxwell A. Cameron. *Making of Nafta: How the Deal Was Done*. Cornell University Press, 2002

Naisbitt, John

American researcher, commentator and consultant (b. 1930)

One of the stars of a generation of futurists that emerged in the 1970s, John Naisbitt, who worked as an executive with IBM and Eastman Kodak, produced work that largely anticipated the Information Age. He is a futurologist whose books have sold in their millions. In *Megatrends* (1982), Naisbitt identified ten 'critical restructurings'. While some have proved accurate predictions of what has happened in intervening years, others have proved less accurate:

'Although we continue to think we live in an industrial society, we have in fact changed to an economy based on the creation and distribution of information.' This is now a hackneyed truism. In the early 1980s, however, Naisbitt was ahead of the game.

'We are moving in the dual directions of high tech/high touch, matching each new technology with a compensatory human response.' This is a theme Naisbitt has returned to and developed in more recent years. 'The acceleration of technological progress has created an urgent need for a counter ballast – for high-touch experiences. Heart transplants have led to new interest in family doctors and neighbourhood clinics; jet airplanes have resulted in more face-to-face meetings. High touch is about getting back to a human scale,' he says.

'No longer do we have the luxury of operating within an isolated, self-sufficient, national economic system; we must now acknowledge that we are part of a global economy. We have begun to let go of the idea that the United States is and must remain the world's industrial leader as we move on to other tasks.' Naisbitt was right to identify the emergence of globalization as a powerful force. His perception of a change in America's perception of itself is open to doubt.

'We are restructuring from a society run by short-term considerations and rewards in favour of dealing with things in much longer-term timeframes.' There is little evidence, some 20 years later, that this trend has become a reality.

'In cities and states, in small organizations and subdivisions, we have rediscovered the ability to act innovatively and to achieve results – from the bottom up.' Naisbitt anticipated the fashion in the late 1980s and early 1990s for empowerment, with responsibility being spread more evenly throughout organizations.

'We are shifting from institutional help to more self-reliance in all aspects of our lives.' Trends in working patterns, such as **employability**, suggest that this is becoming the case for a select few professionals with marketable skills.

'We are discovering that the framework of representative democracy has become obsolete in an era of instantaneously shared information.' **Alvin Toffler** suggested this as far back as 1970 in his book *Future Shock*, though there are few signs of reform.

'We are giving up our dependence on hierarchical structures in favour of informal networks. This will be especially important to the business community.' This has become one of the great trends of the last decade as networks are developed in a bewildering variety of ways – with suppliers, between competitors, internally, globally. Technology has enabled networks never previously anticipated.

'More Americans are living in the South and West, leaving behind the old industrial cities of the North.' In the era of Silicon Valley *et al*, this is stating the obvious, but it was less so in the 1980s.

'From a narrow either/or society with a limited range of personal choices, we are exploding into a free-wheeling multiple-option society.' To this, Naisbitt could have added the *caveat* that this society would offer multiple options but only for a few.

Aside from these trends, Naisbitt has championed the role of small business in generating the wealth of the future. 'Small companies, right down to the individual, can beat big bureaucratic companies ten out of ten times. Unless big companies reconstitute themselves as a collection of small companies, they will just continue to go out of business. It's the small companies that are creating the global company,' he says.

Key texts
- John Naisbitt. *High Tech, High Touch*. Nicholas Brealey, 1999
- John Naisbitt. *Global Paradox*. William Morrow, 1997
- John Naisbitt. *Megatrends*. Warner Books, 1982

NASDAQ (National Association of Securities Dealers Automated Quotation)

NASDAQ is a US stock market. Founded by the National Association of Securities Dealers in 1971, the system started life as a by-product of a US Securities and Exchange Commission report and soon took on a life of its own. The NASDAQ index is heavily weighted in technology stocks and has shared the roller-coaster ride those stocks have experienced through the 1990s and into the new millennium. In 1994, the annual volume of shares traded on the NASDAQ surpassed that of the **NYSE**. Frank Zarb, chairman and CEO since 1997, has steered the National Association of Securities Dealers (NASD) and its stock index, the NASDAQ, through its most turbulent times.

Arriving from Alexander & Alexander Services Inc., the global risk-management consulting firm where he was chairman, CEO and president, Zarb has presided over the astonishing growth of the NASDAQ in recent years. Because of its strong technology bias, the rise and fall of the NASDAQ is taken as a barometer of the health of the New Economy. When the NASDAQ sneezes, the rest of the world's stock markets catch cold. From March 2000 to May of the same year, the NASDAQ index fell from its highest-ever mark of 5000 points to 3500.

Key link
- www.nasdaq.com

Nationalization

Nationalization is the policy that dictates that a country's essential services and industries, and even non-essential industries, are placed under public ownership. It is usually a central policy of a socialist government. It was pursued, for example, by the Labour government in the UK between 1945 and 1951. Assets in the hands of foreign governments or companies may also be nationalized; for example, Iran's oil industry, the Suez Canal and US-owned fruit plantations in Guatemala were nationalized during the 1950s.

Natural Wastage

See Wastage.

Negroponte, Nicholas

Founder, Massachusetts Institute of Technology Media Laboratory (b. 1950)

One of the leading lights of the digital revolution, Nicholas Negroponte can justifiably lay claim to the invention of multimedia through his work at the Massachusetts Institute of Technology (MIT) Media Laboratory.

Negroponte's digital credentials are impressive. A graduate of MIT, where he specialized in **computer-aided design**, he founded MIT's pioneering Architecture Machine Group in 1968 and followed up with the MIT Media Lab. The MIT Media Lab's tech research has paved the way for many of the technologies that define the digital revolution.

Until recently, Negroponte was a regular contributor to *Wired* magazine, which, incidentally and lucratively, he helped fund. He has expounded his views on the digital world in his bestselling book *Being Digital*, which made it to *The New York Times* bestseller list just weeks after its 1995 release.

Key text
• Nicholas Negroponte. *Being Digital.* Knopf, 1995

Nerd

The word 'nerd', which has been appropriated by the computing fraternity and taken on an alternative coolness, was originally used to describe someone square or dull. The word has an interesting history. It was first used in the children's book *If I Ran The Zoo* by Dr Seuss, in the line: 'a Nerkle, a Nerd, and a Seersucker, too!' According to the *American Heritage Dictionary*, the next appearance of the word was in the Sunday Mail in Glasgow, Scotland, in a regular column, 'ABC for SQUARES': 'Nerd – a square, any explanation needed?' Another common term associated with the computer-obsessed is 'geek'. The word is said to be derived from 'geck', meaning

fool. It was originally used to describe a sideshow performer who performed bizarre feats such as, improbably, biting the heads off chickens.

Key text
• Dr Seuss. *If I Ran the Zoo.* Random House, 1950

Net present value (NPV)

Net present value is a method of financial analysis that is based on the notion that money has a time value. Thus, a dollar receivable today is worth more than a dollar receivable tomorrow, because interest can be earned on the dollar received today while interest would be paid on borrowed capital.

For example, suppose an individual is given the opportunity to buy a car by borrowing the entire amount. He has two choices: to pay $11,000 in cash at the time of the sale, or to take an interest-free loan for one year. He would, taking into account the time value of money, choose the second option. Why? Because he would save on a year's interest. But what if he was offered the choice of paying $10,000 cash at the time of the sale or an interest-free loan for one year? To make a useful comparison, we use the 'present value' of money.

With interest at 10 percent, $10,000 will earn $1000 in interest in a year. Therefore, the present value of $11,000 one year from now with an interest of 10 percent is $10,000. The two options are therefore equivalent.

For a true analysis of present value, however, we must consider the possibility of receipts from the alternatives, for example, sums realized on sale for salvage at the end of an item's useful life. The difference between the present value of the receipts and the present value of the expenditures is net present value.

The best financial choice of alternatives is the one with the highest net present value. In reality, net present value calculations can be mathematically complex, involving different timing in receipts of the alternative choices as well as different and changing rates of interest. Nevertheless, any NPV analysis should involve five rudimentary stages: select the discount rate; identify the costs/

benefits to be considered in analysis; establish the timing of the costs/benefits; calculate the net present value of each alternative; and select the alternative with the best net present value.

Net profit

See Profit.

Netiquette

As use of the **Internet** grew, particularly in Usenet groups, e-mail correspondence and chat rooms, an informal Internet etiquette was created through common usage. Guides to polite Internet conduct are posted in many places on the Internet. A good place to start is newsgroup sites, as netiquette prescribes guidelines for best practice when contributing to discussions. Posting a comment in capital letters, for example, is the equivalent of shouting and is considered bad Net manners. New Usenet users should read the frequently asked questions (FAQ) file before asking a question. While there are no official netiquette sanctions, fellow users tend to police the Net fairly effectively, censoring those who cross the boundaries of acceptable behaviour.

Netocracy

The term 'netocracy' was coined by the media and used to refer to the aristocracy of the Internet. Individuals who number among the world's netocracy include such luminaries as Amazon.com's **Jeff Bezos** and Yahoo!'s Jerry Yang and David Filo.

Network

A network is the means by which computers and peripheral devices, such as printers, can be connected in order to share and transfer data. The main types of network are classified by the pattern of the connections – star or ring network,

for example – or by the degree of geographical spread allowed: for example, **local area networks** (LANs) connect computers within a small space, such as a room or building, and wide area networks (WANs) connect LANs. The **Internet** is a worldwide network, used by over 500 million people, which connects university, government, commercial and other computers.

Neuro-linguistic programming (NLP)

Critics of neuro-linguistic programming suggest that it is better suited to a cult than to a business. They may well be right. NLP basically entails systematically using language to exert influence over people. It is built on the recognition that voice quality is 38 percent of the total impact of the communication. Control that, and you control the result of the conversation. The concept was conceived by US mathematician Richard Bandler and linguistics professor John Grinder. The two met at the University of California at Santa Cruz in the 1970s.

NLP has yielded an impressive crop of jargon. There is 'syntactic ambiguity' (an ambiguous sentence where a verb plus *ing* can serve either as an adjective or a verb – such as influencing) and 'tonal marking' ('using your voice to mark out certain words as being significant'). There is also a host of books on the subject and a sizeable and loyal band of followers.

Key text
• Richard Bandler and John Grinder. *Frogs Into Princes: Neuro Linguistic Programming.* Real People Press, 1979

New Economy

The New Economy can be defined as the impact of the information and communications technologies (ICT) sector, or even the Internet, on productivity growth. Another definition specific to the United States is 'the developments that led to the sustained non-inflationary growth in the United States from the early 1990s onwards'. This definition would include new technological developments such as the Internet, the PC and mobile phones; globalization; low unemployment; and better macroeconomic management, particularly with respect to the rate of inflation. The importance of human capital, including knowledge, creativity and social networks, is also a defining characteristic of the New Economy. Physical and financial assets are often far less important. This is in stark contrast with the old economy. For old-economy companies, the key competitive assets are physical and financial assets, such as machinery, goods and property.

New market space

W. Chan Kim and Renée Mauborgne, of the French business school INSEAD, have produced some of the most interesting work in the area of strategy in recent years. Companies, say Kim and Mauborgne, become mired in taking on their competitors in macho, head-to-head battles. If one company jumps ahead, the others follow by doing the same thing. Competitive advantage is short-lived and insubstantial – an incremental improvement here and there. Breaking free of the competition should be every company's objective. Only by creating its own 'market space' can a company achieve significant competitive advantage.

Kim and Mauborgne suggest that only by looking *across* not within traditional boundaries of competition, can companies develop the necessary insights to break free. They have developed a Six Path Framework to creating new market space. It includes: looking across industries – here they point to the example of Home Depot, which looked more broadly at the home-improvement needs of its consumers and recognized that different consumers have different needs; looking across strategic groups; looking across buyer groups; looking across complementary products and services; looking across the functional/ emotional orientation of an industry; and looking across time. By looking at old data in new ways, inspirations and insights may arise.

Key text

- W. Chan Kim and Renée Mauborgne. 'Creating New Market Space.' *Harvard Business Review*, January/February 1999

New York Stock Exchange (NYSE)

The New York Stock Exchange is the principal stock market in the United States. Founded in 1792 under the Buttonwood Agreement (so called because they met under a buttonwood tree), signed by 24 New York City stockbrokers and merchants, the exchange first operated from a rented room at 40 Wall Street. It moved to a 5-storey building at 10 Broad Street in 1817, and was relocated in new buildings on the same site with the address 18 Broad Street. The name 'New York Stock Exchange' was only adopted in 1863. The market suffered the first of several 'black' days when gold speculation resulted in Black Friday in September 1869. Telephones were introduced in 1878, and the market had its first million-share day on 15 December 1886 (28 October 1997 was the first billion-share day). In 1934, the NYSE registered as a national securities exchange with the US **Securities and Exchange Commission** (SEC) and it was incorporated in 1971 as a not-for-profit corporation.

More than 3000 companies are listed for trading on the NYSE. To acquire a listing, a company must be registered with the SEC and meet a range of specific criteria. Listed companies are usually the larger, better-established companies. The first stock traded – underneath the buttonwood tree, back in 1792 – was the Bank of New York. The stock listed for the longest period is Consolidated Edison, first listed in 1824 as the New York Gas Light Company.

Key link

- www.nyse.com

Key text

- James Buck (ed). *The New York Stock Exchange: The First 200 Years*. Greenwich Publishing Group, 1992

Ninety percent club

The ninety percent club is a term coined by the media that refers a group of companies whose share price has fallen by 90 percent or more from its high. Most 'members' of the club are dotcom companies – dot bombs, as they are known – or companies associated with the Internet. Members of the ninety percent club include companies like ICG Communications, a US company whose share price plunged from a peak of $39.25 in 2000 to 25 cents in less than a year, for a drop of 99.4 percent. Other illustrious members include UK companies QXL, Scoot and Affinity Internet.

Nonaka, Ikujiro

Academic and business author

Ikujiro Nonaka's work reached a big audience for the first time with the success of *The Knowledge-Creating Company*, which he co-authored with Hirotaka Takeuchi. His prominence culminated in May 1997 with Nonaka's appointment to the first professorship dedicated to the study of knowledge and its impact on business at the University of California's Haas School of Business. Nonaka is also professor of management at Japan's Hitosubashi University, but is no stranger to the University of California, from which he has both an MBA and a PhD.

Nonaka and Takeuchi's 1995 book was at the vanguard of interest in managing knowledge. In it, the duo argued that Japan's industrial success was grounded on innovation. But why is Japan more innovative than the West? The answer from Nonaka and Takeuchi is that the West emphasizes 'explicit knowledge' – things that can be measured and monitored – while the Japanese value 'tacit knowledge' – the elusive and abstract. The West is hidebound by its faith in rationalism; the East enabled by its 'oneness of body and mind'. Interestingly, Nonaka and Takeuchi also speak up in favour of middle management. Rather than regarding middle managers as the burdensome masses, they suggest that they are vital conduits

for innovation, voices of reason below the chaotic creativity of the top.

Nonaka has gone on to write *Relentless* (with Johny K. Johansson), a populist insight into the art of Japanese marketing.

Key texts

- Ikujiro Nonaka and Hirotaka Takeuchi. *The Knowledge-Creating Company: How Japanese Companies Create the Dynamics of Innovation.* Oxford University Press, 1995
- Johny K. Johansson and Ikujiro Nonaka. *Relentless: The Japanese Way of Marketing.* Harper Business, 1997

Non-disclosure agreement (NDA)

When either party to an agreement, discussion or negotiation wishes for all or part of their dealings to remain confidential, they will require the other to sign a non-disclosure agreement. This is a one-sided or mutually binding agreement in which the parties agree to protect the confidentiality of any discussions that take place or information that exchanges hands. NDAs are frequently requested by **entrepreneurs** wishing to discuss a new business idea with a view to raising finance. Very few **venture capitalists**, however, will agree to sign. NDAs are also often required by manufacturers from programmers, journalists and others in exchange for detailed information or copies of new products in advance of their public launch. For example, a manufacturer might sign an NDA to get a copy of a new operating system in order to have compatible hardware ready for the program's launch. NDAs are often required in order to participate in beta (pre-launch) tests of important pieces of software.

Non-executive director (NXD)

A non-executive director sits on a board in an advisory capacity and is not involved in the day-to-day running of the company. Non-executive directors are usually appointed for their wealth of business experience. They are also appointed by **venture capitalists** to the boards of new ventures.

Non-governmental organization (NGO)

A non-governmental organization is a not-for-profit organization. NGOs are usually issues-driven organizations: they might, for example, focus on environmental matters, human rights or health. Well-known NGOs include Amnesty International, Greenpeace and Oxfam. Governments are involved in the formation of some NGOs, where they appoint panel or board members. These organizations are known as quasi-autonomous non-governmental organizations (QUANGOS) and, while not directly part of a government, may report to a government minister.

Nordström, Kjell and Ridderstråle, Jonas

Funky business gurus (b. 1958 and 1966)

The typical business guru is an American academic in a dull suit who runs through a well-worn presentation and then collects his cheque. Kjell Nordström and his partner Jonas Ridderstråle are different. They are Swedish, young and have shaved heads. They do gigs, not seminars. They are not **Michael Porter**. In fact, the only similarity between the Swedish duo and conventional gurus is their jobs – they are academics at the Stockholm School of Economics. In unconventional times, Nordström and Ridderstråle are building up a sizeable following throughout Scandinavia and increasingly beyond. Their seminars sell out and their book, *Funky Business*, was the first business blockbuster of the new century.

Their ideas focus on globalization and innovation. In a world of suits, Nordström and Ridderstråle's message is refreshingly different.

Key text
- Jonas Ridderstråle, Kjell Nordström. *Funky Business*. Financial Times – Prentice Hall, 2000

Key link
- www.funkybusiness.com

NPR costs

Companies typically spend 20 to 25 percent of sales on third-party suppliers for goods and services not directly related to the end product or services of the business. These non-product related (NPR) costs sometimes exceed those spent directly for the end product. Non-product related goods and services consume considerable budgets and those budgets are usually rising. John Houlihan of consulting firm Booz Allen & Hamilton is one of the experts in the emerging field looking at the dynamics of NPR sourcing.

Its importance is obvious. Managed more rigorously, NPR sourcing's hidden value can be substantial. According to Houlihan, companies can often save approximately 25 percent of their current annual NPR expenditures, with savings of 15 percent achievable within two years. This can be equivalent to around 2 to 4 percent of sales, and may exceed this amount.

Among the organizations that have already reaped the benefits of paying closer attention to NPR costs are a major Dutch bank, which realized annual savings of 21 percent on its printed material; a UK government agency, which saved 23 percent on its cleaning services; and a German electronics company, which saved between 30 and 40 percent on its telecommunications expenditure.

Houlihan emphasizes that there is more to NPR management than mere cost-cutting. Managing the purchasing of NPR goods and services more professionally can have a much broader impact, with improved overall organizational effectiveness and enhanced strategic capabilities, as it encompasses such activities as advertising, transportation, research services and information systems. The wonder is that apparently well-managed companies have overlooked NPR goods and services for so long.

Key text
- John Houlihan. 'How to Capture Hidden Value.' *Strategy & Business*, First Quarter 1999

O

Obsolescence

When a product or service is no longer of any use, or – in the case of many retail goods – out of date, it is termed obsolescent. Consumer perception plays a large part in determining obsolescence, as goods that are perfectly usable become obsolescent because they fall out of fashion. One major reason for this is advances in product technology. Thus, vinyl records became obsolete and were replaced by cassette tapes, which in turn were replaced by CDs. Yet vinyl LPs were and still are perfectly functional. Manufacturers and retailers are often accused of hastening the obsolescence of products to increase profits.

OECD (Organization for Economic Cooperation and Development)

Superseding the Organization for European Economic Cooperation, which was formed to administer the Marshall Plan after World War II, the Organization for Economic Cooperation and Development (OECD) was founded in 1961. It is an organization that provides a forum for its members to discuss, develop and perfect economic and social policy. The OECD headquarters is in Paris and its 29 full members include the most powerful economic powers in the world, including the United States, the United Kingdom and Japan. It has been described as a think-tank, monitoring agency and rich nations' club (its members produce two-thirds of the world's goods and services) and possesses elements of all three. Agencies oper-ating under the auspices of the OECD include the European Nuclear Energy Agency and the Centre for Educational Research and Innovation.

Off-balance-sheet financing

Through complex arrangements, it is possible to legally obtain financing without reflecting the borrowing in the accounts. This makes certain ratios, such as **gearing**, appear better than they actually are. The Accounting Standards Board encourages companies to paint a true picture of their financial position in their accounts and is seeking to control the use of off-balance-sheet financing. The legal structures used to bend the intention of the rules are often referred to as special purpose vehicles (SPV) or special purpose corporations (SPC). Off-balance-sheet financing got a bad name for itself when it was associated with the collapse of US energy company Enron in 2001.

Office of Fair Trading (OFT)

The Office of Fair Trading is an independent organization in the UK set up in 1973 to monitor compliance with the Fair Trading Act (1973). Run by the director-general, the OFT operates in three main areas: competition enforcement, consumer regulation enforcement and markets and policies initiatives. This means that it deals with such issues as monopolies, consumer credit, restrictive trade practices, anti-competitive practices, consumer affairs and takeover bids.

Key link
- www.oft.gov.uk

Ogilvy, David Mackenzie

Advertising wizard; co-founder, Ogilvy & Mather (1911–1999)

David Ogilvy was born on 23 June 1911, the son of a stockbroker. He was educated at Fettes School, a prestigious private school near Edinburgh, Scotland, and Christ Church College at Oxford University, where he secured a scholarship to study history.

After university, Ogilvy sought adventure, trading the dreaming spires of Oxford for the boulevards of Paris, where he worked in the kitchens of the Hotel Majestic. His first assignment was to prepare meals for customers' dogs. Tiring of *la vie Parisienne*, he returned to England to sell a special type of cooking stove, the AGA. He was so successful as a salesman that he was asked to write a manual on how to sell the cooker for the AGA sales force (30 years later, the editors of *Fortune* magazine announced that it was probably the best sales manual of all time). Ogilvy sent the manual to his brother, who worked at London-based advertising agency Mather & Crowther. Impressed, the agency offered him a place as a trainee.

Ogilvy enjoyed the London lifestyle and successfully combined a lavish social life with hard work. He demonstrated a natural aptitude for his new vocation and began to develop his own theories about advertising. 'Concrete figures must be substituted for atmospheric claims; clichés must give way to facts, and empty exhortations to alluring offers,' an enthusiastic Ogilvy wrote in a presentation to his colleagues in the early 1930s.

In 1938, Ogilvy quit his job and set off on another adventure. He travelled to the United States, where he acquired a circle of celebrity friends, including Harpo Marx and Ethel Barrymore. Deciding to stay longer, he moved to Princeton and worked with Dr George Gallup, the man behind the Gallup polls. The experience of working for Gallup provided an invaluable insight into US consumer preferences and the way that they were formed.

The next stop on Ogilvy's haphazard career journey was a position with British intelligence in Washington during World War II. When the war ended, he took to tobacco farming in the heart of the Amish community, in Lancaster County, Pennsylvania. But before long, he was back in New York.

Ogilvy's career in advertising owes much to the endeavours of his brother, who helped Ogilvy secure $45,000 to finance a new agency. He also persuaded another British advertising agency, SH Benson, to invest an additional $45,000 in return for a partnership.

Hewitt, Ogilvy, Benson & Mather opened for business in 1948. The early days were tough. Winning US clients proved difficult for the British Ogilvy, although the addition of Anderson Hewitt, a former employee of J. Walter Thompson, helped. Indeed, Hewitt's uncle, the chairman of J.P. Morgan & Co., lent the agency $100,000 with no security to save the agency at one point. Hewitt also won the first major account, Sun Oil, worth some $3 million.

Although the agency was small, Ogilvy's advertising intuition set the company apart from its competitors. His style was evident in an early campaign for Hathaway shirt makers. Ads featured the man with the eye patch, known as the man from Hathaway, who supported the small shirt makers from Maine in their efforts to take on the giant shirt maker Arrow. Ogilvy used photographs, still a rarity in advertising at that point, featuring a male model, complete with eye patch, performing a variety of unusual tasks. The Hathaway campaign made Ogilvy's reputation and was an early example of his approach to **brand** building and supporting brands through brand image. In a campaign for Schweppes, Ogilvy used the knowledge that he acquired working with Gallup. He assuaged US consumer sensibilities about class by using Commander Edward Whitehead, the distinguished-looking Schweppes boss. Schweppes' sales in the United States bubbled up by 500 percent over the following nine years.

'At 60 miles an hour, the loudest noise in this new Rolls-Royce comes from the electric clock,' was Ogilvy's slogan for his Rolls-Royce campaign. It typified his approach of putting the product centre stage. 'Make your product the hero of the commercial,' Ogilvy famously entreated. As the agency's client list grew, Ogilvy's attempts to alter the advertising industry grew bolder. In 1960, Ogilvy challenged one of the industry's prized but outdated practices: the 15 percent commission. Ogilvy's stance guaranteed publicity. It succeeded in bringing in new clients, such as Shell, who were only too happy to be rid of the 15 percent commission in exchange for a flat fee.

In 1965, the year after his brother's death, Ogilvy's firm merged with Mather & Crowther to form Ogilvy & Mather, creating an agency with total billings of $120 million. In 1966, Ogilvy & Mather became a publicly listed company, only the sixth advertising agency to do so, Ogilvy becoming a wealthy man by selling 61,000 shares of his 161,000-share allotment.

In 1975, Ogilvy & Mather was one of the top 5 advertising agencies in the world, with 1000 clients, offices in 29 countries, and billings of some $800 million. In the same year, Ogilvy stepped down from his position as creative head to spend more time at his twelfth-century chateau in the south of France. In 1989, following a wave of mergers in the industry, Ogilvy's remaining share in the business was acquired by WPP Group. Ogilvy died in 1999.

Key texts
- David Ogilvy. *Ogilvy on Advertising*. Crown, 1983
- David Ogilvy. *Blood, Brains & Beer*. Atheneum, 1978
- David Ogilvy. *Confessions of an Advertising Man*. Atheneum, 1963

Key link
- www.ogilvy.com

Ohmae, Kenichi

Japanese consultant (b. 1943)

There is no doubting that Kenichi Ohmae has the credentials of a modern Renaissance man. He is a graduate of Waseda University and the Tokyo Institute of Technology, and has a PhD in nuclear engineering from the Massachusetts Institute of Technology. He is also a talented flautist and sometime adviser to the former Japanese Prime Minster Nakasone. Ohmae joined **McKinsey** in 1972, becoming managing director of its Tokyo office. McKinsey Americanized him as 'Ken', but the ambitions of his thinking remained resolutely global.

Ohmae's work is important for two reasons. First, he revealed the truth behind Japanese strategizing to an expectant Western audience. Second, Ohmae has explored the ramifications of globalization more extensively than virtually any other thinker.

Ohmae's first contribution was to explode the simplistic Western myth that Japanese management was all about company songs and lifetime employment. There was much more to Japanese management – most notably, the Japanese art of strategic thinking. This, said Ohmae, is 'basically creative and intuitive and rational', though none of these characteristics were evident in the usual Western stereotype of Japanese management.

Ohmae pointed out that unlike large US corporations, Japanese businesses tend not to have large strategic-planning staffs. Instead, they often have a single, naturally talented strategist with 'an idiosyncratic mode of thinking in which company, customers, and competition merge in a dynamic interaction out of which a comprehensive set of objectives and plans for action eventually crystallizes'.

Ohmae also noted that the customer was at the heart of the Japanese approach to strategy and key to corporate values. 'In the construction of any business strategy, three main players must be taken into account: the corporation itself, the customer, and the competition. Each of these "strategic three Cs" is a living entity with its own interests and objectives. We shall call them, collectively, the "strategic triangle",' he said. 'Seen in the context of the strategic triangle, the job of the strategist is to achieve superior performance, relative to competition, in the key factors for success of the business. At the same time, the strategist must be sure that his strategy properly matches the strengths of the corporation with the needs of a clearly defined market. Positive matching of the needs and objectives of the two parties involved is required for a lasting good relationship; without it, the corporation's long-term viability may be at stake.'

The central thrust of Ohmae's arguments was that strategy, as epitomized by the Japanese approach, is irrational and non-linear. (Previously, the Japanese had been fêted in the West for the brilliance of their rationality and the farsighted remorselessness of their thinking.) 'Phenomena and events in the real world do not always fit a linear model. Hence the most reliable means of dissecting a situation into its constituent parts and reassembling them in the desired pattern is not a step-by-step methodology such as systems analysis. Rather, it is that ultimate non-linear thinking tool, the human brain. True strategic thinking thus contrasts sharply with the conventional mechanical systems approach based on linear thinking. But it also contrasts with the approach that stakes everything on intuition, reaching conclusions without any real breakdown or analysis.'

Ohmae went on to suggest that an effective business strategy 'is one by which a company can gain significant ground on its competitors at an acceptable cost to itself'. This can be achieved in four ways: by focusing on the key factors for success (KFSs); by building on relative superiority; through pursuing aggressive initiatives; and by utilizing strategic degrees of freedom. By this, Ohmae means that the company can focus upon innovation in areas that are 'untouched by competitors'.

The second area that Ohmae has greatly influenced is that of globalization. In *Triad Power* (1985), he suggested that the route to global competitiveness is to establish a presence in each area of the Triad (United States; Japan and the Pacific;

Europe). Also, companies must utilize the three Cs of commitment, creativity and competitiveness.

To Ohmae, countries are mere governmental creations. In the Interlinked Economy (also made up of the Triad) consumers are not driven to purchase things through nationalistic sentiments, no matter what politicians suggest or say.

'The essence of business strategy is offering better value to customers than the competition, in the most cost-effective and sustainable way,' Ohmae writes. 'But today, thousands of competitors from every corner of the world are able to serve customers well. To develop effective strategy, we as leaders have to understand what's happening in the rest of the world, and reshape our organization to respond accordingly. No leader can hope to guide an enterprise into the future without understanding the commercial, political, and social impact of the global economy.'

Ohmae suggests that corporate leaders should concentrate on building networks. 'We have to learn to share, sort, and synthesize information, rather than simply direct the work of others. We have to rethink our basic approach to decision making, risk taking, and organizational strategy. And we have to create meaning and uphold values in flatter, more disciplined enterprises,' Ohmae concludes. We will, it seems, have to forget the past in order to create the future.

Key texts

- Kenichi Ohmae. *The End of the Nation State.* HarperCollins, 1995
- Kenichi Ohmae. *The Borderless World.* William Collins, 1990
- Kenichi Ohmae. *Triad Power: The Coming Shape of Global Competition.* Free Press, 1985
- Kenichi Ohmae. *The Mind of the Strategist.* McGraw-Hill, 1982

Old economy

See New Economy.

Oligopoly

Unlike a monopoly, in which one company dominates a market, an oligopoly is a situation in which a few powerful companies control the major part of a particular market. For example, in the United Kingdom, the two largest soap-powder companies – Procter & Gamble and Unilever – control over 85 percent of the market. Firms may fall foul of restrictive trade practice legislation if they are operating in an oligopoly. This is because collusion to fix prices or restrict competition in other ways, such as acting as a **cartel**, is illegal in many countries, including the European Union.

Ollila, Jorma Jaakko

CEO, Nokia (b. 1950)

CEO of one of Europe's high-tech corporate superstars, Jorma Jaakko Ollila was born on 15 August 1950 in Seinäjoki, Finland. He had a slightly unorthodox education: at the age of 17, he obtained a scholarship at Atlantic College. Atlantic College, situated in Wales, is a unique educational establishment founded by Kurt Hahn in 1962, a German national. The educational philosophy is to bring together individuals with leadership qualities who then go on to become political or commercial leaders throughout the world.

After Atlantic College, Ollila studied at the University of Helsinki, obtaining a Master of Political Science degree in 1976, followed by a Master of Science degree in 1978 at the London School of Economics and a Master of Science degree in 1981 from the Helsinki University of Technology. With his academic career over, he joined Citibank, working on the Nokia account. In 1985, he swapped sides, joining the Finnish company as vice-president of international operations. Just one year later, at the age of 35, he was named chief financial officer.

Nokia started life as three separate companies: the Finnish Cable Works; the Finnish Rubber Works; and the Nokia forest products company. The three merged in 1967 and the new company took its name from the timber mill, which in turn took its name from the Nokia River in southern Finland.

Although Scandinavian countries gained a head start in wireless telephony through innovative research, Nokia almost managed to give the market away to Motorola in the 1970s. It was the beginning of a bleak period in the company's history. Nokia's CEO, Kari Kairamo, hedged his bets by investing in a range of high-tech operations, including mobile-phone manufacturing. But Kairamo underestimated the demand for mobile telephones and with its diversified interests, Nokia lost market share to Motorola, which was focused solely on the mass production of mobile phones.

Things went from bad to worse when, in 1988, Kairamo committed suicide. In 1991, the USSR disintegrated, taking one of Nokia's principal markets with it. Ollila stepped into this difficult situation in 1990, when he was put in charge of the mobile-phone business. His first decision was to keep the mobile phone unit rather than sell it to raise much-needed financing. Ollila set about raising morale and reorganizing the mobile phone unit.

When Ollila became CEO in 1992, he embarked on a wholesale rationalization of the company, ditching non-core activities like the paper, rubber, cable, computer and TV businesses. Putting his telecom strategy into action required cash, so Ollila turned to the United States for investment. In 1994, Nokia was listed on the New York Stock Exchange. Between 1994 and 1999, the share price rose over 2000 percent.

One change at Nokia instituted by Ollila is the focus on brand image. Abandoning the existing array of mobile phone brands produced by Nokia, Ollila concentrated on a product line emblazoned with the Nokia name. 'Telecom-oriented, global, focus, value-added' was Ollila's strategy. Competitors might obsess about continually shrinking the size of the mobile phone. Ollila went further, hiring designers to make Nokia's mobile phone a fashion statement. He brought in technicians to create revolutionary scrolling-text displays and other refinements that made the phone as user-friendly as possible. The first digital offering by the company in 1993 was predicted to sell at least 400,000 units. It sold more than 20 million. Profits soared from zero in 1991 to $4 billion in 1999.

As well as non-core businesses, Ollila cut out internal bureaucracy. Out went hierarchical management structures; in came a flat organizational structure. Things get done in the company via networks of individuals. It's an entrepreneurial, innovative environment within a large corporation. Then there is the Nokia Way – a means of tapping into root feeling at the company. Brainstorming at a series of meetings throughout the company is synthesized into a vision statement by the top managers, and this is disseminated back through the organization via a series of presentations. The Nokia Way keeps the employees plugged in to the company.

The year 2000 saw a change in market sentiment toward telecom companies. Used to astonishing growth year-over-year, investors ran for cover when Ollila warned of disappointing third-quarter results in 2000. Shares dropped by 26 percent, wiping out $60 billion worth of market value in a single day. Worse, there was the threat of the mobile Internet and other forms of mobile data transfer. 'It's a big paradigm shift,' said Ollila. 'We have the challenge of sailing in much more uncertain waters.'

Ollila met the many challenges facing Nokia head-on. As a handset manufacturer, Nokia is threatened by commoditization. Some 40 multinationals, more than a dozen companies in China have the ability to manufacture mobile phones. More manufacturers means more phones, which means lower prices and thus lower profits. Ollila is confident that the lure of the Nokia brand and its personalization of phones will outweigh the attraction of low-cost, mass-market clones.

Network business also offers some consolation for Ollila. Twenty-five percent of Nokia's sales in 2000 came from this part of Nokia's operations. Furthermore, the company is still well regarded: in INSEAD business school's 'Competitive Fitness', a study of 67 multinationals in 2001, Nokia was ranked number one. But Ollila can't afford to rest on the company's reputation for long. Difficult challenges lie ahead. Ollila's job at Nokia is far from over. His reputation as a great businessman rests partly on what happens over the next few years.

Key texts

- Dan Steinbock. *The Nokia Revolution: The Story of an Extraordinary Company that Transformed an Industry.* McGraw-Hill, 2001
- Trevor Merriden. *Business the Nokia Way: Secrets of the World's Fastest Moving Company.* John Wiley, 2000

Omidyar, Pierre

Internet entrepreneur and free market philanthropist; founder, eBay (b. 1967)

One of world's most successful **Internet** companies, eBay is the online equivalent of Aladdin's cave, a treasure trove stuffed to the rafters with everything from Beanie Babies to Old Masters. Founder Pierre Omidyar started the business as a hobby, but an **IPO** and 30 million registered users later, Omidyar is one of the richest men in the world.

Omidyar was born in France in 1967 and moved to the United States at the age of 6. His father took up a residency at the Johns Hopkins University Medical Center in Maryland. Omidyar studied Computer Science at Tufts University, Massachusetts. He had already displayed an aptitude for technology. He hired himself out to the school library for six dollars an hour, writing computer programs to print out catalogue cards.

Omidyar went into the computer industry after college, as a software developer first at Claris and then at General Magic Inc. Omidyar's first attempt to start his own company was Ink Development Corporation. The company created software that allowed computers to interpret instructions entered by pen rather than via a keyboard. Later renamed eShop, it was sold to Microsoft in 1996.

The idea for eBay emerged from a conversation with his then-fiancée (now his wife), Pamela, while Omidyar was still at General Magic. A keen collector of Pez dispensers – the candy dispensers with a cartoon character head that tilts back – she was keen to meet other enthusiasts and trade dispensers. Omidyar decided to create a Web site where collectors could meet to buy, sell and discuss their collections with fellow enthusiasts. The centrepiece would be an online consumer-to-consumer auction. 'What I wanted to do was create a marketplace where everyone had access to the same information,' Omidyar later observed.

eBay started life as a home page hosted by a local Internet service provider in 1995. The name eBay stands for 'electronic Bay Area,' after the Bay Area of San Francisco. What began as a small-scale hobby soon blossomed into a business. By 1996, Omidyar had given up his day job to look after eBay. It was soon apparent to Omidyar that there was huge commercial potential for his new business.

Others were persuaded by Omidyar's vision. Venture capital firm Benchmark Capital put in $6.7 million for 22 percent of the new company. By April 1999, the value of its stake had increased to $5.1 billion. Unlike most other dotcom businesses, eBay turned a profit early on, in February 1996. From then on, it was just a question of marking the mileposts. The site sold 3 million items by the end of 1997; was ranked the number-one e-commerce site, based on time spent by users, in May 1998; completed its 10 millionth auction in May 1998; and had more than a million registered users by August 1998. The IPO was in September 1998. From $18, the share price shot up to $53.50. eBay staff danced the conga. Omidyar was worth $274.1 million on paper.

Omidyar had developed one of the best business models on the Net. Revenue comes from the seller's fee plus a commission on the realized price. While commissions may only amount to a few dollars, with more than half a million new items added daily, it soon adds up.

Astute enough to realize when his company had outgrown his ability to manage it single-handedly, Omidyar bought in experienced managers at the right time. First Jeff Skoll, a Stanford MBA and friend of Omidyar's, was brought in as a partner. Then, in 1997, he recruited former Disney marketing executive Meg Whitman from Hasbro to oversee the company's IPO.

eBay is firmly established as one of the Internet's top brands, along with other virtual heavyweights such as Amazon.com and Yahoo! For the nine months ended 30 September 2001, revenues rose 78 percent to $529.4 million. Net income totalled $64.5 million, up from $24.4 million. More than 29.7 million registered eBay users buy and sell items in more than 4500 categories. Millions of items are auctioned off every day.

The company has bought traditional bricks-and-mortar auctioneers to add cachet, build **brand** and increase its user base; aggressively expanded into Europe, all but wiping out competitors such as QXL; and secured alternative revenue streams from business-to-business auction services and fixed-price sales. As eBay shifts upmarket, it is capturing some of the premium auction business and richer clientele by offering goods such as antiques and Old Master paintings.

Omidyar, meanwhile, takes a back seat. Like many wealthy businessmen before him, he has turned into a philanthropist; but this is philanthropy with a twist. In a self-proclaimed drive to rid himself of 99 percent of his fortune during his lifetime, Omidyar has spawned a new form of philanthropy – venture philanthropy. The theory is that Omidyar and his wife will seed a number of causes as they might finance a start-up, favouring those that present a solid business plan and meet key criteria on points such as earnings streams. Then, in a scenario that mirrors the savage world of dotcom business, the non-profits that perform poorly are dropped and the ones that prosper go on to become national organizations. Whether the free market model will prove to be an effective one for non-profit organizations remains to be seen.

Key text
• David Bunnell. *The eBay Phenomenon: Business Secrets Behind the World's Hottest Internet Company*. John Wiley, 2000

Key link
- www.ebay.com

Onassis, Aristotle

Shipping magnate (1900–1975)

To say that Aristotle Onassis's life was colourful would be an understatement. His playboy reputation, marriages, affairs and extravagances are well documented. But there was a good deal more to Onassis than fabulous wealth, Maria Callas and Jackie Kennedy.

Onassis was born in the port of Smyrna, Turkey, on 20 January 1900. By the time Onassis was born, his father was a successful tobacco dealer. Onassis had little time for school, producing consistently poor grades. Instead, he dreamed of becoming a great businessman. 'Great scholars do not make good businessmen and are seldom rich,' he would say. On 27 August 1923, with $250 in his pocket and a third-class ticket, he set sail for Argentina and a new life.

In Argentina, Onassis worked as a telephone operator for a short while. Then, with the help of $700 that he earned playing the stock market, he started his own tobacco business. The business got off to an unpromising start when Greece, the country he was importing tobacco from, announced that it was applying a 1000 percent increase in taxes on those countries with which it did not have a trade agreement. This included Argentina. Onassis boldly drafted a memo to the Greek government complaining. The government didn't change its policy, but it did appoint Onassis as Greece's deputy consul to Argentina.

Onassis's next move was into shipping. Unable to find a decent vessel to purchase in Europe, he was tipped off about some ships belonging to the Canadian National Steamship Company and anchored in the Saint Lawrence River. They were $30,000 apiece. Onassis, in full view of the authorities, crawled over every inch frowning and making lengthy notes. He bought six – for $20,000 each.

When World War II came, it threatened to scupper Onassis's plans for expansion. Two-thirds of his fleet was sequestered in neutral ports. Onassis was forced to do some rapid manoeuvring, sell two cargo ships to Japan, and take a hit on his personal fortune – down from $8 million to $2 million. But he was still in business.

Onassis emerged from the war relatively unscathed. His remaining ships, leased to the US Navy for $250,000 per year, were still intact. Similarly, his oil tankers, impounded in Scandinavia, were undamaged. Of the 450 Greek ships involved in the war, 360 had been sunk. Onassis did not lose a single vessel. His business was in better shape than ever.

After the war, the Liberty Ships built by the US Navy were put up for sale. Onassis unsuccessfully bid for 13 but was cut out by the Greek shipping families who regarded him as a parvenu. Instead, he formed a US company – United States Petroleum Carriers, fronted by prominent US businessmen – purchased a number of oil tankers available only to US companies, and then obtained a controlling interest through his Panama-based holding company. He followed up his audacious coup by arranging a $40 million loan to build five new tankers. His business acumen soon earned him the sobriquet of the 'Golden Greek'.

By 1946, Onassis had the biggest shipping company in the world. In December 1946, he married a Greek-American, Tina Livanos, and settled in New York. For a while, his ships were built in the United States. When shipbuilding became too expensive in America, he turned to Hamburg, where his tankers had been built before the war. The Potsdam Accords limited German-built ship tonnage to 15,000 tons, stifling business in the shipyards of post-war Hamburg. As usual, Onassis and his lawyers found a loophole. There were no restrictions on whaling ships, so Onassis took up whaling.

Until 1954, Onassis operated the largest whaling fleet in the world. However, when the Onassis whaling fleet encroached on Peruvian waters for the second time, the fleet was machine-gunned, bombed and forced to put in at Lima. Four hundred sailors were imprisoned and five ships sequestered. In March 1956, Onassis disbanded his whaling fleet and sold it to Japanese interests.

Master of the waves for two decades, Onassis decided to take to the skies. In 1956, Onassis started Greece's first privately owned national carrier – the first in the world. The airline was named Olympic Airways. The fleet of aircraft was limited to twelve DC-8s, a Dakota, and one DC-4. But Onassis scheduled two international flights: one to Paris and one to London. For agreeing to take over the national fleet, he was rewarded with extremely advantageous terms: a monopoly for 20 years, reimbursement for losses due to strike action, exemption from land taxes and other tax benefits.

In his final years, Onassis suffered a series of business setbacks. His son Alexander died in a freak airplane accident. His business empire, the running of which he had delegated, began to come apart at the seams. The oil crisis of the early 1970s meant that much of his fleet was idle. In January 1975, he was forced to hand over Olympic Airlines to the Greek government after the junta led by the 'colonels' was overthrown. A major property deal turned bad. Onassis's socializing and flamboyant social life had taken the edge off of his formerly razor-sharp business acumen. He had lost his enthusiasm for business and life.

In February 1975, he had an operation to remove his gall bladder but never fully recovered. He died on 15 March 1975.

Key texts
- Peter Evans. *Ari: The Life & Times of Aristotle Socrates Onassis.* Summit Books, 1986
- Nicholas Fraser, Philip Jacobson, Mark Ottaway and Lewis Chester. *Aristotle Onassis.* J.B. Lippincott, 1977

One-to-one marketing

The concept of one-to-one marketing is most closely associated with US consultants Don Pep-

pers and Martha Rogers of the Peppers & Rogers Group. It involves providing services or products to a single customer at a time by identifying and then meeting his individual needs. The aim is to do this on a continuing basis with each customer. The theory is that one-to-one marketing should go beyond the sale of a product or service to the customer and permeate the organization. One-to-one marketing should become part of company culture, part of the vision driving the company. One-to-one marketing offers several benefits, including a concentration on the most profitable customers, obstacles to comparative shopping, lifetime customer relationships, the development of customer feedback and the resulting product improvement, and differentiation from competitors.

Were it not for technology, one-to-one marketing would be an impractical approach for any company other than one serving a niche market of wealthy customers. Modern technology makes it possible to provide mass customization of products.

Key text
- Don Peppers, Martha Rogers and Bob Dorf. *The One to One Fieldbook: The Complete Toolkit for Implementing a Tool Marketing Program.* Doubleday, 1999

OPEC (Organization of the Petroleum Exporting Countries)

Created in 1960, the Organization of the Petroleum Exporting Countries operates to protect its members' interests by manipulating oil production and thus the price of crude oil. Its headquarters are in Vienna. Members include Algeria, Indonesia, Iraq, Iran, Kuwait, Libya, Nigeria, Qatar, Saudi Arabia, United Arab Emirates and Venezuela. Saudi Arabia tends to dominate OPEC and play a major role in its decision-making process. OPEC is in an extremely powerful position, as it controls 40 to 50 percent of the world's crude-oil reserves.

Key link

- www.opec.org

Open question

An open question is a question that does not limit the response to a specific answer. Contrast this with a closed question, such as, 'Is that card red or black?' Only one of a defined number of replies is possible. Open questions are intended to elicit a range of responses to gauge the opinion of the person answering the questions. In a questionnaire, these would be the questions without multiple choices. Open questions are common in job interviews. For example, the interviewer might ask questions such as, 'Why do you think you are a suitable candidate for this position? What made you want to join this company?'

Open source

Open source is usually used to describe source code (the basic building block of software programs) that is freely available and able to be modified by the end user. Open-source code is the antithesis of capitalism and the usual commercial business model, where source code would be a jealously guarded secret, protected by intellectual property laws and licensed for a fee to bring in, in some cases, multimillion dollar revenues.

Instead, open-source code is based on the belief that the open-source, collaborative model is the way to engineer the best software and that commercialism often produces inferior applications. Open source is promoted by a group of computer programmers, who are driven by their philosophical beliefs and collectively known as the open-source movement. Notable examples of open-source software include Linux, Perl, PHP and the Apache Web server. Advocates of the open-source movement include the Swedish inventor of Linux, Linus Torvalds, and American Eric Raymond, author of *The Cathedral & the Bazaar*.

Key text

- Eric S. Raymond. *The Cathedral & the Bazaar: Musings on Linux and Open Source by an Accidental Revolutionary*. O'Reilly & Associates, 1999

Online analytical processing (OLAP)

A company can have all the data in the world, but it's what the company does with the information that matters. An increasing amount of data means that business analysis is becoming ever more important. While data warehousing enables a larger number of people than ever before to carry out detailed and complex analysis of customers, products and markets, online analytical processing (OLAP) gives companies the opportunity to carry out analysis to discover the reasons behind what is happening.

The emergence of analysis is mapped out by Sam Hill, president of Helios Consulting, who is currently writing a book on what he labels 'the age of analysis'. 'Every time we step up to the counter to buy an airline ticket, we step into the age of analysis. The reservation agent quotes a price developed by the airline's yield-management system. Every single night this system analyses the capacity available the following day on every plane and every route. It then sets 20,000 fares to optimize the trade-off between discounting prices or losing passengers to other carriers,' says Hill. 'With every trip to the local supermarket, to the book store, to the doctor's office, we enter the age of analysis. There is as much analysis at work in the supermarket at the corner as in a routine satellite launch. Few of us even give this a passing thought as we wheel our carts down the aisle.' Data warehouses enable companies to carry out this analysis to achieve mass customization. OLAP is the most direct route to tomorrow's customer.

Key link

- www.olapcouncil.org

Operating profit

See Profit.

Operations plan

The operations plan (the operating plan in the US) is the element of the business plan that is all about the internal running of the business. For a start-up to get off the ground, it will need more than just an idea and money. Possible areas covered in this section of the business plan will be:

- **Equipment:** What hardware and software will be needed? Will the company purchase or lease the equipment?
- **Location:** The company will require office space, but how much? Depending on the nature of the business, warehousing and manufacturing premises might also be required.
- **Employees:** The company may need employees. How many? What will they do? How will they be paid?

Option

If an individual or organization has the right to purchase or sell an asset at a specified price by a specified date, it is known as an option. It is important to note that this is a right to purchase and not an obligation to purchase. Thus, if the situation is unfavourable, the holder of the option does not have to exercise it. A right to purchase is known as a call; a right to sell is a put. The price to be paid is called the strike or exercise price. The date by which the option must be used is called the expiry date. Options are a popular method of speculating on moves in the price of an asset over a period of time and of rewarding employees, by granting them options with low exercise process. Equities and commodities such as gold are common assets for which options are issued.

Key text
- Robert Kolb. *Understanding Options*. John Wiley & Sons, 1995

Organic organization

See Mechanistic organization.

Organizational agility

The concept of organizational agility is most closely associated with American management thinker **Richard Pascale**. Pascale argues that even the most successful organizations eventually find themselves grinding to a halt. Inspiration dries up; enthusiasm dissipates; stagnation results. This can only be avoided if an organization pursues seven disciplines of agility, which range from the self-explanatory 'accountability in action' to the more elusive and painful 'course of relentless discomfort'. The organizational future lies in being flexible while strong and moving nimbly but surely.

Interestingly, Pascale is an admirer of the intensive training methods used by the US military, though he admits that converting its methods into the corporate world is handicapped by the fact that 'all it takes is 650,000 acres and a million dollars a day'. Even so, organizational agility means that it is preferable to be a ballet dancer than a muscle-bound Marine.

Organizational chart

An organizational chart is a diagram that depicts the lines of authority and the reporting structure within an organization. If there are many layers of management with reporting lines cascading down from the top, then the structure is a hierarchical one. If there are few layers of management and a high level of employee empowerment, then it is said to be a flat organization. The diagram can also reveal a more esoteric structure, such as a matrix structure.

Outsourcing

During the 1960s, the US **entrepreneur** Ross Perot realized that it was often more efficient to pass the provision of a service or other task previously undertaken by a company to an external third party to perform on its behalf. This process of putting out work became known as outsourcing and Perot, among others, was largely credited with creating the modern outsourcing industry. Outsourcing acknowledges that no organization can excel at everything. Activities that are not associated with the core competencies of the company are best left to specialist companies. An outsourcing agreement allows the provider company to supply a customer with services or processes that the company is currently sourcing in-house and thus removes the need for that company to keep non-core skills and capacity.

Key link
- www.outsourcing.com

Overcapacity

Where total production capability exceeds demand, it is known as overcapacity. Overcapacity may be a temporary situation due to normal market cycles or the result of an economic downturn. The reasons may also be structural, such as the decline of a market. In this case, companies in the market will have to restructure, diversify or go into liquidation.

Over-the-counter market

Not all shares are traded on the major exchanges, such as the **London Stock Exchange** and the **New York Stock Exchange**. Instead of trading through the auction markets, some stocks are traded through a network of computers and over the telephone. This non-exchange market is known as the over-the-counter market. Shares traded in this way are often unlisted because they do not qualify for a listing. They tend to be more thinly traded and more volatile. In the United States, trading in OTC or unlisted securities is monitored by the National Association of Securities Dealers (NASD). Details of OTC shares and their market makers can be found in *The Pink Sheets*, published daily.

Overtime

'Overtime' is the term used to describe the hours worked by an employee in excess of his agreed contractual hours under his terms of employment. In many jobs, employees look upon overtime as a core part of their salary, and indeed, it often makes up a large percentage of that salary. This means that labour difficulties can arise in a situation where the amount of overtime available comes under review by the employer. This happened in the United Kingdom in 2002, when there was talk of withdrawing – in part or in full – overtime entitlement in the police force. The reaction from the employees threatened an industrial dispute.

In some jobs, where there are rigidly set working hours, overtime may be offered as a means for increasing production. Overtime may be paid at a premium rate compared to the normal hourly rate. This is especially true when employees do overtime at unusual times, such as holidays and at night. In companies where there is no rigid definition of hours, there is unlikely to be overtime, as extra hours will fall within the normal job description of employees.

Own brands

See Brands.

P

Packard, David

IT executive and management pioneer; co-founder, Hewlett-Packard (1912–1996)

David Packard, with the help of his friend and fellow student Bill Hewlett, built a multinational technology company, with more than 100,000 employees and annual revenues in excess of $40 billion, from a small engineering company founded in a garage.

Born into a middle-class family on 7 September 1912, Packard grew up in Pueblo, Colorado. From an early age, Packard wanted to be an engineer. His dream was fulfilled when, in 1934, he took a job at General Electric after studying electrical engineering at Stanford University. It was at Stanford that Packard met friend and partner-to-be Bill Hewlett. In 1938, Packard returned to Palo Alto and teamed up with Bill Hewlett. They decided to start their own company.

Founded in a Palo Alto garage in 1939, with just $538 in capital, Hewlett-Packard was to become part of Silicon Valley folklore. It sent a message to all future **entrepreneurs** that great businesses could grow from small beginnings.

The original business plan had Packard as a kind of rent-an-inventor. But his creativity soon ran riot and with Hewlett, he began developing a stream of gadgets. Early designs included an electric shock machine to help people lose weight and an optical device to trigger automatic urinal flushing. The first invention that made money was a piece of equipment to help sound engineers make better recordings.

At the end of their first year in business, Hewlett and Packard had amassed a profit of $1539. They left the garage for more suitable premises in 1940. During World War II, Hewlett joined the Signal Corps, leaving Packard to run the business. Business dropped off in the immediate post-war period, but once Hewlett came back from the military, they hired a number of talented staff and the business began to improve again. Soon, turnover was up to $2 million.

In a division of duties, Packard assumed the managerial role, with Hewlett responsible for engineering and R&D. Packard proved a natural. He introduced a system of management that involved walking among the employees and maintaining a highly visible presence. This was in contrast to the idea, prevalent among companies at the time, that the management and the workforce were a breed apart and should have little to do with each other. It was a practice perpetuated by corporate institutions such as the management dining room, where the great and the good tucked into a three-course culinary extravaganza while the workers huddled around their workstations eating sandwiches.

Packard spurned the trappings of executive status. He maintained a policy of openness, making himself available to speak to employees. His accessibility and the practice of **management by wandering around** (MBWA for short) endeared him to his employees. Packard repaid their respect by empowering staff in their daily work. 'We figured that people will accomplish more,' he said, 'if they are given an opportunity to use their talents and abilities in the way they work best.'

Packard enshrined his enlightened take on worker empowerment and other forward-looking practices in *The HP Way*, written in 1957. In 1970, when the US economy slipped into recession, Packard did not make wholesale redundancies. Instead, he agreed to a new working pattern with the staff. Employees worked nine days out of every two weeks instead of ten. In addition, management and workforce alike took a 10 percent pay cut.

As well as his forward-looking human resource policies, he took an innovative approach to organizational structure. 'I've often thought that after you get organized you ought to throw the chart away,' he opined. It wasn't that Packard didn't believe in organization: it was just that he believed in small, agile units operating within the company. If a division grew cumbersome and unwieldy, Packard broke it into smaller units.

In 1972, Hewlett-Packard introduced a hand-held scientific calculator – the model 35. During the 1970s and 1980s, the company moved into the computer business. Throughout the 1980s, HP was one of the top 5 computer manufacturers in the United States. In the 1990s, however, it struggled as competitors began to out-innovate it. Packard's solution was a return to basics: back to management by wandering around. Although both Packard and Hewlett were approaching 80, they took action to reinvigorate the company. They decided that the HP hierarchy had grown unwieldy and took a scalpel to the organization, cutting out unnecessary layers. The philosophy of small teams and less management was restored, and the company reclaimed its place among America's leading IT corporations.

David Packard died in 1996, safe in the knowledge that his company was once more in shape to compete with the best. Today, HP's future looks less certain, the company is set to merge with Compaq, and it remains to be seen if Packard's enlightened management principles so deeply etched in the company's culture will survive the merger.

Key text

- David Packard. *The HP Way: How Bill Hewlett and I Built Our Company*. Harper Business, 1995

Pacman defence

The Pacman defence is a corporate strategy employed during a hostile takeover bid for a company. Named after the video game, in the Pacman defence, the subject of the bid – the target company – turns the tables and makes a bid for the company proposing the takeover – the predator. The idea of this manoeuvre is to confuse the situation sufficiently to discourage support for the predator's bid while at the same time posing enough of a threat to the predator to make it think twice about its proposed course of action.

Paperless office

Danish businessman Lars Kolind pioneered the paperless office in his audio-technology company, Oticon. The paperless office is an office that literally functions without the use of paper. The idea is that by using IT, networked computers, video conferencing, and other communications technology, paper can be eliminated from the office entirely.

Key text

- David Clutterbuck. *Doing It Different: Lessons for the Imaginative Manager*. Orion, 1999

Parallel imports

Parallel imports are goods imported into a country outside the official distribution network by **entrepreneurs** who are often not official suppliers of a good. Products imported in this way, particularly branded goods such as certain makes of jeans, can be sold more cheaply than the same branded products that are imported through official channels. The market for these unofficially imported goods is known as the grey market. Parallel imports are not the same as counterfeit goods, which are imported to be passed off as the real product. The manufacturers of the branded parallel imports generally take a dim view of parallel imports and have used intellectual property law to prevent the sale of these goods.

Pareto's Rule

Italian political economist and political theorist Vilfredo Pareto (1848–1923) originally developed his 80/20 rule from his observations about the distribution of wealth. He discovered that 80 percent of the land in Italy was owned by 20 percent of the population. Later, while gardening, he discovered that 20 percent of the pea-pods yielded 80 percent of the peas. This principle has since been shown to hold true for a range of distributions and used to show, for example, that 80 percent of a company's profits come from 20 percent of its products or services, or that 80 percent of a company's computer problems stem from 20 percent of its machines.

Parkinson, C. Northcote

Academic business author (1909–1993)

C. Northcote Parkinson studied history at Cambridge and then undertook a PhD at King's College, London. He subsequently held a variety of academic posts in the United Kingdom and the United States, and later in his career was Raffles Professor of History at the University of Malaya. His theories on the machinations of administrative life were developed during five years of army service during World War II.

Parkinson's main ideas are contained in the book *Parkinson's Law*, an amusing interlude in management literature. It was written in the late 1950s, when the human-relations school in the United States was beginning to flower and thinkers were actively questioning the bureaucracy that

had grown up alongside mass production. **Max Weber's** model of a paper-producing bureaucratic machine appeared to have been brought to fruition as the arteries of major organizations became clogged with layer upon layer of managerial administrators.

Parkinson's Law is simply that work expands to fill the time available for its completion. As a result, companies grow without thinking of how much they are producing. Even if growth in numbers doesn't make them more money, companies grow and people become busier and busier. Parkinson observes that 'an official wants to multiply subordinates, not rivals' and 'officials make work for each other'.

Parkinson wryly and accurately debunks the notion of a particular task having an optimum time for completion. There are no rules: everything depends on the person doing the job and his unique situation. 'An elderly lady of leisure can spend an entire day in writing and dispatching a postcard to her niece at Bognor Regis,' writes Parkinson. 'An hour will be spent in finding the postcard, another in hunting for spectacles, half an hour in a search for the address, an hour and a quarter in composition, and twenty minutes in deciding whether or not to take an umbrella when going to the pillar-box in the next street. The total effort, which would occupy a busy man for three minutes all told, may, in this fashion, leave another person prostrate after a day of doubt, anxiety, and toil.'

Parkinson is at his best when describing the life of the humble administrator. Faced with the decreasing energy of age and a feeling of being overworked, he observes that administrators face three options: resign, halve the work with a colleague, or ask for two more subordinates. 'There is probably no instance in civil service history of choosing any but the third alternative,' Parkinson reflects.

The theory is not simply an exercise in superficial cynicism. Parkinson backs it up with statistics. He points out, for example, that the number of admiralty officials in the British Navy increased by 78 percent between 1914 and 1928 while the number of ships fell by 67 percent and the number of officers and men by 31 percent. Parkinson concludes that the expansion of administrators tends to take on a life of its own, explaining, 'The officials would have multiplied at the same rate had there been no actual seamen at all.'

Parkinson does not propose solutions. 'It is not the business of the botanist to eradicate the weeds. Enough for him if he can tell us just how fast they grow,' he says. *Parkinson's Law* is a kind of Catch-22 of the business world, by turns irreverent and humorous, but with a darker underside of acute observation.

Parkinson's sequel to *Parkinson's Law* was *The Law and the Profits* (1960), which introduces Parkinson's Second Law: Expenditure rises to meet income.

Key text
- C. Northcote Parkinson. *Parkinson's Law*. John Murray, 1958

Partnership

A partnership, as opposed to a limited company or sole trader, is defined as two or more persons carrying on a common business for shared profit. It can be any type of business, although the partnership is a popular model for the professions, such as lawyers, accountants, and management consultants.

A partnership differs from a limited company in that the individuals remain separate in identity and are not protected by limited liability, so that each partner is personally responsible for any debts of the partnership.

Pascale, Richard

American educator and consultant (b. 1938)

Richard Pascale was a member of the faculty at Stanford's Graduate School of Business for 20 years. He has since worked as an independent consultant and is the author of *Managing on the Edge* (1990).

Pascale first came to the attention of a large audience with the advent of the **Seven S framework**, one of the most renowned and debated management tools of the 1980s. The framework emerged from a series of meetings during June 1978 between Pascale, Anthony Athos – then of **Harvard Business School** – and the **McKinsey** consultants, **Tom Peters** and Robert Waterman, who were already involved in the research that was to form the basis of *In Search of Excellence*. The Seven 'S's (strategy, structure, skills, staff, shared values, systems and style) are a kind of *aide memoire*, a useful memory jogger of what concerns organizations.

From Pascale's perspective, the Seven 'S's presented a way into comparisons between US and Japanese management. Pascale and Athos concluded that the Japanese succeeded largely because of the attention they gave to the soft 'S's – style, shared values, skills and staff. In contrast, the West remained preoccupied with the hard 'S's of strategy, structure and systems. These conclusions formed the bedrock of *The Art of Japanese Management* (1981), which was one of the first business bestsellers.

In addition to the Seven S framework, Pascale's work is significant for a number of reasons. First, he was among the first researchers to provide original insights into Japanese approaches to business and management.

The second influential area of Pascale's work was that of vision that he and Athos championed. Today, corporate visions are a fact of life. But many fail to match the Japanese practice mapped out by Pascale and Athos, in which visions are dynamic, vivifying *modus operandi* rather than pallid or generic statements of corporate intent.

The third element of Pascale's work is in the related areas of corporate mortality and corporate transformation. In the late 1980s and 1990s, Pascale has drawn attention to the fragile foundations on which our grand corporate assumptions are made. *Managing on the Edge* begins with the line,

'Nothing fails like success.' 'Great strengths are inevitably the root of weakness,' Pascale argues, pausing only to point out that from the *Fortune* 500 of 1985, 143 had departed five years later.

To overcome inertia and survive in a turbulent climate requires a constant commitment to what Pascale labels 'corporate transformation'. Incorporating employees fully into the principal business challenges facing the company is the first 'intervention' required if companies are to thrive. The second is to lead the organization in a way that sharpens and maintains incorporation and 'constructive stress'. Finally, Pascale advocates instilling mental disciplines that will make people behave differently and then help them sustain their new behaviour. In the latter element, Pascale cites the work of the US Army, in which a strong culture allows minds and behaviour to be changed through rigorous and carefully thought-out training.

In his recent work, Pascale has coined the term 'agility' to describe the combination of skills and thinking required of the organizations of the future. Pascale and his co-researchers believe that there are 'four indicators that tell us a great deal about how an organization is likely to perform and adapt'. These are power (whether employees think they can have any influence on the course of events); identity (to what extent individuals identify with the organization as a whole, rather than with a narrow group); contention (whether conflict is brought out into the open and used as a learning tool); and learning (how the organization deals with new ideas).

To survive, says Pascale, companies must continually move on, using the agility engendered by their individuals and culture to ask questions, discuss the undiscussable and shake things up. Case studies of this in practice are few and far between.

Key texts

- Richard Pascale. *Managing on the Edge*. Viking, 1990
- Richard Pascale and Anthony Athos. *The Art of Japanese Management*. Penguin Books, 1981

Patent

See Copyright.

Patterson, John H.

Businessman and industrial welfare pioneer (1844–1922)

Born near Dayton, Ohio, in 1844, Patterson grew up on his family's 2000-acre farm. After attending the local school, Patterson went to Miami University and Dartmouth College, graduating with a BA in 1867. After college, Patterson was determined to go into business on his own. With money saved from a job collecting tolls on the Miami & Erie Canal, he set up as a coal retailer back in his hometown. Next he moved into coal and iron ore mining with his brother Frank, and then, again with his brother, set up a mining supplies store. Stock sold well, but profits failed to materialize. As Patterson was applying a healthy mark-up, something was clearly wrong. Determined to track down the discrepancy, he bought two sales-recording machines invented by a local merchant.

Primitive though the machines were, Patterson immediately appreciated the machines' potential. If he needed one, why didn't every store owner in the country? Moving swiftly, he bought out inventor Jacob Ritty's business in 1884 for $6500, changing the name from the National Manufacturing Company to National Cash Registers. When he looked over the books, he was alarmed to find the business was losing money. Suffering a temporary loss of faith, he offered $2000 to escape the contract. Luckily for Patterson, the seller wasn't interested.

Patterson was forced to make the cash-register business work. Buying premises in a downmarket part of Dayton known as Slidertown, he began manufacturing cash registers on a commercial scale. He was not an enlightened employer, viewing his employees only in terms of production. As a result, his employees, uninspired by their work and their boss, took advantage whenever they could. This led to poor quality – including $50,000 worth of faulty machinery in one year – and poor performance.

Eventually, it dawned on Patterson that if he valued his workers, the quality of his products might improve. He hired architects to design a new factory building that was as suitable for the workforce as it was for the work being done. When the townspeople saw the new building built predominantly from glass and steel, they laughed at Patterson declaring that not one window would be left unbroken before a week was out. But Patterson had the last laugh. His forward-looking building, with its built-in lecture rooms, air conditioning, shower baths and film auditorium, instilled a sense of civic pride in Slidertown and few windows needed replacing.

At times, Patterson's style of leadership was a little paternalistic for the workers' liking. Insisting that workers use the baths provided by the company and attend various entertainments caused considerable resentment. Patterson backed down, but not in time to stop a threatened strike. In a masterly outflanking manoeuvre, he gathered his employees together, reassured them that he understood why they were upset, and declared that everyone could do with a rest. Then he shut down the factory and went travelling. The stunned workers were triumphant at first, but triumph turned first to concern and then to despair as the weeks passed. The workers telegraphed Patterson, begging him to reopen the factory. After two months, he returned to a hero's welcome.

One reason for NCR's success was Patterson's unorthodox sales methods. NCR was one of the first companies in the United States to train a professional sales force. Sales agents were required to memorize a 16-page, 450-word sales primer. Patterson would drop in on the agents unexpectedly and quiz them about the primer. If they failed, he fired them. By 1894, NCR was producing half a million copies of *Hustler*, its sales-newsletter series. Sales conventions were held annually from 1887 on.

Brilliant at promoting sales of NCR cash registers, Patterson was equally effective at squashing the competition. With the help of a promising executive, **Thomas J. Watson** (who went on to found International Business Machines after Patterson fired him), Patterson eliminated the competition through a combination of vigorously defending the cash register patents and acquisitions. Patterson's campaign was so successful that he attracted the unwelcome attention of the US government. Against a backdrop of anti-trust sentiment, he and 28 other executive officers of NCR each received a year's jail sentence and a $5000 fine.

The judgement might have permanently damaged Patterson's reputation, were it not for the Dayton Floods. In March 1913, Dayton was submerged under some 17 feet of water. In the hours before the flood hit, Patterson organized safety and rescue plans and constructed hundreds of makeshift boats at the company's lumberyards, building rafts at the rate of one every seven minutes. For his role in the town's relief efforts, he was titled 'The Saviour of Dayton'. The townsfolk petitioned President Wilson to pardon Patterson and he probably would have been pardoned, had the decision not been overturned by the Court of Appeals in 1915 anyway.

During World War I, Patterson committed NCR's resources to the war effort. He refused to profit from the war, carrying out contracts on a fixed-fee basis, as opposed to a cost-plus basis. Patterson died on 14 May 1922.

Key texts

- Isaac F. Marcosson. *Wherever Men Trade: The Romance of the Cash Register*. Dodd, Mead & Co., 1945
- Samuel Crowther. *John H. Patterson: Pioneer in Industrial Welfare*. Garden City Publishing, 1923

PDF (Portable Document Format)

Portable Document Format is a proprietary file format created by Adobe Systems Inc. for its Acrobat program. It offers advantages over HTML documents, as it retains the entire content of an electronic document (including layouts, graphics, styled text and navigation features) regardless of the computer system on which it is viewed. To a view a PDF file, the user needs the Adobe Acrobat viewer files, which can be downloaded from Adobe's Web site. Because they are platform-independent, PDF files are a good way to send documents over the **Internet**.

P/E ratio (price/earnings ratio)

The P/E ratio is a popular tool in investment analysis, used to assess a share's performance in the market. The ratio is calculated by taking the current share price and dividing by the **earnings per share (EPS)**. The resulting ratio, a number expressed as a multiple, shows how many years it would take the company to earn an amount equal to its share value. A high multiple indicates rapid growth; future earnings are already represented in the share price. A low P/E multiple suggests slow growth. The P/E ratio is a key indicator for analysts and investors determining whether a share is overvalued, fairly priced, or cheap.

Key text
- Jim Slater. *The Zulu Principle: Making Extraordinary Profits from Ordinary Shares*. Orion, 1992

Peer-to-peer (P2P)

Peer-to-peer networking allows network users to exchange information directly without going through a third party. Napster, a clever software program that allowed users to exchange music files over the Internet utilizing Napster's central servers, first brought attention to the possibilities of peer-to-peer, although Napster itself was not true P2P. P2P programs allow one user to directly access information on the hard drive of another user without the need for central servers. Napster was eventually bought out after extensive litigation. It was soon replaced, however, by a number of other true P2P services, such as Gnutella and BearShare.

PEG ratio (price earnings growth ratio)

An investment tool, the PEG ratio was invented by Englishman and financial guru Jim Slater. It is particularly useful for valuing small and midsize growth stocks. The PEG ratio relates the price of a share to growth. It is calculated by dividing the **P/E ratio** by expected per-share earnings growth. A value greater than one implies a stock is overvalued; less than one, that it is undervalued. The figures for the P/E ratio and **earnings per share** used in calculating the PEG ratio are taken from consensus estimates.

Perfect competition

Perfect competition is a theoretical economic model rather than a practical reality. Perfect competition exists when certain underlying assumptions are satisfied. The assumptions are that there are many potential and actual buyers and sellers, each being too small to have an individual influence on the price; there are no barriers to entry or exit; the products being traded are identical; the producers are seeking the maximum profit and consumers the best value for their money; and the consumers have perfect knowledge of the market. Although perfect competition seldom, if ever, exists in the real world, economists often assume perfect competition when stating economic principles, theories, or models.

Perl

Perl (Practical Extraction and Report Language) was developed by US linguist and open-source guru Larry Wall in 1987. It is an open-source programming language for processing text. The language, with a camel as its symbol, is very popular for writing **CGI** scripts for Web pages. Hailed as the 'duct tape' of the Internet, more than half of the sites on the **World Wide Web** use Perl.

Key text
- Larry Wall. *Programming Perl*. O'Reilly, 1992

Permission marketing

The term 'permission marketing' was coined by American marketing innovator **Seth Godin**, former president of Yoyodyne Entertainment and former vice-president of direct marketing at Yahoo! Permission marketing is based on the premise that consumers will voluntarily and willingly give up valuable personal information and also grant permission for marketers to send them product information, so long as they are given sufficient incentive.

The permission marketer must therefore find the appropriate incentive to persuade the consumer to grant permission. Permission marketers must be careful not to abuse the permission granted by the consumer. They also have to manage the relationship to assess whether permission is revoked or to determine if it has lapsed. There is a fine line between e-mailing product information with permission and spamming.

Key text
- Seth Godin. *Permission Marketing: Turning Strangers into Friends, and Friends into Customers*. Simon and Schuster, 1999

Pert analysis

The origins of pert analysis lie in critical-path modelling (CPM), a technique developed by DuPont to map the best trade between cost and completion time for a project. In 1958, the US Navy refined the DuPont technique for the Polaris submarine-construction project. The aim of the project was to complete it as quickly as possible,

allowing for uncertain completion of activity times. With this in mind, they developed pert analysis, which is statistical analysis to determine the best, the most probable, and the worst times for completion of each activity.

PEST analysis

See SLEPT analysis.

Peter, Laurence J.

Canadian academic (1919–1990)

Laurence J. Peter targeted the absurdities of the corporation and of management hierarchies. He observed incompetence everywhere he looked. The result was the Peter Principle, which states that managers in an organization rise to their level of incompetence by being promoted until they fail to do well in their current job. 'For each individual, for you, for me, the final promotion is from a level of competence to a level of incompetence,' wrote Peter.

The greatness of Peter lay in the fact that his humour is grounded solidly in corporate reality. Anyone who has ever worked for an organization can identify with his observations: 'There are two kinds of failures: those who thought and never did, and those who did and never thought'; 'Fortune knocks once, but misfortune has much more patience'; or 'If you don't know where you are going, you will probably end up somewhere else.'

Peter's book, *The Peter Principle* (co-authored with Raymond Hull), was an antidote to the hundreds of books that celebrate corporate success stories. Around his basic joke, Peter weaved a mass of aphorisms and *bon mots*. These included: 'An economist is an expert who will know tomorrow why the things he predicted yesterday didn't happen'; and 'Originality is the fine art of remembering what you hear but forgetting where you heard it.'

Key text

- Laurence J. Peter and Raymond Hull. *The Peter Principle*. William Morrow & Co., 1969

Peters, Thomas J.

American consultant, trainer and commentator (b. 1942)

In 1982, Thomas J. Peters and Robert H. Waterman published *In Search of Excellence*. It marked a watershed in business book publishing. Since 1982, the business book market has exploded into a multimillion-dollar global extravaganza. And, in parallel, the management guru industry has burgeoned.

Tom Peters was born and brought up near Baltimore. He studied engineering at Cornell University and served in Vietnam. He also worked for the Drug Enforcement Agency in Washington. Peters has an MBA and PhD from Stanford, where he encountered a number of influential figures, including Gene Webb and Harold Leavitt. After leaving Stanford, he joined consultancy **McKinsey & Co**. He left the firm prior to the publication of *In Search of Excellence* to work independently.

Tom Peters was both a beneficiary and the instigator of the boom in business books and the rise of the guru business. He was, in effect, the first management guru. While his predecessors were doughty, low-profile academics, Peters was high-profile and media-friendly. A business sprung up around him. First there were the books, then the videos, the consultancy and the conferences.

In Search of Excellence celebrated big companies. Its selection of 43 'excellent' organizations featured such names as IBM, General Electric, Procter & Gamble, Johnson & Johnson and Exxon. The book presented, on the surface at least, the bright side of an American crisis. The Japanese were seemingly taking over the industrial world, unemployment was rising, the recession was a reality and the prospects for the future looked bleak. The management world was ready for good news and Peters and Waterman provided it.

Peters and Waterman's conclusions as to what defines a successful company were distilled down into eight crucial characteristics. These have largely stood the test of time:

- a bias for action
- close to the customer
- autonomy and entrepreneurship
- productivity through people
- hands-on, values-driven
- stick to the knitting
- simple form, lean staff
- simultaneous loose-tight properties

Two years after *In Search of Excellence* was published, *BusinessWeek* magazine covered its front page with a single headline: 'Oops!' It then went on to reveal that the companies featured in *In Search of Excellence* were anything but excellent. The article claimed that about a quarter of the 'excellent' companies were struggling. The single and undeniable fact that the excellent companies of 1982 were no longer all excellent two years later has continued to haunt Peters. 'We started to get beaten up. When the magazine ran the *Oops!* story, it was a bad week,' says Peters. 'I was certain the phone would stop ringing. I wouldn't disagree that I had been on the road too much and in that respect it was a great wake-up call.'

Peters's next two books carried on in much the same vein. *A Passion for Excellence* emphasized the need for leadership. Co-written with Nancy Austin, it was hugely successful but added little in the way of ideas. His next book, *Thriving on Chaos*, was an answer to the big question: How do you become excellent?

Thriving on Chaos opened with the brave proclamation: 'There are no excellent companies.' This is probably the most-quoted single line from Peters's work – either used as proof of his inconsistency, as evidence that he learned from his mistakes, or as a damning indictment of his propensity to write in slogans. *Thriving on Chaos* was a lengthy riposte to all those critics who suggested that Peters's theories could not be turned into reality. Each chapter ended with a short list of suggested action points. '*Thriving on Chaos* was the final, engineering-like, tidying up,' says Peters. 'It was organized in a hyper-organized engineering fashion.'

The major change in Peters's thinking occurred at the beginning of the 1990s. In effect, Peters dismissed the past and heralded in a brave new world of small units, freewheeling project-based structures, and hierarchy-free teams in constant communication. Big was no longer beautiful and corporate structure, previously ignored by Peters, was predominant.

Peters did not mean structure in the traditional hierarchical and functional sense. Indeed, his exemplars of the new organizational structure were notable for their apparent lack of structure. Herein lay Peters's point: companies such as CNN, ABB and The Body Shop thrive by having highly flexible structures, able to change to meet the business needs of the moment. Freeflowing, impossible to pin down, unchartable, simple yet complex – these were the paradoxical structures of the future. 'Tomorrow's effective *organization* will be conjured up anew each day,' Peters pronounced.

Key to the new corporate structures envisaged by Peters were networks with customers, with suppliers and, indeed, anyone else who could help the business deliver. 'Old ideas about size must be scuttled. 'New big', which can be very big indeed, is 'network big'. That is, size measured by market power, say, is a function of the firm's extended family of fleeting and semi-permanent cohorts, not so much a matter of what it owns and directly controls,' he wrote.

If there is a consistent strand through his work, Peters believes it is 'a bias for action'. Forget the theorizing, get on with the job. This is a message that leads academics to shake their heads at its simplicity. With managers, however, it appears to strike a chord.

Key texts

- Stuart Crainer. *The Tom Peters Phenomenon.* Capstone, 1997

- Thomas J. Peters. *Liberation Management.* Alfred Knopf, 1992
- Thomas J. Peters. *Thriving on Chaos.* Macmillan, 1988
- Thomas J. Peters and Nancy Austin. *A Passion for Excellence.* Collins, 1985
- Thomas J. Peters and Robert H. Waterman. *In Search of Excellence.* Harper & Row, 1982

Phillips curve

The Phillips curve was developed by the British economist Alban William Phillips (1914–1975), who graphically plotted wage and unemployment changes between 1861 and 1957. The graph demonstrated that wages rise faster during periods of low unemployment as employers compete for labour. The implication is that the dual objectives of low unemployment and low inflation are incompatible. The concept has been widely questioned since the early 1960s because of the apparent instability of the relationship between wages and unemployment.

Piece rate

Piece rate is the method of payment for work done when an amount is paid per item produced. For example, a worker may be paid 50 cents per shirt stitched by machine. If a worker stitches 100 shirts on Tuesday, then his pay would be $50. If the same worker stitches 150 shirts on Wednesday, the pay would be $75. Piece rates are paid where it is easy to match an end product with the contribution of a worker, usually manual workers.

PLC (public limited company)

In the United Kingdom, a plc is a company registered as such under the provisions of the Companies Act 1980. The act specifies a number of criteria a plc must exhibit. It must have authorized share capital of more than £50,000, with at least

£12,500 paid to the company by the shareholders. It must have the letters plc after its name. Plcs may offer their shares on the open market and are more tightly regulated than limited companies. Converting a private limited company into a public one offers several advantages, such as the ability to raise share capital. It does, however, have potential disadvantages. One such disadvantage is that the company comes under the scrutiny of the financial media and city analysts. The financial markets do not always place a value on a company that the directors and principal shareholders believe reflects the true value of the company. If the founder of a plc perceives the company share price to undervalue the company, they may seek to take the company private again, as Richard Branson did with Virgin in 1989.

Plug-in

A plug-in is a small program that enhances or enables another application. A plug-in may, for example, use one application to launch, display, or interpret a file created using another application. The first plug-ins were made for graphics programs in the 1980s. The practice became widespread in the mid-1990s as a range of plug-ins were produced, mostly by third-party software manufacturers, to enhance the multimedia capabilities of Netscape's Navigator browser. Plug-ins are often created and distributed by independent developers rather than the manufacturer of the program they extend.

Point of sale

The point of sale (POS) is the precise point at which the sale is made. This could be in a retail store, or it could be at home, in the case of door-to-door selling or telephone sales. In some cases, such as **e-commerce** sales over the Internet, it is not always straightforward to determine the point of sale – presumably, it is in cyberspace on a Web site. There are often promotional materials and other inducements to purchase, such as notices of special offers, at the point of sale.

Poison pill

A tactic used to avoid a hostile takeover, a poison pill renders the takeover unpalatable through various actions. It might give one class of shareholders the right to have their shares redeemed at a very good price in the event of the company being taken over, thus causing the potential predator considerable extra cost. Alternatively, a poison pill might issue employment contracts to staff with long notice periods, making it expensive to restructure, or it might contract to sell a key asset, often to a friendly company.

Ponzi scheme

A Ponzi scheme, also known as a pyramid scheme or multilevel marketing, occurs when the person at the beginning of the scheme is promised a return on his investment and frequently receives one, whereas 'investors' further down the pyramid are less likely to receive any return and eventually someone (usually many people) will receive no return whatsoever. The scheme works because each person who joins the scheme recruits a certain number of people to the scheme in order to make money. These people form the next level down on the pyramid. Each person pays a fee to the instigator of the scheme to join and receives a fee for introducing new members. The longer the scheme goes on, the harder it is for existing members to recruit new members. As a result, the people at the bottom of the pyramid usually lose money. As with **pyramid selling**, this type of pyramid scheme is illegal in many countries.

Key texts
- James Walsh. *You Can't Cheat an Honest Man: How Ponzi Schemes & Pyramid Frauds Work.* Silver Lake Publishing, 1998

- Stewart L. Weisman. *Need and Greed: the story of the largest Ponzi scheme in American History.* Syracuse University Press, 1999

Porras, Jerry I.

Academic and business author

Jerry I. Porras is the Lane Family Professor of Organizational Behavior and Change, and Director of the Leading and Managing Change Executive Program at Stanford University's Graduate School of Business where he teaches courses in leadership, interpersonal dynamics and organizational development and change. He also acts as a consultant on organizational development and has worked with companies including Chase Manhattan Bank, Lockheed and Hewlett-Packard.

Porras is best known for his highly influential book *Built To Last: Successful Habits of Visionary Companies* (1994) co-authored with fellow Stanford academic **James Collins**. The culmination of an exhaustive research project analysing the century's most visionary companies, *Built to Last* was the *In Search of Excellence* of the 1990s – a heartening dose of humanity at a time when the cold science of reengineering dominated.

Key text
- James C. Collins and Jerry I. Porras. *Built to Last: Successful Habits of Visionary Companies.* HarperCollins, 1994

Portal

A portal is a Web site designed to be used as a start-up site for Internet-browsing sessions and to provide a gateway to the rest of the Web. To increase their attractiveness, portals expanded in the late 1990s, offering a wide variety of services, such as personalized start-up pages, free e-mail, directories, customized news and weather reports, and free Web space. The first portals were online services such as America Online, which added gateways to the **Internet**. Others have come from different areas: Yahoo! started as a hierarchical guide to Web sites, and Excite as a search engine. CNet's Snap! was the first Web site designed to act as a portal. Traditional portals are under threat from a number of areas. Free ISPs are capturing customers from portals, educated Web users choose to go straight to niche sites that interest them, and satellite and cable companies offer interactive TV with Internet access channelled through their own Web sites.

Porter, Michael

American academic (b. 1947)

Michael Porter is precociously talented and intellectually persuasive. He could have pursued a career as a professional golfer, but chose instead to get a Harvard **MBA**. While completing his PhD at Harvard, Porter was influenced by the economist Richard Caves, who became his **mentor**. He joined the Harvard faculty at the age of 26, becoming one of the youngest tenured professors in the school's history.

In his 1980 book *Competitive Strategy: Techniques for Analyzing Industries and Competitors*, Porter developed the model still regarded as essential reading for strategy makers and MBA students around the world. His timing was impeccable. The publication of his model coincided with a wholesale rethinking of Western business principles. In the 1970s, corporate America had watched in horror as Japanese companies stole market share in industry after industry. Initially, US companies attributed Japanese competitiveness to cheap labour, but by the end of the decade, it was dawning on them that something more fundamental was occurring. Porter encouraged a complete re-evaluation of the nature of competitiveness and changed the way companies thought about strategy forever.

Porter's genius has lain in producing brilliantly researched and cogent models of competitiveness at corporate, industry-wide and national levels. He took an industrial economics framework

– the structure-conduct performance paradigm (SCP) – and translated it into the context of business strategy. From this emerged his best-known model: the five forces framework.

In *Competitive Strategy*, Porter wrote, 'In any industry, whether it is domestic or international or produces a product or a service, the rules of competition are embodied in five competitive forces.' These five competitive forces are:

- **The entry of new competitors:** New competitors necessitate some competitive response that will inevitably use some of your resources, thus reducing profits.
- **The threat of substitutes:** If there are viable alternatives to your product or service in the marketplace, the prices you can charge will be limited.
- **The bargaining power of buyers:** If customers have bargaining power, they will use it. This will reduce profit margins and, as a result, affect profitability.
- **The bargaining power of suppliers:** Given power over you, suppliers will increase their prices and adversely affect your profitability.
- **The rivalry among existing competitors:** Competition leads to the need to invest in marketing, R&D, or price reductions, which will reduce your profits.

The five forces, he asserted, shape the competitive landscape. Initially, they were passively interpreted as valid statements of the facts of competitive life. But by laying them bare, Porter provided a framework for companies to understand and challenge the competitive markets in which they operate. For strategy makers, the five forces represented levers upon which any strategy must act if it is to have an impact on a company's competitive position.

'The collective strength of these five competitive forces determines the ability of firms in an industry to earn, on average, rates of return on investment in excess of the cost of capital. The strength of the five forces varies from industry to industry, and can change as an industry evolves,' Porter observed.

A late addition to his book was the concept of generic strategies. Porter argued that there are three 'generic strategies' that are 'viable approaches to dealing with … competitive forces'. Strategy, in Porter's eyes, was a matter of *how* to compete. The first of Porter's generic strategies was differentiation, competing on the basis of value added to customers (such quality, service, or differentiation) so that customers will pay a premium to cover higher costs. The second was cost-based leadership: offering products or services at the lowest cost. Quality and service are not unimportant, but cost reduction provides focus to the organization. Focus was the third generic strategy identified by Porter. Companies with a clear strategy outperform those whose strategy is unclear or those that attempt to achieve both differentiation and cost leadership.

'Sometimes the firm can successfully pursue more than one approach as its primary target, though this is rarely possible,' he said. 'Effectively implementing any of these generic strategies usually requires total commitment, and organizational arrangements are diluted if there's more than one primary target.'

If a company failed to focus on any of the three generic strategies, it was liable to encounter problems. 'The firm failing to develop its strategy in at least one of the three directions – a firm that is *stuck in the middle* – is in an extremely poor strategic situation,' Porter wrote. 'The firm lacks the market share, capital investment, and resolve to play the low-cost game, the industry-wide differentiation necessary to obviate the need for a low-cost position, or the focus to create differentiation or low cost in a more limited sphere. The firm stuck in the middle is almost guaranteed low profitability. It either loses the high-volume customers who demand low prices or must bid away its profits to get this business away from low-cost firms. Yet it also loses high-margin businesses – the cream – to the firms who are focused on high-margin targets or have achieved differentiation overall. The firm stuck in the middle also probably suffers from a blurred corporate culture and a conflicting set of organizational arrangements and motivation system.'

Key texts

- Michael Porter. *The Competitive Advantage of Nations.* Macmillan, 1990
- Michael Porter. *Competitive Advantage.* Free Press, 1985
- Michael Porter. *Competitive Strategy.* Free Press, 1980

Portfolio analysis

See Branding.

Portfolio career

The portfolio career strategy is one in which an individual undertakes a number of different careers, usually simultaneously, on a part-time basis. He may, for example, do consulting work, write articles and do some gardening. This approach to career development has developed with the end of the job-for-life attitude and the corresponding growth of the **free agent** nation and freelancing.

Positive-sum situation/Positive-sum game

See Game theory.

Pound cost averaging

Pound cost averaging is an investment theory, the purpose of which is to smooth out the fluctuations in price of the equities purchased. It involves the purchasing of equities on a regular basis over time as an alternative to purchasing the same equities in one bulk purchase. If an investor makes a bulk purchase of equities and the price of that equity falls, the investor loses out. If, however, the investor makes his purchase at regular intervals, he will get progressively more shares for his money as the price falls.

Prahalad, C.K.

Business strategy expert (b. 1941)

C.K. Prahalad is Harvey C. Fruehauf Professor of Business Administration and professor of corporate strategy and international business at the University of Michigan, as well as an independent consultant. He has recently announced that he plans to spend more time with his consultancy.

Prahalad is particularly well known for the work he has conducted with fellow strategy expert **Gary Hamel**. This includes the articles 'The Core Competence of the Corporation' (*Harvard Business Review*, May/June, 1990) and 'Competing in the New Economy: Managing Out of Bounds' (*Strategic Management Journal*, Vol. 17, No 3, March, 1996), as well as the bestselling book *Competing for the Future: Breakthrough Strategies for Seizing Control of Your Industry and Creating the Markets of Tomorrow* (1994).

Prahalad's current research interests include the strategic management of large diversified corporations and the role of top management.

Key text

- C.K. Prahalad and Gary Hamel. *Competing for the Future.* Harvard Business School Press, 1994

Predatory pricing

See Pricing.

Preference share

A preference share is issued by a company to give the holder of the preference share rights that are superior in various ways to those of ordinary shares. For example, the holder of a preference share may receive priority to a fixed dividend and priority over ordinary shares in the event of the company being wound up.

Presenteeism

Presenteeism is the phenomenon of an employee's attending work when he should be at home. The culture of presenteeism is linked with an economic climate where redundancies, **downsizing** and delayering are prevalent. To keep their jobs employees feel the need to be seen doing their jobs, even if there is no work to be done. This means working late, going to work even if they are ill, and forgoing holidays. The term was coined by Professor Cary Cooper, a psychologist at Manchester University specializing in organizational management.

Present value

See Net present value.

Pressure group

A pressure group is an association that puts pressure on governments, businesses or political parties to ensure laws and treatment favourable to its own interests. Pressure groups have played an increasingly prominent role in contemporary Western democracies. In general, they fall into two types: groups concerned with a single issue, such as nuclear disarmament, and groups attempting to promote their own interests, such as oil producers.

Price method

US term for Piece rate.

Pricing methods

Companies price their products in many different ways. Pricing methods include contribution pricing, in which a variable pricing strategy is adopted, with different prices charged for the same product depending on the circumstances, and competitive pricing, which sets prices in relation to competitors' prices. Pricing methods can also be cost-based, which includes mark-up pricing, which adds a standard percentage increase to the direct cost price, and cost-plus pricing, in which a percentage increase is added to the full-cost price including an allowance for overhead and other factors.

Predatory pricing is a pricing policy designed to put competitors out of business. Large national companies can operate a differential pricing policy across the country, lowering prices below an economic level where there is intense local competition. The company then cross-subsidizes losses with profits from areas where there is little or no competition. Once local competition is eradicated, the company can raise prices again. Companies operating a predatory pricing policy may fall foul of restrictive trade practice legislation.

By-product pricing is the pricing of products produced incidentally during a production process. Pricing by-products is difficult, as they are an unintended consequence of production and therefore do not have an obvious cost associated with their production. By-products are often priced as high as the market will bear in order to make the overall production process and therefore production of the principal good as competitive as possible.

Often there will be a single company, product or service that is a leader in its market. As the leader, it serves as the pricing benchmark for the rest of the market. This company is known as the price leader. When the price leader sets the price for its product, all of the other products in the market price according to their position relative to the price leader. This pricing policy leads to a stable market and avoids over-competitive pricing, which critics might argue was not in the interests of the consumer. Although this pricing strategy is common, companies, especially in a mature market with a small number of large firms, must be careful not to cross the boundaries of accepted practice by forming a **cartel** and colluding over pricing.

Primary research

See Market research.

Principled negotiation

See BATNA (Best Alternative to a Negotiated Agreement).

Prisoner's dilemma

See Game theory.

Probability

Probability is the likelihood, or chance, that an event will occur. It is often expressed as odds (4 to 1), or in mathematics, numerically as a fraction (1/4), a decimal (.25), or a percentage (25 percent).

The probability that n particular events will happen out of a total of m possible events is n/m. A certainty has a probability of 1; impossibility has a probability of 0.

It is possible to represent probability diagrammatically using a probability tree. For example, a probability tree to calculate the chance of flipping a coin and it landing on heads three times in a row would have three levels: the first reflecting the chances of throwing either heads or tails; the next the chances of throwing heads or tails after throwing heads; and the chances of throwing heads or tails after throwing tails and so on. The series of probabilities can then be multiplied to give the overall probability of a possible event occurring.

Product

A product is the end result of the production process. The period from its conception through to the end of its useful life is known as the product life cycle. The first stage is the development stage, when a product is designed. Then comes the launch of the product, which is likely to be associated with informative **advertising** and promotion because consumers need to be made aware that the product is now available on the market and what its purpose is.

Key to success in the early stages of the product life cycle is product differentiation. This is the practice of making one good markedly different from another. **Branding** is an example of product differentiation. Firms attempt to differentiate their products in order to gain customer loyalty and secure an advantage over their competitors. Product awareness is also crucial. Product awareness is the proportion of individuals within a target market who are aware of a particular product and/or brand. Famous brands with large marketing and advertising budgets, such as Coca-Cola, Microsoft and McDonald's, may have close to 100 percent brand recognition. Brands with very high product awareness are usually brand leaders in their markets.

The next stage is the growth stage, as sales and revenue increase. Then there is a period of maturity for the product, when sales and revenue level off. Competitors may have entered the market, taking away growth of the product, or the market may have become saturated. Finally, the product goes into decline as sales fall. Toward the end of a product's life cycle, the retailers may employ a harvesting strategy. This involves making a short-term profit by cutting marketing expenditures and relying on the impetus from earlier marketing to keep consumers buying the product.

Product placement

Product placement is a form of advertising for goods or services. Instead of billboards or traditional TV ad spots, product placement advertises products through positioning in television and film as props or scenery. Companies pay large sums to have their products endorsed indirectly in popular television programmes and feature films. The star of a film may, for example, shave with a branded razor, or the good guys may drive a particular make of car. Competition for this kind of advertising can be fierce, particularly in popular film franchises like the Bond movies, where a contemporary setting and feel makes product placement easier.

Product recall

If a product from the market is withdrawn, usually due to the discovery of a product defect, it is known as a product recall. Examples of product recalls carried out by major companies include Intel's recall of the Pentium microchip because of a processing flaw, the recall of Perrier mineral water after contamination and Johnson & Johnson's recall of Tylenol after product tampering led to a number of deaths. Plans for a product recall form an essential part of any **crisis management** strategy. The timing and scale of a product recall will have a significant effect on public relations.

Key text
- Howard Abbott. *Managing Product Recall. A Comprehensive Guide to Establishing a Product Recall Plan*. Pitman, 1991

Positioning

In any market, a company must decide how to place its products and services, taking into account the strategies of its competitors. Positioning is the marketing strategy involving the positioning of a company's products or services in the market relative to those of its competitors. Positioning strategies include differentiating the product or service from the competition and positioning a product or service based on low price.

Profit

There are many different definitions of profit. The most general definition is the difference between the selling price and the production cost. This means production cost in its wide sense, i.e. not merely the cost of manufacturing a product, but all of the fixed and variable costs incurred in the process of producing and delivering the product or service.

The gross profit figure is the difference between the revenue from sales and the direct cost of production for a business. It does not take account of the business's overhead. Gross profit is usually shown in the profit and loss account of the company. Dividing gross profit by revenue gives the figure for gross margin. This is the figure that indicates what price a company is getting for its product. Falling gross margins suggest the company is unable to obtain a good price for its products and services.

A more refined definition of profit is that of net profit. Net profit is calculated by taking the gross profit and other receipts and subtracting all costs of the business. The net profit figure may be stated as being before or after tax.

'Operating profit' is a term used to define profit (or loss) arising from the principal trading activity of a company. Operating profit is calculated by deducting operating expenses (expenses vital to core activity) from trading profit (profit before deduction of items such as auditors' fees and interest). If operating costs exceed revenues, there will, of course, be an operating loss.

To find out a company's profit figures, it is best to look at the profit and loss accounts. In many countries, the filing of accounts that include the profit and loss account is required by law. The profit and loss account is a statement of the profit or loss of a company taken from its accounts. Profit and loss accounts comprise three main elements: the trading accounts, detailing sales revenues less production expenses to give a gross profit or loss; an account of any income from other sources, as well as administrative and other expenses/costs (overhead) to give a net profit or loss figure before the deduction of corporation tax; and the appropriation of profits for the payment of dividends and retention of profits in the company after the deduction of corporation tax.

A business or part of a business may also be defined by reference to profit. Thus a part of a business that operates as if it were an individual firm is known as a profit centre. A profit centre may be spun off from the parent company as a company in its own right. This is usually to enable it to raise capital more easily.

Companies may redistribute a distribution of a proportion of a company's profits to its workforce in the form of a bonus payment. This is known as profit share and is designed to give the workforce a vested interest in a company's fortunes. The downside is that if the bonus is a significant part of an employee's pay package and the company fails to pay a bonus in the event of a loss, the employee's morale could be adversely affected. Alternatively, the company may choose to use its profits to pay a dividend to its shareholders.

Project

A project is set of activities designed to achieve a specific goal. Projects may be organized for major works, involving a consortium of companies bringing specific skills. Construction projects, such as bridge and tunnel building, would be an example of this type of project. Most large-scale and many small projects will be overseen by a project manager, the individual responsible for managing the resources necessary to complete the project. A project manager may not carry out any of the tasks the project requires, but he will need to understand all of the processes involved in order to source the right personnel and materials.

Project management will involve matching available resources (time, money and people) against business project aims (early completion date, final cost and so on). The technique originated in the shipbuilding industry during World War I, when Henry Laurence Gantt developed what is now known as the **Gantt chart**, a bar chart deploying use of resources over time. On a smaller scale, projects can be run inside organizations, bringing together teams of people with specific skills to work on a specified task, usually over a fixed period of time.

Promotion (marketing)

A promotion is a tactic used by companies to persuade customers to buy their goods in the short term. There are two main categories of promotion. Above-the-line promotion is advertising, as in television ads or billboards, and is usually designed and carried out by an agency. Below-the-line promotion or **merchandising** covers special offers such as free gifts, discounts, competitions, better value offers (for example, 500 grams for the price of 400 grams) and trade-ins. These may well be devised and implemented by the company itself, although specialist agencies do get involved.

Prospectus

When a company is planning to list on a stock exchange, the investment bank that is handling the flotation will produce a document that contains key information about the company. Part sales brochure, part legal requirement, the prospectus will cover subjects such as the intended business of the company, financial information, a list of proposed managers and a long list of potential risks to the success of the business. In many countries, the prospectus is required by law. In the United Kingdom, for example, if a company is seeking a public listing, the prospectus must comply with the Companies Acts and be lodged with the Companies Registrar. If a company is found to have included misleading information in its prospectus, it is likely to face severe penalties.

Prosumer

In his book *The Third Wave* (1980), US futurist **Alvin Toffler** coined a term that described the connection of production with consumption. The term 'prosumer' was applied to the situation in which interconnected users come together to create products to meet their demands. Prosumer is also used as a contraction of professional and consumer to mean products of a quality suitable for a semi-professional.

Key text
- Alvin Toffler. *The Third Wave*. Morrow, 1980

Psychological contract

The phrase 'psychological contract' was originated by social psychologist **Ed Schein** of the Massachusetts Institute of Technology during the late 1950s. It refers to an unspoken agreement between employee and employer. The agreement or contract described the mutually beneficial position in which the employee gave his loyalty and hard work to an organization in return for job security. The executive gained a fair and virtually guaranteed income and the company acquired a committed workforce. Wholesale **downsizing** in the late 1980s and early 1990s all but put paid to the psychological contract by removing the underlying mutual trust between employer and employee upon which the contract was based. The contract was superseded by concepts such as **employability** and **free agents**.

Psychometric test

A psychometric test is an increasingly popular personality test used by companies to select employees. They are reasonably common in the selection process. The idea is that the tests further help the recruiter to match the individual's characteristics with those required by the position available. Although there are many different types of psychometric testing, they can be loosely divided into two categories – ability (or aptitude) and personality.

- **Ability tests:** Often referred to as tests of maximum performance, ability tests test what the subject can do. They give an indication of reasoning, decision making, problem solving and other skills or aptitudes. Ability tests, such as standard IQ tests, are often encountered early on in the selection process and used as a screening tool.
- **Personality tests:** Often referred to as tests of typical performance, personality tests show what an individual is likely to do. They are not tests in the strict sense; rather, they are indicators of type. There are no incorrect answers as such. However, by demonstrating certain preferences, an individual can manifest a personality that is not suitable, in the recruiter's opinion, for the job. This type of test is often used later on in the selection process to shape and structure second interviews.

Key text
- David Cohen. *How to Succeed in Psychometric Tests*. Sheldon Press, 1999

Public key encryption
See Cryptography.

Public sector

In most economies, the state will own and control

part of that economy, such as central government, local government and government enterprises. Thus, the state may run the health system, cleaning services, road maintenance, the prison service and, almost always, the police and armed services. In a command economy, the public sector allocates most of the resources in the economy. The opposite of the public sector is the private sector, where resources are allocated by private individuals and business organizations.

Pure play

See Internet business models.

Pushing the envelope

The term 'pushing the envelope' is derived from aeronautics to denote going to the edge of existing boundaries. The expression comes from the US Air Force test pilot programme in the 1940s. Companies that push the envelope seek to do things better than before, to extend themselves beyond the **comfort zone**, to out-innovate and out-perform the competition. The phrase was further popularized in the Tom Wolfe's book *The Right Stuff*.

Pyramid selling

Pyramid selling is a scheme in which an entrepreneur sells a franchise to another party together with the goods necessary to carry out the business. That party then does the same, and so on. Eventually the company or individual at the top of the pyramid sells a lot of stock and makes money while those further down the chain are left with surplus stock and often lose money. In many countries, the practice is illegal.

Pyramids of ratios

The pyramids of ratios present the relationship between accounting ratios in a company in a visual form. Usually at the apex of the pyramid is return on capital employed. Beneath are other headings, such as profit margin, profit and revenue. The diagram usually resembles a pyramid in shape.

Q

Qualitative research

Qualitative research is research that relies on opinions and beliefs rather than statistical data. It usually involves interviews with small sample groups from target markets. These are often conducted by a sociologist or psychologist, who endeavours to ascertain the motivation for decisions made by individuals within the group. Why, for example, does one person buy one brand of coffee instead of another? Although expensive to conduct, qualitative research enables companies to keep in touch with their customers' needs.

The origins of qualitative research date back to Austrian psychoanalyst Ernest Dichter, who moved to the United States in the first half of the twentieth century. Dichter applied his psychology skills to marketing and used groups and in-depth interviews as qualitative methods to investigate the motivation of consumers. He set up the Institute of Motivational Studies, which opened a London office in 1959. By the 1970s, the psychoanalytical approach had made way for group discussion without the interpretation of the psychoanalyst.

The parameters of qualitative research have grown considerably since the 1970s. Qualitative research is now far removed from the original psychoanalytical approach, though it continues to draw on many aspects of psychology. It is now much broader in scope, encompassing anything that falls within the umbrella of consumer culture.

Key text
- Hy Mariampolski. *Qualitative market research; a comprehensive guide*. Sage Publications, 2001

Quality circle

A quality circle is a small group of production workers concerned with problems relating to the quality, safety and efficiency of their product. The origins of the quality circle are unclear. Most agree that it originated in Japan during the 1960s. Others, however, argue that the practice began in the US Army in the immediate post-World War II period. Certainly, quality circles were popularized in Japan.

Key characteristics of quality circles are size (8–12 members); voluntary membership; natural work groups, rather than artificially created ones; autonomy in setting their own agenda; access to senior managers; and a relatively permanent existence. Commitment from senior management to the process is vital to ensure its success. An analysis of the steps to implementing a quality circle is discussed in *The Rational Manager*, by US business writers Charles **Kepner** and Ben Tregoe.

Key text
- Charles Kepner and Benjamin Tregoe. *The Rational Manager: A Systematic Approach to Problem Solving and Decision Making*. McGraw-Hill, 1965

Quality function deployment

Quality function deployment is a systems-engineering process that incorporates a visual language and a set of interlinked engineering and management charts. The key to the concept is the 'voice of the customer'. Quality function deployment creates customer value by drawing on the customer's needs as articulated by the customer. The customer's needs are transformed into design and production process characteristics to give a systems-engineering process that delivers product quality as defined by the customer. Planning tools used in QFD include affinity diagrams, relations diagrams, hierarchy trees, Process Decision Program Diagrams (PDPC) and the Analytic Hierarchy Process (AHP).

The concept was introduced in Japan by Dr Yoji Akao in 1966. It was first implemented at the Mitsubishi Heavy Industries Kobe Shipyard in 1972 and taken up by other Japanese industries. It was adopted in the West when its implementation was linked to the success of Toyota, during the late 1970s and early 1980s. One of QFD's early champions in the West was John Hauser, professor of marketing at the MIT Sloan School of Management, who wrote a paper called 'The House of Quality' for the *Harvard Business Review* in 1988.

According to Akao, QFD 'is a method for developing a design quality aimed at satisfying the consumer and then translating the consumer's demand into design targets and major quality assurance points to be used throughout the production phase … [QFD] is a way to assure the design quality while the product is still in the design stage.'

Quality of earnings

To determine a company's quality of earnings is to make an assessment of a company's earnings based on the type of earnings, rather than simply the amount. The aim is to determine in the case of reported earnings whether those earnings are the sign of a healthy, prosperous company or whether there are other factors that need consideration. Some might say that the highest quality earnings are those that can be immediately deposited in the bank, whereas the lowest quality earnings are those that might be turned into cash at some unspecified time in the future. Investment gurus Benjamin Graham and David Dodd wrote in *Security Analysis* that there are different qualities of assets, of which cash is the most dependable. Similarly, it can be argued that there are different qualities of earnings.

An investor can ask certain questions to determine the quality of earnings. First: Are the earnings repeatable? Sales growth is repeatable; cutting costs may be; sales of assets, such as buildings, and onetime receipt of fees are probably not. Second: Are earnings under the company's control? Earnings from currency differential, inflation or a fall in the cost of raw material are not under a company's control and do not improve quality of earnings. Finally: Are earnings in cash or in accounting entries? Earnings in cash are rarely given back, while entries in the account that reflect orders made but not paid may fail to materialize.

Key text

- Benjamin Graham and David Dodd. *Security Analysis: The Classic 1934 Edition.* McGraw-Hill Professional Publishing, 1996

Quantitative research

Quantitative research is research that gives rise to statistically valid data. Quantitative market research uses sufficiently large samples to give statistically meaningful results. It differs from **qualitative research** in that it is more likely to use structured research instruments to gather data; the research results are usually reproducible; research is conducted on large samples, representative of the general population; the research looks less at motivation and behaviour; and analysis of results tends to be more objective. Common quantitative research techniques include surveys, observation and experimentation. For example, it may involve the use of a questionnaire that asks **closed questions**. Quantitative research questionnaires are often based on information derived from previously conducted qualitative research.

Queuing theory

Queuing theory is a mathematical tool used to study and predict delays in networks. Its applications include modelling human behaviour, for example, on highways or in amusement park queues, and optimizing the flow of goods through production lines and the flow of input data in telecommunications and computing systems. It was invented by Danish engineer A.K. Erlang, who was working on a telephone switching system that minimized delays. Queuing theory has a language all its own, in which queues and servers are known as static objects and resources and customers are known as dynamic objects.

Quick ratio

See Liquidity ratio and Acid test ratio.

Quota sample

A quota sample is one selected by the interviewer on the spot. Probably the most common example is the person on the street with a clipboard, who stops passers-by and asks them to complete a questionnaire. The interviewer is usually given a set number of interviewees to obtain. The apparent random sampling of quota sampling is, of course, open to abuse. To begin with, the interviewer could complete the questionnaire himself. Names and addresses of respondents are usually required to prevent this. Alternatively, bias could be introduced depending on factors such as the time of day, the area or the preferences of the interviewer. To combat this, the interviewer will often be required to perform the quota sampling at specified times of the day or to select a certain mix of people. For example, he might be required to take a sample to reflect the constitution of the larger group from which it was selected. If the product was a baby carriage and the target market for carriages was shown to be 80 percent women and 20 percent men, then the sample group would consist of four women for every one man.

Despite its possible flaws, the quota sample has one big factor in its favour: it is cheap. Respondents do not need to be contacted by phone or letter, nor do these contacts need to be followed up. If someone does not wish to participate, the researcher merely moves on to the next person.

R

Rainmaker

'Rainmaker' is a term given to someone who is very successful in business and, in particular, shows a talent for bringing in new business to a company. The association with new business comes from the term's conventional meaning of a person who is able to produce rain through artificial means. The importance of rain to farming is mirrored in the importance of new business to companies.

Ramping

Ramping is the name given to a practice in which a company's stock price is artificially boosted. The boosting is normally a result of the stock being talked up in the media by individuals who will benefit from the increase in price. Ramping of shares is particularly prevalent on investment bulletin boards on the **Internet**, where gossip and rumour are used by investors to inflate a share's price so that they can sell at a profit. The practice is also known as 'pumping and dumping'. Ramping may also involve purchasing shares as part of the strategy to drive the price up.

RAM (random-access memory)

Random-access memory is a memory device in the form of a collection of integrated circuits (chips), frequently used in microcomputers. RAM is much like a person's short-term memory.

Information can be written to and held in RAM, enabling quick access to it and thus enabling the computer to work faster. However, the downside of RAM is that it only holds data while the computer is powered up. When the computer is turned off, the contents of RAM are lost. Also, the amount of information it can hold depends on how much RAM the computer has. If it becomes full of data, the processor will be forced to overwrite the information in RAM each time and this will slow down the computer.

Ratio analysis

Ratio analysis is the comparison of data to examine the performance of a company. Ratios are often used to analyse financial information, such as indebtedness, stock performance and profitability. Analysts can measure ratios against industry benchmarks to compare a company's performance relative to other firms in its market. Common ratios include the current ratio (current assets divided by current liabilities); the liquidity ratio or **acid test ratio** (current assets minus stock divided by current liabilities); the insolvency ratio (shareholders' funds divided by the loss); and return on shareholders' funds ratio (profit before tax divided by 100, then divided again by shareholders' funds).

Rationalization

Rationalization involves the reorganization of a

company to improve efficiency, productivity and profitability. While rationalization could include expanding aspects of a business in the 1980s and 1990s, it has become a byword for **downsizing**. Rationalization may involve any of the following: a contraction of the supply chain, re-evaluation and restructuring of the brand portfolio, whole-sale plant closures, or large-scale redundancies.

Raw data

Raw data consists of the facts and figures collected from surveys, experiments and other sources before they have been processed and meaning or interpretation has been applied. This data is often presented in the form of frequency charts, tables and graphs to make it easier to understand and analyse. For example, meteorological data, such as daily temperature or rainfall, can be collected over long periods of time and then displayed as line graphs so that comparisons can easily be made.

ROM (read-only memory)

Read-only memory is a memory device in the form of a collection of integrated circuits (chips), frequently used in microcomputers. ROM chips are loaded with data and programs during manu-facture. They differ from **RAM** (random-access memory) chips, as they only be read and not writ-ten to by a computer and they retain their contents when the power is switched off.

Recommended retail price

Recommended retail price (RRP) is the price at which the supplier of a product recommends that the retailer sell that product. In many countries, the supplier may go no further than 'recom-mending' a price; insisting on a specified retail price (as in resale-price maintenance), entering into an agreement to fix a price or coercing the

retailer may fall foul of restrictive trade practices legislation.

Redundancy

Redundancy entails the loss of a person's job because the job no longer exists. This may occur because the business is shrinking in size or going bankrupt due, for example, to a recession in the economy. The firm may have introduced labour-saving technology so that fewer workers are now needed to produce the same output as before, or it may be changing its product mix, stopping or reducing production of one line but expanding elsewhere.

The nuances of employment legislation can make it difficult for employers to make staff redundant and can help smart employees survive **downsizing**. Managers in the United Kingdom, for example, have to think very carefully before making an employee redundant. They must use objective criteria, such as skills, qualifications and length of service, to make a decision about which employees to make redundant. Another essential element of the redundancy process is consultation. In the United Kingdom, there must be meaningful consultation with the employees before embarking on a round of redundancies. This means the employer should offer the work-ers an opportunity to suggest how redundancies may be avoided. Finally, before an employee is made redundant, UK companies have a duty to try and find the employee alternative work within the organization. Additionally, in companies making in excess of 20 redundancies, there is a stipulated period of time for which the company must consult. For example, in companies dismiss-ing 20 or more people within 90 days, the period of consultation with the workers must last for a minimum of 30 days.

In the United Kingdom, workers have a right to redundancy payments if they have been with a company for at least two years. As a rule of thumb, workers between ages 22 and 41 get redundancy pay of one week's salary, with a cap at a certain figure (currently around £250) for each year of service. Workers between ages 42 and 64 get slightly more: one and a half weeks' salary for each year. In practice, companies can pay more than the statutory minimum.

Reengineering

Reengineering was the business idea of the early 1990s. It was brought to the fore by American management consultants **James Champy**, co-founder of the consultancy CSC Index, and Michael Hammer, an electrical engineer and former computer science professor at MIT. Champy and Hammer's book, *Reengineering the Corporation*, was a bestseller that produced a plethora of reengineering programmes, the creation of many consulting companies and a deluge of books promoting alternative approaches to reengineering. Thanks to the popularity of reengineering, CSC also became one of the largest consulting firms in the world.

The fundamental idea behind reengineering was that organizations needed to identify their key processes and make them as lean and efficient as possible. Peripheral processes (and, therefore, peripheral people) needed to be discarded. 'Don't automate; obliterate,' said Hammer. A wave of **downsizing** followed as corporations throughout the world obliterated in the name of reengineering. 'I think reengineering follows in the proud footsteps of many dimly remembered management fads. The thing about reengineering is that it produced billions of dollars in consulting revenues and cost thousands of people their jobs,' says Peter Cohan, author of *Net Profit* and formerly with CSC.

The lessons from reengineering are many and varied. First, theorizing is one thing; practice another. The concept of reengineering is simple; turning it into reality is immensely more difficult than its proponents suggested. The blank piece of paper on which companies were supposed to re-map themselves ignored the years, often decades, of cultural evolution that led to an organization doing something in a certain way. Such preconceptions and often justifiable habits were not easily discarded.

The second lesson from reengineering is that businesses really are about people. If companies ride roughshod over people, they lose their trust and goodwill. Reengineering appeared inhumane. Significantly, when the phrase was first invented in 1987, 'transformation' was dismissed as an alternative because it was too 'touchy-feely'.

The third lesson is that corporations were not – and still aren't – natural or even willing revolutionaries. Instead of casting the reengineering net widely, managers tended to reengineer the most readily accessible process and then leave it at that. Related to this – and the subject of Mr Champy's sequel, *Reengineering Management* – reengineering usually failed to impinge on management.

'I do not believe that there will be a long-lasting impact to reengineering because the concept of reengineering depends on changing the way executives manage,' observes Cohan. 'Reengineering has not proven to be a sufficiently compelling reason for executives to change how they behave. If there was a way of recasting reengineering so it became a way to increase managers' compensation and power, then there would be a change in management behaviour and reengineering would have a lasting impact.' Not surprisingly, managers were all too willing to impose the rigours of a process-based view of the business on others, but often unwilling to inflict it on themselves. In retrospect, the mistake of reengineering was that it didn't recommend tackling management first.

Key texts

- Peter S. Cohan. *Net Profit: How to Invest and Compete in the Real World of Internet Business*. Jossey-Bass, 1999
- Michael Hammer and James Champy. *Reengineering the Corporation*. HarperCollins, 1993
- James Champy. *Reengineering Management: The Mandate for New Leadership*. HarperCollins, 1995

Registered users

The term 'registered users' is used in e-commerce to describe the number of users that have signed up to a particular Web site. In an effort to relate the number of Web site users to the value of the company, **e-commerce** has turned to registered users into a valuation tool. By taking the value of the company and dividing it by the number of registered users, it is possible to arrive at a value for each registered user. This figure can then be used as a means of comparing one company to another, although in practice, this is a flawed and crude valuation tool. The problem lies in the quality of the information extracted from the user. In the best cases, demographic, psychographic and technographic information is required in order to register. From this type of information, companies can build up valuable databases of user profiles. However, with other sites, all that is required is a name and e-mail address.

Relationship marketing

The idea behind relationship marketing goes back to the earliest trading times, but the term entered the vocabulary of management during the 1980s. At that time, management writers observed it at work within the high-tech business community of California's Silicon Valley.

In 1985, marketing guru Regis McKenna wrote the first book devoted to the marketing of high-technology companies, *The Regis Touch*. 'Many of the small highly innovative Silicon Valley companies didn't market new products to the larger computer companies on an individual basis in the traditional way,' he observed. Instead, they sought to establish strategic relationships that allowed the smaller company to work almost as a part of the larger organization.

In a very fast-moving industry, the closeness of these relationships was critical to the ability of the smaller firms to develop solutions that met the needs of their customers. It became apparent that their success often depended on personal relationships that had developed into close friendships. Rather than attend to the marketing of products or projects through traditional means, these smaller companies worked extra hard at maintaining ongoing relationships.

Relationship Marketing, McKenna's third book, focused on the interactive relationships vital to market acceptance in the 'age of the customer' and drew wider attention to the concept of relationship marketing.

The logic of relationship marketing is simple. Rather than communicate intermittently with key customers, it makes more sense to develop a relationship of mutual trust so that the dialogue is continuous. Everyone in business has been told that success is all about attracting and retaining customers. But once companies have attracted customers, they often overlook the second half of the equation.

Failing to concentrate on retaining as well as attracting customers costs businesses huge amounts of money annually. It has been estimated that the average company loses between 10 and 30 percent of its customers every year. Organizations are now beginning to wake up to these lost opportunities and calculate the financial implications. Research in the United States found that a 5 percent decrease in the number of defecting customers led to profit increases of between 25 and 85 percent.

Relationship-building programmes now cover a multitude of activities, from magazines targeted at customers to vouchers and gifts. Basically, the programmes aim to persuade a person to use a preferred vendor in order to take advantage of the benefit being offered, whether it is a trip to Acapulco or a price-reduction voucher for a fizzy drink.

Sceptics will say that there is nothing new in this. Indeed, businesses have been giving long-standing customers discounts and inducements since time immemorial. What is now different is the highly organized way in which companies are attempting to build relationships and customer loyalty.

The idea is that if you are constantly aware of what your customers or partners require and keep them informed of developments within your own organization, then the customer-supplier link becomes almost a seamless web. In relationship marketing, the details of the products and services become subservient to the trust that has been established. Why, after all, would a customer go elsewhere if you constantly monitor and adjust what you are doing to meet his needs now and in the future? The advantage of such an arrangement is that problems can be averted before they become a crisis. The only reason for losing the customer is if the relationship breaks down.

Technology is likely to have a marked effect on relationship marketing. On one hand, the emergence of the **Internet** as a global marketplace means that customers are likely to become increasingly promiscuous, able to flirt with suppliers all over the world. At the same time, technology also means that relationship-marketing programmes are becoming ever more sophisticated. When it comes to creating loyal customers, the database is king. Databases mean that companies can target audiences more effectively.

Key texts

- Regis McKenna. *Real Time: Preparing for the Age of the Never Satisfied Customer*. Harvard Business School Press, 1997
- Frederick Reichheld. *The Loyalty Effect*. Harvard Business School Press, 1996
- Tony Cram. *The Power of Relationship Marketing*. FT/Pitman, 1995
- Adrian Payne. *The Essence of Services Marketing*. Prentice Hall, 1993
- Martin Christopher, Adrian Payne and David Ballantyne. *Relationship Marketing*. Butterworth Heinemann, 1991

Remembered pain

See Two-factor theory.

Resale price maintenance (RPM)

Resale price maintenance occurs when a supplier – usually a manufacturer or wholesale supplier – tries to ensure that a retailer does not sell a product below a specified price. RPM may involve an explicit instruction to sell at a particular price, coupled with threats regarding the retailer's access to supply of that good. Alternatively, the supplier may make inducements to the retailer to sell above a specified price, or the supplier may just make it understood that there is a minimum retail price. The idea behind this type of agreement is to maintain profits and discourage competition. If a manufacturer signs an RPM agreement with all of the retailers they supply, they can guarantee their profit margins to a degree. The detrimental effect on competition, however, has led to this type of agreement becoming illegal in many countries, including the United Kingdom and the United States. Penalties can be very severe. In the United States, fines may be as high as $10 million.

Retail price index (RPI)

The retail price index (RPI) is an index compiled by the United Kingdom's Office for National Statistics to reflect the cost of living at any particular time. It is compiled from a national basket of household items called 'indicators', which reflect common items of household expenditure. Each month, the price of these indicators is monitored and adjusted accordingly. The items are altered annually to keep them up to date. For example, in the 2001 review, rainbow trout was replaced by salmon fillets in the food section. The RPI is published a month after it is calculated and used by the government as an indicator of the rate of growth of the economy when making economic decisions and by the **Bank of England** when considering interest rate policy. The index was rebased to 100 in 1987.

The Retail Price Index's history dates back to the Cost of Living Index that preceded it and was published monthly from April 1914. The RPI was introduced in 1947. Today, to avoid confusion, the Cost of Living Index for the years 1914 to 1947 is also referred to as the RPI and the dates given for the RPI are 1914 to the present.

The US equivalent of the RPI is the Consumer Price Index (CPI), compiled on a monthly basis by the Bureau of Labor Statistics (BLS). The CPI was introduced in 1919, following World War I, and was calculated retrospectively starting from the year 1913.

Retention

Retention may refer to a company keeping either its customers or employees. A company's staff retention rate may provide important clues about the general morale of the organization. If the retention rate is poor, **exit interviews** may reveal the reasons. Low customer retention rates can point to factors such as non-competitive pricing, poor after-sales service and lack of product differentiation. Market research can help identify the reasons.

Revans, Reg

Academic and action-learning pioneer (b. 1907)

Unsung and unheralded, British academic Reg Revans is a man with a mission. Now in his late 80s, the creator and champion of **action learning** retains a messianic zeal few younger men could match. 'Unless your ideas are ridiculed by experts, they are worth nothing,' he says. 'I've been talking about action learning for 60 years, but it's not me you should be talking to. Talk to the people putting it into practice.'

The seed of a lifetime's fascination was sown and began to flourish in the 1920s, when Revans worked at Cambridge's Cavendish Laboratories alongside five Nobel Prize winners. In the quest

to split the atom, the eminent scientists tended to champion their own particular fields. To break the logjam, physicist Lord Rutherford decided that the team should hold a meeting every week to discuss their difficulties and ask fresh questions. 'Even though they had won Nobel Prizes, they were willing to acknowledge that things could be going on elsewhere. They asked questions,' Revans remembers.

If leading thinkers could introduce humility and the sharing of knowledge into their working practices, why couldn't others? After World War II, Revans moved on to become the first director of education and training at the National Coal Board and set about applying his ideas. He concluded that colliery managers and miners themselves needed to acknowledge the problems they faced and then attempt to solve them. 'When doctors listen to nurses, patients recover more quickly; if mining engineers pay more attention to their men than to their machinery, the pits are more efficient,' Revans said. 'As in athletics and nuclear research, it is neither books nor seminars from which managers learn much, but from here-and-now exchanges about the operational job in hand.'

With characteristic frankness, Revans announced that he saw no need to employ a team of specialist tutors: 'The ultimate power of a successful general staff lies not in the brilliance of its individual members, but in the cross-fertilization of its collective abilities.' Revans spent two years underground to examine the real problems facing miners. This reinforced his idea that learning comes when problems are aired and shared in small groups of 'comrades in adversity'. (In the 1990s, Nelson Mandela called it 'grassroots collaboration'.) The pits that tried Revans's methods recorded a 30 percent increase in productivity.

Revans's big idea was action learning – a deceptively simple idea. It is concerned with learning to learn by doing, a process for which Revans created a simple equation: $L = P + Q$ (learning occurs through a combination of programmed knowledge (P) and the ability to ask insightful questions

(Q)). 'The essence of action learning is to become better acquainted with the self by trying to observe what one may actually do, to trace the reasons for attempting it and the consequences of what one seemed to be doing,' says Revans.

While programmed knowledge is one-dimensional and rigid, the ability to ask questions opens up other dimensions and is free-flowing. Revans argues that educational institutions remain fixated with programmed knowledge instead of encouraging students to ask questions and roam widely around a subject.

The structure linking the two elements is the small team or set. 'The central idea of this approach to human development, at all levels, in all cultures and for all purposes, is today that of the set, or small group of comrades in adversity, striving to learn with and from each other as they confess failures and expand on victories,' Revans wrote in *Action Learning*.

After his stint at the National Coal Board in the 1960s, Revans and his theories on action learning seemed destined for an academic career. The United Kingdom's first professor of industrial administration at Manchester University, Revans was involved in the debate about the nature of the city's soon-to-be-established business school. Again, action learning ruffled establishment feathers and Revans departed for Belgium to lead an experiment launched by the Foundation Industrie-Université with the support of the country's leading business people and five universities.

Here he found more fertile ground. 'Brussels had been selected as capital of the Common Market, much to everyone's surprise. They decided if they were to be the administrative centre of Europe, they needed to develop international understanding,' he says. The Belgians responded to the idea of action learning with enthusiasm. Top managers were exchanged between organizations to work on each other's problems. 'I wasn't there to teach anyone anything. We got people talking to each other, asking questions. People from the airline business talked to people from

chemical companies. People shared knowledge and experience,' Revans explains. With minimal attention from the rest of the world, the Belgian economy enjoyed a spectacular renaissance. During the 1970s, Belgian industrial productivity rose by 102 percent, compared with 28 percent in the United Kingdom.

Yet again, Revans's success failed to cross the Channel. When his huge book, *Action Learning*, was published, he ended up buying most of the copies. Simple though it may seem, action learning provides a challenge that organizations have found too sizeable even to contemplate. If learning revolves around questioning, there can be no assumption that the manager knows best purely because of his status. When the world was top-down, Revans looked from the bottom up and saw a new world of possibilities.

Many of the fashionable management ideas – teamworking, reengineering, the learning organization – contain elements of action learning. Revans is encouraged, but remains unconvinced: 'What we need now is not a saviour or a guru, but an active movement so that, no matter what their culture, people work together to understand local difficulties. I'm not saying this is the final answer. There is no final answer for anything.'

Key text

- Reg Revans. *Action Learning*. Blond & Briggs, 1980

Reverse takeover

In a reverse takeover, a smaller company takes over a larger one (or a target company takes over a predator). A reverse takeover may be a strategy to avoid a hostile takeover by selling itself to a **white knight**. The term also applies to the situation in which a private company buys a publicly listed company. A private company may do this as a cost-effective method of obtaining a public listing, as it avoids the extensive costs associated with a flotation. The private company may reverse into a 'cash shell' – that is, a company that is publicly listed but no longer actively trades, having sold off the majority of its assets.

Rheingold, Howard

Author and commentator on the digital world (b. 1947)

Pioneer, critic, futurist and public speaker, Howard Rheingold is a member of the board of directors of the highly regarded online community WELL. He was also the founding executive editor of *HotWired*, the pioneering online magazine launched in 1994 by *Wired* magazine.

Rheingold has written a number of books outlining his ideas about how technology is shaping the future. These include *Virtual Reality* (1991) and *The Virtual Community* (1993). Highly regarded on the public-speaking circuit, Rheingold has spoken about the impact of technological change on society to audiences at, among others, the Science Museum of London, the Smithsonian Institute, Apple, Intel and many other top corporations.

Key texts
- Howard Rheingold. *Virtual Reality*. Summit Books, 1991
- Howard Rheingold. *The Virtual Community: Homesteading on the Electronic Frontier*. Perseus, 1993

Key link
- www.rheingold.com

Rich media

A range of technologies that provide an enhanced viewing experience on the **Internet**, rich media includes video, audio, vector graphics, **Java**, dynamic **HTML** and Shockwave. Companies delivering rich media include Real Networks, Macromedia, and Unicast. Examples of the use of rich media online include Unicast's superstitial

pop-up advertising and Macromedia's Flash animations, both of which are commonly used forms of rich-media advertising.

Rightsizing

See Downsizing.

Rights issue

When a publicly traded company wishes to raise financing, one option is to hold a rights issue. In a rights issue, the company raising financing will offer existing shareholders the chance to buy more shares, usually at a discount. For the company to raise the cash it needs, the rights issue must be fully subscribed. Cash calls are unpopular with shareholders because they dilute existing holdings. A rights issue can also be perceived by the market as a sign of weakness in a company's economic position, especially when the cash is used to pay off debt rather than to finance acquisitions.

Ringi

Ringi is a Japanese term meaning to request a decision. A written recommendation suggesting a specific course of action, it is used in *Ringisei*, a Japanese decision-making process that involves circulating proposals within the organization with the participants initialling them. Unlike Western top-down decision-making processes, *Ringi* is an example of the Japanese tradition of consensus decision making from the bottom up. Under this system, any changes in procedures, routines, tactics or even strategies are originated by those directly concerned with the effects of those changes. A final decision is made after an elaborate examination of the proposal through successively higher echelons of the management structure. With this technique, all participants share in the success of a particular decision or, alternatively, share the responsibility for mistakes.

One of the principal drawbacks to *Ringi* is that it can be time-consuming.

Risk-free rate

The risk-free rate is a hypothetical interest rate at which an investor can earn interest without incurring any risk. It is frequently used in financial modelling: For example, it is used in the **Black and Scholes model** for pricing **options**. It is also used in portfolio theory, which postulates the existence of a risk-free asset in addition to a risky asset. In practice, treasury bills are often assumed to be a risk-free investment, assuming they are held forever.

Robbins, Anthony

Motivational speaker (b. 1960)

Anthony Robbins is the master of motivation. Robbins espouses the use of his version of neuro-linguistic programming (NLP) to help achieve peak performance in individuals and organizations. Recipients of his advice range from sports teams, such as the Los Angeles Kings ice-hockey team, to individuals, such as André Agassi and Bill Clinton, and organizations, including Hallmark, Southwestern Bell and the US Army.

Robbins is the bestselling author of many books, including *Unlimited Power* (1986), *Awaken the Giant Within* (1991) and *Giant Steps* (1994). His personal-development audio series, *Personal Power*, has sold 24 million educational audiotapes sold in less than five years.

The toothsome master of motivation, Robbins has carved a highly lucrative niche for himself as the Sylvester Stallone of motivational gurus. Robbins is permanently tanned and grins broadly in every publicity shot ever taken of him. Failure is not on his agenda. Indeed, one of his trading names is The Unlimited Success Group Inc. Through his motivational seminars, he promises the world and more. He is, the hype tells us, 'one of the greatest influencers of this generation'.

Robbins's four infomercials 'have continuously aired on average every 30 minutes, 24 hours a day somewhere in North America since their initial introduction in 1989.'

Robbins speaks and sells in capital letters: 'When you enroll with Anthony Robbins & Associates, you will learn how to get all the MONEY, LOVE, LUCK, CONFIDENCE and SUCCESS you would ever want … IMMEDIATELY!' It may not be subtle, but it works – for Anthony Robbins, at least. His daily rate is a healthy $75,000-plus and he is in demand throughout the world.

Robbins is also founder and dean of Mastery University: 'a year-long educational experience which he facilitates along with a faculty with unmatched qualifications.' Mastery U is not Harvard. Robbins explains: 'We are an entertainment culture, living in an entertainment age. Many educational enterprises fail to achieve the results they desire for lack of one simple idea: most people would much rather be entertained than educated. The 21st century educator must be an Extraordinary Entertainer who Educates people with the finest tools, and empowers them to act upon them. I call this philosophy, E3.' What would you call it?

Key texts

- Anthony Robbins. *Unlimited Power: The New Science of Personal Achievement.* Simon & Schuster, 1986
- Anthony Robbins. *Awaken the Giant Within: How to Take Immediate Control of Your Mental, Emotional, Physical & Financial Destiny!* Summit Books, 1991
- Anthony Robbins. *Giant Steps: Small Changes to Make a Big Difference.* Fireside, 1994

Key link
- www.tonyrobbins.com

ROCE (return on capital employed)

The return on capital employed is a measure of how much money is generated for each unit of currency invested in a company. ROCE is calculated by dividing operating profits by capital employed, multiplied by 100 to give a percentage. Thus, if a company makes an operating profit of $1000 and has used $10,000 to generate that profit, then the company will have an ROCE of 10 percent. The profit figure used is usually the before-tax figure.

ROCE is also known as the primary efficiency ratio and is a key indicator of a company's performance. To make the venture a worthwhile use of capital, the return should be greater than the return an investor can achieve through investments that carry less risk, such as putting the money on deposit or investing in fixed-interest bonds. Otherwise, a company would be better off liquidating its assets and investing the money accordingly. ROCE must be looked at over a period of years, however, as periods of early rapid growth and recessions can skew the figure.

Rock, Arthur

Father of the venture capital industry (b. 1926)

A key figure in post-war economic history, Arthur Rock lit the match that ignited the technology industry in Silicon Valley.

The son of a candy-store owner, Rock passed on life as a confectioner. Instead, he graduated with an **MBA** from **Harvard Business School** in 1951 and went to work for Hayden Stone, a New York-based investment banking firm. Hayden Stone specialized in financing companies. At the time, the **venture capital** industry didn't exist in a formal sense. Venture capital firms existed, but they weren't known as such. They tended to be private family organizations such as that run by the Rockefeller family.

Rock's lucky break came when he was shown a letter sent to Hayden Stone by a client's son: Eugene Kleiner, a research scientist at William Shockley's laboratory in California. Shockley, a brilliant but erratic research scientist, pioneered research on the transistor. Verging on the para-

noid, Shockley's people-management skills were non-existent and the atmosphere at his lab was extremely unpleasant. Key employees decided they could no longer work with Shockley. Kleiner wrote a speculative letter to Hayden Stone asking if anyone knew of a place where the team could continue to work together. Intrigued, Rock flew out to the West Coast with one of Hayden Stone's partners to meet Kleiner and his associates.

Kleiner explained to Rock the research team's new area of research: manufacturing transistors using silicon. If successfully accomplished, it would revolutionize the computer industry. Impressed, Rock agreed that he would help Kleiner raise $1.5 million to set up a separate company. After contacting a long list of potential investors but raising nothing more than a few eyebrows, Rock turned to Sherman Fairchild.

Sherman Fairchild was the largest stockholder in IBM; he had financed Tom Watson Sr when he founded the predecessor company to IBM. He was also an inventor. Fairchild invented the aerial camera – and then had to invent an airplane to go with it. To develop his inventions, he formed two separate companies: Fairchild Camera and Instrument and Fairchild Aviation. Fairchild agreed to invest $1.5 million through Fairchild Camera and Instrument. Kleiner and his associates were given an option to buy out Fairchild for $3 million.

The new company was named Fairchild Semiconductor: the technology gene pool from which the Silicon Valley high-tech phenomenon evolved. Fired up by the Fairchild deal, Rock stayed in California to investigate other investment opportunities. In 1961, he formed investment partnership Rock & Davis with Tommy Davis after Davis left Kern County Land Company, where he had worked as an investment adviser.

Investment in Rock's first partnership fund came largely from Rock's contacts – private individuals on the East Coast. Institutional investors had yet to wake up to the investment opportunity. An investment of roughly $3 million of the fund's capital returned over $70 million to the limited partners. One early investment was in Scientific Data Systems. The company was sold to Xerox in 1969 for some $990 million. In Rock's words: 'A humongous deal in those days.' Rock's approach to venture capital was about more than just investing money. As a board member, Rock worked closely with the companies he invested in to increase their chances of success. Rock was on the board of Teledyne, one of the fund's first investments, for 33 years.

In 1970, Rock formed a new partnership, Arthur Rock & Associates. Fairchild Semiconductor was in a state of flux. Disenchanted with life at Fairchild, Bob Noyce and **Gordon Moore**, two of the key researchers, approached Rock and explained that they wanted to start their own company to research and produce semiconductor memory. Rock raised $2.5 million from 25 investors to invest in the new company, including $300,000 of his own money. The new company was called Intel. The world's largest producer of microprocessors started with a modest $5.5 million of private funding raised on the strength of a business plan written on one and a half pages. Rock remained on Intel's board for more than 30 years.

Rock followed Intel with another seminal computing company – Apple Computers. Tipped off about a small fledgling computer company called Apple by Mike Markkula, ex-VP of Intel, Rock paid a visit to the San Jose Homebrew Computer show to see for himself. He was unable to get anywhere near the Apple stand at the fair because of the crowds desperate to get a glimpse of the new mock-up Apple computer. To the delight of the two young founding entrepreneurs, **Steve Jobs** and Steve Wozniak, Rock invested $57,000. As usual, he assumed a position on the board, a position he only relinquished years later due to a conflict of interest.

Now in his 70s, Rock works in the industry he helped create. Based in San Francisco, he is a director on a number of boards, both profit and non-profit. He still recalls the words of his Harvard professor: 'If you're interested in building a business to make money, forget it. You won't. If you're interested in building a business to make a contribution to society, then let's talk.'

Rockefeller, John D.

Industrialist and oilman (1839–1937)

American industrialist John D. Rockefeller created the modern oil industry. Without the cheap gasoline that Standard Oil produced, it is unlikely that either the wide-scale electrification of the United States or the mass marketing of the car would have happened when they did.

Rockefeller was born in 1839 in Richford, New York. He was brought up on the family farm, where the young Rockefeller displayed a keen business mind. He raised turkeys, sold them for a profit and then lent the proceeds at 7 percent.

At the age of 14, Rockefeller moved to Cleveland, Ohio, with his family. After a year in high school and a spell at Folsom Mercantile College, Rockefeller worked as an office boy and assistant bookkeeper at forwarding and produce-commission merchants Hewitt & Tuttle. Rockefeller didn't receive any payment for 14 weeks, at which time he was handed $50 and put on $25 per month.

Rockefeller was with Hewitt & Tuttle for three years. He left when the firm refused to meet his wage demands of $800 per year. Having spent three years learning how a business is run, Rockefeller started his own.

He borrowed $1000 from his father at 10 percent interest and started a produce business with partner Morris B. Clark. In its first year of business in 1859, the company's revenues were $500,000.

Around this time, several refineries had been opened near Cleveland as oil began to make an impact in Ohio. Rockefeller wasted no time. In 1862 he formed Andrews, Clark and Co., oil refiners. Next he sold his produce-commission interests to Clark and bought out Clark's interest in Andrews, Clark and Co. to form Rockefeller & Andrews.

By 1869, the oil business was going through a tough time. So many firms were trying to get in on the action that the price of oil became severely depressed and many companies went bankrupt. Rockefeller's firm had acquired a number of other, similar small firms and was now called Rockefeller, Andrews & Flagler. Rockefeller saw growth as the way to survive. In 1869, he merged Rockefeller, Andrews & Flagler into the Standard Oil Company of Ohio, with $1 million in capital and Rockefeller as president.

Rockefeller applied the 'combination' strategy to Standard Oil's business that **J.P. Morgan** had so successfully applied to the steel industry. By buying up competitors, both locally and elsewhere in the United States, Rockefeller could spread the risk of operating in such a volatile and risky industry. By 1872, Standard Oil had acquired all of the refining firms in Cleveland. In 1882, after a prosperous decade, all of the businesses in Standard Oil were brought under the single umbrella of the Standard Oil Trust.

Eventually, the dominance of the Trust came to be reviled by both the public and the government. In 1890, a court case was brought against Rockefeller to dissolve the Trust. Rockefeller was put under severe stress; he lost all of his hair, including his eyebrows, and was reputed to have suffered a nervous breakdown. The effects of the court case on Standard Oil were less dramatic. The company simply reformed as the Standard Oil Company (New Jersey) where the laws permitted a parent company to own the stock of other companies. The Standard Oil Company (New Jersey) still controlled three-quarters of the US petroleum business.

It wasn't until 1911 that the US Supreme Court finally ordered the dissolution of Standard Oil, declaring the company in contravention of the country's anti-trust laws. The 38 companies that comprised the oil giant were split into separate entities. Rockefeller stepped down as president of Standard Oil.

During his lifetime, Rockefeller came in for much criticism, as well as some odd mythologizing. It was claimed that he would only eat bread and milk. Another persistent story was of his phenomenal capacity for hard work and long hours, something that Rockefeller denied all knowledge of. 'People persist in thinking that I was a tremendous worker, always at it, early and late, winter and summer,' said Rockefeller. 'The real truth is that I was what would now be called a "slacker" after I reached my middle thirties … . I never, from the time I first entered an office, let business engross all my time and attention.'

Rockefeller's final years were devoted to giving away the bulk of his huge fortune. He gave more than $35 million to the University of Chicago, founded the Rockefeller Institute for Medical Research, the Rockefeller Foundation, and the Rockefeller Sanitary Commission, which eradicated hookworm in the Southern states. At its height, Rockefeller's wealth was $900 million. When he died at the age of 97, on 23 May 1937, at his home in Ormond Beach, he had given away all but $26,410,837.

Key texts

- Ron Chernow. *Titan: The Life of John D. Rockefeller, Sr.* Random House, 1998
- David Freeman Hawke. *John D.: The Founding Father of the Rockefellers.* Harper & Row, 1980
- Allan Nevins. *Study in Power: John D. Rockefeller, Industrialist and Philanthropist.* Scribner, 1953
- Earl Latham. *John D. Rockefeller: Robber Baron or Industrial Statesman?* Heath, 1949
- Allan Nevins. *John D. Rockefeller: The Heroic Age of American Enterprise.* Scribner, 1940

Roddick, Anita

Beauty products and franchise pioneer; founder, The Body Shop (b. 1942)

Born in Sussex in 1942, Anita Roddick was brought up in the sleepy coastal town of Littlehampton, where her parents ran an American-style diner. After finishing secondary school, Roddick turned down a place at the Guildhall School of Music and Drama and a possible career as an actress to go to Newton Park College of Education in Bath and train to be a teacher.

After college, Roddick worked her way around the world. She taught in England and worked for the *International Herald Tribune* in Paris and the

United Nations in Geneva. She was ejected from South Africa for breaking the anti-apartheid laws by attending a jazz club on 'non-whites' night.

Back in Littlehampton, Roddick settled down, married, had children and opened a hotel and restaurant business with her husband, Gordon. When these proved too demanding on family life, the Roddicks sold the restaurant. Roddick's husband disappeared on an ambitious travel expedition: to ride a horse from South America to New York City.

While her husband was away, Roddick looked for another enterprise to concentrate her energy on and earn some money. She came up with the idea of a cosmetics business with a difference: the difference was natural ingredients. Her husband helped arrange a bank loan with the hotel as collateral, and Roddick bought premises next to an undertaker in the nearby town of Brighton.

Roddick opened for business on 27 March 1976, selling socially responsible, environmentally friendly cosmetics. Many of The Body Shop's defining characteristics were decided upon at this early stage, through cost-effectiveness rather than any grand strategic plan. The walls were painted green, not in anticipation of the Green movement, which was yet to blossom, but to hide the damp patches. Product packaging was minimal and recyclable and cost-conscious Roddick wrote out the labels by hand.

Soon, Roddick was planning another store in nearby Chichester. For financing, Roddick turned to local businessman Ian McGlinn, who agreed to put up the full amount of £4000 for a half share of the business. By the time her husband returned in 1977, The Body Shop concept was unstoppable. Requests to set up branches elsewhere in the country were flooding in. To cater for the demand to open shops elsewhere, Roddick and her husband began franchising the concept. Potential franchisees would finance the business and in return would be licensed to use The Body Shop name and agree to buy their stock from Roddick. A high proportion of the early franchisees were women, and Roddick can justifiably claim to have helped change the traditional male-dominated image of entrepreneurs in the United Kingdom.

The Body Shop was different from conventional cosmetics businesses. Roddick made no special claims about her products. She didn't advertise, relying on publicity and then word of mouth to bring the customers through the shop doors. 'Making products that work – that aren't part of the cosmetic industry's lies to women – is all-important,' Roddick has said. 'Making sure we minimalize our impact in our manufacturing processes, clean up our waste, put back into the community … We go where businesses never want to because they don't think it is the role of business to get involved.'

Roddick espouses profits with principles. A celebrated campaigner on a range of ethical issues through The Body Shop, she has supported Greenpeace, Friends of the Earth and Amnesty International, among others. Messages on store bags and Body Shop vehicles often express The Body Shop's support for these causes.

The company went public in April 1984. On the opening day, the share price rocketed and Roddick, her husband and Ian McGlinn all became paper millionaires overnight.

In 1994, Roddick brought in external management help to refocus the business. Unsurprisingly, Roddick found it difficult to adjust to the shift from her hands-on role. In 1998, she stepped down as CEO, remaining co-chairman with her husband. Then, in 2002, Roddick and her husband stepped down as executive directors, remaining involved with the company only on a part-time basis.

From a small shop next to a funeral parlour, The Body Shop network has expanded to more than 1800 shops worldwide, offering more than 400 products. Roddick, now one of the richest women in England, has been showered with awards as a result of both her business endeavours and her social conscience. London's Business Woman of the Year, Retailer of the Year, the United Nations' 'Global 500' environmental award, and even the Order of the British Empire have all come Roddick's way. Now that she is involved with The

Body Shop on a part-time basis, she has more time to champion the causes she so passionately believes in.

Key texts

- Jules Older. *Anita!: The Woman Behind The Body Shop*. Charlesbridge, 1998
- Anita Roddick. *Body and Soul: Profits with Principles: The Amazing Success Story of Anita Roddick & The Body Shop*. Crown, 1991

Key link

- www.thebodyshop.com

ROE (return on equity)

The return on equity is the relationship between a company's net profits and its shareholders' equity, expressed as a ratio. It is calculated by dividing total net profits by total shareholder equity and multiplying by 100. An investor can use the annual or quarterly earnings figures in the company's annual financial report or quarterly filings, or he can use an average of earnings over a longer period than a year. Shareholders' equity can be taken from the balance sheet and is the difference between total assets and liabilities.

The measure can be used as a benchmark to compare companies across industries. A percentage figure in the 10 to 35 percent range indicates a potentially healthy company. Higher numbers suggest rapid growth; the company will need to maintain growth or cut costs to keep the figure high. The main drawback with ROE as a measure is that it takes no account of debt or **gearing**.

Rosenwald, Julius

Former president and chairman, Sears, Roebuck & Co. (1862–1932)

Julius Rosenwald took a promising business and turned it into a great one. That Sears, Roebuck and Co. became the retailing giant it did is largely due to Rosenwald's intervention.

As a child, Rosenwald sold goods door-to-door in Springfield, Illinois – the town where he was born in 1862. An industrious boy, he pumped the bellows on the church organ, peddled pamphlets and sold chromolithographs, the latest consumer craze. During his summer vacation, he worked in a fancy-goods store.

At the age of 16, Rosenwald left school and travelled to New York to work for his uncle's wholesale clothing business. By the age of 21, he saved enough money to buy a small retail-clothing store on Fourth Avenue. One day, the owner of a nearby menswear manufacturer revealed to Rosenwald that he was struggling to keep pace with orders. That same night, Rosenwald decided to abandon his retail store, move to Chicago, and start afresh. Arriving in Chicago, he formed Rosenwald & Weil, manufacturer and wholesaler of summer clothing, with partner Julius E. Weil.

One of Rosenwald's best customers was Richard Warren Sears. A station agent by trade, Sears made a fortune selling watches by mail, retiring once he had accumulated $100,000. Six months later, Sears was out of retirement and soon built a flourishing business based in Chicago under the name Sears, Roebuck and Co. Needing capital to expand his business, he asked if Rosenwald was interested in investing. For $70,000, Rosenwald took a quarter interest in Sears, Roebuck.

Although Rosenwald was a silent partner to begin with, Sears – who ran Sears, Roebuck single-handedly – asked Rosenwald to join him as vice-president in 1896. Over the next 30 years, Rosenwald transformed Sears, Roebuck into one of the largest retailers in the United States.

First, Rosenwald dealt with the Sears, Roebuck catalogue. Mail-order companies were less than honest in their catalogues' wording and illustrations, and it damaged the reputation of the entire industry. Sears, Roebuck was no exception. At times they were guilty of delivering products that didn't correspond to the promises of the lavishly worded and sumptuously illustrated catalogue.

Rosenwald insisted that every illustration and description in the catalogue be carefully compared with the relevant article. Laboratories were built and scientists employed to inspect merchandise received from suppliers. Defective goods were immediately rejected and returned. To increase consumer confidence, he introduced a 'money back if not satisfied' guarantee supported by an advertising campaign. Thus Rosenwald removed the burden of risk from the consumer, placing it squarely on the shoulders of Sears, Roebuck.

Having secured customer confidence, Rosenwald set about broadening the product range available through mail order. Soon, everything from buttons to bungalows was sold by mail. To secure quality supplies, Rosenwald constructed factories employing more than 20,000 workers. Technological innovations such as the conveyor belt increased productivity. The catalogue was further expanded. New goods, like shoes and books, were featured in the catalogue. Shoes, an unlikely candidate for mail order, earned revenues of $1 million per month. Between 1900 and 1906, total sales increased from $11 million to more than $50 million. By 1914, they reached $100 million.

Rosenwald also made changes to the way the company's employees were treated, preferring to think of himself as one of the workers. Asked what it felt like to have so many people working for him, he replied, 'I always think of them as just working *with* me.' To improve the lot of his workers, Rosenwald introduced recreation facilities, as well as an innovative 'employees' savings and profit-sharing scheme.' Eternally cost-conscious, Rosenwald encouraged his workers to be equally parsimonious. Employees who earned less than $1500 per year received a bonus on the anniversary of their joining the company. The bonus was a percentage of the annual salary equal to the number of years an employee had worked for the company. Starting in the fifth year, it rose to 10 percent in the tenth year, and remained at 10 percent thereafter. Rosenwald suggested his employees save the bonus.

Rosenwald became president in 1908 when Sears retired, and chairman in 1925. During the 1920s, he expanded into retail stores. In 1925, Sears opened its first retail store in Chicago. By 1929, there were 324 stores with the name Sears, Roebuck above the doors.

In his final years, Rosenwald concentrated on philanthropy. He established the Julius Rosenwald Fund, a charity for the economic, medical and cultural advancement of African-Americans, with an endowment of $30 million. He gave money to aid the Jews in the Middle East and to help German children after World War I. He also endowed the University of Chicago and helped to establish the Museum of Science and Industry in Chicago. He died in 1932.

Key texts

- Lorin Sorensen. *Sears, Roebuck And Co. 100th Anniversary 1886–1996*. Silverado Publishing, 1985
- Leon Harris. *Merchant Princes*. Harper & Row, 1979
- M.R. Werner. *Julius Rosenwald: The Life of a Practical Humanitarian*. Harper & Brothers, 1939

Router

A router is a device that pushes traffic through a packet-switched network, such as the Internet. The router will be connected to at least two networks and will be located at a gateway where those networks meet. On the **Internet**, traffic travels through a series of routers that relay each packet of data to its destination by the best possible route.

Rubicam, Raymond

Ad man; co-founder, Young & Rubicam (1892–1978)

Raymond Rubicam is known as the 'father of advertising' with good reason. He is one of the men responsible for transforming **advertising** from a crude sales device to a sophisticated marketing tool.

Rubicam was born in Brooklyn, New York, on 16 June 1892. Because of family problems, Rubicam was passed from one relation to another. He spent time with one brother in Texas, a sister in Ohio, and another brother in Denver. The constantly migrating Rubicam had little schooling. Instead, he learned the value of hard work. His putative education came to a premature conclusion when he was 15, at which point he took a full-time job as a shipping clerk's assistant for $5 a week.

For eight years, Rubicam drifted from one job to the next, all the while harbouring a burning ambition to become a writer. In the space of a year, he worked as a door-to-door salesman of photographs, a film projectionist, a theatre usher and a bellhop. Settling in Philadelphia, he wrote a number of short stories and applied to newspapers for the job of a reporter. His persistence paid off when he was offered a job on the *Philadelphia Inquirer* for $12 a week. Rubicam was writing for a living.

His life in advertising started in 1916 as a copywriter at F. Wallis Armstrong, the first company he applied to. It took a little persuasion. After nine days of waiting in the lobby to see the head of the agency, Rubicam 'wrote the boss a furious letter calculated to produce an immediate interview or a couple of black eyes'. Delivered in person, the letter had the desired effect. Tearing out of his office, the agency chief remarked, 'Those ads you wrote didn't amount to much, but this letter has some stuff in it.'

By 1919, Rubicam had moved on to the largest agency of the time, N.W. Ayer & Son. Rubicam wrote some of its best copy. Campaigns for companies such as piano manufacturer Steinway became some of the most famous of the time. Rubicam's slogans for Squib were still being used 70 years later. Rubicam brought ex-colleague and close friend John Orr Young to N.W. Ayer & Son from F. Wallis Armstrong.

Like so many other agencies at the time, N.W. Ayer & Son placed a premium on the quantity and size of advertisements rather than the quality of the copy. Rubicam was convinced that the content

of the ad – design, artwork and copy – were critical factors in the success of any advertising campaign. The last straw came when Rubicam was passed over for promotion after the head of the agency, Wayland Ayer, died in 1922. With just $5000 and one client, Quick Tipper, a company that sold a tool for capping shoelaces, Rubicam and his friend Young founded the agency Young & Rubicam. It was 1923.

Rubicam insisted on promoting creativity at the agency. This approach helped to win the agency's first major client, General Foods. The agency's campaign for General Foods won a mantelpiece full of prestigious awards and the agency was rewarded with more General Foods business – the Grape Nuts and Jell-O accounts. In 1926, Young & Rubicam moved into offices at 285 Madison Avenue, New York.

Rubicam introduced a string of advertising innovations. A firm believer that advertisers should know as much about both the product advertised and the consumer as possible, he hired a professor from Northwestern University to set up a research department investigating consumers' preferences and prejudices. The professor was Dr George H. Gallup, who would go on to found the Gallup Polling organization. Gallup and Rubicam also set up an audience research institute at Princeton, run by a young Englishman, **David Ogilvy**, who would eventually be recognized as one of the great advertising men of his time.

The research findings from this bold experiment encouraged Rubicam to try new types of advertising. The list was extensive: caption bubbles; comic-strip ads that presented an advertisement as a sequential story; the use of a short first paragraph; extensive use of subheadings in long copy; headlines of no more than eleven words in length; scientific audience sampling; and product-recognition and test-advertising research. All of these methods would become standard practice in the industry.

When Young retired in 1927, Rubicam became president, relinquishing the title in 1934 to become chairman. He was a popular boss. The atmosphere at Young & Rubicam was informal, a stark contrast to most businesses of the time, advertising or otherwise. Rubicam retired at the age of 52 in 1944, and moved to Arizona, where he continued to retain his interest in business. He acted as a consultant to the Campbell Soup Company and sat on a number of boards of directors. He also speculated in real estate. He died in 1978 at the age of 85.

Key text

• Julian Lewis Watkins. *The 100 Greatest Advertisements: Who Wrote Them and What They Did.* Dover, 1959

Ryan, John Dennis

Copper king (1864–1933)

John Dennis Ryan showed that it is never too late to chase your dreams. Although mining was in his blood, Ryan only found himself in the industry in his thirties. He used his talents to create the world's biggest copper company.

Ryan was born of mining stock in Hancock, Michigan, in October 1864. His father, who discovered extensive copper deposits in the Lake Superior region, expected his son to follow him into the mining business. But the young Ryan showed no interest in mining at all.

Instead, at the age of 17, he went to work for an uncle in one of the general stores in the Michigan copper-mining district. For eight years, Ryan weighed, measured and wrapped parcels. Then he gave up the grocery store to seek his fortune in Denver where, after a bleak six months of unemployment, he obtained a job as a travelling oil salesman.

At the age of 30, Ryan had carved out of a comfortable niche as a salesman, making somewhere between $100 and $150 a month. But it was a far cry from the achievements of some of the great **entrepreneurs** in business history, many of whom were millionaires by the age of 30. It was marriage that started Ryan on the path to riches.

Ryan married Nettie Gardner when he was 32. She had bigger plans for her husband than life as an itinerant oil salesman. She persuaded Ryan to purchase an interest in a business owned by Marcus Daly, head of Anaconda steel: the Daly Bank & Trust Company. With bluff, bluster, a good deal of money borrowed from friends and all of his savings, Ryan managed to buy out a number of minority shareholders and acquire a controlling interest. Ryan and his wife moved to Montana, where the head office of the Daly banking interests was located.

Ryan ran the business well and gained a reputation as a safe pair of hands. His reputation brought one of **John D. Rockefeller**'s partners knocking at his door with a request to take charge of the affairs of the Amalgamated Copper Co. in Montana. Ryan accepted.

The Amalgamated Copper Co. was in poor shape when Ryan arrived. The company was in litigation with Fritz Augustus Heinze, one of the 'copper kings' and owner of the Montana Ore Purchasing Company. It was also in conflict with the labour force. Ryan became managing director of Amalgamated in 1904. His first task was to negotiate with Heinze.

In his preliminary discussions with Heinze, Ryan sensed an opportunity to buy out all of Heinze's mining interests in Montana. The key to a successful deal, Ryan decided, was protecting Heinze's pride by dressing up the deal to suggest that Heinze was compromising rather than selling out. Ryan's suspicions were confirmed when Heinze refused to meet in public, going out of his way to keep details of the negotiations from his mining workforce. As Ryan recalled, 'After six months negotiating we finally met one night, talked price from one o'clock to three o'clock in the morning, and reached an agreement.'

Heinze signed over virtually all of his mining interests in Montana. With Heinze out of the way, Ryan took on the Western Federation of Miners and the International Workers of the World. Refusing to recognize either union, he declared an open shop. His management skills proved equal to his talent for negotiating, and the amalgamated mines never lost a single day to labour problems.

The mining industry was a rough, tough, often violent world, and Ryan did well to survive, let alone prosper. Take the 34th annual Butte Miner's Union picnic, held at Gregson Hot Springs on Sunday, 11 August 1912. Fourteen thousand people attended, the majority of whom were miners. The main event of the day was the tug-of-war contest between miners from the St Lawrence mine and those from the Buffalo mine. Ryan contributed to the prize money. What started as a tug of war escalated into a punch-up, which turned into a full-scale firefight. Two miners died from gunshot wounds. These were the people Ryan had to manage.

Ryan consolidated many other mines and smelting plants into the Amalgamated Copper Co. In 1910, the entire holdings of Amalgamated were merged into the Anaconda Copper Mining Co. The Amalgamated was dissolved in 1914.

Ryan was in charge of the world's largest copper company.

Ryan spent most of the 1920s wheeling and dealing on Wall Street, a world away from the dirt and grime of the copper mines. When Ryan acquired copper deposits in Chile for some $70 million, it was the largest cash transfer Wall Street had ever witnessed. In 1928, Ryan sold Montana Power for $85 million in stock. He then issued more shares in his company, using the cash to fund speculative investments. When the Wall Street Crash came in October 1929, Ryan was wiped out. His shares, worth $175 each at their height, were valued at a paltry $4. He died broke in 1933 and was buried in a copper coffin, the last of the copper kings.

Key text
- Isaac F. Marcosson. *Anaconda*. Dodd, Mead & Co., 1957

S

Sale and leaseback

In a sale and leaseback, a company will sell an asset, such as a plant, machinery or property, and then purchase the right to use the asset under a lease, either financial or operating. The reason for carrying out such a transaction is usually for cash flow or tax purposes.

Sample

A sample is a small selection of items or people drawn from a larger group and intended to be representative of that group. A sample can be selected by quota, to accurately reflect the composition of the group or market it was drawn from, or randomly. A small group of people chosen as representative of a particular demographic group may be selected as a sample in market research.

The size of a sample will influence the accuracy of the results determined from that sample. A larger sample provides more accurate results, since it more closely reflects the group it was drawn from. It is important to remember when drawing conclusions from a sample that there is always a degree of error involved in sample selection.

The term 'sample' is also used to describe a small amount of a product given to potential retailers and consumers.

Sarnoff, David

Media pioneer (1891–1970)

David Sarnoff pioneered the mass-market enter- tainment industry of radio and television. Born in Uzlian, Russia, in 1891, Sarnoff and his family joined his emigrant father in the United States in 1900. Unfortunately, when Sarnoff arrived in Manhattan on 2 July 1900, it became apparent that his father had struggled to make a living and his health had deteriorated to the point where he was unable to provide for his family. At the age of 9, Sarnoff became the family breadwinner.

Sarnoff sold Yiddish newspapers on street corners, earning a quarter for every 50 papers sold, delivered another paper in the morning, and sang at the local synagogue for a small fee. Somehow, he also managed to attend a local school, the Educational Alliance. At 14, he opened his own newspaper stand, employing his father and brothers.

The road to success for Sarnoff started out at American Marconi Wireless Telegraph. Sarnoff started work there as an office boy. He was to spend the next 60 years there and at its successor, Radio Corporation of America, becoming president before he reached the age of 40.

When the upstart Sarnoff, as the newest employee of the company, introduced himself to Guglielmo Marconi in person, his impudence was rewarded. Sarnoff was promoted first to junior wireless operator and then chief inspector.

It was about this time that Sarnoff met Edwin H. Armstrong, an inventor working on an improved wireless receiver. Armstrong demonstrated his invention to Sarnoff, receiving radio signals from Clifden, Ireland, and a radio station in San Francisco. Sarnoff immediately advised his bosses to explore the possibilities of developing a similar device. His superiors were unimpressed, preferring to stick with existing technology. In

1916, Sarnoff, with considerable foresight, wrote a memo to the board: 'I have in mind a plan of development which would make radio a household utility in the same sense as the piano or the phonograph.'

In 1919, following the end of World War I, a new company, Radio Corporation of America (RCA), was incorporated. This was because the US government was reluctant to hand over the significant technical advances in radio engineering made during the war to an English company like Marconi. The new company held the patents of General Electric and Marconi; Sarnoff was its commercial manager and second-in-command. Sarnoff sent a 28-page 'blueprint for success' to the chairman, lobbying for the production of radios. Sarnoff got his way and RCA began to churn out radio sets, assuring RCA's success as radios became hugely popular.

In 1920, Sarnoff struck a winning deal with Armstrong. RCA received first refusal on Armstrong's innovations and, in return, gave him enough stock in RCA to make him the leading shareholder, as well as some cash.

Despite RCA's domination of its market, the increasing popularity of radio as a form of entertainment, and the creation of the National Broadcasting Company, the Wall Street Crash of 1929 and ensuing financial chaos hit the company badly. In January 1930, after a boardroom shuffle, Sarnoff became president of RCA at the age of 39.

In the late 1930s, Sarnoff directed his attention toward television rather than radio. He introduced television just before World War II, at the 1939 World Fair.

Radio was still to have a significant impact on Sarnoff's life, however. After World War II, Armstrong and Sarnoff fell out over FM (Frequency Modulation), which Armstrong had invented in December 1933. Eventually, after years of dispute, Armstrong was forced to agree a settlement in the courts. In 1954, bitter at the outcome, Armstrong jumped to his death from a thirteenth-story window. Sarnoff's only comment on learning of the death of his onetime friend was that of a man with a guilty conscience: 'I didn't kill Armstrong'.

Sarnoff carried on as usual. Colour television was introduced in 1954. Shrewdly, Sarnoff placed all of RCA's colour television patents in the public domain to avoid damaging litigation, and at the same time tripled spending on colour programming. Now any manufacturer could produce a colour television, but RCA had first-mover advantage in colour broadcasting.

Colour television was Sarnoff's last throw of the dice. The lengthy litigation with Armstrong had taken more of a toll on Sarnoff than he realized. In 1965, Sarnoff's son Robert became president of the company and Sarnoff became chairman.

When son Robert repackaged RCA with a change of name and logo, Sarnoff was roused one last time as he fought successfully to reinstate the old name. It was a hollow victory. The RCA that Sarnoff had created no longer existed. It was now a conglomerate of disparate companies, including Hertz car rentals and Random House Publishing. After a lengthy illness, Sarnoff died in December 1970.

Key texts
- Robert Sobel. *RCA*. Stein and Day, 1986
- Kenneth M. Bilby. *The General: David Sarnoff and the Rise of the Communications Industry*. Harper & Row, 1986
- Carl Dreher. *Sarnoff: An American Success*. Quadrangle/New York Times Books, 1977
- Elisabeth P. Myers. *David Sarnoff: Radio and TV Boy*. Bobbs-Merrill Co., 1972
- *The Wisdom of Sarnoff and the World of RCA*. Wisdom Society for the Advancement of Knowledge, Learning, and Research in Education, 1967
- Eugene Lyons. *David Sarnoff: A Biography*. Harper & Row, 1966

Key link
- www.rca.com

Savings and loans association

See Building society.

Scalable

'Scale up' and 'scalable' are terms that became popular during the dotcom boom of the 1990s. They both refer to the ability to grow a company quickly while keeping the management structures in place. A company can have a profitable business model, but if it's not scalable, then it is of limited interest to venture capitalists. They also refer to being able to take the business model and roll it out on a large scale as the business grows. Scalability is what venture capitalists look for. It is the key to a **killer application**.

Similarly, a scalable solution is one that works for a specific problem and can be extended to work wherever the situation demands. This might be a customer-service solution that is developed in a single branch but can be rolled out across the organization.

Scase, Richard

Trendspotter

Richard Scase is one of the select few who spend their entire working day identifying trends and changes in the working world. Scase, currently professor of organizational behaviour at the University of Kent at Canterbury, is, among other projects, exploring future scenarios for Britain in the year 2010. The future is his domain. And the future, says Scase, will be centred on working flexibly.

'Mobile, flexible organizations require self-confidence,' he says. 'The capabilities to enable homeworking and the like exist, but in too many cases are not being realized.' Scase points out that the barriers to more flexible working practices are mental rather than technical. It can be done. But organizations and, more to the point, managers choose not to. 'The culture of management often still equates commitment, enthusiasm and motivation to being physically around,' Scase says. 'While people could do a great deal more work away from the workplace, not many organizations possess the self-confidence to allow them to do so. If people work out of the office, you can find that their commitment is questioned. The whole politics of promotion often works against people working away from the workplace.'

The end result of this culture of management is that companies are saddled with unnecessarily high overheads – most obviously, expensive and needless office space.

Scase detects that change is in the air. The future will be different. It has to be. 'The culture is changing. We are at a watershed that will lead to fundamental changes in the relationship between our home and working lives,' he predicts, pointing to management consulting firms and high-tech companies where offices have been transformed into attractive meeting places rather than carefully delineated fiefdoms. 'With their more relaxed atmosphere, offices of the future will be where you meet up with clients and colleagues,' says Scase. 'The creative stimulation you get from meeting up with people will still be there, but it will not be static and fixed.'

Scase anticipates that beyond the virtual organization lies the intelligent corporation, at whose heart lies creativity, the source of innovation. He believes the first element of creativity is personal space. 'You can't bureaucratize creativity,' he says. 'You can't tell people to be creative. You need to be able to think and play around with ideas in a comfortable environment.' The second ingredient is social interaction: 'Face-to-face interaction is important. Socializing after work, for example, is extremely powerful and useful. People talk about work in a way they wouldn't do when actually at work.'

The future mapped out by Richard Scase is a world of either/and rather than either/or alternatives. Its aim is to get the best of all possible worlds rather than separating activities into physical and mental compartments.

Key text

- Howard Davis and Richard Scase. *Managing Creativity: The Dynamics of Work and Organization*. Open University Press, 1999

Scenario planning

Scenario planning was invented in the 1940s by Herman Kahn, the famous futurist from the Rand Corporation and the Hudson Institute. The term 'scenario' – meaning a detailed outline for the plot of a future film – was borrowed from Hollywood by Kahn's friend, screenwriter and novelist Leo Rosten.

Kahn was best known for his scenarios about nuclear war and his trademark phrase, 'thinking the unthinkable'. Other early pioneers of scenario thinking also tended to look at the macro level – the future of mankind, for example, or the economy of an entire region.

Although only now coming into wider use, scenario planning has been practised in one form or another in the business world since the early 1960s. It was first used by a farsighted team of planners at oil company Royal/Dutch Shell. They began to build on Kahn's work, developing their own version of the scenario approach as a possible answer to two questions: 'How do we look up to 20 to 30 years ahead?' and 'How can we get people to discuss the "unthinkable" together?' Using the technique, they foresaw the energy crises of 1973 and 1979, the growth of energy conservation, the evolution of the global environmental movement and even the break-up of the Soviet Union years before these events happened.

What Shell realized, however, was that managers need a translation of these grand scenarios into something more recognizable. To have practical use in business, the story needs to be focused on a particular audience or issue. Learning to focus scenarios on a specific business purpose was part of the company's contribution to the practice.

In the 1990s, a string of books, including *The Art of the Long View* by futurist **Peter Schwartz**, *The Living Company* by former Shell manager **Arie de Geus**, and the *Age of Heretics*, based on interviews with Shell managers, by **Art Kleiner**, drew attention to scenario planning, placing it firmly on the management agenda. It is no coincidence, of course, that the technique has came to

the fore at a time when so many seemingly unassailable companies have been wrong-footed by changes in their trading environments.

Key texts
- Gill Ringland. *Scenario Planning*. Wiley, 1998
- Kees Van der Heijden. *Scenarios: The Art of Strategic Conversation*. John Wiley & Sons, 1996

Schein, Edgar H.

American social psychologist (b. 1928)

Edgar H. Schein's work has exerted a steadily growing influence on management theory, particularly over the last 20 years. His thinking on corporate cultures and careers has proved highly important. Schein joined the Massachusetts Institute of Technology (MIT in 1956 and initially worked under the influence of **Douglas McGregor**. He has remained there ever since.

At MIT, Schein soon noted the similarities between the brainwashing of POWs and the corporate indoctrination carried out by the likes of General Electric, at its Crotonville training base, and IBM, at Sands Point. 'There were enormous similarities between the brainwashing of the POWs and the executives I encountered at MIT,' says Schein. 'I didn't see brainwashing as bad. What was bad were the values of the Communists. If we don't like the values, we don't approve of brainwashing.' From this work came Schein's book, *Coercive Persuasion*.

The ability of strong values to influence groups of people is a strand that has continued throughout Schein's work. As he points out, recent trends, such as the learning organization (championed by his MIT colleague **Peter Senge**), are derivatives of brainwashing. 'Organizational learning is a new version of coercive persuasion,' he says.

The dynamics of groups and Schein's knowledge of brainwashing led to a developing interest in corporate culture, a term that Schein is widely credited with inventing. His work on corporate culture culminated in the 1985 book *Organizational Culture and Leadership.* He describes culture as 'a pattern of basic assumptions – invented, discovered, or developed by a given group as it learns to cope with its problems of external adaptation and internal integration – that has worked well enough to be considered valid and, therefore, to be taught to new members as the correct way to perceive, think, and feel in relation to those problems.'

These basic assumptions, says Schein, can be categorized into five dimensions:

- **Humanity's relationship to nature:** While some companies regard themselves as masters of their own destinies, others are submissive, willing to accept the domination of their external environments.
- **The nature of reality and truth:** Organizations and managers adopt a wide variety of methods to reach what becomes accepted as the organizational 'truth' – through debate, dictatorship, or through simple acceptance that if something achieves the objective, it is right.
- **The nature of human nature:** Organizations differ in their views of human nature. Some follow McGregor's Theory X and work on the principle that people will not do their jobs if they can avoid it. Others regard people in a more positive light and attempt to enable them to fulfil their potential for the benefit of both sides.
- **The nature of human activity:** The West has traditionally emphasized tasks and their completion rather than the more philosophical side of work. Achievement is all. Schein suggests an alternative approach – 'being-in-becoming' – emphasizing self-fulfilment and development.
- **The nature of human relationships:** Organizations make a variety of assumptions about how people interact with each other. Some facilitate social interaction, while others regard it as an unnecessary distraction.

These five categories are not mutually exclusive, but are in a constant state of development and flux. Culture does not stand still.

Key to the creation and development of corporate culture are the values embraced by the organization. Schein acknowledges that a single person can shape these values and, as a result, an entire corporate culture. He identifies three stages in the development of a corporate culture: 'birth and early growth', 'organizational mid-life' and 'organizational maturity'.

More recently, Schein's work on culture has identified three cultures of management that he labels 'the key to organizational learning in the twenty-first century'. The three cultures are the operator culture ('an internal culture based on operational success'), the engineering culture (created by 'the designers and technocrats who drive the core technologies of the organization'), and the executive culture (formed by executive management, the **CEO** and their immediate subordinates).

Success is related to how well the three cultures are aligned. It is a precarious balance, easily disturbed. For example, when executives move from one industry to another, cultures are often pushed out of alignment.

Another focus of Schein's attentions in recent years has been the subject of careers. He originated key concepts such as the psychological contract – the unspoken bond between employee and employer – and career anchors. Schein proposed that, once mature, we have a single 'career anchor', which is the underlying career value that we could not surrender. 'Over the last 25 years, because of dual careers and social changes, the emphasis of careers has shifted,' he says. 'The career is no longer overarching. It is probably healthy because it makes people more independent. Lifestyle has become the increasingly important career anchor.'

Key texts

- Edgar H. Schein. *Organizational Culture and Leadership.* Jossey-Bass, 1985

- Edgar H. Schein. *Organizational Psychology.* Third edition, Prentice Hall, 1980
- Edgar H. Schein. *Process Consultation.* Addison-Wesley, 1969

Schwab, Charles R.

Internet stockbroking trailblazer (b. 1937)

Charles R. Schwab is a pioneer of **Internet** stockbroking. More significantly, he helped democratize the stock market via the Internet, proving that large numbers of people would trade online.

Born in Sacramento, California, in 1937, Schwab pursued one moneymaking scheme after another throughout his childhood. He collected walnuts, bagged them up and sold them for $5 each. The walnut business taught Schwab some important business lessons. 'If I wanted to make more money,' he said, 'I had to sell more walnuts.' As a twelve-year-old, Schwab sold eggs door-to-door for a source of income. Soon Schwab had scaled up the business to include ten or more chickens and learned to maximize income by developing multiple revenue streams – selling old chickens as well as chicken fertilizer.

For his next venture, Schwab entered the service industry as a golf caddie. Schwab's enthusiasm for business was matched by his eagerness to study and better himself educationally. A bright student who studied economics at Stanford University, he went on to complete an MBA. Outside the lecture room, he was investing in the stock market, discovering that he had a talent for picking stocks. After he received his **MBA**, he became a partner in a stock newsletter and set up his own mutual fund.

Schwab's own stock brokerage, Charles Schwab Corporation, was launched in 1971. Schwab wanted to bring share ownership to the masses. He also viewed as unethical the heavy-handed sales tactics that many brokerages of the time employed. His idea was to reduce the price of share dealership and make the process quick and simple for the consumer.

By 1975, Schwab's business had become a discount brokerage, with low prices and easy ordering. The **Securities and Exchange Commission**'s abolition of fixed commissions was a catalyst for the move into discount share dealing. Schwab rolled out a revolution in share trading across the United States.

In the 1980s, Schwab took his company to the stock market. Now the public could buy shares in Schwab's business as well. Though Schwab was successful before the advent of the Internet and day trading, those were the factors that propelled Schwab's business into the stratosphere. The Net was the perfect way to take stockbroking to the masses. Schwab recognized that online trading could lower the transaction cost between consumer and company. The Internet offered an alternative means of interacting with the consumer and instant access to large amounts of information, making it possible for day traders to buy and sell stocks from the comfort of their homes. Where most traditional companies were either unconvinced, unwilling to take the risk of damaging their brands, or lacked the imagination to grasp what the new technology could do, Schwab grasped the opportunity with both hands.

With perfect timing Schwab launched the online brokerage eSchwab in 1995. The longest bull market in US history tempted million of Americans to play the stock market, leading to the emergence of the day trader phenomenon. Schwab successfully rode the Internet wave through the 1990s. In just two years, Schwab added 600,000 online accounts. By 1998, the number of accounts had risen to 2.2 million.

Unlike some other Internet stockbrokers, Schwab continued to expand the bricks-and-mortar element of the business, increasing the number of branches in the United States to 400 by 2000. Seventy percent of new accounts were opened through these branches. So although the technology stock sector crash in 2000 and 2001 sank many Internet companies, Schwab survives and thrives with close to 8 million active accounts.

Key texts

- David S. Pottruck and Terry Pearce. *Clicks and Mortar*. Jossey-Bass, 2000
- Charles Schwab. *How To Be Your Own Stock-broker*. Macmillan, 1984

Schwartz, Peter

American futurist

Peter Schwartz is chairman of the **Global Business Network**. He trained as an aeronautical engineer and spent ten years at the Stanford Research Institute. He has written books, including *The Art of the Long View*, and, more intriguingly, acted as a script consultant on the films *War Games* and *Sneakers*. In his previous corporate life, he succeeded Pierre Wack, one of the founding fathers of scenario planning at Royal Dutch/Shell. From 1982 until 1987, Schwartz ran Shell's scenario planning group. He then returned to the United States to set up the Global Business Network with a number of former colleagues, including Stewart Brand.

Described by one magazine as 'an affable, eloquent man with a neat beard and a habit of saying absolutely', Schwartz has created a lucrative niche for himself in the futures markets. He bolstered his reputation in 1982, when he accurately predicted the collapse of oil prices. Shell piled up cash and then bought oilfields when the price collapsed. All companies could do with scenario planners like that.

Less successfully, in the summer of 1997, Schwartz published an article in *Wired* with Peter Leyden entitled 'The Long Boom'. It anticipated a 'boom on a scale never experienced before'. By 1998, Asia was in meltdown and Russia on the verge of collapse. Even so, Schwartz remains the doyen of scenario planning. 'Mr Schwartz owes his cachet to his background as a scenario planner, which is about as respectable as futurology gets,' observed *The Economist*. If Peter Schwartz has anything to do with it, the future may well be rocket science.

Key text

- Peter Schwartz. *The Art of the Long View: The Path to Strategic Insights for Yourself and Your Company*. Currency/Doubleday, 1991

Key links

- www.businesstech.com
- www.gbn.org

Scientific management

The school of scientific management, also known as Taylorism, was started by industrial engineer and inventor **Frederick Winslow Taylor** at the beginning of the twentieth century. Chief engineer at the Midvale Steel Works, Taylor noticed that his fellow workers were engaged in the practice of 'soldiering' – working at a deliberately slow pace. They were able to do this as no one had thought to study how long the tasks the men were carrying out should actually take. Taylor took a stopwatch and set about measuring the time individual tasks should take. Employees were, according to Taylor, nothing more than components in a machine. Taylor's theories about a scientific approach to management, asserting that measurement improves productivity, were outlined in his management classic, *The Principles of Scientific Management*, published in 1911. His studies made him a favourite of managers and an enemy of workers across the globe. Although Taylor's views on management became unpopular as a more humanistic view of management became prevalent with the human relations school, Taylor's work is constantly re-evaluated and reinterpreted to this very day.

Key text

- Frederick Winslow Taylor. *The Principles of Scientific Management*. Harper and Brothers, 1911

Scrip issue

A scrip issue, known as a stock split in the United States, involves the issue of additional shares to shareholders by a company. The shares are usually issued on the basis of a certain number of shares per share held. Under a one-for-one scrip issue, for example, a holder of five shares would receive five more.

One of the main reasons for a scrip issue is to reduce the price of the company's shares in the market. If the share price is particularly high, a scrip issue makes the shares appear more affordable and reasonably priced, although in fact they are effectively worth the same as they were before the scrip issue.

Search engine

A search engine consists of remotely accessible software that helps users find information. Although most common on **Internet** Web sites, they are also found on company intranets. Commercial search engines, such as Google and Lycos, comprise databases of documents, URLs, Usenet articles and more, which can be searched by typing in a key word or phrase. Search engine databases are compiled by a mixture of automated agents (spiders) and Webmasters registering their sites. Web pages are retrieved using software based on complex mathematical modelling. Take Google, for example, founded in 1998 by Sergey Brin and Larry Page: Google's index contains a staggering 2 billion URLs, representing the most comprehensive collection of Web pages on the Internet.

Secondment

An employee is seconded when he is transferred from one part of the workforce to another, from one company division to another, or even from one company to another within a group. Secondment may be for a number of reasons: to further the individual's career development; to meet a recruitment need in the department or company he is seconded to; or to find employment for an individual if he is no longer required to perform his existing job. Secondment is usually temporary, with the employee returning to his original position after a period of time.

SEC (Securities and Exchange Commission)

The Securities and Exchange Commission is the agency in the United States whose primary aim is to protect investors and maintain the integrity of the US securities market. Its headquarters are located in Washington, DC. The SEC was founded in 1934, following the enactment of the Securities Act of 1933 and the Securities Exchange Act of 1934. The legislation and the founding of the SEC were designed to restore investor confidence in the wake of the Wall Street crash and ensuing depression. The first chairman was Joseph P. Kennedy, the father of President John F. Kennedy. The SEC requires public companies to disclose relevant and meaningful information, financial or otherwise, to the public. The agency also monitors the activity of key players in the investment world, including broker-dealers, investment advisers, mutual funds, and stock exchanges. The SEC also acts as an enforcement agency.

Key link
- www.sec.gov

Seed capital

Seed capital is the funding that finances a company through its earliest stages; it is often used to get the idea for the business off of the ground. It may, for example, be used to set up a limited company and conduct the research necessary to draw up a business plan and seek further financing. Although seed capital may be provided by an established **venture capital** firm, more probable sources of seed capital include friends and family and/or **angel investors** – wealthy individuals who use their own capital to provide finance. Venture capital firms are less likely to get involved in a company's very early stages, since providing seed capital is particularly risky. Venture capital firms prefer to invest at a slightly later stage, when the company is established but hasn't started on its rapid growth phase.

Segmentation

See Market segmentation.

Semler, Ricardo

Industrialist and management revolutionary (b. 1959)

If Ricardo Semler were the CEO of a *Fortune* 500 company, he would undoubtedly be one of most celebrated and famous managers of his generation. At his Brazilian company, Semco, Semler has carried out one of the most radical programmes of organizational change ever conducted in an international corporation, with remarkable results.

Semler was born in São Paulo, Brazil, in 1959, where his father, who had emigrated from his native Austria, had built up a thriving engineering company. As a student, Semler possessed natural authority. In high school, he was class president, captain of the track team, and photography editor of the high school yearbook. He also demonstrated a flair for business while running a snack stand intended to raise funds to send students on the class trip the following year. Semler extended opening hours, encouraged competition among suppliers, and charged a commercial price for his goods. The snack stand impresario raised so much money he was able to fly the entire class to a resort.

After a spell at São Paulo State Law School, Semler joined his father at the family firm of Semler & Co. Semler's initial experience of Semler & Co. was one of friction with his father. Their methods of conducting business were worlds apart. Semler was laid-back and happy to work from home; he liked to put his feet up on the desk and generally had a relaxed approach to work. His father was straight out of the old school, kept a regimented schedule and presented a formidable authority figure to employees and clients alike. Worse, he was unwilling to cede authority to his son.

Semler decided to leave but just as he was about to do so, his father transferred a majority of shares into Semler's name. He then went on vacation, telling Semler, 'Whatever changes you want to make in the organization, do them now.' By 6:00 p.m. on Semler's first day in charge, he had fired 60 percent of the top management.

Renaming the company Semco, Semler pledged to diversify from the core business of shipbuilding. He also pledged to strip away the stifling autocratic control exercised by his father. What followed was one of the most remarkable transformations of a company anywhere in the world. In what became something akin to a socio-corporate experiment, Semler introduced a series of fundamental changes at every level of the company.

In terms of structure, Semler settled on a lattice model in which small teams were responsible for all levels of production process. Each group had control of its own budgets and, controversially, its own targets. Although 30 percent of middle managers left between 1985 and 1987 as a result of the apparent stripping of authority and the new way of working, unit costs went down and production soared.

A severe recession in the early 1990s led to severe cost-cutting measures. Remarkably, these were carried out by agreement with the workforce. Under the agreement, management took a 40 percent salary cut. All other wages were also cut, but productivity bonuses went up and the workers were given the right to approve all company expenditures.

The responsible attitude shown by the workforce during this time encouraged Semler to push his experimentation with worker empowerment and participation even further. More power was devolved on workers' teams, which were based on product lines. They could recruit and fire employees at all levels, including their bosses. All decisions were taken democratically. Semler also introduced the idea of the satellite organization. Able employees who might otherwise leave the company were provided with the resources necessary to take an idea and turn it into a business. In return for this freedom, Semco took payment in the form of profits or savings from their individual new ventures. Eventually, the satellite businesses comprised over two-thirds of Semco's business.

There was more: no secretaries, receptionists or personal assistants worked at Semco. All employees, including Semler, handled their own administrative chores and made their own coffee. Job titles were rendered meaningless by the unprecedented workplace democracy. All information in the company was freely available, including all salary information. Management salaries were capped. All non-core competencies were outsourced, often to a satellite company. Employees set their own salaries and recruited new workers. Positions were bid for by workers every six months and accepted or rejected, taking into account skills, salary requested, and other factors. Managers were rated out of 100, and the results made freely available. Consistently falling below 75 would eventually lead to a manager losing his position.

It was an astonishing corporate revolution, especially when you consider the effect on the company's productivity and bottom line. Between 1990 and 1996, sales grew from $35 million to $100 million. By 1998, against a background of recession and hyperinflation, Semco had grown six-fold, productivity had increased nearly seven-fold, and profits had risen five-fold. The company is so popular that Semler has built up a backlog of more than 2000 job applications.

Key texts
- David Clutterbuck. *Doing It Different: Lessons for the Imaginative Manager*. Orion Business Books, 1999
- Ricardo Semler. *Maverick*. Century, 1993

Sen, Amartya

Economist (b. 1933)

Amartya Sen is a Nobel Prize-winning economist with a conscience. His first name means 'one who deserves immortality'. His work on what he calls 'the downside of economics' led to his being called 'economics' answer to Mother Teresa.' This probably says more about the state of economics than Sen's saintliness.

Sen is now Master of Trinity College, Cambridge University, a winding-down position after a glittering academic career. Sen studied at the University of Calcutta and Cambridge. He taught throughout the world and spent ten years at Harvard.

Sen argues that economics has overlooked the fact that there is more to wealth than money and material acquisition. People matter and the standards of living of people matter. Economics has to factor-in the broader impact of its activities. A market collapse in the West may wreak untold havoc among the poorest countries on earth. Sen is the dismal science's voice of conscience.

Key text
- Amartya Sen. *Employment, Technology and Development*. Oxford, 2001

Senge, Peter

American consultant and academic (b. 1947)

Peter Senge is director of the Center for Organizational Learning at the Massachusetts Institute of Technology (MIT). He is founding partner of the training and consulting company Innovation Associates, now part of Arthur D. Little.

Senge studies how firms and other organizations can develop adaptive capabilities in a world of increasing complexity and rapid change. He argues that vision, purpose, alignment, and systems thinking are essential for organizations. In his book *The Fifth Discipline*, Senge gave managers the tools and conceptual archetypes to help them understand the structures and dynamics underlying their organizations' problems.

'As the world becomes more interconnected and business becomes more complex and dynamic, work must become more *learningful*,' wrote Senge. 'It is no longer sufficient to have one person learning for the organization, a Ford or a Sloan or a Watson. It's just not possible any longer to "figure it out" from the top, and have everybody else following the orders of the "grand strategist". The organizations that will truly excel in the future will be the organizations that discover how to tap people's commitment and capacity to learn at all levels in an organization.'

These organizations are what have now been labelled 'learning organizations' and it is for this term that Senge is best known. While the phrase is used with great abandon by other theorists as well as executives, it is rarely fully understood – and it is even more rare actually to find a 'learning organization'. 'In the simplest sense, a learning organization is a group of people who are continually enhancing their capability to create their future,' explains Senge. 'The traditional meaning of the word *learning* is much deeper than just *taking information in*. It is about changing individuals so that they produce results they care about, accomplish things that are important to them.'

He suggests there are five components to a learning organization:

- **Systems thinking:** Senge champions systems thinking, recognizing that things are interconnected. He regards corporations as complex systems. Picking up on the work of some of his MIT colleagues, such as Jay Forrester, Senge introduced the idea of systems archetypes. In practical terms, systems archetypes can help managers spot repetitive patterns, such as the way certain kinds of problem persist or the way systems have their own built-in limits to growth. This has pushed managerial thinking toward contemplating complexity theory, which has spawned numerous books though few go beyond the basic metaphor.

- **Personal mastery:** Senge grounds this idea in the familiar competencies and skills associated with management, but also includes spiritual growth – opening oneself up to a progressively deeper reality – and living life from a creative rather than a reactive viewpoint. This discipline involves two underlying movements: continually learning how to see current reality more clearly and the ensuing gap between vision and reality that produces the creative tension from which learning arises.

- **Mental models:** Mental models essentially deal with an organization's driving and fundamental values and principles. Senge alerts managers to the power of patterns of thinking at the organizational level and the importance of non-defensive inquiry into the nature of these patterns.

- **Shared vision:** Here Senge stresses the importance of co-creation and argues that shared vision can only be built on personal vision. He claims that shared vision is present when the task that follows from the vision is no longer seen by the team members as separate from the self.

- **Team learning:** The discipline of team learning involves two practices: dialogue and discussion. The former is characterized by its exploratory nature, the latter by the opposite process of narrowing down the field to the best alternatives for the decisions that need to be made. The two are mutually complementary, but the benefits of combining them only come from having previously separated them. Most teams lack the ability to distinguish between the two and to move consciously between them.

For the traditional organization, the learning organization poses huge challenges. In the learning organization, managers are researchers and designers rather than controllers and overseers. Senge argues that managers should encourage employees to be open to new ideas, communicate frankly with each other, understand thoroughly how their companies operate, form a collective vision, and work together to achieve their goal.

The trouble is that the learning organization is regarded as an instant solution, yet another fad that can be implemented. Earnest attempts to turn it into reality have floundered. 'I know people who've lost their jobs supporting these theories,' Senge has admitted. 'Yet they go on.'

Change is not viewed by Senge as an organizational phenomenon but as something that must also affect us as individuals. If we do not change, our organizations will not change. This is perhaps where the problem of implementation lies. Organizations regard learning as a route to competitive advantage; individuals regard it as a route to personal advantage. The two extremes have not been bridged.

Key texts

- Peter Senge. *The Fifth Discipline: The Art and Practice of the Learning Organization*. Double-day, 1990
- Peter Senge *et al.* (eds). *The Fifth Discipline Fieldbook: Strategies and Tools for Building a Learning Organization*. Nicholas Brealey, London, 1994

Server

A computer server is a device that manages network resources. File servers, for example, are computers used to store files. Print servers manage printing devices, and network servers deal with network traffic. Web servers will store Web files and serve them up to browsers which connect to that server via the **Internet**. Servers are installed with their own software, such as **UNIX** or Windows NT, which runs the server. Servers may be dedicated to one function or coexist on a multiprocessing system.

Seven-point plan

When recruiters are assessing the qualities of candidates, they may use the seven-point plan conceived by English occupational psychologist Alec Roger. It uses the following criteria: physical (appearance, bearing, health, physique and quality of speech); attainments (achievements, education, training and experience); general intelligence (analytical ability, cognitive ability and creativity); special aptitudes (construction, manual dexterity, mathematical and scientific); interests (intellectual, practical, social and athletic); disposition (compassion, humour, maturity, optimism, passion and self-reliance); and circumstances (geographical mobility and availability at short notice). It does not take into account discriminatory factors, such as marital status or age, unless they are specifically relevant to the job. Once the recruiter has used the seven-point plan to elicit the qualities of the candidate, he can then be compared with a list of the qualities required, as well as with the qualities of other candidates.

Seven S framework

The Seven S framework is no more than a simple distillation of the key elements that make up an organization's personality. Developed around 1980 by two business school academics – Anthony Athos and **Richard Pascale** – and a group of consultants at **McKinsey & Co.** (including **Tom Peters** and Robert Waterman), it provides a useful checklist for thinking about what makes a business tick. It advocates examination in seven basic areas: strategy, structure, systems, style, skills, staff and shared values.

The Seven S model was neatly alliterative, accessible, understandable and, with its logo (later named 'the happy atom'), highly marketable. Managers seemed to like it. The Seven S model was a business theory to fit all occasions which fitted onto a single page.

Pascale and Athos introduced the Seven S model to a mass audience in *The Art of Japanese Management*, published in 1981. Peters and Waterman also featured the framework in *Search of Excellence* when it was published a year later – despite the fact that Tom Peters initially thought the Seven S framework was 'corny'.

The attraction of the Seven S model is that it is memorable and simple. The framework is a model of how organizations achieve success. Inevitably, a model that simplifies something as complex as organizational behaviour is open to abuse, misinterpretation and criticism. Yet, although Japanese management techniques have fallen off their pedestal and the cult of 'excellence' started by Peters and Waterman seems finally to have run its course, it's easy to forget how influential the ideas behind both of these phenomena were. For the first time, the Seven S framework enabled meaningful comparisons between companies from completely different sectors, national cultures and histories. As a way to cover the basics, it remains a useful concept.

Key text
- Thomas J. Peters and Robert H. Waterman. *In Search of Excellence*. Harper & Row, 1982
- Richard Pascale and Anthony Athos. *The Art of Japanese Management*. Penguin Books, 1981

Seybold, Patricia

American IT strategist

Patricia Seybold is noted for her ability to identify cutting-edge technology with the potential to transform business processes. She has more than 20 years' experience in computer industry consulting and is founder and CEO of the Patricia Seybold Group, a worldwide strategic e-business and technology consulting/research firm located in Boston, Massachusetts.

Seybold has written several books. The bestselling *Customers.com* examines how leading companies are designing and implementing **e-business** strategies to build customer relationships. More recently, Seybold looked at how to measure and monitor what matters most to a company's customers in *The Customer Revolution*.

Key texts
- Patricia Seybold. *Customers.com: How to Create a Profitable Business Strategy for the Internet & Beyond*. Times Books, 1998

- Patricia Seybold. *The Customer Revolution*. Crown, 2001

Shamrock organization

The organizational structure most appropriate for the future has been widely discussed in recent years. Irish academic and management guru **Charles Handy** has been one of the most considered participants in this debate. He anticipated that certain models of organization would become dominant. These were the types of organization most readily associated with service industries.

First, and most famously, was Handy's shamrock organization. The concept describes a type of organizational structure with three parts, or leaves: 'A form of organization based around a core of essential executives and workers supported by outside contractors and part-time help.' The consequence of such an organizational form was that companies in the future were likely to resemble consultancy firms, advertising agencies and professional partnerships in their structure.

This model, or variations of it, is often used to explain the move to outsourcing non-core functions. In Handy's analogy, the first leaf of the shamrock represents the core staff of the organization. These people are likely to be highly trained professionals who make up the senior management. The second leaf consists of the contractual fringe – either individuals or other organizations – and may include people who once worked for the organization but now provide it with services. These individuals operate within the broad framework set down by the core but have a high level of discretionary decision-making power to complete projects or deliver contacts. The third leaf includes the flexible labour force. More than simply hired hands, in Handy's model, these workers have to be sufficiently close to the organization to feel a sense of commitment that ensures that their work – although part-time or intermittent – is carried out to a high standard.

The second emergent structure identified by Handy was the 'federal organization', which is not, he emphasized, a synonym for decentralization. He provided a blueprint for federal organizations in which the organizational centre coordinates, influences, advises and suggests. It does not dictate terms or make short-term decisions. The centre is, however, concerned with long-term strategy. It is 'at the middle of things and is not a polite word for the top or even for head office'.

The third type of organization Handy anticipated is what he called 'the triple I' – information, intelligence, and ideas. In such organizations, the demands on personnel management are large. Handy explained, 'The wise organization already knows that its smart people are not to be easily defined as workers or as managers but as individuals, as specialists, as professional or executives, or as leaders (the older terms of manager and worker are dropping out of use), and that they and it need also to be obsessed with the pursuit of learning if they are going to keep up with the pace of change.'

More recently, Handy has suggested that successful organizations of the future will be what he calls 'membership communities'. His logic is that in order to hold people to organizations that can no longer promise them jobs for life, companies have to offer some other form of continuity and sense of belonging. To do this, he suggests, companies have to imbue members with certain rights.

Under Handy's membership community model, the centre is kept small and its primary purpose is to be 'in charge of the future'. Only if the organization is severely threatened does decision-making power revert to the centre. This allows a company to react quickly in a crisis. The rest of the time, decision making is highly decentralized.

Key texts
- Charles Handy. *The Age of Unreason*. Business Books, 1989
- Charles Handy. *The Hungry Spirit*. Random House, 1997

Share options

A share option is the right to buy a certain number of shares in a company at a fixed price on or before a specified time, known as the expiry date. The fixed price is known as the strike price. Share options are different from futures, as the holder of the options is not obligated to exercise them. Share options are often used as part of a benefits package to attract and keep employees, particularly senior executives.

In the United States, there are two main categories of share option, or stock option, as they are also known. Nonqualified Stock Options (NSO) are a traditional type of stock option that will attract taxation – ordinary income tax, Social Security tax, and Medicare tax – on the difference between the fair market value when the option is exercised and the grant price. Incentive Stock Options (ISO) are treated differently by the IRS (Internal Revenue Service); provided that the shares are held at least a year from the exercise date and two years from the grant date, then they will be exempt from income tax. They may, however, attract capital gains tax.

Shareholder power

Ostensibly, shareholders are accorded a number of rights by virtue of their holding shares in a company. These shareholder rights include the right to attend the annual general meeting and to vote on new directors. In reality, for all but a few shareholders, these rights afford very little power to the shareholder to influence corporate policy. Institutional shareholders tend to wield more power than other shareholders because of their ability to influence the financial market's perception of a company. Other shareholders can, and do on rare occasions, band together to force a change in company policy.

Shareholder value

The concept of shareholder value arrived with the sort of trumpeting that usually accompanies a big idea. Yet it really didn't say anything new. Shareholder value simply contends that a company should aim to maximize its value to shareholders; indeed, that this should be the *raison d'être* of a company. The concept gave rise to 'value-based management', which suggested that generating profits was not enough, and that share price performance in particular should be viewed as a key indicator of corporate competence.

This exposes two very different views about the role of companies. It suggests that shareholders are the only ones that count. This overlooks any responsibility to employees and the wider community.

But to large organizations, this perspective can be attractive for a number of reasons. First, it articulates the reasons for a company's existence with commendable clarity. There is none of the vagueness of making *reasonable* profits and pleasing all of the company's stakeholders. It sounds both laudable and achievable – and shareholders are bound to like the idea.

Second, with some adjustments, it fits in with the entire idea of the stakeholder corporation. Shareholders are stakeholders and their numbers are increasingly likely to include other stakeholders, such as employees. Clearly, adding value to the investments of shareholders can have widespread benefits inside and outside an organization.

Advocates of shareholder value claim that it encourages a longer-term view of corporate performance. Instead of desperately seeking to boost quarterly results, executives can channel their energies into creating long-term value growth for shareholders. Institutional investors like the long view and this element was vital in the development of the concept.

What can be said is that value-based management seeks to bridge the gap between the aims of executives and employees and those of shareholders. In the past, companies tended to measure success solely in terms of profits. If profits increased year on year, executives felt they were doing a good job. If, at the same time, the share price underperformed, they offered reassurance to institutional investors but little else.

In contrast, value-based management is as interested in cash and capital invested as in calculations about profitability. 'Cash is a fact, profit is an opinion,' argues one of the creators of the concept, Alfred Rappaport of Northwestern University's Kellogg School of Management.

Key texts

- Andrew Black, Philip Wright and John E. Bachman. *In Search of Shareholder Value: Managing the Drivers of Performance*. Financial Times Management, 1998
- James A. Knight. *Value Based Management: Developing a Systematic Approach to Creating Shareholder Value*. McGraw-Hill, 1997
- Alfred Rappaport. *Creating Shareholder Value: A Guide for Managers and Investors*. Revised edition, Free Press, 1997
- G. Bennett Stewart III. *The Quest for Value: The EVA Management Guide*. Harper Business, 1991

Shareholders

Shareholders are the owners of shares in a company, and therefore the owners of that company. Despite their ostensible status as owners, most shareholders will have little or nothing to do with the day-to-day running of the company. The exception is the directors, who will invariably hold shares in the company they work for. Shareholders do, however, possess certain rights, including the right to attend the annual general meeting, participate in a vote of no-confidence, vote for directors, receive a **dividend** in the event of a dividend payment and receive an **annual report**. In the United States, shareholders are known as stockholders.

Shih, Stan

Electronics magnate; founder, Acer Inc. (b. 1944)

Stan Shih has done more than merely build a globally recognized IT company from a provincial Taiwanese business. He has inculcated a special kind of culture at Acer, his IT products and services company, that reflects his belief in the goodness of human nature. The cynical may scoff, but Shih's trust in human nature has been amply rewarded. Shih has fostered a culture in which risk taking is encouraged and costs incurred through employees' inexperience are written off as 'paying tuition'. The result is a 'tradition of integrity, open-mindedness, partnership, and ownership' that, combined with elements such as a learning culture, innovation and excellent customer service, has created a world-beating IT company.

Shih was born on 18 December 1944. His father died when he was young and he was brought up by his mother, who ran a small grocery store. The business left a lasting impression on Shih. Years later, he recalled that the stationery sold at a profit margin of 50 percent but only turned over every two or three weeks. The sale of duck eggs, although it produced a smaller profit margin, was better business because it turned over every day.

An excellent scholar, Shih first obtained an electrical engineering degree and then a masters degree at the National Chiao-Tung University in Taiwan. Afterward, he went to work for Unitron, a Taiwanese family-run business and the first company in Taiwan to have an R&D department.

Shih's impact at Unitron was immediate. He built the first calculator successfully commercialized by Unitron. A series of promotions followed – first to manager of the semiconductor assembly line, where Shih was in charge of 800 people, then to director – within the space of a year.

Even this early in his career, Shih was beginning to formulate the management theories that would make him famous. 'First, it is important to maintain good relationships among peers and never to take sides with any clique. Conflicts can put you in a disadvantageous position,' he wrote in his autobiography, *Me-Too Is Not My Style*. 'Second, we must have a sense of responsibility.'

After just over a year with Unitron, Shih left to set up another company, Qualitron, backed by the Lin family. Four years at Qualitron, a successful calculator manufacturing company, taught Shih the importance of marketing, a discipline neglected by most Taiwanese companies at the time. While at Qualitron, he developed the first handheld calculator in Taiwan. He also received a painful lesson in the drawbacks of working for a Taiwanese family business. Qualitron was doing well. The Lin family's textile business was not. The Lin family decided to subsidize their ailing textile firm with the profits from Qualitron. Qualitron closed. Shih resolved that any business he ever started would be founded on stable financial management and look after the interests of its employees.

In 1976, Shih founded Multitech, the company that would eventually become Acer. The starting capital was $25,000 and Shih and his wife took a 50 percent share. Initially, industrial design brought in some welcome revenue, but the intention was to focus on the microprocessor industry. Over the following few years, Multitech established a reputation as an innovative electronics company – not just in Taiwan, but around the world. Within five years, Shih and his team had designed 40 applications based on microprocessors.

Selling was difficult because the product was unfamiliar. Bizarrely confused, customers thought Shih was in the low-tech garden machinery business. Salespeople called on Multitech trying to sell them gardening books. Shih took the misunderstanding in good humour. He styled the company the 'gardeners of microprocessor machines' and published a monthly customer magazine titled *Gardener's World*.

In the 1980s, the company had completed its transformation to a PC-focused corporation and secured a growing worldwide reputation with a number of firsts that extended into the 1990s. The company was ahead of IBM with a 32-bit-based PC in 1986. The firm had its **IPO** in 1988. Trading as Acer, the company created the world's first 386SX-33 chip set, led the way in developing recyclable cardboard packaging technology to replace polystyrene, and introduced the dual Pentium to the world in 1994.

As the 1990s drew to a close, Shih had built a world-renowned global IT brand. Shih conquered the market stealthily, by supplying the components that make the guts of the PC. 'I am looking for Acer to be inside [every PC] just like Intel,' says Shih. 'Whether it's a CD-ROM, memory module ROM, memory module, or LCD panel, we'd like to see all computers, no matter what the brand name, have some Acer parts inside.' By 2000, Acer was ranked seventh in the world among PC manufacturers, with $8.5 billion in revenue and more than 120 separate businesses employing 34,000 people around the world. It was the only non-Japanese Asian company in the top 10.

As the new millennium dawned, Shih shook up Acer once again. This time, he refocused the business not on the PC market, as he had 20 years before, but away from the PC toward **Internet** services and software development. Part of the process involved dividing Acer into five independent units. It was a tougher proposition with today's billion-dollar business than with the small local Taiwanese company Shih transformed in the 1980s. But Shih – the eternal optimist, the man who built a company with a corporate culture that rests on the principle that human nature is basically good – is one of the few people who could successfully accomplish such a transformation. Shih has announced that he plans to retire in 2003.

Key texts
- Stan Shih. *Me-Too Is Not My Style: Challenge Difficulties, Break Through Bottlenecks, Create Values*. Acer, 1997 (available from http: //global.acer.com/about/book_meto.htm)
- Robert Chen. *Made in Taiwan: The Story of Acer Computers*. McGraw-Hill, 1997

Shopping cart

A shopping cart is a software program that runs on a Web server and provides functionality to an e-tailing Web site. The program is designed to facilitate **e-commerce** transactions, enabling the user to purchase goods and services over the Internet. A shopping cart may do any or all of the following: allow the purchase of multiple items; allow the shopper to add and remove items as he wishes; provide subtotals including any necessary adjustments for tax; send the appropriate stock adjustment information to the vendor's stock databases; calculate shipping charges; and produce customer invoices.

SMS (short message service)

Short message service is the service for sending text messages to GSM mobile phones. Electronic messages sent in this way are known as g-mail (the word is a combination of GSM and e-mail). GSM (Global System for Mobile communications) is a wireless technology that has rapidly become the world's leading mobile standard, used in more than 170 countries.

With SMS messaging, the user can send up to 160 characters. However, because of the small size of viewing screens on mobiles, users have adapted the English language to create an abbreviated language peculiar to SMS. It is also possible to deliver an SMS message via an Internet Web site called an SMS gateway. SMS messaging has quickly become a popular method of communication. In August 2000, for example, 8 billion g-mails were sent over the airwaves; by 2002, this figure had risen to 30 billion per month.

Key link
- www.gsmworld.com/index.shtml

Short-termism

Short-termism is the adoption of a business strategy that requires results in the short, rather than mid or long, term. Short-termism involves maximizing profits in the near future, usually by cost-cutting (which may involve laying off staff), raising profits to the highest possible level, and cutting back on R&D. Short-termism may be due to the pressures of maximizing shareholder value. The short-term approach is often adopted without sufficient regard as to whether it is in the company's long-term interests.

Silver surfers

Silver surfers are a specific class of **Internet** user comprising the demographic group over the age of 45. Silver surfers are an important group of Internet surfers from a marketing perspective, a fact that was uncovered in a report conducted by Internet analysts Media Metrix when monitoring Internet trends during 1999. Surprisingly, the report showed that silver surfers comprised some 20 percent of online users, compared with 17 percent for the 18- to 24-year-old segment. There were more seniors surfing and they surfed for longer periods of time, more frequently, and more widely than their younger counterparts. These figures exploded a popular myth that the over-50s were the technologically bypassed generation. Online businesses have since reappraised their attitude to this demographic group, paying more attention to its high-spending needs. Web sites aimed specifically at the silver surfers, such as senior.com in the United States and Vavo.com in the United Kingdom, have also increased.

SMTP (simple mail transfer protocol)

Simple mail transfer protocol is the basic protocol for transferring electronic mail between computers. SMTP is an agreed procedure for identifying the host, sending and receiving data and checking e-mail addresses. It is the e-mail delivery mechanism for almost all Internet-based e-mail.

Single-loop learning

The term single-loop learning was introduced by US academics **Chris Argyris** and Donald Schön during the 1970s to describe the attitude toward learning held by a particular type of organization. The organization was referred to as a Model 1 organization. Model 1 organizations are characterized by managers who concentrate on establishing individual goals, who wish to order the world according to their own aspirations and goals, and, although willing to inflict change on others, are unwilling to reappraise their own working or thinking practices. In a Model 1 organization, any learning that takes place will only be in reference to those practices and policies already in place – single-loop learning – rather than re-evaluating those policies, which is termed **double-loop learning**.

Single sourcing

Single sourcing is a practice traditionally adopted by Japanese companies in which services are purchased from a single supplier. Single sourcing might appear to place the company practising it at a distinct disadvantage, as multisourcing from suppliers might be expected to produce more competitive prices. Single sourcing has its own advantages, however, not least that a company can build a strong, mutually beneficial relationship with its supplier. It can also keep prices down by allowing bulk purchasing. The principal downside of single sourcing is that it places complete reliance on that supplier. If the supplier suffers a setback, financially or through an unforeseen event such as a fire or earthquake, it could put a purchaser in great difficulty.

Skimming the market

Skimming the market is the name given to the practice of setting a high price for a product in a new market to maximize profits. New technology will always carry a premium price when it comes to market. This is due to a combination of recouping R&D costs and having few or no competitors in the market. This is why products such as LCD computer screens and plasma televisions are so expensive when they are first released on the market.

Sleeping partner

A sleeping partner is a partner in a business who takes no active role in running the business but still receives benefits from it. Usually an investor in the business, the sleeping partner receives a share of the business's profits in return for his investment. By taking a risk in the first place, a sleeping partner may become very rich, as the garage owner who invested in The Body Shop did when the company was floated on the **London Stock Exchange**. At some point, it may be possible for the other partner(s) in the business to buy out the sleeping partner.

SLEPT analysis

SLEPT analysis is an analysis of environmental influences on a company, beneficial or otherwise. SLEPT is an acronym for social, legal, economic, political and technological. An alternative version is PEST – an acronym for political, economic, social and technological.

Sloan, Alfred P.

American businessman; former CEO, General Motors (1875–1966)

Alfred P. Sloan was the first great professional manager. At General Motors, he created the first management-led modern enterprise and was the arch-exponent of the multidivisional organization. For much of this century, GM has stood as a symbol of the might of corporate America. That it has done so can, to a significant degree, be attributed to Sloan, who was the company's legendary chief during its formative years.

Sloan was also one of the first managers to write an important theoretical book. The rela-

tive dullness of the book, *My Years With General Motors* (1963), should not cloud the size of Sloan's contribution to theory and practice.

When Sloan took over General Motors, the fledgling car market was dominated by Ford. With Ford cornering the mass market, the accepted wisdom was that the only alternative for competitors lay in the negligibly sized luxury market. Sloan thought otherwise and concentrated GM's attentions on the as yet non-existent middle market. His aim was a car for 'every purse and every purpose'.

At the time, GM was an unwieldy combination of companies, with eight models that basically competed against each other as well as against Ford. Sloan cut the eight models down to five, each targeted at a particular segment of the market. The five GM brands – Chevrolet, Oldsmobile, Pontiac, Buick, and Cadillac – were to be updated and changed regularly and came in more than one colour. Ford continued to offer functional, reliable cars; GM offered choice.

While all of this made commercial sense, Sloan inherited an organization ill suited to deliver his aspirations. GM had been built up through the regular and apparently random acquisition of small companies. Sloan set about creating a coherent organization from his motley collection. In the early 1920s, Sloan organized the company into eight divisions – five car divisions and three component divisions. In the jargon invented 50 years later, they were strategic business units (SBUs).

Each of the units was made responsible for all of its commercial operations, with its own engineering, production and sales departments, but was supervised by a central staff responsible for overall policy and finance. The operating units were semi-autonomous, charged with maintaining market share and sustaining profitability in their particular area. In a particularly innovative move, the components divisions not only sold products to other GM companies, but also to external companies. This policy of what Sloan labelled 'federal decentralization' marked the invention of the decentralized, divisionalized organization.

The multidivisional form enabled Sloan to utilize the company's size without making it cumbersome. Executives had more time to concentrate on strategic issues, while operational decisions were made by people in the front line. By 1925, GM had overtaken Ford, which continued to persist with its faithful old Model T. Sloan's segmentation of the market changed the structure of the car industry and provided a model for how firms could do the same in other industries.

After Sloan was lauded as a managerial hero by **Alfred Chandler** and **Peter Drucker**, the deficiencies of his model gradually became apparent. The decentralized structure built up by Sloan revolved around a reporting and committee infrastructure that eventually became unwieldy. Stringent targets and narrow measures of success stultified initiative. By the end of the 1960s, the delicate balance that Sloan had brilliantly maintained between centralization and decentralization was lost. Finance emerged as the dominant function, and GM became paralyzed by what had once made it great.

Key text
- Alfred P. Sloan. *My Years with General Motors.* Doubleday, 1963

Slywotzky, Adrian

American strategy consultant

Adrian Slywotzky is a vice-president at Mercer Management Consulting Inc. His particular areas of expertise include the changing nature of business, strategy, business design, and value migration – a term coined by Slywotzky. His work is at the highly serious end of the guru spectrum. A typical Slywotzky sound bite: 'Pattern thinking is a manager's best tool for communicating as well as making sense of chaotic change.'

Slywotzky is the author of a number of books, including *Profit Patterns* and *Value Migration*. His latest book, *How Digital Is Your Business?* has been particularly well received.

Slywotzky has also written for the *Harvard Business Review* and *The New York Times*. He has degrees from Harvard Law School and **Harvard Business School**.

Key texts
- Adrian Slywotzky and David J. Morrison. *How Digital Is Your Business?: Creating the Company of the Future.* Crown, 2000
- Adrian Slywotzky, David J. Morrison, Ted Moser, Kevin A. Mundt and James A. Quella. *Profit Patterns: 30 Ways to Anticipate and Profit from Strategic Forces Reshaping Your Business.* Random House, 1999
- Adrian Slywotzky. *Value Migration: How To Think Several Moves Ahead of the Competition.* Harvard Business School Press, 1996

SME (small and medium-sized enterprises)

Small and medium-sized enterprises are officially defined under EU legislation as those with fewer than 250 employees. Medium-sized companies have between 50 and 250 employees, and small companies fewer than 50.

Smith, Adam

Scottish social philosopher and economist (1723–1790)

Born in Kirkcaldy, Scotland, Adam Smith entered the University of Glasgow at the age of 14. Strongly influenced by the university's professor of moral philosophy, Smith went to Balliol College, Oxford, in 1740 and began to concentrate on moral philosophy. He returned to Scotland in 1746 and later joined Glasgow University as a professor of logic and then of moral philosophy.

Smith's writing career began in the 1750s and he published his *Theory of Moral Sentiments* in 1759. After leaving the university in 1763, Smith spent time in France, where he met leading thinkers, including Voltaire. There is some evidence to suggest that Smith's *Inquiry into the Nature and Causes of the Wealth of Nations* was begun in Toulouse. The bulk of it, however, was written on Smith's return to Scotland. In 1773, he moved to London, bringing his manuscript with him. When it was published in 1776, *The Wealth of Nations* was instantly successful and influential. Prime Minister Lord North's budget in 1777 and 1778 was influenced by Smith.

Smith returned to Scotland, where he worked as a tax collector and oversaw the destruction of most of his papers before his death in 1790 after a long illness.

Smith's undoubted classic is his book *Inquiry into the Nature and Causes of the Wealth of Nations*. For a book that is more than 200 years old, a great deal of it has a surprisingly modern ring. *The Wealth of Nations* is often viewed as a right-wing manifesto, a gloriously logical exposition of the beauty of market forces. This is only partly true. There is more to *The Wealth of Nations* than a statement of free market *über alles*. Exploration should not be mistaken for advocacy. Published in 1776, *The Wealth of Nations* is a broad-ranging exploration of commercial and economic first principles. Indeed, Smith is often given credit for the founding of economics as a coherent discipline.

For those unversed in the basics of economics, *The Wealth of Nations* remains a useful starting point. Smith lays out the basics with precision. For example, regarding supply and demand, he explains, 'The quantity of every commodity which human industry can either purchase or produce naturally regulates itself in every country according to the effectual demand.' On the rudiments of career management, he points out, 'Every individual is continually exerting himself to find out the most advantageous employment for whatever capital he can command.'

Key to the text is Smith's argument that the value of a particular good or service is determined by the costs of production. If something is expensive to produce, then its value is similarly high.

'What is bought with money or with goods is purchased by labour, as much as what we acquire by the toil of our own body ... They contain the value of a certain quantity of labour which we exchange for what is supposed at the time to contain the value of an equal quantity,' writes Smith.

Smith's logic is remorseless. 'The real price of everything, what everything really costs to the man who wants to acquire it, is the toil and trouble of acquiring it,' he says. 'What everything is really worth to the man who has acquired it, and who wants to dispose of it or exchange it for something else, is the toil and trouble of which it can save himself, and which it can impose on other people.'

It is possible to put a spin on many of Smith's ideas. Agendas can be constructed around them. This is to do them a disservice. *The Wealth of Nations* was the first comprehensive exploration of the foundations, workings and machinations of a free market economy. It was an intellectual triumph, not a manifesto.

Key text

• Adam Smith. *An Inquiry into the Nature and Causes of the Wealth of Nations*. Printed for W. Strahan and T. Cadell, 1776

Socioeconomic group

In marketing, consumers are often classified according to social and economic characteristics. In the United Kingdom, for example, a common classification is the A to E system, which classifies households according to the profession of the head of the household, or principal wage earner. The grades are as follows: A, upper-middle class – professional or director level; B, middle class – senior management; C1, lower-middle class – junior management and clerical; C2 – skilled working class; D, working class – unskilled manual labour; and E – reliant on the state, including pensioners and the long-term unemployed.

Sociotechnical system

The sociotechnical system is a theory that suggests that the organization of work has both an economic and a social element. The theory is largely based on work done by the Tavistock Institute in London. The Tavistock Institute is a social science research, advisory and training organization that was established in 1947. Its work concentrates on 'social, organizational and policy dynamics through action-research, organizational analysis and formative evaluation'. Researchers at the Tavistock Institute examined the effects on employees in the mining industry of a shift from teamworking to mass production. They found that the disruption to the social systems had an adverse effect on employee motivation and concluded that companies should take into consideration social as well as economic factors when implementing change in an organization.

Soft loan

A soft loan is one offered with a non-commercial rate of interest, usually considerably below the commercial rate. Governments often use soft loans to stimulate economic growth in certain areas, offering them to companies operating in specific industries or geographical areas. Soft loans are also made by developed countries and special organizations such as the World Bank to developing countries.

Solvency

A business is solvent when its current assets exceed its current liabilities, meaning that it has positive net current assets or positive working capital. This means that it has enough liquid assets to pay off its debts in the short term. Financial measures used to assess the ability of an organization to cover its debts are called solvency ratios and include gearing and **liquidity ratios**.

Son, Masayoshi

Internet emperor; president and CEO, Softbank Corp. (b. 1957)

Dubbed the 'Emperor of the Internet' by the media, Masayoshi Son – founder, president, and CEO of Softbank Corp. – took the Japanese **keiretsu** business model and applied it to Internet companies. While others stood on the sidelines arguing for caution, Son was putting his money where his vision was. Whether he ultimately fails or succeeds will not alter the fact that he helped breathed life into a dotcom revolution that changed the nature of commerce.

An ethnic Korean, Son was born in Tosu, Japan, on 11 August 1957. Accepted at a prestigious school in Fukuoka, Son showed an early interest in business. Other children idolized musicians or sports stars. Not Son. His hero was Den Fujita, the man who made McDonald's a success in Japan. The resourceful Son telephoned Fujita's office and arranged to meet him in Tokyo. The meeting fired Son's interest in the United States, and in 1973 he headed to California to study English.

Before long, Son was studying for his degree in economics at the University of California. His obsessive nature was already apparent. Many teenagers have pictures up on their bedroom walls: pop stars, sports personalities, pets, family and friends. Son was different. At the age of 19, he saw a picture in a magazine that was to change his life. He cut the picture out, covered it in a see-through plastic wrapper, and put it in his bag, carrying it wherever he went. He even slept with it. The image that had captured the imagination of this economics undergraduate was a microchip.

While in college, Son decided that the best way to make his fortune was to invent something. He vowed to come up with a new idea every day. Son's ideas paid off when electronics giant Sharp bought the patent to a personal organizer that Son invented (which became the Sharp Wizard) for $1 million.

Son banked the money and moved on to his next venture: importing cheap video game machines from Japan. Within six months, Son imported 300 machines, making his company the top games vendor in the area. He then handed the business to a colleague and returned to Japan.

In 1981, with $80,000 of his own money and funds raised from the Japanese Bank Dai-Ichi Kangyo, the 23-year-old Son started software distribution company Softbank. The company soon ballooned into a huge computer services giant. Ten years later, Son had 570 employees, 15,000 dealer outlets, six divisions, five subsidiaries, five joint ventures – and revenues of $350 million a year.

Shortly after Son started Softbank, he fell critically ill with hepatitis, an illness that dogged him for many years. Son shook off the initial effects of the illness and rediscovered his characteristic enthusiasm for business. It was 1994 and a new communication phenomenon was just taking off – the **Internet**. Although global e-commerce revenues were still well below $500 million, Son recognized that the Internet would have a profound impact on people's lives.

Back in the United States, Son backed his instinct with a portfolio of investments in fledgling Internet companies such as buy.com, E*Trade, E-LOAN and Webvan. These included $100 million for a 30 percent stake in an Internet company called Yahoo! By luck or judgement, Son hit the Internet jackpot. Yahoo!, the Internet index-cum-portal, went public in 1996.

In 1999, Son shifted his attention to Japan. In the Japanese market, Son adopted a different approach from that used in the United States. Taking majority stakes in companies and building others from the ground up, he constructed a vertical Internet giant. The key to Son's plan was the acquisition of a majority stake in Yahoo!, through which virtual consumers would be steered to other businesses owned partly or wholly by Softbank, among them the Japanese incarnations of E*Trade, GeoCities, Broadcast.com, Toys.CarPoint, and EToys.

With so much money tied up in the Internet, Son's and Softbank's fortunes are closely tied up with those of the **NASDAQ**. Softbank investors have been on a rollercoaster ride. Son saw his own wealth fall by more than $40 million at one point in 2000, when Softbank's value fell from $190 billion to $23 billion. Son's challenge is to restructure and steer Softbank through the recession. When **e-commerce** revives, as it must, Son will be well placed to take advantage.

In 1997, Son was asked about a target he set himself of building a $10 billion company. Ever ambitious, Son replied, 'The number is not a goal, just a measure, only a milestone. I'm now developing a 300-year plan.' Clearly, Son aims to be in business for a while.

Key link
- www.softbank.com

Soros, George

Financier and speculator (b. 1930)

George Soros is president of Soros Fund Management and one of the most powerful people in the financial world. He has been described as 'one-third hard-nosed financier, one-third philosopher-king, and one-third latter-day Robin Hood'. He came to worldwide attention in 1992 when he made £600 million from selling the pound. As a result, Britain withdrew from the European Exchange Rate Mechanism. Power was at work. The event effectively marked the end for the Conservative government in power. More recently, Soros called for the devaluation of the Russian rouble in 1998. This promptly led to its collapse. Soros has lamented, 'Capitalism was coming apart at the seams.' This has not stopped him rethreading his well-armed needle.

Soros was born in Hungary. He was educated at the London School of Economics, where he came under the spell of Karl Popper, the brilliant philosopher of science, and moved to the United States in 1956. His career has been built around a variety of investment funds. All have reaped impressive dividends: his Quantum Fund racked up 30 percent returns as a matter of routine and exceeded 100 percent on two occasions. 'Sometimes I felt like a gigantic digestive tract, taking in money at one end and pushing it out at the other,' Soros has joked. He has given generously to charitable and other foundations. He has also given long and hard lectures to governments and investors. The difficulty is reconciling the hugely successful investor, the benefactor and the wisdom-laden sage.

Key texts
- George Soros. *The Alchemy of Finance: Reading the Mind of the Market*. Simon and Schuster, 1987
- George Soros. *Soros on Soros: Staying ahead of the Curve*. John Wiley, 1995
- George Soros. *The Crisis of Global Capitalism: Open Society Endangered*. Little Brown, 1998

Spaghetti organization

The term 'spaghetti organization' was coined by Danish businessman Lars Kolind to describe the extremely flexible organizational structure at the company Oticon, where Kolind was CEO. Oticon was stagnating when Kolind took it over. He restructured it along radical lines. In his concept of the perfect corporate organization, he placed the interaction, collaboration and connectivity of people, customers, suppliers and ideas at the company's heart. Kolind called it 'a spaghetti organization of rich strands in a chaotic network'. The key characteristics of a spaghetti organization are choice (staff initiate projects and assemble teams, individuals invited to join a project can decline); multiple roles (the project approach creates multi-disciplined individuals); and transparency (knowledge is shared throughout the organization).

Spam

Spam can loosely be defined as unsolicited e-mail. This definition is quite broad, however, since it does not cover e-mail that is unsolicited but not necessarily unwanted. A better definition is unsolicited and unwanted e-mail (junk mail's cyber-relation). Much spam comprises e-mail ads and promotions, possibly masquerading as e-newsletters that the user once signed up for but then forgot. Spamming, the act of sending spam, is not good **netiquette** and is likely to result in the advertiser being bombarded by flames (angry messages) and 'dumping' (the downloading of large, useless files).

Span of control

The span of control refers to the number of people in an organization who report directly to a particular manager. A board director may have two mangers reporting to him; each of those managers, in turn, may be directly responsible for supervising the work of ten people. Those ten people may have control over other workers lower down in the hierarchy. The greater the span of control, the less likely it is that the person in charge will be able to supervise closely the work of those workers within his span of control.

SSL (secure sockets layer)

The secure sockets layer is a protocol designed by **Internet** company Netscape Communications to allow secure communications over the Internet. SSL involves sending a secure message from a Web browser to a Web server. The sender and recipient both have a digital security certificate. This allows the recipient to decrypt the encrypted message. The entire process is automatic. SSL technology is commonly used in **e-commerce** transactions in which users are purchasing products over the Internet.

Stags

See Bulls, bears and stags.

Stagflation

Stagflation is a combination of *stagnation* and *inflation*. The term was coined by economists during the 1970s to explain an economic situation that violated many of the suppositions of classical economics. When stagflation occurs, there is a combination of rapid inflation, and thus rising prices, with stagnating, even declining, output and increasing unemployment. It is the worst possible scenario – inflation coupled with recession. It is often caused by sharp increases in costs of raw materials and/or labour. The United States and Europe experienced stagflation in the 1970s.

Stakeholders

Stakeholders are those individuals, groups or organizations that have a direct interest in the activities of a business. They include customers, employees, shareholders and members of the community in the geographical locations where the company is located or carries on its work. Popular management theory has it that companies should pay special attention to the needs of their stakeholders. Increasingly, stakeholders are making their companies aware of their views, via methods including the use of pressure groups.

Key texts
* David Wheeler and Maria Sillanpaa. *The Stakeholder Corporation: The Body Shop Blueprint for Maximizing Stakeholder Value*. Financial Times/Prentice Hall, 1997
* Bruce A. Ackerman and Anne Alstott. *The Stakeholder Society*. Yale University Press, 1999

Stallman, Richard

Open-source pioneer (b. 1953)

Richard Stallman is founder of the Free Software

Foundation (FSF) and the GNU Project, and a pioneer of the open-source movement that exploded with the development of Linux by Linus Torvalds.

The FSF is dedicated to eliminating restrictions on copying, redistributing, understanding and modifying computer programs. The foundation does this by promoting the development of all free software, but in particular the GNU operating system.

Stallman, who joined the MIT Artificial Intelligence Lab in 1971, launched the GNU project (an acronym for GNU's Not Unix) in 1984. The project's intent was to develop a free operating system. Today, variants of the GNU system, based on the Linux kernel developed by Torvalds, are widespread.

Stallman has received many plaudits for his work. In 1996, he was awarded an honorary doctorate from the Royal Institute of Technology in Sweden and in 1998 he received the Electronic Frontier Foundation's Pioneer award, together with Linus Torvalds.

Key link
* www.stallman.org

Standard & Poor's

Standard & Poor's is a credit-rating agency that was created in 1941 by the merger of Poor's Publishing, established in 1860 by Henry Varnum Poor, and the Standard Statistics Bureau. The firm provides independent financial analysis and information. It is extremely influential in the financial markets because of its rating of a company's creditworthiness. This rating affects a company's cost of borrowing money and servicing debt.

Key link
* www.standardandpoors.com

Standard deviation

The standard deviation (the symbol for which is Σ or s) is used in statistics to measure the spread of data. The deviation (difference) of each item of data from the **mean** is found, and its value squared. The mean is then calculated for the resulting values. The standard deviation is the square root of this mean.

Standardization

Standardization plays an important role in mass production. It is the regulation of a company's products to ensure that those products are homogeneous. Uniformity and interchangeability of products and parts allows mass production of standardized products, which in turn results in economies of scale. The restrictions that standardization imposes on a product range and the associated inability to deliver highly customized products must be weighed against the benefits that standardization confers.

Start-up

See IPO (initial public offering).

Stewart, Martha

Lifestyle guru; founder, Martha Stewart Living Omnimedia (b. 1941)

Relentlessly driven, incredibly hardworking and an acutely savvy businesswoman, Martha Stewart has made millions from selling people a little slice of her world. Through TV, magazines, product endorsement, consultancy and public speaking, Stewart has transformed her lifestyle into a business as the reigning US queen of homemaking.

Stewart was born in Jersey City, New Jersey, on 3 August 1941. She moved with her family to Nutley, New Jersey, when she was 3. Stewart's business success owes much her childhood. As a girl, she would cook, bake and sew with her mother. Her father, a pharmaceutical salesman, was a keen gardener and taught Stewart about planting, garden design and flower arranging.

Stewart studied history and architectural history at Barnard College on a partial scholarship. While at college, she married Yale law student Andy Stewart. She was 19. When she left Barnard College in 1964, Stewart turned to modelling for full-time work but gave it up in 1965, when she gave birth to her daughter. A change of direction followed in 1967 when, with the help of her father-in-law, she got a job as a stockbroker.

Although Stewart excelled at her new career, earning a salary in excess of $100,000, the timing of her career change was unfortunate. In the early 1970s the oil crisis contributed to an economic slowdown in the United States. In 1973, with Wall Street in the grip of a recession, Stewart and her husband moved to Westport, Connecticut.

Stewart took to rural life with relish. She set about restoring their new house, a farmhouse known locally as 'the Westport Horror'. Soon the house was completely renovated and boasted a fruit tree orchard, vegetable garden, beehives and a variety of livestock. Stewart still lives in the house today and uses it as a base for her business.

With the house in good order, Stewart turned her attention to cooking. Soon she was teaching children and then adults. She opened a small gourmet food business in Westport called Market Basket. She moved the business out of her shared premises and into her home when it began to grow.

After trading in partnership with friend Norma Collier for almost a year, Stewart continued the business on her own, catering for celebrated Connecticut neighbours such as Paul Newman and Robert Redford. Her company was called Martha Stewart Inc.

By raising her profile through teaching, catering and writing articles for publications like *The*

New York Times and *Family Circle* magazine, Stewart's business, which had started as cottage industry, was worth $1 million by 1986. She had also outgrown her house's kitchen and moved into a separate building next to the house. In 1982, Stewart's book *Entertaining* was published. It was one of America's most successful books of its type. Many other books followed, each accompanied by promotional book-signing tours, each garnering plaudits and more fans. In 1988, *Time* magazine referred to her as 'the guru of good taste (and taste buds) in American entertaining, looked to by millions of American women for guidance about everything from weddings to weeding'.

Business continued to grow at a phenomenal rate. In 1987, Stewart signed a $5 million, five-year contract as a consultant to Kmart department stores. The *Martha Stewart Living* magazine and television programmes followed, as did lecturing, personal appearances and a host of accolades. In 1998, she was named among the '50 Most Powerful Women' by *Fortune* magazine. Her company Martha Stewart Living Omnimedia was floated on the **New York Stock Exchange** in 1999, and in 2000 she made the *Forbes* 400 list of billionaires.

Key texts

- Jerry Oppenheimer. *Martha Stewart Just Desserts: The Unauthorized Biography*. Morrow, 1997
- Christopher Byron. *Martha Inc.: The Incredible Story of Martha Stewart Living by Omnimedia*. John Wiley, 2002

Key link

- www.marthastewart.com

Stewart, Thomas A.

Knowledge management guru

A 1970 Harvard University graduate with a degree in English literature, Thomas A. Stewart is one of the leading advocates of knowledge management.

Stewart is a member of the board of editors at *Fortune*, which he joined in 1989 after an 18-year career in book publishing. He has written many cover stories for *Fortune*, covering a wide range of issues from business process reengineering to the Gulf War.

In his book *Intellectual Capital*, Stewart sets out his landmark ideas on **intellectual capital**, which precipitated the knowledge rush in corporations across the globe. Corporations, asserts Stewart, must learn to exploit one of their greatest assets – the specialist skills and knowledge of their employees.

Key texts

- Thomas A. Stewart. *The Wealth of Knowledge: Intellectual Capital and the Twenty-First Century Organization*. Doubleday, 2001
- Thomas A. Stewart. *Intellectual Capital: The New Wealth of Organizations*. DIANE Publishing, 1997

Stickiness

Millions of Web surfers flit from one site to another on a whim, stopping just long enough to gather the information they need. This is not the kind of behaviour that companies are looking for.

Traditional bricks-and-mortar retailers have spent a good deal of money researching customer psychology and shopping patterns to induce them to spend more time and money in their stores. Stickiness, which refers to measures to keep surfers on a particular Web site, is the online equivalent of the smell of fresh bread in the supermarket, the special offer goods at the back of a fashion boutique, or the restaurant at the top of a department store. It's the bait that lures surfers into the Web site and keeps them there.

Common ploys to increase stickiness are chat rooms, where users can mingle virtually and talk to each other in real time; message boards, on which visitors can post comments and discuss issues; e-newsletters, containing a teaser with a link that takes the recipient to the Web site to get the full information; and dynamic content, which can be tailored to an individual's personal interests.

However, millions of users taking up valuable bandwidth are of no commercial use unless they hand over valuable marketing information or spend money. Too many visitors and not enough spending could cause the **e-business** to come unstuck.

Stockholders

See Shareholders.

Stock valuation (inventory)

There are two main accounting methods for stock/inventory valuation: FIFO (First In, First Out) and LIFO (Last In, First Out). The FIFO method of stock valuation assumes that stock is used in the same order that is purchased: the stock that comes in first is the first stock to go out. The LIFO method assumes that the stock that is purchased most recently is used first. Conversely, the stock remaining is the oldest stock and, if the price of stock has increased, the stock with the lowest value. This gives an accurate reflection of a company's profit position but leaves the closing stock undervalued on the balance sheet. LIFO is not permitted in the United Kingdom, France and many other European countries. It is, however, used extensively in the United States.

Straight-line depreciation

Straight-line depreciation is a common accounting method used to depreciate fixed assets. The residual value of the asset is subtracted from the original cost of the asset and the resulting figure divided by the number of years the asset is expected to last for. This gives the amount to be set against income. The result is that an amount

for depreciation is accounted for each year during the life of the asset.

SBU (strategic business unit)

Within large organizations, there are often self-contained business divisions that deal with specific markets. These divisions are known as strategic business units. The SBU may pull together diverse parts of the company, cutting across divisional and geographic lines, in order to serve a particular market more efficiently.

Strategic inflection point

Strategic inflection points occur when a company's competitive position goes through a transition and it adapts to the new situation. The term is associated with **Andy Grove**, chairman of microprocessor company Intel and one of the best-known figures in the computer industry. Strategic inflection points, Grove says, are the points at which an organization must alter the path it is on – adapting itself to a new situation – or risk going into decline. They are concerned with how companies recognize and adapt to 'paradigm shifts'.

'During a strategic inflection point the way a business operates, the very structure and concept of the business undergoes a change,' Grove writes. 'But the irony is that at that point itself nothing much happens. That subtle point is like the eye of a hurricane. There is no wind at the eye of the hurricane but when it moves the wind hits you again. That is what happens in the middle of the transformation from one business model to another. The irony is that, even though these are the most cataclysmic changes that a business can undertake, more often than not those changes are missed.'

The need to spot paradigm shifts is most acute for high-tech companies such as Intel. Indeed, it was IBM's original failure to spot the trend switching from mainframe to personal computers that allowed Intel and Microsoft to create their dominant market positions. Both companies have imbued their cultures with the lesson.

Grove explicitly recognizes that the pace of change in the modern business world is such that entire markets and industries can change almost overnight. This places an increasing burden on strategy makers and involves the ability to discard current assumptions to shape the future of the industry – before someone else does. Grove calls this '10x change' and it can either undermine a business model or create tremendous new growth opportunities.

The trouble with traditional strategic planning approaches is that they tend to extrapolate from the past to create a view of the future. As a result, they often preserve, rather than challenge, industry assumptions. Traditional planning processes tend to analyse external factors individually, therefore missing the power that is unleashed when trends converge. The concept of strategic inflection points recognizes this phenomenon and gives it a name.

Key text
- Andrew S. Grove. *Only the Paranoid Survive.* Currency Doubleday, 1996

Strategic management

The first thinker to conceptualize the role of strategic decision making as a distinct activity for senior management was **Igor Ansoff**. Although Ansoff has been referred to as the 'father' of strategy, it would be an overstatement to say that he invented the concept. However, he did publish the first book specifically devoted to strategy, *Corporate Strategy*, in 1965.

In *Corporate Strategy*, Ansoff addressed the problems facing an organization in terms of the decisions it must make. He identified four standard decision types: decisions regarding strategy; policy; programmes; and standard operating procedures.

The last three of these were similar to earlier ideas on policies and standard procedures: they were designed to resolve recurring issues and problems without requiring significant management time. But strategic decisions, Ansoff said, were different because they had to be applied to new contingencies and therefore had to be completely rethought each time.

Ansoff proposed a completely different classification for decisions. Decisions should be seen as 'strategic' (to do with products and markets), 'administrative' (to do with structure and resource allocation), and 'operating' (to do with budgeting, supervising and controlling). Ansoff completed what has subsequently become the well-known model of strategy–structure–systems.

Ansoff believed that previously, 'concern with strategy had followed an "on-off" cycle attuned to the appearance of major strategic opportunities'. These cycles alternated between an external focus on product markets and an internal preoccupation with operating and administrative efficiencies. Ansoff's concern in 1965 was that the turbulence of the post-war business environment was responsible for a drastic shortening in such cycles. In certain industries, such as electronics, chemicals, pharmaceuticals, plastics, and aerospace, Ansoff felt that change was happening so fast that companies would have to 'continually survey the product-market environment' for new opportunities.

In this new business environment, he argued, no business 'can consider itself immune to threats of product obsolescence and saturation of demand'. Indeed, 'in some industries, surveillance of the environment for strategic threats and opportunities needs to be a continuous process'. Finally, 'at a minimum, firms in all industries need to make regular periodic reviews of product-market strategy'.

Today, these concepts may appear self-evident, but at the time, Ansoff was proposing new imperatives. Ansoff has subsequently been criticized for making too much of turbulence. The point is that, given the levels of satisfaction with the status quo (as evidenced in the writing of his contemporaries), Ansoff was trying to deliver a wake-up call to otherwise complacent managers – something that he succeeded in achieving.

Key texts
- Alfred Chandler. *Strategy & Structure*. MIT Press, 1962
- Henry Mintzberg. *The Rise and Fall of Strategic Planning*. Prentice Hall, 1994
- Igor Ansoff. *Corporate Strategy*. McGraw-Hill, 1965

Strategy Canvas

Companies expend significant time and effort drawing up their yearly strategic plans. Yet, most companies' strategic plans rarely lead to compelling strategies. Instead they tend to be a mishmash of numbers and initiatives or tactics – each of which make sense but which collectively add up to naught. INSEAD business school academics **W. Chan Kim** and **Renée Mauborgne** offer an alternative based not on preparing a document filled with numbers and jargon, but on building the strategic planning process around a picture called the Strategy Canvas. The Strategy Canvas does three things in one picture. First, it shows the strategic profile of an industry by depicting very clearly the factors that affect competition among industry players. Second, it shows the strategic profile of current and potential competitors, showing which factors they invest in strategically. Finally, it shows the company's strategic profile and how it invests in the factors of competition and might invest in them in the future. Through this Strategy Canvas approach, companies can focus their efforts beyond numbers to the big picture, and thereby greatly improve their chances of coming up with a winning future strategy.

Key text:
- W. Chan Kim and Renée Mauborgne. "Charting Your Company's Future." Harvard Business Review, June 2002

Strauss, Levi

Retailing pioneer; founder, Levi Strauss & Co. (1829–1902)

Levi Strauss produced a clothing item that became a national icon. Like Hershey bars and Coca-Cola, Levis are synonymous with American style and culture, and the word 'jeans' was once synonymous with Levi's. Nineteenth century Levi jeans can be worth up to $100,000.

One of seven children, Strauss was born in Buttenheim, Bavaria, on 26 February 1829. The Strauss family moved to New York in 1847, two years after Strauss's father died of tuberculosis. In 1853, Strauss, by now an American citizen, travelled to the West Coast by boat to share in the economic boom generated by the California Gold Rush. Instead of panning for gold, Strauss planned to make his fortune from selling provisions to the prospectors.

It may be apocryphal, but the story has it that when Strauss arrived in San Francisco, a dishevelled miner approached him. The miner grabbed Strauss demanding to know if he had any pants to sell. The rough and tumble of mining meant that miners' pants wore out quickly; pants were valuable commodities. Strauss, spotting an opportunity, replied that although he didn't have any he could make a pair from the one thing he walked off of the boat with – a piece of canvas. He did, the miner was happy, and Strauss started in the pants business. It's probably not true, but it's a nice story.

Strauss did, a little more prosaically, open a San Francisco branch of the family dry goods business. It was located on the waterfront at 90 Sacramento Street under the name 'Levi Strauss'. During the 1850s and the 1860s, Strauss moved addresses several times, each time to larger premises, finally coming to rest at 14–16 Battery Street. It was during this period, in 1863, that the company was renamed Levi Strauss & Co.

It was at this point that prospector Alkali Ike, a miner who worked the Comstock Lode in Nevada, entered the picture. Ike was fed up with his pockets giving way under the weight of the valuable silver nuggets he carried in them. It was a common problem. 'Nothing looks more slouchy in a workman than to see his pockets ripped open and hanging down, and no other part of the clothing is so apt to be torn and ripped as the pockets,' commented *The Pacific Rural Press* on 28 June 1873. Ike was not big on fashion but nonetheless complained bitterly to his local tailor, Jacob W. Davis. Davis, with a flash of inspiration, thought of riveting the material together with copper wire. The result was one happy customer.

Davis, who bought material in bulk from Strauss, wrote to him telling him about his popular new design feature. Unable to afford the patent fee of $68, Davis suggested that Strauss should help him safeguard his new discovery. They filed for a joint patent, which was granted on 20 May 1873. The new Strauss jeans sold for 22 cents a pair.

The riveted 'waist overalls' became so popular throughout the Southwest that Strauss was known as the 'cowboys' tailor'. He brought Davis to San Francisco from Nevada to supervise the cutting operation, scaled up production and opened factories on Fremont and Market Streets.

Levi Strauss & Co. was incorporated in 1890, the same year that the number 501 was used to identify the denim waist overalls. By that point, Strauss had handed over the day-to-day running of his business to his nephews, Jacob, Sigmund, Louis and Abraham. Strauss's later life was devoted to philanthropic work. He was a member of various organizations, including the San Francisco Board of Trade, the Hebrew Board of Relief, the San Francisco Gas and Electric Company and the Liverpool, London, and Globe Insurance Company. When he died in 1902, he left close to $6 million in his estate.

Key text

• Iain Finlayson. *Denim: An American Legend.* Simon & Schuster, 1990

Streaming media

Streaming media is a means by which data can be transferred across a network. Its development was driven by early networks' technological limitations in viewing real-time data, such as audio or video files. The majority of **Internet** users' computers were (and in many cases still are) not powerful enough, or lack access to sufficient bandwidth, to permit the practicable download of large media files. Instead, the user loads a software program called a **plug-in** on his computer that allows him to download video and audio data in a stream over a period of time. The streaming data is then decoded and viewed through the plug-in. Popular streaming media formats include Apple's QuickTime and Real Audio. In practice, limited bandwidth may still result in a non-satisfactory viewing or listening experience.

Stress management

Research has shown that a significant number of working days are lost through illness due to stress. A Families and Work Institute study found that overworked employees are more likely to make mistakes at work, resent their employers for expecting them to do so much, resent co-workers who do not work as hard as they do, and look for new jobs.

While these effects are bad for the employers, it gets worse for the employee. The study also found that employees who feel overworked are more likely to suffer from sleep loss, are more likely to neglect themselves, are less likely to report very good or excellent health, feel less successful in personal relationships, experience more work/life conflict, have higher stress levels, and are less able to cope with everyday life.

Because companies have been successfully sued by employees for damages arising from stress-related illnesses caused in the workplace, the reduction of stress at work has become an important issue. Stress management usually involves a company implementing strategies for reducing stress, such as enforcing work breaks, providing the means for relaxation in the workplace and encouraging managers to identify and deal with stress before it becomes a problem.

Key text
- E. Galinsky, S. Kim and J. Bond. *Feeling Overworked: When Work Becomes Too Much*. Families and Work Institute, 2001

Structural unemployment

See Unemployment.

Substitute brand

See Brand.

Succession planning

Succession planning involves having able understudies in place to step into key positions when they become vacant. Although succession planning is often associated with senior management roles, it is a key issue throughout organizations. In recent years, it has become increasingly evident that the transfer of power from one leader to the next can have a major impact, not just on morale and business performance, but on a company's share price.

Until very recently, most companies of any size created succession plans for senior posts and development plans for key individuals in order to ensure that there was a ready supply of individuals prepared for the top jobs in the future. Usually, this involved accelerated or 'fast-track' programmes for high-potential recruits.

However, it's unclear how appropriate the whole concept of succession planning is in leaner corporate structures. The problem with traditional succession planning – and fast-tracking in particular – is that it creates an expectation of upward progression, even though there are far

fewer rungs on the corporate ladder in today's leaner management structures. It also fails to take account of non-managerial roles – in particular, knowledge workers in creative roles – which may be vital to the future of a business. The question is how to retain a brilliant research scientist or software designer who has no desire for promotion.

In effect, then, traditional fast-tracking and succession planning are likely to be less effective ways of retaining talent in the future. More flexible approaches will be required, customized to suit employees, their families and the changing skills mix of an organization.

In recent years, too, there has been considerable debate about the best way to handle the transfer of power from one **CEO** to the next. Some organizations pride themselves on promoting from within and have a long history of grooming insiders for the top jobs. The best scenario, they believe, is a seamless succession, where the baton is passed from one executive to the next with virtually no interruption to the momentum and style of the business.

Other companies prefer a different succession strategy. Rather than anoint a new CEO in advance, they prefer a Darwinian approach, aiming to create a strong, highly motivated cadre of senior management from which the new CEO will 'emerge' when the time is right.

But the 'succession of the fittest' approach also has some drawbacks. It encourages political intrigue, as senior managers jockey for power to the detriment of the business. A home-grown CEO, of course, isn't always the answer, especially when a company is in trouble. Sometimes a new perspective is required. There is a school of thought, too, that says that regular injections of new blood are necessary to add diversity to the corporate gene pool. Either way, the solution is to bring in an outsider.

An external appointment at the top, on the other hand, can cause disruption through the succession plan lower down, especially if the incoming leader brings his own team along or slashes the management development budget. Such a shortsighted approach can leave holes in the succession plan further down the road, dooming it to failure.

Current trends suggest that many organizations are now actively reinstating succession planning. How appropriate such plans are to the needs of high-flyers and other employees and to the organizations themselves is questionable.

Sull, Don

Management guru (b. 1963)

Don Sull possesses a CV that has 'management guru' written all over it. Armed with a BA, an MBA and a doctorate from Harvard, he has worked with **McKinsey & Co.** as a consultant and was involved in the $1 billion leveraged buyout of tyre-maker Uniroyal Goodrich. Suggesting that he is as much Renaissance Man as New Man, Sull's background also boasts a thirst for philosophy, fluency in German, a spell as a bouncer in a motorcycle bar, authorship of a musical and membership of the Harvard Boxing Club. He is now an assistant professor of strategic and international management at London Business School.

It comes as a surprise, therefore, that Sull's research currently centres on something he calls 'active inertia'. This is a term to describe the corporate tendency for an organization to carry on doing what it has always done when it is faced with a crisis. Rather than freezing rabbit-like in the glare of change, managers and organizations carry on in much the same way as before. 'Inertia is the enemy of progress. Past insights ossify into clichés, processes lapse into routines, and commitments become ties that bind companies to the same course of action. Perhaps the most vital and fulfilling element of a manager's job is to prevent inertia,' Sull concludes.

He brings a historical and philosophical slant to business research and education. Sull contends that talk of visioning and looking toward the future is all very well, so long as it does not forget the past: 'People tend to think of the past as a hindrance. But you can't have a revolution every day. The past also enables and can be a dynamic force. It confers certain advantages such as trust, brands, reputations, and relationships.'

His belief that managers, educators and thinkers require a broader view challenges accepted wisdom. He is critical of the view of management as a social science to which a set of formulas and rules can be universally applied. 'We are starting to see the limits of the model of management as social science. Management is closest to practical and moral philosophy. How do you get people to act in a proactive way to do the right thing?' he says. 'The biggest problem is not that people don't know what to do, just that they don't do it. There is a lack of ambition and imagination.'

But, he observes, such limitations are hardly surprising when one considers a business education system that prefers foolproof models to Stoic philosophy: 'In the United States, business education has been construed more and more narrowly as applied science. Business school professors are engineers and managers are mechanics. Management education is about knowing the right thing to do and getting people to do it. The fundamental assumption is that there are universal laws that can be extracted. I don't believe there are global business laws other than in finance. There are useful generalizations, but in management, context, timing, personality, and history are everything. The challenge lies in developing judgement, knowing which tool to use rather than reaching for the hammer every time.'

Sun Tzu

Chinese soldier (circa 500 B.C.)

The link between the military and business worlds has existed since time immemorial. Its starting point, as far as it is possible to discern, is Sun Tzu's *The Art of War*, written 2500 years ago. The authorship of *The Art of War* remains clouded in mystery. It may have been written by Sun Wu, a military general who was alive around 500 BC. The book is reputed to have led to a meeting between Sun Wu and King Ho-lü of Wu. Sun Wu, not having a flip chart available, argued his case for military discipline by decapitating two of the king's concubines. This proved his point admirably.

The book returned to grace business bookshelves in the 1980s. The attraction of the military analogy is that it is clear who your enemy is. When your enemy is clear, the world appears clearer, whether you are a military general or a managing director. Sun Tzu is an aggressive counterpoint to the confusion of mere theory. After all, most consultants don't offer advice as bold as the following: 'Deploy forces to defend the strategic points; exercise vigilance in preparation; do not be indolent. Deeply investigate the true situation, secretly await their laxity. Wait until they leave their strongholds, then seize what they love.'

Managers lapped up such brazen brutality. Yet *The Art of War* is more sophisticated than that. Why destroy when you can win by stealth and cunning? 'If you are near the enemy, make him believe you are far from him. If you are far from the enemy, make him believe you are near,' wrote the master. 'To subdue the enemy's forces without fighting is the summit of skill. The best approach is to attack the other side's strategy; next best is to attack his alliances; next best is to attack his soldiers; the worst is to attack cities.'

While the imagery of warfare continues to exert influence over managers, it appears to be on the wane. Contemporary business metaphors are as likely to emerge from biology and the environment as from the traditional sources of engineering and warfare.

Key text
- Sun Tzu (trans. Willam B. Griffith). *The Art of War*. Oxford University Press, 1963

Supply chain management

Supply chain management combines logistics with strategy and is of increasingly vital importance to companies. It concerns the management of two-way flows of materials, finance, people and information along the chain from the raw materials to the customer. The concept is founded on the image of a chain with continual links between the different stages.

Traditionally, the nitty-gritty of moving raw materials and products around was regarded as the truly dull side of business. Companies knew that products had to be transported, stored, and distributed, but it hardly set the pulse racing. Competitiveness had little to do with whether raw materials arrived on Tuesday or Friday.

Today, the logistics of moving things around has become an exact science: supply chain management. It has been defined by Bernard La Londe of Ohio State University as 'the delivery of enhanced customer and economic value through synchronized management of the flow of physical goods and associated information from sourcing through consumption'.

Supply chain management has emerged as being of critical importance to the modern organization for a number of reasons. First, the balance of power has shifted. In the past, manufacturers dictated terms to retailers. Now it is retailers who call the shots, with sophisticated systems designed so that they get what they want when they want it. Companies such as Wal-Mart now store massive amounts of information on customers. Manufacturers have to deliver to their increasingly demanding specifications.

Second, time is an increasingly important factor in overall corporate competitiveness. Speed is of the essence, whether in terms of product development, production or distribution. Late deliveries close down production lines or lead to disappointed customers who are all too willing to look elsewhere.

The third factor is the expansion of information technology (IT). IT enables companies to manage the flow of goods, materials, thoughts and information in ways never previously imagined. IT enables each element of the supply chain – whether the manufacturer, retailer or end consumer – to know the others' circumstances. For example, if a supermarket runs out of a particular product line, technology enables it to be automatically reordered.

The final factor bolstering the standing of supply chain management is globalization. Truly global businesses require global supply chains. The right raw materials have to arrive in even the most obscure corporate outpost at the right time in the right amount.

Effective supply chain management can lead to processes, people and materials working more efficiently and so has a significant impact on costs. Removing a link in the supply chain, usually through the use of technology, can often lead to improved services at highly competitive prices – something that computer manufacturer Dell achieved by electing to sell computers directly to the public. For major multinational companies, there is no doubt that global supply chain management is a highly complex challenge, but one critical to their competitiveness.

Key texts
- Douglas Macbeth and Neil Ferguson. *Partnership Sourcing: An Integrated Supply Chain Approach*. FT/Pitman, 1994
- Martin Christopher. *Logistics and Supply Chain Management*. FT/Pitman, 1992
- Richard Schonberger. *Building a Chain of Customers*. Free Press, 1990

Surfing seniors

See Silver surfers.

Sweating assets

When a company is sweating its assets, it is maximizing the profits from those assets. Sweating assets might involve raising prices or cutting production costs and is often a policy employed following a takeover. More radical measures may be taken. It may, for example, pay to close profitable divisions of a company if the capital can be employed more effectively in divisions that have a higher asset turnover.

SWOT analysis

SWOT is a mnemonic for four of the key issues to consider when a company is developing its corporate strategy. S and W stand for strengths and weaknesses: these are internal factors affecting the company in the present. O and T stand for opportunities and threats: these are external factors and are concerned with the future.

Synergy

Synergy arises when two or more distinct entities are combined and the combination is greater than the sum of the parts. Synergy is often a reason given during a merger or takeover. When a retailer merges with a distributor, for example, there are clear synergies relating to supply chain management that mean both companies should benefit. Synergy, however, is often taken to mean overlap. When synergy is used in this manner, it often foreshadows wholesale redundancies in the areas of overlap.

T

24/7 business

A 24/7 business is one that conducts business 24 hours a day, seven days a week. This concept has become more widespread since the focus of companies on customer service, hence the permanently open supermarkets. In practice it may not mean that a good or service can be purchased 24/7 but that customer support is available 24/7. The advent of the **Internet** has made it easier for companies to operate 24/7. Although the physical business may be closed during certain hours the virtual business in the form of a Web site can be permanently available to provide information and facilitate consumer transactions.

Tall hierarchy

A tall hierarchy is a hierarchical organization with many layers. There may be more than ten layers of management, from the chairman and directors at the top through regional and area middle management, down to junior management and the workforce on the shop or factory floor.

Tangible asset

See Asset.

Tapscott, Don

Author and cyber-guru (b. 1947)

Don Tapscott is a consultant and author as well as chairman of the Alliance for Converging Technologies, a think-tank conducting research into the impact of the **Internet** and other forms of new media on business. Former vice-president Al Gore described Tapscott as 'one of the world's leading cyber-gurus'.

He has written a number of books, including the well-received *Paradigm Shift*, which details the transformation of society in the digital age. Other books include *Growing Up Digital* and the recently published *Digital Capital*, which proclaims the arrival of eco-nets as a new business model. His books provide a commentary on the rise of the Net generation. He celebrates the replacement of staid hierarchies with personal chaos.

'Digital technology is a one-on-one medium, unlike past technological revolutions such as TV and the printing press, which were hierarchical and one-way. The new medium is not controlled by anyone,' he says. 'When today's youth enter the workforce they will do so not as ingénues but as authorities. They will find hierarchies in which their boss knows less than they do. They will also find it bizarre how little information sharing goes on, when they are used to exchanging information with strangers online. And they may be puzzled about why it is necessary to go into the office every day.'

Key texts
- Don Tapscott, Alex Lowy and David Ticoll. *Digital Capital: Harnessing the Power of Business Webs.* Harvard Business School Press, 2000

- Don Tapscott. *Growing Up Digital: The Rise of the Net Generation*. McGraw-Hill, 1997
- Don Tapscott and Art Caston. *Paradigm Shift: The New Promise of Information Technology*. McGraw-Hill, 1992

Target market

A target market is that specific segment of a market selected by the marketer for its relevance to a particular product or service. Marketing efforts are then directed at that market. For example, a new ice cream might be marketed at children between the ages of five and twelve. **Market research** is used to determine the appropriate target market.

Taylor, Frederick W.

American inventor and consultant; founder of scientific management (1856–1917)

The son of an affluent family in Philadelphia, Frederick W. Taylor was an engineer and a prolific inventor. At the core of Taylor's view of the working world was his theory of how working life could be made more productive and efficient. This was painfully simple. Taylor was the first and purest believer in command and control. He laid out his route to improved performance in his 1911 book, *The Principles of Scientific Management*.

Taylor's 'science' (which he described as '75 percent science and 25 percent common sense') came from the minute examination of individual workers' tasks. Having identified every single movement and action involved in performing a task, Taylor believed he could determine the optimum time required to complete it. Armed with this information, a manager could decide whether a worker was doing the job well.

The origins of **scientific management** lay in his observations of his fellow workers at the Midvale Steel Company. He noticed that they engaged in what was then called 'soldiering'. Instead of working as hard and as fast as they could, they deliberately slowed down. They had no incentive to go faster or to be more productive. It was in their interest, Taylor said, to keep 'their employers ignorant of how fast work can be done'.

To Taylor, the humble employee was regarded as a robotic automaton. Motivation came in the form of piece work. Employees had to be told the optimum way to do a job and then they had to do it. 'Each employee should receive every day clear-cut, definite instructions as to just what he is to do and how he is to do it, and these instructions should be exactly carried out, whether they are right or wrong,' Taylor advised.

Taylorism was one of the first serious attempts to create a science of management. It elevated the role of managers and negated the role of workers. Armed with their scientifically gathered information, managers dictated terms. The decisions of foremen – based on experience and intuition – were no longer considered to be important.

The man most associated with the application of scientific management was **Henry Ford**, who used it as a basis for his model for mass production. But Taylor's thinking had a profound impact throughout the world. While his theories are now largely disregarded, Taylor's influence can be detected in much of the management literature produced in the last 100 years.

Key texts

- Frederick W. Taylor. *The Principles of Scientific Management*. Harper & Row, 1913
- Frederick W. Taylor. *Shop Management*. Harper & Row, 1903

Telemarketing

Telemarketing is the use of the phone to carry out direct marketing operations. Telemarketers use the phone to contact and market to potential customers. Double glazing and timeshare vacations are good examples of products that are frequently marketed over the phone. Unfortunately, telemarketing has developed a reputation similar to junk mail, limiting its effectiveness.

Ten-bagger

Jargon most closely associated with **Internet** stocks, a ten-bagger is a share that increases value ten-fold, i.e. 1000 percent, in a very short period of time. The term hails from baseball, in which it signifies two home runs and a double. Its use in the investment arena has been attributed to Peter Lynch, fund manager of Fidelity's Magellan Fund from 1977 to 1990 and author of the book *One Up on Wall Street*.

Key text
- Peter Lynch. *One Up on Wall Street*. Simon and Schuster, 1989

Term sheet

A term sheet is a mutually agreed outline of a deal and its terms that can be drafted during preliminary contract negotiations. It contains the details that form the basis of agreements later on. It is particularly common in financing negotiations preceding the financing of a start-up. In such negotiations, the term sheet protects the investment fund and the parties to the agreement, both the **entrepreneur** and the investors, as well as removing the potential for misunderstandings. The reliance placed on term sheets depends on the investor concerned. Some investors see it as an overly aggressive instrument; they would prefer to rely on building a relationship with their entrepreneur partner on a basis of trust. However, term sheets are common practice and the entrepreneur must be satisfied that any term sheet signed accurately reflects his position.

Text message

See SMS (short message service).

Theory X and Theory Y

Even though he died more than 30 years ago, Massachusetts Institute of Technology professor **Douglas McGregor** remains one of the most influential and most quoted thinkers in human relations (or, as it was known in the 1940s and 1950s, behavioural science research). His work influenced and inspired the work of thinkers as diverse as **Rosabeth Moss Kanter**, **Warren Bennis**, and Robert Waterman. Most notably, McGregor is renowned for his motivational models, Theories X and Y.

Theories X and Y were the centrepiece of McGregor's 1960 classic, *The Human Side of Enterprise*. Theory X was traditional carrot-and-stick thinking built on 'the assumption of the mediocrity of the masses'. This assumed that workers were inherently lazy, needed to be supervised and motivated, and regarded work as a necessary evil to provide money.

The premises of Theory X, wrote McGregor, were: '(1) that the average human has an inherent dislike of work and will avoid it if he can; (2) that people, therefore, need to be coerced, controlled, directed, and threatened with punishment to get them to put forward adequate effort toward the organization's ends; and (3) that the typical human prefers to be directed, wants to avoid responsibility, has relatively little ambition, and wants security above all.'

The flip side was described by McGregor as Theory Y, based on the principle that people want and need to work. If this is the case, then organizations need to develop the individual's commitment to its objectives, and then to liberate his abilities on behalf of those objectives. McGregor described the assumptions behind Theory Y as follows: '(1) that the expenditure of physical and mental effort in work is as natural as in play or rest – the typical human doesn't inherently dislike work; (2) external control and threat of punishment are not the only means for bringing about effort toward a company's ends; (3) commitment to objectives is a function of the rewards associated with their achievement – the most important of such rewards is the satisfaction of ego and can be the direct product of effort directed toward an organization's purposes; (4) the average human being learns, under the right conditions, not only to accept but to seek responsibility; and (5) the capacity to exercise a relatively high degree of imagination, ingenuity, and creativity in the solution of organizational problems is widely, not narrowly, distributed in the population.'

Theories X and Y were not simplistic stereotypes. McGregor was realistic: 'It is no more possible to create an organization today that will be a full, effective application of this theory than it was to build an atomic power plant in 1945. There are many formidable obstacles to overcome.'

The common complaint against McGregor's Theories X and Y is that they are mutually exclusive, two incompatible ends of a spectrum. To counter this, before he died in 1964, McGregor was developing **Theory Z**, a theory that synthesized the organizational and personal imperatives.

Key texts
- Robert Waterman. *The Frontiers of Excellence.* Nicholas Brealey, 1994
- Douglas McGregor. *The Human Side of Enterprise.* Twenty-fifth anniversary printing, McGraw-Hill, 1985
- Karl E. Weick. *The Social Psychology of Organizing.* McGraw-Hill, 1979

Theory Z

Before **Douglas McGregor** died in 1964, he was developing Theory Z, which synthesized the organizational and personal imperatives earlier developed in his **Theory X and Theory Y**. The concept of Theory Z was later seized upon by William Ouchi. In his book of the same name, he analysed Japanese working methods. Here, he found fertile ground for many of the ideas McGregor was proposing for Theory Z: lifetime employment, concern for employees including their social lives, informal control, decisions made by consensus, slow promotion, excellent transmission of information from top to bottom and bottom to top with the help of middle management, commitment to the firm, and high concern for quality.

Key text
- William Ouchi. *Theory Z: How American Business Can Meet the Japanese Challenge.* Addison-Wesley, 1981

Therblig

Therblig is an anagram of Gilbreth and refers to a system that divides a task into a number of individual steps. The Gilbreths who coined the term were **Frank and Lillian Gilbreth**, American pioneers of the **scientific management** movement. The Gilbreths invented and refined the system between 1908 and 1924. Its origins were the motion studies they carried out on bricklayers. The method is useful for analysing the way a task is carried out to see if it can be performed more efficiently.

Key text
- Frank B. Gilbreth, Ernestine Gilbreth. *Cheaper By the Dozen.* Thomas Y. Crowell Company, 1948

Thomson, Roy Herbert (Lord Thomson of Fleet)

Media mogul (1894–1976)

One of the great newspaper barons, the mercurial Roy Herbert Thomson (Lord Thomson of Fleet) achieved success on both sides of the Atlantic, first in Canada and then in the United Kingdom. Unlike many of the other famous newspaper proprietors, it seems Thomson was happy to leave the news to his employees, interfering very little in the day-to-day running of his papers.

Born in Toronto, Canada, in 1894, Thomson was a bookish boy, preferring the local library to the athletic field. He left school in 1908 at the age of 14 to work in a coal yard and soon afterward took a job as rope salesman with a youthful **entrepreneur** named Ardagh Scythes.

After an unsuccessful attempt at farming in Saskatchewan, Thomson returned to Toronto, starting a car parts business with his brother. The business was a qualified success. While sales were good – C$700,000 by 1924 – the inexperienced Thomson and his brother overextended the company and ran into financial difficulty. Thomson moved to Ottawa, leaving his brother to salvage the business.

In Ottawa, Thomson obtained a franchise selling radios for the De Forest Crosley Company in North Bay. One big barrier to selling radios was the poor radio reception in the area. To improve matters, Thomson started his own radio station, CFCH North Bay, in March 1931, with a year's rented licence bought for C$1.00 and a transmitter bought on credit.

It was radio that led Thomson to a career in newspapers and his eventual fortune. Following the success of CFCH, he opened two other radio stations further north from North Bay: CKGB in 1932 in Timmins and CJKL in 1933 in Kirkland Lake.

In the same building from which Thomson operated his radio station, his landlord Jim Bartleman ran a local newspaper and renamed it *The Press*. In 1934, Thomson acquired the paper from Bartleman for C$200 and 28 similar monthly payments. By 1936, the paper had moved from a weekly to a daily, and soon Thomson had extended his newspaper holdings further, buying four newspapers in southwestern Ontario for C$900,000.

Over the next few years, Thomson continued to acquire newspapers, often targeting family-run newspapers that had been inefficiently run and faced crippling death duties when the proprietor died. By 1953, Thomson owned 19 publications and a disparate collection of other businesses, including hairdressing salons and an ice cream cone factory. Running out of newspapers to purchase and with rumblings about his monopoly power, Thomson turned his attention to the United Kingdom.

Thomson headed for Britain in 1953. His first target was *The Scotsman*. With the newspaper losing money, the only sticking point for a potential sale to Thomson was management resistance over selling to a non-UK resident. To overcome this objection, Thomson relocated to Scotland in 1954 at the age of 59. 'He's flipped his lid,' said his daughter, Irma, when she heard the news.

It was a bold move. Thomson was not connected to the British establishment. His next deal did nothing to rectify the situation. Borrowing money from the National Commercial Bank of Scotland, he paid £400,000 for the Scottish Television franchise. While critics dismissed the deal as senseless, Thomson saw it as 'a licence to print money'. He was right.

In 1959, Thomson bought out media baron Lord Kemsley's media interests, including regional papers across the United Kingdom plus *The Sunday Times*. These acquisitions were followed by publishing firms Thomas Nelson and Michael Joseph. Thomson received a peerage in 1964, becoming Lord Thomson of Fleet after Fleet Street, the traditional home of British newspapers.

Thomson continued to direct his energies into diversifying his business interests. He set up the travel business Thomson Travel in 1966 and then, in what was to prove one of his most lucrative deals ever, linked up with oil tycoon **John Paul Getty** to exploit the North Sea oilfields with Thomson North Sea. Along the way, he bought a controlling share in *The Times* and sold the idea of the Yellow Pages to the Post Office. He died of a stroke in 1976, at the age of 82.

Key texts
- Russell Braddon. *Roy Thomson of Fleet Street*. Collins, 1965
- Susan Goldenberg. *The Thomson Empire*. Methuen, 1984

Thought leader

A thought leader is an organization or individual that lays claim to an original intellectual concept. In management consultancy, **McKinsey & Co.** and the Boston Consulting Group (BCG) have consistently proven to be thought leaders. **James**

Champy and Michael Hammer are two more examples of thought leaders. The two laid claim to the concept of **reengineering** in their book *Reengineering the Corporation* and subsequently built a consultancy and small industry from it.

Thought leadership

The term thought leadership was coined in the early 1990s by Joel Kurtzman, the editor of the *Harvard Business Review* at the time. In an economy increasingly driven by ideas and concepts, Kurtzman observed, the ability to plant an intellectual flagpole in new territory was a potent source of competitive advantage. In key areas, especially the management consulting and business school sectors, thought leadership conferred **first-mover advantage** to the originator.

Kurtzman subsequently wrote a book, *Thought Leaders*, in which he interviewed leading business thinkers. The term is now generic and denotes what has become a battleground among the leading consulting firms and the growing ranks of management gurus. The power of thought leadership is that it is a more effective way to brand and market intellectual horsepower than traditional advertising.

The term may be relatively new, but as a strategy the origins of thought leadership go back much further. The traditional leader in this field is consultancy **McKinsey & Co**. McKinsey does not advertise. Instead, it relies on its intellectual prowess to carry the brand. It has long been the intellectual benchmark for consulting firms and, largely, continues to be so. 'The firm', as it is affectionately known by McKinsey insiders, bolsters its brand through the *McKinsey Quarterly*, a serious, heavyweight publication that has been around for 35 years and that sometimes makes the *Harvard Business Review* appear frivolous by comparison. Intellectual vigour exudes from every page and this is exactly what McKinsey wants readers to think and experience.

Key text

- Joel Kurtzman. *Thought Leaders*. Jossey-Bass, 1998

Time-based competition

Time-based competition became a management fashion in the early 1990s, largely due to the work of the Boston Consulting Group (BCG). Its chief proponents were two BCG consultants, George Stalk and Thomas Hout. Their book *Competing Against Time* calls on companies to seek to compress time at every stage in every process.

'Time is the secret weapon of business because advantages in response time lever up all other differences that are basic to overall competitive advantage,' write Stalk and Hout. 'Providing the most value for the lowest cost in the least amount of time is the new pattern for corporate success.'

They point to Honda's triumph in the 1980s in its lengthy battle with Yamaha. Honda produced 60 new motorbikes in a year and once managed 113 new models in 18 months. Its speed of development far outstripped Yamaha's and Honda emerged triumphant.

Time-based competition contends that organizations should be structured in the most time-efficient way. The rationale is that processes and systems that are needlessly time-consuming have a direct impact on competitiveness. Being slow costs companies money. Unfortunately, traditional hierarchical organizations are not built with speed in mind. One calculation estimated that over 95 percent of the time products spend in an organization is wasted. Lengthy inventories as well as periods on hold during production cost money.

Stalk and Hout suggest that managers should focus on accomplishing three key tasks. First, they need to 'make the value-delivery systems of the company two to three times more flexible and faster than the value-delivery systems of competitors'.

Second, management needs to 'determine how its customers value variety and responsiveness, focus on those customers with the greatest sensitivity, and price accordingly'. Finally, a company must have 'a strategy for surprising its competitors with the company's time-based advantage'.

Key texts

- James Abegglen and George Stalk Jr. *Kaisha: The Japanese Corporation*. Basic Books, 1988
- George Stalk Jr and Thomas M. Hout. *Competing Against Time: How Time-Based Competition Is Reshaping Global Markets*. Free Press, 1990
- Carl W. Stern and George Stalk Jr (eds). *Perspectives on Strategy From the Boston Consulting Group*. John Wiley, 1998

Toffler, Alvin

American futurist (b. 1928)

Alvin Toffler's first high-impact work was his 1970 book, *Future Shock*. '*Future Shock* suggested that businesses were going to restructure themselves repeatedly,' says Toffler. 'That they would have to reduce hierarchy and [adopt] what we termed **adhocracy**. This sounded sensational to many readers.' It also sounded laughable to many others. In 1970, corporate America was at the height of its powers. The oil crisis was yet to happen; corporate giants appeared to have achieved immortality; economists mapped what would happen decades into the future with apparent confidence. At a time of security and arrogance, Toffler preached insecurity and humility.

Toffler differed from mainstream thought in a number of other ways. First, he was not taken in by the burgeoning overconfidence of the time. His starting point was that things needed to change dramatically. The second crucial area of difference was that Toffler had a keen awareness of the technological potential. The future he envisaged was driven by technology and knowledge. These two themes are constant throughout his work.

While others looked at the impact of technology or the impact of increased amounts of information, Toffler sought out a panoramic view. In 1980, in his book *Third Wave*, he wrote: 'Humanity faces a quantum leap forward. It faces the deepest social upheaval and creative restructuring of all time. Without clearly recognizing it, we are engaged in building a remarkable new civilization from the ground up. This is the meaning of the Third Wave.'

Toffler ushered in the new technological era and bade farewell to the Second Wave of industrialization. 'The death of industrialism and the rise of a new civilization' meant mass customization rather than mass production. 'The essence of Second Wave manufacture was the long "run" of millions of identical standardized products. By contrast, the essence of Third Wave manufacture is the short run of partially or completely customized products,' wrote Toffler. This notion of mass customization has since been picked up by a wide variety of thinkers and, in some areas, is already in existence.

From a technological perspective, Toffler has been amazingly accurate in his predictions. In 1980, for example, Toffler had to explain what a word processor was. Just a few years later, it was an everyday reality for many in the industrialized world (or de-industrialized world, according to Toffler's perspective).

The company of the future, he predicts, will be a 'multipurpose institution,' driven to redefine itself through five forces:

- **Changes in the physical environment:** Companies have to undertake greater responsibility for the effect of their operations on the environment.
- **Changes in the 'line-up of social forces':** The actions of companies now have greater impact on those of other organizations, such as schools, universities, civil groups and political lobbies.
- **Changes in the role of information:** 'As information becomes central to production, as

"information managers" proliferate in industry, the corporation, by necessity, impacts on the informational environment exactly as it impacts on the physical and social environment,' writes Toffler.

- **Changes in government organization:** The profusion of government bodies means that the business and political worlds interact to a far greater degree than ever before.
- **Changes in morality:** The ethics and values of organizations are becoming more closely linked to those of society. 'Behaviour once accepted as normal is suddenly reinterpreted as corrupt, immoral, or scandalous,' says Toffler. 'The corporation is increasingly seen as a producer of moral effects.'

The organization of the future, Toffler envisages, will be concerned with ecological, moral, political, racial, sexual. and social problems, as well as traditional commercial ones.

Toffler's perspective became even broader with his 1990 book, *Powershift*, in which he accurately predicted the growth of regionalism and the profusion of local media.

Key texts

- Alvin Toffler. *Powershift: Knowledge, Wealth, and Violence at the Edge of the 21st Century*. Bantam Doubleday Dell, 1990
- Alvin Toffler. *The Third Wave*. Bantam, 1980
- Alvin Toffler. *Future Shock*. The Bodley Head, 1970

TQM (Total Quality Management)

The quality movement is associated with the Japanese economic renaissance after World War II. Total Quality Management (TQM) is an approach based on the use of quality concepts developed in Japan. By the late 1970s, the diligent application of these techniques by Japanese manufacturing companies had enabled them to overtake many Western manufacturers. Ironically, however, the

quality movement was originally inspired by American ideas.

The aim of TQM is to minimize waste and reworking by achieving 'zero defects' in the production process. TQM is not a single magic bullet, but rather an approach that integrates a group of concepts.

These include many of the concepts associated with lean production, such as **just-in-time** and *kaizen*. Although process-driven, TQM is underpinned by a management philosophy that advocates continuous improvement and a 'right first time' approach to manufacturing.

It was largely due to the application of TQM among a highly disciplined workforce that allowed Japanese companies to catch up with and outperform their rivals in the United States and Europe in the space of just 25 years. One of the first US companies to heed the warning was Xerox. While other parts of corporate America clung to the notion that the Japanese success story was based not on superior process management but on cheap labour costs, Xerox took a long hard look. It quickly realized was that there was more to the superior Japanese performance than the United States wanted to admit. Xerox was one of the first US companies to embrace the new Japanese management techniques that had inflicted the damage.

The company became an enthusiastic convert to the quality movement and set about introducing the 'right first time' philosophy into everything it did. In 1983, 'Leadership Through Quality', the Xerox total-quality process, was unveiled. Important lessons had been learned.

As interest in the quality movement grew, others began to write and consult on how Western companies could adopt the approach. The best known of these Western thinkers were **Joseph Juran** and Philip Crosby. In time, a number of Japanese quality gurus also became better known in the West, including Genichi Taguchi, Taiichi Ohno, and Shigeo Shingo.

By the 1980s, TQM had become a byword for efficiency and success throughout the business world. Indeed, such was the impact of TQM that by the end of this period it was almost possible to divide the world's top manufacturing companies into two categories: those that had introduced TQM and those that were just about to. Reinforcing the trend was the widespread adoption of quality accreditation. International **ISO** 9000 standards created a global quality benchmark.

Key text
- W. Edwards Deming. *Out of the Crisis*. Cambridge University Press, 1988

Townsend, Robert

American businessman, consultant and humorist (b. 1920)

Robert Townsend was highly educated – at Princeton and Columbia – and held a number of important executive positions. But in 1970, he transformed himself into a witty commentator on the excesses of corporate life. His bestseller *Up the Organization* was subtitled *How to Stop the Corporation From Stifling People and Strangling Profits* and was hilariously funny. Most recently, Townsend has written *The B2 Chronicles*, which recounts the story of a company called QuoVadoTron and includes characters such as Crunch, Dooley and Archibald.

Townsend's genius lies in debunking the modern organization for its excess, stupidity and absurdity. He is the ultimate sceptic, by turns playful, indignant, critical and practical. Those with power, or who think they have power, are dangerous beings. 'A personnel man with his arm around an employee is like a treasurer with his hand in the till,' he notes. His quip on consultants – 'They are the people who borrow your watch to tell you what time it is and then walk off with it' – remains one of the most quoted put-downs of an entire industry.

Townsend has no time for the adornments of executive office. His list of no-nos includes reserved parking spaces; special quality stationery for the boss and his elite; muzak; bells and buzzers; company shrinks; outside directorships and trusteeships for the chief executive; and the company plane. He is, in fact, preaching a brand of empowerment and participation 20 years ahead of its time. Humorous it may be but, as with all great humour, there is a serious undercurrent.

Key texts
- Robert Townsend. *The B2 Chronicles: How Not to Butt Heads With the Next Generation*. Pfeiffer & Co., 1994
- Robert Townsend. *Further Up the Organization: How Groups of People Working Together for a Common Purpose Ought to Conduct Themselves for Fun and Profit*. Random House, 1984
- Robert Townsend. *Up the Organization: How to Stop the Corporation From Stifling People and Strangling Profits*. Michael Joseph, 1970

Toyoda, Eiji

Industrialist and automotive engineer (b. 1913)

Eiji Toyoda didn't found the Toyota Motor Corporation, but he did help make it a world-class organization. Through quality and reliability, Toyoda took on the great American car manufacturers at their own game and emerged victorious.

Born on 12 September 1913, Toyoda spent his earliest years surrounded by both business and heavy machinery in and around his father's textile mill near Nagoya. He studied engineering at Tokyo Imperial University in 1933. At the same time, his cousin Kiichiro was setting up an automotive plant at the Toyoda Automatic Loom Works. In 1936, Toyoda joined his cousin in the car plant. It was also the year that the company changed its name from the Toyoda Automatic Loom Works to Toyota.

After organizing the company research facility, Toyoda worked on the shop floor in production planning. To start with, the Toyota Automotive works produced a car built to take parts from American car company Chevrolet. Toyota's first cars rolled off the production line in 1936, but Japan's entry into World War II in December 1941 meant that the Toyota plant's production expertise was channelled into building trucks for the war effort.

When the war was over, Toyoda planned to set up a chinaware business, expecting the Allies to place restrictions on Japanese car production. To his surprise, the Toyota car plant was called upon to build vehicles to help get the country moving again. Trading conditions were still tough, however, and Toyota was driven to the brink of bankruptcy. Toyoda had the unpleasant task of enforcing dramatic cuts in the workforce to save Toyota. To ease cash flow, he created a new company: Toyota Motor Sales.

Toyota's breakthrough as a major car manufacturer came in the 1950s, when Toyoda visited the United States. Toyota had been in the car business for 13 years, and produced just over 2500 vehicles. When Toyoda visited Ford's immense Rouge plant at Dearborn, Michigan, he discovered just how far behind the United States Japanese car production was. The Rouge plant turned out a staggering 8000 vehicles a day. Toyoda realized that if he could combine the best of US and Japanese production methods, Toyota could take on the world.

Back in the United States and with the help of production guru Taiichi Ohno, Toyoda established the Toyota Production System (TPS), also known as **lean production**. A revolutionary approach to manufacturing, lean production consisted of three main elements. The first was **just-in-time** production: production must be linked to the market's requirements. There is no point in producing cars and hoping that customers will buy them. Second, responsibility for quality rests with everyone. Quality defects must be rectified as soon as they are identified. The third element was the 'value stream'. The company should be viewed not as a series of unrelated products and processes but as a continuous and uniform whole, a stream that includes suppliers as well as customers.

Toyota's first full-scale production car to roll off the production line – the Crown – was a success in Japan, but failed to make any impression on the US market when it was introduced in 1957. The problem was that it was designed for Japanese roads, was slow, and prone to overheating problems that made it ill-suited to American highways. Toyota got it right with its next cars, the Corona and the Corolla. The success of the Corolla, launched in 1968, enabled the company to make a big leap forward. By 1975, the Corolla had replaced Volkswagen as America's number one imported car.

In August 1983, Toyoda convened a secret meeting at Toyota, asking those present, 'Can we create a luxury car to challenge the very best?' The answer was a resounding yes. Taking on established luxury brands, including Mercedes and BMW, was a daunting task. Yet Toyoda implemented a cunning strategy to overcome consumer resistance. To create psychological distance from the Toyota value-for-money car models, Toyoda authorized creation of a new brand: the Lexus. Then, to neutralize potential concerns over the reliability and quality of the Lexus, he insisted that the company out-engineer Mercedes and BMW. The result, eventually, was the Lexus LS 400. The car's creation took seven years, $2 billion, 1400 engineers, 2300 technicians, 450 prototypes, and 200 patents. The Lexus was tested in Japan, on mile after mile of carefully built highways that exactly imitated roads in the United States, Germany or the United Kingdom. Toyota even put in the right road signs. It was the Toyota Lexus that finally secured the company's reputation in the United States. For Toyoda, the new brand was a personal triumph.

Toyota is now the third biggest car manufacturer in the world (behind GM and Ford). In Japan, it is the dominant car manufacturer. It now sells close to 1.5 million cars in the United States every year. Toyoda stepped down as president in 1994.

Key texts

- Eiji Toyoda. *Toyota: Fifty Years in Motion.* Kodansha International, 1987

- Russell Braddon. *The Other 100 Years War: Japan's Bid for Supremacy 1941–2041.* Collins, 1983

Key link
- www.toyota.com

TCP/IP (Transmission Control Protocol/ Internet Protocol)

TCP/IP is a set of network protocols for transmitting data. It was developed principally by US research scientists **Vint Cerf** and Bob Kahn during the 1970s, while they were working at the Defense Advanced Research Projects Agency, later known as ARPA. TCP/IP is the protocol used by the Internet and is the technology that underpins **Internet** services like the **World Wide Web**, Internet Relay Chat, and e-mail. TCP/IP has always been the principal networking protocol used by **Unix**, and is now supported by almost all types of operating system.

Trippe, Juan Terry

Founder, Pan American Airways (1899– 1981)

An aviator first and a businessman second, Juan Terry Trippe managed to make the transition from the hands-on management of a small commercial aviation operation to the general management of one of the world's largest passenger airlines. When Trippe started his first fledgling airline, commercial air travel was barely off the ground. By the time he retired, Pan American Airways served 85 nations on six continents.

Born in Seabright, New Jersey, in June 1899, Trippe started flying as a teenager, but could never have imagined the impact he was to have on world travel and commercial flight. In his teens, he flew with the US Navy during World War I. After the war, he graduated from Yale. He did a brief spell in investment banking, but found the world of finance dull. The lure of the skies proved too great

and in 1923, Trippe set up his first company: Long Island Airways.

The company became Colonial Air Transport in 1924, with Trippe as managing director. While at Colonial, Trippe won the first domestic airmail route awarded by the US federal government. The route connected Boston, Hartford and New York. Trippe, however, fell out with the stockholders over his bold plans for expansion. The upshot of the disagreement was that Trippe left Colonial, taking many of the pilots with him to found a new airline: Pan American Airways.

Trippe secured an early coup at Pan Am, when the new airline was awarded the United States–Cuba mail contract. The problem was that to fulfil the terms of the contract Pan Am had to fly the route by 19 October 1927, and the F-7 aircraft Pan Am was intending to use on the route had yet to be delivered. As a stopgap, Trippe chartered a West Indian Aerial Express Fairchild. The Florida–Cuba service commenced on 18 October, flying from Key West to Havana. On 16 January 1928, a Pan Am Fokker F-7 took off from Key West with seven passengers and flew the 90 miles to Cuba. It was the first scheduled commercial passenger service under a US flag.

Pan Am continued to grow under Trippe's stewardship. Trippe secured routes to South America, making a deal with the W.R. Grace airline to create a new airline: PANAGRA, Pan American Grace Airways. PANAGRA served South America from the West Coast until 1968. Trippe also continued to out-innovate competitors. Two-way radios, multi-engine landplanes, on-board navigators, cabin crew, in-flight meals, railway connecting services, and flying boats kept Pan Am ahead of its rivals.

When the Japanese entered the war at the end of 1941, some of Pan Am's clippers in the Pacific were destroyed. Pan Am helped the US war effort by transporting troops and equipment to the war zones using Boeing 314s. The airline also played a key role in the development of the atomic bomb by transporting uranium for the Manhattan Project.

After the war, in 1947, Trippe introduced the first commercial round-the-world flights. The Lockheed 049 left New York carrying 20 passengers and arrived in San Francisco twelve days and 20,000 miles later. Trippe continued to push the bounds of commercial flight technology. In 1955, he acknowledged the potential of jet aircraft to change commercial airlines. 'This is the most important aviation development since Lindbergh's flight. In one fell swoop, we have shrunk the earth,' he said at the time. Within three years, Pan Am jet aircrafts were flying across the Atlantic.

In December 1968, during the Apollo 8 lunar mission, Trippe phoned ABC-TV and made an astonishing offer to the public. Trippe announced that Pan Am would take bookings for the first scheduled moon flights. Pan Am was deluged with inquiries and set up the First Moon Flights Club. When the list was finally closed in 1971, the list numbered 93,000, including one future president, Ronald Reagan. The episode demonstrated both Trippe's willingness to embrace new technology and his marketing genius.

Trippe died in 1981, not long after Pan Am merged with National Airlines. After Trippe's death, Pan Am struggled to survive in a global economic downturn, filing for bankruptcy in 1991. But in another twist to the Pan Am saga, Guildford Transportation revived the company in October 1999 and started a domestic US passenger service from Portsmouth, New Hampshire, to Sanford, Florida. The famous blue globe logo had returned to the skies.

Key texts

- Matthew Josephson. *Empire of the Air: Juan Trippe and the Struggle for World Airways*. Ayer Company Publishing, 1972
- Marylin Bender and Selig Altschul. *Chosen Instrument: Pan Am, Juan Trippe, the Rise and Fall of an American Entrepreneur*. Simon and Schuster, 1982
- Robert Daley. *An American Saga: Juan Trippe and his Pan Am Empire*. Random House, 1980

Key link

- www.flypanam.com

Trompenaars, Fons

Dutch consultant and author (b. 1953)

Brought up by a Dutch father and a French mother, Fons Trompenaars studied at Wharton, one of the top American business schools. He spent three years with Shell, working on a culture-change project, and then worked part-time for the company before founding the Center for International Business Studies. Trompenaars is now developing his research and ideas further through the Trompenaars-Hampden-Turner Group.

Trompenaars's book *Riding the Waves of Culture* was published in 1993. Now in his late 40s, Trompenaars has a troubled relationship with the American business world, which tends to regard his work as concerned with racial and sexual diversity, rather than to do with different cultures. Undeterred, Trompenaars remains dismissive of the American (or any other) managerial model. 'It is my belief that you can never understand other cultures,' he says. 'I started wondering if any of the American management techniques I was brainwashed with in eight years of the best business education money could buy would apply in the Netherlands, where I came from, or indeed in the rest of the world.' The answer he provides is simply that they do not.

Trompenaars has brought enthusiastic vigour to the ethereal world of culture. His books are based around exhaustive and meticulous research. At the heart of Trompenaars's research is a relatively simple proposition: the only positive route forward for individuals, organizations, communities, and societies is through reconciliation. 'Our hypothesis is that those societies that can reconcile better are better at creating wealth. More successful companies are those which reconcile more effectively,' says Trompenaars. The rich don't get even; they get along with each other.

The wide range of basic differences in how different cultures perceive the world provides a daunting array of potential pitfalls. 'We need a certain amount of humility and a sense of humour to discover cultures other than our own; a readiness to enter a room in the dark and stumble over unfamiliar furniture until the pain in our shins reminds us of where things are,' says Trompenaars. Most managers, it seems, are more intent on protecting their shins than blundering through darkened rooms.

Trompenaars's book, *Mastering the Infinite Game* (written with long-term collaborator, Charles Hampden-Turner of Cambridge's Judge Institute of Management Studies), homes in on the dramatic success of the East Asian 'tiger economies'. Not surprisingly, Trompenaars and Hampden-Turner identify fundamental differences in Western and Eastern values. The West believes in rule by laws (universalism) while the East believes in unique and exceptional circumstances (particularism). The West focuses on winning, as opposed to an Eastern concentration on negotiating consensus; the Western belief that success is good opposes the Eastern belief that the good should succeed.

The differences between West and East have been much debated, and there is little to disagree over in Trompenaars and Hampden-Turner's list. But that is not their argument. Instead, their argument remains the same: reconciling different values is the key to success, and it is something that Eastern cultures have proved marvellously adept at achieving. While the East settles the difference, the West remains obsessed with splitting the difference. It is a cultural imponderable that is enough to make even Trompenaars despair.

Key texts

- Fons Trompenaars. *Did the Pedestrian Die?* John Wiley, 2003
- Fons Trompenaars and Charles Hampden-Turner. *The Seven Cultures of Capitalism.* Piatkus, 1994
- Fons Trompenaars. *Riding the Waves of Culture.* Nicholas Brealey, 1993

Key link

- www.thtconsulting.com

Trump, Donald

Property tycoon; founder, Trump Hotels & Casino Resorts Inc. (b. 1946)

With chutzpah and Machiavellian-like cunning, comeback king Donald Trump built a billion-dollar property empire only to see it crumble at the beginning of the 1990s. That the irrepressible Trump mounted a comeback and rebounded from the severe financial difficulties he encountered only cements his reputation as a resilient businessman and brilliant negotiator.

Trump, born in 1946, had property development in his blood. His grandfather and father were both successful real estate developers. At the age of 8, Trump was building skyscrapers with his brother's building blocks. At 13, he attended the New York Military Academy in Cornwall-on-Hudson. His athletic prowess – he was captain of the baseball team – helped Trump survive a tough education. In 1964, Trump took a place at Fordham University but transferred in 1966 to the Wharton School of Finance and Commerce, where he studied economics, graduating top of his class in 1968.

In 1971, Donald Trump moved to Manhattan and took a small apartment in a prime location. Trump scouted the property of Manhattan, noting the position and condition of the millions of dollars' worth of real estate lining the streets. He also cultivated a network of contacts that might help him when the time came to invest. To augment his networking, Trump made a pitch for membership of an exclusive Manhattan club: Le Club. As membership was granted by introduction, the impetuous Trump circumvented the normal procedure, telephoning the manager of the club and inviting him for a drink. Trump was eventually invited to become a member of Le Club and so gained access to its prestigious clientele.

By 1973, Trump was on a roll. Having assumed control of his father's real estate company, he had sole responsibility for development decisions. In the five years he had worked for his father, the business had grown from a $40 million to $200 million business. Rent on Trump properties in New York alone was bringing in more than $50 million a year. Showing a steely nerve when it came to risk taking, Trump demonstrated an uncanny ability to predict the direction of the real estate market.

In 1976, by the age of 30, Trump was one of the most talked-about property developers in the United States. The Trump organization employed more than a thousand people and consisted of a complex network of more than 60 companies. As his reputation grew, he found it easier to clear a path through the regulations surrounding property development. In 1982, he obtained a gambling licence in New Jersey and planned to expand into the casino and gaming industry by building a hotel and casino in Atlantic City.

The pinnacle of Trump's property development career was the construction of the eponymous 68-storey Trump Tower on Fifth Avenue. It was a testimony to Trump's fearsome negotiating and marketing skills that he refused to lower prices in spite of intense competition in the rentals market. Perversely, he raised them. The rich, who strangely attributed a certain cachet to paying over the odds, were happy to pay extra. Such an acute perception of human psychology has served Trump well in business.

At its peak, at the end of the 1980s, Trump's empire included the Trump Shuttle airline; casinos in Atlantic City, New Jersey; Trump Parc, with more than 24,000 rental and co-op apartments; the New Jersey Generals American football team; and a riverboat casino in Indiana.

The end of the booming 1980s brought apparently insurmountable problems for Trump. It became apparent that Trump had overextended himself. Increasing interest rates, falling property prices, and poor gambling revenues left Trump vulnerable, unable to service the $2 billion debt the Trump organization was burdened with. Trump was saved by the banks, who themselves had inadequate security for many of their loans, leaving them equally exposed if the Trump empire collapsed. Trump temporarily handed over control of many his properties to the banks in return

for restructured debt. It was an escape act that Houdini would have been proud of.

Trump said at the time that 'anyone who thinks my story is anywhere near over is sadly mistaken' and time has proved the charismatic Trump right. In one of the biggest business comebacks of all time, Trump fought his way back into the business limelight. Back in real estate development, the business he knows best, Trump is involved in purchasing the Empire State Building as well as the gigantic 76-acre West Side railyards project in Manhattan.

Key texts

- Donald J. Trump. *Trump: The Art of the Comeback*. Random House, 1997
- Harry Hurt III. *Lost Tycoon: The Many Lives of Donald Trump*. Weidenfeld & Nicolson, 1993
- Wayne Barrett. *Trump: The Deals and the Downfall*. Harper Collins, 1992
- John R. O'Donnell. *Trumped! The Inside Story of the Real Donald Trump: His Cunning Rise and His Spectacular Fall*. Simon & Schuster, 1991
- Donald J. Trump and Chester Leerhsen. *Trump: Surviving at the Top*. Random House, 1990
- Donald J. Trump and Tony Schwartz. *The Art of The Deal*. Random House, 1987
- Jerome Tuccille. *Trump: A Biography*. Donald I. Fine, 1987

Key link

- www.trumponline.com

Trademark

See Copyright.

Transactional leadership

Transactional leadership is a concept that was developed by management academic Bernard M. Bass and later expanded by Bass and fellow academic Bruce Avolio. It is based on the idea that the relationship between leaders and their followers develops from the exchange of some reward, such as performance ratings, pay, recognition or praise. It involves leaders ensuring that wider organizational goals are met by clarifying goals and objectives, and communicating to organize tasks and activities with the cooperation of their employees.

Key text
- B.M. Bass. *Leadership and performance beyond expectations.* Free Press, 1985

Transnational corporation

The transnational corporation is a concept developed by Harvard Business School's **Christopher Bartlett** and London Business School's **Sumantra Ghoshal**. At the heart of their work during the late 1980s and early 1990s is the demise of the divisionalized corporation exemplified by **Alfred P. Sloan's** General Motors.

Bartlett and Ghoshal's work on globalization and organizational forms came to prominence with the book *Managing Across Borders* (1989), one of the boldest and most accurate pronouncements of the arrival of a new era of global competition and truly global organizations. Bartlett and Ghoshal suggest that new, revitalizing, organizational forms can – and are – emerging. Crucial to this is the recognition that multinational corporations from different regions of the world have their own management heritages, each with a distinctive source of competitive advantage.

The first multinational form identified by Bartlett and Ghoshal is the *multinational* or *multidomestic* firm. Its strength lies in a high degree of local responsiveness. It is a decentralized federation of local firms (such as Unilever or Philips) linked together by a web of personal controls (often expatriates from the home country firm who occupy key positions abroad).

The second is the *global* firm, typified by US corporations such as Ford earlier in this century and Japanese enterprises such as Matsushita. Its strengths are scale efficiencies and cost advan-

tages. Global-scale facilities, often centralized in the home country, produce standardized products, while overseas operations are considered as delivery pipelines to tap into global market opportunities. There is tight control of strategic decisions, resources and information by the global hub.

The *international* firm is the third type. Its competitive strength is its ability to transfer knowledge and expertise to overseas environments that are less advanced. It is a coordinated federation of local firms, controlled by sophisticated management systems and corporate staff. The attitude of the parent company tends to be parochial, fostered by the superior know-how at the centre.

Bartlett and Ghoshal argue that global competition is now forcing many of these firms to shift to a fourth model, which they call *transnational*. The transnational firm has to combine local responsiveness with global efficiency and the ability to transfer know-how – better, cheaper, and faster.

The transnational firm is a network of specialized or differentiated units, with attention paid to managing integrative linkages between local firms as well as with the centre. The subsidiary becomes a distinctive asset rather than simply an arm of the parent company. Manufacturing and technology development are located wherever it makes sense, but there is an explicit focus on leveraging local know-how to exploit worldwide opportunities.

Ghoshal and Bartlett conclude that, in the flux of global businesses, traditional solutions are no longer applicable. They point to the difficulties in managing growth through acquisitions and the dangerously high level of diversity in businesses that have acquired companies indiscriminately in the quest for growth. They have also declared obsolete the assumption of independence among different businesses, technologies and geographic markets that is central to the design of most divisionalized corporations. Such independence, they say, actively works against the prime need: integration and the creation of 'a coherent system for value delivery'.

Key texts

- Christopher Bartlett and Sumantra Ghoshal. *The Individualized Corporation.* Harvard Business School Press, 1997
- Christopher Bartlett and Sumantra Ghoshal. *Managing Across Borders.* Harvard Business School Press, 1989

Treasury bill

A treasury bill is a financial security issued by the **Bank of England.** Treasury bills are short-term and redeemable. Usually issued for a three-month period, they are sold at a discount to par, and do not carry interest. They are usually bought by discount houses in a competitive tender and then resold in the discount market, principally to commercial banks. Treasury bills are also issued by the US Treasury, and usually referred to as T-bills.

Trojan virus

A small computer program resident on a computer user's hard disk, a Trojan virus allows a third party to control that computer remotely over a network by operating as a **server.** The Trojan disguises itself as a common file, although unusual computer activity, such as opening and closing of the CD tray or applications opening automatically, may betray the Trojan. It is usually delivered to the user's computer via an infected e-mail attachment. There are thousands of Trojans in existence. The most potent, such as Back Orifice and Sub-seven, allow a remote user to set up an interface, enabling him to assume complete control of the infected computer and access all information contained on it or, worse still, carry out malicious acts.

Troubleshooter

A troubleshooter is manager, usually with considerable general management experience across a range of businesses, brought into a company to deal with a specific problem. Troubleshooters differ from management consultants, as they have a mandate to take any actions they think appropriate. A famous example of a troubleshooter in the United Kingdom is **Sir John Harvey-Jones**, former chairman of ICI.

Turner, Robert Edward III

Media magnate and 24-hour news pioneer; founder, Turner Broadcasting System (b. 1938)

With a relentless drive, an uncanny ability to predict consumer demand, and a supreme confidence in his own vision, Robert Edward (Ted) Turner III is one of the greatest media tycoons of all time. Above all, it has been his willingness to go against the grain and back his hunches regardless of conventional wisdom and the critics, that has made him so successful.

Born in Cincinnati, Ohio, in 1938, Turner had a chequered academic career. Turner was an unruly pupil. McCallie, an exclusive school for boys in Chattanooga, Tennessee, punished errant pupils by issuing demerits. A demerit required the offender to walk a quarter of a mile. Turner earned more than 1000 demerits in his first year – further than any pupil could walk in the time available. The school was forced to reinvent its disciplinary methods especially for Turner.

Turner's anti-authoritarian attitude continued at Brown University where, caught with a woman in his room against the rules, he was asked to leave, but not before he had made a name for himself on the university sailing team. Sailing remained an abiding passion. In 1977, Turner won the America's Cup with his yacht *Courageous*.

After university, Turner returned home, married, and settled down to a tough schedule working 15 hours a day in his father's advertising billboard business. A natural salesman, Turner made fast progress in the business and was soon promoted to manager of the firm's operation in Macon, Georgia. In March 1963, when Turner was just 24, his father, under severe pressure at work, shot himself in the head. In these terrible circumstances, Turner became president and CEO of the Turner Advertising Company.

Turner wasted no time expanding the company with a series of audacious moves – not least the move into television, acquiring UHF station Channel 17 in 1970. Channel 17 was the worst placed of the major television channels in Atlanta. Turner engineered a deal to take Turner Advertising public, acquiring the assets of Channel 17 and forming a new company: Turner Communications.

To change the station's fortunes, Turner fed viewers a diet of reruns – classic shows and black-and-white movies. The outspoken critics were silenced as the viewing figures shot up and the advertising revenue flooded in. In 1976, the station went nationwide, transmitting to cable systems across the United States via satellite. It was the start of the 'superstation' concept.

Turner's diversification continued. In 1976, he bought a major league baseball team, the Atlanta Braves, and in 1977 the Atlanta Hawks of the National Basketball Association. Once again, Turner was ahead of the game. His instincts told him that televised sports would bring in big television audiences.

In 1980, Turner was doing the unexpected again. He used profits from Turner Broadcasting Systems to launch CNN (Cable News Network). As usual, the critics were scathing, predicting that a 24-hour all-news network would never work. Once again, they were wrong and Turner was right. 'I am the right man in the right place at the right time,' Turner said. 'Not me alone, but all the people who think the world can be brought together by telecommunications.' CNN was a great success, cementing its reputation with coverage of the Gulf War when, for the first time, a TV audience could watch a war in real time, from the comfort of their armchairs.

Turner amassed television stations: Headline News (1982), CNN International (1985), TNT (1988), SportsSouth (1990), The Cartoon

Network (1992), Turner Classic Movies (1994), CNNfn (1995) and CNN SI (1997) were all added to the network. Shortly after Castle Rock Entertainment joined Turner Broadcasting in 1993, Turner merged TBS with New Line Cinema.

But Turner wasn't infallible: his hostile takeover bid for CBS failed. The 'Checkout Channel', providing in-store news and information, proved a disappointment. Turner also paid $1.6 billion for the MGM film library, a sum many commentators considered over-generous.

In 1996, Turner oversaw the merger of TBS with Time Warner. With 10 percent of Time Warner stock, he had the largest single shareholding. It left Turner well placed to profit from the development of a new communication phenomenon: the Internet. Turner became vice-chairman in the new organization, taking responsibility for Time Warner's Cable Networks division, which included the assets of Turner Broadcasting System (TBS), Home Box Office, Cinemax, and Time Warner's interests in Comedy Central and Court TV. He was also responsible for New Line Cinema and the company's professional sports teams.

Then in 2001, Turner was involved in one of the biggest mergers of the era, when AOL merged with Time Warner to create the largest entertainment conglomerate in the world. Time Warner's shareholders received 45 percent of the new company to AOL's 55 percent. Turner became vice-chairman and senior adviser of AOL-Time Warner.

Key texts
- Roger Vaughan. *Ted Turner: The Man Behind the Mouth.* Sail Books, 1978
- Christian Williams. *Lead, Follow, or Get Out Of The Way: The Story of Ted Turner.* Times Books, 1981
- Hank Whittemore. *CNN: The Inside Story.* Little, Brown & Co., 1990
- Porter Bibb. *It Ain't as Easy as It Looks: Ted Turner's Amazing Story.* Crown, 1993

Key link
- www.cnn.com

Turnkey project

A turnkey project is a large-scale project. The term is usually used to refer to the construction of a plant or building. The supplier builds, installs and tests production processes before handing the plant over. The plant is then ready to start 'at the turn of a key' – hence the term. In IT, the term is used to describe an IT system that is delivered and installed ready to run from day one.

Two-factor theory

The two-factor theory is the result of research carried out by US psychologist **Frederick Herzberg** during the 1950s. The theory suggests that motivation factors in the workplace can be divided into two types. The first type includes those factors that tend to lead to increased job satisfaction, such as achievement, recognition and responsibility. The second includes those factors that tend to lead to job dissatisfaction, including work conditions, salary and company policies. Herzberg used the concept of remembered pain to illustrate that, in his two-factor theory, demotivation is as important as motivation. Remembered pain is an event that so deeply affects the employee that he continues to hold a grievance against the employer for a long time afterward.

Type A personality

Phrase coined by US cardiologist Meyer Friedman in the 1950s to describe 'uptight' people who, his research showed, were more likely to suffer from heart attacks. One clue to the existence of a type A personality turned out to be the state of the armchairs in the waiting room of Friedman's practice. Uncharacteristically, the chairs were worn not on the back of the seat but on the armrest and front of the seats. The reason – Friedman's heart patients anxiously fidgeting and rising from their chair to demand how long they would have to wait. Type A personality traits include: strong need to be an expert on a subject, doing everything rapidly, feeling of guilt when relaxing, frequent knee-jiggling or finger tapping, determination to win every game, even when playing with those that are less skilled or experienced, and speech characterized by explosive acceleration and accentuation of the last few words of a sentence. Type A personalities can take some comfort from the fact that other research conducted by Friedman suggested counselling could help reduce some of the risk. Friedman was a victim of his own success early in his career. He suffered angina aged just 45 and two heart attacks, the first aged 55. He took his own advice however and learned to chill out successfully making the transition from Type A to Type B personality. He continued working way past retirement until shortly before his death aged 90.

Key text
- Meyer Friedman and Ray Rosenman. *Type A Behavior and Your Heart*. Knopf, 1974

U

Uberrima fides

Uberrima fides is Latin for 'utmost good faith'. The doctrine of utmost good faith is the over-riding principle governing insurance contracts. For example, when a risk is discussed with an insurance broker, the proposed insured is obliged to make a full disclosure of all facts that might materially affect the underwriting of a risk. The insurance broker is also bound by that duty when proposing the risk to a prospective insurer. Material facts include those that are not revealed by the questions on a proposal form. Similarly, if circumstances that might affect the underwriting of the risk change during the period of insurance, they must be disclosed to the insurer. Failure to disclose a material fact will render the policy void and any claims will not be met by the insurer.

Ultra vires

Latin for 'beyond the powers,' an *ultra vires* act is one made by a public authority, company, or other agency that goes beyond the limits of its powers. In administrative law, the doctrine of *ultra vires* governs all delegated legislation. Where an act is found to be *ultra vires*, it will have no legal effect.

Ulrich, Dave

American consultant and executive coach

Dave Ulrich has been listed by *Forbes* magazine as one of the 'top 5 executive coaches' and by *BusinessWeek* as one of the 'top 10 educators' in management. He is a leading thinker in the field of human resource management and has done significant research on how organizations can best be structured to add value to their stakeholders. Professor of business administration at the University of Michigan, Ulrich is on the core faculty of the Michigan Executive Program and co-director of Michigan's Human Resource Executive Program. He has written a number of books, including *Human Resource Champions* (1997).

Ulrich is also a fellow in the National Academy of Human Resources and editor of the *American Human Resource Management Journal*. He has carried out consultancy and research work for more than a hundred *Fortune* 200 companies.

Key texts
- Brian E. Becker, Mark A. Huselid and Dave Ulrich. *HR Scorecard: Linking People, Strategy, and Performance*. Harvard Business School Press, 2001
- Dave Ulrich, Jack Zenger and Norm Smallwood. *Results-Based Leadership: How Leaders Build the Business and Improve the Bottom Line*. Harvard Business School Press, 1999
- Arthur K. Yeung, David O. Ulrich, Stephen W. Nason and Mary Ann Von Glinow. *Organizational Learning Capability: Generating and Generalizing Ideas with Impact*. Oxford University Press, 1998
- Dave Ulrich, Michael R. Losey and Gerry Lake (eds). *Tomorrow's HR Management: 48 Thought Leaders Call for Change*. John Wiley, 1997
- Dave Ulrich. *Human Resource Champions: The Next Agenda for Adding Value and Delivering Results*. Harvard Business School Press, 1997

- Ron Ashkenas, Dave Ulrich, Todd Jick and Steve Kerr. *The Boundaryless Organization: Breaking the Chains of Organizational Structure.* Jossey-Bass, 1995
- Dave Ulrich and Dale Lake. *Organizational Capability: Competing from the Inside Out.* John Wiley, 1990

Unbundling

For a retailer of a good or service, it makes sense to tie products and/or services together where possible. This is usually only possible where one of those goods or services is a leader in its market, and especially where the retailer has a quasi-monopoly position. The packaging of products and services together is known as bundling. For example, Microsoft famously bundled its Internet browser, Explorer, with its Windows operating system. In the United Kingdom, British Telecom had control of the telecommunications infrastructure and was therefore originally able to supply Internet services without competitors obtaining access.

In situations such as these, which may have a significant anti-competitive effect, there is often a move by national government or competition authorities to unbundle the packaged goods or services. In the United States, there was an investigation into Microsoft's market position and whether it should be forced to unbundle its browser from its operating system. In the United Kingdom, regulators have forced BT to unbundle control over the telecom lines that connect the home to the local exchange. This separating out of connected goods and services is known as unbundling.

Underwriting

Underwriting is the acceptance of a business risk for a fee. The fee is often referred to as a premium. In insurance, for example, an underwriter will assesses an insurable risk, decide on an appropriate premium for that risk, and then underwrite all or part of that risk on behalf of his company or syndicate. During an IPO, an investment bank may underwrite the

issue of shares for a fee. The bank will agree to purchase any shares that are not taken up by the public, thus assuming the risk of an unsuccessful flotation. In most cases where a business risk is underwritten, the underwriter lays off that risk. This means that all or part of the risk is passed on to third parties, such as re-insurers in the case of insurance.

Unemployment

While unemployment – being out of work – seems like a simple concept, closer inspection reveals it is a little more complex. For example, is someone who works a very small number of hours but is actively seeking full-time employment unemployed? Is someone who is disabled and unable to work unemployed? In order for unemployment statistics to be compared in any meaningful way, they must be defined in a similar manner. It is for this purpose that the International Labour Organization (ILO), an agency of United Nations, provides an internationally agreed-upon definition of unemployment. The ILO guidelines place all people over 16 into one of three classes: in employment; unemployed; or economically inactive. For the purposes of the ILO definition, unemployed people are those who are out of work, wish to have a job, have actively sought work in the previous four weeks, and are available to start work in the following two weeks; or those individuals who are out of work, have obtained a job, and are waiting to start that job within the following two weeks.

From a wider economic perspective, there are several different types of unemployment. Structural unemployment is the type of unemployment that occurs when there is a change in demand or when a new technology renders an industry redundant, creating long-term unemployment. The end of coal mining in the Welsh valleys and the middle and the north of England, for example, created long-term structural unemployment. Frictional unemployment occurs as a result of the delay between losing one job and finding another. Demand-deficient unemployment occurs because the economy is depressed and demand is insufficient to require output at full capacity. Technological unemployment occurs when technological advances occur in labour-intensive industries, rendering them less labour-intensive.

Unique selling proposition

Unique selling proposition (USP) is the term coined by US advertising executive Rosser Reeves and explained in his 1961 book *Reality in Advertising*. Along with **David Ogilvy**, Reeves was probably the leading copywriter of his generation. According to Reeves, the unique selling proposition consists of three distinct elements:

- Each advertisement should make a proposition to the consumer of the 'buy this product and you will get this specific benefit' kind.
- The proposition must be unique in that it is either not offered, or cannot be offered by the competition.
- The proposition must be 'so strong it can move the mass millions'. In other words, it must be persuasive enough to cause a significant number of consumers to purchase a product.

The USP was an advance over **advertising** theory at the time because it encouraged the creation of a distinct and unique identity for the brand and/or product. So convinced was Reeves of the merits of the USP that he even defined advertising as 'the art of getting a Unique Selling Proposition into the heads of the most people at the least possible cost'.

An example of a USP might include advertising that emphasizes the characteristic air bubbles in Aero chocolate bars, which make the chocolate light in texture.

Key text
- Rosser Reeves. *Reality in Advertising*. Random House, 1961

Unit cost

The unit cost is the average cost of an individual unit of production. It is calculated by dividing the total cost by the number of units produced. Unit costs are comprised of two elements: variable costs and fixed unit costs. When using unit costs to predict the total cost of producing a certain number of units, it is important to remember to take into account the fixed element.

UNIX

UNIX is a multi-user operating system with a hierarchical file system normally written in programming language C. The name 'UNIX' was originally 'Unics', for UNiplexed Information and Computing System. First designed for minicomputers, UNIX has become increasingly popular on microcomputers, workstations, mainframes and supercomputers. It is the product of more than 30 years' continuous development by users across the globe – so much so that it is no longer possible to say there is just one version of UNIX, as any two UNIX operating systems are unlikely to be identical. However, UNIX's trademark is owned by the international consortium the Open Group.

URL (uniform resource locator)

URL is an abbreviation for uniform resource locator, a series of letters and/or numbers specifying the location of a resource, such as an HTML page or image file on the World Wide Web. Each URL comprises the protocol of the resource (e.g., http: or ftp:), a domain name, a description of the document's location within the host computer, and the name of the document itself, separated by full stops and backslashes. Thus, *The Times* Web site can be found at www.the-times.co.uk/news/pages/home.html, and an online exhibition of the Dead Sea Scrolls at www.ibiblio.org/expo/deadsea.scrolls.exhibit/intro.html. The complexity of URLs explains why bookmarks and links, which save the user from the chore of typing them in, are so popular.

V

Vail, Theodore Newton

Telecommunications pioneer (1845–1920)

Theodore Newton Vail was one of a generation of entrepreneurs who helped change the face of America and the world at the turn of the twentieth century. Born in 1845 in Carroll County, Ohio, Vail spent the majority of his childhood in New Jersey. When his family moved to a farm in Iowa in 1866, the young Vail continued west, landing a job as an operator in a Union Pacific boxcar.

It was when Vail moved out of the boxcar and into the railway's mail delivery service that his talents began to shine. Vail pored over railway timetables and train connections, calculating the quickest routes. He used this knowledge to construct a railway mail guide and improve the region's mail transportation system, which was a disorganized shambles.

Vail's ingenuity brought him to the attention of the US government. Vail was summoned to Washington and handed the task of reforming the entire country's mail service. Vail swiftly rose from assistant superintendent of the mail service to general superintendent. Rescheduling the entire country's delivery service cut into the revenues of some railway companies. Yet despite the powerful vested interests of the railway companies ranged against him, Vail succeeded in reorganizing the mail.

His indomitable nature also brought him to the attention of Gardiner G. Hubbard, father-in-law of Alexander Graham Bell, inventor of the telephone. Hubbard needed a man with a forceful personality and uncompromising drive to build a company on the back of the telephone's invention. Vail was that man. Vail had the vision to see how the telephone could revolutionize communications – not only on a regional but also on a national level.

In 1878, Vail accepted the position of general manager at the American Bell Telephone Company, newly founded by Bell and Hubbard, who were the subject of much ridicule. *The Times* called the new invention 'the latest American humbug'. 'I gave up a $3500 salary for no salary,' Vail remarked at the time.

At Bell, he devoted his entire energy and passion to rolling out the telephone nationwide. In 1882, Vail oversaw the purchase of the Western Electric Co. of Chicago, one of the premier manufacturers of telephone equipment. In 1885, the group of companies Vail presided over was incorporated as AT&T (the American Telephone and Telegraph Company). Vail stayed with Bell until it was sufficiently established to secure enough capital to expand across the country, city by city. When that moment had arrived, in 1887, he left Bell and bought a 200-acre farm in Vermont.

Before settling down on his farm, Vail toured South America, transformed the horse-drawn trams in Buenos Aires to electric lines, opened offices in London, spent time in France and Italy, and installed electric lighting and telephone systems in numerous other cities.

In 1907, a financial crisis struck the United States. Companies were overburdened with debt. Banks withdrew credit, capital dried up, stocks withered and new share issues failed. The AT&T Company was no exception. AT&T was also under threat from the federal government, which was threatening to break up the 'telephone trust'. The directors, in their hour of need, turned to Vail. They travelled to Vail's Lyndon ranch in Vermont, pleading for him to help save the company.

Vail agreed and swiftly raised $21 million in new capital, followed by $250 million over the next six years. To defeat the trustbusters, Vail fought his war on several fronts. He continued to pursue a policy of consolidating the telephone networks under the AT&T umbrella by buying up competitors. At the same time, he campaigned under the 'One System, One Policy, Universal Service' slogan to persuade the public that a single telephone service was the best way. To placate the government, he agreed to regulatory supervision. It was a masterful performance. AT&T emerged from the financial crisis of October–November 1907 as the dominant force in telephony.

Having developed a taste for business again, Vail was reluctant to return to a quiet farming life. He pursued new ventures into his seventies. In 1910, he bought control of the Western Union Telegraph Company for $30 million, intending to introduce the 'tel-letter': mail delivered over the wire at a nominal cost. His plans were cut short when the Department of Justice stepped in to break up the telegraph–telephone combination. Vail was forced to sell Western Union and agree that AT&T would not buy any more independents. Vail retired from AT&T for the second and final time in 1919, dying a year later, on 16 April 1920.

Key texts
- Albert Bigelow Paine. *In One Man's Life: Chapters From the Personal & Business Career of Theodore N. Vail.* Harper & Brothers, 1921
- H.M. Boettinger. *The Telephone Book: Bell, Watson, Vail and American Life, 1876–1976.* Riverwood Publishers, 1977

Valorization

Valorization occurs when the value of a currency or commodity is artificially raised or maintained by a government or other organization. One method of achieving this is through controlling the quantity of a commodity produced or released onto the market, as **OPEC** does with oil production.

Value chain

A value chain involves several companies working together to meet market demands. The chain will usually consist of a small number of primary value suppliers of a product or service and a larger number of tertiary value suppliers that increase the value of the product or service to the consumer. An example often used to illustrate the way a value chain operates is that of **Microsoft**. Microsoft is a primary value supplier, supplying the Windows operating system for personal computers. However, if it were not for all the other companies who add value by producing software to run on the Windows OS, Microsoft's product would be far less attractive to the consumer. Management consultants **McKinsey & Co.** once estimated that in the case of the value chain predicated on the Windows OS and controlled by Microsoft, worth some $383 billion, Microsoft only had a 4 percent share of the total value.

Key text
- Harvard Business Review. *Harvard Business Review On Managing The Value Chain.* McGraw-Hill, 2000

Value-chain integration

There are three distinct elements to value-chain integration: the interface with the customer, the supply chain in the back room, and the connection of the two.

ERP, or enterprise resource planning, was the early 1990s attempt at optimizing the supply chain. Advances in software development and networking meant that companies could connect their empires and automate and coordinate their procurement programmes. Software manufacturers such as PeopleSoft, SAP and Oracle provided the technologies.

ERP applications have now moved on to Web-based solutions. Industry-specific procurement sites have been set up on the **Internet** and the flexibility of the Web-based approach has allowed companies to source more efficiently from a range of suppliers.

At the front end, the Internet should provide an excellent way to interact with the customer. The best Web sites allow customers to find what they are looking for easily and, where possible, to add their own specifications. Companies like **Dell**, for example, allow customers to configure their own computers to a degree. Ordering, too, should be as immediate as possible. It is always surprising how many companies fail to realize the importance of getting this part of the value chain right.

The last part of the chain is the connection between the Web site and the back room. It should work like this. The customer arrives at the Web site and purchases a product – a set of golf clubs, say. The order is processed internally. An order is sent to the warehouse or supplier and the goods are dispatched. The software makes the appropriate stock adjustments and orders in a replacement set of clubs if required.

However, in many companies this is the least efficient part of the value chain. Often the front and back ends are processed on separate networks, frequently because of software incompatibility. Instead of overhauling the system when they introduced the front end Web site, many companies patched the back end and front end together the best they could. Only when this last part of the chain is properly addressed will companies reap the full benefits of value-chain integration.

Value innovation

Value innovation is a business concept invented by INSEAD business school academics W. Chan Kim and **Renée Mauborgne** the late 1990s. It involves looking at corporate strategy from the perspective of creating entirely new markets or redefining existing markets by simultaneously pursuing exceptional value and the lowest costs. There are five dimensions in which value innovators challenge conventional competitors:

- **Industry assumptions:** Value innovators challenge and leapfrog them.
- **Strategic focus:** Value innovators don't follow but create new markets.
- **Customers:** Rather than looking for differences, value innovators look for commonalities between customers.
- **Assets and capabilities:** Value innovators build capabilities to fit the market, rather than defining the market according to their capabilities.
- **Product and service offerings:** Value innovators provide goods and services that customers really value, even if it means moving outside their established business.

Key Text
- W. Chan Kim and Renée Mauborgne. 'Value Innovation: The Strategic Logic of High Growth.' *Harvard Business Review*, January/February 1997

Value investing

Value investing is an investment strategy oriented to selecting stocks with prices that are cheap relative to their fundamentals. The aim is that the investment should be worth substantially more than the price paid for it. Although Benjamin Graham is often cited as the man who invented value investing, the practice goes back further than Graham's contribution, to other investors such as Bernard Baruch. Graham, however, spent many years researching the practice and disseminating his knowledge to the public, and for this reason he is known as the father of value investing. Another major figure in the investment world associated with the practice is the Sage of Omaha, investment guru **Warren Buffet**.

When investors look for value in investment, they may use a number of financial indicators, including the P/E ratio, the dividend yield and the dividend/earnings ratio.

Vanderbilt, Cornelius

Transportation king (1794–1877)

Cornelius Vanderbilt was simply the most brilliant businessman of his generation. He combined an innate understanding of the principles of economics with a consummate grasp of business strategy. Vanderbilt understood that delivering a reasonable service at a low cost would always win out over a government-subsidized monopoly. Rather than fleece consumers by providing a substandard, outdated, expensive service, Vanderbilt gave his customers innovation and value for money. In his lifetime, Vanderbilt amassed fabulous wealth – some $105 million, an unimaginable amount in the nineteenth century.

Vanderbilt was born on 27 May 1794, on Staten Island, New York. Vanderbilt bypassed school, preferring the outdoor life. Although he could barely read and write, he did take a keen interest in business. In 1810, Vanderbilt's mother gave the 16-year-old $100 to clear and plant an 8-acre field. Vanderbilt used his profits to buy a small flat-bottomed sailboat and started a ferry business between Staten Island and New York City.

The ferry business taught Vanderbilt some important commercial lessons. By taking any fare, no matter what the weather conditions, Vanderbilt gained a reputation as reliable and customer-friendly. He also learned the simple economics of low costs and high turnover. Undercutting the competition increased passenger numbers.

The war with England in 1812 turned out to be an opportunity to improve his business. Vanderbilt continued to sail his normal routes and make extra money ferrying food along the Hudson River to a blockaded New York City. He used the profits to buy an interest in two more boats.

By 1817, Vanderbilt's business was doing well. He had expanded to include the coastal routes between Chesapeake Bay and New York, developed a retail business selling provisions to ships in the harbour, and owned interests in a number of boats.

Then the steamboats arrived. Entrepreneurs Robert Fulton and Robert R. Livingston introduced their new technology to New York. They obtained a monopoly on all steamboat traffic for a period of 30 years. Vanderbilt realized that the days of sailboats were numbered. Rather than persisting with outdated technology, he sold his boats. Vanderbilt set out to learn about steamboats, joining steamboat operator Thomas Gibbons, a wealthy attorney and plantation owner. As soon as he was able, he began ferrying passengers from New Jersey to Manhattan in direct contravention to the monopoly. To persuade passengers to use his service, he only charged one dollar, undercutting Fulton and Livingston's four dollar ticket price. He made the money back by selling food and drinks.

In 1824, Vanderbilt got the chance he had waited for when the US Supreme Court declared the Fulton and Livingston monopoly illegal. The end of the monopoly brought dramatic changes in the steamboat business. Prices came down, competitors entered the market and boat technology improved. Vanderbilt thrived in this competitive environment. In 1829, he started his own steamboat business, introducing a through service – steamboat, stagecoach, steamboat – from New York City to Philadelphia. In classic Vanderbilt business fashion, he immediately slashed prices. The competition, fearing a price war, clubbed together to pay Vanderbilt to go away.

It was the same story on the Hudson River. Vanderbilt savagely cut fares until he was carrying passengers for free and, as before, making up the losses on the food. It wasn't long before the Hudson River Steamboat Association, whose cosy **cartel** Vanderbilt had disturbed, caved in, agreeing to pay Vanderbilt $100,000 as well as ten annual payments of $5000 each in return for his leaving the area.

Soon Vanderbilt owned a fleet in excess of 100 steamboats. Always keen to serve consumer demand, he created a new shipping route across the mainland to serve the gold rush inspired by the 1848 discovery of gold in California. The usual chain of events followed. Vanderbilt formed the Accessory Transit Company, struck a deal with the Nicaraguan government, constructed a port on the Pacific Coast and in 1851 started sailing the new route. As usual, his fares were cheaper – $400 compared to the competition's $600. The competition offered Vanderbilt $672,000 not to operate a route to California.

Remarkably, when he was in his sixties and had amassed a fortune of $40 million – enough to retire comfortably – Vanderbilt switched his business interests from water to land. Once again abandoning soon-to-be-outdated technology, Vanderbilt moved into the railway business.

By 1869, Vanderbilt had taken control of the Hudson River Railroad and the New York Central system. He merged the two companies, gained control of railroad lines from New York to Chicago, and created a consolidated railroad system between the two cities. Unrelenting, he upgraded iron rails with steel imported from England, doubled tracks, and built the Grand Central Depot in New York City – the largest rail terminal in the world.

When Vanderbilt died on 4 January 1877, his railroad empire extended over 740 miles of track and included 486 locomotives and 9000 freight cars. Every year, 7000 passengers were transported courtesy of Vanderbilt.

Key texts
- Arthur D. Howden Smith. *Commodore Vanderbilt: An Epic of American Achievement.* Robert McBride, 1927
- Gustav Metzman. *Commodore Vanderbilt (1794–1877): Forefather of the New York Central.* The Newcomen Society of England, 1946

Variance

Variance is a concept used in budgeting and the control of costs. It is the difference between expected or predicted costs and actual costs. The practice of examining variances in budgeting and costing and determining their causes is known as variance analysis. In variance analysis, differences are not referred to as positive or negative but as favourable or adverse – that is, the variance either contributes to or reduces profits.

VAT (value-added tax)

A general consumption tax, value-added tax is assessed on the value of goods and services. It is general because the tax covers all commercial activities that involve the production and distribution of goods and the provision of services. It is called a consumption tax because the burden falls on the consumer. VAT is charged as a percentage of price.

VAT was introduced in Europe by the First VAT Directive of 11 April 1967. This required each member of the European Union to replace its general indirect taxes with a system of value-added tax. However, while the European Union is still moving toward a uniform VAT system and rate, VAT remains a tax determined and regulated by national laws.

The United States has a different approach to sales tax. Individual states impose their own sales taxes as they see fit. A 2001 initiative that has broad state approval – the Streamlined Sales Tax Project – aims to 'simplify and modernize sales and use tax collection and administration'.

Venture capital

Venture capital is the financing provided by professional investors to aid the development of young, fast-growing companies, often start-up businesses, or to expand existing companies. Venture capital firms are generally arranged as private partnerships with a small number of general partners, as well as a number of external limited partners who also provide money toward the establishment of venture capital funds. In return for a venture capital firm's investment in another company, it will receive equity in that company. If the company has an **IPO**, the equity will convert to traded stock and the venture capital firm can realize its investment. The venture capital industry was pioneered by figures such as **Arthur Rock** and Eugene Kleiner. Some of the best-known companies in the world received venture capital in the early stages, including Microsoft, Intel, Genentech, Apple and Sun Microsystems.

Viral marketing

Viral marketing is word-of-mouth advertising carried out in cyberspace, usually by e-mail. It works when one friend sends another an e-mail with a clickable link that takes the recipient through to the host Web site, where the product or service is sold.

It's been a while since **Internet** guru Michael Tchong called 'viral marketing' the buzzword of the year in 1998. The term was originally coined by venture capitalist Steve Jurvetson, who backed Hotmail. Coincidentally, Hotmail is the example most often cited by proponents of viral marketing. Spending less than $500,000, Hotmail managed to sign up more than 12 million users in less than 18 months. How did it accomplish this prodigious feat? Every e-mail sent by a Hotmail subscriber invites the recipient to sign up for an account. It's infectious stuff. To succeed, the marketing virus must spread quickly. The most successful viruses tend to be fun or useful.

Virtual organization

The notion of the virtual organization has more than one interpretation. To some people, 'virtual' refers simply to companies' ability to use IT to allow people in remote locations, even on different continents, to work together effectively. For others, the definition goes further, describing an amorphous organization made up of project teams that form to fulfil a specific purpose and disband at a moment's notice.

The theory on which the concept is built is perfectly sensible. Technology enables companies to dismantle their cumbersome headquarters buildings – the costly bricks and mortar of the conventional business. Employees can work at home or occasionally in satellite offices when required. Linked by networks of computers, communicating by e-mail and modems, people become more productive when they are freed from the burdens of commuting and the regularity of office life. With no expensive tower blocks to support, organizations make massive cuts in operating costs. The virtual organization is life-enhancing and profit-enhancing.

Employees' technological ability to communicate and share information also means that patterns of decision making are fundamentally altered, with no necessity for coordination from the centre. If individual workers are dots on the organizational map, then one justification for traditional structures was to provide a framework to direct their efforts. But as soon as you can connect each dot – or computer terminal – to any other, the need for a formal structure disappears. Take it a step further and think of those dots as light bulbs connected with the power of communication. Theoretically, at least, a virtual organization can instantly light up any pattern or configuration of skills required, and can switch it off just as quickly.

The virtual organization is well understood and a logical extension of technology. But virtual organizations are, as yet, notable mainly for their absence. If the arguments for the virtual organization are so persuasive, why are so few decision makers convinced?

It might be because virtual organizations are perceived as merely trendy. They remain associated with smart and creative companies. Yet a manufacturer in Pittsburgh can benefit from organizing itself in a virtual way as much as one in Palo Alto.

Another stumbling block is that the virtual organization requires a quantum leap rather than steady evolution. Making it work requires more than short-term enthusiasm on the part of senior managers. It requires some understanding of the technical possibilities – as well as a harmonious and respectful relationship with corporate IT specialists.

Finally, the virtual organization uses IT as a primary corporate resource. The trouble is that many organizations continue to regard IT as a function rather than a dynamic organizational tool.

Given the apparent difficulties in creating truly virtual organizations, the way forward may rest with compromise solutions, such as hot-desking or the use of virtual teams – groups that are accountable for the achievement of transient or short-term objectives. For most companies, true virtual working is still some way off.

Key texts

- Raymond Grenier and George Metes. *Going Virtual*. Prentice Hall Computer Books, 1995
- Jessica Lipnack and Jeffrey Stamps. *The Age of the Network*. John Wiley, 1996
- Charles Savage. *Fifth Generation Management*. Butterworth-Heinemann, 1996

Virus

US computer security guru Fred Cohen, who coined the term computer virus, defined it as 'a computer program that can affect other computer programs by modifying them in such a way as to include a (possibly evolved) copy of itself'. The first viruses released into the wild – to the general public – were the Apple viruses, spread on Apple II floppy disks in 1981. The virus was known as Elk Cloner. The term was officially coined by Cohen in 1983, and from 1986, when the Brain virus was written by two brothers from Pakistan, the creators of viruses continued to perfect their techniques and stay one step ahead of the anti-virus software writers. By 1990, the virus problem was sufficiently widespread to make the production of commercial anti-virus software viable. Norton AntiVirus by Symantec was one of the first. Common viruses in the wild since 1990 include Michelangelo, Melissa, ILOVEYOU, Anna Kournikova, and HomePage.

Key link

- http://all.net/

Volatility

Volatility, in investment parlance, is the amount by which an equity's price moves up and down beyond the market's average range. It is calculated by taking the annualized standard deviation of daily change in price. An equity's volatility is normally related to the risk associated with the company. In turn, the associated risk is related to such things as **gearing**, type of business and company size. The shares of a small company with high debt operating in a new and unproven market are likely to be highly volatile.

Some share traders rely on volatility to make money. This is particularly true of day traders, who often aim to be in and out of a stock in the space of an hour, let alone a day. An indication of a stock's volatility can be found in its **beta**, which is often quoted in the financial press and on financial Web sites.

Voluntary liquidation

A voluntary liquidation is the situation in which the shareholders apply to wind up the company while the company is still solvent – the directors may even have to make a statement to that effect. If it appears to the liquidator that the company will be unable to meet its debts, then they will call a meeting of the creditors and a compulsory liquidation will take place. Contrast voluntary liquidation with the situation in a **Chapter 7 bankruptcy**, for example, in which a company is put into involuntary liquidation after bankruptcy.

Vortals

A vortal is a specific type of **Internet** portal. A contraction of 'vertical portal', vortals are Web sites that aggregate industry-specific content and tailor it to the needs of that particular industry. One example is VerticalNet, a collection of industry-specific communities like nurses.com. Vortals are not exclusively business-to-business. Sites like Expedia (travel) and Greenfingers (gardening) are examples of business-to-consumer vortals. Vortals obtain revenue in a number of ways. Online catalogues are a common feature, where the different products of different contributors to the vortal can be combined in a single catalogue. The vortal might also facilitate procurement, taking a fee along the way.

Vulture capitalists

The term vulture capitalists was coined to describe the situation in which companies pick over the bones of troubled dotcom businesses. Administrators, other dotcom companies and online auction sites are examples of the kind of companies that have benefited from the demise of dotcom companies. The term is also used to describe **venture capital** firms who see the plight of dotcom companies as an opportunity to leverage their investment by securing better terms.

W

Walton, Samuel Moore

Retail pioneer; founder, Wal-Mart Corp.
(1918–1992)

The **Frank Woolworth** of his generation, Samuel Moore Walton died one of the richest men in the world, having built an empire of more than 1000 mass-merchandise discount stores under the Wal-Mart name.

Walton was born in Oklahoma on 29 March 1918, and spent much of his childhood moving with his family from town to town in Missouri as his father pursued work. The family finally settled in Columbia, Missouri, in 1933, where Walton took on several jobs to bolster the family income.

A bright student, Walton studied for a business degree at the University of Missouri at Columbia, from which he graduated in 1940. In addition to his studies, he ran a large paper route, with revenues of some $4000 (the equivalent of more than $40,000 in 1998 dollars). This earned him the nickname 'Hustler' Walton. After college, Walton took a position as a management trainee in Des Moines, Iowa, at the retail store JCPenney. It was there that he learned many of the management techniques that he was to apply later, including fostering a sense of inclusion by calling his employees 'associates' and managing by walking around or, in Walton's case, by flying around.

Walton spent World War II serving in the US military police. When he returned to civilian life at the end of the war, he borrowed $20,000 from his father-in-law and bought a Ben Franklin store in Newport, Arkansas. The store opened on 1 September 1945, when Walton was 27.

In 1950, Walton was forced to sell his Newport store because of problems renewing the lease. Rather than quit, Walton moved to nearby Bentonville and bought another Ben Franklin store, calling it 'Walton's Five and Dime'. He soon owned a string of stores in the region. The stores were spread out over a wide geographic area, and Walton found a novel means of visiting them: he flew his own decrepit pre-war airplane from one store to the next.

Walton's next move was to introduce self-service. The concept of self-service was a new one, and the fact that it enabled the owner of the store to pass on cheaper prices to the customer appealed to Walton. One of Walton's greatest strengths was that he was always willing to embrace innovation. In the early 1960s, Walton pressed the Ben Franklin management to let him introduce the discount store concept. Ben Franklin stalled, so Walton opened up his own store, Wal-Mart, which owed much to the K-mart store in Chicago, a store that Walton had visited to observe its operation first-hand. Walton's first Wal-Mart discount store was opened on 2 July 1962, in Rogers, Arkansas. Walton was still earning the bulk of his income from his chain of Ben Franklin stores but spent much of his time on the Wal-Mart store, experimenting with different layouts and mixes of stock to create the perfect discount store.

The second Wal-Mart opened in 1964 in the town of Harrison, Arkansas. The first day was a disaster. The temperature was 115 degrees. Manure from the donkeys providing donkey rides was trodden through the store. The watermelons outside popped in the heat. Tarmac melted. Local businessman David Glass uttered the legendary observation: 'It was the worst retail store I've ever seen.' Glass eventually became president of the Wal-Mart Corporation.

Unable to finance expansion of the Wal-Mart empire adequately from profits alone, Walton raised $5 million on the stock market through a public offering of Wal-Mart stock in 1970. The money enabled Walton to roll his high-volume, low-profit-margin strategy to six more stores as well as a distribution centre. From the 1970s onward, Walton's construction of new stores grew at a phenomenal rate, with 452 built during the 1970s and 1237 in the 1980s.

Somehow, Walton still managed to keep in touch with his thousands of employees. He travelled from store to store by plane and, when he found a store that didn't meet his high standards, closed it on the spot, only reopening it when it came up to scratch. He wrote a monthly column in the company newspaper, *Wal-Mart World*, personally replied to letters from staff raising questions or suggesting ideas, and insisted on attending the opening of new stores whenever possible. In 1983, he promised to dance down Wall Street in a grass skirt if the company reached its profit targets. It did, and Wall Street was privy to the sight of Walton dancing the hula.

Walton retired in 1974. Yet two years later, in June 1976, he was back as **CEO**. By 1987, Wal-Mart had opened its thousandth store and was an early adopter of network technology, linking all of the stores through a satellite system. Loyal investors had much to thank Walton for. One hundred shares purchased for a mere $1650 in 1970 were, by the time of Walton's death in 1992, worth a staggering $2.6 million.

Diagnosed with leukaemia in 1982, Walton continued running his company and, after treatment in a Texas hospital, he returned to work. In 1988, he was diagnosed with bone marrow cancer. He died on 6 April 1992.

Key text

- Sam Walton with John Huey. *Sam Walton; Made in America; My Story*. Doubleday, 1992

WAP (wireless application protocol)

When wireless application protocol, a standard for delivering Web-like applications on mobile phones and other wireless devices, was first introduced, it was hailed as the mobile **Internet**. WAP was started as the Wireless Application Protocol Initiative in the 1990s by Unwired Planet and mobile phone manufacturers Motorola, Nokia and Ericsson. In theory, WAP phones can be used for e-mail and messaging, reading Web pages, shopping, booking tickets and making other financial transactions, as well as for phone calls. Despite all the hype, however, WAP has been superseded to some extent by 3G mobile phone technology.

Warburg, Paul Moritz

Banker; co-creator, US central banking system (1868–1932)

Born into a wealthy banking family in Hamburg in 1868, Paul Moritz Warburg received the finest education money could buy, with an emphasis on banking and finance. After university, he gained hands-on work experience in Europe's major financial centres. He worked in London, Paris and Hamburg before travelling around the world in 1893, taking in India, China, Japan and the United States. In the United States, he met Nina J. Loeb, daughter of Solomon Loeb, one of the most powerful men on Wall Street and a partner in international banking house Kuhn, Loeb and Co.

Back in Hamburg, Warburg was set to become a partner in the family firm, M.M. Warburg & Co. Yet he passed up his banking birthright for love. He returned to the United States in 1895 to marry Nina Loeb. At first, the couple returned to live in Germany. Nina's parents fell ill, however, and wanted their daughter nearby, so Warburg accepted a job in New York City at Kuhn, Loeb and Co.

Warburg kept his head down and worked hard. He was involved in a number of multimillion-dollar deals, including the financing of the Pennsylvania Railroad's development of the railway in New York, which involved the tunnels in Manhattan. A scholarly man, Warburg was unimpressed by the US banking system. Compared with the sophisticated banking system in Europe, US banking and finance were in a shambles. An outsider with poor spoken English, Warburg was reluctant to voice his thoughts publicly. Instead, he wrote down his thoughts on the system in an essay that he locked away in a drawer. But in 1907, with a severe financial crisis looming, urged on by colleagues and acquaintances, Warburg went on the record with his opinions about the shortcomings of the US financial system.

'The United States is at about the same point that had been reached by Europe at the time of the Medicis,' Warburg wrote. 'We have been shown bricks of the time of Hammurabi, the Babylonian monarch, evidencing the sale of a crop and similar transactions, and I am inclined to believe that it was as easy to transfer ownership of these bricks from one person to another as it is today for an American bank to realize upon its discounted paper, if indeed it was not easier.' Americans didn't take kindly to being compared to the Babylonians, but the normally unassuming Warburg had a point and they knew it.

Warburg's technical papers on the subject, such as 'Plans for a Modified Central Bank', attracted the interest of Senator Nelson Aldrich. Aldrich was in charge of the Aldrich Committee, which was convened to investigate the possibility of transforming the US banking system. In November 1910, Aldrich organized a 'duck hunt' on a small island off the coast of Georgia.

Four men were invited on the duck hunt with Aldrich – Frank, Harry, Piatt and Paul. Because of the secrecy of the mission, it was first names only. The full names were: Frank Vanderlip, president of National City Bank; Harry P. Davison, a partner in J.P. Morgan; A. Piatt Andrew, assistant secretary of the Treasury; and Paul Warburg.

The cleverest and most powerful men in US finance were assembled on the tiny Jekyll Island. Despite the rifles (Warburg had to borrow his), hunting clothes, and other paraphernalia, the true purpose of the trip had nothing to do with ducks. The reason for the men's presence on the island was to develop a plan to be put before Congress for banking and currency reform. For ten days, the five men burned the midnight oil, thrashing out the basis for a new banking system founded on a central bank.

The result was the Aldrich plan, a proposal document that called for a central bank based in Washington, known as the 'National Reserve Association', as well as 15 branches throughout the United States. Publicly, it was proclaimed a team effort. but Warburg was credited with the most significant contribution to its formulation before, during and after the Jekyll Island meeting. The plan was presented to the public in January 1911, and endorsed by the National Monetary Commission in January 1912.

After Jekyll Island, Warburg spearheaded a crusade to educate the business community and the public. A persuasive advocate for the new banking system, he was appointed head of The National Citizens League for the Promotion of Sound Banking. Bipartisan Warburg worked with both Republicans and Democrats. Although Democrat President Woodrow Wilson came to power before the Aldrich plan became legislation, he agreed to use the plan as the foundation for reform. Furthermore, Wilson appointed Warburg to the **Federal Reserve** Board after the Federal Reserve Act was passed in December 1913. Warburg resigned from his partnerships at Kuhn, Loeb and Co. and M.M. Warburg, happily trading a salary of some $500,000 for one of $12,000.

Events conspired against Warburg. With the likelihood of a war against Germany growing, the Federal Reserve Board was no place for a man that many still regarded with suspicion due to his German background. Warburg was forced to resign from the Federal Reserve Board when Woodrow Wilson refused to renew his term of office. He went on to found the International Acceptance Bank but never recovered from his perceived betrayal at the hands of the US politicians. He died on 24 January 1932.

Key text
- Ron Chernow. *The Warburgs: The Twentieth-Century Odyssey of a Remarkable Jewish Family.* Vintage Books, 1994

Warrant

A warrant is a type of financial security that gives the purchaser the right to buy a stock at a fixed price on a specified date. Like most financial securities, warrants can be traded on the financial markets in a manner similar to stocks. Warrant holders do not receive a dividend. Rather, they expect to profit from both capital growth and the difference between the purchase price and the exercise price.

Wastage

During most production processes, there will be a degree of loss of resource.

This loss is known as wastage. It may be that the wastage is inevitable or that it is caused by poor workmanship or an inefficient production process. Other examples of wastage include damaged goods subsequently sold at a discount, if at all, and goods that are past their sell-by date. Wastage doesn't have to related to products; it may refer to people. In human resource terms, for example, wastage refers to the turnover of staff.

Watson, Thomas J. Sr

IT empire builder; founder, International Business Machines (1874–1956)

The history of computing is about more than just the scientists. It is about the men who manage the creativity and innovation and transform the wildest dreams of scientists into commercial reality. Thomas J. Watson Sr was one such man who managed the growth of a small company with a promising technology into a billion-dollar company with a technology that changed the world.

Watson is gone; the company he created, IBM, is one of America's most enduring companies.

Born in Campbell, New York, on 17 February 1874, Watson's upbringing was a traditional nineteenth century rural one. Dignity, respect for others, self-respect, conscientious work, optimism and loyalty were values impressed upon Watson throughout his childhood. He carried the values throughout his life, both private and public.

At 18, Watson was driving a horse and buggy across New York State, hawking an unlikely combination of pianos and sewing machines to farmers. Watson took all manner of goods in trade: animals, farm equipment and produce were all exchanged and then sold again by him. He learned that if he kept his customers happy, more people would buy his goods on recommendation.

Watson's lucky break came when he went to work for the National Cash Register Company in 1898. Watson joined NCR, known universally as 'the cash', as a salesman. Once he had the first few sales under his belt, he made swift progress. He was promoted to manager of the company's Rochester branch in 1899 and then to general sales manager – right-hand man of NCR's founder, **John H. Patterson**, an eccentric, charismatic businessman and a remarkable business pioneer. While at NCR, Watson came up with the slogan that would later become firmly associated with IBM: 'THINK!' The motto was originally conceived to revitalize a dispirited NCR sales force.

After a series of run-ins with Patterson, Watson was fired from NCR. In 1914, he joined the Computing-Tabulating-Recording Company (CTR) as general manager. The company eventually became International Business Machines – IBM. As a newcomer brought into shake things up, Watson was disliked by the staff, who feared for their jobs. But Watson didn't fire a single employee. Instead, he decided to improve employee performance and productivity. It was the foundation of IBM's famous policy of job security. It was a policy IBM stuck to throughout the Great Depression. Twenty-five percent of the US labour force was out of work, but IBM carried on expanding, producing excess inventory and stockpiling it, a gamble that ultimately paid off.

Watson used many ideas from Patterson's liberal working practices to create an enthusiastic working atmosphere at IBM. This included staging concerts, picnics, and other entertainments, as well as giving rousing speeches. Watson also instituted an open-door policy, making himself available in person to see his employees whenever they wished and actively encouraging their visits. Another key element of Watson's management strategy at IBM, the practice only lapsed after his death, when the size of the company made it impracticable.

Watson went out of his way to keep his employees happy. At IBM Day at the World's Fair in 1939, Watson took 10,000 people to the fair at the company's expense. Sales conventions became increasingly extravagant affairs. A visit by General Eisenhower to IBM in July 1948 was extended, at the insistence of Watson, to allow Eisenhower to address workers at the IBM plant.

Watson's management style had the desired effect. Between 1914 and 1946, IBM's profits grew 38-fold. After World War II, revenues grew from $115 million in 1946 to $1.7 billion by 1961, with the number of employees increasing from 17,000 to 80,000 during the same period. One hundred shares bought in 1914 would have cost $2740. By 1962, shortly after Watson's death, they were worth $5,455,000.

IBM's post-war success was in large part due to a new breed of computing machine. The world's first large-scale computer was IBM's Mach 1, built in collaboration with Dr Howard Aiken and presented to Harvard University in 1944. The Mach 1 was followed by the first commercially available IBM computer, the 701, in 1952. Thomas Watson Sr died four years later on 19 June 1956. A month before his death, he passed control of the company to his eldest son, Thomas J. Watson Jr.

Key texts

- Thomas J. Watson Jr and Peter Petre. *Father, Son & Co: My Life at IBM and Beyond*. Bantam, 1990

- F.G. Buck Rodgers with Robert L. Shook. *The IBM Way*. Harper & Row, 1987
- William Rodgers. *THINK: A Biography of the Watsons and IBM*. Stein and Day, 1969

Weber, Max

German sociologist (1864–1920)

In terms of management theorizing, Max Weber has become something of a *bête noire*, the sociological twin of **Frederick Taylor**, the king of **scientific management**. Weber observed emerging organizations in the fledgling industrial world. He argued that the most efficient form of organization resembled a machine. It was characterized by strict rules, controls and hierarchies, and driven by bureaucracy. Weber termed this type of organization the 'rational-legal model'.

At the opposite extreme was the 'charismatic' model, in which a single dominant figure ran the organization. Weber dismissed this as a long-term solution. Once again, Weber was the first to discuss this phenomenon and examine its ramifications. No matter what **Tom Peters** and Robert Waterman say, history bears Weber out: an organization built around a single charismatic figure is unsustainable in the long term.

The final organizational form Weber identified was the traditional model, in which things are done as they always have been done, such as in family firms, in which power is passed down from one generation to the next.

If an organization required pure efficiency, there was, said Weber, only one choice: 'Experience tends universally to show that the purely bureaucratic type of administrative organization – that is, the monocratic variety of bureaucracy – is, from a purely technical point of view, capable of attaining the highest degree of efficiency and is in this sense formally the most rational known means of carrying our imperative control over human beings.'

In *The Theory of Social and Economic Organization*, Weber outlined the 'structure of authority' around seven points:

1   It comprises a continuous organization of official functions bound by rules.

2   It operates in a specified sphere of competence.

3   The organization of offices follows the principle of hierarchy.

4   The rules that regulate the conduct of an office may be technical rules or norms. In both cases, if their application is to be fully traditional, specialized training is necessary.

5   In the rational type of organization, it is a matter of principle that the members of the administrative staff should be completely separated from the ownership of the means of production or administration.

6   In the case of the rational type, there is also a complete absence of appropriation of his official position by the incumbent.

7   Administrative acts, decisions and rules are formulated and recorded in writing, even in cases where oral discussion is the rule or is even mandatory.

Modern commentators usually cannot resist the urge to scoff at Weber's insights. It was undoubtedly a narrow way of doing things and one that seems out of step with our times. Yet, in the early part of the twentieth century it was a plausible and effective means of doing business. Like all great insights, it worked, for a while at least.

Key texts

- Max Weber. *The Protestant Ethic and the Spirit of Capitalism*. Scribner's, 1958
- Max Weber. *The Theory of Social and Economic Organization*. Free Press, 1947

Weighted average cost of capital (WACC)

The weighted average cost of capital is a technique used to assist companies in calculating the cost of raising financing. First, the cost of each element of capital such as debt (loans or bonds) and equity (common or preferred stock) is multiplied by its percentage of the total capital. The figures for every element of capital are then added together. The result is the weighted average cost of capital, a rough guide to the rate of interest per monetary unit of capital.

To illustrate, if a company raises capital with £5 million of stock with an expected rate of return of 5 percent and £15 million of debt through a bond issue with a coupon of 10 percent, the WACC is as follows:

- equity (£5 million) divided by total capital (£20 million) = 25%
- multiplied by cost of equity (5%) = 1.25%
- debt (£15 million) divided by total capital (£20 million) = 75%
- multiplied by cost of debt (10%) = 7.5%

Added together, this gives a WACC of 8.75%.

Welch, Jack Francis Jr

Celebrated manager; former CEO, General Electric (b. 1935)

One of most celebrated managers and leaders of the twentieth century, Jack Francis Welch Jr, was born on 19 November 1935, in Peabody, Massachusetts. He grew up in Salem, Massachusetts, where his father worked as a railroad conductor.

After high school, Welch studied chemistry at the University of Massachusetts, where he worked hard and played hard, graduating with honours. A PhD in chemical engineering from the University of Illinois came next. Finishing his studies, Welch moved to Pittsfield, Massachusetts, to start his first real job at General Electric.

Welch's meteoric career at GE almost didn't happen. He quit in 1961, sick of the cumbersome bureaucracy at the company. Fortunately for GE, Welch's boss persuaded him to stay, offering more money and a better position. Welch's decision was rewarded when, in 1968 at the age of 33, he became GE's youngest general manager ever. He was divisional vice-president by 1972 and had his sights set even higher. His employee evaluation form stated his long-term ambition – to become **CEO**.

By 1979, he was vice-chairman and executive officer. Along the way, he built the plastics division into a formidable $2 billion business; turned around the medical diagnostics business; and began the development of GE Capital. In December 1980, Welch was announced as the new CEO and chairman of GE. At 45, he was the youngest chief the company had ever appointed and only the eighth CEO in 92 years.

When Welch took over, GE was in reasonable shape. That year, *Fortune* magazine voted it the best managed company in America, yet GE's stock was performing badly. The Japanese were posing a real threat to US manufacturers with new production systems such as 'lean manufacturing', and the world economy was beginning to stall. Recognizing that GE would have to change in order to compete successfully on the world stage, Welch spent the 1980s stamping his mark on GE through a series of radical changes.

Welch declared his intention to make GE the world's most valuable company. From then on, there was no room for unprofitable areas. Every GE business would have to be number one or number two in its industry or be scrapped. Focus was shifted to service industries. This exercise created a raft of new businesses – more than 1000 – and resulted in the disposal of 70 existing businesses.

Next, Welch thinned out the organization, granting power to the individual business units and taking it away from the centre. 'Fight it. Hate it. Kick it. Break it,' was Welch's anti-bureaucracy battle-cry.

The cuts went deep. Nearly 200,000 GE employees left the company, mostly through redundancies, and the company saved $6 billion. The media dubbed Welch 'Neutron Jack'. But it wasn't all destructive. By the end of the 1980s, Welch was on Stage Two: rebuilding a company fit for the twenty-first century. Welch vowed to create what he called a 'boundaryless' organization. 'Knock down the walls that separate us from each other on the inside and from our key constituents on the outside,' was the way he put it. The intention was to encourage innovation and the communication

of ideas. Pre-Welch era employees with a good idea would hang on to it, keen to claim it as their own and receive the ensuing praise. In Welch's GE, employees would be willing to share ideas and the company made sure that employees received the praise they deserved.

Another important element of corporate culture utilized by Welch was corporate values. He used them to give guidance to employees and ensure they were pulling in the same direction. Corporate values were so important to Welch that he famously carried a copy of the values around with him printed on a card.

In the mid-1990s, Welch adopted the concept of 'Six Sigma' developed by Motorola in 1985. A statistical term, Six Sigma refers to products with a 99.9998 percent perfection rate. Implementation of Six Sigma within an organization relies on rigorous measurement and testing to deliver results. Welch got management 100 percent behind the adoption of Six Sigma. In the period between 1995 and 1999, a 3 percent increase in profit margins was attributed to the rollout of Six Sigma at GE.

A raft of figures demonstrates the success of Jack Welch's time as CEO of GE. Between March 1981 and November 1999 the GE stock price rose from just over $4 to $133, allowing for four stock splits – an increase of 3200 percent. From 1980 onward, the average total return of GE shares was about 27 percent and the company has returned 100 consecutive quarters of increased earnings from continuing operations. To put the company's performance in context: if you bought $10,000 worth of General Electric shares in March 1981 and reinvested the dividends, by the end of 1999 they would have been worth $640,000. Since 1981, GE sales have risen from $27.2 billion to $173.2 billion. Over the same period, profits rose from $1.6 billion to $10.7 billion. By 1999, General Electric was the second most profitable company in the world. Whichever way you cut the cake, Welch is one of the greatest corporate leaders of the twentieth century.

Welch finally stepped down as head of GE on 7 September 2001. It was a little later than planned, as Welch had delayed his retirement to carry off a mega-merger between GE and Honeywell. The deal was approved by the US Department of Justice but sunk by the European Union regulators. Welch left GE planning to see his autobiography, *Jack: Straight from the Gut*, published and carry out some consultancy work.

Key texts

- Jack Welch with John A. Byrne. *Jack: Straight From the Gut*. Warner Books, 2001
- Stuart Crainer. *Business the Jack Welch Way*. AMACOM, 1999
- Noel M. Tichy and Sherman Stratford. *Control Your Destiny or Someone Else Will: How Jack Welch is Making General Electric the World's Most Competitive Corporation*. Currency/Doubleday, 1993
- Robert Slater. *The New GE: How Jack Welch Revived An American Institution*. McGraw-Hill, 1992

Key link

- www.ge.com

Weyerhaeuser, Frederick

Lumberman; founder, Weyerhaeuser Timber Co. (1834–1914)

Through hard work, entrepreneurial endeavour, and brilliant management, Frederick Weyerhaeuser brought together the rivermen, the loggers, the millers, and the other diverse trades involved in the timber industry, and built the biggest timber company in the world.

Weyerhaeuser was born in 1834 in Niedersaulheim, Rhein Hessen, Germany. As a young man, he left Europe for America to seek his fortune. When he arrived in America in 1852 at the age of 18, he had no money, no skills to speak of and no valuable possessions to sell.

Strong and willing to work hard, Weyerhaeuser got a job was as a labourer in Erie, Pennsylvania. He married his wife, Elisabeth, in Erie. Weyerhaeuser then moved to Rock Island, Illinois, and worked on the railroad. In 1856, at the age of 22, Wey-erhaeuser obtained work at local sawmill, Mead, Smith and Marsh. Weyerhaeuser applied himself to the dirty, difficult business and impressed the mill owner sufficiently to earn a promotion. In 1857, he was chosen to head Mead, Smith and Marsh's operations at Coal Valley, Illinois. It was the beginning of his career in the timber industry, which would see him rise from labourer to multimillionaire.

When the Mead, Smith and Marsh mill went bankrupt in 1858, Weyerhaeuser was out of a job. But instead of crumbling at the first sight of adversity, Weyerhaeuser turned this setback into an opportunity. In 1860, with his brother-in-law Frederick Denkmann, he bought the sawmill for $3500.

The new venture was called Weyerhaeuser & Denkmann. Denkmann ran the sawmill and Weyerhaeuser went out to rebuild the debt-riddled business. 'I went around among the farmers,' Weyerhaeuser said, 'exchanging lumber for horses, oxen, hogs, eggs, anything they had, which I then traded to the raftsmen for logs.' Weyerhaeuser travelled upriver to meet the rivermen, visited the loggers in their camps, and learned how to fell trees and scale logs.

Traditionally, logs felled in pine forests to the north were transported down the Mississippi River with giant log rafts manned by crews of up to 35 rivermen using oars to steer the cumbersome vessels. This changed when a boatyard owner adapted a steamboat to tow the logs. To exploit this commercial opportunity, in 1871, Weyerhaeuser formed a coalition of sawmill owners – the Mississippi River Logging Company – with Weyerhaeuser as president. At its peak, the Mississippi River Logging Company had 75 steamboats towing logs on the upper Mississippi and employed some 1500 men. With long-time business partner Denkmann, Weyerhaeuser dramatically expanded his business, acquiring other sawmills, founding the Rock Island Lumber and Manufacturing Co. in 1878, and purchasing tracts of pine forest in Wisconsin. Through the 1870s and 1880s, Weyerhaeuser bought more than 200,000 acres in Wisconsin from Cornell University.

By the end of the nineteenth century, Weyerhaeuser headed the largest lumbering enterprise in the United States. Weyerhaeuser had logged much of the old forests of the Great Lakes region and now turned his attention to other American states. Leaving daughter Apollonia in the family house on Rock Island in 1899, Weyerhaeuser moved to St Paul, Minneapolis, where he moved into 266 Summit Avenue – one of the city's most prestigious addresses.

One neighbour was **James J. Hill**, a long-time St Paul resident and president of the Great Northern Railway who was then in the process of completing the railroad from St Paul to Seattle. Weyerhaeuser and Hill became firm friends. Hill's company had acquired a controlling interest in the Northern Pacific Railway, Great Northern's principal competitor, and the possession of vast swathes of land came along with the railroad interests. The land was originally donated by the federal government in the 1880s for the construction of the transcontinental railroad. (A substantial portion of the original allotment, the land covered an area of 44 million acres, equivalent to 68,750 square miles.)

Over dinner one evening, Weyerhaeuser and Hill got to haggling over the sale of the 900,000 acres to Weyerhaeuser. Weyerhaeuser suggested five dollars an acre; Hill suggested seven; they agreed on six. For $3 million up front and eight payments of $300,000 plus interest, Weyerhaeuser had bought 900,000 acres of prime forestry land. 'There is a great lot of it,' said Weyerhaeuser, commenting on the quantity of timber, 'in every conceivable direction.' As part of the deal, he negotiated shipping rates that were way below commercial rates for transporting the timber with Hill.

Due to the size of the deal, Weyerhaeuser was forced to turn to other timber men to help raise the down payment. It took nearly all of the lumbermen of the upper Mississippi River to raise the money. In 1900, Weyerhaeuser and the other investors founded the Weyerhaeuser Timber Company with Weyerhaeuser as president. By 1905, Weyerhaeuser owned 1.5 million acres of timber. He died in 1914, having built the largest timber company in the world.

Key texts

- Joni Sensel. *Traditions Through the Trees: Weyerhaeuser's First 100 Years.* Documentary Book Publishers Corporation, 1999
- Ralph Hidy, Frank Ernest Hill and Allan Nevins. *Timber and Men: The Weyerhaeuser Story.* Macmillan, 1963

Whistleblowing

Whistleblowing refers to exposing malpractice within an organization, whether to the management, the media or the appropriate authorities. Most companies profess to support whistleblowing when it occurs. In practice, however, whistleblowers put themselves at considerable personal risk, particularly in terms of their careers. While whistleblowers often benefit society by exposing illegal or anti-competitive practices, they are often cast as troublemakers by corporations and ostracized by fellow employees and find it impossible to continue working for the same employer, or even in the same industry.

In the United Kingdom, the Public Disclosure Act 1998, also known as the Whistleblowers' Charter, has sought to remedy this stigma, with some success. Whistleblowing is often related to discriminatory practices within the workplace and often occurs in public-service organizations, such as the police or the health system. One of the most famous whistleblowing cases of recent times is that of Sherron Watkins, who exposed the true implications of the off-balance-sheet transactions carried out at US energy company Enron.

White goods

White goods are consumer durables such as refrigerators, washing machines, and dishwashers. They get their name from the white enamel in which they were traditionally finished. Confusingly, many white goods are today any colour but white – as, indeed, many **brown goods** are black or silver.

White knight

If a company is the subject of a hostile takeover bid, it has a number of potential defences at its disposal. One such defence is to invite a white knight to ride to its aid. The white knight is in this instance a company, usually one that is already on good terms with the target company, which is invited by the target of a takeover bid to make a rival bid.

Whyte, William H.

Editor and author (1918–1999)

William H. Whyte was an editor at the magazine *Fortune* at the time he wrote his best-known work, *The Organization Man.* The bulk of his career was spent as an 'urbanologist', studying people's movements and behaviour in a city environment. Among his revealing findings was that a large percentage of companies that moved from New York City ended up in locations less than eight miles from the homes of their chief executives. His other books included *The Last Landscape* (1968); *The Social Life of Small Urban Spaces* (1980); and *City* (1989).

During the more stable times of the 1950s and 1960s, the careers enjoyed by corporate executives were built on solid foundations. This was the era of corporate man (there was no such thing as corporate woman at this time). Grey-suited and obedient, corporate man was unstintingly loyal to his employer. He spent his life with a single company and rose slowly, but quietly, up the hierarchy.

The life of corporate man was brilliantly and poignantly described by Whyte in his 1956 book *The Organization Man.* Reviewing the book in *The New York Times*, C. Wright Mills wrote that Whyte 'understands that the work-and-thrift ethic of success has grievously declined – except in the rhetoric of top executives; that the entrepreneurial scramble to success has been largely replaced by the organizational crawl.'

Implicit to the organizational crawl was the understanding that loyalty and solid performance brought job security. This was mutually beneficial. The executive gained a respectable income and a high degree of security. The company gained loyal, hardworking executives.

Loyalty was key. 'The most important single contribution required of an executive, certainly the most universal qualification, is loyalty [allowing] domination by the organization personality,' noted **Chester Barnard** in *The Functions of the Executive* (1938). (The word 'domination' suggests which way Barnard saw the balance of power falling.) While loyalty is a positive quality, it can easily become blind. What if the corporate strategy is wrong or the company is engaged in unlawful or immoral acts? Also, there is the question of loyal to what? At the time of *The Organization Man*, corporate values were assumed rather than explored.

In the world described by Whyte, the corporation becomes a self-contained and self-perpetuating world, supported by a complex array of checks, systems, and hierarchies. The company is right. Customers, who exist in the ethereal world outside the organization, are often regarded as peripheral. In the 1950s, 1960s and 1970s, no executive ever lost his job by delivering poor quality or indifferent service. Indeed, in some organizations, executives only lost their jobs by defrauding their employer or insulting their boss. 'Jobs for life' was the refrain and, to a large extent for executives, the reality. The world of *The Organization Man* rewarded the steady foot soldier, the safe pair of hands.

The last word on Whyte goes to *Fortune*'s founder, **Henry Luce**:

'It was *Fortune*'s William H. Whyte Jr who made the 'Organization Man' a household word – and the organization wife too. His was a fine achievement in sociological reporting. In it he related the phenomenon of the business organization to questions of human personality and values. The kind of people who are eager to hear the worst about American society assumed that Mr White was predicting the destruction of individualism by the organization. Whyte was not a doomsayer. True, he was uneasy about corporate life, which seemed to stifle creativity and individualism. He was uneasy about the subtle pressures in the office and at home that called for smooth perform-ance rather than daring creativity. But he did not urge the organization man to leave his secure environment. Rather he urged them to fight the organization when neces-sary and he was optimistic that the battle could be successful.'

Key text
• William H. Whyte. *The Organization Man.* Simon & Schuster, 1956

Window dressing

Window dressing refers to using creative account-ing practices to make the financial situation in the accounts appear better than the position in reality. Various tactics may be employed to achieve this aim. Off-balance-sheet transactions may hide a multitude of sins. Executing a **sale and leaseback** deal just before the end of the financial year, for example, results in a quick cash injection, artifi-cially improving the **liquidity ratio**.

Winfrey, Oprah

Talk show queen (b. 1954)

From a childhood marked by abuse and discrimi-nation, Oprah Winfrey has become an American icon, a black woman who has conquered US tele-vision and found a place in the hearts of the US public. She has succeeded by being herself.

To say that Winfrey had a tough childhood would be an understatement. Born to unmar-

ried teenagers on 29 July 1954, she was initially brought up by her grandmother. At the age of four, she moved to Milwaukee, Wisconsin, to live with her mother. She then went to her father, before once again settling with her mother in Milwaukee in 1963.

She was raped at the age of 9 and narrowly avoided being sent to a home for juvenile delin-quents by her mother. Finally, Winfrey was dispatched back to live with her father, Vernon Winfrey, a businessman in Nashville, Tennessee. Luckily for Winfrey, her father was a strict disci-plinarian and with his help Winfrey began to get control of her life.

At 16, she got her first big break. The first black girl to win a national beauty contest, Winfrey was invited on a tour of a local radio station to pick up her prize. Out of this trip came the opportunity to read the radio news after school. This in turn led to a job as a reporter on a Nashville radio station, WVOL. Winfrey also enrolled at Tennessee State University to study performing arts.

Initially, Winfrey turned down the first TV job she was offered, but her college professor persuaded her to change her mind. Winfrey became the first African-American news anchor at WTVF-TV in Nashville. On television, she was a natural.

In 1976, Winfrey moved to Baltimore to work at WJZ-TV as a news co-anchor. After a bumpy start when she was demoted to a morning spot, station executive Phil Baker offered her an opportunity to co-host a talk show on the station. Putting a black woman on as host of the station's principal talk show was a risk for the studio. It was also a risk for Winfrey, who had planned a career in news. The show, *People Are Talking*, was a success and soon it was Winfrey and her down-to-earth style that people were talking about. Along with a rise in her Nielsen ratings came a move to Chicago's morning show, *AM Chicago*, where in 1984 she went head-to-head with Phil Donahue, America's top-rated talk show host.

Still only 30 years old, Winfrey continued to wear her heart on her sleeve. Her openness struck a chord with her audience. She elevated *AM Chi-*

cago from the lowest-rated talk show to the top of the ratings in just eight weeks. She even beat Phil Donahue's ratings.

Her increased media coverage paid off when she was asked to audition for the part of Sophia in Steven Spielberg's 1985 film *The Color Purple,* an adaptation of the book by Alice Walker. She got the part, and subsequently received an Oscar nomination for Best Supporting Actress.

It was great timing for Winfrey, who was about to launch a nationally syndicated talk show, titled *The Oprah Winfrey Show.* It was this show, launched in 1986, that propelled Winfrey into the big time. She soon racked up 10 million viewers across the United States.

In 1988, Winfrey formed Harpo Productions – her name spelled backward – acquiring the rights to her show from Capital Cities/ABC. She was only the third woman to own a major studio, following in the footsteps of Mary Pickford and Lucille Ball.

Throughout Winfrey's successful professional life, she maintained an ongoing and often very public struggle with unwanted pounds. Attempts to keep her weight down varied from exercise to a radical, four-month-long liquid diet. Eventually she managed to come to terms with herself and her weight, something that helped her self-esteem and her bank balance, as the book *In the Kitchen with Rosie* (Rosie was her chef) became the fastest-selling book in the United States.

Chasing Winfrey's success, talk shows sprang up on every TV station. What started as a frank discussion of personal problems soon became sensationalist television prying into the private lives of individuals, exposing the underbelly of human life. Appealing to the lowest common denominator, at times such programmes seemed little more than a licence to televise sleaze. The downward spiral in programme quality and subject matter began to tarnish Winfrey by association. In 1994, Winfrey attempted to distance herself from the excesses of the genre by repositioning herself in the marketplace. She vowed to concentrate on more uplifting, highbrow issues: 'change your life' TV. Impressively, Winfrey succeeded in redefining herself and differentiating her show in the talk show market place. This shift of emphasis secured another series run for her through to 2004.

Key texts

- George Mair. *Oprah Winfrey: The Real Story.* Birch Lane Press, 1994
- Robert Waldron. *Oprah!* St Martin's Press, 1988

Key link

- www.oprah.com

Win-lose (adversarial) approach

See Game theory.

Win-win (cooperative or problem-solving) approach

See Game theory.

Win-win situation

See Game theory.

Withholding tax

When a non-resident of a country receives income, he may be subject to a withholding tax. Withholding tax is deducted at source to ensure that the income doesn't leave the country within which it is earned without being taxed. Dividends paid on US stocks held by a UK resident would be subject to a withholding tax, for example. As with most tax legislation, however, there are ways around this tax, usually involving the transition of income into capital before it is received by the non-resident. Where countries have reciprocal double-taxation arrangements, the tax may be reclaimable.

Woodruff, Robert Winship

Soft-drink magnate; former CEO, Coca-Cola (1889–1985)

Robert Winship Woodruff was the man behind one of the biggest corporate success stories of the last century, Coca-Cola. A restless, driven, controlling figurehead, he was responsible for aggressively marketing Coca-Cola to a thirsty world and for taking a caramel-based soft drink and turning it into an American icon.

Born on 6 December 1889, in Columbus, Georgia, Woodruff was the son of Ernest Woodruff, president of the Trust Company of Georgia, the company that, as part of a syndicate, bought control of The Coca-Cola Company. Ernest Woodruff became the president.

Despite being a poor student, Woodruff was popular with the head of his school, the Georgia Military Academy. Why? Because when the Atlanta National Bank was about to foreclose on the school's mortgage, it was Woodruff who visited the bank's vice-president and, through a combination of bluffing and name-dropping, persuaded them to back off.

At Emory College, Woodruff's next educational port of call, he paid other students to complete his homework. Asked later in life for tips on being a successful manager, Woodruff offered, 'If you can get someone to do something better than yourself it is always a good idea.' He may have successfully delegated his college work, but he still failed to complete his degree.

At first, to Woodruff's surprise, his working life was a perplexing failure. He was dismissed from a series of jobs for no obvious reason. It transpired that Woodruff was not responsible for his appalling employment record. His father was. To teach Woodruff that a rich father was not a passport to an easy life, Woodruff Sr had arranged for his son to be fired on each occasion. When Woodruff discovered that his father was interfering in his career, he was furious and vowed never to work for his father again.

He made sure his next job was out of his father's influence, signing on as a truck salesman at the White Motor Company. He must have inherited some of his father's business acumen, however, as he was swiftly promoted through the company, becoming vice-president and then general manager.

In 1919, Woodruff's father put together an investment group that bought out the Candler family's interests in The Coca-Cola Company for $25 million. The deal was structured so that 500,000 shares of Coca-Cola common stock were sold on the stock market for $40 a share. Asked by his father if he wished to participate in the syndicate, Woodruff picked up a large parcel of the company's stock at a knockdown price of $5 per share.

Woodruff was reconciled with his father when he accepted the position of president of The Coca-Cola Company in 1923, at the age of 33. He took a substantial pay cut to do so, turning down the opportunity to move to Standard Oil at an annual salary of $250,000. Woodruff said in his defence that he took the job at Coca-Cola as it was the only way he could boost the value of his stock in the company.

For the next six decades, Woodruff transformed Coca-Cola from a promising US soft-drinks manufacturer into a global giant that dominated its market. His influence extended into every aspect of the company's operations. He started with the company's marketing strategy. Only positive images were to be associated with the product. All negative connotations were banished. Coca-Cola's medicinal roots were severed.

In production and distribution, Woodruff set in motion a drive for quality. In 1928, soda fountains exceeded sales of bottles. Woodruff made sure the service engineers for the soda fountains were highly trained and could pass on their knowledge to the storekeepers operating the fountains. He set up a Fountain Training School where salesman could learn how to mix Coca-Cola properly. He also introduced a standard procedure manual. He introduced quality standards in the bottling plants, stipulating that all employees were to wear uniforms and that hygiene and quality checks should be introduced. These measures were an essential part of Coca-Cola's success.

Woodruff's most important contribution to the company was probably his move to expand into international markets. Although Asa Candler had exported Coca-Cola in 1900, the company's approach to export was a disorganized process, lacking coordinating management.

In 1926, Woodruff set up the Foreign Department, which in 1930 became a full-blown subsidiary, The Coca-Cola Export Corporation. With Woodruff in charge, Coca-Cola's march to global domination was relentless. He brokered a deal with the Olympic committee, which took Coca-Cola to Holland to be sold at the 1928 Olympics in Amsterdam. Wherever Coca-Cola was sold abroad, Woodruff secured the position of the drink by investing in the local economy, building bottling plants, and employing locals for the distribution. This way, the brand acquired goodwill in the countries to which it was exported.

Woodruff resigned as president in 1939 but played an active role for some time afterward. World War II helped proliferate Coca-Cola throughout the world. Woodruff promised that 'every man in every uniform gets a bottle of Coca-Cola for five cents wherever he is and whatever it costs the country.'

In the post-war period, Woodruff concentrated on battling rival Pepsi-Cola. He remained an extremely influential force at Coca-Cola right up until and even beyond his retirement in 1965. He even groomed potential CEOs, such as **Roberto Goizueta**, from behind the scenes. He died on 7 March 1985, at the age of 95.

Key texts

- Mark Pendergrast. *For God, Country, and Coca-Cola: The Unauthorized History of the Great American Soft Drink and the Company That Makes It.* Scribner, 1993
- Thomas Oliver. *The Real Coke, the Real Story.* Random House, 1986

Key link

- www.coca-cola.com

Woolworth, Frank Winfield

Retail pioneer; founder, F.W. Woolworth Co. (1852–1919)

Frank Winfield Woolworth was the pioneer of price-driven retail. Laying down a tradition of value for money that was later followed by companies such as Wal-Mart, Woolworth was one of the first merchants to build a retail empire founded on chain stores and volume retailing.

Born at the family home in Rodman, New York, Woolworth and his family moved to a 108-acre farm near Great Bend, New York, in late 1858 when Woolworth was seven years old.

With only a single schoolroom in the small town, Woolworth's opportunity for education was limited. Much of Woolworth's time was taken up helping his father with the family's eight-cow dairy herd. After attending commercial college for a brief period, Woolworth went to work as a clerk in Dan McNeil's general store in Great Bend. In 1873, Woolworth went to work for William Moore, the owner of Augsbury & Moore, a leading dry goods store in Watertown, New York, with a personal recommendation from Dan McNeil.

Woolworth started at the bottom. He swept floors, created window displays, and delivered goods. The hours were long: six days a week, 7:00 a.m. to 9:00 p.m., with little pay. At first, Woolworth was expected to work for a year with no salary, but Woolworth managed to persuade his employers to pay him $3.50 a week after three months of working for nothing.

Two years later, Woolworth moved on to another store, Bushnall's Department Store, as a senior clerk. In 1876, he married Jennie Creighton, a Canadian, and purchased a four-acre farm. Unfortunately, the tough conditions and lack of support at work meant Woolworth suffered from fever and stress-related illness, which forced him to give up his position at Bushnall's and kept him at home for a year, unable to work. As he was recovering, his old employer, William Moore, came knocking at Woolworth's door with a request to return to work at the now-renamed

Moore & Smiths. Woolworth accepted, at a salary of $10 a week.

In 1878, Woolworth's daughter was born and his mother died. But it was also a year of radical change in the world of retailing. In the Midwest, a new tactic in retailing had made its debut – the five cent table. Surplus merchandise was marked down to a nickel by retailers and displayed on a five cent table. Customers snapped up the bargains and were then drawn into buying other goods at full price. Moore travelled to New York and snapped up $100 worth of five cent goods for Moore & Smith. Woolworth arranged the counter and they were sold out in a day.

With goods supplied by Moore, Woolworth next opened his own store in Utica, New York, selling only five cent goods. 'The Great Five Cent Store' opened for business on a Saturday evening in February 1879 with $321-worth of five cent goods. The first ever Woolworth sale was a fire shovel. The store, however, was a failure and soon closed. Undaunted, Woolworth opened another in June of the same year in Lancaster, Pennsylvania. Now Woolworth sold goods for five and ten cents. The Lancaster store was a success. In November 1880, he opened a second store in Scranton, Pennsylvania. This too was a success and Woolworth never looked back.

Woolworth brought in family members to help expand his empire. By 1895, Woolworth had 28 stores, including that of his ex-boss William Moore, and revenues of more than $1 million. The growth continued at breakneck speed. There were 35 stores in 1900, 189 stores by 1908, and 600 stores by 1911. In January 1918, the thousandth store opened on Fifth Avenue in New York City.

Woolworth's one-man retail business had burgeoned into a global enterprise. In 1905, Woolworth, bowing to commercial pressures, incorporated F.W. Woolworth & Co., issuing 50,000 shares to executives and employees. Corporate offices were first located in New York City's Stewart Building, overlooking City Hall Park. Then, in April 1913, the company moved into the Woolworth Building, the tallest skyscraper of its time. Woolworth's office was situated on the twenty-fourth floor. Thirty feet square, its design was based on Napoleon's famous Empire Room and contained the clock and other articles from the original room.

In 1916, the F.W. Woolworth stores served more than 700 million customers and had revenues of more than $87 million. Every town in the United States with a population of over 8000 had a Woolworth's store.

By the time Woolworth was installed in the Woolworth Building, he was approaching the end of his career. With his health failing, he took to periods of rest in Europe. His wife Jennie was suffering from premature senility. Woolworth's own health continued to decline steadily, partly due to a refusal to care for his teeth. On 4 April 1919 he fell desperately ill, dying four days later.

Key texts

- Karen Plunkett-Powell. *Remembering Woolworth's: A Nostalgic History of the World's Most Famous Five-and-Dime.* St Martin's Press, 1999
- John P. Nichols. *Skyline Queen and the Merchant Prince: The Woolworth Story.* Trident Press, 1973
- John Kennedy Winkler. *Five and Ten: The Fabulous Life of F.W. Woolworth.* Books for Libraries Press, 1970
- *Woolworth's First 75 Years: The Story of Everybody's Store.* F.W. Woolworth Company, 1954
- Nina Brown Baker. *Nickels and Dimes: The Story of F.W. Woolworth.* Harcourt, Brace & World, 1954

Work in progress

Work in progress is the unfinished goods, parts, and other materials in the production process. Together with raw materials and finished goods, work in progress is classed as stock. In some production systems, work in progress is minimal, particularly where production methods such as **just-in-time** are employed. In other systems, where production of the finished good takes a long time, such as aircraft manufacturing, work in progress constitutes a high proportion of a company's stock.

Work/life balance

Work/life balance is the term used to describe the time devoted by an individual to his work in relation to the time devoted to non-work activities. Companies are increasingly recognizing the importance of employees' maintaining a healthy work/life balance, e.g., not neglecting family life at the expense of work. Research has suggested that striking the right work/life balance leads to a more motivated, less stressed workforce and reduces **burnout**. Yet employees around the world continue to work increasingly long hours. The average American worker clocks up nearly 2000 hours at work every year. Despite the heady speed of technological innovation, American working hours have actually increased by 4 percent since 1980. **Bill Gates** once observed: 'I personally work long hours, but not as long as I used to ... Most days I don't work more than 12 hours. On weekends I rarely work more than 8 hours.'

Work study

A work study involves the observation, recording, analysis, and evaluation of how a task is carried out by workers. Work studies, such as time and motion studies, are associated with **Frederick W. Taylor** and the scientific school of management. By observing and measuring how workers perform a task, the person conducting the study can recommend ways in which that task could be performed more efficiently.

Working capital

Working capital is calculated by subtracting a company's current assets from its current liabilities. The result is either positive or negative. A company with plenty of working capital has sufficient funds to finance its corporate strategy, buy property and equipment, and hire new staff. Ample working capital also means the company can move quickly to take advantage of a beneficial situation rather than have to arrange financing.

The ratio of current assets to current liabilities is known as the working capital ratio – a general indication of the solvency of a company, the adequacy of its working capital, and its ability to meet day-to-day demands upon it.

World Trade Organization (WTO)

The World Trade Organization was founded in 1995, and replaced the **GATT** agency. Headquartered in Geneva, Switzerland, the WTO has more than 140 member countries and a budget in excess of 120 million Swiss francs. Its functions include handling trade disputes, providing a forum for trade negotiations, providing technical assistance and training for developing countries, administering WTO agreements and monitoring national trade policies. WTO decision making is by consensus, although majority voting is possible. The top-level decision-making body is known as the Ministerial Conference and meets at least once every two years.

Key link
- www.wto.org

World Wide Web

The World Wide Web is a hypertext system for publishing information on the **Internet**. It was developed by UK academic and research scientist **Tim Berners-Lee** while working at the CERN particle physics laboratory in Geneva in 1989. Berners-Lee also wrote the first Web client (browser-editor) and server in 1990.

World Wide Web documents ('Web pages') are text files coded using **HTML** to include text and graphics, and are stored on a Web server connected to the Internet. Web pages may also contain dynamic objects and **Java** applets for enhanced animation, video, sound and interactivity. In 2000, it was estimated that there were more than one billion pages on the Web.

Wrongful trading

When a company is unable to avoid insolvency, it must not continue to trade. Should it do so, it will be guilty of wrongful trading. Under UK law, in the event of a liquidation, creditors can apply to a court to have a director of a company held personally responsible for the debts of that company. If it can be shown that the director was aware that the company would become insolvent yet continued trading, then the court may order the director to make a contribution to the company's assets.

X / Y / Z

XML (eXstensible Mark-up Language)

XML is a simplified subset of SGML (Standard Generalized Mark-up Language) used for defining languages for specific purposes or specific industries for use on the **World Wide Web**. SGML is a standardized language developed by the **International Organization for Standardization (ISO)** in 1986. It specifies rules for tags that can be attached to a document and instructs elements of a document to be interpreted in different ways. **HTML (Hypertext Mark-up Language)** is also derived from SGML.

XML differs from HTML in that it is an extensible language, allowing the user to create new commands or tags as they wish. HTML is a fixed language: the user can only use those commands or tags that already exist. Thus XML is more powerful than HTML, and less cumbersome than SGML. XML has been developed through the W3 Consortium, which first published XML 1.0 in December 1997, and was issued as a 'recommendation' in 1998. Although it was envisaged that XML would largely replace HTML, that has not happened and XML has made only relatively small inroads into the use of the ubiquitous HTML.

Key link
- www.xml.com/index.csp

Zero-sum game

A zero-sum game is a situation in which one party can only benefit at the expense of another.

If one negotiator wins, the other must lose. This would be the case, for example, where two companies wished to acquire the same target or where two companies wanted the majority of a finite resource. The concept was originated by US mathematician John von Neumann. Take the simple game of 'Odds and Evens'. Two children each have a penny. One child agrees to be 'odds', the other to be 'evens'. The children cover their pennies and reveal them at the same time. If the two coins show the same face, both heads or both tails, then 'evens' wins the coins. If the coins show different faces, then 'odds' wins the coins. The different possibilities for the game are as follows, with a win as 1 and a loss as −1.

- Head/Head: Even 1 Odd −1
- Tail/Tail: Even 1 Odd −1
- Head/Tail: Even −1 Odd 1
- Tail/Head: Even −1 Odd 1

In each case, sum total is zero. It is impossible for both parties to win or for both parties to lose.

The zero-sum approach, often adopted as an aggressive strategy in negotiations, is also referred to as a win-lose approach. However, strictly speaking, most negotiations are not true zero-sum games, as a win-win solution is theoretically possible.

Zip

Zipping refers to the compression of data files to enable them to be transferred more efficiently. Data is compressed in a particular format, sent, and then decompressed. Specialist software programs, such as WinZip, are available to zip and unzip files.

Zipf's Law

Zipf's Law is the unusual observation that the frequency of occurrence of an event (P), as a function of the rank (i) when the rank is determined by the above frequency of occurrence, is a power-law function:

$$P_i \sim 1/i^a$$

with the exponent (a) close to unity.

For the non-mathematically minded, the rule states, essentially, that the probability of the occurrence of a word in a selection of text or item in a collection of items starts high and tapers off. So, for example, the tenth most frequent word would appear roughly one-tenth as many times as the most frequent. The law is named after American Harvard University linguistics professor George Kingsley Zipf (1902–1950), who proposed it after studying the frequency of words appearing in selected passages of text. Zipf made detailed examination of James Joyce's *Ulysses*, not a task for the faint of heart. He discovered that the tenth most frequent word occurred 2653 times, the hundredth most frequent word 265 times, the two hundredth word 133 times, and so on. What he discovered is that the rank of the word multiplied by its frequency equals a constant that approximates to 26,500.

Zipf's Law is true for other observations of frequency and rank, such as a revenue of a company as a function of its rank. This is an observation that **Vilfredo Pareto** had also made some time before.

Key texts

- G.K. Zipf. *Human Behavior and the Principle of Least Effort.* Addison-Wesley, 1949
- G.K. Zipf. *Psycho-Biology of Languages.* Houghton-Mifflin, 1935; MIT Press, 1965
- G.K. Zipf. *Selective Studies and the Principle of Relative Frequency in Language.* Harvard University Press, 1932

Z score

The Z score is a single-figure indicator of a company's financial position obtained from a weighted average of accounting metrics. Z-score analysis was developed during the 1960s by Edward I. Altman, now a professor at New York's Stern School of Business. Altman developed the Z score from his research into the financial position of 33 manufacturing companies that had filed for bankruptcy under Chapter X of the National Bankruptcy Act between 1946 and 1965, as well as 33 control companies.

The ratios used to calculate the Z score are: return on total assets; sales to total assets; equity to debt; working capital to total assets; and retained earnings to total assets. These ratios are then multiplied by a weighted figure and added together. The result is a number between –4 and +8. According to Altman, a Z score below 1.81 is an indication of financial difficulty, while a score above 2.99 indicates financial safety.

Key texts

- Edward I. Altman. *Corporate Financial Distress and Bankruptcy.* Second edition, John Wiley, 1993
- Edward I. Altman. *The Z-Score Bankruptcy Model: Past, Present, and Future.* John Wiley, 1977

INDEX